PERSUASION

RECEPTION AND RESPONSIBILITY

8TH EDITION

Persuasion

RECEPTION AND RESPONSIBILITY

Charles U. Larson
Northern Illinois University

Wadsworth Publishing Company

I(T)P® An International Thomson Publishing Company

Belmont, CA • Albany, NY • Bonn • Boston • Cincinnati • Detroit • Johannesburg • London
Madrid • Melbourne • Mexico City • New York • Paris • Singapore • Tokyo • Toronto • Washington

Communications Editor: Randall Adams
Assistant Editor: Michael Gillespie
Editorial Assistant: Megan Gilbert
Marketing Manager: Mike Dew
Project Editor: Dianne Jensis
Print Buyer: Barbara Britton
Permissions Editor: Robert Kauser

Production: Del Mar Associates
Designer: Penna Design
Copy Editor: Kevin Gleason
Cover: John Odam
Compositor: ColorType, San Diego
Printer: The Maple-Vail Book Manufacturing Group

Cover Photos:
© TSM/Mug Shots, 1998
© TSM/Jon Feingersh, 1998

Printed in the United States of America
3 4 5 6 7 8 9 10

For more information, contact Wadsworth Publishing Company, 10 Davis Drive, Belmont, CA 94002,
or electronically at http://www.wadsworth.com/wadsworth.html

International Thomson Publishing Europe
Berkshire House 168-173
High Holborn
London, WC1V 7AA, England

International Thomson Editores
Campos Eliseos 385, Piso 7
Col. Polanco
11560 México D.F. México

Thomas Nelson Australia
102 Dodds Street
South Melbourne 3205
Victoria, Australia

International Thomson Publishing Asia
221 Henderson Road
#05-10 Henderson Building
Singapore 0315

Nelson Canada
1120 Birchmount Road
Scarborough, Ontario
Canada M1K 5G4

International Thomson Publishing Japan
Hirakawacho Kyowa Building, 3F
2-2-1 Hirakawacho
Chiyoda-ku, Tokyo 102, Japan

International Thomson Publishing GmbH
Königswinterer Strasse 418
53227 Bonn, Germany

International Thomson Publishing Southern Africa
Building 18, Constantia Park
240 Old Pretoria Road
Halfway House, 1685 South Africa

Library of Congress Cataloging-in-Publication Data

Larson, Charles U.
    Persuasion: reception and responsibility/Charles U. Larson. — 8th ed.
        p.   cm
    Includes bibliographical references (p.   ) and index.
    ISBN 0-534-52281-5
    1. Persuasion (Psychology)   I. Title.
BF637.P4L36   1998
303.3'42 — dc21   97–18841

For Mary, without whom . . .

Preface

It has been twenty-five years since the first edition of *Persuasion: Reception and Responsibility* was published. At that time, the United States was on the verge of a national nervous breakdown, having endured the Vietnam war, the assassinations of Robert Kennedy and Martin Luther King, Jr., corruption in high places, a counterculture promoting drugs and sex, the rejection of traditional values, and the splitting of the generations. The background for these disturbing events was an information, communication, and technology explosion the extent of which was just beginning to be perceived. The public was vulnerable to overwhelming amounts of persuasion — ethical and unethical — that were beginning to engulf modern society.

Published in the midst of this context, the first edition of *Persuasion: Reception and Responsibility* received a warm welcome. In 1973 most college students were idealistic baby boomers who refused to trust anyone over thirty (which was fine with me since I was still a few years away from that age myself). They believed that the sheer moral force of their collective wills could change the course of history. (And perhaps it did — they toppled two presidents, advanced the rights of women and mi-

norities, and brought government under increasing scrutiny.) They — and their professors, my colleagues in the discipline — were ready for a book that was receiver-oriented and that encouraged critical reception and acceptance/rejection of persuasive messages, judged from a perspective of what we called "ethical behavior."

With each revision of the book since then, I have tried to respond to the communication/persuasion milieu that I believed was (or soon would be) facing the generation of students who would be using the book — just as I tried to respond to the needs of an antiwar generation of student receivers that first time around. This eighth edition has been no exception.

Today we face problems at least as difficult, perplexing, and challenging as those faced by students of persuasion back in the 70s. In spite of the fact that the cold war appears over, that we are making progress against pollution, and that the economy appears to be heading in a healthy direction, things still appear out of control in many areas, and it still seems as if "events are in the saddle and ride mankind." We can't stop the spread of AIDS; brutal and bloody revolutions and ethnic and religious slaughter have broken out in Africa, the Balkans, South America, the former Soviet Union, and Asia, and the United Nations and the United States are being called on now more than ever to help maintain peace and freedom throughout the world. Domestically, we have reason to worry about the drug epidemic, the graying of America, the seemingly uncontrollable deficit, challenges in health care, new technologies, and a host of other issues.

Now, more than ever, we need to be trained as critical consumers of persuasion who are on guard not to be persuaded by every political, religious, or profit-motivated huckster that comes along. There is at least as great a need in 1998 for the study of *Persuasion: Reception and Responsibility* as there was two decades ago, and this eighth edition has been in preparation with those challenges in mind. The examples have been updated, new models of persuasion have been included, and several chapters have undergone major revisions. I hope the additions and changes will help you in your attempts to become responsible and critical receiver/consumers of the myriad persuasive messages coming at you.

Acknowledgments

No book ever reaches print without the help of many talented and sharing persons: colleagues, students, editors, and critics, all of whom deserve thanks. First and foremost, I thank the graduate and undergraduate students who keep challenging my sometimes old-fashioned and limited view of persuasion; I have learned as much from them as they have from me. I would also like to thank those who formally critiqued the manuscript while in progress: Loren Dickinson, Walla Walla College; Walter G. Kirkpatrick, University of Memphis; Robert Payne, East Central University; Gayle M. Pohl, University of Northern Iowa; Laurinda W. Porter, St. Cloud State University; and Richard L. Stovall, Southwest Missouri State University. You have all offered valuable advice and continue to lead me to new sources of and perspectives on persuasion.

Finally, the eighth edition would not have been possible without the staff at Wadsworth: Becky Hayden, who first recognized the need for a receiver-oriented textbook in persuasion; Todd Armstrong, Michael Gillespie, and Nancy Sjoberg, who kept me on task and on schedule; and all the other Wadsworth staffers and freelancers who helped make this eighth edition possible. Most especially, though, I offer thanks to you teachers and students who have used earlier editions and who will use this edition. I welcome your suggestions and advice for further revisions, and I hope that, in some way, this book will help make us all critical receivers of the persuasion of the next millennium. Feel free to write to me in care of the publisher.

Contents

PERSUASION

RECEPTION AND RESPONSIBILITY

PART ONE

Theoretical Premises

The 1990s were ushered in with a breathtaking set of megachanges. Consider a few of them: the collapse and final bankruptcy of over seventy years of Marxist/Leninist socialism in Eastern Europe and the Soviet Union; the end of the cold war; huge federal deficits; a massive savings and loan industry scandal that will cost us and our children thousands of dollars each; political elections à la bash and smear, complete with innuendo and name-calling; and the worsening of the AIDS and drug epidemics, to name but a few. Underlying all of this change is a constant — the permanent presence of persuasion from all sides. Persuasion has been a common denominator in the arenas of economics, politics, religion, business, and interpersonal relations ever since humans began to interact. Never before, however, has it had such great potential as a tool for affecting our daily lives, as a means to many ends — both good and not so good — and as a presence in nearly every moment of our waking lives. Our world today and the world we will face as we approach the millennium rest on the power of various kinds of persuasion.

We need to approach this prominence of persuasion in our everyday lives keeping in mind that at its core, persuasion is a symbolic act for both persuaders and receivers. It is also basically a democratic and humanistic attempt to influence others. In other words, persuasion attempts not to coerce others into taking a certain action but rather to move them toward considering taking that action by giving them good logical, emotional, and cultural reasons for taking the action. Additionally, the good reasons for action must be delivered to the receivers via an appropriate medium, whether "one-to-one" interpersonal communication or "one-to-many" forms of communication, such as contemporary electronic and print media. And there are new media on the horizon to carry this multitude of persuasive messages. For example, we will soon be ushered into

an age of "virtual reality," using a medium that simulates real experiences and that has awesome potential for both good and bad.

As you read and use this book to study persuasion, I hope you will change in important ways. We live in a world in which persuasive messages of various types continually compete for our attention and favor. What's more, the exciting times in which we live depend heavily on successful persuasion, whether in rebuilding Eastern Europe and the fragments of the former Soviet Union and stopping the slaughter in the former Yugoslavia, or in electing a president of the United States. On less global levels, persuasion affects consumer behavior, interpersonal behavior, and intrapersonal behavior — self-persuasion. Most of the time, we do not send persuasive messages; instead, we are predominantly in the role of the persuadee, or receiver and consumer, of persuasive messages. The goal of this book and class is to make you more critical and responsible consumers of persuasion.

In some ways, you are already a critical receiver, but you can improve your reception skills; that is what this book should teach you to do. You will need to identify how critical a receiver you are: How easily are you persuaded? How does persuasion work on you? What tactics are most effective with you? with others? Which are least effective? Part I investigates these questions and establishes a perspective for you. Part II is a search for fundamental persuasive premises that can sway most receivers. These are the foundations on which persuaders build their arguments. We need to understand how and why persuaders appeal to these premises. Why do we respond to certain psychological appeals and not to others? Why are some lines of reasoning more convincing than others? Why do persuadees in some cultures respond to certain appeals and not to others? These are the questions Part II will try to answer. Finally, Part III explores some of the contexts in which persuasion operates—campaigns, public speeches, interpersonal persuasion, some parts of the mass media, propaganda, and advertising.

Chapter 1 looks at the degree to which persuasion dominates our lives. We will examine several definitions of persuasion, ranging from those rooted in ancient Greece to those derived from the contemporary media age. We will discuss a useful model suggested by Hugh Rank, a scholar of persuasion and propaganda. The model was an outgrowth of Rank's work with the National Council of Teachers of English (NCTE) and their concern over the increase in "doublespeak," the attempt to use words to confuse and mislead an audience. In Chapter 2, Richard L. Johannesen provides a variety of approaches to the ethical issues that arise whenever persuasion occurs. Keep in mind that these approaches and issues involve both persuaders and persuadees—senders and receivers, advertisers and consumers, politicians and their constituents, governments and citizens.

Chapter 3 looks at a variety of theories that explain how persuasion operates from different perspectives. This summary of theories is intended to whet your appetites for more in-depth study of these perspectives—a sampler of views for you to try. Chapter 4 examines the raw material of persuasion—human symbolic behavior—especially as it occurs in language. Part I concludes with Chapter 5, which describes and demonstrates several alternative ways receivers can analyze, interpret, decode, and finally critique persuasive language. It is not important that you find one approach that you prefer, but that you consider the various alternatives.

Part I sets the stage for a deeper investigation of persuasion and its applications. Exploration of this field can be traced back to Aristotle and beyond and the study of persuasion in Greek democracy. He knew that by establishing common ground, persuaders could get audiences to identify with them. Thus, it was the persuader's task to find areas of common beliefs and preferences. Aristotle believed that having identified this common ground, persuaders could develop arguments in which the audience participates by providing a part of the argument—usually a widely held major premise. He called these participative arguments *enthymemes,* or abbreviated syllogisms. Our search in Part II for those premises that seem persuasive to large numbers of persuadees thus reflects Aristotle's teaching.

When you finish this book and course, I hope you will find that you have changed from a somewhat uncritical persuadee to a responsible and analytical receiver, ready to face the persuasion blitz of the 1990s and approaching millennium.

1

Persuasion in Today's World

It has been a quarter century since the first edition of *Persuasion: Reception and Responsibility* was published. Naturally, the world is quite a different place from what it was in 1973, during the Vietnam war, with its angry demonstrations and revolutionary rhetoric. Yet some things remain constant, especially in regard to the dynamics of persuasion.

Consider just a few of the changes that we have experienced during the past twenty-five years. We abandoned a major war in Vietnam; the Democratic party returned to dominance; the national debt passed $1 trillion; the age of the personal computer dawned; Americans were forced to directly address questions of health care, deficit reduction, and the end of the cold war; we witnessed the transition of U.S. presidential power from a veteran of World War II to a veteran of the antiwar movement of the Vietnam era; and we saw the rise of a potentially terrifying militia movement willing to engage in urban terrorism.

We have also incorporated a host of technological innovations into our daily lives — video cameras and recorders, cable and satellite television options, new telephone systems, and automatic teller machines, personal computers, and two totally new media — the Internet and e-mail. On the political/economic front, we were each billed several thousand dollars to bail out the savings and loan industry; America found itself unable to dictate its will in Latin America, Europe, the Middle East, or anywhere else; Marxist/Leninist socialism crumbled from within, and a new age of electronic information dawned.

At the same time, some things have remained the same. We are still faced with processing more persuasion than ever. People still respond to persuasive appeals from advertisers, politicians, and ideologues; we still esteem traditional institutions and values such as the family, success, and education; and we still play politics on campus, on the job, in our organizations, and in our families. Unfortunately, we also continue to face an energy crisis, we continue to foul our environment, and world peace eludes us.

What do you think?

How many persuasive messages do you think you've seen today?

4

Persuasion in an Information Age

In one way or another, everything just cited has been related to persuasion. During the past decade we have been persuaded that the United States is no longer the world's number one economic power, and we have been persuaded that we cannot live without items such as ATM cards, plastic credit, remote control devices, personal computers, home pages, and "surfing the net." As voters and consumers, we need to be persuaded to support candidates or to buy products. Whether as individuals, corporations, or governments, we need to be persuaded to do our part in saving and restoring the environment. For these and many other reasons, it is more important than ever to train ourselves to become responsible and critical receivers of persuasion.

Let's consider just a few of the areas in which we need to become better persuadees. *Advertising Age* magazine estimates that the average American is exposed to over 5000 persuasive messages a day. These messages appear in many formats. A prime example is the television spot, with its high-tech artistry utilizing computer graphics, sophisticated special effects, and digital sound. At the same time as these ads gain in sophistication, they are also shrinking in duration. Whereas 30- and 60-second spots were long the staples of television advertising, the 15-second spot, the 10-second reinforcement spot, and soon 7½-second spots will dominate television advertising. Other formats containing persuasive messages include newspaper or magazine advertisements in all their artistic and nonartistic forms, billboards and signs along the roadside, radio spots, T-shirts with product names imprinted on them, home pages, faxes, and so on. Even the packaging of the various products we use is persuasive, as are the "shelf talkers" in the supermarkets and the coupons or rebate forms that accompany products today.

Most recently we have been deluged with direct-marketing messages, ranging from catalogs and direct-mail appeals to telephone solicitations and direct-response television ads.

Furthermore, as you read these words, newer and more sophisticated forms of advertising are being devised. For example, computer billboards and networks are now exploited by persuaders, and interfaces between home computers, electronic mail, and computer-generated graphics and filing systems make it possible for individuals to receive their own personalized "newspaper," which includes only subjects of interest to them, or to hyperlink to more new information than we can handle.

Although the thought of receiving totally individualized information and services is widely appealing, little serious consideration has been given to the implications of this kind of deep segmentation. A primary concern is the fact that we must divulge much of our individual and group identity—demographics, interests, age, political and sexual preferences, religion, income, media habits, and a host of other "private" information—in order to get these individualized products.

In fact, in the eyes of the advertising industry, this relinquishing of intimate data has already been achieved. **Brand scanning,** for instance, is advertising's newest tool for analyzing consumers, segmenting the market, and designing ads to persuade them. In brand-scan market research, consumers are given a "consumer card," similar to a credit card, which entitles the consumer to "special" prices on a few products. When purchases are presented at the computerized cash register, they are recorded and compared with the information the consumer has volunteered (television viewing habits and demographic and psychographic information, for example). For the first time, advertisers have a direct link between advertising exposure and actual product purchase. And what do we guinea pig consumers get in return for giving away large chunks of our private selves? A small discount on our groceries.

Thus the intimate details of our lives are becoming increasingly available to marketers who want to sell us everything from politicians to beer. Some of the sources from which marketers obtain personal data include census information, sold to advertisers by the federal government, and demographic and biographical information drawn from driver's license bureaus, hunting and fishing licenses, tax departments, highway patrol records, vehicle registration bureaus, and more, all sold regularly by state and local governments. And each time we fill out a product-warranty questionnaire, we give away information that is also sold to marketers. In short, we are rapidly losing our privacy and our individuality as we are "packaged" into market segments or potential consumer groups.

Nowhere has this sort of information been so cleverly and completely exploited than in the burgeoning casino industry. Here, "brand-scan type" room keys and special casino cards can be used to charge almost anything from meals and drinks to gambling chips and shows. This information taken together with customer surveys, hotel registration information, and other data bases allows the casino to track the customers' eating, drinking, and gambling habits and preferences, as well as their use of time and even the paths they take through the casino. This information allows the marketing departments to situate the right persuasive message to the right customer in the right place and at the right time, whether that means a direct mail announcement that the customer has won a "free" room at Harrahs or an in-room notice on the television announcing a show or meal special or a score of other appeals. And you can be certain that this sophistication will soon be copied by other industries, and that it will

> **What do you think?**
>
> How many "frequent user" or "preferred customer" cards do you have?

become even more sophisticated and detailed. In an information society we soon lose a significant degree of privacy, and there is little we can do about it. It is like saying, "I refuse to cooperate with Universal Product Codes — I won't buy anything that has a UPC code on it!!!" This information age will not go away, so as persuadees we need to get ready to deal with it. We can't afford to be like the horse and carriage lovers of yesteryear who refused to throw away their buggy whips because horseless carriages "just won't catch on."

Persuasion in a Technological World

Today, more than ever before in human history, persuasion pervades our everyday lives. We are in the midst of what Alvin Toffler (1980) calls "the third wave" of great change experienced by humanity — the technological revolution. Although persuasion was useful in instituting change in the first two "waves" of great innovation — the agricultural wave and the industrial wave — it will be essential in inducing people to try, accept, and finally adopt the many new ways of thinking, believing, and behaving that go hand in hand with the worldwide shift to the technological age. We are seeing but the first vague dimensions of only a few of the changes that will be facing us. Children no longer take their parents' word as law — they need to be motivated to avoid drugs, to take core subjects at school, to turn down the volume of their Walkman to avoid damage to their hearing. The U.S. government has discovered that it must make increasing use of persuasion to convince the citizenry to conserve energy, to "find themselves" in the Army, or to be honest when filling out their income tax reports. Social institutions, such as churches, educational groups, and community organizations, are finding it more necessary than ever to use persuasion to gain or even to maintain membership levels and financial support for their projects. Meanwhile marketers must convince consumers that a product will add excitement to life—that it will make consumers more successful, sexier, or more secure. In education, we find persuasion becoming more important in motivating students to achieve, to listen, and to participate. All of these persuaders vie for our attention and for our loyalties and support.

We could go on and on. Clearly, persuasion pervades our world. Clearly, too, in such a world we need training in persuasion: not only in how to persuade others but in how to—and how not to—be persuaded.

Of course, you could decide to simply reject all the persuasion directed at you. But, if you reject all persuasion by politicians, how will you know for whom to vote? If you reject all advertising, how will you compare brands or learn about new products? If you reject the persuasion of your teachers, how will you know what courses to take or what to choose as a major? Perhaps you could personally investigate the record of every politician on the ballot or personally test every detergent or motor oil or ski wax on the market. Maybe you could even take one of every kind of course and evaluate its career possibilities. But if you did, you would have little time for anything else!

The world around us tells us that we need to be persuaded, if only to reduce our alternatives before making choices. At the same time, we need to be prepared for the many potent and perhaps mistaken—even negative—things our persuasion world can do to us. Noted communications expert Neil Postman (1981) called attention to just one aspect of persuasion and its potency in shaping our values: the television commercial. According to Postman, by the time you're twenty you're likely to have seen about a *million* commercials. That averages out to a thousand a week. Imagine what we would think if a propaganda artist were pumping persuasion down our throats that often every week. Some would

call us robots. What impressions do we get from these commercials? Here is Postman's analysis:

> This makes the TV commercial the most voluminous information source in the education of youth. . . . A commercial teaches a child three interesting things. The first is that all problems are resolvable. The second is that all problems are resolvable fast. And the third is that all problems are resolvable fast through the agency of some technology. It may be a drug. It may be a detergent. It may be an airplane or some piece of machinery. . . .
>
> The essential message is that the problems that beset people—whether it is lack of self-confidence or boredom or even money problems—are entirely solvable if only we will allow ourselves to be ministered to by a technology. (p. 4)

How often have we been affected by this simple little belief? How often have we bought that bottle of Obsession or Ban, or those Hanes stockings, because we subconsciously believe that they will make us more attractive to the opposite sex and give us a successful love life? or help us land a job or impress a teacher? How many of us believe that the environment will be saved by technology?

One of the purposes of this book is to make you at least aware of what is happening to you in this persuasion world. The title of this book, *Persuasion: Reception and Responsibility*, suggests the direction we will take. Our focus is on the training of *persuadees*—those on the receiving end of all the persuasion. People need to learn to be critical, to observe and judge the persuasion coming at them.

Of course, persuasion is not a recent discovery, and it would have been good in past times for people to have been aware of the persuasion going on around them. If they had been, perhaps many tyrants of history might not have risen to power; wars might have been avoided; diseases might have been cured or avoided. But today, in a technological age in which the means through which persuasion can be designed and disseminated are extremely sophisticated, being an aware and cautious persuadee is more essential than ever. The National Council of Teachers of English (NCTE) recognized this need when it instituted its regular conferences on "doublespeak" and when it began to announce an annual "doublespeak award," to be given to the persuader(s) whose language was most "grossly unfactual, deceptive, evasive, confusing, or self-contradictory."

Doublespeak in a Persuasion-Filled World

Even in a persuasion-riddled world such as ours, you would not need defensive training if all persuaders stayed out in the open and talked straight. Too many, however, speak in doublespeak. **Doublespeak** is the opposite of straightforward language: It tries to miscommunicate; it tries to conceal the truth and to confuse. The word is related to "newspeak," a term George Orwell coined in his chilling description of the world he anticipated in his novel *1984.* "Newspeak" was used to shift meanings for words and concepts in order to confuse the citizenry. For example, "war" meant "peace" and "freedom" meant "slavery." Although Orwell's frightening future view has not come to pass, enough of it has come true to make us all take a second look at the doublespeak of our times. Consider the "peacekeeping" missions the United States has engaged in around the world: Kuwait, Somalia, the Balkans, and elsewhere. Or consider Bill Clinton's campaign vow to cut the deficit while increasing taxes on the rich and providing tax relief for the poor. Yet one of his earliest tax proposals increased the cost of gasoline, which taxed rich and poor alike. In other cases he

What do you think?

What kind of a house is advertised as a "Handyman's Special"?

instituted "user fees" for services previously covered by taxes. His predecessor, George Bush, had promised "No new taxes!" and then labeled subsequent tax increases as "revenue enhancers." So both were guilty of using doublespeak. In the former Yugoslavia, the term "ethnic cleansing" provides a key example of doublespeak — it was used to camouflage the existence of concentration camps, as well as the raping, pillaging, and killing of thousands of innocent victims. The concept is not very far from Adolf Hitler's "Final Solution," in which millions of victims lost their lives.

Of course, doublespeak isn't confined to the world of politics. A real estate ad indicating that a house is "convenient to the interstate" probably means that you will hear cars whoosh by day and night. College administrators who refer to "more liberal admission standards" when they mean falling enrollments are using doublespeak, as are used-car dealers who use the words "good work car" when they mean a junker.

You can identify numerous examples of doublespeak once you get started. One of the most humorous, which received the NCTE award for doublespeak from a foreign source, was made by General Joao Baptista Figueiredo, then president of Brazil. He told reporters, "I intend to open this country to democracy, and anyone who is against that I will jail; I will crush!"

Unfortunately, doublespeak seems to be on the increase; the average American eighteen-year-old has seen over 20,000 hours of television and views scores of commercials per week (Nielson, 1993). In short, we are rapidly becoming numbed by doublespeak (see Figure 1.1).

Defining Persuasion—From Aristotle to Burke

Let us begin our study of the persuasion process by looking at how it has been defined at various times and by various experts.

Berry's World

"Not the truth AGAIN!"

© 1990 by NEA, Inc.   2-A

Figure 1.1. *In a world of doublespeak, even the truth becomes a victim of audience doubt and skepticism. (Berry's World reprinted by permission of NEA, Inc.)*

The field of modern communication can trace its roots to the ancient Greeks, who were the first to systematize the use of persuasion, calling it "rhetoric." They studied it in their schools, using it in their courts and in implementing the first democracies in the Greek city-states. Primary among the ancient theorists was Aristotle, who defined rhetoric as "the faculty of observing in any given case, the available means of persuasion." According to Aristotle, persuasion is made up of *artistic* and *inartistic* proofs, both of which we will explore in more depth. Persuasion, according to Aristotle, can be based on a source's credibility (*ethos*), emotional appeals (*pathos*), and/or logical appeals (*logos*) (Roberts, 1924). He also thought that persuasion is most effective when based on the *common ground* existing between persuader and persuadee. This common ground permits persuaders to make certain assumptions about the audience and its beliefs. Knowing these beliefs, the persuader can use the *enthymeme*, a form of argument in which the first or major premise in the proof remains unstated by the persuader and, instead, is supplied by the audience. The task of the persuader, then, is to identify common ground, those first or major premises held by the audience, and to use them in enthymematic arguments (see Figure 1.2).

Roman students of persuasion added specific advice on what a persuasive speech ought to include. The Roman orator Cicero identified five elements of persuasive speaking: inventing or discovering evidence and arguments, organizing them, styling them artistically, memorizing them, and finally delivering them skillfully. Another Roman theorist, Quintilian, added that a persuader has to be a "good man" as well as a good speaker.

Those early definitions clearly focused on the sources of messages and on persuaders' skill and art in building a speech. Later students of persuasion reflected the changes that accompanied an emerging mass-media world. Winston Brembeck and William Howell (1952), two communication professors, described persuasion as "the conscious attempt to modify thought and action by manipulating the motives of men toward predetermined ends" (p. 24). In their definition, we see a notable shift from the use of logic toward the internal motives of the audience. By the time Brembeck and

What do you think?

Which of Brembeck and Howell's definitions do you prefer and why?

Figure 1.2. In this advertisement, which appeared in a hunting and fishing magazine, common ground is established with all fathers who feel somewhat estranged from their grown sons. The common ground is then used to promote the purchase of a Johnson motor so that the father and son can get away together on a fishing trip. (Reprinted by permission of Outboard Marine Corporation.)

Howell wrote their second edition, in the 1970s, they had changed their definition of persuasion to "communication intended to influence choice" (1976, p. 19). In the mid-1960s, Wallace Fotheringham, another communication professor, defined persuasion as "that body of effects in receivers" that had been caused by a persuader's message (1966, p. 7). Here the focus is almost entirely on the receiver, who actually determines whether persuasion has occurred. By this standard, even unintended messages, such as gossip overheard on a bus, could be persuasive if they caused changes in their receivers' attitudes, beliefs, or actions.

Kenneth Burke (1970), literary critic and theorist, defines persuasion as the artful use of the "resources of ambiguity." Burke believes that the degree to which persuadees feel that they are being spoken to in their "own language" is critical to creating a sense of **identification** — a concept close to Aristotle's "common ground." In Burke's theory, when true identification occurs, the persuaders of the world try to act, believe, and talk like the audience.

In the first edition of this book, I defined persuasion as "a process" that changes attitudes, beliefs, opinions, or behaviors. In that definition, the *process* of persuasion gets the attention. Persuasion occurs only through cooperation between source and receiver. Following Burke's lead, my definition is now: **persuasion** is *the co-creation of a state of identification between a source and a receiver that results from the use of symbols.* Once you identify with the kind of world a huckster wants you to like — say, *Marlboro Country* — persuasion has occurred. You may never smoke, but you have been changed. The world of Marlboro Country has become attractive to you. Maybe you'll respond to the appeal of the attitude and begin to value ruggedness and individualism, or perhaps you'll try to emulate the Marlboro Man's dress and demeanor, or perhaps you'll vote for a candidate who projects a "Marlboro" image.

During the 1996 Arizona presidential primary, only Pat Buchanan chose to project this image by wearing cowboy boots and Western-style clothes. In this definition, the focus of persuasion is not on the source, the message, or the receiver, but on *all* of them equally. They all *cooperate* to make a persuasive process. The idea of **co-creation** means that what is inside the receiver is just as important as the source's intent or the content of messages. In one sense, *all* persuasion is **self-persuasion** — we are rarely persuaded unless we *participate* in the process.

The words "co-created" and "self-persuasion" are central. Persuasion is the result of the combined efforts of source and receiver. Even in cases of terrorism and hostage taking, some hostages begin to identify with their captors and may even embrace the terrorists' cause. We now know, for example, that many of the Branch Davidians sect led by David Koresh identified so much with Koresh and his beliefs that they willingly went to their deaths when their Texas compound caught fire. Thus, even in bizarre and potentially coercive situations, persuasion — and especially self-persuasion — operates.

Criteria for Responsible Persuasion

How does this cooperative persuasion happen? What makes it work? Although persuasion can occur under the most unlikely circumstances (in the midst of an emotional argument, during a riot, and even in a concentration camp), three circumstances seem to increase the chances that responsible receivers can be rationally and ethically persuaded.

First, persuasion is most likely to occur in a responsible and fair way *if both sides have an equal opportunity to persuade and if each has approximately equivalent ability and access to the media of communication.* If a gag rule is imposed on the proponents of one side of a question while advocates of the other side have freedom to persuade, then receivers will get a one-sided and biased view of the issue.

What do you think?

Is there ever real "equal opportunity" for both sides to persuade?

Second, *there should be a revelation of agendas*. Each side should notify the audience of its true aims and goals and say how it intends to go about achieving them. Candidates ought to admit how they intend to attack their opponents' credibility, or how their tax proposal works. Thus, auto manufacturers ought to tell us that they build reliable cars, not excitement. Of course, if we receivers knew the hidden agendas of many persuaders, we would quickly be put on guard against their appeals. In many cases, this criterion is met only partially. But even having a hint of the real goal of a persuader can make us more responsible receivers, so it is useful to try to determine a persuader's intentions before acting on his or her advice.

Third, and most important, is *the presence of critical receivers*—receivers who test the assertions and evidence presented to them. They look for information from all sides in a debate and withhold final judgment until they have sufficient data. If we have such a set of receivers, the first two criteria are minimal, and responsible persuasion can still occur. In the election of 1996, the press pointed out many examples of negative TV ads, which then seemed to boomerang. Shortly thereafter, candidates began to pull negative ads.

Because the receiver is central to persuasion, it's a good idea for you to study the process of persuasion from that point of view. You need to observe yourself being persuaded and try to see why and how persuasion happens. This knowledge will allow you to be more critical and therefore more effective in rejecting persuasive messages when appropriate—and in accepting others when that is wise.

The SMCR Model of Persuasion

The simplest model of communication, and the one most widely referred to, is the **SMCR model** (see Figure 1.3), suggested by Claude Shannon and Warren Weaver in 1949 and modified since that time by others such as David Berlo (1960). The model contains four essential elements:

- A **source** (S), who or which is the encoder of the message. The code may be verbal, nonverbal, visual, musical, or in some other modality.

- A **message** (M), which is meant to convey the source's meaning through any of the codes.

- A **channel** (C), which carries the message and which may have distracting noise.

- A **receiver** (R), who decodes the message, trying to sift out channel noise and adding his or her own interpretation.

To illustrate the components of the SMCR model, let's suppose that your young niece or nephew is watching an ad for a "complete set of Power Rangers" and is promised by the advertiser that owning the set can practically guarantee instant popularity and acceptance by his or her peers. You want the child to be a more discriminating consumer, so you point out that the sponsor is actually interested in profit, not peer popularity. In this case, you are explaining a *source-related* aspect of persuasion. Then you alert your young friend to the doublespeak going on in the ad—the product "virtually guarantees" popularity. You ask what the word "virtually" means in this advertising claim and by doing so focus attention on the *message* itself and not the motives of the persuader. Finally, you point out that clever camera work and skillful editing have made the Rangers seem almost alive, when in reality they

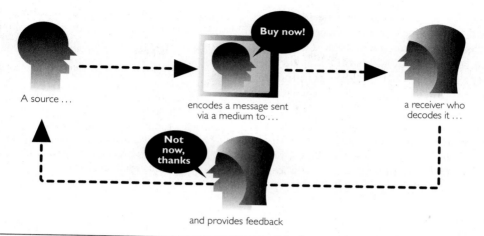

Figure 1.3. *The SMCR model.*

are composed of flimsy plastic. Now you have focused on the persuasive impact of the medium of transmitting the message, the *channel*. Then you might ask your young friend whether there is some internal or unstated reason he or she wants to be popular, thus focusing on the *receiver* element of this model.

These elements are also part of the persuasive process that is the focus of our definition of persuasion. Being prepared for persuasion involves being critical of all four elements. We must be alert to the motives of the source, whether they are obvious or disguised. We must pay attention to the message — its symbolic meaning. It is also a good idea to think about the channel, or medium, being used to send the message — what kinds of effects does it have? Finally, we need to be aware of our own role in persuasion — what are we adding?

We can use a number of tools to try to determine a source's **motives.** Language choice, for example, can tip us off to source intent. The ideas the source thinks will be persuasive to the audience are often expressed in the words the source chooses, the metaphors the source uses, and even

the kinds of sentences in the message. Are they questions? Exclamations? Short and punchy? Long and soothing?

For example, several years ago the Schick razor company came out with a "cosmetic" razor called Personal Touch. What do the words *cosmetic, personal,* and *touch* tell you about the Schick company's view of its potential customers? Is it aiming at a "macho" man? A business tycoon? A sports enthusiast? Or is it aiming at women who feel they deserve special attention and haven't been getting it lately?

Analyzing the source has two benefits. First, it alerts us to the persuasion being aimed at us. Second, it tells us things about the source that can help us when the source becomes our persuadee. In a way, sources tip us off to their *own* persuasive weaknesses. If you hear a friend trying to persuade you by using statistics, for instance, you can pretty safely bet that statistics will be a big help when you are trying to persuade that person.

We have other tools that allow us to analyze the **message** and what it is intended to say. In later chapters we will look at the organization of the message, its style, and the appeals it makes. You will learn to look at the evidence contained in the message and at how it relates to the persuasive goal. You may want to look at the nonverbal as well as the verbal elements in the message to see which of these codes has what kinds of effects.

For example, consider the wording of an ad placed in newspapers across the country by the International Fund for Animal Welfare (IFAW), which was opposing the harvest of baby seals in Canada—a highly emotional issue because the young seals are clubbed to death. As shown in Figure 1.4, the ad reads:

Do you really know what can go into a simple fish sandwich?
Fish caught by Canadian Fishermen who also kill the baby seals. Your purchase of a McDonald's or Burger King Fish Sandwich could help buy the boats, hard wooden clubs, and guns used by the seal hunters as they turn from fishing to the cruelty of killing adult and baby seals.

Figure 1.4. *Ad encouraging people to boycott fish sandwiches in order to stop the killing of harp seals. (Used by permission of IFAW.)*

By looking at the symbolic impact of the pictures and words such as "hard wooden clubs," receivers can be alerted to investigate more fully. Such an investigation might reveal that only a few Canadian fishermen are also seal hunters, that clubbing the seals is actually the least painful, most humane means of killing them (a claim made by the hunters), or that the flesh of the seal is not used in the fishwich as the picture suggests. By looking at the message carefully, receivers can be alerted to get other sides of the story or can identify places where the full story is not given or even where the argument is deceptive.

We can also train ourselves to be alert to the kinds of effects that various **channels** have on persuasion. Does the influence of TV, for example, make a message more or less effective? Has TV made us more vulnerable to certain message types? What are the effects of other media, such as radio and billboards? Are certain kinds of ballyhoo more useful or persuasive than others? Why do some media use certain techniques and others use different ones? By looking at the persuasive effects of this element in the SMCR model, receivers can begin to understand how a persuasive message works — what its goals are.

What do you think?

Why do you think Energizer uses so much television for its "Rabbit" ads?

Finally, you need to look at yourself, the **receiver** in the persuasive transaction, to determine what kinds of motives, biases, and perspectives *you* bring to the persuasive situation. What fascinations, needs, and desires do you bring to the world of persuasion? The answer, of course, is continually being sought by persuaders, whether they are politicians, ideologues, advertisers, propagandists, or even our co-workers, friends, and colleagues. Knowing even a part of the answer makes us more critical and responsible receivers.

Try to think of persuaders as persons who want to achieve certain *goals*. These goals are directed by one or more *strategies* and are put into action by specific *tactics*. Communication researcher Patricia Sullivan (1993) describes these steps in her analysis of a speech given by Reverend Jesse Jackson at a convention of the Democratic party. Jackson had a *goal* of uniting the party in his keynote speech. One of his strategies was to stress the common ground among the various factions of the party and another was to get the audience involved in the message. He used several *tactics* to put his strategies into action. For example, he titled his speech "Common Ground and Common Sense," thus creating the issue of unity as one that would be supported by all because it made sense. Jackson also used a call-response format for parts of the speech (uttering a phrase or sentence that the audience then repeats in unison) to unite and get audience involvement.

Rank's Model of Persuasion

As part of the National Council of Teachers of English (NCTE) Project on Doublespeak, several persons were asked to suggest ways of teaching people to be critical receivers of persuasion. Hugh Rank (1976), a researcher on the project, put the challenge this way:

> These kids are growing up in a propaganda blitz unparalleled in human history. . . . Schools should shift their emphasis in order to train the larger segment of our population in a new kind of literacy so that more citizens can recognize the more sophisticated techniques and patterns of persuasion. (p. 5)

Rank outlined a model of persuasion that could help teach people to be critical receivers. He called it the **intensify/downplay schema** and tried to keep it as simple as possible. It can serve as a good overall model for you.

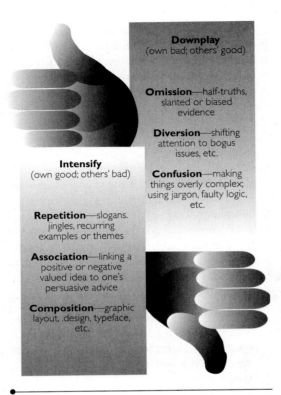

Downplay
(own bad; others' good)

Omission—half-truths, slanted or biased evidence

Diversion—shifting attention to bogus issues, etc.

Intensify
(own good; others' bad)

Confusion—making things overly complex; using jargon, faulty logic, etc.

Repetition—slogans. jingles, recurring examples or themes

Association—linking a positive or negative valued idea to one's persuasive advice

Composition—graphic layout, design, typeface, etc.

Figure 1.5. The intensify/downplay schema. (Adapted by permission of Hugh Rank.)

The basic idea behind Rank's model is that persuaders usually use two major strategies to achieve their goals. They either *intensify* certain aspects of their product, candidate, or ideology, or they *downplay* certain aspects. Often they do both. Like a magician, they want to draw attention away from some things and toward others in order to pull off the illusion. Figure 1.5 illustrates this model.

On the strategic level of the model, persuaders can choose to

1. Intensify their own good points.

2. Intensify the weak points of the opposition.

3. Downplay their own bad or weak points.

4. Downplay the good points of the opposition.

On the tactical level, persuaders can use **repetition, association,** and **composition** to intensify their own good points or the bad points of the opposition, while they can use **omission, diversion,** and **confusion** to downplay their own bad points or the good points of the opposition.

Persuasive strategy, then, is the overall step-by-step program for reaching one's goal. Strategy relies on tactics, which are the specific kinds of arguments or points one tries to make. Thus, if a candidate wants to persuade voters to support her (that is, her goal), she can try to make them feel good about her candidacy (her strategy of intensifying her own good), which she will accomplish by associating herself with forthright stands on issues; by repeating her campaign slogan on signs, buttons, bumperstickers, and advertisements; and by using the state capitol building in the background of all her ads and photos (her tactics of repetition, association, and composition). Let's explore the strategies and tactics of the Rank model in more depth.

Intensification

The first strategy in the Rank model is intensification. Within this strategy are the two substrategies of intensifying either one's own strong or good points or the weak or bad points of the opposition. Basic to all of us is the desire to look good in the eyes of the world. Some of the tactics that can be used to intensify our own good points and the other's bad points (making us look good by comparison) are *repetition, association,* and *composition.*

Repetition. One way we can intensify good or bad points about a product, person, or candidate is by repeating them over and over. Consider a series of Bud Lite TV ads, popular several years back. The basic format of these ads was to have the central character—a naive but good-natured and attractive young male—enter a bar and say, "Gimme a Lite," whereupon he was faced with one of a variety of "lights" he didn't intend, such as a flaming hoop or a blowtorch. His response was always the same, too—"I mean a Bud Lite," whereupon he was served the sponsor's product.

The harp seal advertisement repeatedly intensifies the bad aspects of the seal hunt through its brutal images and language and through the helpless- and innocent-looking baby seal. It also repeatedly puts you, the reader, into the story. Notice the words "your purchase," "if you made a pledge today," "you have it in your hands to save the baby seals today." This repetition intensifies IFAW's good possibilities if only each individual reader would make a commitment.

Association. Another tactic for intensification suggested by the Rank model is association, which relies on a three-part process: (1) a cause, product, or candidate is linked (2) to something already liked or disliked by (3) the audience; thus, the cause, product, or candidate picks up or is identified with the thing liked or disliked. In the harp seal ad, the hunters are associated with cruelty and brutality. When we first see the ad, most of us are shocked by the thought that baby seal meat might be mixed into the fish sandwich. The sandwich is pictured next to the baby seal. The clubbing scene provides negative association. Some of the minor details drive home the point (15,000 seals clubbed to death in twenty-eight days).

What do you think?

Why would Dennis Rodman be a good spokesperson for a tattoo parlor?

Persuaders engage in careful audience analysis to identify the fears, wants, and biases of their target audience. They then mesh their goals with this set of alignments. For example, politicians know that we have fears about cyberspace, so they tie these fears to their own cause by stating that, if elected, they will enact strict controls over the use of cyberspace. An advertiser might associate a product—a certain kind of athletic shoe—with a well-known professional athlete who uses them. The ad might also associate the shoes with everyday people who are athletic—with joggers, tennis players, or, as Nike did, even with a person in a wheelchair. This set of associations intensifies the good aspects of the shoe and demonstrates that one doesn't have to be an athlete to benefit from its features.

Composition. The third and final tactic of intensification is composition, which means emphasizing one's own good characteristics or the other's bad characteristics by changing the physical makeup of the message. This change is frequently accomplished nonverbally and can take several forms. For example, the makeup of the printed word can be altered, as in changing "U.S.A." to "U.$.A." or "America" to "Amerika," to send messages on several levels. The makeup, or composition, of a candidate's publicity photo can be manipulated. For example, by using the device of a low camera angle, a candidate can be made to look larger than he or she really is. The low angle also tells us to look up to the candidate. The layout of an advertisement can also be used for purposes of intensification.

Composition is also used by persuaders who create comparison and contrast in the media. Marshall McLuhan (1964) called this technique the "brushing of information against information." One bit of information about a candidate for political office is pictured against some dramatic setting—say, the Vietnam War Memorial in Washington, D.C. Perhaps music on the soundtrack is a muted version of "America the Beautiful," and a voiceover talks about the candidate's determination. The camera zooms back to show the true size of the memorial as the music now swells and the announcer says, "Senator Jones — a dedicated veteran, a dedicated senator, and a dedicated American." The ad might then end with its disclaimer: "This ad is paid for by thousands of dedicated Americans for Senator Jones — Vote for Jones on November 3 and you vote for dedication." The background, the music, the voiceover, and the printed words of the disclaimer on the screen all "compose" the ad's meaning. Change the background to the Lincoln Memorial and you change the meaning of the ad to some degree. Use a different kind of music, such as a military march, and again meaning is affected. So the brushing of information against other information creates sophisticated nuances of meaning through the tactics of intensification. In this case, both association and composition are central to the creation of meaning.

As noted earlier, juxtaposing the baby seal with the fishwich in the harp seal ad creates a dramatic effect — an innocent victim becomes part of your fishburger. Of course, this is not the case, but the initial association and the headline make the point emphatically enough to gross out the average McDonald's or Burger King customer. In the lower right-hand corner of the ad, the "Save the Seals" logo also uses a composition by superimposing the killing of a seal with the words "NØ to Canadian Fish." Further, the letter "Ø" with the slash through it looks like the international highway sign that we frequently see warning us not to turn left or not to park in a certain place. The composition of both the logo and picture, as well as the altering of the print, creates negative feelings toward Canadian fish.

As you can see, by using Rank's model for intensification as a starting place in becoming a critical receiver, you can gain insights into how a particular piece of persuasion works. You can do the same thing with the other component of the Rank model, downplaying.

Downplaying

Sometimes persuaders do not want to intensify or call attention to something (their own shortcomings, for example), because doing so would defeat their persuasive purpose. Likewise, it would not be useful to advertise the strong points of your competition. What the persuader does is to *downplay* his or her own bad points and the competitor's good points.

For example, in the presidential primaries of 1996, Steven Forbes downplayed his business experience and access to family wealth, while Lamar Alexander intensified his business experience and downplayed his wealth. In the meanwhile, Patrick Buchanan downplayed his part in the Watergate scandal twenty years earlier and intensified his positions on immigration and abortion, and Robert Dole downplayed his shifts on issues like abortion and prayer in the schools while intensifying his war experience and his leadership in the U.S. Senate. In another case of downplaying, both Ford and General Motors initially downplayed a number of industry innovations introduced by Chrysler Corporation — rebates, 7/70,000 warranties, the invention of the minivan, the reintroduction of the convertible, the introduction of the driver's (and later passenger's) air bag, and the promotion of the four-wheel-drive Jeep Cherokee as a vehicle for upscale owners as opposed to a macho outdoorsman. While both Ford and G.M. later tried to match Chrysler's efforts, the initial downplaying left the two latecomers with a "me too" image which had to be downplayed because Chrysler's preemptive innovations forced the issue. Let's look now at the specific tactics of downplaying: *omission, diversion,* and *confusion.*

Omission. Omission is simply the leaving out of critical information to avoid highlighting one's own shortcomings. For example, the Claussen company intensifies its own good when it advertises that its pickles are refrigerated rather than cooked and are therefore much crisper than Vlasic pickles, its major competition. However, Claussen *omits* telling the consumer that in order to extend the pickles' shelf life, they are relatively higher in sodium than Vlasic pickles (their own bad) and that refrigeration isn't necessary for Vlasic pickles (other's good). On the political front, in the 1992 presidential campaign, Bill Clinton omitted revealing that he had avoided military service.

Diversion. Diversion, another downplaying tactic, consists of shifting attention away from another's good points or one's own bad points. The basic purpose is to provide a substitute issue — sometimes called a "stalking horse" — to draw attention or fire from the opposition in order to divert their efforts from one's "own bad," or in another variation to divert attention away from "their good" points or issues.

For example, in the presidential primary campaigns of 1996, diversion was used in several ways. To divert attention from Patrick Buchanan's surprising popular appeal, the opposition provided information about Buchanan's statements of admiration for Hitler. In another case, Lamar Alexander wore wading boots to draw attention to his refusal to use negative ads and hence away from his failing campaign.

Humor can also be used to divert attention. For instance, the Energizer battery ads use humor by depicting a toy bunny that "keeps going and going" to divert attention from the fact that all alkaline batteries wear out in about the same period of time. During World War II, President Franklin Roosevelt was accused of misusing his war powers by sending a destroyer to retrieve his dog Fala. The Republicans and the press attacked him in a variety of ways. Finally, FDR used humor to divert attention from the issue and called a press conference at which he announced that while he could handle criticisms of himself and his family, he was putting his foot down when it came to picking on Fala. The warship issue quickly faded from public attention.

Another tactic is to use emotional appeals that rely on an opponent's personality or appearance, sometimes called the *ad hominem argument.* In this argument, the persuader diverts attention from the real issue by attacking the personality or character of his or her opponent. For example, consider the political cartoon in Figure 1.6.

A hot issue during the 1996 presidential primaries was the proposal for a "flat tax" first put forth by Steven Forbes, the multimillionaire son of the founder/publisher of *Forbes* magazine. His opposition quickly recognized the persuasive potential of this proposal — no more complicated tax forms, deductions, credits, and other details, and the simpler tax would permit a huge downsizing of the IRS. Soon Forbes' opponents floated their own versions of a flat tax, and the debate turned to the fine points of each alternative (e.g., whether one version permitted a deduction for interest on home mortgages or whether another version permitted a deduction for contribution to nonprofit charities). Splitting hairs on the proposals diverted attention away from the major question: Is a flat tax feasible, practical, and fairer than the present system? Finally, *splitting hairs* over certain arguments in many controversies can divert attention from the major issues of the debate and can consume valuable time from discussion of the central issues.

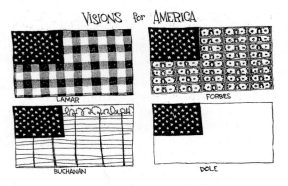

Figure 1.6. *This political cartoon uses composition to differentiate the styles and philosophies of four candidates for the GOP presidential nomination. Lamar Alexander, sending a down-home image, wore black-and-red checked woodsman-type wool shirts on the campaign trail. Steven Forbes spent $25 million of his own money in the primaries, while arch-conservative Pat Buchanan wanted to stop illegal immigration, particularly from Mexico, and to stop free-trade agreements. Robert Dole was rather dull. (© 1996, Washington Post Writers Group. Reprinted with permission.)*

Confusion. A final tactic for downplaying one's own weak points or the competition's strengths is to create *confusion*. This can be done either by using highly technical terminology or jargon that the receiver doesn't understand or by weaving an intricate and wandering answer that confuses the listener. For example, most Americans knew that the *Challenger* catastrophe had been caused by a faulty O-ring on the space shuttle's rocket boosters. Consider the following testimony before a special Presidential Commission given by a key executive of the company that made the O-rings. Commission member and former astronaut Neil Armstrong asked the executive about ice forming on the shuttle's outer surface (a symptom that the O-ring might fail). The executive responded:

> Apparently the facility in the original design did not have protection for this kind of consideration, although it may have been intended, and I think the freeze protection plan that was put into place was expected to handle the conditions with much less free water than was found as a result of going through that experience for the first time under real conditions.

While not using technical terms, the executive certainly used bureaucratic jargon that few of us could translate into a meaningful answer to Armstrong's question (Kowinski, 1987).

Consider the advertisement for a Canon A-1 camera shown in Figure 1.7. Note that the headline confuses through the use of jargon. What in blazes does "hexa-photo-cybernetic" mean? By looking more closely, you see that the Canon A-1 has six supposed advantages. That explains "hexa" (as in hexagon). Then we see that it has several automatic devices to match shutter speed with lens opening, which involves some mathematical programming of the apparatus; moreover, the settings are digitally displayed. So the word "cybernetic" can be honestly used. And "photo" simply relates to camera. Nevertheless, "hexa-photo-cybernetic" is pseudoscientific ad lingo intended to impress if not to confuse. The ad omits mentioning that many cameras in the same price range have similar features, and Canon is not alone among cameras in having some kind of automatic exposure sensors. Although Canon's having all the automatic features on a single camera was unique at the time the ad was published, the invented term "hexa-photo-cybernetic" is confusing, especially if it is intended for photographers interested in automatic features — they tend to be amateurs who prefer the camera to do the work while they merely point and shoot.

Figure 1.7. How is Rank's confusion used here? (Used by permission of Canon U.S.A., Inc.)

Another device for downplaying one's own weaknesses or the competition's strengths through confusion is the use of *faulty logic.* "She's Beautiful! She's Engaged! She Uses Earth Balsam Hand Creme!" is one example. The supposed logical flow is that because "she" uses the hand cream, she is beautiful, and because she is beautiful, she met and won the man of her dreams and is now engaged. Not even fairly naive consumers are likely to buy this whole package, but the idea that the hand cream will make the user more attractive to men is fairly likely to stick.

Rank cites a number of other ways to confuse, including *being inconsistent, contradicting,* and *talking in circles*—"V.O. is V.O." or "So Advanced, It's Simple."

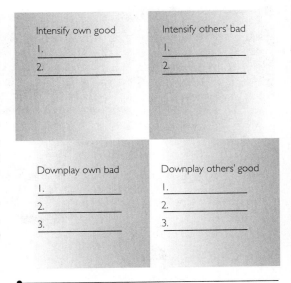

Figure 1.8. *Intensify/downplay scorecard.* (*By permission of Hugh Rank.*)

Self-Protection: A Method

In his discussion of doublespeak, Rank offers some general advice on how to detect the flaws of persuaders who use various tactics to intensify or downplay: "When they intensify, downplay." That is, when we recognize a propaganda blitz, we should be cool, detached, and skeptically alert not only to the inflated puffery of advertising with its dreams and promises, but also to intensified attack propaganda—the threats and exploitation of fears by a demagogue or government agent, elected or appointed. Rank also says, "When they downplay, intensify." A way to do so systematically is to divide a sheet of paper into quarters, as shown in Figure 1.8, and then enter the kinds of downplaying and intensifying being practiced. Simply by seeing these items, you can become more alert to what kind of manipulation is going on.

Let's try this technique with a brief example. Consider the ad for Smirnoff vodka in Figure 1.9. First let's look at the intensification used in the ad. Remember that the persuader may intensify by repeating, by using association, and by manipulating the composition of the message.

Notice the *repetition* of the product name in the ad. (This is also *intensification* of the product's own good, because consumer folklore includes the belief that the only true or authentic vodka must be Russian—and the name Smirnoff does seem Russian.) Then the ad uses *association* in its copy. Smirnoff vodka is associated with "Europe's elite," "proper food," a "delicious evening," being "impeccable," being "memorable," and fine crystal. So association is used to intensify the own-good aspect of the message. *Composition* is used to intensify in several ways. Look at how the picture is organized: The wine glasses are untouched, whereas the highball glasses are in people's hands and clearly have been sampled. *Word choice is*

Figure 1.9. Intensification and downplaying in a persuasive message. (Courtesy Ste. Pierre Smirnoff, a division of Heublein.)

used to intensify—another example of composition. The ad also intensifies the opposition's bad points: The wine just sat there. Wine can ruin your palate. Again, word choice intensifies the "badness" of wine. Wine is made to seem disreputable because it "plays with your palate," because it is "forceful."

Now, does the persuader *downplay* anything? Vodka can be potent, especially if you drink it like water during a dinner party. That fact is omitted. Instead we are told that it "leaves you breathless"—no one can smell that you've been drinking. There is some faulty logic here as well. Why is it amusing that while the Smirnoff flowed, the wine only "sat there"? Why is that "not surprising"? With all these allusions, the ad *confuses* the reader. By identifying the many tactics at work, persuadees can become alert to and critical of the persuasive messages that come their way.

We will discuss a number of other tools of analysis as we proceed, but Rank's intensify/ downplay tool is a useful general one to employ at first. You will want to try it with a variety of persuasive messages that you encounter. In future chapters, we will discuss the role of language as it is used to persuade. We will also look at how our own internal motives and drives can be exploited by those who wish to persuade us. Our preferences for certain kinds of logic can be used by the persuader who designs the message. Cultural premises that are trained into us from birth are the bases for many persuasive appeals. Finally, we are also affected by the way we respond to the different media used in persuasion.

Review and Conclusion

If you are now more alert to the possible ways you are being manipulated, you are well on your way to becoming a critical receiver. You are ready to arm yourself with some of the tools of analysis that make wise consumers, and there is a bonus for learning them. In learning how you are persuaded and in exploring the tactics that other persuaders use, you can become a more skillful persuader yourself. Seeing what works, in what circumstances, with what kinds of people, will be useful as you prepare to become a persuader. Skillful consumers of messages learn to be more effective producers of messages. As we move ahead, it will be useful to apply the tools of persuasion on your own or through using the study questions and exercises outlined at the end of each chapter.

It is also useful to examine the ways in which you are persuaded on the interpersonal level. Every day you make decisions in nonpublic settings. You decide to heed or reject your parents' advice on the basis of your interpersonal communication with them. They try to persuade you to major in a certain field, to seek a summer job, or to continue or cease dating a certain person. Rank's model can be helpful here, too. Identify what your parents intensify and downplay. You can do the same thing with other interpersonal relationships in which persuasion is used—with roommates, friends, or colleagues, or with your boss. You can also see whether identification or alignment is occurring between you and the other individuals, and spot the kinds of symbols that lead to or discourage identification. Critical analysis of interpersonal persuasion can help you make decisions and improve your critical reception skills in many situations. People are persuaded daily in the public arena through advertisements, speeches, radio or television programs, and newspaper or magazine articles; they need to remember that significant persuasion also frequently takes place in their personal lives.

Questions for Further Thought

1. If you or someone you know recently made a major purchase (for example, an auto, a CD player, or a word processor), identify the context in which you or your friend was persuaded. Where did the persuasion take place? In the showroom? through a television ad? interpersonally, such as in discussing the purchase with a friend? What kinds of appeals were made? What characteristics were intensified? downplayed?

2. Much persuasion occurs in interpersonal contexts. Examine one of your interpersonal relationships, such as that between you and your parents, your roommate, a teammate, or a fellow member of an organization or church. Describe how, when, and where persuasion has been used in the relationship. What characteristics about yourself have you intensified? downplayed? What characteristics has the other person intensified? downplayed? Has repetition been used? association? omission?

3. Beginning with the definition of *persuasion* offered in Chapter 1, attempt to create a model that reflects all the important elements of the definition.

4. Identify three types of persuasion you have seen recently (such as advertisements or speeches), and analyze each according to the definition offered in this chapter. What are the symbols? What is the persuader's intent? What does the persuasion say about the persuadee's probable frame of reference?

5. What are the tactics of intensification? How do they work? Give examples of their use on television, in print, on radio, by politicians, and by advertisers.

6. What are the tactics of downplay? How do they work? Give examples of their use on television, in print, on radio, by politicians, and by advertisers.

7. What is a "propaganda blitz"? Identify one currently going on in media coverage of an event or in regard to some political issue. Give an example of one that has been or is now being used on your campus.

8. Identify some current examples of the strategies of intensification and downplaying being used in Russia as it continues to struggle for a sound economic system.

9. Where are some of the tactics of intensification and downplaying being used in regard to environmental issues?

References

Berlo, F. K. (1960). *The process of persuasion*. New York: Holt, Rinehart & Winston.

Brembeck, W., & Howell, W. S. (1952). *Persuasion: A means of social control*. Englewood Cliffs, NJ: Prentice-Hall.

Brembeck, W., & Howell, W. S. (1976). *Persuasion: A means of social control* (2nd ed.). Englewood Cliffs, NJ: Prentice-Hall.

Burke, K. (1970). *A grammar of motives*. Berkeley: University of California Press.

Fotheringham, W. (1966). *Perspectives on persuasion*. Boston: Allyn & Bacon.

Kowinski, W. (1987). Jargon—just say no. *Metamorphoses, 5*, 16–19.

McLuhan, M. (1964). *Understanding media: The extensions of man*. New York: Signet Books.

Nielsen, A. C. (1993). *The 1993 Nielsen report on television*. Northbrook, IL: Nielsen Media Research.

Postman, N. (1981). Interview. *U.S. News & World Report*, January 19, 1981, 43.

Rank, H. (1976). Teaching about public persuasion. In D. Dieterich (Ed.), *Teaching and Doublespeak*. Urbana, IL: National Council of Teachers of English.

Roberts, R. (1924). *The works of Aristotle*. Oxford, Eng.: Clarendon Press.

Shannon, C. E., & Weaver, W. (1949). *The mathematical theory of communication*. Urbana: University of Illinois Press.

Sullivan, P. A. (1993). Signification and Afro-American rhetoric: A case study of Jesse Jackson's "Common ground and common sense" speech. *Communication Quarterly, 41*, 1–15.

2

Perspectives on Ethics in Persuasion

Richard L. Johannesen
Northern Illinois University

Evidence mounted during the 1980s and 1990s of citizen concern with the decline of ethical behavior, especially of persons in positions of significant public or private responsibility. "What Ever Happened to Ethics?" asked the cover story of *Time* (May 25, 1987). "A Nation of Liars?" inquired *U.S. News and World Report* (February 23, 1987). A poll in February 1987 by *U.S. News* and the Cable News Network showed that more than half of the persons surveyed believed that people were less honest than ten years earlier. According to *Time:* "Large sections of the nation's ethical roofing have been sagging badly, from the White House to churches, schools, industries, medical centers, law firms and stock brokerages." *Time* concluded: "Ethics, often dismissed as a prissy Sunday School word, now is at the center of a new national debate." Political commentators and private citizens continued to debate the issue of "character" as it applied to ethics in the public and private lives of President Bill Clinton, Speaker of the House Newt Gingrich, and other political leaders. Magazine articles explored the decline of an appropriate "sense of shame" as a norm in American culture (*Atlantic Monthly,*

February 1992, pp. 40–70; *Newsweek,* February 6, 1995, pp. 21–25). A national survey of 3600 college students at twenty-three colleges (*Washington Post National Weekly Edition,* December 7–13, 1992, p. 36) revealed that one in six college students had lied on a résumé or job application or during a job interview; that two out of five had lied to a boss and one out of three had lied to a customer during the past year; and that one out of five admitted cheating on an exam. *Time* magazine devoted seven pages to the topic of "Lies, Lies, Lies" (October 5, 1992).*

Imagine that you are an audience member listening to a speaker—call him Mr. Bronson. His aim is to persuade you to contribute money to the cancer research program of a major medical research center. Suppose that, with one exception,

---

*This chapter, in whole or in part, may not be reproduced without written permission from the publisher and from the author. For a much more extensive exploration of the perspectives, standards, and issues discussed in this chapter and identification of relevant resource materials, see Johannesen (1996). My personal view of ethical persuasion is rooted in the political perspective of American representative democracy and in Martin Buber's conception of dialogue.

all the evidence, reasoning, and motivational appeals he employs are valid and above ethical suspicion. However, at one point in his speech, Bronson *consciously* chooses to use a set of *false* statistics to scare you into believing that, during your lifetime, there is a much greater probability of your getting some form of cancer than actually is true.

To promote analysis of the ethics of this hypothetical persuasive situation, consider these issues. If you, or the society at large, view Bronson's persuasive end, or goal, as worthwhile, does the worth of his end justify his use of false statistics as one means to achieve that end? Does the fact that he consciously chose to use false statistics make a difference in your evaluation? If he used the false statistics out of ignorance or out of failure to check his sources, how might your ethical judgment be altered? Should he be condemned as an unethical person, as an unethical speaker, or, in this instance, for use of a specific unethical technique?

Carefully consider the standards, and the reasons behind those standards, that you would employ to make your ethical judgment of Bronson. Are the standards purely pragmatic? (In other words, should he avoid the false statistics because he might get caught?) Are they societal in origin? (If he gets caught, his credibility as a representative would be weakened with this and future audiences, or his getting caught might weaken the credibility of other cancer society representatives.) Should he be ethically criticized for violating an implied agreement between you and him? (You might not expect a representative of a famous research institute to use questionable techniques, and thus you would be especially vulnerable.) Finally, should Bronson's conscious use of false statistics be considered unethical because you are denied accurate, relevant information you need in order to make an intelligent decision on a public issue?

As receivers and senders of persuasion, we have the responsibility to uphold appropriate ethical standards for persuasion, to encourage freedom of inquiry and expression, and to promote the health of public debate as crucial to democratic decision making. To achieve these goals, we must understand their complexity and recognize the difficulty of achieving them.

In this chapter, I do not intend to argue my own case for the merit of any one particular ethical perspective or set of criteria as *the best one*. Rather, I view my role here, as I do in the classroom, as one of providing information, examples, and insights and of raising questions for discussion. The purpose is to stimulate you to make reasoned choices among ethical options in developing your own position or judgment.

Ethical issues focus on value judgments concerning degrees of right and wrong, goodness and badness, in human conduct. Persuasion, as one type of human behavior, always contains *potential* ethical issues because

1. It involves one person, or a group of people, attempting to influence other people by altering their beliefs, attitudes, values, and overt actions.

2. It involves conscious choices among ends sought and rhetorical means used to achieve the ends.

3. It necessarily involves a potential judge (any or all of the receivers, the persuader, or an independent observer).

As a receiver and sender of persuasion, how you evaluate the ethics of a persuasive instance will differ, depending on the ethical standards you are using. You may even choose to ignore ethical judgment entirely. Several justifications are often used to avoid direct analysis and resolution of ethical issues in persuasion:

1. Everyone knows this appeal or tactic obviously is unethical, so there is nothing to talk about.

2. Only success matters, so ethics are irrelevant to persuasion.

3. After all, ethical judgments are only matters of our individual personal opinion, so there are no final answers.

Nevertheless, potential ethical questions exist, regardless of how they are answered. Whether you wish it or not, consumers of persuasion generally will judge your effort, formally or informally, in part by their relevant ethical criteria. If for none other than the pragmatic reason of enhancing chances of success, you would do well to consider the ethical standards held by your audience.

Ethical Responsibility

Persuaders' ethical responsibilities may stem from a status or position they have earned or have been granted, from commitments (promises, pledges, agreements) they have made, or from the consequences (effects) of their communication for others. Responsibility includes the elements of fulfilling duties and obligations, of being accountable to other individuals and groups, of being accountable as evaluated by agreed upon standards, and of being accountable to one's own conscience. But an essential element of responsible communication, for both sender and receiver, is exercise of thoughtful and deliberate judgment. That is, the responsible communicator carefully analyzes claims, soundly assesses probable consequences, and conscientiously weighs relevant values. In a sense, a responsible communicator is *response-able*. She or he exercises the ability to respond (is responsive) to the needs and communication of others in sensitive, thoughtful, fitting ways.*

Whether persuaders seem *intentionally and knowingly* to use particular content or techniques is a factor that most of us take into account in judg-

---

*This discussion of responsibility is based on Pennock (1960), Freund (1960), Niebuhr (1963), and Pincoffs (1975).

ing degree of communication ethicality. If a dubious communication behavior seems to stem more from accident, from an unintentional slip of the tongue, or even from ignorance, we are often less harsh in our ethical assessment. For most of us, it is the intentional use of ethically questionable tactics that merits our harshest condemnation.

In contrast, it might be contended that, in argumentative and persuasive situations, communicators have an ethical obligation to doublecheck the soundness of their evidence and reasoning before they present it to others; sloppy preparation is not an adequate excuse to lessen the harshness of our ethical judgment. A similar view might be advanced concerning elected or appointed government officials. If they use obscure or jargon-laden language that clouds the accurate and clear representation of ideas, even if it is not intended to deceive or hide, they are ethically irresponsible. Such officials, according to this view, should be obligated to communicate clearly and accurately with citizens in fulfillment of their governmental duties. As a related question we can ask, does *sincerity* of intent release a persuader from ethical responsibility concerning means and effects? Could we say that *if* Adolf Hitler's fellow Germans judged him to be sincere, they should not have assessed the ethics of his persuasion? In such cases, evaluations are probably best carried out if we appraise sincerity and ethicality separately. For example, a persuader sincere in intent may use an unethical strategy.

What are the ethics of audience adaptation? (See Figure 2.1.) Most persuaders seek to secure some kind of response from receivers. To what degree is it ethical for them to alter their ideas and proposals to adapt to the needs, capacities, desires, and expectations of an audience? To secure acceptance, some persuaders adapt to an audience to the extent of so changing their ideas that the idea is no longer really theirs. These persuaders merely say what the audience wants to hear, regardless of their *own* convictions.

Figure 2.1. *How are the ethics of audience adaptation at issue here? (Calvin & Hobbes Copyright 1989 Universal Press Syndicate. Reprinted with permission. All rights reserved.)*

On the other hand, some measure of adaptation in language choice, supporting materials, organization, and message transmission to reflect the specific nature of the audience is a crucial part of successful communication. No ironclad rule can be set down here. Persuaders must decide the ethical balance point between their idea in its pure form and that idea modified to achieve maximum impact with the audience.

The Importance of Ethics

"A society without ethics is a society doomed to extinction," argues philosopher S. Jack Odell (in Merrill and Odell, 1983). According to Odell, the "basic concepts and theories of ethics provide the framework necessary for working out one's own moral or ethical code." Odell believes that "ethical principles are necessary preconditions for the existence of a social community. Without ethical principles it would be impossible for human beings to live in harmony and without fear, despair, hopelessness, anxiety, apprehension, and uncertainty" (p. 95).

A societal or personal system of ethics is not a magic or automatic cure-all for individual or collective ills. What can ethical theory and systematic reflection on ethics contribute? One answer is suggested by philosopher Carl Wellman (1988):

> An ethical system does not solve all one's practical problems, but one cannot choose and act rationally without some explicit or implicit ethical system. An ethical theory does not tell a person what to do in any given situation, but neither is it completely silent; it tells one what to consider in making up one's mind what to do. The practical function of an ethical system is primarily to direct our attention to the relevant considerations, the reasons that determine the rightness or wrongness of any act (p. 305).

Responsibilities of Receivers

What are your ethical responsibilities as a receiver or respondent in persuasion? An answer to this question stems in part from the image we hold of the persuasion process. Receivers bear little responsibility if audience members are viewed as inert, passive, defenseless receptacles, as mindless blotters uncritically accepting ideas and arguments. In contrast, persuasion can be viewed as a transaction in which both persuaders and persuadees bear mutual responsibility to participate actively in the process. This image of persuadees as active participants suggests several responsibilities, perhaps captured by two phrases: reasoned skepticism and appropriate feedback.

Reasoned skepticism includes a number of elements. It represents a balanced position between the undesirable extremes of being too open-minded or gullible, on the one hand, and being too closed-minded or dogmatic, on the other. You are not simply an unthinking blotter "soaking up" ideas and arguments. Rather, you ex-

What do you think?

What are some of a receiver's "response-abilities"?

ercise your capacities actively to search for meaning, to analyze and synthesize, and to judge soundness and worth. You do something to and with the information you receive: You process, interpret, and evaluate it. Also, you inform yourself about issues being discussed, and you tolerate, even seek out, divergent and controversial viewpoints, the better to assess what is being presented.

As a receiver of persuasion, you must realize that accurate understanding of a persuader's message may be hindered by attempting to impose your own ethical standards on that persuader. Your immediate "gut-level" ethical judgments may cause you to distort the intended meaning. Only after reaching an accurate understanding of the persuader's ideas can you reasonably evaluate the ethics of his or her persuasive strategies or purposes.

In this era of distrust of the truthfulness of public communication, reasoned skepticism also requires that we combat the automatic assumption that most public communication is untrustworthy. Just because a communication is of a certain type or comes from a certain source (government, candidate, news media, advertiser), it must not automatically, without evaluation, be rejected as tainted or untruthful. Clearly, you must always exercise caution in acceptance and care in evaluation, as emphasized throughout this book. Using the best evidence available, you arrive at your best judgment. However, to condemn a message as untruthful or unethical solely because it stems from a suspect source and before directly assessing it is to exhibit decision-making behavior detrimental to our political, social, and economic system. Rejection of the message, if such be the judgment, must come after, not before, evaluation of it. As with a defendant in the courtroom, public communication must be presumed ethically innocent until it has been proven "guilty." However, when techniques of persuasion do weaken or undermine the confidence and trust necessary for intelligent public decision making, they can be condemned as unethical.

As an active participant in the persuasion process, you need to provide **appropriate feedback** to persuaders. Your response, in most situations, should be an honest and accurate reflection of your true comprehension, belief, feeling, or judgment. Otherwise, persuaders are denied the relevant and accurate information they need to make decisions. Your response might be verbal or nonverbal, oral or written, immediate or delayed. A response of understanding, puzzlement, agreement, or disagreement could be reflected through your facial expression, gestures, posture, inquiries, statements during a question-answer period, and letters to editors or advertisers. In some cases, because of your special expertise on a subject, you even may have the obligation to respond, to provide feedback, while other receivers remain silent. You need to decide whether the degree and type of your feedback are appropriate for the subject, audience, and occasion of the persuasion. For instance, to interrupt with questions, or even to heckle, might be appropriate in a few situations but irresponsible in many others.

Disagreement and conflict sometimes occur in intimate and informal interpersonal settings. In such situations, when at least one participant may be emotionally vulnerable, individual personalities often affect each other in direct and powerful ways. When you as a receiver in such a situation decide to respond by expressing strong disagreement, you should avoid "unfair" tactics of verbal conflict because they are irresponsible (Ross & Ross, 1982): Avoid monopolizing the talk with the intent of preventing others from expressing their position. Avoid entrapment, in which you lure someone into saying something that you intend to use later to embarrass or hurt them. Avoid verbally "hitting below the belt" by taking unfair advantage of what you know to be the other person's special psychological vulnerability. Avoid stockpiling or accumulating numer-

ous grievances so that you can overwhelm others by dumping the complaints on them all at once. Finally, avoid dragging in numerous irrelevant or trivial issues and arguments in order to pile up an advantage.

Some Ethical Perspectives

We will briefly explain six major ethical perspectives as potential viewpoints for analyzing ethical issues in persuasion. As categories, these perspectives are not exhaustive, mutually exclusive, or given in any order of precedence.

As a receiver of persuasion, you can use one or a combination of such perspectives to evaluate the ethical level of a persuader's use of language (such as metaphors, ambiguity) or of evidence and reasoning. We also can use them to assess the ethics of psychological techniques, such as appeals to needs and values, the stimulation and resolution of dissonance and imbalance, or the appeal to widely held cultural images and myths. The persuasive tactics of campaigns and social movements can also (indeed must) be subjected to ethical scrutiny.

Religious Perspectives

Religious perspectives stem from the moral guidelines and the "thou shalt nots" embodied in the ideology and sacred literature of various religions. For instance, the Bible warns against lying, slander, and bearing false witness. Taoist religion stresses empathy and insight, rather than reason and logic, as roads to truth. Citing facts and demonstrating logical conclusions are minimized in Taoism in favor of feeling and intuition. These and other religiously derived criteria could be used to assess the ethics of persuasion.

On two weekends in January 1987, evangelist Oral Roberts recounted on his syndicated television program an encounter with God the previous year. God told Roberts that he would not be allowed to live beyond March 1987 unless he raised $8 million to be used for sixty-nine scholarships for medical students at Oral Roberts University to allow them to serve in medical clinics overseas. In an emotion-laden plea to his viewers, Roberts asked, "Will you help me extend my life?" Roberts's chief spokesperson, Jan Dargatz, defended Roberts's motives to reporters but conceded that his "methods have hit the fan." Dargatz said that Roberts sincerely believed the fund drive was a "do-or-die effort" and believed it "from the very core of his being." The Reverend John Wolf, senior minister of Tulsa's All Souls Unitarian Church, condemned the appeal as "emotional blackmail" and as an "act of desperation" (Buursma, 1987). Another news report revealed that in 1986 Roberts had made a similar appeal. Roberts told a Dallas audience that his "life is on the line" and that God "would take me this year" if he did not raise necessary funds to finance "holy missionary teams." "Because if I don't do it," Roberts said, "I'm going to be gone before the year is out. I'll be with the Father. I know it as much as I'm standing here." Roberts failed to raise the necessary money (*Chicago Tribune*, February 26, 1987).

To assess the ethicality of Roberts's appeals, you might bring to bear an ethic for Christian evangelism developed by Emory Griffin (1976). For example, to what degree could Roberts's persuasion be condemned as that of a rhetorical "rapist" who used psychological coercion to force a commitment? Intense emotional appeals, such as to guilt, effectively "remove the element of conscious choice." Or is Roberts's persuasion more that of a rhetorical "seducer" who uses deception, flattery, or irrelevant appeals to success, money, duty, patriotism, popularity, or comfort to entice an audience? What other ethical standards rooted in Christian doctrine or scripture might be used to evaluate Roberts's appeals, and how might those standards be applied?

Human Nature Perspectives

Human nature perspectives probe the *essence* of human nature by asking what makes a human fundamentally human. They identify unique characteristics of human nature that distinguish us from "lower" forms of life. Such characteristics can then be used as standards for judging the ethics of persuasion. Among some of the suggested characteristics are capacity to reason, capacity to create and use symbols, capacity for mutual appreciative understanding, and capacity to make value judgments. The assumption is that uniquely human attributes should be promoted, thereby promoting fulfillment of maximum individual potential. A determination could be made of the degree to which a persuader's appeals and techniques either foster or undermine the development of a fundamental human characteristic. A technique that *de*humanizes, that makes a person less than human, would be unethical. Whatever the political, religious, or cultural context, a person would be assumed to possess certain uniquely human attributes worthy of promotion through communication.

In 1990 in Florida, a U.S. District Court judge declared obscene the album *As Nasty As They Wanna Be* by the rap group 2 Live Crew. But in a local trial in Florida that year, three members of 2 Live Crew were acquitted of obscenity charges for performing the songs. These incidents are part of a larger controversy concerning lyrics for music and rap songs that explicitly refer to the sexual and violent abuse and debasement of women and that attack ethnic groups. For example, lyrics on the *Nasty* album vividly describe the bursting of vaginal walls, forcing women to have anal or oral sex, forcing them to lick feces, and such acts as urination, incest, and group sex. Similarly sexually violent lyrics can be found in songs by such individuals and groups as Judas Priest, Great White, Ice-T, and Guns N' Roses. And bigotry against immigrants, homosexuals, and

African Americans surfaces in Guns N' Roses song, "One in a Million."

Regardless of whether such lyrics are judged obscene or whether they are protected by the freedom-of-speech clause of the First Amendment, many would say that they should be condemned as unethical (Johannesen, 1997). Such lyrics treat women not as persons but as objects or body parts to be manipulated for selfish satisfaction of males. These lyrics dehumanize, depersonalize, and trivialize women and celebrate violence against them, and they reinforce inaccurate and unfair stereotypes of women, homosexuals, and ethnic groups. How do *you* believe a human nature perspective on communication ethics might be used to assess such lyrics?

Political Perspectives

The implicit or explicit values and procedures accepted as crucial to the health and growth of a particular political-governmental system are the focus of political perspectives. Once these essential values are identified for that political system, they can be used for evaluating the ethics of persuasive means and ends within that system. The assumption is that public communication should foster achievement of these values; persuasive techniques that retard, subvert, or circumvent these basic political values would be condemned as unethical. Different political systems usually embody differing values leading to differing ethical judgments. Within the context of American representative democracy, for example, various analysts pinpoint values and procedures they deem fundamental to healthy functioning of our political system and, thus, values that can guide ethical scrutiny of persuasion therein. Such values and procedures include enhancement of citizen capacity to reach rational decisions, access to channels of public communication, access to relevant and accurate information on public issues,

maximization of freedom of choice, toleration of dissent, honesty in presenting motivations and consequences, and thoroughness and accuracy in presenting evidence and alternatives.

In the late 1980s and early 1990s, the issue of "hate speech" on college and university campuses illustrated the tension between the right of freedom of speech and the ethically responsible exercise of that right. On one campus eight Asian American students were harassed for almost an hour by a group of football players who called them "Oriental faggots." On another campus white fraternity members harassed a black student by chanting, "Coon," "Nigger," and "Porch monkey." At a different school a white male freshman was charged under the school's speech code with racial harassment for calling five black female students "water buffaloes."

In response to hate-speech incidents, numerous colleges and universities have instituted speech codes to punish hateful and offensive public messages. Among the forms of expression punishable at various schools are:

- Use of derogatory names, inappropriately directed laughter, inconsiderate jokes, and conspicuous exclusion of another person from conversation

- Language that stigmatizes or victimizes individuals or that creates an intimidating or offensive environment

- Face-to-face use of epithets, obscenities, and other forms of expression that by accepted community standards degrade, victimize, stigmatize, or pejoratively depict persons based on their personal, intellectual, or cultural diversity

- Extreme or outrageous acts or communications intended to harass, intimidate, or humiliate a student on the basis of race, color, or national origin, thus reasonably causing him or her severe emotional distress

Whether hate speech is protected by the First Amendment or whether campus speech codes are constitutionally legal, specific instances of hate speech should be evaluated for their degree of ethicality (Johannesen, 1997). Although hate speech could be assessed according to various ethical perspectives (such as human nature), how might values and procedures central to an American democratic political perspective be used to judge hate speech?

Situational Perspectives

To make ethical judgments, situational perspectives focus *regularly* and *primarily* on the elements of the specific persuasive situation at hand. Virtually all perspectives (those mentioned here and others) make some allowances, on occasion, for the modified application of ethical criteria in special circumstances. However, an extreme situational perspective *routinely* makes judgments *only* in light of *each different context*. Criteria from broad political, human nature, religious, or other perspectives are minimized; absolute and universal standards are avoided (see Figure 2.2). Among the concrete contextual factors relevant to making a purely situational ethical evaluation are:

1. Role or function of the persuader for the audience

2. Expectations held by receivers concerning such matters as appropriateness and reasonableness

3. Degree of receiver awareness of the persuader's techniques

4. Goals and values held by receivers

5. Degree of urgency for implementing the persuader's proposal

6. Ethical standards for communication held by receivers

"ROCCO, ARE YOU LISTENING?"

Figure 2.2. *How might situational ethics apply here? (© 1993 by Sidney Harris,* Hemispheres *Magazine.)*

From an extreme situational perspective, for instance, it might be argued that an acknowledged leader in a time of clear crisis has a responsibility to rally support and thus could employ so-called emotional appeals that circumvent human processes of rational, reflective decision making. Or it might be argued that a persuader may ethically use techniques such as innuendo, guilt by association, and unfounded name calling as long as the receivers both recognize and approve of those methods.

Legal Perspectives

A legal perspective would take the general position that illegal human communication behavior also is unethical. That which is not specifically illegal is viewed as ethical. In other words, legality and ethicality are made synonymous. Such an approach certainly has the advantage of allowing simple ethical decisions. We would only need to measure communication techniques against current laws and regulations to determine whether a technique is ethical. We might, for example, turn for ethical guidance to the regulations governing advertising set forth by the Federal Trade Commission or the Federal Communications Commission. Or we might use Supreme Court criteria, or state legislation, defining obscenity, pornography, libel, or slander to judge whether a particular message is unethical on those grounds.

However, many people would feel uneasy with this legalistic approach to communication ethics. They would contend that obviously there are some things that are legal but are ethically dubious. And some social protesters for civil rights and against the Vietnam War during the 1960s and 1970s admitted that their actions then were illegal but contended they were justifiable on ethical and moral grounds. Persons holding such views would reject any conception of ethicality and legality as synonymous, would view ethics as much broader than legality, and would argue that not everything that is unethical should be made illegal.

How should we answer the question, to what degree can or should we enforce ethical standards for communication through government law or regulation? What degrees of soundness might there be in two old but seemingly contrary sayings: "You can't legislate morality" and "There ought to be a law"? In twentieth-century society in the United States, very few ethical standards for communication are codified in governmental laws or regulations. As indicated earlier, FCC or FTC regulations on the content of advertising and laws and court decisions on obscenity and libel represent the governmental approach. But such examples are rare compared to the large number of laws and court decisions specifying the boundaries of freedom of speech and press in our society. Rather, our society applies ethical standards for communication through the more indirect avenues of group consensus, social pressure,

persuasion, and formal-but-voluntary codes of ethics.

Controversies surrounding computer communication on the Internet and World Wide Web illustrate not only the tension between freedom and responsibility but also pressures for legalistic approaches to ethics and for the formation of formal codes of ethics. Should you be free to say or depict anything you want, without restriction, on the Internet, e-mail, or WWW? The freedom-responsibility tension is underscored by Frank Connolly, a professor of computer science at American University (*Washington Post National Weekly Edition*, Oct. 30–Nov. 5, 1995, p. 36): "With the Internet, we are in the situation where there are no controls, no cyber-cops, no speed limits. The other side of these freedoms is that individuals have to exercise responsibility for their actions." But there are pressures for controls and for formal rules of responsibility. In February 1996 Congress passed the Communications Decency Act to punish the publishing of "indecent" or "patently offensive" material on the Internet—material that could be available to children as well as adults. But in June 1996 a three-judge U.S. Court of Appeals decision declared the Decency Act unconstitutional. University officials debated whether to apply existing campus speech codes that prohibit "hate speech" and harassment to the Internet and e-mail activities of students or whether to formulate special codes of computer communication ethics to guide student use. Virginia Tech University, for example, instituted a student code that prohibited abusive conduct, in words or actions, that "demeans, intimidates, threatens, or otherwise interferes with another person's rightful action or comfort," *both online and elsewhere on campus*. The dean of students at Virginia Tech said the university's position was that "if you use our server, then you have some responsibility because you associate the name of the institution with what you say." (See, for example, *Washington Post National Weekly Edition*,

Oct. 30–Nov. 5, 1995, p. 36; Nov. 6–12, 1995, p. 27; *Chicago Tribune*, Nov. 24, 1995, sec. 1, p. 30.) What is your view on how ethical responsibility for computer communication on the Internet should be promoted? On your campus, what official policies (set how and by whom?) govern ethically responsible communication on the Internet and World Wide Web? How adequately and appropriately do these policies speak to specific issues of communication ethics? Do these policies actually seem to address matters of legality more than ethicality?

Dialogical Perspectives

Dialogical perspectives emerge from current scholarship on the nature of communication as dialogue rather than as mono-logue.* Such perspectives contend that the attitudes toward each other among participants in a communication situation are an index of the ethical level of that communication. Some attitudes are held to be more fully human, humane, and facilitative of personal self-fulfillment than are other attitudes.

What do you think?

Which of the perspectives seems most useful to you?

Communication as *dialogue* is characterized by such attitudes as honesty, concern for the welfare and improvement of others, trust, genuineness, open-mindedness, equality, mutual respect, empathy, humility, directness, lack of pretense, nonmanipulative intent, sincerity, encouragement of free expression, and acceptance of others as individuals with intrinsic worth regardless of differences over belief or behavior.

Communication as *monologue*, in contrast, is marked by such qualities as deception, superiority,

exploitation, dogmatism, domination, insincerity, pretense, personal self-display, self-aggrandizement, judgmentalism that stifles free expression, coercion, possessiveness, condescension, self-defensiveness, and viewing others as objects to be manipulated. In the case of persuasion, then, the techniques and presentation of the persuader would be scrutinized to determine the degree to which they reveal an ethical dialogical attitude or an unethical monological attitude toward receivers.

How might ethical standards rooted in a dialogical perspective be applied to political campaign persuasion? Consider the face-to-face question-and-answer "citizen forums" held by Bill Clinton with voters during the 1992 presidential campaign. For any particular forum, you could assess the degree to which the communication of participants reflected and promoted dialogical rather than monological attitudes. How might a dialogical ethical perspective apply to intimate interpersonal communication situations such as between friends, family, lovers, and spouses? Earlier in the section on responsibilities of receivers, some "unfair" tactics of verbal conflict in interpersonal communication were summarized. How would you assess those tactics from a dialogical perspective?

With the preceding ethical perspectives (religious, human nature, political, situational, legal, dialogical), we can confront a variety of questions that underscore difficult issues relevant to ethical problems in persuasion. As receivers constantly bombarded with a variety of verbal and nonverbal persuasive messages, we continually face resolution of one or another of these fundamental issues.

Ethics, Propaganda, and the Demagogue

Is propaganda unethical? The answer to this question in part depends on how propaganda is defined. As Larson will emphasize in a later chapter,

---

*For a general analysis of communication as dialogue and monologue, see Johannesen (1971). See also Friedman (1960).

numerous, often widely divergent, definitions abound. Originally, the term "propaganda" was associated with the efforts of the Roman Catholic church to persuade people to accept the church's doctrine. Such efforts were institutionalized in 1622 by Pope Gregory XV when he created the Sacred Congregation for Propagating the Faith. The word "propaganda" soon came to designate not only institutions seeking to propagate a doctrine but also the doctrine itself and the communication techniques employed.

Today one cluster of definitions of propaganda presents a *neutral* position toward the ethical nature of propaganda. A definition combining the key elements of such neutral views might be: *Propaganda is a campaign of mass persuasion.* According to this view, propaganda represents an organized, continuous effort to persuade a mass audience, primarily using the mass media (see Qualter, 1962; Kecskemeti, 1973). Propaganda would thus include advertising and public relations efforts; national political election campaigns; the persuasive campaigns of some social reform movements; and the organized efforts of national governments to win friends abroad, maintain domestic morale, and undermine an opponent's morale both in "hot" and "cold" war. Such a view stresses communication channels and audiences and categorizes propaganda as one species of persuasion. Just as persuasion may be sound or unsound, ethical or unethical, so, too, may propaganda.

Another cluster of definitions takes a *negative* stance toward the ethical nature of propaganda. Definitions in this cluster probably typify the view held by many average American citizens. A definition combining the key elements of such negative views might be: *Propaganda is the intentional use of suggestion, irrelevant emotional appeals, and pseudoproof to circumvent human rational decision-making processes* (see Werkmeister, 1957; Chase, 1956). Such a view stresses communica-

tion techniques and sees propaganda as *inherently* unethical.

Are the traditional propaganda devices always to be viewed as unethical? Later Larson will describe the traditional list: name-calling, glittering generality, transfer, testimonial, plain folks, card stacking, and bandwagon. Such a list, however, does not constitute a surefire guide, a "handy-dandy" checklist, for exposing unethical persuasion. The ethics of at least some of these techniques depends on how they are used in a given context.

The *plain folks* technique stresses humble origins and modest backgrounds shared by the communicator and audience. The persuader emphasizes to the audience, although usually not in these words, that "we're all just plain folks." In his whistle-stop speeches to predominantly rural, Republican audiences during the 1948 presidential campaign, Democrat Harry Truman typically used the plain folks appeal to establish common ground in introductions to his speeches. He used the device to accomplish one of the purposes of the introductory segment of most speeches—namely, to establish rapport; he did not rely on it for proof in the main body of his speeches. If a politician relied primarily on the plain folks appeal as pseudoproof in *justifying* the policy he or she advocated, such usage could be condemned as unethical. Furthermore, Truman really was the kind of person who could legitimately capitalize on his actual plain folks background. A politician of a more privileged and patrician background, such as Edward Kennedy, could be condemned for using an unethical technique *if* he were to appeal to farmers and factory workers by saying "you and I are just plain folks."

Today the label "demagogue" is frequently used to render a negative ethical judgment of a communicator. Too often, the label is only vaguely defined—the criteria used to evaluate a person as a demagogue are unspecified. In ancient

Greece, a demagogue simply was a leader or orator who championed the cause of the common people.

You are now invited to consider the following five characteristics collectively as possible appropriate guides for determining to what degree a persuader merits the label "demagogue":*

1. A demagogue wields popular or mass leadership over an extensive number of people.

2. A demagogue exerts primary influence through the medium of the spoken word—through public speaking—whether directly to an audience or by means of radio or television.

3. A demagogue relies heavily on propaganda defined in the negative sense of intentional use of suggestion, irrelevant emotional appeals, and pseudoproof to circumvent rational decision-making processes.

4. A demagogue capitalizes on the availability of a major contemporary social issue or problem.

5. A demagogue is hypocritical; the social cause serves as a front or persuasive leverage point, whereas the actual primary motive is selfish interest and personal gain.

Several cautions are in order in applying these guidelines. A persuader may reflect each of these characteristics to a greater or lesser degree and only in certain instances. A persuader might

---

*The basic formulation from which these guidelines have been adapted first was suggested to me by Professor William Conboy of the University of Kansas. These five characteristics generally are compatible with the standard scholarly attempts to define a demagogue, for instance, Reinhard Luthin (1959) and Barnet Baskerville (1967).

fulfill several of these criteria (such as items 1, 2, and 4) and yet not be called a demagogue; characteristics 3 and 5 seem to be central to a conception of a demagogue.

Ethical Standards for Political Persuasion

Directly or indirectly, we are daily exposed to political and governmental persuasion in varied forms. The president appeals on national television for public support of a diplomatic treaty. A senator argues in Congress against ratification of a treaty. A government bureaucrat announces a new regulation and presents reasons to justify it. A federal official contends that information requested by a citizen action group cannot be revealed for national security reasons. At any given moment, somewhere, a national, state, or local politician is campaigning for election. At a city council meeting, a citizen protests a proposed property-tax rate increase. What ethical criteria should we apply to judge the many kinds of political/governmental persuasion? We will consider several potential sets of criteria in the hope that among them you will find ones especially useful in your own life.

Traditional American textbook discussions of the ethics of persuasion, rhetoric, and argument often include lists of standards suggested for evaluating the ethicality of an instance of persuasion. Such criteria often are rooted, implicitly if not explicitly, in what we earlier in this chapter described as a political perspective for judging the ethics of persuasion. The criteria usually stem from a commitment to values and procedures deemed essential to the health and growth of the American political/governmental system of representative democracy. Obviously, other cultures and other governmental systems may embrace basic values that lead to quite different ethical standards for persuasion.

What follows is my synthesis and adaptation of a number of such typical traditional lists of ethical criteria for persuasion.* Within the context of our own society, the following criteria are not necessarily the only or best ones possible; they are suggested as general guidelines rather than inflexible rules, and they may stimulate discussion on the complexity of judging the ethics of persuasion. Consider, for example, under what circumstances there may be justifiable exceptions to some of these criteria. Also bear in mind that one difficulty in applying these criteria in concrete situations stems from differing standards and meanings people may have for such key terms as *distort, falsify, rational, reasonable, conceal, misrepresent, irrelevant,* and *deceive*.

1. Do not use false, fabricated, misrepresented, distorted, or irrelevant evidence to support arguments or claims.

2. Do not intentionally use specious, unsupported, or illogical reasoning.

3. Do not represent yourself as informed or as an "expert" on a subject when you are not.

4. Do not use irrelevant appeals to divert attention or scrutiny from the issue at hand. Among the appeals that commonly serve such a purpose are "smear" attacks on an opponent's character, appeals to hatred and bigotry, innuendo, and God or Devil terms that cause intense but unreflective positive or negative reactions.

5. Do not ask your audience to link your idea or proposal to emotion-laden values, motives, or goals to which it actually is not related.

6. Do not deceive your audience by concealing your real purpose, self-interest, the group you represent, or your position as an advocate of a viewpoint.

7. Do not distort, hide, or misrepresent the number, scope, intensity, or undesirable features of consequences or effects.

8. Do not use "emotional appeals" that lack a supporting basis of evidence or reasoning, or that would not be accepted if the audience had time and opportunity to examine the subject themselves.

9. Do not oversimplify complex, gradation-laden situations into simplistic two-valued, either/or, polar views or choices.

10. Do not pretend certainty where tentativeness and degrees of probability would be more accurate.

11. Do not advocate something in which you do not believe yourself.

During the 1980s, political analysts in the mass media often criticized President Ronald Reagan for misstating and misusing examples, statistics, and illustrative stories. They charged that he did this not just on rare occasions but with routine frequency in his news conferences, informal comments, and sometimes in speeches (Johannesen, 1985; Green and MacColl, 1987). The glaring misuse of facts and anecdotes in ethically suspect ways continues in recent national political discourse. For example, syndicated columnist Joseph Spear takes to task House Speaker Newt Gingrich for this habit ("Third-wave Newt comes unglued," DeKalb, IL *Daily Chronicle*, March 17, 1995, p. 4). Spear observes: "We know that Newt doesn't care that his facts are often not factual. He spoke about a

*For example, see the following sources: Buehler and Linkugel (1975), Oliver (1957), Minnick (1968), Ewbank and Auer (1951), Thompson (1975), Bradley (1988), Nilsen (1974), and Wallace (1955).

ten-year-old student in St. Louis who was suspended for asking God's blessings on his cafeteria meals. It was not true. He told how the FDA refused to approve an innovative heart pump. It was not true. He rattled on and on about a 'federal shelter' in Denver that was outperformed by a private facility down the street. It was not true." Spear's judgment is that "Newt is a prattler, a careless accuser, an irresponsible teller of tales." An editorial in the *Washington Post National Weekly Edition* (March 13–19, 1995, p. 27) contends that trying "to get the story straight, whether you're in our business or Speaker Gingrich's, is not a luxury, but a responsibility." To assess the ethicality of such misstatements and misuse in current political discourse, you are encouraged to apply our previous discussions concerning intention, sincerity, responsibility, the political perspective, and suggested standards for political persuasion.

Ethical Standards for Commercial Advertising

Consumers, academic experts, and advertisers themselves clearly do not agree on any one set of ethical standards as appropriate for assessing commercial advertising. Here we will simply survey some of the widely varied criteria that have been suggested. Among them you may find guidelines that will aid your own assessments.

Using a kind of religious perspective, John McMillan (1963) contends that the first responsibility of an advertiser is not to either business or society but rather to God and principles higher than self, society, or business. Thus, advertisers are responsible to multiple neighbors — to owners, employees, clients, customers, and the general public. Second, they have a responsibility for objective truth. Third, they are responsible for preparing advertising messages with a sense of respect for their audience. Finally, argues McMil-

lan, advertisers are responsible for seeking product improvements.

Several writers on the ethics of advertising suggest the applicability of perspectives rooted in the essence of human nature. Thomas Garrett (1961) holds that a person becomes more truly human in proportion as his or her behavior becomes more conscious and reflective. Because of the human capacity for reason and because of the equally distinctive fact of human dependence on other people for development of potential, Garrett suggests several ethical obligations. As humans, we are obliged, among other things, to behave rationally ourselves, to help others behave rationally, and to provide truthful information. Suggestive advertising, in Garrett's view, is that which seeks to bypass human powers of reason or to some degree render them inoperative. Such advertising is unethical, not just because it uses emotional appeal, Garrett believes, but because it demeans a fundamental human attribute and makes people less than human.

Theodore Levitt (1974) uses a human nature position to *defend* advertising techniques often viewed by others as ethically suspect. While admitting that the line between distortion and falsehood is difficult to establish, his central argument is that "embellishment and distortion are among advertising's legitimate and socially desirable purposes; . . . illegitimacy in advertising consists only of falsification with larcenous intent" (p. 279). Levitt grounds his defense in a "pervasive, . . . *universal*, characteristic of human nature — the human audience *demands* symbolic interpretation of everything it sees and knows. If it doesn't get it, it will return a verdict of 'no interest' " (p. 284). Because Levitt sees humans essentially as symbolizers, as converters of raw sensory experience through symbolic interpretation to satisfy needs, he can justify "legitimate" embellishment and distortion. He contends:

> Many of the so-called distortions of advertising, product design, and packaging may be viewed as a

paradigm of the many responses that man makes to the conditions of survival in the environment. Without distortion, embellishment, and elaboration, life would be drab, dull, anguished, and at its existential worst. (p. 285)

Sometimes advertisers adopt what we earlier in this chapter called legal perspectives, in which ethicality is equated with legality. However, Harold Williams (1974) observes:

What is legal and what is ethical are not synonymous, and neither are what is legal and what is honest. We tend to resort to legality often as our guideline. This is in effect what happens often when we turn to the lawyers for confirmation that a course of action is an appropriate one.

We must recognize that we are getting a legal opinion, but not necessarily an ethical or moral one. The public, the public advocates, and many of the legislative and administrative authorities recognize it even if we do not. (pp. 285–288)

Typically, commercial advertising has been viewed as persuasion that argues a case or demonstrates a claim concerning the actual nature or merits of a product. Many of the traditional ethical standards for "truthfulness" and "rationality" have been applied to such attempts at arguing the quality of a product. For instance, are the evidence and the reasoning supporting the claim clear, accurate, relevant, and sufficient in quantity? Are the emotional and motivational appeals directly relevant to the product? The techniques that Larson will discuss as "weasel words" and as "deceptive claims" might be judged unethical according to this standard of truthfulness.

What do you think?

Have you ever been fooled by an unethical advertisement?

The American Association of Advertising Agencies' code of ethics was revised in 1990. As you read the following standards, consider their degree of adequacy, the degree to which they still are relevant and appropriate today, and the extent to which they are being followed by advertisers. Association members agree to avoid intentionally producing advertising that contains

1. false or misleading statements or exaggerations, visual or verbal

2. testimonials that do not reflect the real choice of the individuals involved

3. price claims that are misleading

4. comparisons that unfairly disparage a competitive product or service

5. claims insufficiently supported or that distort the true meaning or practicable application of statements made by professional or scientific authority

6. statements, suggestions, or pictures offensive to public decency or to minority segments of the population

What if ethical standards of truthfulness and rationality are *irrelevant* to most commercial advertising? What if the primary purpose of most ads is *not* to prove a claim? Then the ethical standards we apply may stem from whatever alternative view of the nature and purpose of advertising we do hold. Some advertisements function primarily to capture and sustain consumer attention, to announce a product, to create consumer awareness of the name of a product. What ethical criteria are most appropriate for such attention-getting ads?

Finally, consider Tony Schwartz's (1974) resonance theory of electronic media persuasion, which Larson discusses in Chapter 12. He argues that because our conceptions of truth, honesty, and clarity are products of our print-oriented culture, they are appropriate in judging the content of printed messages. In contrast, he contends that the "question of truth is largely irrelevant when dealing with electronic media content" (p. 19). In assessing the ethics of advertising by means of electronic media, Schwartz thinks that the Federal Trade Commission should focus not on truth and clarity of content but on the effects of the advertisement on receivers. He laments, however, that at present "we have no generally agreed-upon social values and/or rules that can be readily applied in judging whether the effects of electronic communication are beneficial, acceptable, or harmful" (p. 22). Schwartz summarizes his argument by concluding that

> truth is a print ethic, not a standard for ethical behavior in electronic communication. In addition, the influence of electronic media on print advertising (particularly the substitution of photographic techniques for copy to achieve an effect) raises the question of whether truth is any longer an issue magazine or newspaper ads. (p. 22)

The Ethics of Subliminal Persuasion

In Chapter 14, Larson describes the nature and some possible uses of subliminal persuasion. Such persuasion involves words or pictures flashed on a movie or television screen so rapidly, played on an audio channel so softly, or disguised in a magazine ad so skillfully that viewers or listeners do not consciously recognize them. However, the subliminal messages, it is claimed, are absorbed subconsciously by the receivers. Larson also notes that use of such techniques might raise ethical issues.

In the late 1950s, at the federal and state levels, a number of bills were introduced to make the use of subliminal techniques in commercial or political advertisements illegal. None of these bills ever became state or federal law. In January 1974, the Federal Communications Commission did issue a Public Notice warning broadcasters that because such subliminal perception techniques

were intentionally deceptive, they were contrary to the obligation of stations to serve the public interest; revocation of a broadcast license might result from using them. Both the Television Code and the Radio Code of the National Association of Broadcasters voluntarily pledge member stations not to use any techniques that attempt to convey information "by transmitting messages below the threshold of normal awareness."

In the 1980s, companies started marketing subliminal self-persuasion programs for voluntary self-improvement. One of these firms offered for sale a series of audiocassettes containing subliminal suggestions to help a person lose weight, stop smoking, and improve memory. Another firm advertised videocassettes for home television that included subliminal messages on such topics as stress control, alcohol control, career motivation, golf expertise, and sexual confidence. This latter company emphasized the voluntary nature of using its programs and the fact that viewers could replay the videotapes in slow motion if they wished to see the messages consciously.

What judgments might be made concerning the ethicality of subliminal persuasion? From the human nature perspective described earlier in this chapter, the unique capacities for conscious value judgment and for rational processing of information could be stressed for protection. In addition, the right of privacy of an individual's mental processes might justify declaring that use of subliminal techniques in situations of involuntary and unconscious exposure is ethically irresponsible. An individual should have the freedom, in the view of Olivia Goodkin and Maureen Phillips (1981), "to choose the time, circumstances, and extent to which his attitudes, beliefs, behavior, and opinions are to be influenced and shaped by another" (p. 1104). Thus, because hidden use of subliminal persuasion circumvents and undermines capacities and freedoms that are essential to human self-fulfillment, it could be condemned as unethical.

Negative ethical judgments of subliminal persuasion might also grow from one version of the political perspective described earlier. The values fundamental to the health of American representative democracy as a system of self-government could provide standards for ethical assessment. Essential to this democratic system is the development of a person's ability to be consciously aware of her or his own mental activities, "to question their validity, to judge them critically, to alter or correct them" (Branden, 1969). Franklyn Haiman (1958) sees promotion of our capacity to reason logically as a value necessary for adequate functioning of our system of representative democracy. The ethical standard advocated by Haiman is the degree of rationality, the degree of conscious free choice, reflected in and promoted by any specific persuasive technique or appeal. Condemned as unethical in Haiman's view (especially in political campaigning, governmental communication, and commercial advertising) are techniques that influence the receiver "by short-circuiting his conscious thought processes and planting suggestions or exerting pressures on the periphery of his consciousness which are intended to produce automatic, nonreflective behavior" (p. 385). Unannounced use of subliminal persuasion would particularly warrant ethical condemnation because it attempts to circumvent the human mind and reason and to elicit nonreflective, semiconscious, or unconscious responses.

From the legal perspective, society's negative ethical judgments of subliminal persuasion could be formalized by making specific types of subliminal techniques illegal. Haiman (1981) sees "no First Amendment barrier to outlawing" subliminal stimuli when used on unconsenting persons (p. 233). Goodkin and Phillips (1981) reject as legal remedies, on the one hand, the total prohibition of the manufacture, sale, and use of subliminal persuasion devices, or, on the other hand, regulation restricting uses to those deemed beneficial to society. Instead they advocate laws requiring disclosure of any public or private use of subliminal techniques and disclosure of the content subliminally transmitted.

The Ethics of Intentional Ambiguity and Vagueness

"Language that is of doubtful or uncertain meaning" might be a typical definition of ambiguous language. **Ambiguous** language is open to two or more legitimate interpretations. **Vague** language lacks definiteness, explicitness, or preciseness of meaning. Clear communication of intended meaning usually is one major aim of an ethical communicator, whether that person seeks to enhance receiver understanding or to influence belief, attitude, or action. Textbooks on oral and written communication typically warn against ambiguity and vagueness; often they directly or indirectly take the position that intentional ambiguity is an unethical communication tactic. For example, later in this book Larson discusses ambiguity as a functional device of style, as a stylistic technique that is often successful while ethically questionable.

Most people probably would agree that intentional ambiguity is unethical in situations where accurate instruction or efficient transmission of precise information is the acknowledged purpose. Even in most so-called persuasive communication situations, intentional ambiguity would be ethically suspect. However, in some situations communicators may believe that the intentional creation of ambiguity or vagueness is necessary, accepted, expected as normal, and even ethically justified. Such might be the case, for example, in religious discourse, in some advertising, in some legal discourse, in labor-management bargaining, in political campaigning, or in international diplomatic negotiations.

We can itemize a number of specific purposes for which communicators might believe that intentional ambiguity is ethically justified: (1) to heighten receiver attention through puzzlement; (2) to allow flexibility in interpretation of legal concepts; (3) to use ambiguity on secondary issues to allow for precise understanding and agreement on the primary issue; (4) to promote maximum receiver psychological participation in the communication transaction by letting receivers create their own relevant meanings; (5) to promote maximum latitude for revision of a position in later dealings with opponents or with constituents by avoiding being "locked into" a single absolute stance.

In political communication, whether during campaigns or by government officials, several circumstances might be used to justify intentional ambiguity. First, a president or presidential candidate must often communicate to multiple audiences through a single message via a mass medium such as television or radio. Different parts of the message may appeal to specific audiences, and intentional ambiguity in some message elements avoids offending any of the audiences. Lewis Froman (1966) describes a second circumstance: A candidate "cannot take stands on specific issues because he doesn't know what the specific choices will be until he is faced with the necessity for concrete decision. Also, specific commitments would be too binding in a political process that depends upon negotiation and compromise" (p. 9). Third, groups of voters increasingly make decisions about whether to support or oppose a candidate on the basis of that candidate's stand on a single issue of paramount importance to those groups. The candidate's position on a variety of other public issues is often ignored or dismissed. "Single-issue politics" is the phrase frequently used to characterize this trend. A candidate may be intentionally ambiguous on one emotion-packed issue in order to get a fair hearing for his or her stands on many other issues.

In his *Law Dictionary for Non-Lawyers,* Daniel Oran (1975) warns against use of vague language but also notes

> Some legal words have a "built-in" vagueness. They are used when the writer or speaker does not want to be pinned down. For example, when a law talks about "*reasonable* speed" or "*due* care," it is deliberately imprecise about the meaning of the words because it wants the amount of speed allowed or care required to be decided situation by situation, rather than by an exact formula. (pp. 330–331)

In some advertising, intentional ambiguity seems to be understood as such by consumers and even accepted by them. Consider the possible ethical implications of the Noxzema shaving cream commercial that urged (accompanied by a beautiful woman watching a man shave in rhythm with strip-tease music): "Take it off. Take it *all* off." Or recall the sexy woman in the after-shave commercial who says, "All my men wear English Leather, or they wear *nothing at all.*"

The Ethics of Nonverbal Communication

Nonverbal factors play an important role in the persuasion process. In a magazine advertisement, for example, the use of certain colors, pictures, layout patterns, and typefaces influences how the words in the advertisement are received. Later in this book, Larson provides examples of what he terms nonverbal "bias" in photo selection, camera angle and movement, and editing in news presentation. In *The Importance of Lying*, Arnold Ludwig (1965) underscores the ethical implications of some dimensions of nonverbal communication:

> Lies are not only found in verbal statements. When a person nods affirmatively in response to something he does not believe or when he feigns

attention to a conversation he finds boring, he is equally guilty of lying. . . . A false shrug of the shoulders, the seductive batting of eyelashes, an eyewink, or a smile may all be employed as nonverbal forms of deception. (p. 5)

Silence, too, may carry ethical implications. If to be responsible in fulfilling our role or position demands that we speak out on a subject, to remain silent may be judged unethical. On the other hand, if the only way that we can successfully persuade others on a subject is to employ unethical communication techniques or appeals, the ethical decision probably would be to remain silent.

Spiro T. Agnew (1969), when vice-president of the United States, catalogued numerous nonverbal elements of television news broadcasts that he believed carried ethical implications: facial expressions, sarcastic tone of voice, raised eyebrow, and vocal inflection. In the context of contemporary American political campaigns, Dan Nimmo (1981) questions the ethicality of electronically induced voice compression in radio or television advertisements for candidates: "A slow-talking, drawling Southerner can be made to speak at the rate of a clipped-word New Englander. A hesitant, shy-sounding speaker becomes decisive and assured" (p. 196).

In *Harper's* magazine, Earl Shorris (1977) condemns as unethical the nonverbal tactics of the *New York Times* in opposing Bella Abzug as a candidate for mayor of New York City:

The *Times*, having announced its preference for almost anyone but Mrs. Abzug in the mayoral election, published a vicious photograph of her taken the night of her winning the endorsement of the New Democratic Coalition. In the photograph, printed on page 1, Mrs. Abzug sits alone on a stage under the New Democratic Coalition banner. There are three empty chairs to her right and five empty chairs to her left. In this forlorn scene the camera literally looks up Mrs. Abzug's dress to show the heavy calves and thighs of an overweight woman in her middle years.

While the editorial judgment may be right, in that Bella Abzug is probably not the best choice or even a good choice for mayor of New York, the photograph is an example of journalism at its lowest (p. 106).

To further explore ethical standards for nonverbal communication, you are urged to read several sources that are especially rich in extended case studies. The entire issue of the *Journal of Mass Media Ethics*, 2 (Spring/Summer 1987) is devoted to ethics in photojournalism. Some contributors suggest concrete ethical guidelines (pp. 34, 71–73). Others discuss photos as claims and the nonobjectivity of photos (pp. 50, 52). A photo as a reflection of the photographer's formed ethical character is probed (p. 9). Three essays in the *Journal of Mass Media Ethics*, 6 (no. 3, 1991) examine the ethics of computer digital alteration of photos and video.

The Ethics of Racist/Sexist Language

In *The Language of Oppression*, Haig Bosmajian (1983) demonstrates how names, labels, definitions, and stereotypes have been used to degrade, dehumanize, and suppress Jews, blacks, Native Americans, and women. His goal is to expose the "decadence in our language, the inhumane uses of language," that have been used "to justify the unjustifiable, to make palatable the unpalatable, to make reasonable the unreasonable, to make decent the indecent." Bosmajian reminds us: "Our identities, who and what we are, how others see us, are greatly affected by the names we are called and the words with which we are labeled. The names, labels, and phrases employed to 'identify' a people may in the end determine their survival" (pp. 5, 9).

"Every language reflects the prejudices of the society in which it evolved. Since English, through most of its history, evolved in a white,

Anglo-Saxon, patriarchal society, no one should be surprised that its vocabulary and grammar frequently reflect attitudes that exclude or demean minorities and women" (Miller & Swift, 1981, pp. 2–3). Such is the fundamental position of Casey Miller and Kate Swift, authors of *The Handbook of Nonsexist Writing*. Conventional English usage, they believe, "often obscures the actions, the contributions, and sometimes the very presence of women" (p. 8). Because such language usage is misleading and inaccurate, they see ethical implications in it. "In this respect, continuing to use English in ways that have become misleading is no different from misusing data, whether the misuse is inadvertent or planned" (p. 8).

To what degree is the use of racist/sexist language unethical, and by what standards? At the least, racist/sexist terms place people in artificial and irrelevant categories. At worst, such terms intentionally demean and "put down" other people through embodying unfair negative value judgments concerning traits, capacities, and accomplishments. What are the ethical implications, for instance, of calling a Jewish person a "kike," a black person a "nigger" or "boy," an Italian person a "wop," an Asian person a "gook" or "slant-eye," or a thirty-year-old woman a "girl" or "chick"? Here is one possible answer: "In the war in Southeast Asia, our military fostered a linguistic environment in which the Vietnamese people were called such names as *slopes, dink, slant, gook,* and *zip;* those names made it much easier to despise, to fear, to kill them. When we call women in our own society by the names of *gash, slut, dyke, bitch,* or *girl,* we—men and women alike—have put ourselves in a position to demean and abuse them" (Bailey, 1984).

Within a particular political perspective, we might value access to the relevant and accurate information needed to make reasonable decisions on public issues. Racist/sexist language, however, by reinforcing stereotypes, conveys inaccurate depictions of people, dismisses taking serious account of people, or even makes them invisible for purposes of the decision. Such language denies us access to necessary accurate information and thus is ethically suspect. From human nature perspectives, such language is ethically suspect because it dehumanizes by undermining and circumventing the uniquely human capacity for rational thought or for using symbols. From a dialogical perspective, racist/sexist language is ethically suspect because it reflects a superior, exploitative, inhumane attitude toward others, thus hindering equal opportunity for self-fulfillment for some people.

Some Feminist Views on Persuasion

Feminism is not a concept with a single, universally accepted definition. For our purposes, elements of definitions provided by Barbara Bate (1992) and by Julia Wood (1994) are helpful. Feminism holds that both women and men are complete and important human beings and that societal barriers (typically constructed through language processes) have prevented women from being perceived and treated as valued persons of equal worth with men. Feminism involves commitment to equality and respect for life. Feminism rejects oppression and domination as desirable values and believes that difference need not be equated with inferiority or undesirability.

"My indictment of our discipline of rhetoric springs from my belief that any intent to persuade is an act of violence." Thus Sally Miller Gearhart (1979) opens her attack on rhetoric-as-persuasion because it reflects a masculine-oriented, "conquest/conversion mentality." Traditional views of rhetoric have assumed that "it is a proper and even a necessary function to attempt to change others." The conquest/conversion model for persuasion is subtle and insidious, says

Gearhart, "because it gives the illusion of integrity. . . . In the conversion model we work very hard not simply to conquer but to give every assurance that our conquest of the victim is really giving her what she wants." Gearhart contends that the rational discourse of traditional rhetoric actually is a "subtle form of Might Makes Right." Teachers of rhetoric, she argues, "have been training a competent breed of weapons specialists who are skilled in emotional maneuvers, experts in intellectual logistics. . . ."

Working from feminist assumptions, Gearhart offers a particular view of "communication" as a more desirable and ethical alternative. This view of communication involves "deliberate creation or co-creation of an atmosphere in which people and things, if and only if they have the internal basis for change, may change themselves; it can be a milieu in which those who are ready to be persuaded persuade themselves, may choose to hear or choose to learn." Participants entering into this kind of interaction would try to develop an atmosphere where change for all participants can take place, would recognize that participants may differ in knowledge of subject matter and in basic beliefs, would look beyond these differences to attempt to create a sense of equal power for all, would be committed to working hard to achieve communication, and would be willing at a fundamental level to "yield her/his position entirely to the other(s)." This view of communication, believes Gearhart, moves away from a male-dominated model that assumes that all power was in the speaker/conqueror. Instead, the "womanization of rhetoric" focuses on atmosphere, listening, receiving, and a "collective rather than a competitive mode."

While they accept much of Gearhart's critique of a speaker-centered rhetoric of conquest, conversion, domination, and control, Sonja Foss and Cindy Griffin (1995) believe that such persuasion should remain one among several rhetorics available to humans for selection in varying contexts. They do not want to characterize such a view of rhetoric as inaccurate or misguided. But as one alternative, Foss and Griffin develop an "invitational rhetoric" rooted in the feminist assumptions that relationships of equality are usually more desirable than ones of domination and elitism, that every human being has value because she or he is unique and is an integral part of the pattern of the universe, and that individuals have a right to self-determination concerning the conditions of their lives (they are expert about their lives).

"Invitational rhetoric," say Foss and Griffin, invites "the audience to enter the rhetor's world and to see it as the rhetor does." The invitational rhetor "does not judge or denigrate others' perspectives but is open to and tries to appreciate and validate those perspectives, even if they differ dramatically from the rhetor's own." The goal is to establish a "nonhierarchical, nonjudgmental, nonadversarial framework" for the interaction and to develop toward the audience "a relationship of equality, respect, and appreciation." Invitational rhetors make no assumption that their "experiences or perspectives are superior to those of audience members and refuse to impose their perspectives on them." While change is not the intent of invitational rhetoric, change may be a result. Change may occur in the "audience or rhetor or both as a result of new understandings and insights gained in the exchange of ideas."

In the process of invitational rhetoric, Foss and Griffin contend, the rhetoric "offers" perspectives without advocating their support or seeking their acceptance. In invitational rhetoric, individual perspectives are expressed "as carefully, completely, and passionately as possible" to invite their full consideration. In offering perspectives, "rhetors tell what they currently know or understand; they present their vision of the world and how it works for them." Rhetors in invitational rhetoric "communicate a willingness to call into question the beliefs they consider most inviolate and to relax a grip on these beliefs." Invitational rhetors strive to create the conditions of safety, value, and freedom in interaction with audience members. *Safety* involves "the creation of a feeling of security and freedom from danger for the audience." Participants do not "fear rebuttal of or retribution for their most fundamental beliefs." *Value* involves acknowledging the intrinsic worth of audience members as human beings. In interaction, attitudes that are "distancing, depersonalizing, or paternalistic" are avoided. In invitational rhetoric, "listeners do not interrupt, confront, or insert anything of their own as others tell of their experiences." *Freedom* involves the power to choose or decide. Restrictions are not placed on the interaction. Participants may introduce for consideration any and all matters; "no subject matter is off limits, and all presuppositions can be challenged." Furthermore, in invitational rhetoric the "rhetor's ideas are not privileged over those of the audience. . . ."

In concluding their explication of an invitational rhetoric, Foss and Griffin suggest that this rhetoric requires "a new scheme of ethics to fit interactional goals other than inducement of others to adherence to the rhetor's own beliefs." What might be some appropriate ethical guidelines for invitational rhetoric? What ethical standards seem already implied by the dimensions or constituents of such rhetoric described by them?

From her stance as a feminist teacher and scholar of communication, Lana Rakow (1994) spoke to an audience of students and teachers of communication at The Ohio State University. She employed the norms of "trust, mutuality, justice, and reciprocity" as touchstones for communication relationships. As a part of a wide-ranging address on the "mission" of the field of communication study, Rakow contends that we must develop a communication ethic to guide our "relations between individuals, between cultures, between organizations, between countries." She asks, "What kind of 'ground-rules' would work

across multiple contexts to achieve relationships that are healthy and egalitarian, and respectful?" She suggests three:

1. *Inclusiveness* means openness to multiple perspectives on truth, an encouragement of them, and a willingness to listen. Persons are not dehumanized because of their gender, race, ethnicity, sexual orientation, country, or culture.

2. *Participation* means ensuring that all persons must have the "means and ability to participate, to be heard, to speak, to have voice, to have their opinions count in public decision making." All persons "have a right to participate in naming the world, to be part of the discussion in naming and speaking our truths."

3. *Reciprocity* assumes that participants be considered equal partners in a communication transaction. There should be a "reciprocity of speaking and listening, of knowing and being known as you wish to be known."

In what respects, and why, do you agree or disagree with the positions advocated by these feminist scholars? What contributions do their viewpoints make to our better understanding of the process of persuasion as it *does* function and as it *ought to* function?

Ethical Standards for Interpersonal Communication

As Larson discusses elsewhere in this text, varying degrees of persuasion are attempted in two-person and small-group settings. One difficulty in assessing the ethics of persuasion in such interpersonal situations is that most standards for ethical persuasion are intended specifically for public persuasion. Are these ethical standards also applicable to private, face-to-face communication?

Or are ethical standards needed that apply uniquely and most appropriately to interpersonal communication? Here are several sets of ethical guidelines that have been proposed for interpersonal communication.

John Condon (1977) explores a wide array of ethical issues that typically emerge in interpersonal communication settings: candor, social harmony, accuracy, deception, consistency of word and act, keeping confidences, and blocking communication. In discussing these ethical themes, Condon stresses that any particular theme may come into conflict with other themes and that we may have to choose one over the other in a given situation. Although Condon does not formulate specific ethical criteria, perhaps we can restate some of his views in the form of potential guidelines that we may want to consider.

1. Be candid and frank in sharing personal beliefs and feelings. Ideally, "we would like *no* to mean *no*, we would like a person who does not understand to say so, and a person who disagrees to express that disagreement directly."

2. In groups or cultures in which interdependence is valued over individualism, keeping social relationships harmonious may be more ethical than speaking our minds.

3. Communicate information accurately, with minimal loss or distortion of meaning.

4. Avoid intentional deception, which generally is unethical.

5. Make verbal and nonverbal cues, words and actions consistent in the meanings they communicate.

6. Avoid intentionally blocking the communication process—such as by cutting off persons before they have made their point, changing the subject when the other person obviously has more to say, or nonverbally distracting others from the intended subject—because this is usually unethical.

Ernest Bormann (1990) suggests ethical standards for task-oriented small-group discussions. These ethical guidelines are rooted in a political perspective based on values central to American representative democracy. In summary and paraphrased form, they are:

1. Participants should be allowed to make up their own minds without being coerced, duped, or manipulated.

2. Participants should be encouraged to grow and to develop their own potential.

3. Sound reasoning and relevant value judgments should be encouraged.

4. Conflicts and disagreements that focus on participants as persons rather than on ideas or information should be avoided.

5. Participants should not manipulate group members solely or primarily for their own selfish ends.

6. When in the adviser role, participants should present information honestly, fairly, and accurately. They should reveal their sources. They should allow others to scrutinize their evidence and arguments. They should not lie, because lying breaks the trust necessary for participants to assess information.

7. With respect to external groups or individuals, participants within the group should be committed to defending true statements of fact, praiseworthy value statements, and sound advice.

8. Participants should communicate with each other as they would want others to communicate with them.

9. Communication practices in the group should be judged within a framework of all

relevant values and ethical criteria, not solely or primarily by the worth of the end or goal to be reached. Gandhi's ethical touchstone is sound: "Evil means, even for a good end, produce evil results."

Ethics and Personal Character

Ethical persuasion is not simply a series of careful and reflective decisions, instance by instance, to persuade in ethically responsible ways. Deliberate application of ethical rules is sometimes impossible. Pressure for a decision may be so great or a deadline so near that there is insufficient time for careful deliberation. We may be unsure what ethical criteria are relevant or how they apply. The situation may seem so unusual that applicable criteria do not readily come to mind. In such times of crisis or uncertainty, our decision concerning ethical persuasion stems less from deliberation than from our formed "character." Furthermore, our ethical character influences the terms with which we describe a situation and whether we believe the situation contains ethical implications (Lebacqz, 1985; Klaidman & Beauchamp, 1987; Hauerwas, 1977).

Consider the nature of moral character as described by ethicists Richard DeGeorge and Karen Lebacqz. According to DeGeorge (1986):

> As human beings develop, they tend to adopt patterns of actions, and dispositions to act in certain ways. These dispositions, when viewed collectively, are sometimes called character. A person who habitually tends to act as he morally should has a good character. If he resists strong temptation, he has a strong character. If he habitually acts immorally, he has a morally bad charac-

What do you think?

Is telling a "little white lie" in order to protect the feelings of a friend a breach of ethics?

ter. If despite good intentions he frequently succumbs to temptation, he has a weak character. Because character is formed by conscious actions, in general people are morally responsible for their characters as well as for their individual actions. (p. 89)

And Lebacqz (1985) believes:

> Indeed, when we act, we not only *do* something, we also shape our own character. Our choices about what to do are also choices about whom to be. A single lie does not necessarily make us a liar; but a series of lies may. And so each choice about what to *do* is also a choice about whom to *be* — or, more accurately, whom to become. (p. 83)

In Judeo-Christian or Western cultures, good moral character is usually associated with habitual embodiment of such virtues as courage, temperance, wisdom, justice, fairness, generosity, gentleness, patience, truthfulness, and trustworthiness. Other cultures may praise additional or different virtues that they believe constitute good ethical character. Instilled in us as habitual dispositions to act, these virtues guide the ethics of our communication behavior when careful or clear deliberation is not possible.

In what ways does the issue of "ethical character" apply to the 1992 and 1996 presidential campaigns of Bill Clinton and to his communication during his presidency? Consider the arguments in some of the national press commentary. During the 1992 campaign, political columnist Paul Greenberg (1992) contended: "The character issues just won't go away no matter how many times Bill Clinton assures us, word of honor, that his is fine. His stock response to questions about his character or absence of same is to say that nobody's perfect, admit he's not, and therefore imply that he's no better or worse than anybody else." Economist and syndicated columnist Robert J. Samuelson (1994, 1995) was especially critical of Clinton's communication as it reflects character. Samuelson argued that Clinton routinely exaggerates, fibs, and misstates on both foreign and domestic policy. "Everywhere, he seems to dissemble" (1994). *Washington Post* political analyst David Broder (1994) observed: "Meantime, the questions about his strength of character and his candor that emerged in the campaign have been deepened by both the personal and official controversies of the first year. At the root of many of them is his habit of rewriting history, including his own words and actions, to suit his current needs." In 1996 a *U.S. News* survey (Borger and Kulman, 1996) concluded: "Yet character remains the president's Achilles heel. The poll found that while 70 percent of voters describe Dole as moral, only 41 percent describe Clinton that way." While respondents in the poll could not identify concrete "best aspects" of Clinton's character, they included "deceptive, cheater, and indecisive" among "worst aspects" of his character (p. 36). In what ways and why do you agree or disagree with the judgments of these critics? What might be some differences between the concept of "character" generally and the concept of "ethical character" more specifically?

Columnist Stephen Chapman (1987) suggests three reasons that media scrutiny of the character issue is so intense on presidential candidates. First, voters are imposing increasingly higher ethical standards. Second, "personal integrity is one of the few matters that lend themselves to firsthand judgments by the voters. Most voters may feel unable to judge whether a politician is right about the defense appropriations bill. But they are able to consider evidence about a politician's ethics and reach a verdict, since they make similar evaluations about people every day" (p. 3). Third, voters "tend to vote for general themes, trusting candidates to apply them in specific cases. A politician who creates doubt about his personal honesty doesn't merely sow fear that he will steal from the petty cash. He creates doubt that his concrete policies will match his applause lines" (p. 3).

To aid in assessing the ethical character of any person in a position of responsibility or any person who seeks a position of trust, we can modify guidelines suggested by journalists. We can ask: Is it probable that the recent or current ethically suspect communication behavior will continue? Does it seem to be habitual? Even if a particular incident seems minor in itself, does it "fit into a familiar pattern that illuminates more serious shortcomings?" If the person does something inconsistent with his or her public image, "is it a small miscue or a sign of hypocrisy?" (Alter, 1987; Johannesen, 1991).

Improving Ethical Judgment

One purpose of this book is to make you a more discerning receiver and consumer of communication by encouraging ethical judgments of communication that are specifically focused and carefully considered. In making judgments of the ethics of your own communication and the communication to which you are exposed, your aim should be specific rather than vague assessments, and carefully considered rather than reflex-response "gut level" reactions.

The following framework of questions is offered as a means of making more systematic and firmly grounded judgments of communication ethics.* At the same time, we should bear in mind philosopher Stephen Toulmin's (1950) observation that "moral reasoning is so complex, and has to cover such a variety of types of situations, that no one logical test . . . can be expected to meet every case" (p. 148). In underscoring the complexity of making ethical judgments, in *The Virtuous Journalist* Klaidman and Beauchamp

*For some of these questions I have freely adapted the discussions of Goodwin (1987), pp. 14–15; Christians, et al. (1991), pp. 21–23; and Perelman and Olbrechts-Tyteca (1969), pp. 25, 483.

(1987) reject the "false premise that the world is a tidy place of truth and falsity, right and wrong, without the ragged edges of uncertainty and risk." Rather, they argue: "Making moral judgments and handling moral dilemmas require the balancing of often ill-defined competing claims, usually in untidy circumstances" (p. 20). How might you apply this framework of questions? (Also see Figure 2.3.)

1. Can I *specify exactly* what ethical criteria, standards, or perspectives are being applied by me or others? What is the concrete grounding of the ethical judgment?

2. Can I justify the *reasonableness and relevancy* of these standards for this particular case? Why are these the most appropriate ethical criteria among the potential ones? Why do these take *priority* (at least temporarily) over other relevant ones?

3. Can I indicate clearly in what respects the communication being evaluated *succeeds or fails in measuring up* to the standards? What judgment is justified in this case about the *degree* of ethicality? Is the most appropriate judgment a specifically targeted and narrowly focused one rather than a broad, generalized, and encompassing one?

4. In this case, to whom *is ethical responsibility owed* — to which individuals, groups, organizations, or professions? In what ways and to what extent? Which responsibilities take precedence over others? What is the communicator's responsibility to herself or himself and to society at large? Are the ones to whom primary responsibilities are owed the ones who most appropriately should decide the ethics of this case?

5. *How do I feel about myself* after this ethical choice? Can I continue to "live with myself" in good conscience? Would I want my parents or spouse to know of this choice?

© CREATIVE MEDIA SERVICES   Box 5955   Berkeley, Ca. 94705

Figure 2.3. *How might the guidelines for ethical judgment help to evaluate this situation?*

6. Can the ethicality of this communication be justified as a *coherent reflection of the communicator's personal character*? To what degree is the choice ethically "out of character"?

7. If called upon *in public to justify* the ethics of my communication, how adequately could I do so? What generally accepted reasons or rationale could I appropriately offer?

8. *Are there precedents* or *similar previous cases* to which I can turn for ethical guidance? Are there significant aspects of this instance that set it apart from all others?

9. How thoroughly have *alternatives been explored* before settling on this particular choice? Might this choice be less ethical

than some of the workable but hastily rejected or ignored alternatives? If the only avenue to successful achievement of the communicator's goal requires use of unethical communication techniques, is there a realistic choice (at least temporarily) of *refraining* from communication — of not communicating at all?

Review and Conclusion

The process of persuasion demands that you make choices about the methods and content you will use in influencing receivers to accept the alternative you advocate. These choices involve issues of desirability and of personal and societal good. What ethical standards will you use in making or judging these choices among techniques, content, and purposes? What should be the ethical responsibility of a persuader in contemporary American society?

Obviously, answers to these questions have not been clearly or universally established. However, the questions are ones we must face squarely. In this chapter, we have explored some perspectives, issues, and examples useful in evaluating the ethics of persuasion. Our interest in the nature and effectiveness of persuasive techniques must not overshadow our concern for the ethical use of such techniques. We must examine not only *how* to, but also *whether* to, use persuasive techniques. The issue of "whether to" is both one of audience adaptation and one of ethics. We should formulate meaningful ethical guidelines, not inflexible rules, for our own persuasive behavior and for use in evaluating the persuasion to which we are exposed.

Questions for Further Thought

1. What standards do *you* believe are most appropriate for judging the ethics of political/governmental persuasion?

2. What ethical standards do *you* think should be used to evaluate advertising?

3. When might intentional use of ambiguity be ethically justified?

4. To what degree is use of racist/sexist language unethical? Why?

5. Do the ethical standards commonly applied to verbal persuasion apply equally appropriately to nonverbal elements in persuasion? Should there be a special ethic for nonverbal persuasion?

6. What should be the role of personal character in ethical persuasion?

References

Agnew, S. (1969). Television news coverage. *Vital Speeches of the Day*, Dec. 1, 98–101.

Alter, J. (1987). The search for personal flaws. *Newsweek*, Oct. 19, p. 79.

Bailey, R. W. (1984). George Orwell and the English language. In E. J. Jensen (Ed.), *The future of nineteen eighty-four* (pp. 23–46). Ann Arbor: University of Michigan Press.

Baskerville, B. (1967). Joseph McCarthy: Briefcase demagogue. In H. Bosmajian (Ed.), *The rhetoric of the speaker*. New York: D. C. Heath.

Bate, B. (1992). *Communication and the sexes*. (Reissue) Prospect Heights, IL: Waveland.

Borger, G., & Kulman, L. (1996). Does character count? *U.S. News and World Report*, June 24, 35–41.

Bormann, E. G. (1990). *Small group communication* (3rd ed.). New York: Harper/Collins.

Bosmajian, H. (1983). *The language of oppression* (rpt. ed.). Lanham, MD: University Press of America.

Bradley, B. E. (1988). *Fundamentals of speech communication* (5th ed.). Dubuque, IA: Wm. C. Brown.

Branden, N. (1969). Free will, moral responsibility, and the law. *Southern California Law Review, 42,* 264–291.

Broder, D. S. (1994). Clinton's report card. *Washington Post National Weekly Edition,* January 24–30, 4.

Buehler, E. C., & Linkugel, W. A. (1975). *Speech communication for the contemporary student* (3rd ed.). New York: Harper & Row.

Buursma, B. (1987). Do-or-die deadline rallies Roberts' flock. *Chicago Tribune,* Jan. 17, sec. 1, pp. 1, 10.

Chapman, S. (1987). How seriously has Joe Biden hurt his presidential effort? *Chicago Tribune,* Sept. 20, sec. 4, p. 3.

Chase, S. (1956). *Guides to straight thinking.* New York: Harper & Row.

Christians, C., Rotzoll, K. B., & Fackler, M. (1991). *Media ethics* (3rd ed.). New York: Longman.

Coffey, R. (1987). Biden's borrowed eloquence beats the real thing. *Chicago Tribune,* Sept. 18, sec. 1, p. 23.

Condon, J. C. (1977). *Interpersonal communication,* New York: Macmillan.

DeGeorge, R. (1986). *Business ethics* (2nd ed.). New York: Macmillan.

Ewbank, H. L., & Auer, J. J. (1951). *Discussion and debate* (2nd ed.). New York: Appleton-Century-Crofts.

Foss, S. K., & Griffin, C. (1995). Beyond persuasion: A proposal for an invitational rhetoric. *Communication Monographs, 62,* 2–18.

Freund, L. (1960). Responsibility — Definitions, distinctions, and applications. In J. Friedrich (Ed.), *Nomos III: Responsibility* (pp. 28–42). New York: Liberal Arts Press.

Friedman, M. S. (1960). *Martin Buber: The life of dialogue.* New York: Harper Torchbooks.

Froman, L. A. (1966). A realistic approach to campaign strategies and tactics. In M. K. Jennings & L. H. Ziegler (Eds.), *The electoral process.* Englewood Cliffs, NJ: Prentice-Hall.

Garrett, T. M. (1961). *An introduction to some ethical problems of modern American advertising.* Rome: Gregorian University Press.

Gearhart, S. M. (1979). The womanization of rhetoric. *Women's Studies International Quarterly, 2,* 195–201.

Goodkin, O., & Phillips, M. A. (1981). The subconscious taken captive: A social, ethical, and legal analysis of subliminal communication technology. *Southern California Law Review, 54,* 1077–1140.

Goodwin, H. E. (1987). *Groping for ethics in journalism* (2nd ed.). Ames: Iowa State University Press.

Green, M., & MacColl, G. (1987). *There he goes again: Ronald Reagan's reign of error* (rev. & updated ed.). New York: Pantheon.

Greenberg, P. (1992). Character and other details on the Clinton watch. *Chicago Tribune,* March 20, sec. 1, 25.

Griffin, E. A. (1976). *The mind changers: The art of Christian persuasion.* Wheaton, IL: Tyndale House.

Haiman, F. S. (1958). Democratic ethics and the hidden persuaders. *Quarterly Journal of Speech, 44,* 385–392.

Haiman, F. S. (1981). *Speech and law in a free society.* Chicago: University of Chicago Press.

Hauerwas, S. (1977). *Truthfulness and tragedy.* Notre Dame, IN: University of Notre Dame Press.

Johannesen, R. L. (1971). The emerging concept of communication as dialogue. *Quarterly Journal of Speech, 57,* 373–382.

Johannesen, R. L. (1985). An ethical assessment of the Reagan rhetoric: 1981–1982. In K. R. Sanders, L. L. Kaid, & D. Nimmo (Eds.), *Political communication yearbook 1984* (pp. 226–241). Carbondale: Southern Illinois University Press.

Johannesen, R. L. (1991). Virtue ethics, character, and political communication. In R. E. Denton, Jr. (Ed.), *Ethical dimensions of political communication* (pp. 69–90). New York: Praeger.

Johannesen, R. L. (1996). *Ethics in human communication* (4th ed.). Prospect Heights, IL: Waveland.

Johannesen, R. L. (1997). Diversity, freedom, and responsibility. In J. Makau and R. C. Arnett (Eds.), *Communication ethics in an age of diversity,* (pp. 155–186). Champaign: University of Illinois Press.

Kaus, M. (1987). Biden's belly flop. *Newsweek,* Sept. 28, 23–24.

Kecskemeti, P. (1973). Propaganda. In I. de S. Pool, W. Schram, F. W. Frey, N. Maccoby, & E. B. Parker (Eds.), *Handbook of communication* (pp. 844–870). Chicago: Rand McNally.

Klaidman, S., & Beauchamp, T. L. (1987). *The virtuous journalist.* New York: Oxford University Press.

Lebacqz, K. (1985). *Professional ethics*. Nashville, TN: Abingdon Press.

Levitt, T. (1974). The morality (?) of advertising. In J. S. Wright & D. S. Mertes (Eds.), *Advertising's role in society* (pp. 278–289). St. Paul, MN: West.

Ludwig, A. (1965). *The importance of lying*. Springfield, IL: Charles C. Thomas.

Luthin, R. (1959). *American demagogues* (rpt. ed.). Gloucester, MA: Peter Smith.

McMillan, J. E. (1963). Ethics and advertising. In J. S. Wright & D. S. Warner (Eds.), *Speaking of advertising* (pp. 453–458). New York: McGraw-Hill.

Merrill, J. C., & Odell, S. J. (1983). *Philosophy and journalism*. New York: Longman.

Miller, C., & Swift, K. (1981). *The handbook of nonsexist writing*. New York: Barnes and Noble.

Minnick, W. C. (1968). *The art of persuasion* (2nd ed.). Boston: Houghton Mifflin.

Niebuhr, H. R. (1963). *The responsible self*. New York: Harper & Row.

Nilsen, T. R. (1974). *Ethics of speech communication* (2nd ed.). Indianapolis, IN: Bobbs-Merrill.

Nimmo, D. (1981). Ethical issues in political communication. *Communication, 6*, 187–206.

1974/75 roster and organization of the American Association of Advertising Agencies. (1974). New York: AAAA.

Oliver, R. T. (1957). *The psychology of persuasive speech* (2nd ed.). New York: Longmans, Green.

Oran, D. (1975). *Law dictionary for nonlawyers*. St. Paul, MN: West.

Pennock, J. R. (1960). The problem of responsibility. In C. J. Friedrich (Ed.), *Nomos III: Responsibility* (pp. 3–27). New York: Liberal Arts Press.

Perelman, C., & Olbrechts-Tyteca, L. (1969). *The new rhetoric*. Notre Dame, IN: University of Notre Dame Press.

Pincoffs, E. L. (1975). On being responsible for what one says. Paper presented at Speech Communication Association convention, Dec. Houston, TX.

Qualter, T. H. (1962). *Propaganda and psychological warfare*. New York: Random House.

Rakow, L. (1994). The future of the field: Finding our mission. Address presented at Ohio State University, May 13.

Ross, R. S., & Ross, M. G. (1982). *Relating and interacting*. Englewood Cliffs, NJ: Prentice-Hall.

Rothwell, J. D. (1982). *Telling it like it isn't: Language misuse and malpractice*. Englewood Cliffs, NJ: Spectrum Books.

Samuelson, R. J. (1994). Clinton—passionate hypocrite. *Washington Post National Weekly Edition*, January 24–30, 28.

Samuelson, R. J. (1995). Clinton, the deficit and the truth. *Washington Post National Weekly Edition*, November 27–December 3, 5.

Schwartz, T. (1974). *The responsive chord*. Garden City, NY: Anchor Books.

Shorris, E. (1977). The fourth estate. *Harper's*, Oct., p. 106.

Thompson, W. (1975). *The process of persuasion*. New York: Harper & Row.

Toulmin, S. (1950). *An examination of the place of reason in ethics*. Cambridge, Eng.: Cambridge University Press.

Wallace, K. R. (1955). An ethical basis of communication. *Speech Teacher, 4*, 1–9.

Wellman, C. (1988). *Morals and ethics* (2nd ed.). Englewood Cliffs, NJ: Prentice-Hall.

Werkmeister, W. H. (1957). *An introduction to critical thinking* (rev. ed.). Lincoln, NE: Johnson.

Williams, H. M. (1974) What do we do now, boss? Marketing and advertising. *Vital Speeches of the Day, 40*, 285–288.

Wood, J. T. (1994). *Gendered lives: Communication, gender, and culture*. Belmont, CA: Wadsworth.

3

Approaches to Research in Persuasion

Permanence and change exist in the world of persuasion, and the same holds true for research in persuasion — some ancient theories and concepts have current validity and usefulness, while new theories and concepts continue to emerge as explanations for persuasive events. Knowledge of these established and emerging theories should help you to become a more critical persuadee and hence a more effective persuader. As we focus on these explanations, try to keep in mind that research exists along a continuum from qualitative/"artistic" research on one end to quantitative/"scientific" research on the other (see Table 3.1). We will explore samples of the theory and research typical of various points along the continuum. The purpose of the continuum is to provide a simple means for you to "borrow" theories to evaluate the many persuasive messages aimed at you every day by family, friends, advertisers, politicians, government, and mass media.

The Persuasion Research Continuum

At the qualitative end of our research continuum are theories that trace their origins to the analysis of persuasion (frequently referred to as "rhetoric") as an "artistic" activity. At the quantitative end are theories that trace their origins to the rise of the social sciences. They approach persuasion research and theory as a "scientific" enterprise. Table 3.1 lists several typical characteristics of each approach. Additionally, the research cited may give you a few clues or ideas in the search for the widely held major premises in what Aristotle called the *enthymeme* — the assumption supplied by the audience or persuadee while the persuader provides the minor premise that leads to the audience-drawn conclusion. Human beings have been trying to explain how and why persuasion works, and to define its ethics and its values as well as its dangers for most of human history. The age-old questions concerning the ethical and unethical uses of persuasion have become even more central to modern life in a highly sophisticated technocracy such as ours and will continue to be raised as we approach the twenty-first century. Such questions will probably be increasingly difficult to answer because of the awesome powers of various new and old technologies for human communication.

Qualitative Characteristics	Quantitative Characteristics
Individual interpretation of communication event	Group interpretation of communication event
Persuasion = Art	Persuasion = Science
Evaluation/prediction	Explanation/prediction
Looks for patterns of messages/communication	Looks for patterns of receiver response
Examines types of communication	Examines amounts or quantity of communication

Table 3.1. *The continuum of research theories and methods*

Qualitative Research Theory and Methods

We begin our study of contemporary persuasion by returning to the roots of persuasion research, ancient Greece: where persuasion was essential to all citizens because they had to represent themselves and their interests before the Greek courts. The Greek city-states were democratic, and the citizenry had the right to speak out on issues of the day. Greek philosophers like Aristotle tried to describe what happened when persuasion occurred, and much of what they said on the subject is as true today as it was then.

Interests in persuasion continued through the works of Roman philosophers such as Cicero and Quintilian. Their interests also focused on persuasion in the courts and government. Persuasion is still a central part of everyday life, particularly in democracies. And the ethical concerns of the ancients have not changed much either.

Keep in mind that our central focus is on the search for "first premises," or the "common ground" on which persuasion is built. In Aristotle's day, the habits of Greek democracy determined the nature of important first premises. Today, the stresses and emerging habits of a developing technological world will determine which first premises are important. The process by which we are persuaded, however, has remained amazingly constant.

Aristotelian Theory and Research

Aristotle was a remarkable person. His father had been the court physician to Philip, the King of Macedonia, so Aristotle received the finest education. He studied for twenty years with Plato and was then selected by Philip's son, Alexander the Great, to be what we might call the secretary of education. Not only did Aristotle develop schools using the methods of Platonic dialogue, but he also set 1000 men to work to catalog everything known about the world at that time. He was thus the first great librarian and researcher of Greece. He also wrote up the findings of his 1000 researchers in over 400 books covering a variety of topics, including his *Rhetoric*, considered by some to be the single most important work on the study of speech making.

Aristotle developed his theory on which today's persuasion theory is based, by observing many persuaders at work in Athens—in the law courts, the government, and the marketplace. In the *Rhetoric*, Aristotle focused on what he called the *artistic proofs* or *appeals* that the persuader could create or manipulate. *Inartistic* proofs are those that are not under the control of the persuader (for example, situational factors such as the place where the persuasion occurs or the speaker's height or physical attractiveness). Recall from Chapter 1 that Aristotle identified three major types of artistic proof, which he called *ethos, pathos,* and *logos.* He also identified *topoi* (topics or places where one might find logical persuasive appeals) and saw emotional appeals as the "virtues" that the Greek citizenry valued.

Because Aristotle's ideas still apply in today's complex world of persuasion, it is useful to explore them more closely.

Ethos — Charisma and Credibility. **Ethos,** the first element in Aristotle's theory of persuasion, has several dimensions. Before actually making a persuasive presentation, all persons are perceived in some way by their audience. Even if a persuader is totally unknown to the audience, audience members will draw certain conclusions about him or her based on what they see — the speaker's body type, height, complexion, how the speaker moves or dresses, whether he or she is well groomed or disheveled, and a host of other nonverbal messages. In cases where the persuader is known, he or she has a reputation, for example, for honesty, knowledge, experience, or a sense of humor. A good example of how these various factors affect ethos is the differences in the ethos of O. J. Simpson before the murder of Nicole Brown Simpson and after. The same kinds of observations about ethos can be made regarding various candidates and even products and/or services — What is the ethos of Bill Clinton and/or McDonald's, for example?

Additional characteristics become apparent as the speech is delivered that add to or detract from ethos — for example, vocal quality, cleverness of argument, word choice, eye contact, gestures, and so on. More recently, researchers have added other dimensions — sincerity, trustworthiness, expertise, and dynamism or potency. Today, press releases, image consultants, flattering photography, and a host of other devices can be used to develop a speaker's "ethos" to an audience. Consider the impact of the persuader's reputation

for recent persuaders such as Saddam Hussein or Rush Limbaugh. The second dimension of persuasion consists of artistic proofs — the speaker controls them. For example, a persuader might use powerful language, figures of speech, or strategically planned gestures. The speaker might make a point of using eye contact to touch on various areas of the audience or might make direct eye contact with the television cameras. All of these and other artistic proofs make up a person's *image, charisma,* or *ethos.*

What do you think?

Who is a particularly credible persuader on the present political scene?

At times, one element in ethos may outperform the others. For instance, in the early 1990s, Tommy Lasorda was a spokesperson for Ultra Slim-Fast. He was not a diet expert, so the expertise factor did not have a bearing on his value as a user of Ultra Slim-Fast. However, Lasorda *had* lost a lot of weight using the product. In this case, change in physical appearance was the critical factor in his credibility.

Sometimes a person's reputation might be the critical factor. For example, Bill Clinton's reputation as a "womanizer" was especially vexing to him in the 1992 presidential campaign, South African political leader Nelson Mandela's reputation as an unjustly jailed black leader surely affected his return to power after twenty years' imprisonment, and David Koresh's reputation as the militant leader of a religious cult probably had something to do with the FBI raiding his group's enclave. Thus, *ethos,* or credibility, is a shifting quality depending on circumstantial factors as well as on sincerity, expertise, and dynamism.

Pathos and the Virtues. **Pathos** relates to the emotions. It includes appeals to the passions or the will. Persuasion is aimed at our emotional "hot buttons." Bell Telephone recognizes this fact with its slogan "Reach Out, Reach Out and Touch Someone."

In today's terms, pathos equates with psychological appeals. Persuaders assess the emotional state of the audience and design artistic appeals aimed at those states. Knowing that the audience feels helpless in the face of events, a persuader can succeed by reassuring them. For example, the "Good Times" virus hoax periodically pops up on the Internet, and every time some people believe it and are afraid that their computer will be ruined by it. The persuader who reassures them that the virus is an "urban legend" level hoax will be successful and respected thereafter as a person "in the know."

The following list describes several of the deep-seated values, or *virtues*, cited by Aristotle as appeals to the emotions. As you consider them, try to think of contemporary examples for each.

1. *Justice* involves respect for laws, people's right to have what belongs to them, tolerance, and related attributes.

2. *Prudence* relates to how one gives advice or demonstrates good judgment. For example, Dennis Rodman seems to lack prudence, or good judgment, whereas, a seemingly humble athlete such as Michael Jordan is thought of as having good judgment — as being prudent.

3. *Generosity* involves not only giving money to good causes but having an unselfish attitude at home, at work, in one's community, in government, or in international relations. This virtue lies behind the ongoing debate over America's role in the world in the coming millennium. Are we to be the world's police force? How much leadership can we give to efforts to save the environment?

4. *Courage* is a virtue that is quite obvious in today's world. To Aristotle it meant doing what you think is right, even under pressure — not backing away from unpopular issues or positions. A recent example might be the President's veto of a popular bill because it runs against some principle of fairness or wisdom.

5. *Temperance* was associated by Aristotle with qualities such as self-restraint and moderation in all areas of human conduct. The temperate person is in control of his or her emotions and desires. Such people aren't self-indulgent in their opinions, nor are they likely to be excessive in giving advice. They are open-minded and willing to consider all sides of a situation and try to be empathic with the other person's point of view.

6. *Magnanimity* was felt by Aristotle to be a willingness to forgive and forget, a desire to seek ways to better the world, and the ability to rise above pettiness. The ability to be as gracious in losing as in winning is a sign of magnanimity. Politicians must appear magnanimous — when they win, they compliment their opponents, and when they lose, they must congratulate and vow to support the winner.

7. *Magnificence* is the ability to recognize and be committed to the better qualities in human beings and to encourage them in oneself. History abounds with examples of magnificent persuaders — Washington, Lincoln, Barbara Jordan, Crazy Horse, Martin Luther King Jr., and others. Their magnificence came from the ability to encourage the best in themselves and others.

8. *Wisdom* was never really defined by Aristotle, but it is obvious that he conceived it to be more than just knowledge or intelligence. He seems to have associated it with good judgment, character, and experience.

This list of virtues doesn't exhaust the potential kinds of emotional argument, but it does show that this "artistic" form of proof still works in our current technocracy.

Logos and Topoi or "Places of Argument." Logos refers to appeals to the intellect, or to the rational side of humans. It relies on the audience's ability to process statistical data, examples, or testimony in logical ways and to arrive at some conclusion. The persuader must predict how the audience will do this and thus must assess their information-processing and conclusion-drawing patterns. Aristotle and other ancients most frequently combined information syllogistically.

Syllogisms begin with a major premise such as:

The chemical PCB is dangerous to humans.

This major premise is then associated with a minor premise:

Cattle raised near chemical plants absorb PCB.

Which leads to the conclusion:

Cattle raised near chemical plants are dangerous to humans.

Of course, the persuader then offers a course of action for consumers, such as identifying the origin of the meat they eat or perhaps avoiding beef altogether. In any case, to use this kind of proof, the persuader must predict how the audience will logically assemble the information. Consider how the persuadee in Figure 3.1 is responding.

Clearly, being able to identify these patterns of information processing and being able to design arguments and use evidence effectively is an artistic proof. You can find logical appeals operating in your daily life. Your parents, for example, might use data about the cost of tuition, living in a dormitory, and travel to and from college to persuade you to attend one school as opposed to another. Politicians use statistics and examples to persuade you to believe in a certain view or to vote in a certain way. Advertisers use graphs and tables to persuade you to smoke their cigarette, drive their make of car, or add a new appliance to your home. In each of these cases, the persuader is bet-

Figure 3.1. *How effective is this appeal: Does it have credibility? Is there anything "logical" about it? (© 1987 FarWorks, Inc./Distributed by Universal Press Syndicate.)*

ting that you will process the information logically and predictably. In these cases, there has been a co-creation of meaning using the syllogistic form of reasoning.

Much of contemporary market research attempts to identify the major premises held by consumers. With these in mind, marketers design products, packaging, and advertising that effectively develop "common ground" and hence the co-creation of persuasive meaning. From my experiences at a mid-sized ad agency, I learned how effective this common ground is and, equally important, how disastrous not knowing it can be. For example, a client manufactured contact lenses that could change the wearer's eye color. Who are the typical customers for this product—

vain yuppies concerned about appearance? Which media would you choose to reach these customers—cable television? On what programs would you advertise—health and exercise shows? The agency advised the client to conduct some market research to learn about their current users. The research revealed that the largest portion of the customer pool was made up of black males. Our intuitive guess about users would probably have overlooked this market segment and thus would have resulted in wasted advertising dollars and a failed advertising campaign. The client decided to use black radio stations and direct mail based on lists drawn from subscriptions for magazines such as *Jet* and *Ebony*.

Consider the cartoon in Figure 3.2. There is obviously a hidden premise that causes the reac-

tion in the last panel—probably something like "Being forced to pay for the mistakes of the government is unfair." By stating the minor premise ("Every man, woman, and child will have to pay over $1000 for the savings and loan scandal"), the cartoonist persuades the reader to co-create the conclusion: "This is an important issue."

The ancient concept of the enthymeme remains a foundation of persuasion. This is especially true when enthymemes are coupled with audience involvement—the co-creation of proof or meaning. This shared creation forms what Aristotle called "common ground." Aristotle thought that a good way to find such common ground was to categorize the *topoi*—places or topics of argument. Persuaders identify these "places" and try to determine whether they will work for a partic-

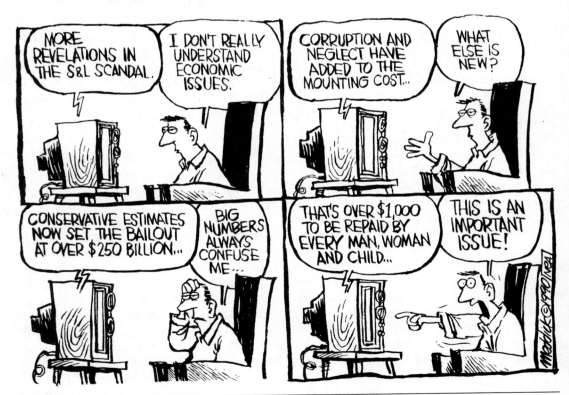

Figure 3.2. What is the hidden premise here? (Reprinted by permission of NEA, Inc.)

ular audience. Let's look at a few of these places as Aristotle saw them. Again, you will probably find them remarkably contemporary.

1. *Arguments as to degree, or "more or less."* Is it more or less just to demand life imprisonment or the death sentence for serial killers? Will it profit me more or less to sell my inventory at reduced rates rather than to store it? Will candidate A be more or less trustworthy than candidate B? Are Guess jeans more or less durable than Levis? Are they more or less fashionable than Levis? Is durability more or less important than style or brand?

2. *Arguments of possibility versus impossibility.* Is it possible for Third World countries to live in ecologically sound ways? Will the Japanese continue to dominate the electronics industry? Will the Internet and e-mail cause the U.S. Postal Service to go out of business? All these questions reflect the topoi of possibility versus impossibility.

3. *Past fact: Has an event really occurred?* This topoi is very important in the courts, where it must be proved that a crime actually occurred. A corporation that is trying to decide whether it should close a factory needs to look at past facts—Was the factory profitable? Was it efficient? Was it environmentally sound?

4. *Future fact: Is something likely to occur in the future?* This differs from the argument of possibility versus impossibility in that it focuses on probabilities, not possibilities. Will the new factory be more profitable? Efficient? Environmentally sound?

5. *Size and magnifying or minifying.* Is something important or unimportant? Will it result in a significant or insignificant change? In another example, will a large or a small amount of our leisure time be consumed by "surfing" the Web? To what degree will e-mail be integrated into college instruction?

Again, these forms of persuasion seem remarkably contemporary. In fact, we could argue that most contemporary persuasion research is derived from the work of Aristotle in some way or another.

Researchers using Aristotle's theory explain a given persuasive message by exploring the persuader's *ethos, pathos,* and *logos* as well as the uses made of various virtues and topoi. They also frequently look at "canons" (or stages) of the persuasion process (the *invention* of various arguments or "proofs"; the *organization* or "disposition" of these proofs; the *style* used by the persuader; and finally the *delivery* of the message).

Much of the research done in the early years of the communication discipline (1915–1960) used the methods or the theories of the ancient rhetorical theorists. Most of the persuasion analyzed using this method consisted of public speeches usually delivered by either political/populist speakers (such as Abraham Lincoln, Chief Tecumseh, or Carrie Nation). These studies fall along the qualitative/artistic side of the research continuum.

Other Qualitative Approaches

We now briefly examine three other qualitative research methods that exemplify the qualitative, interpretive, "artistic" approach: narrative, genre, and focus group methods.

Narrative Theories and Research. Several persuasion theorists base their work on the idea that the drama or story is the most powerful and pervasive metaphor that humans use to persuade and explain events.

In his particularly comprehensive narrative theory, communication theorist Walter Fisher (1987) suggests that all rational (and perhaps some irrational) behavior can be understood using the story, drama, or narrative as an analytical device by casting the persuasive event in narrative terms: Who are the persons in the narrative? What do they do in it? Why do they do what they do? What are the results? For example, a presidential campaign is a story being acted out on the national stage for us, the voters. The narrative begins with the candidates announcing their intention to run for office and continues to election day. The candidates are the characters—some liberal and others conservative, some Easterners and others Westerners, some attractive and others less so, and so on. They take certain positions on issues (abortion, immigration, gun control). They adopt unique and individual styles of communicating with voters (such as using short political television spots or longer infomercials). They characterize their opponents in certain ways ("Tax-and-spend liberals"). And they face campaign events (a scandal, a primary victory, plunging popularity in the polls) in their own ways and for their own reasons. The stages on which they perform their roles include party rallies, parades, news interviews, their families, and TV talk shows.

Fisher maintains that narratives succeed, or persuade, or fail depending on whether they have coherence and fidelity. *Coherence* is the way the story hangs together and thus has meaning or impact. *Fidelity* is the probability or believability of a story.

With a coherent story, almost everyone understands its premises or the points it tries to make. The story is told artistically, and it is believable. Coherence relies on the degree to which the story is internally and externally consistent. *Structural or argumentative consistency* means that the story is logically organized or told—it's internally consistent. In other words, we generally don't know the end of the story or the fate of the characters until the story is complete (that is, it has a beginning, middle, and end in the most traditional cases). In structurally consistent narratives, the characters have good reasons for doing what they do, and the impact of the situation or setting of the story also makes sense. For example, the biographical video stories shown at national political conventions must hang together in logical ways. We see how the candidate's formative years led him or her to this nomination. The actions of various characters (parents, spouse, children, longtime friends, enemies, the press) seem logical, as do the candidate's actions at various important times in his or her life. In the opinion of many, O. J. Simpson's narrative about what he did or didn't do on the night Nicole Brown Simpson and Ron Goldman were murdered lacked structural coherency. It seemed internally inconsistent in many ways. The same kind of inconsistency can affect the coherence of public relations efforts and advertising. The narratives told by tobacco company officials regarding their lying when testifying about the known effects of nicotine and the industry's manipulation of the substance is a PR example that boomeranged because of a lack of structural coherence. The narratives about battery life acted out by the Energizer bunny succeeded because they had internal consistency—he always kept going and going. Successful candidate "stories" are internally structurally consistent, whereas unsuccessful (and hence unpersuasive) stories or narratives aren't, and characters in them "wouldn't act that way in real life."

Consider the structural coherence in the advertisement in Figure 3.3, taken from *Advertising Age* (a publication aimed at persuaders who use advertising to shape purchase behaviors and brand loyalty). Who is/are the main "character(s)"? What is the "plot"? Does the ad make sense and seem to make a persuasive "argument"? Does the persuasive premise "ring true"? These kinds of questions can be used to test the structural coherence of any persuasive narrative.

Material coherence is the degree to which the narrative matches, "fits" with, or resonates with other similar narratives that we have heard, learned, and believed. It seems complete; there are no loose ends. So the candidate's video biography matches or is similar to the story or stories of prior nominees. A fund appeal for getting food and medicine to starving refugees from a war or natural disaster fits with similar appeals made in other circumstances. The narrative or story used in a shampoo advertisement shows the characters having problems or experiences similar to those in the "real world." For example, in a shampoo ad, a boy meets a girl in an elevator; the girl notices dandruff on his blazer and ignores him; the boy's boss tells him about Head and Shoulders; he uses the brand that night; the boy again sees the girl in the elevator the next day, and this time she notices him. How typical is this kind of event in the "real world"? The activities of Timothy McVeigh, the accused Oklahoma City bomber, seemed to fit a pattern that would materially coincide with a person who was a mad bomber. Consider various speeches, television or print advertisements, editorials, and other forms of persuasion to determine their material coherence.

Characterological coherence is the degree to which the characters in the narrative are believable. The portrayal of Hannibal "The Cannibal" Lecter by Anthony Hopkins in *Silence of the Lambs* and of Richard Milhous Nixon in *Nixon* are both good examples of characterological coherence. He is bone-chillingly believable. In the world of persuasion we might ask whether a political candidate would be likely or unlikely to have the kinds of values a video biography of him or her suggests. In looking at television advertising, we might ask whether the person giving the endorsement, such as actress Candice Bergen for Sprint, would be likely to use such products or brands. For instance, former Chicago Bears coach Mike Ditka appeared in an advertisement endorsing the services of one bank over another. Was the ad likely to have characterological coherence, given what Coach Ditka might know about the banking industry?

Figure 3.3. *Consider the structural coherence of this advertisement. (Reprinted by permission of Modern Talking Picture Service, Inc.)*

Fidelity in a narrative is similar to coherence but focuses more on the reliability or truthfulness of the story—does the story "ring true" to us? A story with good fidelity is like a compact disc as compared to a cheap portable radio. It presents a rationale or "logic of good reasons" (Fisher, 1987) for the setting, plot, characters, and outcome of the narrative. Fisher gives us some benchmarks of narratives that have good fidelity: They deal with human values that seem appropriate for the point or moral of the story and for the actions taken by the characters; the values seem to lead to positive outcomes for the characters and are "in synch" with our own experiences; and the values form an ideal philosophy or vision for our future. In a 1996 debate over repealing the ban on assault weapons, Congressman Kennedy, nephew of President John Kennedy and Senator Robert Kennedy, both of whom were assassinated, delivered an impassioned speech against repealing the ban. He argued that a killing doesn't affect just the person slain, but his or her entire family for generations, and in some cases even the nation. Because of his experience, his narrative had high fidelity — it rang true and was "in synch" with our values. Figure 3.4 demonstrates what can happen when fidelity is lacking in a given event.

Persuasive narratives cut across a broad expanse of human behavior. For example, they can be applied to topics as lofty as religious values and

What do you think?
Which advertising narratives seem to have the best fidelity?

as sordid as child pornography. They can be applied to both logical and emotional causes. They appeal to our native imagination and feelings. Furthermore, they have an easy "access code" in that we don't need to know a complicated system to understand them. Like the silent movies, they are easy to understand.

Narratives can also form communities of identification that together form a common world view. Because of this, narratives have been a central part of most if not all ideological movements throughout history: Early Christians told a story of salvation, America's founding fathers promoted a narrative of freedom, and pro-life advocates tell a narrative of the sanctity of life. The narrative form of persuasive strategy will likely continue to pervade human affairs in the future. As we proceed with our study of persuasive reception and responsibility, we will encounter other narrative theories.

Generic Theory and Methods. The French word *genre* refers to a distinct group, type, class, or category (Foss, 1989). Thus, "generic criticism" refers to criticism of particular groups, types, or categories of communication. A major assumption of generic persuasion theory is that important situational factors constrain and perhaps even dictate

Figure 3.4. *Politicians frequently include spending cuts in their "story" for their program. How much do these promises of cuts have or lack fidelity? (Frank and Ernest reprinted by permission of NEA, Inc.)*

the use of certain persuasive strategies and tactics. For example, the kind of persuasion used to justify a flat tax clearly differs from the kind of persuasion used to convince your college administration to alter the starting dates of semesters. Obviously there also are similarities between these persuasive messages (both use language, make claims or assertions, and offer evidence). But the kind of persuasion needed to justify tax reform to an entire nation is far different from the persuasion needed to convince a bureaucracy like a college. Generic theory tries to identify the unique and salient demands of given types of persuasive situation(s). Foss (1989) describes three characteristics on which genres of persuasion are built: situational factors, substantive factors, and stylistic characteristics.

Situational factors are those events and expectations that imply a certain kind of persuasive communication. For example, the Inaugural Address of an incoming or returning president carries with it the expectation that the speech will be delivered in a dramatic, perhaps patriotic, setting. Thus, past presidents have chosen such sites as the steps of the Capitol looking down the mall toward the Lincoln Monument or the Custis Mansion overlooking Arlington Cemetery. The situational factors implied by a speaker delivering a eulogy would obviously differ from those for the inauguration speech and would share characteristics with other eulogies.

Substantive and stylistic characteristics also typify distinct persuasive genres. For example, some speeches try to warn the audience of impending doom. They are called "Jeremiads" after the Old Testament prophet of doom, Jeremiah. Obviously their substance (warnings of disaster) differentiates them from messages that try to reassure or that try to lay blame.

Persuasion messages called "apologia" intend to apologize for some past act and have four strategies: denial, bolstering, differentiation, and transcendence (Ware and Linkugal, 1973).

In *denial* the persuader may directly deny the allegations or intentions regarding the charges. With *bolstering* the persuader tries to identify with some value (such as patriotism) or some group (such as the family) that has positive connotations in the mind of the audience, thus leading the audience to trust or identify with the persuader. In *differentiation*, the persuader tries to put a new perspective on events and asks the audience to suspend its judgment until the whole story has been told — especially the accused persuader's side of the story. In *transcendence*, the persuader attempts to "rise above" the charges being made and to shift the audience's attention to a larger or more noble purpose. Richard Nixon's apologia on the Watergate scandal used transcendence by claiming that the cover-up was necessary to protect national security. You can imagine the variations in style that persuaders might use when applying one or more of these substantive strategies.

Other persuasive genres include gallows speeches made by those about to die, Fourth of July speeches, political campaign speeches, sermons, and resignation speeches.

This discussion of qualitative persuasion research should give you an idea of the breadth of the types of research, and there are other approaches that you may want to explore.

Focus-Group Theory and Research. Another kind of qualitative persuasion research involves collecting nonnumerical symbolic information (words, images, metaphors, and sometimes nonverbal behavior) from groups of persons recruited to participate in *focus groups*. The data extracted from these discussions may then be further tested using quantitative methods. Thus, focus-group methodology bridges the two major halves of the research

What do you think?

Does the use of focus groups by advertisers bother you?

continuum. The basic idea in focus-group methodology is to motivate the group members to freely discuss a given topic about which persuasion is to be constructed (a candidate's image, a brand name, perceptions of a religion, a nonprofit organization). A skilled discussion leader then shapes or focuses the discussion along various themes or selling points. The discussions are taped. Researchers then analyze the tapes looking for patterns of recurring images, words, actions and interactions, themes, and other potentially meaningful symbolic data. This is the qualitative side of the bridge. These findings are then further studied on the quantitative side of the bridge using approaches such as surveys, interviews, or experiments.

In response to the findings, a candidate may alter his or her image, or a company may alter brand names, the organization's goals, packaging, or slogans. Even candidate hairstyles have been altered based on focus group data.

A brief example may help you to understand the art and science of focus-group methods. Consider the development of the "I've got a secret — in the refrigerator" campaign for Arm & Hammer baking soda. At the time of the research, the major uses for the product were as an antacid, for brushing teeth, for eliminating acid from automobile battery terminals, for bathing and cleaning — especially refrigerators — and as a leavening agent, mainly for chocolate chip cookies. Even though Arm & Hammer had a 97 percent share of the market, they wanted to stimulate further customer usage. After all, one box could make about 400 batches of chocolate chip cookies, and very little is needed to brush one's teeth.

In focus-group interviews homemakers discussed their uses of and attitudes toward baking soda. After repeatedly analyzing many such groups, the researchers discovered a sophisticated concept in the minds of many of the homemakers. The concept was that of "refrigerator guilt," caused by not cleaning the refrigerator as often as they remembered their mothers doing so — once a month. The busy homemakers were lucky to get at the job twice a year, always finding several withered vegetables and various unidentifiable and disgusting substances.

The campaign gave homemakers a way to dispel refrigerator guilt by telling them that putting a box of Arm & Hammer in the refrigerator was nearly as effective as a thorough cleaning to absorb odors and keep it smelling sweet. For years the idea had been listed on the Arm & Hammer box as one of the uses for the product, but now it was being marketed from the *consumers'* perspective. The initial ads sometimes featured two homemakers discussing how busy they were and how one seemed to have such a clean refrigerator. She finally admitted that "I've got a secret — in the refrigerator," and the TV viewer would be shown the box inside the refrigerator with vapors — presumably the bad odors — being sucked into it. The second homemaker was duly impressed, vowing to go out and buy the product right away. Later spots needed only to use the slogan and the video showing the vapors getting sucked into the Arm & Hammer box. These commercials were reinforced with print ads depicting the same idea.

The approach was so successful that Arm & Hammer had to postpone a nationwide campaign using it because quantitative market tests showed that they would never be able to meet the increased nationwide demand without building new factories. A year later, with the new factories in operation, the nationwide rollout took place and was a phenomenal success. Today most of us have a box of Arm & Hammer in the refrigerator and one in the freezer, and we pour it down the garbage disposal every two months to "sweeten" the drain. The chocolate chip cookie factor now accounts for only a minuscule slice of annual sales.

The critical factor here was identifying the reason(s) given by consumers who purchased the product and how they used it. Market researchers using such approaches are becoming more and more sophisticated at identifying our vulnerabilities to clever persuasion (Honomichil, 1984).

Quantitative Research Methods and Theory

The following overview of quantitative theoretical perspectives on persuasion should help you see how "scientific" researchers try to identify and explain the effects and uses of the major premises held by audiences. Sometimes the major premise is a need for social approval or to identify with a certain reference group. At other times, the audience's major premise is the need to feel internally consistent. Or the premise may be a shift in attitudes or values or the degree to which one trusts a given persuader.

We can mark the beginning of such perspectives and approaches with the end of World War II. The years before and during the war showed the awesome power of persuasion and propaganda, particularly when conveyed to the masses via the new electronic media. Entire societies could be powerfully manipulated through skillful persuasion. The same kind of mass persuasion was happening in the everyday marketplace as well. In politics, religion, and commerce, effective persuaders were reaching mass audiences in unprecedented numbers and kinds, thanks to the new media of the postwar years. In the social sciences—especially in psychology and sociology—researchers were trying to explain, predict, and ultimately control human behavior. Much of this activity focused on persuasion and on identifying what variables seemed most effective in getting people to change their voting, purchasing, and other behaviors.

This body of quantitative research can be divided into at least five distinct types of research theory and methods: (1) "single-shot" attitude change theory, (2) learning theory, (3) tension-reduction theory, (4) information-processing theory, and (5) mass-media effects theory. There are other scientific approaches to the study of persuasion, but these five should give you a good feel for and a fairly broad perspective concerning contemporary persuasion research.

"Single-Shot" Attitude Change

Single-shot attitude change theory grew out of an ambitious research project conducted by the Yale Communication and Attitude Change Program (Hovland, Janis, & Kelley, 1953). This theory maintains that human behavior is guided by certain constraints or harnesses, and that among the most important of these are attitudes. Thus, if a persuader could change a receiver's attitudes, a change in behavior would result. For instance, if I can change a positive attitude toward smoking (it's a cool thing to do) to a negative attitude (it's an unhealthy, expensive, and filthy thing to do), the receiver ought to change behavior by quitting smoking. The question for the research then becomes: What factors in the persuasive process are most important in changing people's attitudes?

Because the Yale studies were rooted in learning theory and information processing, the researchers assumed that people would change their attitudes if they were provided with sufficient reinforcement or evidence for the change. In other words, people must be motivated to process information that will change their existing attitudes and hence the actions that flow from those attitudes. The researchers maintained that persuasion passes through a chain of five steps or stages (see Figure 3.5):

1. *Attention*. If persuadees do not attend to a message, they cannot be persuaded by it.

2. *Comprehension*. If persuadees do not understand or comprehend a message, they cannot be persuaded by it.

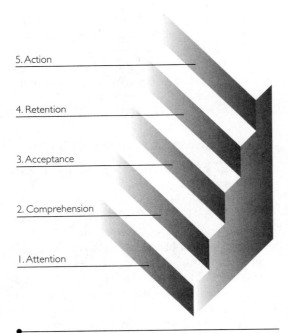

5. Action

4. Retention

3. Acceptance

2. Comprehension

1. Attention

Figure 3.5. *According to information-processing theory, attitude change occurs in five steps.*

3. *Acceptance.* If persuadees reject the message after attending to and comprehending it, they will not be persuaded.

4. *Retention.* Most of the time, persuadees have to withhold action for some time after comprehending and accepting the message. They therefore must retain or remember the message and its advice until the time comes to act on it.

5. *Action.* The specific behavioral change or action requested in the message must be in accordance with the accepted and retained appeals. The Yale approach assumes people act in logical ways that are consistent with the argument of the persuader.

Although each of these elements in the persuasive process is important to the success or fail-

ure of a message, most of the researchers who have conducted studies in the Yale tradition have focused on the third step, the *acceptance* stage. In other words, they tried to discover what factors most powerfully lead to acceptance or rejection of a message. These factors can be grouped into four categories: those related to the source of the persuasive message, those related to the message itself, those related to the channel in which the message was sent, and those related to the receivers who got and responded to the message.

Source. The **source** is an important factor in the acceptance stage in two ways: first is the source's *credibility* or *believability*, which we touched on in our discussion of ethos; second is the source's *attractiveness* to the receiver. Much of the early credibility research relied on the Aristotelian notion of *reputation*. In source-varied studies, the same message was attributed to persuaders having various kinds of reputations. A message about smoking and lung cancer, for example, was attributed either to a college sophomore or to a doctor from the surgeon general's office. Not surprisingly, greater attitude change occurred when the audience believed the message was coming from the doctor than when they thought it was coming from the student. However, with time this "reputation" effect on credibility declined. Hovland and his colleagues called this a "sleeper effect." Thus, reputation affected the immediate acceptance or rejection of a message but had little or no effect on *retention*.

Other source studies have focused on such questions as whether the height of a source leads to more or less attitude change, whether the rate of delivery has effects, whether eye contact has effects, and so on. Researchers have found that perceived height *is* a factor in source attractiveness; taller persuaders are rated as more believable and more trustworthy than shorter ones. Also, if persuaders deliver their messages in halting or introverted ways, they exert less effect on attitudes than those who deliver their speech in smooth and extroverted ways. Gender also influences acceptance; attractive but same-sex persuaders are rated as having less credibility than attractive but opposite-sex persuaders.

An important factor in determining attractiveness or likability in a source seems to be the degree to which the source is similar to ourselves. Most of us probably think of ourselves as nice, likable persons. That is probably why we believe the testimonials of Michael Jordan for various products. Despite his highly successful career, he is still a humble, down-to-earth person. So credibility as a source variable seems to be related to attractiveness and likability. But there are other dimensions to source credibility—honesty, for example.

The overall conclusion of the Yale studies on credibility is that sometimes reputation is a critical factor and sometimes it interacts with attractiveness, similarity, or other variables.

Message. Another factor in persuasion is the nature of the **message.** For example, researchers have studied such variables as the order of presentation of the message—should the most important piece of evidence be presented first or last (Hovland, 1959)? Once again, the considerable body of research on this question has not produced any clear-cut conclusions. Sometimes it is better to place the most controversial or important piece of evidence first in the message; at other times it is better to present it later. One significant finding, however, is that receivers play an important part in determining whether particular evidence affects their attitudes. When the evidence is in line with the receiver's beliefs, it will be accepted and will cause a greater shift in attitudes than when it runs counter to the receiver's beliefs (Petty and Cacioppo, 1986). Of course, that makes perfect sense—we all like to hear, and we remember, things that confirm our beliefs.

Another aspect of the message is whether the persuader presents one side or two sides of a particular topic. Many studies using varied topics have concluded that two-sided messages seem to be more effective in the long run, especially with people who are opposed to your side of the story.

Using appeals to fear in the message has also received research attention. The overall conclusion is that the use of moderate fear appeals seems to produce the most enduring and significant changes in attitudes and behavior. Receivers quit smoking more often when given moderately frightening reasons for doing so (for example, "You run a risk of contracting lung cancer, heart disease, or emphysema and dying at a young age if you smoke") than when given highly frightening reasons (for example, "You will die a painful and horrible death"). High-fear appeals seem to produce a "boomerang effect"—the persuadees reject the message because it is too frightening (McGuire, 1968).

Other aspects of messages, such as amount of evidence, use of visual aids, and so on, have also been studied. The results are not conclusive, suggesting that change is caused by multiple variables.

Channel. The **channel** is studied in several ways. An obvious approach is to compare the effects of an identical message transmitted over different channels—the print medium versus the audiovisual medium, for instance. Usually, messages presented via the audiovisual medium result in greater attitude change than do those on the audio channel alone, and messages on the audio channel in turn produce greater acceptance and attitude change than printed versions of the same message—*as long as the message is simple.* Once a certain level of complexity is reached, the written channel is most effective. And with the introduction and widespread adoption of e-mail and the Internet, a totally new set of variables enters the picture. Does the ability to have immediate interactivity alter the persuasion ratios? How critical is the loss of nonverbal information for the interactive word? Does the interactive word affect our feelings about what it means to be a member of an audience? These are just a few of the many other questions which remain to be addressed, let alone answered.

An interesting aspect of the channel effect in attitude change is *noise*. In noise studies, an attempt is made to distract the receivers. The distractions can be caused by showing one thing visually (on a screen, for instance) while telling another thing in the auditory channel. In the short run, such distractions accompany more attitude change when the topics run counter to the original attitudes of the receivers. The short-term change associated with the distraction quickly fades, however (Watts & Holt, 1979). Again, it is the receiver who makes the difference. If the message resonates with the receiver, one result occurs; if it clashes with the receiver's position, another result occurs.

Receiver. Although numerous attitude-change studies explore the various aspects of the **receiver** that affect persuasion, they tend to cluster around two central issues: *personality variables*, such as self-esteem, confidence, anxiety, or ego defensiveness, and the degree to which the receiver is *ego involved* with or committed to the issue at hand. Generally speaking, high self-esteem makes us willing and able to comprehend and weigh messages, but it also makes us somewhat immune to persuasion. Low self-esteem makes people vulnerable to being influenced and to shifting their attitudes. This makes sense. A lack of certainty about the self will deter you from coming to grips with difficult issues, contradictory facts, and differing opinions. On the other hand, high self-esteem gives you the confidence to risk analyzing opposing views or entering into arguments. This makes you less vulnerable to persuaders.

Self-esteem seems to work hand-in-hand with one's degree of ego involvement with a topic. If you are deeply involved in some issue — say the environment — not only will you devote time and resources to the issue but you will be able to remember and produce many counter-arguments to a opponent and supporting data for your position. As Figure 3.6 demonstrates, when faced with opposition to a topic with which we are highly ego involved, we are likely to try to defend our position, as the postmaster seems ready to do. Further, because of our commitment, we will have more persuasive ammunition than an uninvolved persuadee. However, when the other's persuasion is consistent with our position, we process this information efficiently and respond with greater attitude change than do those having less involvement.

What do you think?

Which type of variable in the SMCR model seems to have the most effect?

Other Variables. Apparently, attitudes are not the only constraint on behavior — or perhaps they interact in varied ways with other variables. This problem will resurface when we discuss tension-reduction theories and the social judgment—involvement theories.

It isn't strange that researchers find it difficult to consistently demonstrate attitude-behavior relationships, because attitudes involve a complex set of beliefs. Values are even more complex. When I value free enterprise, I base my value on many attitudes — attitudes toward profit, capitalism, laws of supply and demand, and competition. Just as each attitude is made up of a complex set of beliefs, each value is made up of a complex set of attitudes.

Social psychologist Martin Fishbein suggests measuring the effects of various persuasive variables on the persuadees' behavioral intentions and not on their attitudes. Instead of asking people to rate their attitude toward recycling, for example, Fishbein would ask them to rate their in-

Figure 3.6. *Here the receiver is determining "meaning." Does the cartoon resonate with your experiences? If so, how does that affect the credibility of the U.S. Postal Service?* (Frank and Ernest *reprinted by permission of NEA, Inc.*)

tentions to actually *engage in* recycling. Following this initial response, the persuasion variable—say evidence—is introduced. After hearing about how many thousands of years it takes for a plastic bleach bottle to decompose, how much longer present landfills would last with recycling, how much usable material could be recycled, what it would be worth, and other evidence about the issue, the subjects would again rate their intentions to recycle. Not only does this approach focus on a less fickle measure, but it seems to be better at predicting actual behavior (Fishbein and Ajzen, 1975). It follows that if you want to test the effects of a certain advertising or public relations campaign, you need to test behavioral intentions, not attitudes. Ask the consumer "Do you intend to try the new brand?" instead of asking them "How positive or negative do you feel about the new brand?" Even the act of saying "Yes, I intend to try the brand" is a kind of commitment that is likely to lead to actual purchase behavior.

Rokeach's Belief Hierarchy. Another researcher interested in the effects of attitudes on behavior is social psychologist Milton Rokeach (1973). Rokeach's theory assumes a hierarchy of beliefs, attitudes (which are stronger and more complex than beliefs), and values (which are stronger and more complex than both beliefs and attitudes). He examines beliefs as the building blocks for attitudes. Thus, any attitude carries with it several, perhaps many, beliefs, and these attitudes cluster around the strongest element in Rokeach's hierarchy—values. In other words, each person has countless beliefs, far fewer attitudes, and probably a rather limited number of true values.

Beliefs can be general or specific, significant or insignificant. They are the statements each of us makes about himself or herself and the world each of us perceives. For example, I have lots of beliefs about the sport of fishing. They relate to lure selection, water temperature, how I really relax when fishing, and many more aspects of fishing. These and related beliefs lead to a positive attitude toward fishing, and as a result I try to go out fishing (a behavior) as often as possible.

We can have attitudes about objects or things and attitudes about situations, and the two types can interact. For example, my positive attitude toward fishing sometimes clashes with my attitude toward accomplishment and job responsibility. When these attitudes clash, I must choose between them or find some way to satisfy both attitudinal positions. In other words, I may choose to go fishing and forget about work, I may postpone the fishing trip and go to work, or I may take some work with me on the fishing trip.

Many attitudes are related to the most important and powerful concepts in Rokeach's hierarchy — human values. *Values* are specific sets of beliefs and attitudes that act as long-term goals. There are two types of such values: terminal values and instrumental values. *Terminal values* are ultimate life goals and would be expressed in statements such as the following: "I want to be a success," "I want freedom," "I want true friends," "I want a sense of accomplishment," "I want to be a world-class fisherman," "I want inner peace." *Instrumental values*, on the other hand, are the tools with which one hopes to achieve one's terminal values and life goals. They could be expressed in statements such as the following: "I will be efficient," "I will be polite and cheerful," "I will read about fishing."

Rokeach speculates that attitudes, beliefs, and values are interwoven and ranked in various hierarchies into a single belief system that receivers bring to the persuasive situation. Like the layers of an onion, some are at the core, or center, of the system, whereas others are at the periphery. The outer layers are much easier to alter than the ones at the center, and as we get closer and closer to the core, change becomes nearly impossible. Rokeach postulates five levels of belief:

1. *Primitive beliefs (unanimous consensus)*. These core beliefs come from our direct experience of the world. We find consensus about them from our peers. An example might be that the sun sets in the west. These beliefs rarely change and are almost axiomatic. When they are challenged, we find life to be very disturbing. If you've ever been lost and confused about direction and then discovered that what you thought was east is actually west, you know how disturbing that can be. Many persons your parents' age had almost primitive beliefs about job security until

the early '90s when "downsizing" came in and they found themselves unemployed at age fifty-something.

2. *Primitive beliefs (zero consensus)*. These beliefs are also learned by direct experience but are private and sometimes idiosyncratic. They are personal, and we don't get direct outside confirmation. An example might be a belief that we are basically a certain kind of person — lazy, energetic, selfish, or generous. Another might relate to our perceptions of how others feel about us, such as "Most people like me." These beliefs also rarely change.

3. *Authority beliefs*. These beliefs are sometimes controversial and depend on our interchange with others — usually our parents or peers. "It's best to tell the truth — then you don't have to remember" is an example I received from my parents. These beliefs are changeable, but only with much experience or persuasion.

4. *Derived beliefs*. These are beliefs we develop from our interchanges with sources we trust, but in a secondhand fashion instead of directly. Examples might be beliefs we develop from reading books, hearing news reports, or listening to persons whose credibility is high (editors, political leaders, or perhaps religious leaders). These are easier to change than any of the deeper beliefs.

5. *Inconsequential beliefs*. These beliefs relate to individual preferences and tastes and are relatively easy to change because we don't have to alter our self-identity to change them. "I prefer living where there is a change of seasons" is an example.

Values, taken together with our attitudes and beliefs, result in what Rokeach called our *self-concept*. We all want to be satisfied with ourselves, and we work hard to achieve this sense of well-being. Although shifts in beliefs or attitudes

Berry's World

"Next week, try to identify with BART Simpson, instead of Homer."

Figure 3.7. How would this patient's self-concept differ if he identified with Bart? Would any of his terminal values be changed? What about his instrumental values? (Berry's World reprinted by permission of NEA, Inc.)

might result in short-term changes in behavior, only values serve as life guides that dictate a lifelong set of behaviors in either terminal or instrumental ways (see Figure 3.7).

Learning Theory and Research

Some researchers define *persuasion* as a specialized kind of learning. We *learn* to believe in a certain religion. We *learn* to set certain goals for our-

selves. We *learn* to behave in a certain way and to vary our behavior according to the situation. There are many learning theories, and most contemporary ones are rooted in the behavioral tradition. Their goal is to predict and ultimately to control behavior through such methods as conditioning.

Skinnerian Behaviorism. The name most identified with the word "behaviorism" is of course B. F. Skinner, and much of Skinner's work is applicable to the study of persuasion (Skinner, 1957). For example, Skinner identified what he called **schedules of reinforcement** (Le Francois, 1980). This refers to how frequently and for what kind of behavior positive or negative stimuli (or what most of us call rewards or punishments) are presented. If a positive stimulus (or reinforcer) is presented for every instance of a specified behavior, the schedule is a *continuous* one. We all behave in conformity with such schedules in our everyday lives. Vending machines, for example, regularly give us items whenever we deposit money (unless they are not functioning properly).

Skinner called his second kind of reinforcement *intermittent reinforcement,* indicating that not all correct responses result in reinforcement. Skinner further suggested that these intermittent schedules could occur on either a *ratio* or *interval* basis and further that the ratio or interval could be *fixed* or *variable* (see Figure 3.8). With a *fixed ratio* schedule, a correct response is reinforced after so many specific responses; piecework in a factory is an example. With a *random,* or *variable,* ratio schedule, the number of correct responses or lever presses resulting in reinforcement is not predictable (a behavior might be reinforced after the 5th, then 19th, then 11th response, and so on). With a *fixed interval* schedule, the subject is reinforced at predictable time intervals (such as every 5 minutes), while with a *random (variable) interval* schedule, the length of time between reinforcements is not predictable (after 5 minutes,

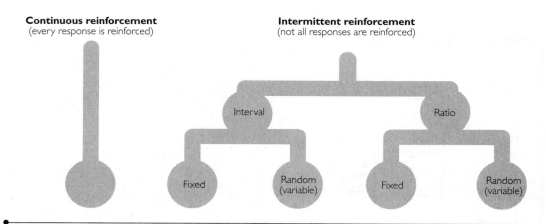

Continuous reinforcement
(every response is reinforced)

Intermittent reinforcement
(not all responses are reinforced)

Interval

Ratio

Fixed

Random
(variable)

Fixed

Random
(variable)

Figure 3.8. *The five basic schedules of reinforcement: continuous, fixed-interval, random interval, fixed ratio, and random ratio. These may be combined in a variety of ways. (Reprinted by permission of Guy R. Le Francois and Wadsworth Publishing Co.)*

then after 20 minutes, then after 1 minute, then after 28 minutes, and so on).

None of this is very complicated when you think of it. B. F. Skinner merely systematized and labeled the process of reinforcement. But his work was extremely important because it helped people in a wide variety of contexts determine analytically whether they were appropriately reinforcing others. For example, Skinner worked with the Emery Air Freight company to increase employee productivity and accuracy. Giving verbal rewards to employees for answering the phone within two rings, for routing deliveries efficiently, and for packaging items efficiently, Skinner got extremely significant improvements in a short time. We could say that he used praise to "persuade" the workers to improve. Many parents wonder if they have "spoiled" their children by giving too much positive reinforcement.

Let's look to the world of advertising for some examples of how schedules of reinforcement are used or appealed to in order to persuade. Consider the ad for Chivas Regal scotch in Figure 3.9. The six panels depict a repeated gesture — the giving

and receiving of Chivas on special occasions. The ad is intended not for the person getting the Chivas but for the person who gives it. Everyone knows the good feelings one gets for bringing the perfect gift, and the reward for being considered thoughtful and clever by others. That is the positive reinforcement. On the other hand, if I see a character in an ad for deodorant get rejected because he or she has BO, I will try to avoid this negative reinforcement by using the brand.

In the world of politics, the persuader's task is to determine the voter's pattern of reinforcement. This is why candidates engage in so much polling: to determine whether their stimuli — speeches, ads, position papers, and so forth — are making a difference with the voters. Getting "dissed" on a computer chat group is a kind of negative reinforcement.

As receivers/voters, we need to evaluate the reinforcements politicians offer us. Are the campaign promises positive or negative

What do you think?

Name a reinforcement that is particularly effective with you?

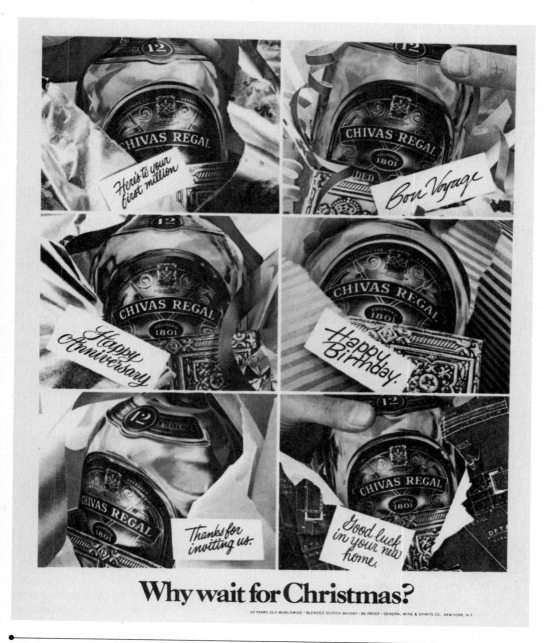

Figure 3.9. *What reward does this ad imply that purchasers of Chivas Regal will receive? What is the reward for the recipients? (Used by permission of General Wine and Spirits Corp.)*

stimuli? What will we have to do to get the positive reinforcements and to avoid the negative ones? Unlike the theories discussed earlier, traditional learning theory places less emphasis on the receiver than on the source. In fact, Skinner would not admit to the testing of any **black-box constructs.** By this he meant mental states such as drives, motives, instincts, attitudes, values, or beliefs. All of these were unknowable to Skinner because they are all internal in a person's mind and body — they are inside the "black box." For him, correlation of the subject's behavior with the researcher's manipulation of the environment was the only real observation that could be recorded. Behavior could thus relate to things outside the persuadee, such as room color, rather than internal things, such as mood.

Social Learning Theory and Research. Albert Bandura's social learning theory is not as restrictive as Skinnerian behaviorism and does permit concepts that are inside the "black box" to explain how change occurs (1972). Bandura believes that humans respond to the continuous interaction between their internal state and the social reinforcements that follow from their behavior with others. Thus we learn how to behave from our social interactions. When we perceive that a certain behavior is not socially rewarding or perhaps even leads to social punishment, we learn (or are persuaded) to continue the behavior or to cease it. The reinforcers come from two major sources: external information, in the form of direct or vicarious experience, and internally developed, self-reinforcing systems such as our self-concept.

From the external world, we may get direct rewards or punishment for our behavior and as a result discover a social rule and behave accordingly. For example, let's suppose that you become a member of an Internet chat group or network. You will soon discover the social rules of the Web, or "Netiquette" as it is known. You may be

reprimanded for sending personal messages to one member of the network using the entire network or for posting excessively long messages. These social rules will soon alter your Internet behavior, and the same pattern of learning occurs for other behaviors. Most of the social rules we follow are learned through direct experience, and, although many of them are formed in our early years, we continue to discover new social rules throughout our lives.

Another external source through which we learn acceptable social behavior is **role playing.** We all do this every day — we imagine ourselves in the position of some other person or in some other situation. In this safe context — the imaginary role — we can try various alternatives without risk. We can imagine, for example, what other persons will say or do in response to us. Once we have perfected the script in the role-playing context, we can then test it out in the real world with real participants. In many companies, management personnel are asked to role-play the person they may have to fire the next week or the person with whom they will have a performance appraisal interview. In these uses of the technique, we learn or persuade ourselves to behave in socially acceptable ways.

A final external source of reinforcement identified by Bandura is the use of **role models.** We all admire certain individuals — sports heroes, successful persons, leaders, and others. Because we admire them, we emulate their behavior or take their advice. Candice Bergen tells us that Sprint is the telephone service that will allow us to stay in contact with grandma. The screen dissolves to an attractive young mother calling her mother and letting the kids talk to grandma. The message of the ad is that calling grandma is socially desirable behavior. We also get many examples of acceptable behavior from our family and peers. We model our behavior after theirs and in so doing persuade ourselves to value that kind of behavior. Many of these models come to us through the mass media and can persuade large groups to behave in similar ways.

Role models also seem to be more important at some times in our lives and less important at other times. Junior high school seems to be a time when peer role models heavily influence behavior. Early adulthood, the much-talked-about "midlife crisis" at age thirty-five or forty, and retirement are others. During each of these periods, we persuade ourselves to alter our behavior in conformity to, or sometimes in defiance of, socially approved patterns.

The second major source of reinforcements comes from within each person. These self-given reinforcements develop early and continue to develop and shift throughout life. They are closely tied to one's self-concept. For example, one thing I value about myself is that I am blunt. I don't like people who beat around the bush when discussing an issue. Although my bluntness is sometimes positively reinforced and sometimes punished by external sources, the most powerful reinforcer for bluntness is my own evaluation of whether it is generally a good thing to be blunt. In fact, I interpret the reactions of others to my bluntness as being positive—sometimes people thank me for getting all the cards on the table or for telling it like it is. But even when I get hostile responses from others, I tell myself that it was worth it to cut through all the baloney.

Persons with low self-esteem give themselves little internal self-reinforcement for their actions; persons with high self-esteem give themselves lots of self-reinforcement. Of course, if I run into repeated negative responses and maybe even censure, I may shift my behavior and correspondingly alter my internal reward systems.

Tension-Reduction Theory and Research

Tension-reduction theories (also referred to as *consistency theories*), as the name implies, rest on the assumption that human beings want to reduce psychic tension in their lives. Often this tension arises from differences between two sets of information (the one you have in your head and the one a persuader introduces) or between your behavior and a set of information that a persuader presents to you, as when a smoker continues the habit in the face of evidence showing the unhealthy effects of smoking. The inconsistency might also be between your behavior and the behavior that is expected of you by another person in a given situation. Your professor expects certain behavior from you (being prompt, meeting deadlines, or taking pride in work done) and may experience inconsistency when a student doesn't exhibit the expected behavior. The professor may try to resolve these inconsistencies through counseling or perhaps a reprimand.

Balance Theory. The earliest consistency theory was proposed by Fritz Heider (1946, 1958) and later elaborated by Theodore Newcomb (1953), who applied it to the simplest form of human communication: one person communicating with another about a single topic. In this extremely simple situation, inconsistencies may arise when you hold a certain belief or opinion about the topic and the other person holds a slightly different position.

Such disagreements are common. You have probably experienced this type of recurring but never-resolved argument frequently. The discomfort that arises provides the human dynamics for the Heider-Newcomb explanation of **balance theory.** When tensions arise either between or within individuals, they try to reduce these tensions, by self-persuasion, changing beliefs, or trying to persuade others. Here is where balance theory offers strategies for persuasion.

Let's look at how such instances of balance or imbalance might be diagrammed. Attitudes between two persons (the persuader and the persuadee) can be represented by positive signs (+)

or by negative signs (−). Thus, the two persons could like (+) or dislike (−) one another. They could agree that the issue they are dealing with has bad (−) or good (+) values. One person may feel good (+) about the topic whereas the other feels bad (−) toward it. Notice in Figure 3.10 that both the receiver and the source have good feelings about each other. Because they agree on the topic and relate positively toward each other, they have a feeling of comfort—in Heider's word, *balance*.

There are three ways in which a person can feel this balance:

1. The source and receiver can have a negative attitude toward the object or idea and a positive attitudinal set toward one another, as in Figure 3.10. (You and I can both dislike politics and like each other, so we experience comfort and balance.)

2. The source and receiver can have a positive attitude toward the object or idea and can have good feelings toward one another. (You and I like fishing and like each other, thus experiencing comfort and balance.)

3. The source and receiver can disagree about the idea or object and can dislike each other. (You and I dislike each other, so it is comforting to know that we don't agree on the topic.) It is nice to know that those we respect and like have the same values and ideas as we do. It is also nice to know that those nincompoops we dislike don't agree with us.

The persuader who tries to strengthen pre-existing beliefs in an audience can do so by creating a *balanced* situation for the receiver. As persuadees, we need to be aware of this strategy. When persuaders tell you what you already know or believe (for example, that living in a suburb is bad, that the price of food is skyrocketing, that recycling is good), you ought to realize that creating balance is their strategy.

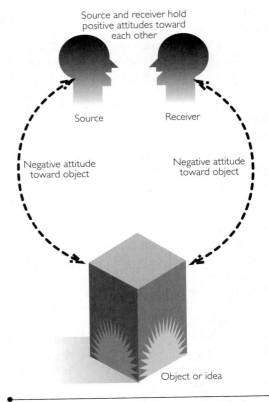

Source and receiver hold positive attitudes toward each other

Source   Receiver

Negative attitude toward object   Negative attitude toward object

Object or idea

Figure 3.10. *The Heider-Newcomb model of balance.*

Suppose that the persuader wants to *change* beliefs and attitudes. It would be foolish to try to create balance for the persuadees. Instead, persuaders will try to throw our view of the world out of whack by creating imbalance, in which our beliefs are shaken. Consider Figure 3.11. In this situation, someone I do not respect dislikes the same things I dislike. I am bound to feel uncomfortable, or in a state of imbalance, in such a case. How can I agree with such an idiot?

I think my next-door neighbor is a jackass. If we agreed about a topic, issue, candidate, or brand, I would feel "dis-ease." Given that situation, I would have to alter either my opinion of my neighbor or my opinion about the topic to achieve balance. Thus, to persuade persons to change their minds, persuaders need to create imbalance. The sense of inconsistency forces the receiver to shift evaluations to achieve balance and thus psychological comfort.

There are probably only two ways in which imbalance in persuasive situations can be created:

1. If the source and receiver favor each other but disagree about an object or idea, the receiver will experience imbalance.

2. If the source and receiver disfavor each other but agree on attitudes toward an object or idea, the receiver will experience imbalance.

Again, a principle we already know is operating. We want the world to live up to our expectations of it. If it does not, we experience imbalance; if it does, we experience balance.

Persuaders who want to get receivers to change their minds about an idea or object create feelings of psychological imbalance, or discomfort. When persuaders try to destroy your beliefs (for example, that joining a fraternity will detract from your studies), you ought to realize that they are creating imbalance for you. They want to change your opinion by relying on your need for psychological balance, or comfort.

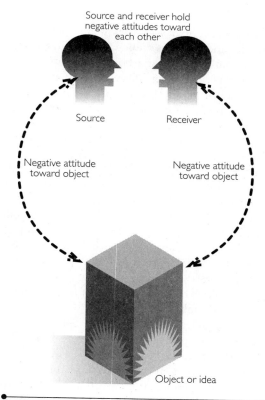

Figure 3.11. *The Heider-Newcomb model of imbalance.*

Cognitive Dissonance Theory. A problem for balance theory relates to the degree of difference between the two people or the two instances to be judged. In other words, although the theory accounts for *qualitative* differences between judgments, it doesn't deal with *quantitative* differences. At first glance, this may seem to be a minor problem, but when you consider the amount of difference that might exist between persons or between concepts in regard to controversial topics such as abortion or school prayer, you can see the need to take into account how far persons are from one another on a topic. **Cognitive disso-** nance theory, first suggested by Leon Festinger (1962), addresses this problem of quantitative as well as qualitative differences between persons and ideas. Unlike balance theory, which predicts *changes* in attitudes, judgments, or evaluations, dissonance theory predicts that when we experience psychological tension, we try to *reduce* it in some way. **Tension reduction** involves more than just change; it has a *quantitative* dimension. In other words, we can change our evaluations or judgments a little, a moderate amount, a lot, or not at all. Another feature of dissonance theory is that the tension is produced by dissonance within an individual's *psychological* system.

Balance theory relies more on *logical* inconsistencies than on *psychological* ones. However, our attitudes and opinions are made up of how we *feel* about various ideas and how that relates to our prior experience, our idiosyncrasies, and so on. Dissonance theory allows us to take those things into consideration. Let us examine its major tenets in more detail.

Festinger defines dissonance as a feeling resulting from the existence of two nonfitting pieces of knowledge about the world. As in balance theory, there are times when things fit, or "go together." This is *consonance*, from the Latin "to sound together, harmonize, agree." Festinger's term for balance exists when "considering a pair of elements either one [of which] does follow from the other." Although I may greatly dislike telemarketers as a group, I might like a certain salesperson. This may create slight feelings of dissonance or imbalance.

Festinger says that any two beliefs can be shown as two parallel lines (see Figure 3.12). The bottom bar shows belief A, and the X above it marks a position on that belief. The top bar represents other information about A. The Y above this bar represents our position on the new information, which we might call belief B. The distance between these two points—X and Y—is the amount of *dissonance* we feel. The world is not acting as it should. The dissonance must be reduced, providing the basis for many actions. Some persons change dissonant cognitions

by moving their beliefs closer to one another. Others rationalize the problem away by discrediting the source of the cognitions. Others escape from feelings of dissonance by the process of selective perception, selective retention, or selective exposure; in other words, they choose to forget, not to receive/perceive, or not to be exposed to the information.

Today a new sense of "dis-ease" is filling everyone who is sexually active, and most intelligent persons know that the major causes of infection by the AIDS virus are unsafe sex practices, the sharing of needles among drug users, and, to some degree, blood transfusions or accidental exposure of one's blood to the blood of AIDS carriers.

What can sexually active people do to reduce these feelings of psychological "dis-ease"? They have a variety of options:

1. They may devalue their initial beliefs about the most appropriate methods of birth control and use condoms.

2. They may devalue the AIDS information by telling themselves that this news blitz is just a scare tactic dreamed up to cut down on the promiscuity of the younger generation.

3. They may selectively perceive the information, telling themselves that their sexual partners are not likely carriers of the AIDS virus. This process is called *selective perception*.

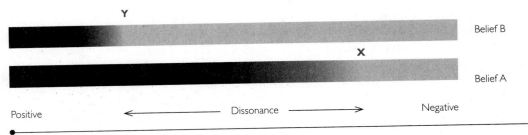

Figure 3.12. Festinger's model of dissonance.

4. They may try to forget the frightening information about AIDS. This process, called *selective retention,* means remembering or forgetting whatever you want to.

5. They may try to rationalize the problem away by telling themselves that a cure for AIDS is just around the corner.

6. They may become celibate or have fewer partners.

7. They may do more than one of the above.

Although Festinger does not deal in depth with the notion of consonance, it seems clear that we seek it. We listen to the candidate of our choice but more often than not avoid listening to the person we will not vote for. Conservative people read conservative newspapers; liberal people read liberal newspapers. The most avid readers of ads for Fords are persons who just bought a Ford. Chicago Cubs fans try not to expect a winning season so they won't feel disappointed, while Chicago Bulls fans not only expect a winning season, they expect a championship. Let's suppose you decided to major in communication and then discover that the jobs in that field are plentiful and well paid. You experience consonance, especially because it was the attractive job opportunities that lured you into the field anyway.

Experiences like this are common; we find information confirming our position, and that makes our belief stronger. We can take many actions as a result of feelings of consonance:

1. We can revalue our initial beliefs, making them stronger in all likelihood—"It really *was* a good idea to major in communication."

2. We can revalue the source of the information input. "Boy! Those other communication students are really sharp and on the ball. They'll go far in this world!"

3. We can perceive the information as stronger than it actually is and focus on the strongest parts of it.

4. We may remember the most positive parts of the information and choose to highlight those that best support our belief—the high salaries, maybe.

5. We may seek more supporting information by going to the placement office, for instance, and copying down the starting salaries of communication graduates.

6. We may do several of the above.

The tactic of creating consonance, then, is used to strengthen attitudes, to gird existing cognitions, and to increase one's source of credibility. Consonance probably is used as frequently in persuasion as is dissonance, for persuaders often want to reinforce people's opinions, attitudes, beliefs, or behaviors.

Unfortunately, Festinger's theory and the myriad resulting research studies focus mainly on those cases in which dissonance arises. Another shortcoming of the theory is that it, like its predecessors, oversimplifies the human situation. Nonetheless, we know a great deal more about persuasion today as a result of Festinger's theory. Most important, Festinger's work emphasizes what the receiver does with the persuasion aimed at him or her. It is the receiver's internal state and psychological mechanisms that determine the outcome of persuasive appeals at least as much as does the source's skill at designing and delivering the message. In Figure 3.13, Moses seems to know the internal state of the children of Israel better than Jehovah does. As a result, Moses offers advice on message design.

What do you think?

What causes feelings of dissonance for you?

Figure 3.13. *What kind of imbalance, incongruity, or dissonance is Moses feeling in this cartoon? Why?* (Frank and Ernest *reprinted by permission of NEA, Inc.*)

Information-Processing Theory and Research

In a sense, all communication and hence all persuasion basically relies on the processing of information. Among the information-processing theories are social judgment/social involvement theory and elaboration/likelihood theory.

Social Judgment/Social Involvement Theory and Research. Social judgment/social involvement theory claims that two elements in a persuasion situation shape how we process persuasive information prior to making a decision (Sherif & Sherif, 1965, 1967).

The first of these elements is the "anchor point," or the internal reference point with which we compare persons, issues, products, and so on that we encounter in the "real world." For example, "concentrated" or "ultra" detergent brands were promoted as being "new and improved" because less detergent was needed for a load of laundry. When consumers first encountered these products, what would they have used as a criterion for judging the effectiveness of the concentrated soap? They probably used the "regular" version of the brand they had used in the past. If the new and improved version was as effective as the

old, they probably switched to the concentrate, simply because it was lighter to carry and took less space—both benefits to the average consumer. If, however, the new and improved version seemed to be less effective, they probably stayed with their traditional form of the product. Their anchor point for the purchase decision was the "old," familiar product form. Our anchor points are always present when we make decisions, and they always influence our decisions in some way. The stronger the anchor point, the more influence it has.

The second element in the social judgment/social involvement model is the receiver's "ego involvement" in the brand, issue, candidate, or whatever is under consideration. Many brand-loyal consumers are highly ego-involved with their "favorite" brand. With more significant choices facing the persuadee, his or her ego involvement increases. For example, the children of Republican voters are quite likely to vote for G.O.P candidates regularly because their ego involvement regarding political preference is high. Some consumers purchase only General Electric or Ford or Magnavox products because of their experience with the brand in the past. It is very difficult to get people to donate money to a new or unfamiliar "good cause" because they have no ego involvement in the issue. For example, when few persons knew what the initials AIDS even stood for, it was difficult to solicit donations for foundations trying to get at the causes and a possible cure for the disease. The average citizen had no ego involvement with the disease. After substantial publicity about AIDS victims who hadn't been needle sharers or homosexuals, it became easier for people to donate to the foundations, because they were more ego involved with the disease and realized that everyone was at risk to some degree.

Surrounding our various anchor points are sets of decisions at varying levels of commitment or sacrifice. The Sherifs identified three clusters of such commitment or sacrifice. The first, one's *latitude of acceptance*, consists of those options that one might likely accept. Some might be more or less acceptable than others, but all are tolerable in some measure. The *latitude of rejection* consists of those options that one would not accept (see Figure 3.14). Again, some are more intolerable, but all options are unacceptable in this region. Between the latitudes of acceptance and rejection is the *latitude of noncommitment*. These are options we don't feel all that strongly about, and we are willing to consider the pros and cons about them.

The various methods proposed for reducing the federal deficit and the national debt exemplify the dynamics of these latitudes. Some of the proposals—such as a ten-cents-a-gallon increase in the tax on fuel used for nonbusiness transportation—may be within our latitude of acceptance. Others—such as a tax on heating fuel—may be outside our latitude of acceptance but inside our latitude of noncommitment—we are willing to consider the arguments in favor of and against this option. Other options—such as an increase in gasoline prices to European levels—are probably in the latitude of rejection for most U.S. citizens.

You can see how a person's anchor points and latitudes of acceptance, rejection, and noncom-

"In order to avoid contracting AIDS, I . . ."

Latitude of acceptance
(positive/compliant)

A = ". . . will ignore the warnings."

B = ". . . will use condoms when engaging in sex."

C = ". . . will bank my own blood when scheduled for surgery."

Latitude of noncommitment
(neutral/will consider)

D = ". . . will probably limit the number of partners I have."

E = ". . . will ask my partners if they have been tested positive for HIV."

Latitude of rejection
(neutral/noncompliant)

F = ". . . will severely limit the number of sex partners I have."

G = ". . . will become monogamous."

H = ". . . will become celibate."

Figure 3.14. *Social judgment/social involvement latitudes and options.*

mitment can interact and determine which persuasive messages succeed. Put another way, receivers are almost immune from persuasion in their latitude of rejection, and open to persuasion and objective about issues in their latitude of noncommitment, as Figure 3.15 demonstrates. For some of us, the latitude of acceptance on a given issue is wide, whereas for others it is narrow. The same is true of the latitudes of rejection and noncommitment—they vary from issue to issue and from person to person.

Our **ego involvement** with a particular brand, issue, candidate, or good cause can also affect the options we choose. As defined by the

"You'll start work on Monday, Miss Finley....
And please, no blue jeans or halter tops."

Figure 3.15. *The boss here is talking about the company's latitude of rejection. In terms of social judgment/social involvement theory, explain the humor in the rules of dress.* (Reprinted from the Saturday Evening Post © 1990.)

Sherifs and fellow researchers, ego involvement is an attitude that persuadees incorporate as part of themselves. If people's involvement is particularly strong, they may even *label* themselves with the position, as in "I'm a feminist" or "I'm an environmentalist" or "I'm a militiaman."

The Sherifs thought that social affiliation with like thinkers is a critical factor in determining the degree of ego involvement a person has in a given issue — "birds of a feather. . . ." Whatever the degree of involvement, it will lead to message distortion. Highly involved persons see things as either pro or con — there is no middle ground for them. Less-involved persons do not polarize as much, and for them there are probably shades of gray and areas where they can see both sides of the story. Highly involved persons may judge an issue as so close to their anchors that they incorporate the position as their own. The Sherifs call this phenomenon **assimilation,** or minimiz-

ing the difference between one's anchors and new information. Highly involved persons also compare and distort positions that differ from their own; they see a greater discrepancy than there really is. This is called the **contrast effect.** It is usually impossible to change highly ego-involved persons and, for this reason, most persuasion is aimed not at them but at persons with low to moderate involvement.

Again, we see that the receiver is central in the explanation of persuasive effects in social judgment/social involvement theory. An important difference here, however, is that social commitments to or identifications with a particular peer group enter in and are especially important if the receiver has become highly involved in the issue by making a public commitment to the issue.

Put another way, receivers are extremely vulnerable to persuasion within their latitude of acceptance, almost immune from persuasion in their latitude of rejection, and open to persuasion and objective about issues in their latitude of noncommitment. It is critical that persuaders know what are audiences' latitudes of acceptance, rejection, and noncommitment in order to shape messages that really persuade.

In summary, social judgment/social involvement theory has several implications for the reception of persuasive messages:

1. Messages that fall within one's latitude of acceptance will probably lead to a good deal of attitude change and perhaps behavioral change.

2. Messages that fall within one's latitude of rejection are not likely to lead to attitude or behavior change.

3. Messages that fall within one's latitude of noncommitment will be considered and may lead to attitude and behavior change depending on other variables, especially one's level of ego involvement.

Elaboration Likelihood Theory and Research.
Social psychologists Richard Petty and John Cacioppo (1986) have suggested what they call elaboration likelihood theory as a possible approach to information processing in persuasive situations. They argue that human beings exhibit one or more kinds of reactions to information: They can *cognitively* know and understand it; they can *affectively,* or emotionally, feel about it; and they can *exhibit behavior* toward it.

The elaboration likelihood model highlights two critical concepts: the receiver's *thought process* (how much thinking goes into making decisions based on persuasion) and, more important, the receiver's *involvement with the topic or decision* — in other words, how likely it is that the decision will affect the person's life. High-involvement issues or decisions are processed centrally, whereas low-involvement decisions are processed peripherally. Persuasion in the central-processing route occurs "as a result of a person's careful and thoughtful considerations of the true merits of the information present" (p. 3). Persuasion in the peripheral processing route occurs "as the result of some simple cue in the persuasion context (for example, an attractive source)" (p. 3).

To simplify things, let's say that we can either think "a little" or "a lot" about a topic, depending on our motivation and our ability to process information. If the decision to be made is complex and personally involving — which kind of computer to buy, for example — then "a lot" of careful thinking will go on. Price won't be the only thing we consider and compare. We might compare megs of memory, modem speed, software, warranty, service, and other complex factors. Our thinking will involve reasoning, scrutiny of evidence, and an evaluation of our computing needs, to name a few. This information will be centrally processed. If, on the other hand, the decision to be made is trivial — between two kinds of household bleach, for example — we are not likely to think a lot about the decision. After all, most

brands are about the same, so there is little "risk to substitutability," and we are likely to make a purchase decision based on price, packaging, who endorses the product, sales promotion, or some other minor element. In other words, choosing a computer will involve the cognitive and central processing route, while choosing a bleach will rely on the affective, emotional, peripheral route.

Petty and Cacioppo also believe that people want to hold correct attitudes and are willing to process information about their attitudes and change them as a result. In other words, even if they hold a belief that flag burning is OK, they are willing to hear arguments against that position. Petty and Cacioppo also believe that various factors can affect the direction and number of one's attitudes and can enhance or reduce argument strength. If an attractive or highly credible source is against flag burning, that factor could increase or decrease the weight you might give to the Supreme Court's decision that flag burning is not prohibited by the Constitution. Petty and Cacioppo also believe that increased scrutiny of one's attitudes lessens the impact of peripheral cues, and vice versa. That is, as you investigate the flag-burning issue, it becomes more and more unlikely that a source's appearance will have an effect on you. Petty and Cacioppo also believe that attitudes can be affected by bias. If you are already biased against the Supreme Court, this bias could affect your attitude toward its decision on flag burning.

Mass-Media Effects Theory and Research

Although we will be looking at the mass media, especially electronic media, in detail in a later chapter, several common threads run through the literature on the effects of mass media and offer another explanation for persuasion. The common themes in **mass-media effects theories** are (1) that by sharing a common pool of experience, we become vulnerable to distortion and propaganda, (2) that we are selective about the media messages to which we expose ourselves, and (3) that mass-mediated messages have become so pervasive that we are on the verge of being overwhelmed by them.

Until the 1980s, most research on the mass media was done from the descriptive, scientific, quantitative perspective. Any subjective, artistic, qualitative criticism of mass media was being published in film magazines or the popular press, not television or mass communication journals. Thus, our focus here will be primarily on the quantitative research. Keep in mind, however, that important qualitative media research has and is being done and reported. There are two benchmarks for this body of research. One was the publication in 1984 of *Critical Studies in Mass Communication Research,* a professional journal devoted to the reporting of qualitative studies of the mass media. The other benchmark was the broadcast of the highly acclaimed television series *Hill Street Blues,* which prompted much needed qualitative theory, research, and criticism of mass communication, especially television.

Technological Determinism Theory

Technological determinism theory partially explains contemporary persuasion. It maintains that the technology of any given era is the major determinant of the cultural patterns of that era. The late Marshall McLuhan (1964) was a controversial technological determinist. As he put it, "the message of any medium or technology is the change of scale or pace or pattern that it introduces into human affairs," or, in briefer terms, "the medium is the message" (p. 24). In our era, the dominant technology is electronic communication, via television, radio, telephone, recordings, computers, and the Internet, to name a few. These media provide us with access to a huge pool of common information and experience.

To get a feeling for the range of information and experience we all share, consider the similar if not identical answers we would probably get to the following questions if we were to interview a hundred people on any downtown street:

1. What NFL running back holds the all-time record for yards gained rushing?

2. Who spins *The Wheel of Fortune?*

3. What is the major product sold at the Golden Arches?

4. What is Dolly Parton's most noticeable physical feature?

5. What are at least two meanings of "macintosh"?

6. Which realtors wear gold-colored jackets?

7. What technique was used to create the California Raisins?

8. What happened to the Berlin Wall in 1989?

9. What NBA basketball team won a record seventy-two games in one season?

10. What television family features a trouble-making child named Bart?

11. What character did Madonna portray in the movie *Dick Tracy?*

12. What black leader was released from prison in South Africa after many years, and what effect did his release have?

13. Which fashion model has a mole on her face?

14. Which NBA basketball player tested positive for HIV?

15. What is the name of Murphy Brown's house-painter?

16. Who are the unwed soap opera mothers and on which soap operas?

17. Who is Rush Limbaugh and what does he believe?

18. What are "Lunchables"?

19. Who is Ted Kazynski?

20. Who uses the slogan "Smart. Very Smart"?

These are just a few of the many questions we could ask, but they demonstrate how much we all share and from a variety of contexts, all due to the mass media. But what does that have to do with persuasion? Given the importance of Aristotle's concept of common ground, or identification, we can readily imagine how some of this pool of common knowledge and experience could be used to create enthymemes. Bart Simpson, for example, became such an effective emblem of rebellion that some school systems outlawed the wearing of any Bart Simpson paraphernalia (T-shirts, buttons, hats, and so on). Most believe Marxism is unworkable, and we know that the Soviet Union is defunct. Because of the power and pervasiveness of electronic media, receivers become vulnerable to mass persuasion through appeals to shared information and experience. Each of us is part of a mass target for advertisers, politicians, religious spokespersons, demagogues, and other persuaders.

Our electronic technology not only provides us with this vast store of cultural icons, it also shapes the way we think about things—even abstract things. Communication researcher James Carey (1982) has pointed out that with the invention of the telegraph and later the wireless, *time* became a critical factor in human affairs. Desperados had to cut the telegraph lines as they left town to give them more *time* for their getaway.

Because the telegraph made it easy for commodity buyers to almost instantly know prices paid for wheat in faraway Kansas, the margin for profit between purchase and sales of the wheat shrank so drastically that it was necessary to invent what we know of today as the "futures market." In it you buy wheat not yet planted, you sell it before it is harvested, you never take physical charge of a product that you will never see, yet you may have invested thousands of dollars! What a remarkable change in thinking about time.

The use of the telephone sped things up even more, and, to this day, telephones are not permitted in the pits of the major stock and commodity exchanges, to provide a thin sliver of *time* for the traders—which means the margin between profit and loss. A student runner for the Chicago Board of Trade was cautioned not to stop for anything on his trip to the trading floor with a sell order. His message was to sell over forty boxcars of a precious metal. One minute's delay might have meant millions of dollars of extra profit or additional loss. And the Internet has caused us to think differently about time. E-mail is instantaneous. Some of my "snail mail" recently took ten days to get to California—the Pony Express guaranteed that kind of speed! And a secretary can now send a letter to a mailing list of several hundred names in just a few seconds instead of the hours it used to take.

Of course, time isn't the only concept affected by our electronic technology. My family owns four personal computers, and we are shopping for replacements. I save money on my long-distance calls by telephoning a computer that relays my call by satellite to another computer in the city I'm calling. We throw away a credit-card-sized calculator that we purchased a few years ago for $10. Why throw it away? Not because it doesn't work, but because a replacement battery for it costs more than a new, solar-powered calculator.

It is estimated that, for the foreseeable future, the cost of home and other computers will be halved every three years or less, whereas their capabilities will double. One expert has estimated that if the automobile industry had maintained the same rate, the Rolls Royce would now cost about $2.50 and would get over 1000 miles per gallon (Dizzard, 1975). It's mindboggling to imagine the many ways in which what McLuhan called the "change of scale, pace, or pattern" has affected our culture in the past five years, and that mindboggle is dwarfed if we try to imagine the next five. All the changes of scale, pace, and pattern influence us as persuadees, shifting the ways we are affected by messages and, probably, increasing our vulnerabilities.

Running almost counter to the pervasive effects posited by the technological determinists is a well-documented trend on the part of receivers to engage in individual, nonmass selectivity. Thus, although it is true that electronic media dominate our era, that the total number of books read per capita has dropped dramatically, and that the number of persons who rely on newspapers or news weeklies for their information has also dropped, it is also true that people are becoming increasingly selective in choosing which media — electronic or print — to patronize (Schwartz, 1973). Thus, although fewer persons read newspapers, the number of different newspapers being published has increased. One trip to your local newsstand will confirm this. You can find a periodical publication for almost any narrow interest you can imagine — a publication for those interested in monsters; for those who like to shoot muzzle-loading, black-powder shotguns and rifles; for those who jog; for those who grow only amaryllis bulbs; and so on. The same increase in options is occurring in the electronic media, especially with the growth of cable TV, dish-satellite-antennae, videotaped programs or movies, pornography (and other topics) on the Web, and so on. This proliferation has led to the concept of **narrowcasting,** the design of electronic messages for specific clusters of people who have certain interests, hobbies, or activities. Thus, although our technology is increasingly altering the scale, pace, and pattern of our lives, it is also providing us with more alternatives to choose from. And the new offering of HDTV will bring us unique and at the same time mass persuasion.

Uses and Gratifications Theory and Research

One approach to the persuasive effects of mass media is uses and gratification theory. It focuses on the receiver of communication, maintaining that "the audience is actively utilizing media contents rather than being passively acted upon by the media" (Katz, Blunder, & Gurevitch, 1974, p. 11). Until its introduction, little attention had been paid to the role of the receiver in mass communication research or theory. For the most part, it was assumed that receivers were message sponges who merely absorbed media messages until they were motivated to act and then went out and purchased, voted, or joined in accord with the various media pitches.

Simply put, the theory assumes that receivers have various needs, ranging from low-order basic needs, such as food, shelter, or sex, to high-order, complex needs, such as self-identity. There are many ways in which to meet those needs, and receivers make choices from among them. Some of these choices — in fact many of them — involve using the mass media. As a result, a particular mass medium competes with other mediated and nonmediated methods of gratifying needs.

For example, suppose I need to perceive myself as "sports-minded." So I develop an interest in outdoor sports such as hunting and fishing as well as spectator sports such as football and baseball. There are several ways I can meet this high-order self-identity need. I could watch *Monday Night Football* and focus on the halftime review of Sunday's games so I will be able to enter the football pool at work and not look like an idiot. Or I could read the sports section of the newspaper, again focusing on the details, reviews, and commentaries on the weekend's games. This will also allow me to fill in the football pool and look good, and I can still make it to my meeting at the YMCA. Well and good, as long as it is Monday night. But suppose it is Sunday afternoon and my hunting or fishing partner calls up and suggests going out to the fields or lake for several hours. Now my self-identity needs can be met in either mediated or nonmediated ways: I can go out and maybe bag my limit or catch a lunker and be able to brag about it at work and also enjoy the companionship of my friend today. As for the football pool? Well, it's just a dollar, and I can choose the same picks as my morning paper and still appear to be informed. My self-image (and I hope others' image of me) will now include not only being a knowledgeable fan of pro football but being an active outdoor-sports enthusiast as well. Note that, in this example, not only do media compete with nonmedia activities to meet the receiver's needs, they also compete with one another.

From a persuasive point of view, advertisers must compete with one another to capture my time so that they can insert their appeals between the pages of the sports section or throughout the broadcast of the halftime show on *Monday Night Football* or on a hunting or fishing show.

Jay Blumler (1979), one of the originators of uses and gratifications theory, outlines four kinds of needs that motivate people to turn to media. The first he calls **surveillance,** the need to keep track of our environment. We look to media to find out what's happening that might be of use to us. Even though you may think your college newspaper is worthless, you probably still glance through it to find out what is going on. You notice not only campus and local news and sports, but some of the advertisements, the announcements from organizations on campus, and the personals column.

The second kind of need is **curiosity,** the need to discover new and previously unknown information. We frequently see appeals to this need in sensationalist publications like the *National Enquirer.* Headlines like "O. J.'s Secret Diary Reveals Who Did It" or "Elvis Seen Peeping on Lisa and Jacko" are designed to tickle our *need to know* and to get us to buy the paper. Most frequently, the story doesn't live up to the promise of the headline, but apparently that doesn't matter to the curious reader. Of course, there are less dramatic examples of curiosity at work. For example, most direct mail marketing appeals have a "teaser" printed on the envelope—something like "Cashier's Check Inside!" to prompt what direct marketers call an "open up." Other curiosity-arousing tactics in direct mail marketing include the "Cracker Jacks" theory, which advises putting something lumpy in the envelope. The assumption is that, just as everyone who opens a Cracker Jacks box immediately looks for the "prize," even though they know that there has never been a good prize in a Cracker Jacks box, they will open the lumpy package to discover the contents. Curiosity lies at the heart of this kind of behavior.

A third kind of need identified by Blumler is **diversion.** We need relief from our day-in, day-out routines and use media to escape. The need for escape is met in many mediated and nonmediated ways, such as by reading mystery novels, watching TV shows, or going to the movies. This powerful need to check out of the here-and-now and into the there-and-then is most easily met by media, especially electronic media.

Finally, Blumler identifies the need for **personal identity,** which is closely related to Rokeach's self-concept. Media help us identify who we are, through our reading, listening, or viewing. Blumler and his colleagues found a fascinating difference between the print and electronic media. For example, persons who are sure of themselves and are outgoing, social, and interactive tend to get a sense of who they are through reading, whereas less socially interactive and perhaps less self-assured persons rely on viewing TV to get a sense of who they are or to find a substitute for social activities. This sense of identity may come from role models we see on television, from political views written in newspapers, or from a certain type of music that we listen to and identify with our own lifestyle. Country-and-western fans, for example, are likely to have different personal identities than do opera fans.

The uses and gratifications approach to mass-media persuasion also places the consumer or receiver at the center of the persuasive act. Receivers can and do select from the mediated and non-mediated alternatives for meeting their surveillance, curiosity, diversion, and personal-identity needs; their selections may make the difference between the profit and loss, victory and defeat, or success and failure of a persuader.

Cultivation Theory and Research

Another scientific explanation of mass-media effects, cultivation analysis, grows out of the work of George Gerbner and his colleagues (1986). They hold that

> Television is a centralized system of storytelling. It is part and parcel of our lives. . . . Television cultivates from early infancy the very predispositions and preferences that used to be acquired from other primary sources. . . . television has become the primary common source of socialization. (p. 18)

In other words, the common experience pool contains, within its overwhelming flood of messages, certain images and patterns that we take as reflecting reality, as Figure 3.16 demonstrates. In earlier times, these images and patterns were learned from parents, peers, the community, schools, churches, and other sources. Since the advent of

television, these sources have been replaced by the stories, characters, news events, and other information brought to us on the "tube of plenty." Cultivation theory predicts that the more one watches television, the more one comes to believe that the things shown on the screen reflect reality. Thus, heavy television viewers will live as if that reality exists and operates in the "real" world. Furthermore, because the televisual "reality" portrays many social values and prejudices, successful business leaders are male not female on television, and most characters are physically attractive. You can imagine the kinds of biases and values such reinforcement is likely to "cultivate." Most important, heavy viewers will begin to behave in ways consistent with the televisual reality they watch. Thus social values, biases, and stereotypes begin, develop, and endure.

What do you think?

What "lessons" about lifestyle have you learned from the mass media?

In a typical cultivation theory–based study, the content of television programs of a particular type (sitcoms, children's programs, soap operas, news, sports) is analyzed to see how many show a certain kind of reality (such as physical and psychological violence; seductions; racial, physical, or family conflict). Then a group of heavy television viewers and a paired group of light television viewers respond to a series of questions regarding their viewing patterns and how they feel about the particular reality under study. The results might then show that heavy viewers of prime-time crime shows believe there is more violence in the streets than there really is, and that they are handgun owners, have multiple locks on their doors, have burglar alarms or private security service, and so on. Light viewers, on the other hand, might not believe that society is as violent as depicted on television. The researchers' conclusion is that television "cultivates" or "grows" percep-

Perception. Reality.

 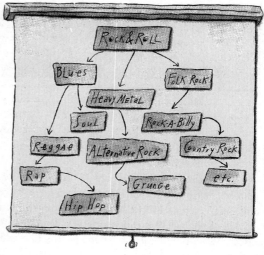

For a new generation of Rolling Stone readers, it's more than rock & roll, and they like it. For every branch on the rock & roll family tree, we have thousands of readers climbing aboard. If you want to reach 8 million people whose attitudes, ideas and lifestyles are changing the world, sink your roots into the pages of Rolling Stone.

Rolling Stone

Figure 3.16. *Sometimes a mediated reality (perception) cultivates a sense of the world that is inaccurate, biased, or stereotypical. (© Straight Arrow Publishers, Inc., 1994. All rights reserved. Reprinted by permission.)*

tions of violence. Other "realities" might include sexual promiscuity, alcohol and cigarette consumption, and unwed motherhood.

The result of the cultivation is a homogeneous audience whose members live and believe much more like one another than in earlier times. As Figure 3.17 implies, the medium is our primary teacher regarding social behavior. Try to examine your own viewing habits and the possible effects that are being cultivated in you. Let us now turn to a qualitative approach to mass media — the in-

terpretation of mass-mediated messages as if they were reflections of our culture.

Mass Media as Cultural Texts

In recent years, scholars have begun to examine communication events (speeches, interviews, news broadcasts, interpersonal interactions, works of literature, and films, to name a few) as "texts" that are meant to be "read" by audiences and analysts.

Figure 3.17. *Looking young and attractive is but one of many values that the mass media "cultivate" in each of us.* (Frank and Ernest *reprinted by permission of NEA, Inc.*)

Imagine that 5000 years from now a researcher finds a time capsule containing a huge collection of television commercials from the last decade of the twentieth century. What might the researcher conclude about what life was like way back then? What did people do for a living? What did they believe in? What kinds of values did they have? One conclusion would probably be that twentieth-century people were powerfully influenced by and tied to the automobile. There seem to have been two levels at which this influence occurred. Apparently you couldn't have lived in the twentieth century without an automobile, and local dealers thought the customer was a fool, for in spite of their transparent insincerity, dealers repeatedly went on the air as their own spokespersons instead of using famous athletes or entertainers.

Many other cultural details would also be discernible in the ads (color and style preferences, physical characteristics of the vehicles, lucky outcomes from owning this or that car, and so on). And that would be a tiny tip of the iceberg, for there are many other categories of commercials. For example, twentieth-century people must have been incredibly filthy: Witness the numerous ads for laundry detergents, room and personal deodorants, anti-dandruff shampoos, toothpastes, mouthwashes, douches, toilet paper, and so on. All in all, the newfound commercials would serve as a set of texts that illuminate the nature of twentieth-century America.

This recent approach to mass-media messages as "cultural texts" is fascinating and has identified a great number of significant patterns in our culture, such as our compulsion to consume products, energy, and various raw materials. This compulsion draws fire from various critics, among them the Marxists.

Marxist Theory and Research. Another interpretation of the function of mass media has been advanced by Marxist critics. Marxist theorists address the issue of economic power as it exists in capitalistic countries such as the United States, Japan, and Germany. They believe that those who control the means of production (the *bourgeoisie*) control and determine the nature of society. This results in a power elite, or *hegemony*. The major economic motive in capitalism is profit. Profit is naturally tied to the production *but* also the consumption of "things" or products. The bourgeoisie achieve production and profit by exploiting the abilities of the workers (the *proletariat*) and thus dominate and oppress them in a variety of ways. For example, the workers are attracted to produce "things" in order to earn wages, which then permits them to purchase the essentials (and later the nonessentials) of life. This produce-earn-purchase cycle creates a never-ending and ever-increasing necessity to work in order to produce "things" in order to earn wages in order to buy things. This process, which Marx called "wage slavery," will not be overcome until the proletariat rises up and challenges the dominant power group and its philosophy and gets control of the means of production.

We have seen this model become enacted in varying degrees, ranging from communism to socialism and to socialistic programs enacted or being considered in our own country.

How does this all relate to our study of persuasion? Well, some ways are fairly obvious. Because political power is needed to maintain economic power, the bourgeoisie must find members willing to run for political office and support their races with money, volunteers, and other things necessary for political persuasion. A Marxist critic might note that the profit motive and its resulting cycle of consumption is instilled in the citizenry through subtle forms of persuasion. The value of earning money begins in childhood (having a lemonade stand, taking out the garbage to earn an allowance, and so on). The profit motive is dominant throughout youth and early adolescence (having a paper route, getting paid for good grades) and throughout adulthood (getting a well-paid job, accumulating wages to purchase "things"). This emphasis on money and what it can buy is constantly reinforced in the media.

Marxist critics might also identify news reporting as promoting the prevailing political and economic ideology. They would argue that the mass media depict terrorists as outlaws, whereas a perfectly valid argument could be made for the position that terrorists represent the proletariat and that terrorism is merely a strategy to dramatically state an opposing ideology.

Marxist critics of mass media note the news programs contain advertising and that they also persuade people that financially successful persons (such as Michael Jordan, Steffi Graf, Spike Lee, Madonna, Donald Trump) lead the most interesting lives and that therefore such success should be everyone's goal. Television programming is also controlled by the power elite, who make certain that the content of entertainment programming reinforces the dominant ideology (capitalism). It is therefore not surprising that TV game shows *emphasize* prizes and that all the TV businesspersons are financially if not emotionally successful.

The Marxist critic's role is to "unmask" the forces of hegemony, to reveal and perhaps to subvert the dominant ideology. To Marxist critics, the mass media in general serve to communicate a view of reality that supports the status quo. Naturally, such critiques are controversial; however, they may be useful if only to alert us to potential persuasive strategies that we as receivers may face.

Feminist Theory and Research. Feminist theory provides another important approach to the study of mass-media effects. It holds that a variety of aspects of current life can best be explained by looking at how gender issues are dealt with in modern mass media. Feminist research deals with how the prevailing order and status relationships are continually being reinforced by the mass media. As a result, certain groups (such as females) are being exploited by those in control (males). Feminist theorists argue that the first thing one must do when investigating any messages in our society (including mass-mediated messages but others as well) is to ask, "And what about the women?" (Lengermann and Niebrugge-Brantley, 1992). In other words, what is happening to women in the mass-media messages and, as a result, to women in general? What do the messages really mean from the woman's perspective? And what effects on women are generated by mass-mediated or other messages?

Consider the highly popular, long-lived, and simple-minded game show *Wheel of Fortune*. On the surface it seems innocuous enough. Three contestants are asked to figure out a phrase or saying by guessing the arrangement of various letters of the alphabet. The host spins a wheel that has various dollar values printed on it. These dollar values are multiplied by the number of times the correctly guessed letter appears in the phrase or saying. The contestant who guesses a phrase correctly wins the amount he or she has accumulated. The winner is the contestant who ends up with the most money and as a result gets to go for the big prizes — trips, furs, jewelry, automobiles, furniture, boats, and so on. Now, "What about the women?" Note that it is a male, Pat Sajak, who is "in charge." Further, this male figure is depicted as personable, articulate, talkative, intelligent, and capable. His assistant, however, is a different story. Vanna White seems to be the ultimate "Barbie doll," whose major duty on the program is to walk back and forth in front of the billboard containing the phrase or saying, all the while displaying her new (and usually suggestive) outfit. She smiles continuously as she reveals the hidden letters. Vanna rarely speaks, and when she does (usually at the end of the show), her comments are usually insipid or related to the outfit she is wearing. She seems to depict the stereotypical attractive, not-too-intelligent, servile "girl next door."

A feminist critique of this show would focus on the values being communicated and how they attempt to "persuade" the male and female audience members. Some of the messages being sent by the show include

1. Men are capable and women are not.

2. Men are far more intelligent than women.

3. One of women's major roles is to be servants to men — to do the simple and menial tasks.

4. Men are in charge in contemporary society.

5. Women should have extensive wardrobes and rarely wear the same outfit more than once.

6. Women are shy and don't speak up much.

7. When women speak, their comments are naive, perhaps even insipid.

8. Womanly prizes are things to improve one's appearance, such as jewelry, furs, spas, cosmetics, furniture, and trips to romantic places.

9. Manly prizes include items that test manhood — boats, sports cars, and so on.

10. Women rarely initiate conversations; instead they respond when asked to, mainly by men.

11. Women are mainly thought of as sex objects — appearance and being attractive to men is what *really* counts.

According to the feminist perspective, as a result of receiving these messages and many others from media dominated by the prevailing male power holders, women have been taught to think that they are less than men. Hence, women have come to believe that they can't hold jobs that require an outgoing and even assertive personality, and that they are best at breeding and nurturing children. They aren't worth talking to about serious topics, and they are submissive and shy and focused on their appearance. And because all these behaviors are characteristic of females, they are less valued than the activities typifying men.

Feminist researchers aim at uncovering, discovering, and revealing the sexist nature of much of modern life and then arguing for equality as it is viewed in an ideal democracy. They want women to have the same opportunities as men to self-actualize, both on and off the job, and they want equitable pay for women. The strategy has accounted for significant gains for women, such as affirmative action, an increased number of women moving into leadership roles in various venues in society, and a number of other real advances. Liberal feminists have also had a major impact on our use of language. We now use "chairperson" instead of "chairman," "mail carrier" instead of "mailman," "law enforcement officer" instead of "policeman," "TV news anchor" instead of "TV news anchorman," and so on. We are also seeing increasing use of gender-free or gender-equitable language, especially when it comes to pronouns (loss of the generic use of "he" and "him" to refer to people in general). Numerous other gains could be readily identified. A negative reaction to these advances seems to be underway, with programs like affirmative action recently coming under fire.

Radical feminists see a need to reinvent our society and culture. They maintain that gender equity, increased opportunities for women, job and pay equity, and other recent gains for women are not sufficient to create a genderless society. Instead, we need a complete alteration in the ways we think and act. As we saw in Chapter 2, radical feminists attack the field of communication (and most other disciplines), and especially persuasion, as being male focused — more studies focus on great male persuaders than on great female persuaders; researchers study persuasion as it is used in male-dominated roles in organizations, groups, and interpersonal communication; and so on. Not only would the radical feminist perspective encourage more feminist research, but it would maintain that we need to redefine the whole concept of communication/persuasion.

Although still in its infancy, mass-media criticism is likely to grow into an important means of defining our culture and of identifying ways in which consumers are lured into purchasing products. From the point of view of persuasion, these mass-media "texts" certainly must indicate the kinds of first premises that operate in convincing enthymemes. They demonstrate what kinds of appeals succeed and what strategies and tactics persuaders will use to convince us to buy their products, vote for a certain candidate, or support a given cause. The study of media messages as texts can do a lot to inform persuadees.

Review and Conclusion

Our continuum of theoretical approaches to the study of persuasion began with the ancient Greeks and Romans as the originators of the subjective or artistic approach to persuasion. Generic and narrative approaches to persuasion also focus on this subjective end of the research continuum. At the midpoint, we considered focus-group research — a hybrid approach that employs both the artistic and scientific approaches. Then we began to move to the scientific end of the continuum with attitude change theory, Rokeach's belief hierarchy, learning theory, and tension-reduction theories. We then investigated information-processing theories and concluded with theory, research, and criticism of the mass media of contemporary culture. These theories are only representative of the many approaches to explaining the process of persuasion, but they should give you some idea of how varied are the ways in which researchers study this phenomenon that dominates our lives.

Questions for Further Thought

1. What are the virtues, and how do they relate to both ethos and pathos? Can you identify any of these virtues in our nation's leaders? in professional athletes? in film or television characters?

2. What are "topoi"? How do they work? Can you identify any ways in which today's political leaders use them? Are they apparent in any television spots you have seen recently? in any of the catalogs and other

direct-mail pieces you have received? in any print ads? on any Web sites?

3. What is the significance of having a "common experience pool," and how does it relate to the Aristotelian concept of the enthymeme?

4. Identify a current issue on your campus. How does narrative theory help your understanding of the issue?

5. What are some generic categories of persuasive communication? What criteria seem to unite them?

6. How did the "refrigerator guilt" concept affect the average American homemaker? What did Arm & Hammer use to discover this concept? How might this example be related to the consistency theories discussed in this chapter?

7. What was the major focus of attitude researchers such as Hovland and his associates?

8. What is meant by "behavioral intention" as used by Fishbein? Give some examples. How do behavioral intentions relate to attitudes? to behaviors? What is the difference between a belief *in* something and a belief *about* something?

9. What are the primitive beliefs according to Rokeach's perspectives? What are authority beliefs? Give examples. What is the difference between one's attitude toward an object or a topic and one's attitude toward a situation? What is the difference between terminal and instrumental values? Which is strongest: a belief, an attitude, or a value? Which is easiest to change?

10. How does learning theory relate to persuasion?

11. Explain the following from the perspective of social learning theory as postulated by Bandura: external sources of reinforcement,

self-reinforcement, role playing, and role modeling.

12. What are some shortcomings of the Heider-Newcomb balance theory? How does dissonance theory go beyond the balance models?

13. What is the latitude of acceptance? How does it work? What is the latitude of rejection? the latitude of noncommitment? What is ego involvement as defined by the Sherifs? What does it do to information that runs counter to one's position?

14. What are the three dimensions or ways in which human beings exhibit reactions to information as presented in persuasive messages? What is the difference between the central- and peripheral-processing routes in elaboration likelihood theory?

15. What is the "uses and gratifications" explanation of the functions of mass media? How might it apply to political persuasion during election times? How might it apply to advertising? How might the mass-media function of determining a personal identity relate to political persuasion and advertising?

16. Explain the phrase "mass-media messages are texts."

17. If you were a cultural anthropologist examining the repository of television spots from the 1990s, what kinds of values (beyond the fixation on the automobile and cleanliness) might you identify as typical of consumers in the last decade of the twentieth century?

18. Why does cultivation theory use the "growth" concept to explain why people learn social roles from television?

19. What are the differences between light and heavy watchers of television in terms of how much violence they perceive to exist in the world?

20. How do Marxist critics view the mass media? Do you agree with their assessment? If so, why? If not, why not?

21. What is the relationship between Marxist and feminist criticism? between radical and liberal feminist positions on critical research in communication?

References

Bardeau, A. (1972). *Social learning theory.* Englewood Cliffs, NJ: Prentice-Hall.

Blumer, J. (1979). The role of theory in uses and gratifications studies. *Communication Research, 6,* 9–34.

Carey, J. (1982). The telegraph and its effects. Speech delivered at Northern Illinois University, Spring 1982.

Chaiken, S., & Eagly, A. H. (1976). Communication modality as a determinant of message persuasiveness and message comprehensibility. *Journal of Personality and Social Psychology, 34,* 605–614.

Dizzard, W. P. (1975). *The coming information age: Overview of technology, economics, and politics.* New York: Longman.

Festinger, L. (1962). *A theory of cognitive dissonance.* Stanford, CA: Stanford University Press.

Fishbein, M., & Ajzen, I. (1975). *Belief, attitude, intention, and behavior.* Reading, MA: Addison-Wesley.

Fisher, W. R. (1987). *Human communication as narration: Towards a philosophy of reason, value, and action.* Columbia: University of South Carolina Press.

Foss, S. K. (1989). *Rhetorical criticism: Exploration and practice.* Prospect Heights, IL: Waveland Press.

Gerbner, G., Gross, L., Morgan, M., & Signorelli, S. (1986). Living with television: The dynamics of the cultivation process. In J. Bryant & D. Zillman (Eds.), *Perspectives on media effects.* Hillsdale, NJ: Erlbaum.

Heider, F. (1946). Attitudes and cognitive organization. *Journal of Psychology, 21,* 107–112.

Heider, F. (1958). *The psychology of interpersonal relations.* New York: Wiley.

Honomichil, J. (1984). *Marketing research people: Their behind-the-scenes stories.* Chicago: Crain Books.

Hovland, C. I. (1959). *The order of presentation in persuasion.* New Haven, CT: Yale University Press.

Hovland, C. I., Janis, I. L., & Kelley, H. H. (1953). *Communication and persuasion.* New Haven, CT: Yale University Press.

Le Francois, G. (1980). *Of children* (3rd ed.). Belmont, CA: Wadsworth.

Littlejohn, S. W. (1983). *Theories of human communication* (2nd ed.). Belmont, CA: Wadsworth.

McGuire, W. J. (1968). Personality and attitude change. In A. G. Greenwald, T. C. Brock, & T. M. Ostrum (Eds.), *Psychological foundations of attitudes.* New York: Academic Press.

McLuhan, M. (1964). *Understanding media.* New York: Signet Books.

Newcomb, T. (1953). An approach to the study of communicative acts. *Psychological Review, 60,* 393–404.

Osgood, C., & Tannenbaum, P. (1955). The principle of congruity in the prediction of attitudes. *Psychological Review, 62,* 42–55.

Petty, R. E., & Cacioppo, J. T. (1986). *Communication and persuasion: Central and peripheral routes to attitude change.* New York: Springer-Verlag.

Rokeach, M. (1973). *The nature of human values.* New York: Free Press.

Schwartz, T. (1973). *The responsive chord.* New York: Anchor Press.

Sherif, M., & Sherif, C. (1967). *Attitude, ego involvement and change.* New York: Wiley.

Skinner, B. F. (1957). *Verbal behavior.* New York: Appleton-Century-Crofts.

Ware, B. L., & Linkugal, W. A. (1973). They spoke in defense of themselves: On the generic criticism of apologia. *Quarterly Journal of Speech, 59,* 273–283.

4

The Making, Use, and Misuse of Symbols

"The boundary between human and animal — between the most primitive savage and the highest ape — is the language line. . . . The birth of language is the dawn of humanity; in our beginning was the word. We have always been endowed with language because before we had words, we were not human beings. [We] grapple with the mystery of life by trying to find words to say what it is. [Words] tell us that we must never take for granted the miracle of language" (Lederer, 1991).

Throughout history the uniquely human ability to create symbols has made possible major cultural advances. Before the development of the spoken word, humans were not much different from beasts, but the ability to use symbols for communication enabled us to live cooperatively. Tribes were formed using the communicative power of symbols. Communication facilitated the specialization of labor and allowed humans to create cultures. As with the opening of Pandora's box, however, the use of symbols to communicate also allowed humans to engage in less constructive behaviors, such as teasing, breaking promises, deceiving, scolding, demeaning, and lying. And with the development of the written word and movable type, people found that treaties could be both made and broken, legal contracts could destructively bind people for years, and laws could be used for evil as well as good. As the title of a recent book, *Deeds Done With Words*, indicates, language is a frequent surrogate for action — "sticks and stones can break your bones, but words can really hurt you!" Language theorist Kenneth Burke (1986) put it best when he said that humans are "symbol making, symbol using, and symbol misusing" creatures.

This ability to use symbols — verbal, pictorial, gestural, musical — lies at the heart of persuasion and so deserves our attention. As receivers, we need to get to the bottom of persuasive meanings; carefully analyzing the symbols used or misused by persuaders can help us get there. For instance, imagine a television advertisement for any brand of beer. It probably uses verbal, visual, gestural, musical, and other symbols to indicate that truly "in" people use the brand, have a certain lifestyle, and live happily ever after.

By examining the various kinds of symbols used in persuasion, we can

1. discover the persuader's use or misuse of symbols.

2. discover the persuader's stylistic preferences and what they may reveal about his or her motives.

3. anticipate the kinds of messages likely to come from this source in the future.

How can a careful examination of a persuader's symbols reveal so much? The answer is that making symbols is a creative act, and, as such, is ego involving, thus revealing a good deal about the persuader's modes of expression.

Author and language critic Richard Lederer (1991) offers many examples to help us avoid taking the English language for granted. Consider just a few of them:

1. Of almost 3000 languages in existence today, only ten are the native language of more than a hundred million people, and English ranks second in the list only behind Chinese, which has more native users (pp. 19–20).

2. Users of English as a second language outnumber native users (p. 20).

3. English is the first language of forty-five countries (p. 20).

4. One out of every seven people alive today speaks English (p. 20).

5. Most of the world's books, newspapers, and magazines are written in English, and two-thirds of all scientific publications and 80 percent of all stored computer texts are written in English (p. 20–21).

6. English has one of the richest vocabularies — 615,000 words in the *Oxford English Dictionary* (which doesn't include slang, many technical and scientific terms, and newly invented words) compared to French, which has about 100,000 words; Russian, which has about 130,000; and German, which has about 185,000 words (p. 24). And at the same time that it is so rich in vocabulary, English is remarkably economical (e.g., it re-

> **What do you think?**
>
> Which of these facts about the English language surprises you most?

quires far fewer syllables to translate Mark's gospel in English than it does in any of the Romance, Germanic, or Slavic languages) (p. 29).

7. English is now the international language of science, business, politics, diplomacy, literature, tourism, and pop culture — Japanese pilots flying Japanese airliners over Japanese air space must communicate with Japanese flight controllers in English, not their native Japanese (p. 30).

8. It would take 10 trillion years to utter all the possible English sentences that use twenty words (p. 17).

9. English is a hospitable language — more than 70 percent of our words come from other languages (e.g., boss, kindergarten, polka, sauna, canoe, zebra, alcohol, jukebox, camel, tycoon, tundra, ketchup, pal, vodka, sugar, tattoo, and flannel, to name a few) (pp. 24–25).

10. English is probably the easiest language for nonnative speakers to learn (p. 28).

Lederer also demonstrates an enduring and perhaps permanent element of the English language by asking students to arrange the five words describing a group of *scholars* whose focus of study is *Shakespeare,* who also happen to be from *Lithuania,* and all *five* of whom are *old.* Try this exercise and discover that you and most, if not all, of your classmates will come up with "five old Lithuanian Shakespearean scholars." Our language use is also very sophisticated. InwritingandreadingtheEnglishlanguage,weneedvisualcuestodeciphermessages. There are two visual cues in that string of syllables — the comma and the capital letter E — and both shout out, "Here is a word break!" Yet in spoken English, we don't have visual cues and consequently might be baffled when trying to hear the difference between "no notion" and "known ocean," between "buys ink" and "buys zinc," between "meteorologist" and

Figure 4.1. *Compare these statistics with the fact that the King James version of the Bible uses only about 8000 words, the entire works of Homer contain about 9000, and all of Milton has only about 10,000 words. Other words coined by Shakespeare include "amazement," "bump," "clangor," "dwindle," "fitful," "lonely," "majestic," "obscene," "pious," "road," and "useless." (Used by permission of Wide World Photos.)*

"meaty urologist," and between "cat's skills," "cats' kills," and "Catskills."

Lederer also calls to our attention how creative each of us is when using language. "Incredible as it may seem . . . practically every sentence that you speak and write during your lifetime has never been spoken or written before in human history," with the exception of stock phrases like "have a good day" (p. 16). Probably each of us "invents" words, though not as prolifically as Shakespeare did (see Figure 4.1).

Language and Its Roots

Eloquent persuasion is unique and fresh. It strikes us as having caught the moment; it may even prophesy the future. The speech made by Martin Luther King Jr., the night before he was killed had elements of prophecy. He said that God had allowed him "to go up to the mountain," that he had "seen the promised land," and that he doubted that he would get there with his follow-

ers. He concluded, "And I am happy tonight! I'm not fearing any man! Mine eyes have seen the glory of the coming of the Lord!" Although the words were drawn from the Old Testament and Julia Ward Howe's "Battle Hymn of the Republic," King's use of them was unique in the context of the movement he was leading. After his assassination, they seemed prophetic.

When we think about persuasion, then, we are inevitably faced with the artistic process of making word symbols. These are symbolic *acts*— like the assassination of a president or pope, which express rejection of authority, outrage at capitalism or Catholicism, or some other objection. But these are not the usual stuff of persuasion—language is.

By the age of two, a child's brain is ready to learn language and the child talks ceaselessly and discovers two very powerful words: "No!" and "Why?" They call this age the "terrible twos" because the power of language, the power of the negative, and the power of the question have been unleashed almost simultaneously. This "word power" or "magic" can kill or cure, as we know from the voodoo spell or the chant of the medicine man. Modern-day witch doctors of language include advertising copywriters, radio talk show hosts, politicians, and others.

Today we find many groups responding to symbols in dramatic ways. Some people use buttons, badges, or bumper stickers to make their symbolic point. "Think Globally; Act Locally," "Guns Don't Kill; People Do," or "Da Bulls." Others use their license plates to make declarations about themselves and their philosophies: "IM N RN," "REV BOB," "COACH," "I M SX C," "MR X TC," or "TACKY." Each of these messages is a symbolic act that makes a highly ego involving and revealing statement about its user. Researchers know that persons displaying bumper stickers, wearing T-shirts with a product label imprinted on it, or sporting campaign buttons will be far more likely to vote for a candidate, buy the product, or join the cause they are promoting. This is because by making their symbolic "statements," they have already "acted" and their words have become deeds.

Language can also be misused, as we discovered in looking at doublespeak and euphemisms back in Chapter 1. The deaths of Iraqi civilians in Operation Desert Storm became "collateral damage," while tax increases are now "user fees." Misuse of language is not always so treacherous. For example, *Newsweek* regularly carries a feature called "Buzzwords," which describes the names people in various occupations use to describe their clients. Telephone operators, for example, use the terms "captive customer" (for prison inmates who make collect calls), or "TUIs" (for drunks who use the phone). Movers refer to odds and ends as "chowder," because they just toss the items together in one box. "Lumpers" are the muscle men who actually move the stuff into or out of the truck.

The symbols and language used in advertising also frequently border on misuse. Market researchers decided to use the words "Recipe for Success," for example, to assure working women who use Crisco that they are indeed "cooks" and not just "microwavers" who merely thaw and reheat meals.

The receiver of persuasive messages can learn a lot about a persuader's motives by paying careful attention not only to the whole message but also to its particular words. Consider the language used by Hitler and other German Nazis of the 1930s in referring to the Jews: "vermin," "sludge," "garbage," "lice," "sewage," "insects," and "bloodsuckers." Those words were red flags signaling Hitler's march toward a "final solution"—concentration camps and gas chambers. Words became deeds, and as a result more than 6 million Jews were treated exactly like vermin or lice—they were simply exterminated. Lest we think that such a possibility is just ancient history, we need to remember that "ethnic cleansing" is still occurring in many places in the world, and that many opinionated persons and groups in this country believe that certain subgroups and minorities deserve similar treatment. The major weapon for instigating dehumanization is language. Words seem to blunt the edge of their true meaning when put into action, and seem to sanitize the brutality lurking behind them. We will certainly encounter such terms in the future. A warning to receivers: Linguistic camouflage can be dangerous stuff.

Even in less dramatic settings, we find that words create emotional responses and can demean people. Consider the term "lady doctor." What is the person using those words implying? That the doctor is not as good as a male physician? That the doctor is in the business only for the fun or sport of it? Why does the use of "lady" carry so much meaning and emotional response? On my campus the word "greasers" sparked a heated debate on an e-mail network chat group between persons familiar with the prejudicial use of the word in referring to Hispanics, who were outraged that the word was used in the group, and others who thought the word was harmless. They were familiar with a meaning for "greaser" that equated with tough, cocky, and arrogant high-school-aged males during the 1950s and 60s who wore leather jackets, rode motorcycles, smoked cigarettes in school, and had long hair combed (and greased) back into what were called "duck-tails." Only recently have we become sensitized to the use (and misuse) of Native American references in athletics—the Braves, the Redskins, the Chiefs, and so on. These examples show how word usage can persuade as well as outrage. The world of marketing provides many examples.

Brand names often reveal producers' attitudes toward their customers, or even toward the public in general. Oster Corporation has a "food crafter" instead of a "food chopper." This choice of words tells us that Oster is taking a gourmet approach. (*Chopping* sounds like work. *Crafting?* Now, that's art.) In the status and power-conscious 1950s and 1960s, new brands of cigarettes took "classy," even elitist names—Viceroy, Marlboro, Winston, Tareyton, while those coming on the market in the socially conscious 1970s and 1980s, however, had names like Fact, True, and Merit, and smoking some brands was supposed to be a way of making a gender statement—Eves and Virginia Slims, for example. At one time, the brand names of American-made automobiles suggested status, luxury, power, and speed: Road-master, Continental, Coupe de Ville, Imperial. In the 1970s and 1980s, new car brands coming on the American market suggested technology, speed, and economy: Rabbit, Colt, Fox, Jetta, Laser, and 6000 LE. When the baby boomers started hitting midlife in the 1990s, auto brand names suggested wealth, quality, durability, and long lives—Sterling, Infiniti, Sable, Probe, LeBaron, Towncar. In the world of food, fast, easy preparation is suggested by names like Lunchables, Budget Gourmet, and Bagel Bites. The rest of this decade will bring us more examples from the worlds of both packaged and durable goods.

Indeed, the language of brand names is a critical element of persuasion for a variety of product lines.

By understanding the many ways in which language can be manipulated, persuadees can look beyond the surface to delve deeper into the meaning of the message and the motives of the source. Persuaders, on the other hand, can analyze receivers and craft their words and phrases to appeal to them. They can "listen" to their audience for clues to what receivers need and want to hear.

How can we learn to identify the uses and misuses of symbols, especially in the language used by politicians, advertisers, employers, customers, and other persuaders? One way is to investigate how language scholars view the power and use of words. A useful approach to the study of language is based on the work of philosopher Suzanne K. Langer.

Langer's Approach to Language Use

Suzanne Langer (1951) recognized the power of language symbols. Like Lederer and others, Langer believed that the ability to create symbols is what distinguishes humans from beasts. In addition to being able to experience feelings, events, and objects, we are able to talk and think about them, even when the actual feelings, events, or things are not present. Two terms are used to describe this distinction: signs and symbols.

Signs indicate the presence of an event, feeling, or object. Thunder is a *sign* of lightning and usually of rain. That's why my dog goes into a panic at the sound of thunder—having had lightning strike close to her as a pup, she frantically tries to hide from it. If she could use *symbols,* I could talk to her about thunder and explain the futility of trying to hide from it. Only the comforting sound of my voice seems to calm her down, and then it is the tone of the voice (another *sign*, from Langer's perspective), not the words, that gives her comfort.

Another sign might be the red light at an intersection, indicating potentially dangerous cross-traffic. Leader dogs can recognize the red light by its location on the top of the traffic light and can even be taught to stop the person they are leading, but they cannot be taught to recognize the symbolic link between the red light and danger—that is a much more complex notion. As Langer (1951) put it, "Symbols are not proxy of their objects, but are vehicles for the conception of objects" (p. 60). Because of our ability to use symbols, you and I can understand the presence of danger by such means as the color red, the word "danger," or the skull and crossbones on a bottle of poison. Further, Langer maintains that the power to use symbols is a basic need; even persons unable to write or speak can't avoid making symbols.

Some symbols have a *common meaning* that most agree on. Langer calls such symbols *concepts*, in contrast to *conceptions*, which she uses to refer to particular individuals' meanings for the concept. All human communication (and hence persuasion) involves concepts and conceptions. Therefore, the possibility of misunderstanding is always present, as noted earlier. Some persons' conception of the symbol "greaser" differed vastly from others' conception of the same symbol. For that reason, Langer introduced three terms to be used when discussing meaning—signification, denotation, and connotation. *Signification* is what the thunder means to my dog and what the red top light on the traffic signal means to a leader dog. *Denotation* is the common meaning we have for the concept of danger. *Connotation* is my or your private conception of danger. Langer also maintained that meaning can be discursive or presentational. *Discursive meaning* is the combination (usually sequential) of smaller bits of meaning (usually language). *Presentational meaning* occurs all at once and must be experienced in its entirety (looking at a painting or statue or experiencing a ritual, a ballet, or a piece of music). Thus, some of the "meaning" in any advertisement is discursive (the slogans, the jingles, the ad copy), and some is presentational (graphic layout, font, and pictures). Similarly, some of the meaning of a political campaign is discursive (the speeches, press releases, interviews) while some is presentational (the way the candidate looks, his or her "image," the pictorial and musical elements in campaign spot ads). Responsible receivers of persuasion will try to identify the common meanings or concepts being communicated, their individual conceptions of those meanings, and the difference between their individual connotation and the unique connotations of other receivers.

The Semantic Approach to Language Use

Beginning in 1933, with the landmark work *Science and Sanity* by Count Alfred Korzybski (1947), scholars called **general semanticists** began a careful and systematic study of the use and meaning of language. Their purpose was to improve understanding about human communication problems and to encourage careful and precise uses of language. They wanted to train people to be very specific about sending and receiving words, in order to avoid such pitfalls as the stereotyping typical of Fascist propaganda in Europe and the United States. Hitler, Franco, and Mussolini had risen swiftly to prominence and had gained enough early public support to institute dangerous regimes. The general semanticists believed that an effective way to prevent such dictatorships would be to teach people to be aware that the appeals of demagogues were "maps" (inner perceptions) and not "territories" (realities).

Even when based on observed traits, stereotypes are unreliable, simply because no member of a class or group is exactly like any other member.

Berry's World

© 1988 by NEA, Inc.

"I'm a value-free yuppie. You're a value-free yuppie. Let's do something that calls for some MORAL RELATIVISM!"

Figure 4.2. *What is your map for "yuppie"? What is the actual territory for today's "yuppie"? (Berry's* World *reprinted by permission of NEA, Inc.)*

As Korzybski suggested, and as Figure 4.2 demonstrates, *the map is not the territory.* In other words, the internal perceptions or conceptions of persons, groups, things, and ideas we carry around in our heads are likely to be different from the real persons, groups, things, and ideas. Like Langer, Korzybski and his colleagues recognized the difference between an event, object, or experience and an individual's conception of it. Their use of the word "map" is equivalent to Langer's "conception," while their use of the word "territory" would be equal to "objective reality" and close to Langer's use of the word "concept." Our faulty maps are usually expressed through the language we create to convey them.

For the general semanticists, the real problem occurs when people act as if their maps represent the territory and thus turn the map into the territory, a mistake Korzybski believed to be potentially dangerous. He believed that we all carry thousands of maps around in our heads that represent nonexistent, or at least unreal, territories. To demonstrate this concept for yourself, write down the name of a food you have never eaten, a place you have never been, and an experience you have never had. Associated with these names are maps for unknown territories. For example, you may think that fried brains are slimy and gooshy, when in reality they feel like well-scrambled eggs. What is your map for skydiving? being a rock star? How do these maps match up with the real territories? In some aspects, the territory will agree with your map, which is probably a result of the *media exposure* you have had to other countries, foods, and activities. But in most cases, your maps will be very different from the territories as they really are.

Our mental and word maps represent a real problem in communication, especially in persuasion. Just as persuaders have to discover the common ground of ideas in order to persuade you to adopt their point of view, they also have to identify the maps you carry around in your head. Then they must either play on those maps, using your misperceptions to their advantage, or try to get you to correct your faulty maps. Only then can they persuade you to buy, vote, join, or change your behavior.

Our faulty maps frequently are expressed through language; we create and use words to express our maps. We react to them as if they are true representations of the territories we imagine. To the semanticists, this "signal response" is equivalent to my dog trying to hide from lightning whenever she experiences the "sign" (also "signal") of thunder. Signal responses are emotionally triggered reactions to symbolic acts (including language use) as if the actual act were being committed. The congressional debate over a proposed amendment to ban flag burning was nearly evenly divided between those who felt that flag burning (the "map") was equivalent to destroying the country and those who felt that the "territory" (the ideas behind the flag—the Constitution, the Bill of Rights, freedom of expression, and so on) was more important than the flag itself. Those who opposed flag burning often exhibited violent *signal responses*, such as physically attacking flag burners.

> **What do you think?**
>
> Which of your "maps" do you think is closest to the "territory"?

The semanticist approach to language is to train senders and receivers to be continually alert to the difference between signals and symbols. As Figure 4.3 demonstrates, symbols (such as the words Frank uses in the job interview) can even be self-effacing.

Semanticists isolate meaning in concrete terms. For example, suppose I tell you that "Generation X college students are conservative, selfish, and lazy." Your response will probably be negative because of the connotations of some of the words used—"selfish" and "lazy" for sure, and maybe "conservative" as well. You might well respond that "Ancient, ivory tower, egghead professors are spaced-out, vindictive, and uncaring!" Neither of us has much chance of establishing common ground and persuading the other.

Semanticists would advise both of us to use what they call **extensional devices,** techniques for getting outside of the emotional connotations that often accompany words. One extensional device I could use to modify my language would be to identify the specific college students I have in mind. This is called **indexing.** In this case I would alter my statement to something like "Generation X college students who have everything paid for by their parents are conservative, selfish, and lazy." That would calm down some of you—at least a little—because you probably know fellow students who get everything paid for, including lots of extras you don't get. But I still would not be as clear as I could be, according to the semanticists.

They would further urge me to use an extensional device called **dating,** or letting you know the time frame of my judgment about college students. Using dating, I would alter my sentence

JOB COUNSELOR

WELL, I MAY NOT BE ABOVE REPROACH, BUT DOES IT HELP IF I'M BENEATH CONTEMPT?

© 1987 by NEA, Inc. THAVES / 2

Figure 4.3. *What would a semanticist think of this cartoon? The words "reproach" and "beneath contempt" might be likely to prompt a signal response. Why? (Frank and Ernest reprinted by permission of NEA, Inc.)*

further by saying something like "Generation X college students of the nineties who have everything paid for by their parents are conservative, selfish, and lazy." That might cool you down a little more, unless, of course, you are one of those college students whose expenses are paid for by their parents. Here is where the extensional device semanticists call **Etc.** comes into play. This device is meant to indicate that I can never tell the *whole story* about any person, event, place, or thing. Using this device, I would alter my sentence to something like "Generation X college students of the nineties who have everything paid for by their parents are conservative, selfish, and lazy, *among other things*." Now I have suggested that conservatism, selfishness, and laziness aren't the students' only attributes. For example, they also might be "societally concerned about environmental issues," "concerned about honesty," or any of a number of other positive attributes.

Finally, Korzybski and his colleagues advised using an extensional device called **quotation marks,** a way to indicate that I am using those flag words in a particular way—my way—that isn't necessarily your way. For example, my meaning of the word "selfish" might relate to the students' unwillingness to help other students succeed in class. Or it could mean their unwillingness to get involved in volunteer experiences for the good of the community, or any of a number of meanings that wouldn't necessarily match your meaning for the word "selfish." My sentence might now read "Generation X college students of the nineties who have everything paid for by their parents are 'conservative,' 'selfish,' and 'lazy,' among other things." Now how would you react to the sentence? You would probably probe for my meanings for the emotional words, or you might even agree with me if your meanings of those words were similar to mine.

The result of using extensional devices is to make the maps in our heads more closely resem-

ble the territory to which we are referring. It would be wise for persuaders to design careful, specific, and concrete extensional messages, especially when using emotionally charged words or abstract words for which there can be many meanings—but frequently they don't. Abstract words such as "power," "democracy," "freedom," "morals," and "truth" are particularly vulnerable to misunderstanding. Unethical persuaders often intentionally use abstract or emotionally charged language to achieve their purposes. It is our task to remember the map-territory distinction and use the extensional devices as we listen for the uses and misuses of symbols. We must remember that as receivers, we, too, have "response-ability."

Kenneth Burke's Approach to Language Use

Perhaps no language theorist or critic has written as many treatises in as wide a variety of fields nor with as broad a knowledge of human symbolic behavior as Kenneth Burke, who died in 1994. A self-educated intellectual who once said he was merely footnoting Aristotle, Burke focused on the use of language to persuade people to action. He defined persuasion as "the use of language as a symbolic means of inducing cooperation in beings that by nature respond to symbols" (1950, p. 43). This active cooperation is induced by what he termed *identification*, a concept tied to Aristotle's common ground. The development of identification occurs through the linguistic sharing of what Burke called *substances*, or the raw material of our self-concepts.

Our self-concepts are made up of various kinds of symbolic and real possessions, including physical (clothing, cars), experiential (work, activities), and philosophical possessions (beliefs, attitudes, values). Identification with others develops to the degree that we *symbolically* share these possessions. In other words, we identify with persons who have the same view of life as we do, who enjoy the same kinds of activities, who have similar physical possessions, who live similar lifestyles, and so on.

If we think of the word "substance" as having the prefix "sub," meaning *beneath*, and the root word "stance," meaning one's mental and emotional position on an issue, then the dictionary definition of substance as "the essential part of a thing—its essence" is especially meaningful in regard to identification. We identify with others because we share their *essential* beliefs, values, experiences, and so on. I am like you, and you are like me to some degree; hence, I will believe you when you persuade me. For example, in the movie *Natural Born Killers*, Mickey and Mallory, the two mass murderers, forge a powerful identification with one another via shared sub-stances. They share the experience of being abused by parents. They share the murder of Mallory's father and later the murders of many other persons. They share physical belongings such as each other's blood, each other's bodies, and identical rattlesnake rings, to cite a few. And they share lifestyles, from the first scenes in the movie where they go on a killing binge in a small restaurant to the final scenes when, after a bloody escape during a prison riot, they are seen some time later as nomads in a large motor home with their children playing while Mickey comforts Mallory, who is once again pregnant.

Burke argued that the sharing of "substances" or "identification" is equivalent to persuasion. To Burke, most persuasion attempts to describe our "essential parts," and this description is always revealing. All words have emotional loadings and reveal the feelings, attitudes, values, and judgments of the user. Examining persuasive language can tell us about ourselves *and* the persuaders who appeal to our interest, support, and commitment.

Burke also thought that the symbolic activities (such as the use of language) inevitably lead to feelings of *guilt*. He reasoned that language automatically leads to rule making and moralizing, and since we all break the rules or don't live up to the morals at some time, we all experience some degree of guilt. Burke argued that all human cultures exhibit patterns that help explain guilt. First is the invention of the *negative*, or what something is not. Obviously the word "puppy" is not a puppy, so language that identifies what something is inherently leads to the idea of what something is not—the negative. The negative leads to sets of "Thou shalt nots" (whether supernatural, parental, spousal, or societal). Inevitably we fail to obey some of these negatives and experience guilt. "No" is one of the first things we learn as children, and we realize that it means we have displeased someone. Our own use of the negative usually emerges at about age two, when we start to take control of our own lives. We have heard "No, no, no," but now we begin to use it ourselves. It gives us power, and we go about testing the extent of that power throughout the "terrible twos" and in fact throughout the rest of life. The second pattern that contributes to guilt is the principle of a hierarchy, or "pecking order." It happens in all societies and groups, and it leads to either jealousy of others higher in the pecking order or to competition with them. We rarely, perhaps never, reach the top of the pecking order and feel guilty about that. A third source of guilt is our innate need for *perfection*; we all fall short of our goals and feel inadequate and ashamed of our shortcomings. This shame makes us feel guilty about not living up to our own or others' expectations.

How do we rid ourselves of guilt? In most cases guilt is purged symbolically—we offer up a sacrifice, or we engage in self-inflicted suffering, penance, and so on. But the most handy, flexible, creative, artistic, and universal means is

> **What do you think?**
>
> Name a "sub-stance" that unites you with a group to which you belong.

language—we usually try to get rid of guilt by talking about it—in prayer, to ourselves, to some sort of authority, or to someone with whom we share substances and with whom we identify. Consider how frequently persuaders offer us symbolic ways to alleviate our guilt. The imperfect mother rids her guilt by having Betty Crocker refrigerated cookie dough on hand. The imperfect dad takes his family on a vacation or coaches his kids' baseball team. The imperfect child tries to do better at school or apologizes and starts over.

Persuasion through identification works because we all share substances and because we all experience guilt. In processing persuasion, try to recognize that persuaders create identification by referring to shared substances—preferred beliefs, lifestyles, and values. They motivate you by appealing to your internal and inevitable feelings of inadequacy or guilt. Examine the language and images used in advertisements, sermons, political appeals, and other persuasive messages, reminding yourself of the strategies being used to create identification and guilt.

The Semiotic Approach to Language Use

Like other approaches to language use we've discussed, semiotics is concerned with the generation and conveyance of meaning. A number of scholars are associated with this "science" of meaning (Ferdinand de Saussure, Charles Sanders Peirce, Roland Barthes, Umberto Eco, and others). Semiologists apply the tools of linguistics to a wide variety of "texts" (a concept we dealt with briefly in Chapter 3). Viewing almost anything as a text, a semiotician can talk about the "meaning" of a doctor's office, a meal, a television program, a circus, or any other verbal or nonverbal symbolic "texts." According to semiotic theory, all texts convey meaning through signs or *signifiers* that refer to objects, concepts, or events

called *signifieds*. These signifiers interact with one another in meaningful and sophisticated but not obvious relationships, or *sign systems*, which make up the "language," or "code," of the text.

These codes can be inferred from a text. For example, consider your classroom as a text having its own signifiers and signifieds, some linguistic and some nonverbal. The room usually has an *institutional* "meaning," signified by the plain concrete or plaster walls, fluorescent lighting, and black or green boards. Blackboards and plaster walls usually signify that the building is an old one. Green boards and cinder block walls signify a younger building. The kinds of student desks (with or without arms), the arrangement of the room (e.g., desks in rows vs. groups), the physical objects (an overhead vs. video projector), all are signifiers that tell us about what to expect when entering this "text."

Or consider several of the codes embedded in various texts. For example, a simple code is the use of black and white hats in old cowboy movies to indicate the good guy and the bad guy. Pages being blown off a calendar signify the passage of time. What meanings are conveyed by drinking out of mugs, as opposed to Styrofoam cups or fine china? Each type of cup is a signifier, and each coffee drinker, consciously or unconsciously, is conveying a different kind of message. Yet words aren't even involved. In a semiotic approach to the study of meaning, we try to "read" each message from several perspectives: from the words that are or are not spoken, from the context in which or from which they are spoken, and from the other signifiers included in and with the message—visuals, colors, tone of voice, and so on.

The semiotician approaches any communication event as if it were a "text" to be "read" by the receiver/analyst. Language scholar Arthur

What do you think?

What are some important signifiers that you carry in your billfold?

Asa Berger (1984) uses Sherlock Holmes' unique abilities to infer meaning from minute clues as an example of semiotics at work in the "real world." In the story "The Blue Carbuncle," for example, Holmes explains a series of meanings that he infers from several signifiers identified in a hat left behind by the criminal. Though the hat is of the best quality, it is in disrepair, thus signifying that its owner has had a decline in his fortunes. House dust versus street dust on the hat signifies that the man doesn't go out much and that his wife doesn't love him anymore. Holmes explains that if she did love him, she would clean his hat (of course, this story predates the recent feminist movement in Western culture). And a wax spot on the hat indicates that the man still lights with candles versus gaslights. Holmes's poor baffled assistant is told that such a semiotic analysis is "Elementary, my dear Watson, elementary."

More and more marketing and advertising research is being conducted from a semiological approach, according to Curt Suplee (1987) of the *Washington Post*. He quotes advertising/design celebrity George Lois as saying, "When advertising is great advertising, it fastens on the myths, signs, and symbols of our common experience and becomes, quite literally, a benefit of the product. . . . As a result of great advertising, food tastes better, clothes feel snugger, cars ride smoother. The stuff of semiotics becomes the magic of advertising" (p. 3). In a recent commercial for a bank (described by one of its ad-agency creators), "An oddly modern-faced caveman is running across a barren rockscape. He is breathing hard, glancing around as if fearing pursuit. Finally he comes to a ledge and leaps . . . to become a snugly space-suited astronaut floating above the earth." The voice-over for these actions says, "You don't need a bank that keeps pace. You need a bank that sets it. Perpetual. What your bank is going to be" (Suplee, 1987). Compare your reading of the ad/text with what its designers have to say about it. They explain, in order to suggest that the bank

is forward looking and pace setting, "we show early man — by analogy the viewer and his 'primitive' banking system — and the various things he has to react to. Then we show him taking a literal leap of faith into the future with Perpetual as his bank" (Suplee, 1987).

What is the semiotic meaning of the following letter sent to the Communication Studies chair of my department?

Dear Professor Jones,

I am interested in directives as to how one may proficiency out of the speech requirement. Having been advised to seek counsel from you "specifically"—I sincerely hope you will not be displeased with my enthusiasm by asking this indulgence. There is a basis for my pursuing this inquisition as I am an adept speaker with substantiating merits. I will be overburdened with more difficult courses this fall—at least they will be concomitant with my educational objectives in the fields of Fine Arts and Languages. It would be a ludicrous exercise in futility to be mired in an unfecund speech course when I have already distinguished myself in that arena. I maintained an "A" average in an elite "advanced" speech course in High School. I am quite noted for my bursts of oratory and my verbal dexterity in the public "reality"—quite a different platform than the pseudo realism of the college environs. There is a small matter of age—I shall be twenty-two this fall. I am four years older than the average college freshman. I am afraid that I would dissipate with boredom, if confined with a bunch of teenagers. Surely you can advise something that would be a more palatable alternative?

Yours sincerely,

P.S. Please do not misconstrue this "inquiry" as the enterprise of an arrogant student, but one who will be so immersed in serious intellectual pursuits that the "speech" requirement will be too nonsensical and burdensome.

If ever a student needed to know about communication, it was this person. But what does the language usage here tell you about the writer of the letter? She (yes, it's written by a female) uses sixty-four-dollar words — perhaps a code for insecurity — but she seems unsure about her choice of words: Several times she puts words into quotation marks, a code for her own "special" meaning. She uses italics to signify the same thing — this word has a special meaning. She also misuses some words. For example, she says that she is pursuing an "inquisition" when she means an "inquiry." (An inquisition is a tribunal for suppressing religious heresy.) She says she has "substantiating merits" when she probably means that she has "substantial reasons" for being excused from the course. These and other signifiers add up to the semiotic meaning of the letter.

Semiotics can be applied to far more serious matters than such letters, however. For example, what was the meaning of the O. J. Simpson criminal trial for American opinions about race, and what signifiers conveyed those meanings? Did the outcome of the trial signify reverse racism on the part of black jurors, or did it signify that minorities can get a fair verdict even in widely publicized and sensationalized cases? Why were there so many O. J. jokes at the time? Why did one person say, "If an NFL star had to murder his wife,

why couldn't it have been Frank Gifford?" What other meanings might the event have had? What code(s) operated in the event and in world response to it? What signifiers defined what signifieds? Semiotic analysis can help you uncover these and a host of other meanings.

Review and Conclusion

This chapter should have given you a deeper appreciation for human symbol making, using, and misusing and for the power of language as a tool of persuasion — especially the English language. Perhaps you are beginning to realize how much meaning you can discover when you begin to critically analyze the various verbal and nonverbal symbols in persuasion. It takes time and care to discover discursive and presentational persuasion; to identify the means being used to create a state of identification; to determine the difference between the map and the territory; and to learn the many codes operating in various kinds of texts. To be a responsible persuadee, you need tools to assist you in analyzing the many persuasive messages targeted at you. Chapter 5 focuses on tools for the analysis of language and other symbols.

Questions for Further Thought

1. Why is symbol making such a powerful human activity? Give several examples of how symbols create high involvement in people.

2. What is meant by Burke's phrase "symbol misusing"? Give some examples of the misuse of symbols.

3. Why is the English language so powerful?

4. Why is a red stoplight a sign to a leader dog, and how is that "meaning" different from the

words "red stoplight" or "dangerous cross-traffic"?

5. What did Suzanne Langer mean when she said that symbols are the "vehicles for the conception of objects"?

6. What is the difference between signification, denotation, and connotation?

7. What is the difference between a presentational and a discursive symbol?

8. What is the difference between a "map" and a "territory" according to the general semanticists? What is an example of one of your food maps? one of your geographic maps? one of your experience maps?

9. What is a "signal response"? Give several examples.

10. What are the extensional devices recommended by general semanticists? What purpose do these devices serve? Give examples.

11. What does Kenneth Burke mean by "identification"? "substance"? the "need for hierarchy"? "guilt"? How do these concepts explain why language is so important in persuasion and in living life?

12. What is the difference between a signifier and a signified? What is a code? Give examples of simple codes from the worlds of sports, politics, and advertising.

References

Berger, A. A. (1982). *Media analysis techniques*. Beverly Hills, CA: Sage Publications.

Berger, A. A. (1984). *Signs in contemporary society*. New York: Longman.

Burke, K. (1950). *A rhetoric of motives*. Berkeley: University of California Press.

Burke, K. (1986). *Language as symbolic action*. Berkeley: University of California Press.

Korzybski, A. (1947). *Science and sanity*. Lakeville, CT: The Non-Aristotelean Library.

Langer, S. K. (1951). *Philosophy in a new key*. New York: New American Library.

Lederer, R. (1991). *The miracle of language*. New York: Pocket Books.

Suplee, K. (1987). Semiotics: In search of more perfect persuasion. *The Washington Post*, January 18, 1987, Outposts sec., pp. 1–3.

5

Tools for Analyzing Language and Other Symbols

Now you have some perspective on the making, using, and misusing of symbols and a greater appreciation for the power of the English language. We now consider several ways to analyze both verbal and nonverbal persuasive symbols. We begin by looking at several dimensions of language.

Dimensions of Language

The cube in Figure 5.1 represents three major dimensions of language: the **semantic dimension,** or all the possible meanings for a word; the **functional dimension,** or the various jobs that words can do (naming, modifying, activating); and the **thematic dimension,** or the feel and texture of words (for example, the word "swoosh" sounds or feels like its meaning). Imagine that this cube consists of many smaller cubes, each representing a word or set of words (such as a phrase or sentence) having its own unique semantic, functional, and thematic dimensions or meanings. Then consider this line of ad copy: "Sudden Tan from Coppertone tans on touch for a tan that lasts for days." On the *functional dimension*, the words "Sudden Tan" name a product. *Semanti-*

cally, however, much more is involved. The word "sudden" indicates an almost instantaneous tan, and indeed the product dyes your skin "tan" on contact. The ad's headline is "Got a Minute? Get a Tan" and is superimposed over before-and-after photos of an attractive blonde who has been (presumably) dyed tan by the product. On a *textural*, or *thematic*, level, the words that name the product do even more. The word "sudden" sounds or feels like the word "sun," so the product name sounds like the word "suntan." The *s* and *t* sounds are repeated in the line of copy, reinforcing the notion of a suntan. Try to describe how the message would make you feel if the meanings of the words disappeared and only their sounds remained.

Here are some more examples of the thematic, or textural, qualities language can have:

- The Presto Corporation named its new corn popper The Big Poppa! in the hope that our minds would establish a thematic link with the sounds of popping corn while we chuckle at the takeoff on the familiar "Big Daddy" cliché and the popper/poppa play on words.

- The Kero-Sun heater burns kerosene and warms your house like the sun.

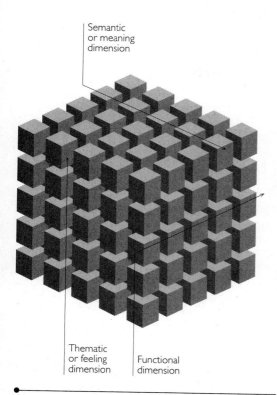

Semantic or meaning dimension

Thematic or feeling dimension

Functional dimension

Figure 5.1. *This figure showing the dimensions of language is based on a description of a model for meaning suggested by Charles E. Osgood, George J. Suci, and Percy H. Tannenbaum.*

- You can have a Soup-erb Supper with a package of Hamburger Helper's beef-vegetable soup.

- And then there is the product that will make every woman Smooth, Soft, and Sexy.

The Functional Dimension: What Do the Words Do?

Examine the following language used during a trial in which the accused—an abortionist and the woman who had the abortion—faced charges

of manslaughter because the abortion occurred late in pregnancy. The defense attorney referred to previous attempts to abort the fetus by saying, "after two unsuccessful attempts." The prosecutor used active verbs and identifying nouns, saying "they tried twice . . . they were unsuccessful," to focus the blame on the woman and the doctor. In the one case, the function of the words was to blunt the accusation; in the other it was to focus blame. The functional dimension has powerful persuasive potential; if nothing else, it can simply shift our focus (Andrews, 1984). So an important dimension of persuasive language is the functions, tasks, or jobs that the words perform.

What do you think?

What function does the phrase "Aw, gimme a break!" serve?

The Semantic Dimension: What Do the Words Mean?

The semantic dimension explains the various shadings of meaning that can be given to certain words. For example, in the same abortion case, the defense succeeded in getting a ruling censoring the prosecution's use of the terms "baby boy" and "human being" and having the word "fetus" substituted throughout the trial. What is the difference in the meaning or connotation of these words? Clearly, choosing the word with the proper semantic meaning can be critical for the persuader, and persuadees need to focus on word choice. It can provide a clue about the source's underlying intentions and, perhaps, believability. For example, mock jurors rated witnesses who used hypercorrect speech as less convincing, less competent, and less intelligent than witnesses who chose less formal words and phrases (Andrews, 1984).

The meaning of a specific word may be critical. In the trial of John Hinckley for the attempted assassination of Ronald Reagan, the

Figure 5.2. *Are the functional and semantic dimensions of language shown here? (Reprinted by permission of Journal Sentinel Inc.)*

defense and prosecution disagreed about whether Hinckley's poetry was "bizarre" versus "eccentric." If it was bizarre, it meant the author was probably insane. However, if the poetry was merely "eccentric," its author might be a little odd, but he was certainly not insane. The jury thought the dilemma could be resolved by a dictionary definition of "poetry." Interestingly, the judge in the trial refused to let the jury have a dictionary (Andrews, 1984).

Although we do not know exactly what happened during the deliberations, in all likelihood, there was a lot of discussion in the jury's deliberations on the different shades of meaning between the words "bizarre" and "eccentric."

And most bureaucrats, such as those shown in Figure 5.2, try to use language to reduce the emotional feelings of certain words. Or consider the following language used on the first page of a four-page fold-out ad for the Chevrolet Camaro: "Laser Cameras. Hotlight Inspections. Robogates. Sonic Tests. What Are We Building Here, A Cruise Missile?" Unfolding the ad reveals the answer, "You Might Say That." The first quote

clearly demonstrates the power of the naming *function* of nouns, as it cites the various tests performed on the vehicle. And three of these noun names are modified by adjectives, each of which *semantically* suggests state-of-the-art technology: "Laser," "Hotlight," and "Sonic."

You may want to experiment with how words can be used and how subtle differences in meaning can occur through word choice and the semantic dimension of language.

The Thematic Dimension: How Do the Words Feel?

In addition to having function and semantic meaning, some words also have a feeling, texture, and theme to them. You can almost sense them. All onomatopoeic words (words that sound like their meaning, such as "shush," "rustle," "buzz," "hum," "ding," or "boom") are obvious examples of the theme or texture of language.

Somewhat less obvious thematic examples rely on assonance, or the repetition of vowels or vowel sounds (for example, "the low moans of our own soldiers rolled across the battlefield like the groans of the doomed"). Alliteration is similar except that it relies on the repetition of consonants. For example, a *Sesame Street* cartoon about the letter "w" says that "Wanda the wicked witch washes her wire wig in a wishing well on windy Wednesdays." An advertising example might be "Make me meatload like my mother used to make — get Mom's Meatloaf Magician!" Both alliteration and assonance are favorite tools of the copy writer. Once you are attuned to these techniques, you will find many examples in print and electronic advertisements.

Sometimes the style of the persuader has a texture or theme to it. For example, after saying he was "going to kick a little ass" in his 1984 debate with vice-presidential candidate Geraldine Ferraro, then vice-president George Bush appeared in a highly publicized 1988 news interview with Dan Rather, in which Bush let slip that Rather "makes Leslie Stahl [another of CBS's *Face the Nation* interviewers] look like a pussy!" The comment was recorded on tape and leaked. Bush was forced to apologize to numerous women's groups, explaining he had only meant that Stahl was as harmless as "a pussy cat." Bush lost most of the female vote in 1992.

Thematic meaning or texture can be created by the use of powerful metaphors. According to communication researcher Michael Osborn (1967), one of the best-known persuaders of the twentieth century, British prime minister Winston Churchill, repeatedly used what Osborn termed archetypal "light" metaphors to characterize the British military and citizenry and "dark" metaphors for the Nazi leaders. In a radio speech during the Battle of Britain, Churchill said,

> If we stand up to him [Hitler], all Europe may be free and the life of the world may move forward into broad, sunlit uplands. But if we fail, then the whole world, including the United States, including all that we have known and cared for, will sink into the abyss of a new Dark Age made more sinister, and perhaps protracted, by the lights of perverted science. . . . Good night then: sleep to gather strength for the morning. For the morning will come. Brightly will it shine on the brave and the true, kindly upon all who suffer for the cause, glorious upon the tombs of heroes. Thus will shine the dawn. (Osborn, 1967)

During the presidential primaries of 1996, several interesting metaphors were developed by various candidates to create thematic or textural meaning. Millionaire candidate Steven Forbes wanted a "flat tax" and depicted the present tax system as something that we needed to kill and "drive a stake through its heart." Conservative columnist Patrick Buchanan was for "America First" and a "New Conservatism of the Heart." Candidate Lamar Alexander decided to use nonverbal symbols that had thematic meaning when he wore a red-and-black checked "lumberjack"

shirt and hip boots during a particularly mud-slinging part of the campaign.

By carefully considering the functional, semantic, and thematic dimensions of any persuasive message, we can exercise our response-ability as receivers. Even if our interpretation of the ad doesn't match that of the ad's creators, the process of identifying the symbols and trying to interpret what they mean is a positive step in preparing us for responsible reception of persuasion. It can alert us to the uses and misuses of persuasive symbols.

The Power of Symbolic Expression

Symbolic expression has power to affect us and others both mentally and physically. For example, the kinds of symbols people use and respond to can affect their health. People who use expressions such as "I can't stomach it" or "I'm fed up" or "It's been eating away at me now for a year" have more stomach ulcers than others. Symbolic days, such as birthdays, can also have dramatic effects. In nursing homes, more persons die during the two months after their birthday than during the two months before. Thomas Jefferson and John Adams both died on the Fourth of July, a date of tremendous significance for both of them. Jefferson is even reported to have awakened from a deathlike coma on the third to ask his doctor if it was the fourth yet. Some people die soon after the death of a loved one—and from the same disease. In other words, symbolic sympathy pains can become real (Koenig, 1972). And many survivors and family members of victims of the bombing of the Murrah building in Oklahoma City in 1995 experienced such serious physical and psychological malaise that they required prolonged medical and psychological treatment.

Not only do symbols deeply affect individuals, but they also serve as a kind of psychological cement for holding a society or culture together. The central symbol for the Lakota Indians was a sacred hoop representing the four seasons of the Earth and the four directions from which weather might come. In the center of the hoop were crossed thongs that symbolized the sacred tree of life and the crossroads of life. Shortly after the hoop was broken during the Wounded Knee massacre of 1890, the tribe disintegrated. A Lakota wise man named Black Elk explained the symbolic power of the circle for his tribe:

> You have noticed that everything an Indian does is in a circle, and that is because the Power of the World always works in circles, and everything tries to be round. In the old days when we were a strong and happy people, all our power came to us from the sacred hoop of the nation and so long as the hoop was unbroken the people flourished. . . . Everything the Power of the World does is done in a circle. The Sky is round and I have heard that the Earth is round like a ball and so are all the stars. The Wind, in its greatest power, whirls. Birds make their nests in circles, for theirs is the same religion as ours. The sun comes forth and goes down again in a circle. The moon does the same, and both are round.
>
> Even the seasons form a great circle in their changing and always come back again to where they were. The life of a man is a circle from childhood to childhood and so it is in everything where power moves. Our tipis were round like the nests of birds and these were always set in a circle, the nation's hoop, a nest of many nests where the Great Spirit meant for us to hatch our children. (Black Elk, 1971)

Black Elk believed that his tribe had lost all their power or medicine when the whites forced the Indians out of their traditional round tepees and into the square houses on the reservation.

What symbols serve as the cultural cement for our way of life? A good place to identify some of the central symbols in our culture is in advertisements. Consider the verbal and nonverbal symbols in Figure 5.3. How do they reflect the central values of our culture?

We can also look to political rhetoric to find symbolic evidence of our cultural values. Since the breakup of the communist world, two important words used by politicians are "freedom" and "equality." As columnist David Broder (1984) noted, "Words are important symbols, and . . . 'freedom' and 'equality' have defined the twin guideposts of American Democracy" (p. 41). The words have the thematic qualities to stir patriotic emotions. Interestingly, however, they are not rated the same by all persons. As several sociological researchers have noted, "Socialists rank both words high, while persons with fascist tendencies rank both low; communists rank 'equality' high but 'freedom' low and conservatives rate 'freedom' high but 'equality' low" (p. 41). What do these word preferences tell us about their users?

It is easy to see that the power of symbols in their functional, semantic, and thematic dimensions is considerable. Not only can they reveal motives, they can also affect our self-image and express our cultural ideals and national character.

We now turn to examine tools for analyzing the functional dimension of language in persuasion. Let's keep the power of the semantic and thematic dimensions in mind for no single word can be charted in semantic space without referring to all three dimensions.

Tools for Analyzing Persuasive Symbols

Being aware of the functional, semantic, and thematic dimensions of language and nonverbal symbols is helpful in our roles as responsible receivers of persuasion. However, these dimensions are broad and somewhat general. Tools for the analysis of persuasion help us focus our critical eyes and ears to more specific aspects of language symbols. Below are several such tools.

Figure 5.3. How do nonverbal cues function in this ad? (Reprinted by permission of Northern Illinois Gas Co.)

Tools for the Functional Dimension

Two tools for analyzing the functional dimension of language symbols in persuasion are language critic Richard Weaver's grammatical categories (especially regarding sentence types), and consideration of the effects of word order, or syntax, in sentences.

Weaver's Grammatical Categories. Language theorist and critic Richard Weaver (1953) suggests that the type of sentence format preferred by a person can offer clues as to that person's world view, the way he or she uses information, and how he or she come to conclusions. Weaver discusses the implications indicated by a persuader's preference for simple sentences, compound sentences, or complex sentences.

Simple sentences usually express a single complete thought or point, and they must have at least one subject or noun and one action word or verb (for example, "He hit"). They sometimes have objects or words that receive the action ("He hit the ball"). They might even have several subjects ("Juan and Kim hit the ball") or several verbs ("Juan and Kim kicked, screamed, and pointed at the ball"). Examples of incomplete simple sentences might be "Behind the ball" and "And ran fast," because neither expresses a complete thought. There are a variety of other possibilities involving modification of both subject and verb.

Persuaders who prefer using simple sentences do not perceive the world as a very complex place. As Weaver puts it, such a person "sees the world as a conglomerate of things . . . [and] seeks to present certain things as eminent against a background of matter uniform or flat" (p. 120). The simple sentence sets the subject off from the verb and object; it sees *causes* that *act* to have *effects* on *objects*. When a persuader uses this form, the persuadee ought to look at what is being highlighted, at what affects what, and at how ac-

tion occurs. For example, consider the use of the simple sentence in these words spoken by Jimmy Carter: "Our country is made up of pluralism or diversity. . . . But that's not a sign of weakness. It's a sign of strength. Some people have said that our nation is a melting pot. It's not. . . . The point is why we came to this country. . . . we become not a melting pot but a beautiful mosaic." (There is a clear foreground and background in most of them. Subjects are set off from verbs and objects, and cause and effect are highlighted.)

Compound sentences are made up of two or more simple sentences joined by a conjunction (for example, "She ran, and she jumped"). Weaver says that the compound sentence sets things either in balance (for example, "He ran, and he ran fast") or in opposition ("He ran, but she walked"). It expresses some kind of tension—whether resolved or unresolved. Weaver says it "conveys that completeness and symmetry which the world ought to have, and which we manage to get, in some measure, into our most satisfactory explanations of it" (p. 127). Persuaders who use compound sentences see the world divided into polar opposites or similarities—totally against one another or in concert with one another. The union leader, for example, says, "You are either against us, or you are with us!" and thus oversimplifies a complex world by using a compound sentence. Each of the two elements (simple sentences) in the example is complete and could stand alone.

Though ungrammatical, the first two sentences in Mark Twain's classic novel *Huckleberry Finn* are compound ones:

> You don't know about me, without you have read a book by the name of *The Adventures of Tom Sawyer*, but that ain't no matter. That book was made by Mr. Mark Twain, and he told the truth, mainly.

What do you think?

Identify a contemporary talk show host's sentence preference.

The elements before and after the conjunctions "but" and "and" could stand alone as single complete thoughts. Notice how both sentences convey resolved tension, completeness, and symmetry (you wouldn't know who Huck is, but that's okay/Mark Twain wrote the book, and he was basically truthful). When you encounter compound sentences in persuasion, it is important to try to identify the resolved or unresolved tension, the completeness, and the symmetry.

Complex sentences are similar to compound sentences in that they may have two or more distinct components, but not all of them can stand alone as complete simple or compound sentences. In other words, some of the elements in the sentences rely on (or are *dependent* on) another element in the sentence and cannot stand alone. Once, in speaking about word choice, Mark Twain used a complex sentence: "Whenever we come upon one of these intensely right words in a book or a newspaper, the resulting effect is physical as well as spiritual and electrically prompt" (Lederer, 1991, p. 128).

The complex sentence features a more complex world—several causes and several effects at the same time. Weaver (1953) says that it "is the utterance of a reflective mind" that tries "to express some sort of hierarchy" (p. 121). Persuaders who use complex sentences express basic principles and relationships, with the independent clauses more important than the dependent clauses. For example, consider the following paragraph describing the entrance of new words and meaning into our language during the 1980s:

A *baby boomer* . . . tired of life in the *fast track* spent *networking* with *yuppies, yumpies,* or *dinks*, disconnected her *cellular phone* and paid some *megabucks,* to go to a *fat farm.* Feeling like a *couch potato,* she stopped her *feeding frenzies* with calzone and *chimichanga* and gave the *high five* to *grazing* on *nouvelle cuisine.* . . . the computer had thoroughly befuddled her sense of *back up, bit, boot,*

crack, disk, hacker, mail, memory, menu, mouse, park, scroll, virus, and *window.* No wonder that *Boomer* began feeling like a *no-brainer gomer,* a totally *loose cannon,* and a *ditzy airhead.* (Lederer, 1991, pp. 44–45).

Look for elements that are dependent on others to express a complete thought (such as "feeling like a couch potato," "and gave the high five to . . ."). In all likelihood, they rank lower in importance than the independent elements.

Weaver also had some observations about types of words. For example, nouns, because they are thought of as words for things and as labels for naming, are often reacted to *as if they were the things they name.* They "express things whose being is completed, not whose being is in process, or whose being depends upon some other being" (p. 128). Thus, when people call police officers pigs, they make the enemy into an object—a thing. It is easy to spit on a pig. The pig is an object. Looking at persuaders' nouns may give us clues as to their perceptions of things. When persuaders reduce persons to things or objects, they do so for a reason: Usually it is to deal with people as objects, not as human beings.

The function of adjectives is to add to the noun, to make it special. To Weaver, adjectives are second-class citizens. He calls them "question begging" and says they show an uncertain persuader. If you have to modify a noun, Weaver would say you are not certain about the noun. In Weaver's opinion, the only adjectives that are not uncertain are *dialectical* (good and bad, hot and cold, light and dark). Examining adjectives used by persuaders may reveal what the persuaders are uncertain about and what they see in opposition to what.

Adverbs, to Weaver, are words of *judgment.* Unlike adjectives, they represent a community judgment—one with which others can agree and that reflects what the persuader thinks the audience believes. For example, adverbs such as "surely," "certainly," or "probably" suggest agreement. When persuaders say, "Surely we all know and believe that thus-and-such is so," they suggest that the audience agrees with them.

Syntax as an Analytical Tool. In contrast to using grammatical categories and sentence types to analyze persuaders' messages, we can look at syntax.

Syntax is defined in the *Random House College Dictionary* as "the pattern or structure of the word order in sentences or phrases." How on earth can that have a persuasive effect? Word order can either *alert* or *divert* the reader/listener. Consider the difference between these pairs of sentences:

- Before bombing the terrorist headquarters, we made sure the target was the right one.

- We were sure the target was the right one before bombing the terrorist headquarters.

  or

- After thinking the proposition over, I've decided to buy another brand.

- I've decided to buy another brand after thinking the proposition over.

In the first sentence in each pair, the dependent element occurs at the beginning of the sentence ("Before . . ." and "After . . ."). This *alerts* the reader or listener to the conditions needing to be satisfied before taking or not taking the action (checking the target and thinking over the proposition). The main point of the sentence is expressed in the independent element. In the second sentence in each pair, the action comes first, and the dependent element now diverts the attention of the listener or reader to the justification for taking the action or to the action itself (changing the brand, bombing the target). Some persuaders use emotional or surprising words by placing them at the beginning of a sentence to defuse the impact of the evidence to follow—the audience is *alerted* by the emotionality of the claim to focus on the details of the evidence. For example, the speaker might say, "There is no greater hypocrite than the animal rightist who opposed use of animals in research labs during the day and then goes home and has beef, fish, or chicken for supper!" The reader knows beforehand that the claim or theme is about hypocrisy, and he or she then focuses on the reasons for making the claim. The sentence is dramatic and creates a puzzle for the listener/reader, thus focusing his or her attention. The other side of the coin is the speaker who *diverts* the audience from the evidence by hiding the claim at the end of the sentence, making the listener/reader wonder where all this evidence is leading. For example, the speaker says, "The animal rightist who opposes the use of rats in the research lab and then goes home to eat beef, fish, or chicken is the kind of hypocrite this country doesn't need and who causes more than their share of trouble." Not only is the drama of the sentence reduced, but the power of the evidence is also overlooked because the audience is in search of the speaker's destination.

Pictorial Design/Camera Language. Some of the *nonverbal* symbols—both visual and auditory—used in persuasion (especially in advertising) can convey powerful symbolic meanings. The elements of good pictorial design, as well as of music, sound effects, special effects, camera angle, and movement, can all convey functional meaning. Let's consider a few of these nonverbal functional symbols. Imagine a blank television screen on which you are going to project a message—say an ad for a car dealer. The ad will have verbal meaning through the words printed on the screen and said on the voiceover, but further meaning will develop through such things as balance and mass, lines and angles, tone and color, and camera perspective and movement.

Visual balance and mass refer to the degree to which various parts of the screen or page are taken up by visual symbols such as pictures, logos, or blocks of copy (see Figure 5.4). Asymmetrical

Slogan

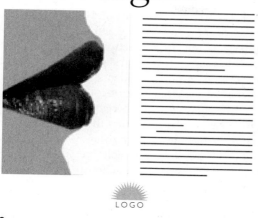

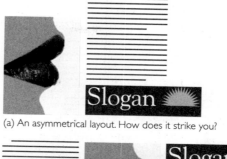

(a) An asymmetrical layout. How does it strike you?

(b) A symmetrical layout. How does it strike you?

Figure 5.4. *Pictures, blocks of copy, slogans, and other nonverbal elements in advertising can either create balance (symmetry) or asymmetry.*

Figure 5.5. *(a) This is an asymmetrical one. How does it strike you? (b) This demonstrates symmetrical balance. How does it strike you?*

balance is usually preferred because it is more visually interesting and has more creative potential (see Figure 5.5). A heavy mass at the bottom (see Figure 5.6) "implies firmness, solidarity, support, and importance" (Burrows, Wood, & Gross, 1992, p. 254). A heavy mass at the top (see Figure 5.7), on the other hand, conveys uneasiness, "instability, suspense and/or impermanence" (p. 254).

You can imagine the various ways in which balance could be used in a TV car ad, with video footage showing the car swooping through curves in one of the blocks, price being featured in another, plus aerial footage showing the huge selection of new models on the dealership lot, all adding functional meaning to the spoken and written words in the ad.

The use of various kinds of *lines* in an ad can communicate further functional meanings. For example, straight lines suggest firmness, rigidity, directness, or strength, while curved or rounded lines imply softness, elegance and movement

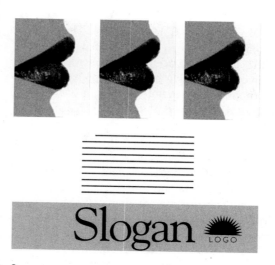

Figure 5.6. *A heavy mass at the bottom indicates security, firmness, and importance.*

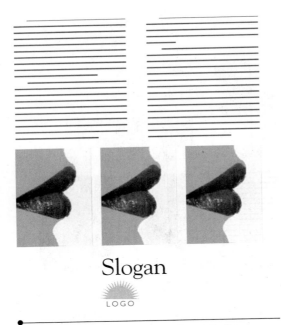

Figure 5.7. *A heavy mass at the top indicates instability, suspense, and impermanence.*

(Burrows, Wood, & Gross, 1992). Thus, if your automobile ad is for a sportier model, show it handling curves in a graceful way while more conservative models might appear on the straightaway. Horizontal lines connote serenity, inactivity, and openness, while vertical lines are dignified, important, and strong. Diagonals imply action, imbalance, instability, and insecurity.

Tone and color communicate emotions. Color communicates mood and mass or weight. The warm colors of the spectrum (yellow, orange, red) communicate exciting feelings, while the cooler colors (blue, green, or turquoise) communicate tranquillity and peace. Similarly, "light tones result in a delicate, cheerful, happy, trivial, feeling, whereas dark tones result in a feeling that is heavy, somber, serious, [and] forceful" (Burrows, Wood, & Gross, p. 254). Darker colors ap-

pear heavier and carry more mass. You feel more secure and solid when a dark blue color takes up the bottom third of a page or screen, and you probably feel more trapped and depressed when the dark color covers the top third of the screen or page. Notice how expensive products such as jewelry are frequently packaged in dark colors, whereas more trivial products such as breakfast cereals are packaged in light-colored boxes.

Camera shots and movement also communicate meaning. For example, the long or "establishing" shots are far enough away that people's faces are not distinguishable, yet they set the mood for the message or action to be seen, and they often relate the involved persons to the setting and circumstances. For example, in *Apocalypse Now* the long shot of the strange armed village in Cambodia where Kurtz (Marlon Brando) has set up headquarters, establishes and prepares the viewer for the mood, tone, and action that is to follow. Medium shots, which include most of a person's body and distinguishable faces, are used to carry dialogue or interaction between characters; the scene in *Forrest Gump* at the White House, where Forrest meets President Kennedy, is a good example. Close-ups usually include only the characters' faces, and may be accomplished by slow zooming in; they usually are meant to tell the viewers that they are now looking into the characters' minds in very intimate and personal ways. In *Schindler's List*, the close-up is used to show Schindler's emotion and tension when he decides to wet down the cattle cars loaded with Jews being sent to concentration camps.

Other nonverbal means of expression such as music, color, and special effects imply various levels of meaning and can frequently provide the most important functional meaning in the message. For example, in *Schindler's List*, a little girl is highlighted because her coat is colored rose while the rest of the screen is in documentary black and white. The viewer is introduced to her and follows her step-by-step to her ultimate death. Color draws our attention to her and serves to provide continuity for the enormous horror of the story.

Tools for the Semantic Dimension

Although the functional dimension of language bears important verbal and nonverbal meanings, the semantic dimension of language probably carries the bulk of meaning for most messages. Let us examine some tools for analyzing this dimension of language symbols.

Strategic Uses of Ambiguity. It may seem like heresy for persuaders to intentionally be ambiguous in designing their persuasive messages, but they often do just that—they try to be somewhat unclear, vague, and general. They do so in order to allow for the widest possible degree of common ground or identification. In other words, they want each potential persuadee to fill in his or her own private meanings or connotations for the particular word or symbol. This strategy results in the largest number of potential interpretations and thus creates the largest potential audience for the persuader's brands, candidates, or causes. It also provides the persuader with an "escape hatch" if questioned on the way a word or other symbol is being used, and thus helps the persuader please as many and offend as few persons as possible. As a receiver, you need to identify such cases of intentional ambiguity and analyze the reason(s) persuaders try to be unclear.

Persuaders use several methods to create strategic ambiguity. One method is to carefully choose words that can be interpreted in many, often contradictory, ways. For example, a politician may favor "responsibility in taxation and the education of our youngsters." Those who think teachers are underpaid and need substantial raises might hear this as a call for *spending* tax dollars.

Those who hold a reverse view could as easily interpret the statement as saying that educational spending needs to be *cut*. There are other possible interpretations as well. The key word, the one that increases the ambiguity, is "responsibility." It sets up the rest of the sentence.

Though Steven Forbes first used the term "flat tax" in the presidential primaries of 1996, it was soon adopted by practically every other candidate for the G.O.P. nomination, no two of whom interpreted it in exactly the same way. It was attractive because it was ambiguous and mushy. How flat should the tax tables be? What could be deductible? Should there be several degrees of "flatness" or just one? "Family values" was another such term. Did it mean subsidizing single mothers so they could keep their families together and not have to work so they could nurture the family? Or did it mean ending legal abortions? Or did it mean making divorced parents pay child support? Or did it mean taking the kids to church? The ambiguity of the term was its strength.

Ambiguity can be created by *juxtaposing or combining words or phrases in startling ways or by presenting issues in a new light.* For example, the term "born again" became familiar in the 1980s and was persuasive to many people. It referred to people who claimed to have been converted to Christianity, even if they were members of Christian denominations before their conversion. The term "born again" suggests that the earlier beliefs are forgotten or incorrect and that the conversion causes them to be revitalized and re-created.

Some born-again lobbyists labeled their political group the "moral majority," creating highly persuasive and intentional ambiguity. The term was ambiguous first because the group did not constitute a majority but actually was a minority.

> **What do you think?**
>
> Identify a particularly ambiguous claim being made in advertising today.

The term also implies that, because most people try to behave morally, almost anyone could be a member. This ambiguous term had great persuasive appeal. Media preachers created what political researchers Dan Nimmo and James Combs (1984) call "The Electronic Church." "*Moral decay*" became another highly persuasive and also ambiguous term. We respond to "moral decay" in the same way we respond to tooth decay. Rush Limbaugh coined a term that juxtaposes meanings to create a powerful kind of ambiguity about a group of persons whom he calls "FemiNazis." The positivity of "feminine" clashes with the negativity of "Nazis" and shocks the audience into a new way of thinking.

How can we defend ourselves against ambiguous language? The semanticists advise using more specific and concrete elaborations on any ambiguous term. The semioticians advise us to seek the full meanings in persuasive "texts" by delving into various verbal and nonverbal "signifiers" to determine what is really being "signified." Using both the semantic and the semiotic approaches, you can reduce ambiguity in language.

Examining the denotations and connotations of persuasive symbols is another tool for studying the semantic dimension of language. There are other tools for approaching the semantic dimension of language. Among the more useful is the dramatistic approach suggested by philosopher and literary critic Kenneth Burke.

Kenneth Burke's Dramatism. In addition to his theoretical ideas on language discussed in Chapters 3 and 4, Kenneth Burke offers students of persuasion a theory and a tool for analyzing the semantic dimension of language. He called his method "dramatism" and his tool of analysis the "dramatistic pentad."

Like the other theories we discussed in Chapter 3, dramatism maintains that the basic model that humans use to deal with and to explain various situations is the drama. Burke

(1960) thought of it as "a philosophy of language" capable of describing and analyzing a wide variety of human motivations as they are expressed in symbolic acts such as human language use. Burke said that a central concept in this approach to language and motivation is the idea of action (which is motivated) as opposed to motion (which is not motivated). Basic bodily functions such as sweating or digestion occur without us willing them to occur—they are nonsymbolic acts. Action, on the other hand, requires the ability to use language symbolically—we must will it into being. In other words language use is a kind of symbolic action because it is motivated.

Burke believed that when we communicate, we choose words because of their dramatic potential, and that different individuals find some elements in the drama more potent than others. Some, for example, may believe that great people affect the outcome of events; when persuading, such persons give examples of individual effort winning the day. Burke described their persuasion as based on the *agent*, or actor. For other persons, the *scene*, or setting, may be the motivating element; they choose scenic words and phrases to persuade. Burke's model, the dramatistic pentad, has five central elements, as its name implies: scene, act, agent, agency, and purpose (see Figure 5.8).

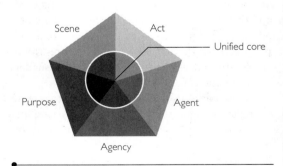

Figure 5.8. *The five elements of dramatism ultimately affect one another and each emerge from a common unified core—the drama itself.*

Scene is the place where action occurs. It includes not only physical location but situation, time, social place, occasion, and other elements of the setting. The scene could be something like "Campaign '96," "Ruby Ridge," "a Web site," "an inauguration," or *The Oprah Winfrey Show*." People for whom this is a key element are likely to believe that a change in the scene will cause other things to occur. They might believe, for example, that if gays are permitted to join the armed forces, there will be less discrimination and hostility toward them. The scene should be a "fit container" for the act. For example, the Lincoln Memorial was a "fit" scene for Martin Luther King's "I Have a Dream" speech, which is what made the speech so memorable and successful. The roadside diner is an "unfit" scene for a mass murder in *Natural Born Killers,* which is why the audience gasps when the guns start blazing. Burke believes that persons favoring scene as a key element have a *materialist* philosophy of life. They think that the physical, social, and psychological environment in which action occurs can be the cause of good or bad outcomes.

Act in Burke's model refers to any motivated or purposeful action. In persuasive messages, the verb is the best indicator of the act. High comedy or high tragedy result when the act is not appropriate for the scene. A Charlie Chaplin film in which the snooty society hostess gets hit in the face with a cream pie is funny because the act doesn't "fit" the social scene. The assassination of a political leader while attending church is tragic because the act doesn't "fit" the physical scene. Burke suggests that *realism* is the philosophy of life associated with an emphasis on act. What is the act in Figure 5.9?

Agent is Burke's term for the person or group of persons who take action in the scene — they are the actors or characters (the police officer, the corrupt politician, the Unabomber, Bill Clinton, Howard Stern, Madonna, and so on). Figure 5.9 expresses an agent focus. Motives (such as hatred

Figure 5.9. *The agent is the focus of this ad, as can be easily seen, but other elements of the pentad are apparent also. (Reprinted by permission of Southern Comfort Company.)*

of Serbian minorities, instincts, greed, or jealousy) sometimes act as agents. Countries and organizations (militia groups, UN peacekeeping forces, the National Rifle Association, pro-choice groups) frequently act as agents. Persuaders who emphasize agent as a key element tend to have *idealism* as their philosophy of life, according to Burke. They believe that strong individuals determine the outcome of events.

Agency is the tool, method, or means used by persuaders to accomplish their ends. For example, Arm & Hammer baking soda used "focus-group research methods" as the agency to conduct market research. Steve Forbes used the flat tax in his 1996 primary bid. Hamlet uses the play within a play as the agency to determine guilt. Energizer uses a mechanical bunny to send the message that its battery "keeps on going and going and . . ." Calvin Klein uses nudity and prepubescent, anorexic-appearing females as agencies to get attention for Obsession perfume. And Wheaties uses famous athletes to promote the brand as "The Breakfast of Champions." Communication strategies also act as agencies (such as intensifying one's own good points or others' bad ones). Persuaders emphasizing agency tend to have *pragmatism* as a philosophy of life.

Purpose is the reason an agent acts in a given scene using a particular agency. Sometimes the persuader's purpose is quite apparent, while at other times it is covert. The U.S. Army says you can "Be All You Can Be in the Army," thus suggesting a purpose for an individual to enlist. The U.S. government sends food and other humanitarian aid for the apparent purpose of avoiding the starvation of millions of people and anarchy. Pro-life advocates have as a purpose the overturning of *Roe v. Wade.* These are all apparent purposes, but what are the true purposes? Why did Magic Johnson reveal that he was infected with HIV? Why were Infiniti automobiles never shown in the advertisements that introduced the new vehicle to the marketplace? The purposes of these actions aren't very clear. Burke believed that persuaders favoring purpose as a key element tend to have *mysticism* as a philosophy of life — they believe that something greater than the individual (God, the Constitution, the American spirit) determines the outcome of human affairs.

These five elements can be used to develop a persuasive strategy (see Figure 5.10). For example, if you were trying to get a date for a rock concert, you might emphasize the *scene,* describing the auditorium, crowd, sounds, costumes, lighting, exciting colors, and similar elements. An alternative strategy would be to focus on the *act,* describing the kinds of music and the interactions between the performers and the audience. You might also choose to focus on the *agent,* describing the musicians, their reputations, and their appearance. If you chose to feature *agency,* you might mention the sound system, the unique instruments, and special effects such as explosions on stage. Finally, you could feature *purpose* by telling your prospective date that "To be really 'in,' you shouldn't miss attending a live rock concert, and you might meet other interesting people from the audience."

In any situation, all of these elements of the pentad operate simultaneously to greater or lesser degree. Burke suggested that if you compare them in pairs, or **ratios,** you can identify a persuader's "key" emphases. In *Hamlet,* for example, the dramatic tension created in the **scene-act ratio** comes from the fact that Hamlet's mother has married his uncle following the mysterious death of Hamlet's father, the king. Worse, the marriage followed the funeral by less than one month, hardly the proper act for a scene in which extended mourning for a deceased king should be occurring. Hamlet is disturbed by this imbalance in the scene-act ratio and curses his mother and uncle in a soliloquy, saying, "She married. O, most wicked speed, to post with such dexterity to incestuous sheets!" Later, Hamlet teases his friend Horatio, asking whether he had visited court for the funeral or the wedding. Hamlet expresses his anger ironically in these bitter words, which reflect his reaction to the imbalance of the scene-act ratio: "Thrift, thrift, Horatio! The funeral baked meats did coldly furnish the marriage tables." We can almost hear him ready to use more damning language, yelling, "Whore! Slut."

We also frequently see the persuasive power of the scene-act ratio in advertisements. For

What do you think?

Which is your key element of the pentad?

She goes
two blocks to
pre-school.
But college is
just around
the corner.

Your tomorrows depend on the consistent performance of your long-term investments. And that's why investors have made Kemper one of America's largest asset managers. For over forty years, the Kemper Family of Mutual Funds has been dedicated to the kind of steady, long-term performance that builds tomorrows today. To learn more, talk to your financial representative at this location.

We're Building Tomorrows Today™

Figure 5.10. *The scene here is a childhood home. The agents are father and daughter. The act is nurturing, and the purpose is planning for the future. As is often the case, the product is the agency. This ad was designed in response to an ad Kemper had run in which a father is planning for his son to go to college. What might be the hidden purpose and agency here? (Used by permission of Kemper Financial Services.)*

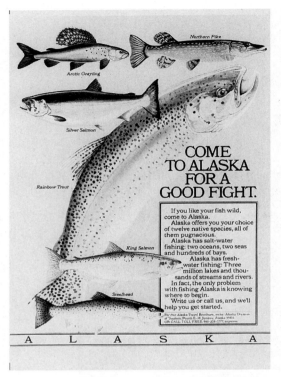

Figure 5.11. *How are the scene and the act balanced in this ad? (Used by permission of the Alaska Division of Tourism.)*

example, in Figure 5.11, the scene — the state of Alaska — offers tourists great fishing with the words "If you like your fish wild" and "twelve native species, all of them pugnacious." It adds that the Alaska scene has "two oceans, two seas, and hundreds of bays," thereby furthering the scene-act balance — after all, where but in the largest state would you expect the biggest fight with a fish?

Scene can also interact with the other elements of the pentad. In the **scene-agent ratio,** balance or imbalance again can indicate potent

persuasion or high drama — comedy, tragedy, or melodrama. In the film *Psycho,* one of Alfred Hitchcock's masterpieces, viewers instinctively note a scene-agent imbalance when Anthony Perkins tells Janet Leigh that he has stuffed all the taxidermic specimens in the office of the Bates Motel. The imbalance is intensified when we see him spy on her through the secret peephole in the eye of one of the specimens. The imbalance here implies the strong possibility of danger, and we may subconsciously whisper "Don't stay at this motel — find another one down the road!" The tension caused by the scene-agent imbalance is increased when we hear Perkins and his "mother" arguing at the Victorian house near the motel — again we want to warn Leigh to "close and lock the bathroom door whenever you take a shower!" Her murder is later "discovered" by Perkins, who is shocked at the scene-agent disparity of someone as kind as his "mother" stabbing a young girl to death. Hitchcock uses scene-agent tension throughout the rest of the film as well as in his other films to keep the audience on the edge of their seats.

The ad for Goodyear tires in Figure 5.12 uses the scene-agency ratio to persuade us to purchase the brand. The scene is the "great outdoors" as the headline tells us, and the agency is the tire that will assure you of a good bass expedition. Notice that the agent is the least important thing in the ad — you can barely see him. The act of landing or retrieving a boat is complete, while the agency — the Goodyear tire — is at the center of the ad. Any of the other ten possible pairs of elements of the pentad might be examined to discover a persuader's key term or element.

Burke believed that a persuader's key term infuses every aspect of life — home, family, job, political choices, and philosophy of life to name a few. As a result, identifying a persuader's key terms or elements can alert you to the underlying motives of the persuasion and help you to predict

Figure 5.12. An example of a scene-agency ratio. (Reprinted by permission of The Goodyear Tire & Rubber Company.)

his or her future persuasive appeals. As you encounter persuasion in any of its many forms, try to listen for the key term being used, and process your response to the persuasion accordingly.

Tools for the Thematic Dimension

As noted earlier in this chapter, the thematic dimension of language is that quality in certain words or sets of words that gives them a texture or "feel." Although the words do have a semantic meaning and a syntactical function, their most important persuasive aspect is their ability to set a mood, develop a feeling, or generate a tone or theme for the persuasion—hence the term "thematic." For example, Lincoln set the theme for his famous Gettysburg Address with his words

> Fourscore and seven years ago our fathers brought forth on this continent a new nation, conceived in liberty and dedicated to the proposition that all men are created equal.

How far less stirring the speech would have been if he had said:

> Eighty-seven years ago the signers of the Declaration of Independence started a new country designed to assure us of freedom and equality.

The two sentences have nearly equivalent semantic and functional meanings; the obvious difference between them lies in their texture.

Earlier we noted how the repetition of consonants (alliteration) or vowels (assonance) carries thematic meaning. The advertisements for Satin cigarettes, for example, use alliteration to create a thematic meaning for the brand—"Smooth. Silky. Satin Cigarettes." Sometimes parallel sentence structure communicates a thematic meaning. For example, consider the no-nonsense theme or texture contained in the parallel sentences used in the following print ad promoting MTV as a channel to target a specific audience. The ad features a male in his twenties slouching in an easychair holding a TV remote control device. The headline reads "Buy this 24-year-old and get all his friends absolutely free." The copy reads:

> If this guy doesn't know about you, you're toast. He's an opinion leader. He watches MTV. Which means he knows a lot more than just what CDs to buy and what movies to see. He knows what

clothes to wear, and what credit card to buy them with. And he's no loner. He heads up a pack. What he eats, his friends eat. What he wears, they wear. What he likes, they like. And what's he never heard of . . . well . . . you get the idea. **MTV. A darn good way to influence the MTV Generation.** (*Advertising Age*, July 5, 1993, p. S-3)

We also noted earlier that thematic differences also come from the metaphors persuaders create or from the use of **onomatopoeia** (words that sound like their meaning, such as "swish," "swoosh," "burp," "rustle," or "clap"). Let's turn now to several other tools for discovering the thematic meaning in persuasive messages. They include finding metaphorical themes; noting the use of sensory language; looking for god, devil, and charismatic terms; seeking the pragmatic and unifying styles; and using semiotics to determine the thematic meanings communicated by nonverbal symbols or "signifiers" in a text.

Metaphorical Style. Persuaders can convey a great deal of their message by setting the mood for the persuadees. They can depict a setting appropriate for the message by repeatedly using certain sounds and images. Michael Osborn (1967) has studied the use of *archetypal metaphors* (universal and primal images consistent within and even across cultures), in particular the light-dark comparison. He maintains that, traditionally, we identify light with the sun, warmth, growth, comfort, and so on; we associate dark with mystery, night, cold, and other uncomfortable and troubling things. Osborn points out that persuaders often use repeated references to this dichotomy. John F. Kennedy, in his inaugural address, used this archetypal metaphor when he talked about passing a torch from one generation to another and predicted that the light from this symbolic torch could illuminate the world for freedom; the light was depicted as good, warm, friendly, and virtuous. Elsewhere, the world was filled with darkness and poverty.

There are other archetypal metaphors. For example, the power of the sea and the life-giving and cleansing power of water may explain the holy or magical powers traditionally ascribed to it (as in the fountain of youth or baptism). Mircea Eliade (1971) is convinced that there is also an archetypal metaphor of "the center." In his view, we repeatedly look for a central point—a symbolic navel for our world. For some groups, it is even a specific place (Mecca for Moslems, Munich for Nazis, Jerusalem for Jews and Christians). He also identifies a metaphor of returning to a previous time or place that is sacred or profane.

Most such archetypal metaphors relate to life experiences that all people—primitive as well as modern—can relate to. The light-dark metaphor probably emerged eons ago from a fear of the unseen dangers that lurked in the darkness of night and the lessening of fears that came with light. Another powerful image is fire—burning, destroying, warming, and cleansing are its central metaphorical features.

What are some other universal experiences that humans share from culture to culture and from age to age? When you discover them, you will see that they are often used in advertising and political persuasion and that perhaps you may also use them in your interpersonal encounters as you try to persuade others.

Sensory Language. A courtroom communication expert, Stephanie L. Swanson (1987), maintains that the most effective lawyers rely on words relating to the senses. She speculates that jurors can be categorized as (1) auditorily dependent; that is, relating best to words that are tied to sound; (2) visually dependent; that is, relating best to words that are tied to sight; or (3) kinesthetically dependent; that is, relating best to words that are tied to the sense of touch. For example, an attorney might ask three witnesses to describe an automobile accident. The auditorily dependent witness might answer by saying, "I was walking down

Oak Street *listening* to my Walkman, when I *heard* the screech of brakes, and then there was a sickening *sound of crashing* glass and metal, and someone *screamed*." The visually dependent witness might say, "I *saw* this brown Ford coming around the corner practically on two wheels. Then he must have hit the brakes, because it *looked* like the car slid sideways toward me, and then I *saw* the front end of the Ford *make a mess* of the little Geo." The kinesthetically dependent witness might say, "I had this *feeling* that something was about to happen, and when it did I *felt* frightened and helpless and I *cringed* as the cars crumpled up like scrap paper." Swanson advises attorneys to "listen closely to the sensory language used by your clients . . . try to respond in kind—matching the sensory language of the other person" (p. 211). She advises them to carefully listen to the kinds of words used by prospective jurors during the *voire dire* process and to then "tailor your language to your listeners' primary sensory channel. You can 'paint a picture' for a visual person, 'orchestrate the testimony' for an auditory person, and 'touch the heart' of the kinesthetic individual. By using sensory language, you let the jurors feel that your discourse is directed toward them individually" (p. 211).

Thus, in trying to identify a persuader's use of the thematic dimension of language, another aspect to explore is the sensory language used in the persuasion.

God, Devil, and Charismatic Terms. Another thematic or textural characteristic of style often used in persuasion is the development of **families of terms.** Persuaders like to see the world as divided into neat categories that can be used to persuade others. One of these category sets is made up of *god terms* and *devil terms,* as noted by Richard Weaver (1953). Weaver said that terms or labels are really only parts of propositions. However, they are often linked with other terms or labels to shape a message or a persuasive argument. He de-

fines "god term" as an expression "about which all other expressions are ranked as subordinate and serving dominations and powers. Its force imparts to the others their lesser degree of force" (p. 211). Weaver sees a god term as an unchallenged term that demands sacrifice or obedience in its name. He uses three terms as examples of god terms: *progress, fact,* and *science.* Progress still has persuasive power, but it is hampered by some of the things associated with it—pollution, for example. Science has lost some of its credibility, for science has produced, along with constructive marvels, nuclear weapons and technology that may destroy the earth through pollution.

The first *Newsweek* issue of 1988 declared, "The 80s Are Over: Greed Goes Out of Style." The magazine went on, in an extensive article, to describe the "god terms" of the "me generation/decade," as symbolized by Madonna's *Material Girl*, Rambo, and *Lifestyles of the Rich and Famous* with its "aptly named" host Robin Leach (Barol, 1988). These god terms have been displaced.

What are the god and devil terms of the '90s? Some are the environment, green, "the family," security, balanced, terrorism, deficit spending, politically correct, technology, feminazis, dittoheads, surfing the Web, and others. What are the god and devil terms of your subculture or other subcultures? Explore them, for they will alert you to potential persuasive appeals that could persuade you or that you might use.

What do you think? What is a god term for our culture today?

The use of god and devil terms is evident in advertisements for consumer goods. For example, consider a few recently popular god terms in ads for food: "lite," "light," "low sodium," "no sodium," "low calorie," "clear," "organically grown," and "with fiber" to name a few. Candidates for devil terms include "artificial preservatives," "salt," "gas guzzler," "herbicides," "pesticides," and "toxic."

You will be able to discover more as you search contemporary advertising "texts" for the thematic dimensions of words or terms.

Weaver points out that the connotations of certain negative terms can sometimes be reversed, making the terms neutral or even positive. Take, for example, the expression "wasted" or "getting wasted." Its use during the 1970s referred to killing Viet Cong or others perceived to be the enemy during the Vietnam War. Later, it referred to getting drunk or doped up.

Weaver also described **charismatic terms**—"terms of considerable potency whose referents it is virtually impossible to discover. . . . Their meaning seems inexplicable unless we accept the hypothesis that their content proceeds out of a popular will that they *shall* mean something" (p. 48). His example is the word "freedom," which has no apparent concrete referent but which seems, many years after Weaver discussed it, to still have great potency.

Perhaps because so many things are being questioned in this skeptical last decade of the century, we have fewer examples of charismatic terms, but there are some good candidates. Take "market economy," which became a charismatic term for many in the early '90s with the fall of the former Soviet Union and of the communist governments there and in Russia's satellite states. Few knew exactly what "market economy" meant, yet almost any change in those countries was justified if it somehow reflected a market economy. Opening a fast-food franchise, putting advertising on the sides of vehicles, and purchasing a previously government-owned business were all praised because they mirrored things found in "market economies." Unfortunately, these changes did not lead to improvement overnight; as a result, there was a loss of faith in the concept/term of "market economy."

Another 1990s candidate for a charismatic term is "recycling." With growing awareness of declining natural resources, the concept of recycling has been applied to a host of things—paper, aluminum, glass, even people. A logo consisting of arrows acting as the three sides of a triangle is imprinted on grocery sacks, product containers, newspapers, aluminum cans, and a host of other items. Thousands of communities, schools, corporations, churches, and other groups have gone on recycling kicks, even though some of the recycled material is either warehoused or discarded because there is now a surplus of the stuff. The term has nonetheless had the power to motivate impressive numbers of persons and convince them that it is their duty as a human being to wash out and crush aluminum cans, collapse 2-liter bottles and milk jugs, and carefully save miscellaneous paper, from used envelopes and junk mail to empty cereal boxes.

Pragmatic and Unifying Styles. Another characteristic that builds a thematic wholeness or gives a texture to persuasion is the reliance of a persuader on one of two kinds of styles—the **pragmatic style** or the **unifying style.** These styles can be thought of as signifying two separate strategies; however, persuaders can use the tactics of either strategy, or they can combine the two extremes.

Pragmatic persuaders usually find it necessary to convince listeners who do not necessarily support their position. As a result, they must try to change minds as opposed to reinforcing beliefs, and they must choose appropriate tactics. A politician speaking at a public event (e.g., a college convocation or a news conference) as opposed to a party event (e.g., a rally of supporters) is faced with using the pragmatic style. *Unifying persuaders* are in a much more comfortable position. They talk to people who already believe what is going to be said. They don't need to change minds; they need only reinforce beliefs—to whip up enthusiasm and dedication or to give encouragement. Rush Limbaugh speaking to his television and studio audiences would be likely to use the tactics of the unifying speaker — his audiences already believe what he is going to say. These two styles demonstrate two opposing situations, and they describe the problems facing the persuader in these situations. The problems for pragmatic persuaders are clear — they must change opinion before they can expect action. Unifying persuaders can be much more idealistic — they can usually afford to be more bombastic without offending the audience. These persuaders can be more emotional and less objective than the persuader faced with a questioning audience. What are the stylistic devices of these extremes?

The unifying persuader is able to focus on the then-and-there — on the past or on the future — when things were ideal or when they can become ideal. The position of unifying persuaders is that things look better in the future, particularly if we compare them with the present. Because the audience will fill in the blanks, language choice can be abstract. It is usually poetic and filled with imagery that excites the audience's imagination. Although there may be little that is intellectually stimulating (or that requires careful logical examination) about what unifying persuaders say, there is much that is emotionally stimulating. The words and images offered by such persuaders are precisely the words listeners believe *they* would have said if they were doing the talking. The unifying persuader is thus the sounding board for the entire group, providing them with the cues, but not the details, of the message. The audience can participate with the persuaders in the creation of the message; in fact, audiences sometimes participate actively by yelling encouragement to unifying persuaders or by repeating shibboleths to underscore their words — "Right on" or "Amen, brother" or "Tell it like it is."

Pragmatic persuaders, because they must win an audience, cannot afford to take the risk of appealing to abstract ideals. They must be concrete, focusing on facts instead of images, emphasizing what cannot be disputed or interpreted so easily. They do not try to depict an ideal situation in subjective there-and-then terms. Instead, they have to focus on real aspects of immediate problems familiar to the audience — problems of the here-and-now that are realistic, not idealistic. Their orientation is to the present instead of the future. Because pragmatic persuaders are forced to be concrete and realistic, their language is concrete and prosaic. Lofty thoughts are of little value, especially if they are expressed in equally lofty words. These persuaders tend to focus on facts and statistics instead of imagery.

Clearly, these two extremes are not an either/or proposition — persuaders may, on occasion, use the tactics of both perspectives. When they do, they are probably responding to their audience's level of doubt or acceptance. In the following excerpt, the author is using the pragmatic style. Note the use of here-and-now references, the down-to-earth prosaic language, and concrete examples and references in the following:

> I came here 26 years ago to teach, and like many of my friends, I really didn't expect to stay. I like to think we're all still here because we found a place that only asks us to be whatever we can manage. Call it refuge, an escape from the hurly burly of the rest of the country. Now the West is confronting epic changes. We're growing faster than any other region; people from . . . all over America. People who can are running to enclaves like Montana in search of an unthreatening life. . . . So it's no wonder that a lot of Montanans way down the economic ladder are feeling alienated. A few of them—the militant ones we're reading about—are furious. . . . In Montana, this wave of crazies is regarded as bad luck we don't deserve. On the other hand some of us are guilty . . . of ignoring conditions that drove such folks to think

they have to pursue their political objectives with guns and bombs (Kittredge, 1996, p. 43).

The persuader here is a Montana professor who is trying to convince his audiences (primarily Montanans, but also other readers of *Newsweek*) that his state is not as filled with militant lunatics as it appears and that such folks need to be convinced that violence is unacceptable. With the audience spread out and bipolar at the least, he needs to be down-to-earth, prosaic, practical, and present-oriented. Notice his use of common expressions such as "hurly burly" and "wave of crazies." He also uses concrete examples and references and is very present-oriented — focusing on what needs to be done now to save the situation. He has assessed his audience accurately as one that needs persuasion, not reinforcement; as a bipolar versus a unipolar one, and his style fits the audience's needs.

Contrast that bit of persuasion with the following example of a unifying persuader attempting to reinforce and energize an audience to action. The speaker is Georgia governor Zell "Give 'Em Hell" Miller. The occasion is the Democratic National Convention of 1992, where Miller is giving the keynote speech opening the convention. The audience is made up of party regulars, delegates to the convention and their guests, members of the press, and others. Miller's purpose is to unify and activate the party faithful in the hall and in the television audience for the upcoming national campaign for the presidency and other offices:

> We are gathered here to nominate a man from a remote, rural corner of Arkansas. . . . That is powerful proof that the American Dream still lives. Bill Clinton . . . feels our pain, shares our hope and will work his heart out to fulfill our dreams. You see, I understand why Bill Clinton is so eager to see the American Dream kept alive for a new generation. Because I too was a product of that dream. I was born during the worst of the Depression on a cold winter's day in the drafty bed-

room of a rented house, and I was my parents' hope for the future. Franklin Roosevelt was elected that year and would soon replace generations of neglect with a whirlwind of activity. . . . But what of the kids of today? Who fights for the child of a single mother? Because without a government that is on their side, those children have no hope. And when a child has no hope, a nation has no future. I am a Democrat because we are the party of hope. . . . Robbed of hope, the voices of anger rise up, rise up from working Americans who are tired of paying more in taxes and getting less in services. And George Bush doesn't get it? Americans cannot understand why the rich can buy the best health care in the world, but all the rest of us get is [sic] rising costs and cuts in coverage—or no health insurance at all. And George Bush doesn't get it? Americans cannot walk our streets . . . and George Bush doesn't get it? . . . He doesn't see it; he doesn't feel it; and he's done nothing about it. . . . And so the choice in this election is clear. We've got us a race between an aristocrat, an autocrat, and a Democrat. . . . We have a leader and a party and a platform that says to everyday working people of this country: We will fight your fight. We will ease your burden. We will carry your cause. We will hear all the voices of America . . . from the silky harmonies of the gospel choirs to the rough-edged rhythms of a hot country band . . . from the razor's edge rap of the inner city to the soaring beauty of the finest soprano. We hear your voice, America. We hear your voice. We will answer your call. We will keep your faith. And we will restore your hope.

Notice the past and future references and the metaphors of the shattered dream, robbed hope, and voices of America. The repeated phrases act as refrains, some of which the audience picks up in a call-response pattern ("And George Bush doesn't get it?"). The parallel sentence structures are also similar to poetic refrains ("We will fight your fight. We will ease your burdens" or "We hear your voice, America. . . . We will answer your call"). And while the language is simple, it has elements of poetry to it (the "silky harmonies," "razor's edge," and "soaring beauty"). It relies on emotions rather than reason, and it reinforces and energizes the audience, as audio and video transcriptions of the speech clearly show (people jumping from their seats, wild applause, tears, and so on).

The pragmatic and unifying styles are a function of the audience and its needs and not of the speaker. We can learn something about persuaders by observing which style they choose for which kinds of audiences. Persuadees can gain insight into how they are being seen by the persuader by identifying the style of the message.

Semiotics as a Tool For Decoding Persuasion

We have briefly referred to the field of semiotics as a way to study meaning. Although the origin of this approach goes back to the work of Charles Morris and Charles Sanders Peirce in the late 1940s and 1950s, its most important contemporary theorist is Umberto Eco, known for his bestselling novels *The Name of the Rose* and *Foucault's Pendulum*. Eco (1984) holds that the process of "signification" (or the giving of meaning to a "sign") involves four elements: (1) the objects or conditions that exist in the world, (2) the signs that are available to represent these objects or conditions, (3) a set of choices among signs, or a *repertoire* of responses, and (4) a set of rules of correspondence that we use to encode and decode the signs we make and interpret.

It is this final characteristic that most directly addresses the goal of this course. The discovery of the various codes used by persuaders and understood by persuadees characterizes *cooperatively* created meanings. In other words, we participate in our own persuasion by "agreeing with" the code(s) persuaders use. Most important, we can become critical consumers of persuasion

by continually striving to discover and reveal these codes (Eco, 1979). The work of semiotician and former circus owner and ringmaster Paul Buissac (1976) offers some fascinating examples of codes in his semiotic analysis of circus acts that demonstrates this idea of an easily discernible code that is understood by "children of all ages" around the world:

> Wild animal, tightrope, and trapeze acts never occur back to back in the circus . . . they are always interspersed with clown acts, small animal acts, magic acts, or the like. If a daring act is canceled, the entire order of acts needs to be altered because of audience expectations, the need for tension reduction, and to communicate that the world is alternately serious and comedic.
>
> . . . Death-defying acts also have a code — usually a five-step sequence. First, there is the introduction of the act by the ringmaster (a godlike figure able to control not only the dangers but the chaos of the circus). This introduction, with its music, lights, and revelation of dazzling and daring costumes, is followed by the "warm-up," in which minor qualifying tests occur: The animal trainer, dressed as a big-game hunter, gets all the animals to their proper positions; the trapeze artist, with his beautiful assistants, can easily swing out and switch trapeze bars in mid-air; the tightrope walker dances across the rope with ease. Then comes the major tests or tricks: getting the tiger to dance with the lion, double trapeze switches, and walking the wire blindfolded. Having passed these tests, the circus performer then attempts the "glorifying," or "death-defying," test. It is always accompanied by the ringmaster's request for absolute silence and, ironically, by the band breaking the critical silence with a nerve-tingling drumroll. Then comes the feat itself: The animal tamer puts his head into the lion's mouth; the trapeze artist holds up a pair of beautiful assistants with his teeth, demonstrating his amazing strength; and the tightrope walker puts a passenger on his shoulders and rides a bicycle backward and blindfolded across the high wire. Frequently

there is a close call: An unruly tiger tries to interfere with the "head-in-the-mouth" trick; there is a near miss on the trapeze, a stumble on the high wire, and so on. Once the glorifying test is passed, the ringmaster calls for applause as the act exits and then returns for a curtain call. This sequence is a "code" we all understand.

More subtle examples of codes are frequently found in advertising. For example, consider the ad for Bostonian shoes in Figure 5.13. What codes are operating in this ad? Some are rather obvious, but others are more subtle. In fact, some codes in the ad are embedded within other codes. The most obvious code is that the ad is trying to sell a product. However, what kind of product is not so clear. Finding out requires more detailed decoding, but we soon discover that the product is men's shoes. Another less obvious code is that the product is an upscale one, as indicated by the composition and copy of the ad and by the price of the shoes—$105. The ad is understated; there is little actual ad copy. Finally, the photography is distinctively "fine art" in its composition.

Within these codes is an even more subtle code—one that is only implied, never directly stated. This code signifies the lifestyle that goes with the product. The shoes are merely an emblem of that lifestyle. What do we see in this photograph? Clearly, it is the "morning after" a very satisfying night of lovemaking (notice the coffee cups and pastries on the bed, the negligee on the well-rumpled bedding, the indentations on both pillows). The lifestyle includes a fine home (notice the expensive furniture and the framed photographs on the nightstand in the upper left corner). This lifestyle includes expensive accessories (a Rolex watch and a Mont Blanc pen are on the dresser), stylish suspenders, theater tickets slipped into the frame of the mirror, a beautiful wife in the picture under the tickets, and being physically attractive (note the snapshot of him, bare chested and muscular). It is clear that this ad carries a lot of meaning and that this meaning is

"signified" by the verbal and nonverbal symbols being used (or perhaps misused, depending on one's perspective).

Although analyses like these may be intriguing, they are difficult to carry out without some kind of systematic methodology. The fields of theoretic semiotics and applied semiotics (for example, advertising and image/political consulting) are rapidly expanding, and you as a receiver need a simplified way to pin down these uses (or misuses) of symbols. A methodology for doing this kind or semiotic analysis has been developed by communication scholar Arthur Asa Berger, whom we met briefly in Chapter 4. Berger (1984) provides a fairly simple checklist for doing such an analysis that my students find useful. First, consider the pieces of persuasion aimed at you as if they are "texts" to be read, and then put on your Sherlock Holmes hat and start looking for clues. Using the following steps, analyze the meaning of the ad for Ms. magazine in Figure 5.14.

A. Isolate and analyze the important signs in your text.

1. What are the important signifiers?

2. What do they signify?

3. Is there a system that unifies them?

4. What codes can be found (for example, symbols of status, colors, music)?

5. Are ideological or sociological issues being addressed?

6. How are they conveyed or hinted at?

B. Identify the central structure, theme, or model of the text.

1. What forces are in opposition?

2. What forces are teamed with each other?

3. Do the oppositions or teams have psychological or sociological meanings? What are they?

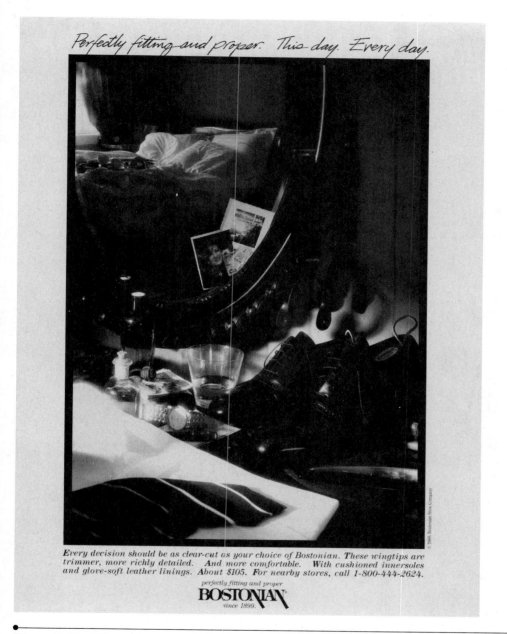

Perfectly fitting and proper. This day. Every day.

Every decision should be as clear-cut as your choice of Bostonian. These wingtips are trimmer, more richly detailed. And more comfortable. With cushioned innersoles and glove-soft leather linings. About $105. For nearby stores, call 1-800-444-2624.

perfectly fitting and proper

BOSTONIAN

since 1899.

Figure 5.13. *What messages are implied by the "code" of physical objects in this ad (theater tickets, rumpled bedclothes, articles of clothing that seem to have been hurriedly discarded, an empty cocktail glass, and so on)? (Reprinted by permission of the Bostonian Shoe Company.)*

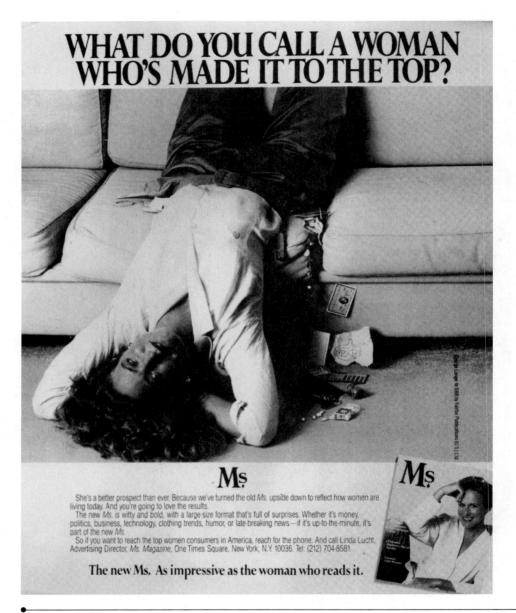

Figure 5.14. *Using the semiotic approach to uncovering meaning as outlined by Berger, uncover the meaning of this ad/text. Note that the woman has "lost" items from her pockets—a passport, the keys to an Audi, credit cards, a picture of herself drawn by her child, jewelry, aspirin, a champagne cork, a $100 bill, and other signs. What do they signify? How old is this woman? Is she sentimental? Stressed? Busy? (Used by permission.)*

C. What is the narrative structure of the text? (That is, if a "story" is being told, what are its elements?)

1. How does the sequential arrangement of events affect meaning? What changes in meaning would result if they were altered?

2. Are there any "formulaic" aspects to the text (for example, hard work leads to success, justice prevails, honesty gets its reward)?

D. Does the medium being used affect the text? How?

1. Use of shots, camera angles, editing, dissolves, and so on.

2. Use of lighting, color, music, sound, special effects, and so on.

3. Paper quality, typefaces, graphics, colors, and so on.

4. How do the speaker's words, gestures, and facial expressions affect meaning?

E. How does the application of semiotic theory alter the original meaning you might have ascribed to the text? (You may want to do further reading in semiotics to answer this question effectively.)

Of course, this discussion of the semiotic approach to language and meaning is brief and necessarily simplified. Nonetheless, it should give you another tool for discovering the important first premises that emerge from our language preferences and the images molded from them.

Gender and Style

In an article titled "He: This Is an Okay (Lovely) Analysis (Emotional Investigation) of Our Words (Deepest Corridors of Meaning)," language critic and English professor Edwin Bruell (1986) considers how gender affects our use of language and style. As you may have guessed from the way the title of the article is written, the words inside the parentheses represent the feminine mode of expression, while the words outside the parentheses represent the masculine mode of expression. As Bruell notes, "There seems to be a form of poverty in America that is strictly a masculine phenomenon: poverty of expression" (p. 12). He goes on to point out some differences between male and female word choice. For example, women can characterize clothing, dolls, furniture, or sunsets with words like "lovely," "darling," "sweet," "adorable," or "cute," whereas men rarely use such words. Men may perhaps use the word "lovely" to express their assessment of a new dress on their spouse or another woman, but they would never use it to describe the new suit of clothes on another man. Bruell claims that "men shy away from all such usages because they passionately fear being labeled sissified. Their superlatives are likely to be far less flowery" (p. 12). Instead they tend to limit their superlatives to words like "fine," "great," "good," and occasionally "grand" if they are talking about a sports event. Also, according to Bruell, "Women will speak of 'fragrance' and 'scent' and 'aromatic, seductive' concoctions. A man will speak of 'smell' . . . and . . . a shutout defeat just 'stinks.'" To men, locker room jokes are "dirty stories," but at cocktail parties women listen to the same stories but label them "risqué" party stories. An orderly desk is "tidy" to a woman, but it is "neat and organized" to a man. An attractive, well-dressed, carefully groomed woman may be described as "dainty" or "fetching" by another woman, but she will be "nice," "okay," or "swell" to a man. Bruell recounts an encounter with a female confidant who exclaimed, "How cunning they are! How positively ravishing!" which he thought referred to stereotypes that "frighten me (no, make that 'scare the —— out of me')." Actually she was rhapsodizing about her first view of a set of burly tag-team wrestlers (p. 12).

Other researchers have identified several additional gender-related characteristics of language use. For example, authors Diane Dunaway and her husband Jonathan Kramer (1990) note that, because of their training, men avoid using more words than necessary and try to get to the point right away. As a result, many men view conversations between females as "superfluous chatter." Women see language use as a kind of social glue, and they don't have to transfer information in their conversations. They view conversation as an aid to developing relationships. Dunaway and Kramer attribute this characteristic of what they call "malespeak" (which prevents men from being able to express affection and to forge satisfying intimate relationships) to gender training.

Another researcher in gender-related differences in language use, Deborah Tanner (1990), maintains that unless women are very direct in their conversations with men, they are likely to be misunderstood and perceived as manipulative. She also advises women to avoid personal anecdotes and references when conversing with men, as they are likely to be uncomfortable with such references. Men are also likely to interpret interrupters such as "Uh huh" and "okay" as indicating agreement, so women should avoid those when conversing with men.

With the advent of the World Wide Web and e-mail, it may be that other differences between men and women in language use will begin to appear. Men seem to be more assertive in a net chat group on my campus and more argumentative. A smaller proportion of women are members of and interact with this group, and those who do are frequently perceived as assertive. Men seem to send and forward more humorous messages than women.

Language choices can reveal much information about persuaders: their cultural heritage, their political inclinations, their philosophy, the nature of their audiences, their gender, and a host of other kinds of meanings and interpretations. It becomes essential, therefore, for critical and ethical receivers of messages to look beyond the substance of the message for deeper indications of the persuader's attitudes and world view as well as his or her potential future actions. How do we go about this?

Tuning Your Ears for Language Cues

The overall message here is that consumers of persuasion should be vigilant when processing and responding to persuasive messages. In the course of this vigilance, one of the most important things you can do is to *tune your ears* to language for various clues to style and motives. Using some of the tools described in this chapter is one way. If you have thought about these tools, or if you have tried to apply these tools to the persuasion around you, you have already started the tuning process. Applying the study questions at the end of this and other chapters is another good way to continue.

There are at least three specific strategies you might use to make yourself more critical of style and to "decode" or "psych out" persuaders:

1. *Role-play the persuader.* Assume that you are the persuader. How would you shape the persuasion you wish to present? For example, if you favor high salaries for ballplayers, how would you frame a pragmatic message for half-hearted believers, those who are neutral, or others who are only moderately opposed? Would you mention the shortness of most players' careers (hence they receive a low

overall salary across a lifetime, despite high yearly salaries). You might compare ballplayers to entertainers, who also make several million dollars per year for relatively little actual work time. If your audience happened to be the Association of Professional Baseball Players, you could afford to bypass the numbers and use highly emotional and abstract language to motivate the audience. You might create images of club owners as filthy-rich bloodsuckers who mindlessly use up the best years of an athlete's life. Your language would probably be there-and-then — referring to new goals of the group or past abuses.

2. *Restate a persuasive message in various ways.* Ask yourself, "What are other ways to say this?" Then try to determine how these alternatives will change the intent of the message and its final effects. You might, for example, try using the parts of the pentad.

For example, take the following slogan for Grand Marnier Liqueur: "There Are Still Places on Earth Where Grand Marnier Isn't Offered After Dinner." The slogan is printed on a photo of a deserted island. The appeal is scenic. An agent-oriented version of this slogan might be "People of Taste Offer Grand Marnier." A purpose-oriented version might read "Want to Finish the Conference? Offer Grand Marnier." An agency-oriented version might say "Grand Marnier — From a Triple-Sec-ret Recipe," stressing the method of production. The act might be emphasized by saying "Make a Move — Offer Grand Marnier." Of course, each slogan would accompany appropriate visuals.

3. *Attend to language features in discourse.* Don't allow yourself to passively buy into any persuasive advice that is being hawked. Instead, get into the habit of looking at a message's style. Analyze messages on billboards and in TV commercials, the language used by your parents when they try to persuade you, the wording on packages you purchase, or the phrases used in discussions between you and friends, enemies, or salespersons. In other words, start listening not only to *ideas* but to *word* strategies, the packaging of those ideas. Try it on me. What kinds of words do I use? Why? How does my style differ from that of other textbook writers? Focusing on these features will give you an intriguing pastime, and you will develop an ear for stylistic tipoffs, a skill that will prove valuable in helping you to predict and respond to the communication of others.

Review and Conclusion

Responsible receivers of persuasion relate to the language a particular persuader chooses. They gain general insight by looking at the semantic connotations of the words chosen. They look at word order, or syntax, and at how frequently various parts of speech are chosen. The degree of ambiguity used by the persuader is often revealing, as in a dramatistic analysis such as that suggested by Burke. The motifs and metaphors chosen by a persuader often reveal motive. And persuadees can look at the god, devil, and charismatic terms used, as well as the choice of pragmatic versus unifying style. Finally, we can apply the semiotic approach to the interpretation of persuasive messages, identifying as many of the signifiers in a persuasive message as possible.

All these critical devices are enhanced by role playing, restating, and developing awareness of the words and style as well as the ideas used in a persuasive speech, a TV documentary, a film, a political slogan, a social movement, a package design, or a friend's request.

Questions for Further Thought

1. Transcribe the lyrics of a popular song. Now analyze them according to the functional tools presented in this chapter. Is there a preference for a certain word type? A certain sentence structure? Is the message ambiguous or concrete? Explain.

2. Describe several semantic tools. What do you think is the pentadic perspective of the President of the United States? Of your instructor?

3. Describe the tools for a thematic or textural analysis of language and use some of them to analyze the persuasion occurring in a recent political campaign. What do these analyses tell you about the candidate?

4. What are the god terms of your parents? What are their devil terms? As an experiment, shape a request for something from your parents, expressed in their god terms.

5. How does a unifying persuader differ from a pragmatic one? Find examples of each type of persuader in your class, in persuasive attempts of the past, or in defenders of some persuasive issue being discussed in your community. Are there other differences between these two types? What are they?

6. What are the differences between *semantics* and *semiotics*? Which is more objective? When might it be appropriate to use each approach? How do you use semantics and semiotics to both analyze and create persuasive messages?

7. What is the difference between a text and a symbol? What is the difference between a signifier and the signified?

8. How does gender affect how we use language? Can you give examples beyond those cited in this chapter?

References

Andrews, L. A. (1984). Exhibit A: Language. *Psychology Today*, February 1984, p. 30.

Barol, B. (1988). The eighties are over. *Newsweek*, January 4, 1988, pp. 40–48.

Berger, A. (1984). *Signs in contemporary culture*. New York: Longman.

Black Elk. (1971). *Touch the earth*. New York: Outerbridge and Dienstfrey.

Broder, D. (1984). Quoted in S. J. Ball-Rokeach & M. Rokeach. The great American values test. *Psychology Today*, November 1984, p. 41.

Bruell, E. (1986). He: This is an okay (lovely) analysis (emotional investigation) of our words (deepest corridors of meaning). *The Chicago Tribune*, December 31, 1986, sec. 7, p. 12.

Buissac, P. (1976). *Circus and culture: A semiotic approach*. Bloomington: Indiana University Press.

Burke, K. (1960). *A grammar of motives*. Berkeley: University of California Press.

Burrows, T. D., Wood, D. N., & Gross, L. S. (1992). *Television production*. Dubuque, IA: William C. Brown.

Carter, J. (1977). *A government as good as its people*. New York: Simon & Schuster.

Dunaway, D., & Kramer, J. (1990). *Why men don't get enough sex and women don't get enough love*. New York: Pocket Books.

Eco, U. (1979). *The role of the reader*. Bloomington: Indiana University Press.

Eco, U. (1984). *Semiotics and the philosophy of language*. London: Macmillan Press Ltd.

Eliade, M. (1971). *The myth of the eternal return*. Princeton, NJ: Princeton University Press.

Kittredge, W. (1996). The war for Montana's soul. *Newsweek*, April 15, 1996, p. 43.

Koenig, P. (1972). Death doth defer. *Psychology Today*, November 1972, p. 83.

Lederer, R. (1991). *The miracle of language*. New York: Pocket Books.

Nimmo, D., & Combs, J. (1984). *Mediated political realities*. New York: Longman.

Osborn, M. (1967). Archetypal metaphors in rhetoric: The light-dark family. *Quarterly Journal of Speech*, April 1967, 115–126.

Osgood, C. E., Suci, G. J., & Tannenbaum, P. H. (1957). *The measurement of meaning*. Urbana: University of Illinois Press.

Swanson, S. L. (1981). Sensory language in the courtroom. *Trial Diplomacy Journal*, Winter 1981, 37–43.

Tannen, D. (1990). *You just don't understand: Men and women in conversation*. New York: William Morrow.

Weaver, R. (1953). *The ethics of rhetoric*. Chicago: Regnery.

PART TWO

Identifying Persuasive First Premises

As we saw in Part I, there are many ways to define, explain, and interpret persuasive messages and the symbols used to convey them. The critical question of ethics enters into every persuasive decision we make, whether as receivers or as persuaders. As we continue our study, you should refer to what we learned in Part I about the foundations of persuasion theory, the many theoretical explanations of persuasive phenomena, and the various means of analyzing the verbal and nonverbal symbols used in persuasive language, regardless of their source.

Underlying all means of analytically processing the symbols of persuasion is the ancient Aristotelian concept of the *enthymeme*, which we discussed in Chapter 3, where we examined Aristotle's triad of ethos, pathos, and logos. The enthymeme will serve as the analytical metaphor or organizational device for Part II. It is useful to think of Part II as a search for the types of major premises in enthymemes.

In Part II we identify those major premises that audiences already believe and those that audiences can be convinced of in order to prompt the desired conclusion. We look at certain major categories of premises that audiences believe — we hunt for major premises.

The first category of major premise is the *process premise*, covered in Chapter 6. Process premises rely on psychological factors that operate in nearly all persuadees. Persuaders tie their product, candidate, or idea to these process premises, which are then used as the major premises in enthymemic arguments that have wide appeal.

In Chapter 7, we look at the second category of major premises: *content premises*. Their persuasiveness lies in the audience's belief in the truth or validity of the argument.

For example, if the audience believes that history repeats itself and that as a result we can avoid the mistakes of the past, the persuader merely has to draw a convincing analogy between the past and the present. This is what happened when Iraq invaded its neighbor Kuwait in the summer of 1990, taking foreigners as hostages and inflicting brutal treatment on Kuwait's citizenry. The invasion bore a striking resemblance to Hitler's 1938 invasion of his neighbor Austria. Iraq's leader, Saddam Hussein, also reminded people of Hitler in his complete dictatorship over the people of Iraq. President George Bush used this analogy to muster world opinion against Hussein. The analogy was so convincing that the United Nations passed a number of resolutions condemning the invasion and authorizing a massive trade embargo against Iraq. The UN even voted to authorize the use of military force if necessary. It was the first time the UN had voted such extreme measures with such unity. The audience supplied the logically based major, or content, premise and drew the desired conclusion: Stop Hussein now and avoid a repeat of World War II.

You have probably noticed that there is considerable similarity between process premises and content premises. Process premises rely on *psychological* or *emotional* needs, whereas content premises rely on *logical* or *rational* patterns. We have been trained in these patterns of inference since early childhood; they have been reinforced throughout our lives. For instance, when we tell two-year-old children that if they continue to cry they will have to go without television or a particular toy, we are using "If . . . then . . ." reasoning.

The third major category of major premises, discussed in Chapter 8, is the *cultural premise*. This kind of premise relies on patterns of behavior or beliefs that resemble articles of faith for audiences and that have been passed on to them by their culture or society. For example, Americans learn that when faced with a problem they must seek a solution to it, perhaps by establishing a task force or swallowing a pill. This seems so obvious that we are dumbstruck to discover that people from some other cultures prefer to accept the inevitable when faced with a problem. Problem solving is a culturally transmitted pattern for us. Knowing that, persuaders motivate us to take actions by portraying the actions as solutions. Even if we don't perceive that there is a problem, and thus are not searching for solutions, clever persuaders can create problems and sell us a cure. Cultural premises consist of the myths and values our society holds dear.

In Chapter 9, we explore *nonverbal premises*, which are similar to cultural premises in that they vary from culture to culture as well as from sub-

culture to subculture. These nonverbal premises are sometimes more potent than sophisticated verbal premises. Often, nonverbal premises result in the ultimate success or failure of persuasion.

As you read Part II, think of yourself as searching for major premises that you and an audience hold in common. By identifying these major premises you can not only become a more skillful persuader but also, and more important, you can more effectively evaluate the persuasion aimed at you.

6

Process Premises:
The Tools of Motivation

Some persuasion theorists draw a distinction between logical and emotional appeals, arguing that they represent opposite ends of a continuum and that the "better" appeals are the logical ones. Others characterize these two types of appeals along a rational versus irrational continuum and assume that rational appeals are "better." Both of these explanations assume that persuasive appeals are either one thing or another and that the two types of appeals operate separately and independently. They also carry with them the sense that persuasion occurs all at once as a result of some key phrases, statistics, the charisma of the persuader, or some other factor. It is true that some persuasion seems to occur all at once. For example, Patrick Henry's "Give Me Liberty or Give Me Death" speech probably converted some members of his audience on the spot, but Henry's audience was probably already leaning toward his position before he even spoke.

In fact, most persuasion involves self-persuasion, usually occurs incrementally or bit by bit across time, and frequently involves many kinds of persuasive communication. One "emotional" appeal might accomplish a slight change

in persuadees that is then reinforced by a series of "logical" arguments that lead to the final behavior that proves the persuasion was successful. For example, an automobile company trying to sell you a new car uses some clearly emotional appeals ("We build excitement!"), some clearly logical appeals ("Economical—up to 50 miles per gallon on the highway"), and some hybrid appeals—they are emotional and logical—("Now equipped with life-saving airbags on the driver's *and* the passenger's side").

In this chapter we examine appeals that tap into the *psychological processes* operating in persuadees and that rely on human emotions, drives, or instincts—appeals we rarely ponder over. We call these appeals **process premises** because they target psychological processes that seem to operate in most people. For example, most of us have fears of some kind and will eagerly take action to dispel those fears. As a result, persuaders make appeals to alleviate fears about one's health or grooming ("Now—with Fiber." "Got halitosis? Listerine mouthwash makes your breath kissing sweet"). Process premises are operating when we buy a product because of brand loyalty, brand name, a memorable slogan, catchy jingles, or even packaging. Process premises also operate in more serious situations, such as listening to political speeches or appeals from social movements. For example, pro-life advocates are using process premises when they show the film *The Silent Scream*, which claims that the tiny skulls of unborn fetuses are crushed during an abortion.

In the early 1990s, process premises appealing to attitudes and beliefs were used to bring about the collapse of communist governments in Poland, East Germany, Czechoslovakia, Hungary, Romania, Bulgaria, and Russia. In these appeals, the major premise was that marketplace economics are good. Minor premises such as the desirability of private ownership of property led audiences to the conclusion that communism was bankrupt.

And, of course, emotional appeals that rely on psychological processes are evident in interpersonal persuasion between spouses, parents and children, siblings, lovers, and bosses and employees. Psychological appeals are seen in business, marketing, advertising, sales promotion, and ideological advocacy on behalf of emotionally loaded issues.

Needs: The First Process Premise

Each of us has a set of individual **needs.** Some of them are critical to us—we can't live without them; others are not critical—we can get along without them for awhile. Not everyone's priorities are identical, but our needs resemble one another's enough that various theories of motivation can identify those that typify audiences. Some theories identify needs that are physiologically based, such as our needs for the staples of survival and physical security. Other theories focus on less concrete needs, ones that lead to our overall sense of well-being (success on the job, or the need for religious

belief, for example). Without them or some substitute, we feel frustrated, anxious, afraid, or even angry. These needs are hard to measure, so they are inferred from patterns of behavior that people exhibit. For instance, because people seem concerned about being successful, we can infer a need for symbols of success.

Such symbols become representations of the fulfillment of people's need to succeed. For the most part, persuasion in today's changing world is aimed at promoting or selling symbolic ways to meet people's physiological and emotional needs. Although there *are* some products (such as self-improvement courses) that really can help you make a better impression on the boss, for the most part what people buy and support doesn't have a direct effect. They buy and use Binaca breath spray not because it ensures a better impression but because they hope it will prevent bad breath.

Effective persuaders must successfully determine their audience's needs. If they analyze these needs incorrectly, persuasion can boomerang. For example, a well-known luggage manufacturer once spent thousands of dollars to produce an impressive and clever TV ad. The spot opens with luggage being handled roughly as it is loaded into the cargo bay of a huge airliner. (The central piece of luggage was made by the sponsor). The plane is next seen in flight, but someone has failed to latch the cargo bay door. As the plane banks, our star piece of luggage falls out of the now-open door. The camera follows the suitcase as it falls 30,000 feet and lands with a huge thud on some rocks. Then the case is opened to reveal the undamaged contents. Now, that ought to be a pretty convincing ad. However, airing of the commercial in a test market was followed by a tremendous drop in sales. Why? Using focus-group interviews, researchers found that most

What do you think?

What is the difference between a true need and a symbolic one?

people, even regular airline travelers, fear a plane crash. They resent the implication that their luggage will survive them in the event of a crash.

Some of the motivation research done on behalf of advertisers appeared in a book titled *The Hidden Persuaders* by Vance Packard (1964). It was promoted with sentences like these:

> In this book you'll discover a world of psychology professors turned merchandisers. You'll learn how they operate, what they know about you and your neighbors, and how they are using that knowledge to sell you cake mixes, cigarettes, soaps and even ideas. (p. 5)

Packard reported that a majority of the hundred largest ad firms in the country had been using psychoanalytic research. He noted that other professional persuaders—public relations executives, fund raisers, politicians, and others—were turning to psychological theorists to discover customers' motives. They then tied their products, candidates, and causes to these motives. Packard quotes one ad executive as saying:

> Motivation research . . . seeks to learn what motivates people in making choices. It employs techniques designed to reach the subconscious mind because preferences generally are determined by factors of which the individual is not conscious. . . . Actually in the buying situation the consumer acts emotionally and compulsively, unconsciously reacting to images and designs which in the subconscious are associated with the product. (p. 5)

Another advertiser gave some examples of how the research was used:

> The cosmetic manufacturers are not selling lanolin; they are selling hope. . . . We no longer buy oranges, we buy vitality. We do not buy just an auto; we buy prestige. (p. 5)

Clearly, psychology had entered the field of advertising. According to Packard, market researchers operating from this perspective had three assumptions about people. First, they assumed that people don't always know what they want when they make a purchase. Second, they assumed that one cannot rely on what people say about what they like and dislike. Finally, they assumed that people do not act logically or rationally. Packard gave several examples of how these assumptions operate. For instance, motivation researchers wondered what made people buy laundry detergent. Purchasers *said* they bought it because of its cleaning power. A sample group of consumers was given three boxes of detergent. They were asked to test the three types and report back. Actually, the three boxes contained the same detergent—only the color of the boxes was different. The test group reported that the detergent in the yellow box was too harsh, the one in the blue box was too weak—it left clothes gray after washing—but the stuff in the yellow-and-blue box was great.

The psychoanalytic approach to marketing most closely reflects the symbolistic tradition of psychology. Indeed, much of the in-depth research that Packard describes is like psychoanalysis. The researchers used focus-group interviews that encouraged customers to describe the fears, pleasures, nightmares, fantasies, and lusts they associated with the product or the ad for it. Other researchers used complex psychological tests like the Minnesota Multiphasic Personality Inventory (MMPI). Still others used projective tests in which people completed sentences about the product or described the "real meaning" behind cartoon vignettes related to the product.

The trend continues, more than forty years after Packard first described it. In fact, the "hidden persuaders" are using increasingly sophisticated methods to fight against the new technologies for skipping commercials by "zapping" them with a fast-forward remote control:

> Advertisers aren't about to take this lying down. Desperate to keep you tuned to their pitches, they're trying some new tricks. If that's news to

you, it may be because these new techniques are manipulating you in ways you're not aware of. "Many of these commercials have more impact on the subconscious level," charges New York University media professor Neil Postman. Perhaps more disturbing, ad agencies often enlist psychologists and neurophysiologists to make sure the pitches have the desired effect. (Freedman, 1988)

Packard's Eight "Hidden Needs"

In his research, Packard found eight "compelling needs" that were frequently used in selling products. We still use them today, although probably with more sophistication.

Advertisers discovered the hidden needs that Packard described by using the focus-group interviews or projective tests to identify "compelling needs." Merchandisers designed their ads to promise that the product or service would provide some degree of real or symbolic fulfillment of the compelling need. You can almost imagine Freud himself probing even deeper into the consumer's subconscious, looking for the "hot" buttons that will turn people on to products and avoiding the "cold" ones that will turn them against a product. We still see such pitches in advertising, politics, propaganda, and elsewhere aimed at Packard's eight "hidden needs."

Need for Emotional Security. We are living in one of the most insecure eras in human history. Terrorism seems unstoppable. Militia groups are armed. Our environment is becoming more and more polluted. The protective ozone layer surrounding our planet is disintegrating. The world economy is delicately poised on the edge of disaster. AIDS threatens many countries—in some parts of Africa, over half the population is infected. Our national debt appears to be so out of control that even with tax increases and budget cuts we may still face financial disaster. On the world scene, no one knows what will replace the

bankruptcy of communism in Eastern Europe and the former Soviet Union. Ours is a very insecure and unpredictable world. Little wonder that we search for substitute symbols of security.

Deodorants promise us "social security." Self-improvement courses promise better job security. Retirement planning programs offer financial security in one's "golden years." And politicians promise economic security (and almost every other kind of security) if they are elected. All of these examples serve as minor premises in enthymemes that begin with the major premise "Security or permanence is good" and that lead us to buy the product, adopt the service, or support the cause. At a time when we need permanence, we face unpredictable change, and that makes us vulnerable to persuasion aimed at assuring or reassuring us of some semblance of security.

Need for Reassurance of Worth. We live in a highly competitive and impersonal society in which it is easy to feel like mere cogs in a machine. Packard noted that people need to feel valued for what they do. Housewives, factory workers, and public service workers need to feel that they are accomplishing something of value, are needed by their families and organizations, and are appreciated by others. In other words, people need to feel that they make a difference. This need forms the basis of many persuasive appeals by volunteer organizations, by self-help tapes promoting self-esteem, by companies selling products that purportedly help us to be better parents (Bactine), better spouses ("Remember her with flowers"), and more successful at work (matchbook advertisements for career training). This need was demonstrated in an interesting study in which managers and workers were asked to rate ten factors in job satisfaction. Managers rated "wages," "fringe benefits," and "working conditions" as the top three. Workers placed those three at the bottom. Their top three were "appreciation for work done," "my boss listens to

"GReaT PaRTY? WHO DID YouR DEMOGRaPHICS?"

Figure 6.1. *Apparently, being a successful hostess is considered a "compelling need" by some people. The humor of the cartoon underscores the degree to which hidden persuaders in the form of various advertising technologies (for example, demographic analysis) are perceived in our culture. (Freeze Frame cartoon from Advertising Age, December 28, 1987. Copyright Crain Communications, Inc. Reprinted by permission of Crain Communications and Bill Whitehead.)*

me," and "fellow workers." As seen in Figure 6.1, even hostesses need reassurance of worth.

We need to feel assured of our worth in the world. At a time when skepticism is "in," when people don't seem to really communicate with one another, many people believe that "they no longer live in a world of friends and neighbors and families, but in a world of associates, clients, and customers who will look them in the eye, smile — and lie like a rug" (Marquand, 1988).

This skeptical outlook was carefully chronicled in a best-selling study of American society titled *Habits of the Heart: Individualism and Commitment in American Life.* Robert Bellah and his coauthors (1985) set out to study the degree to which contemporary middle-class individuals felt commitment to things other than themselves. They interviewed over 200 persons in depth. Their findings are disturbing. Most of the interviewees found reassurance of worth in material things. In a section titled "The Poverty of Affluence," Bellah and his colleagues concluded that most contemporary Americans see themselves in a race for material goods, prestige, power, and influence. And in this race they separate themselves from others and find little emotional security in "the lonely crowd." Small wonder that we have become a "culture of consumption," seeking in the ownership of material goods the self-worth we can really only derive from being committed to and relating with others in our personal and public lives.

Need for Ego Gratification. Packard found that many of the consumers he studied not only needed to be reassured of their basic worth but also needed their egos "stroked" as if they were really special — a step beyond mere self-worth (see Figure 6.2). This need for ego gratification can come from a variety of sources: friends, co-workers, neighbors, parents, groups, institutions, and, most important, ourselves. Packard refers to a heavy-road-equipment manufacturer that increased sales by featuring drivers rather than machines in magazine ads. Operators have a major say-so in purchase decisions — that is, when contractors buy heavy equipment, they ask those who operate the machines for their opinions.

Persuaders often target a group whose members feel they have been put down for some time — teachers, police, or social workers, for instance. It is easy to sell products, ideas, or candidates by hooking into the out-group's ego needs in personal ways that appeal to an individual's self-perception. For example, for years the traditional family was out of style as divorce rates soared and couples chose to live together instead

Figure 6.2. Hagar is giving himself ego gratification here, but realizes that it goes only so far before reality intrudes. (Reprinted with special permission of King Features Syndicate.)

of getting married. Those who remained committed to the ideal of the traditional family and its associated values felt like outcasts. This was the perfect time for a persuasive "pro-family" appeal, which is precisely what happened on both sides in the most recent three presidential campaigns with all candidates promising to restore the family to its prior place of respect.

Ego gratification needs are potent. A good example of an ad based on this need is shown in Figure 6.3. Note that the ad copy stresses the importance Hyatt places on the individual—in this case the woman executive, whose needs have been largely overlooked by the hotel industry until recently. Hyatt offers her thoughtful extras—

skirt hangers, shampoo, and even hair dryers in the room. She must be pretty special to have a large hotel chain go out of its way to provide her with such amenities.

Need for Creative Outlets. In our modern technocracy, few products can be identified with a single artisan. This was not always so. For example, craftsmen such as cabinetmakers created a piece of furniture from beginning to end—it was their unique product. The same applied to bakers, farmers, and housewives who did the weaving, knitting, sewing, and cooking. But with the advent of mass production, more and more people became only a part of the production cycle—

Figure 6.3. *Hyatt promises to fulfill the need for ego gratification. (Used by permission of Hyatt Corporation.)*

first, second, and third drafts for style and mechanics; and artists create the diagrams and illustrations. Most advertising, news releases, public relations efforts, films, television programs, political speeches, and other familiar forms of persuasion are also the product of many hands.

Meanwhile, more and more work formerly done by people is now being done by technology—robots, computers, word processors, food processors, microwave ovens, and so on. And the outlook for the future indicates the trend to be growing, not lessening. Yet people still seem to need to demonstrate their own handicraft skills. Given this need, gardening, cooking, home improvement, and other hobby-type activities are bound to succeed. Even with prepared foods, from which the art of cooking has been almost totally removed, creativity still sells. Hamburger Helper leaves room for you, the cook, to add your own touch. Noodles Romanoff makes you a chef worthy of the czar. Old El Paso taco dinner allows you to add all the creative toppings for a taco shell.

Need for Love Objects. People whose children have grown up need to replace the child love object—a situation called the empty-nest syndrome. For some, the replacement is a pet; for others, it might be a foster grandchild. Persuaders understand this need and strive to meet it in a variety of ways. Television producers, for example, provide us with childlike entertainment personalities who serve as "substitute" children.

Many older persons have pets as substitute love objects. They coddle them, spoil them, and even dress them up. The pet food industry knows this and targets the "gourmet" level of their product lines to such persons. These pet lovers would never buy "generic" dog or cat food or even "standard" brands like Redheart or Alpo, but they proudly bring home gobs of "Premium Cuts," "Tender Vittles," "Beef 'n Gravy," "Tuna Surprise,"

cogs in the machine. They had less and less that they could point to as their own unique product, and they felt less and less "creative" in many ways. Packard identified a need for expressing one's own unique creativity.

In today's quickly evolving world, the opportunity for creative outlets is further reduced as more and more people work in service occupations in which no actual construction of products occurs. This trend is likely to continue beyond the year 2000. Even a book such as this one is not the result of one individual's work and creativity—critics make suggestions, editors alter the and "Chicken Spectacular." The food sounds like human food, and it even looks appetizing. In ads, it is always served up with a piece of fine silverware and in bite-sized pieces. The substitute love object generates lots of sales these days.

Need for a Sense of Power. If you have ever driven a motorcycle on the open road, you know what it is like to feel powerful. We Americans, perhaps more than members of any other culture, seem to be programmed to chase potency and power and to gratify our need for them symbolically. The bigger the engine, the better. Snowmobiles and dune buggies are marketed by the sense of power they give. Whether the product is a double-triggered chainsaw or a garden tractor, power is the emphasis. Stanley tools doesn't sell any wimpy "light duty" hammers and wrenches — the consumer wants "heavy duty" powerful tools. We don't elect many non-macho politicians. In fact, every major candidate for the presidency has to demonstrate physical and psychological strength or power. An owner of a tow-truck business whom I know told me that over half his calls came from owners of four-wheel-drive vehicles — the very vehicles that are supposed to be able to go through anything and never get stuck. That, apparently, is the problem. The owners of these vehicles satisfy their need for power by finding impossibly tough terrain through which to take their vehicles. Often, they get bogged down and have to call for a tow.

Need for Roots. One of the predominant features of our times is increasing mobility. If you are employed by any large firm, chances are you will have to move several times during your career. During the ten years following college graduation, the average American moves at least a dozen times, and several of the moves involve crossing county lines; at least one involves a move across a state line. IBM moved its young

executives so frequently that the company was jokingly referred to by employees as "I've Been Moved." When you do move, especially if it is some distance from home, there are several "pieces of home" you can bring with you to keep you from getting too lonely. One is brand loyalty; recent college graduates have one of the strongest levels of brand loyalty. If you have ever moved to another state, you will have noticed how disconcerting it is to not find familiar supermarket chains or your favorite service-station chain. Advertisers make appeals to these feelings.

This need for roots and brand loyalty also helps explain the concept of "line extension" in the development of new products. We feel more at home buying the new Quaker Oats Squares rather than another brand because of the familiar old-fashioned face of the Quaker promising "An honest taste from an honest face." He is an emblem of our youth and our roots.

What do you think?

Can you identify how you fill your need for roots?

Brand names are portable — we can take them to a new home to remind us of our roots. Nabisco, for example, not long ago increased its nationwide shelf space by twenty miles by using line extension for "New Stars," an eighteen-item cookie and cracker product. The old and familiar name of the manufacturer helped establish the credibility of the new product (Friedman and Dagnoli, 1988). The need for roots can also be appealed to using emotional ties to "home." The Lane furniture company, for example, offers newlyweds a Lane cedar chest to "take part of home with you" when you marry or move off to that new job.

We see the appeal to roots in ads for the "old-fashioned," whether apple pies, Heartland Cereal, or stockbrokers who earn their money "the old-fashioned way." We've already noted the appeal politicians make to the value of family. It is surprising how many politicians manage to hold their marriages together just until they win an election.

This trend of increasing mobility and fragmentation of our lives probably will continue into the future. As a result, the need for roots that Packard described many years ago is still with us and is still an important touchstone. It is a responsive chord that advertisers, politicians, and ideologues will continue to strike in their many persuasive appeals to us.

Need for Immortality. None of us believes in our own mortality. Packard suggested that the fear of dying and the need to believe in an ongoing influence on the lives of others underlies many kinds of psychological appeals. The breadwinner is made to feel that in buying insurance, for instance, he or she buys "life after death" in the form of financial control over the family. The buyer can help the kids go to college even if he or she isn't there.

Other products make similar appeals to the fear of death. Promise margarine will keep you healthy longer because "Promise is at the heart of eating right." And Nivea's Visage face cream keeps your skin "firmer, healthier, and younger" for only pennies a day. As the ad executive noted in an earlier quote, we aren't buying lanolin, we are buying hope — hope for a chunk of immortality and youth.

This need for immortality seems particularly relevant in our modern technocracy. Perhaps people now feel even more helpless to control their lives than they did when Packard conducted his research. The much-talked-about "midlife crisis," when people get divorced, quit their jobs, buy a red convertible, run off with an 18-year-old stud or dolly, and engage in daring experiences (such as bungee jumping), may be symptomatic of the fears people have as they re-alize that they have passed the probable midpoint of their lives and want to be young again or at least capture some of the experiences they missed along the way.

Maslow's Pyramid of Needs

Abraham Maslow (1954), a well-known psychologist, offered a starting point for examining people's needs. He noted that people have various kinds of needs that emerge, subside, and then reemerge. In his pyramid of needs, the lower levels represent the stronger needs and the higher levels represent the weaker needs (Figure 6.4). Keep in mind that this pyramid is only a model and that the lines between needs are not as distinct as the picture suggests. Also note that higher needs are not *superior* to lower ones. They are just different and, in all likelihood, weaker and less likely to emerge until stronger needs are met. Recall our metaphor from Chapter 3 describing an individual's belief system as being like an onion, where peeling away layers eventually

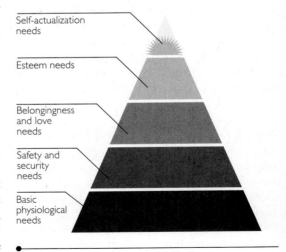

Figure 6.4. *Maslow's pyramid of needs.*

Self-actualization needs

Esteem needs

Belongingness and love needs

Safety and security needs

Basic physiological needs

leads to the core, or primitive, beliefs, on which there is unanimous agreement (for example, the sun rises in the east). In Maslow's pyramid of needs, the core of the onion is the base of the pyramid — needs or beliefs about which there is unanimous agreement. As we move up the pyramid or out from the core, we find needs or beliefs on which there may not be unanimous agreement and on which individuals may place varying degrees of value. So there is an upward or outward dynamic in Maslow's hierarchy of needs: As more powerful needs are met, less potent needs emerge.

As time passes, the earlier needs emerge again as they are or are not met. For example, the need for food or water emerges and then recedes as we eat or drink. Maslow argued that these needs have a **prepotency** — that is, they are tied together so that weaker needs, such as ones for self-respect, emerge only after stronger needs, like ones for food, have been filled. We probably could not persuade a dehydrated desert wanderer to clean up a little before drinking from our well. He had better fulfill the need for H_2O first. The need to slake thirst is prepotent; until it is fulfilled, it is impossible for one to consider other ideas.

This concept is similar to Rokeach's belief hierarchy, which we discussed in Chapter 3. Advertisers appeal to consumers' using human needs as an underlying assumption.

Basic Needs. The bottom level of Maslow's pyramid contains the strongest needs we have — basic needs. These are the physiological needs for regular access to air, food, water, sex, sleep, and elimination of wastes. Until these needs are met, we cannot concern ourselves with other, higher needs. The basic needs are too strong to be forgotten in favor of other needs. At the same time, they can be used to motivate behavior. The person who is starving can be motivated to do all sorts of unusual things to secure food, ranging

from stealing it to eating insects. And we know that the need for air can cause drowning victims to panic and drown not only themselves but their would-be rescuers as well.

Security Needs. The second level of Maslow's pyramid contains our needs for security. There are several ways one might look at these needs. We may want to feel secure in our ability to satisfy basic needs. If we feel that our job may end shortly, we have a strong need to obtain income security. We may want to get another, more secure job. Or we might want to save money for hard times. This is one kind of security. At the same time, we might look at this need level in another light. Let us suppose that we have job security — our boss assures us that we will be the last to be let go. We still may feel insecure because of the rising crime rates in our neighborhood. We might take drastic action to ward off thieves, such as installing a burglar alarm system, or sleeping with a loaded pistol under the pillow. Even when we feel secure about our home, we still may feel insecure about world politics. We may feel that our country needs more missiles or antimissile missiles. Or, a person may have social insecurity and as a result spend money on self-improvement classes, deodorant, hair transplants, and mouthwash.

Those who are not technically trained to meet the requirements of the computer age realistically fear falling by the wayside. Global competition has eaten into the market share of U.S. industries, leaving thousands unemployed. Many analysts have explained several election results as related to fears of economic displacement and the resulting loss of jobs. According to Maslow's model, this fear emerged in response to current economic conditions. In other words, the need for security emerges and reemerges as various threats to our security become evident and must be met. Once the need is met, it redefines itself and thus is always present to some degree.

More recently, the awesome changes occurring in previously communist countries have introduced a new source of insecurity.

Today, insecurity, like change, is one of the few *predictable* things. Eight of every ten jobs that will be filled by tomorrow's students after they graduate do not even exist today, so it's almost impossible to prepare for the future. New computer technology becomes obsolete in two to three years. No one can keep up with the new (and frequently essential) information about jobs, health (as seen in Figure 6.5), communities, and a host of other personal and social issues. We live in a time when very little is secure. It is not surprising that so many security-oriented products, politicians, and organizations appeal to us on a daily basis.

Belongingness and Love Needs. Once our security needs are met, at least in part, we become aware of needs on the third level: belonging or association needs and love needs. A number of options are open to us in meeting our need for association. Usually, individuals go beyond family and job and seek groups with which to fill this need—they are the joiners of our society. They become members of dozens of groups such as the PTA, bowling leagues, churches, golf clubs, or service groups. Usually, we keep the number of groups we join small and, although we may be members of several organizations, we are active members in only a few. Whatever the case, we meet our belonging needs only partially. However, there is growing concern over the tendency of people to isolate themselves. In his article "Bowling Alone," Robert Putnam (1995) observed that more and more persons are joining what he calls "check book groups" such as the Sierra Club or AARP—all you have to do to belong is to write the check: The groups rarely if ever meet. At the same time membership is going down in traditional groups like the Lions, Elks, and so on, and fewer people bowl in organized leagues, preferring to "bowl alone."

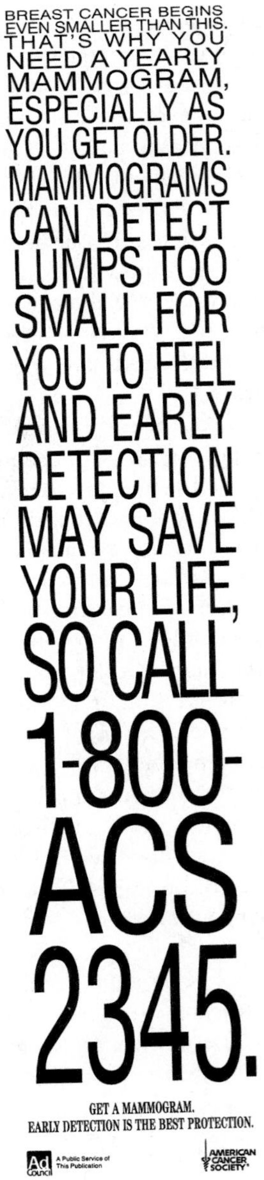
BREAST CANCER BEGINS EVEN SMALLER THAN THIS. THAT'S WHY YOU NEED A YEARLY MAMMOGRAM, ESPECIALLY AS YOU GET OLDER. MAMMOGRAMS CAN DETECT LUMPS TOO SMALL FOR YOU TO FEEL AND EARLY DETECTION MAY SAVE YOUR LIFE, SO CALL 1-800-ACS-2345.
GET A MAMMOGRAM.
EARLY DETECTION IS THE BEST PROTECTION.
Ad Council
A Public Service of This Publication
AMERICAN CANCER SOCIETY

Figure 6.5. *The need for security is the appeal used in this ad from the American Cancer Society. (Reprinted by permission of the American Cancer Society.)*

Like basic and security needs, the need to belong often interacts with these other needs and continues to reemerge throughout our lives. Also, what fulfills our belonging needs differs at various points in our lives. But the need to belong will always be with us, and going hand-in-hand with a need to feel a part of some groups is the need to feel loved or esteemed by the members of those groups, be they family, fraternity, team, church, or political party. As persuadees we need to recognize when this need is being appealed to by persuaders so that we can critically evaluate their appeals.

Esteem Needs. Once we satisfy belongingness needs, we feel the emergence of needs in level four of Maslow's model: the needs for esteem. Once we are part of a group, we want to feel that the group values us as a member. We want to feel wanted and valued as human beings. We are happy when our families understand and admire the things we do. The esteem need is also a reemerging need. That is, if we find that we are needed and esteemed by our family, our need for esteem does not fade away. Instead, its focus shifts. We want now to feel needed by our co-workers, our boss, and our friends. Many product appeals offer a kind of symbolic substitute for esteem. As Figure 6.6 shows, your kids will hold you in high esteem if you use a Char-Broil gas grill to whip up a great meal.

Cultural trends also influence our esteem needs. For example, during the 1980s, esteem came from *conspicuous consumption*, consumption engaged in for purposes of display. But, as noted earlier, several important things happened to change the way people satisfied esteem needs. Political, financial, and religious scandals shook people's faith in traditional institutions, and the "me first" mentality seemed to fade in the late '80s.

The '90s have sounded a different note. There seems to be communal concern for the environment. Young and old, producers and con-sumers, conservatives and liberals are pitching in in a variety of ways to clean up our air, land, and water resources. People seem to realize that working in community can help meet our esteem needs. In fact, "community" has become a god term in the 1990s.

Self-Actualization Needs. Although Maslow initially put the need for self-actualization at the top of his pyramid, thereby implying that it would rarely emerge, he later came to believe that in a way, the need to live up to one's potential is an integral part of everyone's life. At first, Maslow believed that individuals could live up to their potential only when all four of the lower needs were fulfilled.

In many ways, Maslow's initial ideas were accurate. It is hard for a young person on the way up to think about self-actualization, just as it is hard to meet love or esteem needs if you do not belong to some group that can give you love or esteem. Yet Maslow's later thinking about all these needs and their prepotency is valid, too. He came to see self-actualization as occurring through what he called "peak experiences"—events in which people can enjoy themselves, learn about themselves, or experience something they have only dreamed of before. Thus, the person who goes out into the Boundary Waters Canoe Area wilderness and learns to be self-reliant and not to fear isolation has enjoyed a peak, or self-actualizing, experience. The same might apply to people who learn something about themselves when they take their first job after high school or college and discover that they have abilities that are of value to a company or to fellow workers.

Cultural trends can affect the ways in which we seek to satisfy our self-actualization needs. Social critic T. J. Jackson Lears (1983) has noted that the search for ways of identifying one's self and one's potential came about when the United States shifted from being a culture of production to a culture of consumption. We shifted from secure

THE GRILLER: MARATHON MOM

No time to waste, right? So a gas grill has to perform quickly, easily. Enter MasterFlame². It's built with your schedule in mind: easy push button ignition, sturdy shelves for extra work space, a cooking system that virtually eliminates uneven heat, and multi-level cooking to prepare the main course and side dishes at one time. Give it a try... you'll find you've made a delicious dinner for your family and it wasn't a chore at all. In fact, it's our guess you'll find you even had fun.

To locate Char-Broil MasterFlame² gas grills, and find out about a free gift with purchase, just call

1-800-477-0118

THE GRILL: MASTERFLAME²™ FROM
Char-Broil

Figure 6.6. Esteem needs are the key appeal in this ad. (Reprinted by permission of Char-Broil.)

farm living to an unsettling urban loneliness, a shift away from traditional values, and chaotic changes in our lifestyles. The result, Lears claims, was the search for a "therapeutic ethos," or an identity that would let individuals be at ease with themselves— that would permit them to self-actualize. To a large extent, this therapeutic ethos of-fered in-ner harmony, a reduction of feelings of empti-ness, and a hope for self-realization through patterns of consumption. As we approach a new century, what will be the means for achieving self-actualization—our own true potential? It is certain that there will be persuaders offering a variety of means for achieving this final prepotent need.

As you encounter various persuasive events and opportunities (public and interpersonal), apply Maslow's model to them. See whether it sheds

What do you think?

How are you trying to self-actualize?

light on the needs that people feel and that may motivate their actions. You may want to experiment with persuading another person using several levels of Maslow's model. If the person doesn't seem motivated by appeals to security, try appealing to basic or belonging needs.

Uses of the Needs Process Premise

In our search for the first premises that serve as springboards for persuasion in enthymemes, psychological processes show us promising possibilities in the area of human needs. These needs, whether identified by Packard's list or Maslow's pyramid or some other model, are strongly felt by audiences. Persuaders frequently tie other minor premises to them to allow audience members to complete the argument by drawing the conclusion. For example, feeling the need for job security, a college student decides to major in a field that holds the promise of job openings after graduation. It is only common sense. Yet what we call "common sense" is common only because so many of us have the same or similar needs.

We may wish to relabel our needs in terms other than those used by Maslow or Packard, but their categories serve as good general descriptions. We ought to consider the requests persuaders make of us from the perspective of our own needs. And as persuaders, we ought to examine the current needs of those we wish to influence. If we do that, not only are we more likely to succeed, we are more likely to do our audience a service by giving them a means to satisfy their needs.

A good way to train yourself to evaluate appeals from this critical perspective — as persuadee or persuader — is to restate persuasive messages, such as television commercials, from the perspective of the Packard and Maslow models. In our search for first premises on which persuasion may be built, it is clear that human psychological and physiological needs are powerful motivators. As you will see, attitudes — the second type of process premise — operate in similar ways.

Attitudes: The Second Process Premise

When we surveyed the theoretical perspectives on persuasion, we looked at how various researchers explain attitudes using a variety of theories. One unifying element among these theories is the fact that attitudes can serve as the unstated major premises in persuasive enthymemes.

We noted in Chapter 3 that attitudes are considered predispositions to behave and that confusion exists as to the degree to which attitudes can reliably predict behavior. A better predictor of behavior seems to be one's "intention to behave," discussed by Fishbein and Ajzen (1975). Psychologists Alice H. Eagley and Shelley Chaiken (1993) have defined an **attitude** as "a psychological tendency that is expressed by evaluating a particular entity with some degree of favor or disfavor" (p. 1). According to them, *evaluating* includes all classes of responding — "overt or covert, cognitive, affective, or behavioral." The important word in their definition is "tendency," by which they mean "an internal state that lasts for at least a short time" (p. 2). Because it is internal, we cannot observe it directly, so we try to observe it in "evaluative responses." Examples of evaluative responses include expressing "approval or disapproval, favor or disfavor, liking or disliking, approach or avoidance, attraction or aversion, or similar reactions" (p. 3). According to Eagley and Chaiken, we make such evaluations concerning "attitude objects," which include "virtually anything that is discriminable" (p. 3).

Take, for example, the attitudes surrounding vegetarian eating habits. Vegetarians usually justify their eating preferences in one or both of two ways: (1) eating only vegetables and grains is healthier and more ecologically sound, and (2) vegetarian habits do not bring pain to animals—it is a "kinder" way of living. Both of those justifications are evaluative responses to the attitude object called "vegetarianism." We try to predict the behavior of vegetarians based on those evaluations. We wouldn't, for example, offer steak tartare to them as an hors d'oeuvre, because we predict that they won't try it and may in fact consider the offer an insult.

For our purposes, attitude objects are usually found in the persuader's request for action or offer of products, ideas, beliefs, and so on. If the persuadee evaluates the actions or offers positively, he or she will be more likely to act as requested or to accept the offer being made.

Attitudes and Opinions

From another point of view, communication researcher Milton Rokeach (1968) pointed out that individual beliefs range from those that are primitive and strongly held to those that are based on authority and are not as strongly held. These belief sets cluster and form attitudes, which, according to Rokeach, fall into two categories: *attitudes toward objects or issues* and *attitudes toward situations*.

Both classes of attitudes can predispose us to action, but they can also confuse us, especially when they conflict with each other. Such conflict can be seen when parents protest the presence of AIDS-infected students in public schools. The parents' attitudes toward the object (the infected student) and their attitudes toward the situation (the possibility that their own children will be infected) may either conflict or converge. These attitudes, in turn, probably emerge from complex sets of beliefs about both the object and situation: The parents may sympathize with the innocent victim while at the same time holding certain neg-

ative beliefs about the situation—the epidemic proportions of sexually transmitted diseases (STDs) and the deadly outcome of the AIDS virus. A persuader on either side of this controversy would need to address both sets of beliefs.

Opinions resemble beliefs but are far more fickle; as opinion polls demonstrate, opinions change rapidly and often dramatically. We all have opinions about politicians and what they say in a campaign and about what they do after taking office. These opinions can change, however, especially if a president makes a few key errors: a foolish statement, losing to Congress on a particular issue, or choosing to support a friend who turns out to be corrupt. The Gallup and Harris polls record such shifts of opinion on a regular basis. Remember, however, that opinions may not influence the behavior of persons who hold them. For instance, although our opinions about a president may slip toward the negative over a period of a few months, we may still vote for that person in the next election. This is not to say that opinions do not at all affect behavior—only that they sometimes exert a weak influence (Larson and Sanders, 1975). Given a large enough change in opinion, however, we *may not* support a president in the next campaign; or, given enough small shifts in our opinions, we may change our overall attitude toward that president.

We have an *attitude* toward smoking composed of many *opinions*: that it is costly; that it is unhealthy; that it is dirty; that it bothers others; that it destroys the body's supply of vitamin C, and so on. Philip Zimbardo, a prominent social psychologist, and his colleagues (1976) note that attitudes are "either mental readiness or implicit predispositions that exert some general and consistent influence on a fairly large class of evaluative responses" (p. 20).

Notice that Zimbardo stresses the enduring quality of attitude shifts. There is even a school of advertising research, known by the acronym

DAGMAR, holding that ad agencies ought to *Define Advertising Goals for Measured Advertising Results* (Colley, 1961). In other words, the goal of advertising may be only *attitudinal change* toward the brand and not change in purchase behavior. It is hoped that if we have an improved image of a product—say Rice Chex—we will buy more of the product. Unfortunately, this attitude-behavior link has been difficult to demonstrate, perhaps because of the many intervening variables that might also affect consumer behavior. Simple awareness of a product's name, packaging, display location in the store, special offers, or kind of background music being played may cause us to buy it. Other factors, such as time of day or gender, may be the key. Even in carefully controlled experiments with many of these causes filtered out, attitude and behavior do not consistently link up (Zimbardo, Ebbesen, and Maslich, 1976).

Functions of Attitudes

Another way to think about attitudes is to focus on their various persuasive functions, dimensions, or effects. Attitudes have a **cognitive function** or dimension: they are *learned.* Consider the environment: Our attitudes toward air and water pollution, recycling, and endangered species are all part of *what we know* about these issues. Some advertisements are aimed at cognitions. A mutual fund company advertises that it is "no load"—customers don't have to pay commissions when they purchase shares. This is knowledge that is learned and hopefully persuades the consumer to select this fund over others that do charge commissions. The same function is met by some political advertisements as well.

Attitudes also have an **affective function:** they affect our emotions and feelings. In other words, attitudes toward recycling and air and water pollution affect *how we feel* about these issues. Again, some ads are aimed at the affective dimension, or emotions. These ads might be image ads such as Nike's "Sorry, our spokesman's a little busy right now," shown during the 1996 N.B.A. playoffs. In the ad, those words appeared on the screen accompanied by shots of Michael Jordan playing in the various championship games.

Finally, and most important, attitudes have a **behavioral function:** They predispose us to take certain actions. Because we hold certain attitudes about air and water pollution, we do or do not buy gas guzzlers, we do or do not use detergents, and we do or do not recycle our garbage. In other words, the behavioral function of attitudes affects *what we do* about these issues. And some ads are aimed at prompting actual behavior. One goal of advertising, for example, is to "induce trial" or to get the consumer to try the brand. Such ads might include a free sample or might offer a rebate with purchase of the brand.

Attitudes and Intention

The work of Martin Fishbein and Icek Ajzen (1975) has added another concept to research on attitude and behavior change. This concept, labeled **behavioral intention,** relates to what one *intends* to do about something, regardless of what action one finally takes. Here, a fairly consistent set of results emerges: Attitude change *does* seem to precede what people say they *intend* to do about the environment—as a result of attitude change, we *say* that we *intend* to recycle, that we *intend* to conserve water, or that we *intend* to purchase, join, try, vote, or donate. When people describe what they intend to do, they have, in a sense, already symbolically enacted the behavior. Thus a person who displays a bumper sticker in favor of a certain candidate is stating a behavioral intention, and it is likely that this person will vote for that candidate. Politicians know this and urge potential voters to display buttons, bumper stickers, and signs, in order to guarantee their votes on election day.

Attitudes and Interpersonal Communication

There are several other dimensions to the attitude change and subsequent behavior puzzle. One of these dimensions is the degree to which attitudes function as tools of interpersonal communication. In other words, do expressions of attitudes have more to do with fitting oneself into a comfortable position with those with whom we are interacting than they have to do with our ultimate behavior? For example, I have a hunting and fishing partner who is much more politically conservative than I am. When I express political attitudes or even opinions about political issues of the day to him, I am very careful about the exact words I use. His friendship is worth more to me than my need to express my attitudes bluntly. J. R. Eiser (1987), a critic of much of the attitude research that has been conducted, puts it this way:

> One of the main shortcomings of many attitude theories is their emphasis on individualistic, intrapsychic factors to the relative neglect of the social and communicative context within which attitudes are acquired and expressed. Not only the expression but also the experience of attitude is shaped by how we have learnt to anticipate what we say and do. For this reason, attitude is both a subjective experience and a social product, and the expression of an attitude is a social act (p. 2).

In other words, we express attitudes in ways that help us get along with persons who are significant to us. As a result, there sometimes may be logical discrepancies between expressed attitudes and subsequent behavior.

Attitudes and Information Processing

Closely related to the behavioral intentions approach is the focus on human information processing. The idea here is that you can't look at

attitudes and behavior without also looking at what information in the persuasive message is processed by the audience, how it is stored, and how it is retrieved. When trying to look at this process, one of the first questions one must ask is: Can the audience comprehend this message? The next step is to determine how the message is stored in the audience members' long-term memory (LTM). It may be entirely new information to the audience, or it may fit with an existing network or several networks ("nets") of information already stored in LTM.

Take, for example, the "cents off" coupons appearing in newspapers, circulars, and magazines. As persuasive information, they fit with several memory networks in our minds: whether we already use the brand in our house, how often we use it, and whether the value of the coupon is sufficient to justify taking the time to "clip" it. To someone else, the coupons mesh with different nets that might include totally different information.

Research into how information is stored in LTM is in its infancy, but most theorists agree that it is usually stored in networks and in the form of key words, symbols, and relationships.

Joseph Cappella and Joseph Folger (1980) use an interesting example of a stored network based on the following sentences: "Gigolos are despicable creatures. They deceive women and steal their money." Here the concept of "gigolos" is linked with "creatures" (modified by "despicable"), who then "steal" (objectified by "money"), and "deceive" (the object being "women"). If you drew such a network, you would discover that the central concept/word is "gigolos," about which audiences have affective or emotional feelings that can be retrieved when the key concept is stated. This is one way "nets" can be built.

Another organizing device for LTM may be *episodic* in nature. That is, we remember things that are presented to us in episodic or dramatic segments that then become integrated with LTM networks relating to one of the numerous personal episode types such as being deceived, winning over the odds, revealing the culprit, and others. If you can identify the episodic types that people have, these could serve as vital first premises in persuasive enthymemes. As we will see later, another theorist, Tony Schwartz, provides a model for resonating with or "evoking" such experiences from audiences.

At the behavior stage of the information-processing model (for example, voting, buying, joining, saluting, smiling, expressing one's view), the critical concepts or episodes are retrieved from LTM and provide the persuadees with good "reasons" for taking action.

Petty and Cacioppo (1986) present an insightful application of their information-processing model to persuasion. You will recall from Chapter 3 that Petty and Cacioppo presented an "elaboration likelihood" explanation for persuasion, particularly as seen in highly "logical" and "reasoned" persuasion as opposed to "emotional" or "affective" kinds of persuasion. Their explanation of persuasive effects postulates two routes of persuasion. Logical/reasoned persuasion flows through a *central processing* path that requires lots of evidence and reasoning and is frequently used when making major purchase decisions (a personal computer, or a new car). Emotional persuasion flows through a *peripheral processing* path and relies on simple cues (advertising, packaging, coupons, or other sales promotions). This path is usually associated with making less important decisions (whether to eat at Burger King or Subway). Their explanation rests on a set of basic assumptions:

1. Although people want to have "correct" attitudes, the degree to which they will elaborate on an issue/decision will vary from individual to individual and from situation to situation.

2. A variety of variables can affect attitude change and can act as persuasive arguments,

peripheral cues, or attitudinal positions (interests, motivation to research an issue or elaborate on it, and so on).

3. When motivation or ability to elaborate decreases, peripheral cues become more important and carry the load of persuasion/attitude change (for example, "I don't know much about the Internet, and I'm not that interested anyway"). Conversely, as motivation or ability to elaborate on a claim increases, peripheral cues lose impact ("After hearing that the Internet includes libraries, companies, and governmental groups, I wanted to get more info").

What do you think?

Have you made any recent purchases that involved elaboration?

4. Persuaders can affect a consumer's motivation or ability to process information/arguments by either encouraging or discouraging careful examination of the argument/claim ("April 15 is only a week away, so you'd better bone up on the new tax laws" versus "At your income level, you may as well use the short tax form 1040EZ").

5. Issues/arguments that flow from the central processing path are more likely to persist, predict actual behavior, and be resistant to counterpersuasion (deciding to purchase a camcorder after doing lots of research versus brand preference in deciding to purchase breakfast cereal).

For our purposes, persuasion relying on process premises is likely to be processed in the peripheral path, whereas persuasion that relies on reasoned premises (which we will discuss in Chapter 7) is likely to be processed in the central path. Petty and Cacioppo offer a flowchart depicting the various options available and routes taken in any persuasive transaction—see Figure 6.7.

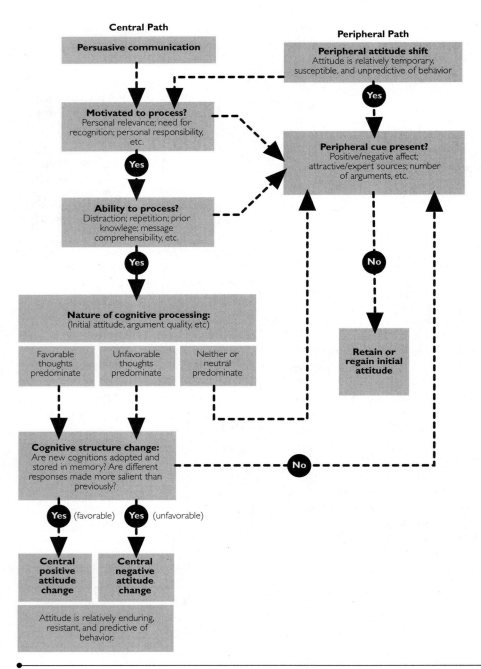

Figure 6.7. Decision flow in the elaboration likelihood model.

Notice that the various options in the model rest on the motivation to process a persuasive message. In the first step, we see that persuadees must want to investigate a given product, candidate, or cause. The process is short-circuited if the *motivation* isn't there. In the second step we see that if motivated to process an offer/appeal/claim, a persuadee must also possess the *ability* to process the persuasion in one of the two paths. From that point on, the nature of the attitude change depends on which path is followed. If the peripheral path is used, the resulting attitude change will be weak, short-lived, and less likely to result in behavior, whereas if the central processing path is used, the resulting attitude change will be potent, long-lived, and likely lead to change in behavior.

There are several other approaches to studying the message-attitude-behavior chain, each of which has its strengths and weaknesses. But all agree that attitudes have something to do with behavior and that attitudes can be altered via persuasive messages. The presumption then is that the suggested behavior will ultimately follow.

What does all this mean to the persuadee who is in the business of listening critically in a world of doublespeak? What can we do to uncover persuaders' intentions and beliefs about the audience? Being aware of attitudes helps us to second-guess what the persuader thinks of us. For example, what kind of attitude, long-term memory, or episode is the customer presumed to have for an ad for sunglasses showing a macho man on a motorcycle. The persuader obviously believes that members of the target market have high image needs, have strong feelings about the importance of power, are somewhat snobbish, and are not conformists. Are these the people who read *Vanity Fair,* the magazine in which the ad appeared? How would the company advertise in another kind of magazine — say, *Playboy* or *Outdoor Life?* By seeking to identify the attitudes that persuaders assume we have, we become more critical

receivers. We can become conscious of our attitudes and can see how persuaders use them to get us to follow their advice.

Consistency: The Third Process Premise

In Chapter 3 we looked at several of the theories that explain human behavior in terms of people's need for balance, consistency, or consonance. These theories posit that human beings feel comfortable when the world lives up to or operates consistently with their perceptions of or predictions about events. When this consistency is not evident, people are predisposed to change either themselves or their interpretations of events to bring the world into a more balanced state. Knowing where and when this phenomenon is likely to occur, persuaders can offer a means to return to consistency and thus comfort. For example, persuaders attempting to change public attitudes toward the health care crisis usually try to create dissonance in health care users ("Your employer's group insurance plan won't begin to cover the costs of major surgery" or "With an HMO you don't get to go to the best surgeon").

If humans seek out psychological equilibrium, it is valuable for us as receivers to try to identify what puts us into states of imbalance, making us then vulnerable to persuasion. Conversely, if psychological equilibrium is our goal, we ought to identify those circumstances that make us comfortable and can be targeted for persuasion that reinforces attitudes. Consistency theory researchers Charles Osgood and Percy Tannenbaum (1955) put it this way: "Changes in evaluation are always in the direction of increased congruity with the existing frame of reference."

As Eiser (1987) points out, defining "the existing frame of reference" is a critical factor in predicting attitude shifts. One must identify the

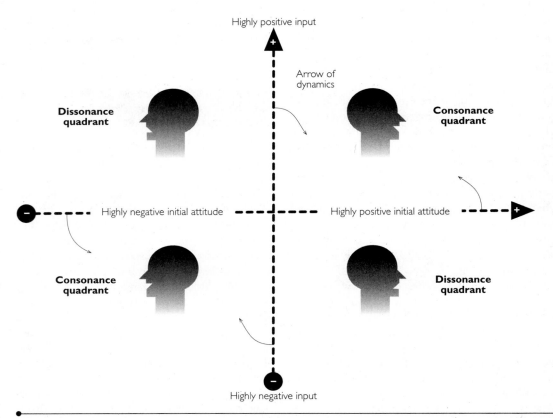

Figure 6.8. *The quadrant model of cognitive consonance and cognitive dissonance. The advantages of this model over the ones examined in Chapter 3 are clear. Not only can we represent the kind of psychic comfort or discomfort being experienced, we can represent the amount of comfort or discomfort experienced, plus the dynamics of dissonance and consonance.*

receiver's current frame of reference to create the kind of incongruity or inconsistency that will prompt feelings of psychological "dis-ease" that will then lead to movement along an attitude scale. According to Eiser, these "evaluative frames of reference . . . are more general than the specific objects of judgment being evaluated" (p. 27).

What are some of these frames of reference for groups of potential persuadees? In other words,

what are some of the sources of dissonance and consonance? Both are important. Sources of dissonance are critical when persuaders want to *change* attitudes. Sources of consonance are important when persuaders want to *strengthen* or *reinforce* existing attitudes.

Another way to think about consonance and dissonance is shown in Figure 6.8. The horizontal axis of the model represents our initial attitude toward a topic — say, subscribing to America

Online. Notice that this attitude can range from highly positive on the right to highly negative on the left. The vertical axis represents any kind of input that we might receive concerning the topic (something we read, a discussion we have regarding Internet access). Again, the input can range from highly positive at the top to highly negative at the bottom.

The arrows on both axes indicate the dynamics of the model. Notice that the positive end of the initial attitude axis has an arrow pointing at the positive end of the input axis. If you have positive initial attitudes toward America Online, you will seek, agree with, or relate to information, experience, and other evidence that supports this point of view. Conversely, if you have negative initial attitudes toward the provider, you will seek, agree with, or relate to information, experience, and other evidence that supports this point of view. Because of the dynamics of the model, the upper right and lower left quadrants of the model each depict persuasion that relies upon consonance; conversely, the quadrants at the upper left and lower right depict persuasion that plays on feelings of dissonance.

Try charting your own initial attitudes toward a variety of given topics and how you relate to various kinds of inputs that create either dissonance or consonance. The model applies to such varied persuasive situations as voting for a candidate, switching brands, and choosing to donate money to a good cause.

Sources of Dissonance

What kinds of situations or events can cause you to feel a sense of imbalance? Some of them are unique to you, of course, but many of them are similar — even identical — for large groups of people. These are likely targets for persuaders because the predictable inconsistencies in life are potent first premises in persuasive arguments.

Loss of Group Prestige. One way for persuaders to make us feel discomfort is to cause us to perceive a loss of **group prestige.** For example, the behavior of not only the prosecution and defense teams but also the judge in the O. J. Simpson criminal trial must have caused a loss of prestige for attorneys and judges at large. The legal community reacted to this loss in prestige quickly by referring to F. Lee Bailey as "Flea" Bailey, and Judge Ito jokes emerged throughout the trial. Police officers around the country must have felt a similar loss of prestige when Mark Fuhrman testified about not using the "n" word and then being repeatedly refuted on this by other witnesses and by an audio tape. And the citizenry of Los Angeles must have felt some loss of prestige as a result of the year-long spectacle and its accompanying ballyhoo in the tabloid press.

The loss of group prestige can apply to small and large groups alike, ranging from a fraternity or sorority to an entire profession or region of the country. The loss can even cause dissonance for an entire nation, as must have been the case when genocide was revealed in the former Yugoslavia. Institutions like the FBI or Congress experience a loss of group prestige when they can't identify a terrorist or when they "gridlock" the government. In such cases of a loss of group prestige, members of the concerned institution usually move quickly to reduce dissonance by such means as humor, apologies, and explanations.

Economic Loss. Another kind of fear frequently exploited by persuaders is the fear of **economic loss.** When we perceive that our economic value (measured in savings, property, salary, or whatever) is in danger of being reduced, we feel psychic dissonance and insecurity. For example, in the late '90s, many persons were "downsized" or "merged" out of their jobs — jobs that they had assumed would be theirs until retirement. The obvious dissonance caused by such loss was dealt with in a number of ways. Some of the displaced workers "chose" to take "early" retirement; others returned to school; some accepted jobs with much lower salaries, and yet others went into business for themselves.

Persuaders can appeal to this fear of losing one's job to induce Americans to vote for politicians who promise to reduce inflation, budget deficits, or wasteful spending. Persuaders can sell us investment schemes to protect our financial security. We can be induced to join organizations or causes to protect our economic well-being. An allegedly nonprofit lobbying organization set up to prevent Social Security benefits from being cut was revealed to have spent next to nothing on lobbying efforts and merely gave out handsome salaries and plush expense accounts to its officers.

Loss of Personal Prestige. Whenever we perceive that we are losing the respect of others — our **personal prestige** — and feel helpless to do anything about it, dissonance is bound to emerge — regardless of the situation or the degree to which we feel responsible. This source of dissonance is used to appeal to parents whose children aren't achieving to their ability. For example, an ad for a series of motivational programs said, "If your child comes home with bad grades from grade school, refuses to practice the piano, watches too much television, and seems bored with school, then the responsible thing for a parent to do is to send the child to Chicago's Motivational Institute." In other words, parents could regain lost self-respect by being responsible and enrolling their child. Ads promoting hair restorers or weight reduction plans also play on the loss of personal prestige. And we are all familiar with ads warning that if people see dandruff on your collar in the elevator on Monday morning, your personal stock at work will drop out of sight. Other fears related to loss of prestige include fears about loss of youth, loss of health, or deteriorating appearance. All such fears make us vulnerable to appeals related to our need for consistency.

Uncertainty of Prediction. We also feel discomfort when we are unable to **predict** people's behavior or the course of events with any degree of certainty. A dramatic example of this is recorded in Viktor Frankl's book *Man's Search for Meaning* (1962). Frankl reported that some former concentration camp inmates found it impossible to reenter the world of normalcy. They turned away from the open gates of the unpredictable, free world. They needed the predictability of the camp schedule and personnel in order to cope.

We find the same reaction in much less vivid but more personalized examples whenever we change our environment: when we change schools, when we move to a new job, when we break up with a spouse or lover, when we join the armed services, or when we move into any other unpredictable context. One of the most powerful weapons of any terrorist organization is the unpredictability of its target selection. For example, America seemed insulated from terrorism, at least within its borders, until the bombings of the World Trade Center in New York and the Murrah Building in Oklahoma City. America was now vulnerable to terrorism and would have to come to terms with a new kind of unpredictability.

Today we are in a national state of dissonance caused by our inability to predict our lives and count on the accuracy of the predictions. Products that promise to "protect" us from some negative circumstance (illness, job loss, financial difficulties) use the inability to predict as a "hook" to persuade us. This inability often serves as the missing premise in an enthymeme.

Sense of Guilt. A final source of dissonance is **guilt.** It springs from the potential disapproving judgments of important others such as our parents, peers, or world opinion. News pictures of starving prisoners and ruined homes in the former Yugoslavia can cause a national sense of guilt in Americans, and probably helps prompt our government to send troops, food, medicine, and other forms of aid to various locations around the globe.

Such self-imposed and internalized feelings of dissonance can be explained in various ways. Freudian psychoanalysts would say that we are afraid of reprimands from our symbolic parents, incorporated in our conscience, or superego. These fears lead to shame or self-hatred, and guilt is a symptom of that shame. Transactional psychology offers a similar explanation for guilt: The *child* in us fears a reprimand from the *parent* in us, which the *adult* in us handles by taking action to alleviate the feelings of guilt.

In any case, this source of dissonance is frequently used in persuasion. Kenneth Burke (1961) explained the process using a religious allegory. In the epilogue of his book *The Rhetoric of Religion,* Burke narrates an argument between God and the Devil about human motivation. God explains that he will ultimately win out over the Devil, who has introduced sin into the world. His explanation hangs on the development of guilt as an inevitable result of sinning. This guilt will then have to be purged. The purgation will have to set things right with God, against whom the mortals have sinned, and the result of the purgation will be some sense of redemption.

Of course, we have seen this pattern repeated in various religions, but we ought not overlook more mundane examples of this sin-guilt-purgation-redemption chain. Politicians who urge us to return to the principles "that made this country great" are using the religious model. Our sin lies in disregarding those principles. Our guilt is the sense of dissonance we feel. Our purgation is whatever action is suggested to return us to the tried-and-true principles—prayer in the schools, abolishing affirmative action, or a constitutional amendment banning abortion on demand.

Numerous product pitches rely on the sin-guilt-purgation-redemption pattern. For example, most health-related products (such as nighttime cold medicines) show a sick child coughing and sneezing—the sin. Then the parent goes to the medicine cabinet only to discover that the Pertussin container is empty, and the parent is guilty.

But the all-night supermarket has more on its shelves, so the parent goes out in the middle of the night to get some—the means of purgation. The next morning the child awakens refreshed and perky as a cricket, to go off to school—the resulting redemption. The consumer is urged to avoid the sin, guilt, and purgation steps by making sure that there is enough medicine on hand. Auto manufacturers use a similar technique to persuade consumers to buy safe cars with air bags for *both* the driver and the passenger. Even the humble washday detergent identifies dull, drab, and dirty clothes as a sin that can be redeemed by using the right detergent, resulting in a whiter, brighter, fluffier, and better-smelling batch of laundry. You can no doubt identify numerous other examples of the use of guilt to sell products.

Sources of Consonance

Some appeals are made to give receivers a sense of consonance, and are made more frequently than those aimed at creating dissonance. Consonance-producing appeals are used to reinforce existing beliefs, attitudes, or behaviors and frequently to activate receivers. What are some of the means used to create consonance?

> **What do you think?**
>
> Why might choosing an occupation cause someone dissonance?

Reassurance of Security. One of the ways to appeal to our need for equilibrium or balance is to reassure us that we are **secure.** As noted in both Maslow's and Packard's lists of needs, security needs are basic and can have several dimensions. To feel assured that we are secure from terrorist attacks, police stations, airports, courthouses, and other public buildings are protected with metal detectors and even armed guards. Promises of job security are powerful persuaders for persons making career choices. And IRA accounts offer retirement security. Politicians promise to stop the export of factory jobs to offshore employers and to balance the budget to assure the viability of Social Security and Medicare.

Sometimes we see ideological persuaders use this tactic as well. Religious leaders convince their followers that by remaining true to the faith, by participating in rituals, or maybe by increasing their donations they can avoid damnation. And good causes also promise security: MADD will get drunk drivers off the roads; one's church will offer the security of salvation; and the Citizen's Utility Board promises to fight increases in utility costs on our behalf.

Demonstration of Predictability. A consonance-producing tactic related to reassurance of security is to demonstrate that the world operates in **predictable** ways. Following the 1929 crash of the U.S. stock market, predictability went out the window, causing several other devastating drops in the value of the market. Only after the market had bottomed out and the government was able to demonstrate predictability by insuring savings through the FDIC did the small investor reenter the market.

Manufacturers also rely on the appeal to predictability: "You Can Be Sure If It's Westinghouse." Anytime we see warranties emphasized, we are probably being persuaded by a consonance-producing appeal regarding predictability. The Canon Sure Shot camera ad shown in Figure 6.9 demonstrates another appeal to predictability. Note the unpredictable snapshots taken by other cameras at the top of the ad. Then look at the features that assure the amateur photographer of predictably good results: auto loading, auto winding, auto focus, and auto exposure. You can't make a mistake with Sure Shot: "perfect pictures every time."

Use of Rewards. A third consonance-producing tactic is the use of **rewards,** or positive reinforcements. You may remember from our discussion of learning theory in Chapter 3 that reinforcement increases the probability that a behavior will be repeated. Persuaders often use positive and complimentary statements to reinforce behavior. In one of his most famous books, *How to Win Friends and Influence People*, Dale Carnegie (1952) offered this advice to his readers:

> Let's cease thinking about our accomplishments, our wants. Let's try to figure out the other man's good points. Then forget flattery. Give honest sincere appreciation. Be "hearty in your approbation and lavish in your praise," and people will cherish your words and treasure them and repeat them over a lifetime — repeat them years after you have forgotten them. (p. 38)

As you can see, Carnegie had put his finger on ways to make one's audience feel good about themselves. This is a good approach to persuading audiences or, as Carnegie put it, *influencing people.*

Ads for products frequently use positive pitches to prompt feelings of consonance and thus reinforce behavior. Look at the travel section from the Sunday newspaper and you'll find numerous examples, such as the ad for a Midwest ski resort that advises the reader to "Go Ahead. This Year Give Yourself the Best Ski Vacation of Your Life — You Deserve It" or the American Express ad that promises "Our London. Now You Can Afford to be Penny Wise and Pound Foolish." These claims and others like them build feelings of psychological comfort in the readers, who now perceive that they deserve the ski vacation they have wanted or that they can now afford to go to London. These offers are persuasive because they reward persuadees and convince them that they deserve good treatment. Even something as cost free as offering appreciation for work done or favor given is rewarding to receivers and tends to increase the probability that similar behavior will occur in the future. That's why successful supervisors seem to be good at giving rewards as well as offering criticisms and why such things as "Customer Appreciation Days" tend to reinforce brand and customer loyalty.

Figure 6.9. *Canon provides predictable results if you use this camera. (Used by permission of Canon U.S.A., Inc.)*

What are some examples of such persuasion in your world? Chances are you can identify numerous examples of consonance-producing persuasion in your everyday life.

Review and Conclusion

In Part II of this book, we are searching for various kinds of unstated and nearly universally held major premises that can serve in persuasive enthymemes. One of these kinds of premises, the process premise, relates to appeals to the emotions and the will—to the psychological processes operating daily in each of us.

One kind of process premise involves our needs and wants. We can see needs and wants operating in Maslow's hierarchy of needs model and in Packard's (sometimes Freudian) listing of human needs. There are other models of human need states as well. A second kind of process premise that can predispose us to action involves our attitudes and beliefs. If persuaders change our beliefs and attitudes about fuel efficiency, they predispose us to buy fuel-efficient autos, furnaces, and hot water heaters. If persuaders want us to continue voting for a certain party, they reinforce our existing beliefs and attitudes. Both of these persuasive types can be used with either attitudes toward objects/issues or attitudes toward situations. It may be important for persuaders to reinforce or change our behavioral intentions. If persuaders can get us to clip a product coupon, their job is more than half done because we intend to buy the product when we clip the coupon.

We further explored the impact of attitudes on very important and less important purchases, voting, and joining decisions as they operate in the Petty and Cacioppo elaboration likelihood model.

Finally, closely related to both attitudes and needs is the human desire for psychological consonance. We seek a world in which our predictions are verified, in which people we like approve of the same things we do, and in which our values and attitudes do not conflict with our behavior. If we feel a lack of balance, we actively seek ways to bring our world into congruity. If we perceive balance to exist, we experience ease and can be easily motivated to continue to act as we have been doing. Persuaders try to create dissonance if they want us to *change* our behavior and try to create consonance if they want us to *maintain* our behavior. Although each of us is unique, our need states, attitudinal clusterings, and desires for psychological balance are similar enough that persuaders can use these processes as first premises for large groups of people.

Questions for Further Thought

1. What is a process premise? Explain.

2. What is the difference between an attitude and a need? Give examples.

3. What does Maslow mean when he calls his hierarchy of needs "prepotent"?

4. Which needs described by Packard are the most ego involving or personal in nature?

5. Give an example of the need for emotional security.

6. Give an example of how advertisers use the need for ego gratification.

7. Give an example of the need for a sense of power.

8. What are three functions of an attitude?

9. What is the difference between an attitude and an opinion?

10. What is the difference between a behavior and a behavioral intention?

11. According to the elaboration likelihood model, which decision path will be used when we consider purchasing ice cream?

12. According to the elaboration likelihood model, what happens if the audience can't be motivated regarding the processing of information in a voting decision (such as reasons to vote for or against a school bond referendum)?

13. According to the elaboration likelihood model, what happens to a joining decision if the audience does not have the ability to respond?

14. Using the elaboration likelihood model as depicted in Figure 6.8, explain the flow of information regarding a current issue.

15. What are some sources of dissonance?

16. What are some sources of consonance?

References

Bellah, R. N., Madsen, R., Sullivan, W. M., Swoder, A., & Tipton, S. M. (1985). *Habits of the heart: Individualism and commitment in American life*. New York: Harper & Row.

Burke, K. (1961). *The rhetoric of religion: Studies in logology*. Boston: Beacon Press.

Cappella, J. N., & Folger, J. P. (1980). An information-processing explanation of attitude behavior inconsistency. In Cushman, D. P., & McPhee, R. D. (Eds.). *Message-attitude-behavior: Theory, methodology, and application*. New York: Academic Press.

Carnegie, D. (1952). *How to win friends and influence people*. New York: Simon & Schuster.

Colley, R. H. (1961). *Defining advertising goals for measured attitude results*. New York: Association of National Advertisers.

Eagley, A. H., & Chaiken, S. (1993). *The psychology of attitudes*. New York: Harcourt Brace Jovanovich.

Eiser, R. J. (1987). *The expression of attitude*. New York: Springer-Verlag.

Fishbein, M., & Ajzen, I. (1975). *Belief, attitude, intention, and behavior: An introduction to theory and research*. Reading, MA: Addison-Wesley.

Frankl, V. (1962). *Man's search for meaning: An introduction to logotherapy*. New York: Washington Square Press.

Freedman, D. H. (1988). Why you watch some commercials—whether you want to or not. *TV Guide*, February 20.

Friedman, J. L., & Dagnoli, J. (1988). Brand name spreading: Line extensions are marketers' lifeline. *Advertising Age*, February 22.

Larson, C. U., & Sanders, R. (1975). Faith, mystery, and data: An analysis of "scientific" studies of persuasion. *Quarterly Journal of Speech, 61*, 178–194.

Lears, T. J. J. (1983). From salvation to self-realization: Advertising and the therapeutic roots of the consumer culture. *The culture of consumption: Critical essays in American culture, 1880–1980*. New York: Pantheon.

Marquand, R. (1988). Needed: Curriculum with character. *The Chicago Tribune*, January 24, p. 5.

Maslow, A. (1954). *Motivation and personality*. New York: Harper & Row.

Osgood, C. E., & Tannenbaum, P. H. (1955). The principle of congruity in the prediction of attitude change. *Psychological Review, 62*, 43.

Packard, V. (1964). *The hidden persuaders*. New York: Pocket Books.

Petty, R., & Cacioppo, J. (1986). *Communication and persuasion*. New York: Springer-Verlag.

Putnam, R. (1995). Bowling Alone: America's declining social capital. *Journal of Democracy* 6 (1), 65–68.

Rokeach, M. (1968). *Beliefs, attitudes, and values: A theory of organization and change.* San Francisco: Jossey-Bass.

Zimbardo, P. G., Ebbesen, E. E., & Maslach, C. (1976). *Influencing attitudes and changing behavior.* Reading, MA: Addison-Wesley.

Zimbardo, P. G., & Leippe, M. R. (1991). *The psychology of attitude change and social influence.* New York: McGraw-Hill.

7

Content Premises in Persuasion

Another type of premise that frequently operates in enthymemes is based on people's ability to think logically or rationally. The elaboration likelihood model suggests that this kind of persuasion utilizes the central processing route and involves considerable analysis and the ability to use our intellectual abilities. Premises relying on logical and analytical abilities are called *content premises*. Many such premises are perceived as valid and true by large segments of the audience and hence serve as major premises in enthymemes. Some persuasion theorists call these premises "arguments," or propositions. Marketers call them "offers." Whatever the label, this chapter examines persuasion that operates by using the persuadee's logical, reasoned, and intellectual abilities.

For example, suppose I want to persuade you to support legalized prostitution. What would you consider good and sufficient reasons for doing so? For some persons, there aren't any good (let alone sufficient) reasons for such a policy—there is no way to persuade this segment of the audience. For others, the policy seems so sensible on the face of it that you don't need to persuade them—they already approve. But what about those who neither approve nor disapprove—the undecided members of the audience? They require more information, evidence, discussion, and debate on the issue before taking a side. In other words, they are asking for proof or some good and sufficient reasons for supporting the proposition. You might tell them about how legalized prostitution would reduce the rate at which people contract AIDS. You might discuss the tax revenues that could be generated by having governmental licensing of prostitutes. And you might point out that such a policy would remove criminal elements from the practice of prostitution. The success or failure of any of these "arguments," "claims," or "propositions" relies on underlying premises believed by the audience: that AIDS is epidemic and deadly, that tax revenues are needed, and that criminal elements in any activity are undesirable. Those widely held beliefs are content premises and serve as parts of enthymemes.

We have all learned certain logical patterns because we have encountered them repeatedly over time. Most of us believe, for example, that events have causes and that when certain things occur, other things invariably follow. Problems also have causes, and when these causes are removed, the problem seems to be eliminated. This particular pattern of rational and intellectual reasoning—called **cause-effect reasoning**—is a powerful first premise often used in persuasion. For example, evidence could be presented to prove that a certain baseball team's pitching staff had experienced many training camp and early season injuries. A logical "effect" of this "cause" would be that the team would end the season with a poor record. It would not be necessary to convince an audience that injuries lead to losses; it would be necessary only to list the various injuries and then conclude that a losing record was likely. This example shows that the cause-effect pattern can be a potent first premise.

This pattern is a type of content premise frequently used by politicians and government officials, in the courts, in business, and even in consumer advertising to some degree. All first premises use assumptions already in the audience's mind as the implicit major premise in an enthymeme. Content premises rely on the patterns by which the *content* of messages is connected with what are believed to be accepted patterns of logical or rational thought. In other words, content premises "sell" because they are assumed to be logical.

The power of the content premise lies not in its ability to stir the emotions, to create psychic "dis-ease," or to appeal to hidden needs. Rather, its power lies in eliciting a rational or logical response from or conclusion by the persuadee.

What Is Proof?

Proof varies from *situation to situation*. What may "prove" a point to people in a weekly fraternity meeting may not "prove" the same point to a university administrator. Several books and at least one film—*J.F.K.*—in the last three decades have tried to "prove" that President John F. Kennedy's assassination was the result of a complex conspiracy. They have successfully persuaded some people but failed with others. Thus, proof varies from *person to person* as well. The Clinton Administration tried to "prove" that cutting the deficit would spur economic growth. Their evidence convinced some people but did not convince others. Proof can thus vary from group to group. In general, though, we can say that proof consists of enough evidence that can be connected through reasoning to lead typical audience members to take the persuader's advice or to believe in what he or she says.

Aristotle identified "places of argument," *topoi*, or topics. Sometimes, for instance, the topic might be some sort of precedent that the audience recognizes as the way things have always been done. The precedent sets a guide for the future, and, unless the audience is given numerous good reasons for breaking the precedent, the precedent controls future instances of similar issues.

What do you think?
What is "proof" for you?

For example, a precedent that you take for granted is that school, from the primary grades to high school, is typically a September-to-June affair. Why? From an economic standpoint, this schedule is foolish, given the expense of heating school buildings during the winter months in most of the United States. However, we all know that there is a precedent for the September-to-June model. It was originally devised during the agrarian phase of our society, when young people's help was essential to get the crops planted, tended, and harvested. Today, the same precedent operates, but with a slightly different twist—June, July, and August are months in which lots of public and private construction and repair work occurs, people go on vacation and need to be temporarily replaced, and many summer service industries (swimming pools, state and national parks, golf courses, and so on) need additional help to serve their customers. Students can fill these temporary jobs. For these and other reasons, the agrarian precedent still serves as our model, even though the need for it is no longer critical and even though it is costly.

Most contemporary theorists agree that proof is composed of two factors: **reasoning** and **evidence.** In the proper mix, these two will lead persuadees to adopt the changes a persuader advocates. There are several ways to look at evidence and reasoning. By examining what persuaders do — how they operate — we can infer motives and discover what they are up to. For example, suppose I wished to persuade you that smoking causes lung cancer. The thrust of my message — the *strategy* of it, so to speak — is to create a cause-effect argument. I want to prove to you that a given effect — lung cancer — has a given cause — cigarette smoking. Along the way I might engage in a variety of tactics (for example, I might show slides of cancerous lung cells, I might give vivid testimony of the pain and suffering involved in lung cancer deaths, or I might offer statistical correlations of the relation between smoking and cancer), but they would all be related to my general strategy or intention. These *tactics* are the source from which proof will ultimately emerge for you as persuadee. Somewhere along the line, I will reach the threshold for you and will have "proved" to you that smoking causes lung cancer. This, of course, may persuade you to stop smoking. In other situations, other elements will persuade you to stop — the key proof may not even be planned by a persuader but can still be the threshold for change. Thus, we see that the nature of evidence and reasoning has remained quite stable. What has changed dramatically in the information age are the *kinds and amount of evidence.*

Before the advent of electronic media, modern advertising, and contemporary propaganda, audiences were accustomed to receiving very specific, verifiable evidence. For example, if you used a person's testimony to prove a point, it was crit-ical to tell the audience why that person qualified as a good source of evidence. Audiences were suspicious of some kinds of evidence — analogies, for example. Today, however, we accept the testimony of a pro athlete when he endorses an investment plan, even though he does not qualify as an expert on economics. And we frequently accept analogies as evidence — animated automobile tires depicted as having cat's claws to grip the road, for instance. Or we see news photos of damage from a flood, tornado, or hurricane, and the pictorial evidence persuades us that we need to support individual, group, and governmental emergency aid to the victims. And politicians offer us evidence supporting a policy or their own incumbency or candidacy. Parents supply what they think are good and sufficient evidence and reasons for not having a roomie of the opposite gender. And students frequently counter with their own evidence and reasons in favor of having such a living arrangement. In all of these cases, proof varies from person to person and from situation to situation. Underlying all of these examples, however, is a pattern of enough evidence combined with reasoning resulting in what we call proof.

Types of Evidence

Different kinds of evidence vary in strength or persuasive power, depending on the context in which they are used. In some situations, for instance, statistics are used to powerful effect; in others, pictorial evidence is relied on; and in yet others, retold or vicarious experience most effectively delivers the persuasive message of the content premise. In all of these instances, persuasion relies on the assumption that one can learn about and act on information gained indirectly and vicariously. This is why stories about the experiences of others are such effective evidence and why they are favored as persuasive devices. Frequently, advertisers use testimonials from well-known people who endorse products. The advertisers assume that consumers will vicariously absorb the experience that the movie star or athlete relates and will buy the product.

But even when we do not learn by or become swayed by the experience of others, our own experience is usually enough to cause us to change. The Lakota Indians were aware of this. As a baby crawled close to the campfire, they did not pull it away with shouts of "Hot! Stay away, baby! Hot!" as we do in our culture. Instead, they watched the baby's progress very closely and allowed the baby to reach into the fire and touch a hot coal, burning itself mildly. They then quickly pulled the baby away and treated the burn. The experience "persuaded" the child to be careful with fire.

Generally, there are two broad forms of evidence: dramatic and rational. The following sections explore these two forms of evidence in more detail.

Dramatic Evidence

Dramatic evidence relies on our tendency to structure our lives in narrative or story form. In previous chapters, we looked at some research theorists who present this case convincingly—Burke and Fisher, for example. Here we will examine several kinds of dramatic evidence, including narratives, testimonials, anecdotes, and participation/demonstration.

Narratives. People have always been fascinated by stories—myths, legends, and ballads, carried on in an oral/aural tradition. With the advent of literate society—writing and later print—other forms of narratives emerged, such as plays, poetry, novels, and most recently, the short story. Technology brought us still other forms, including radio programs, movies, cartoons, soap operas, documentaries, evening news shows, game shows, talk shows, news stories, and athletic events—all with their roots in storytelling.

Evidence that is dramatic in nature invites and encourages vicarious experience on the part of persuadees in an attempt to persuade them to a certain course of action. Such persuasion relies on the persuadees' ability to project themselves into the context or situation described by the persuader—to "feel" what others feel, to "live" the problem vicariously. This type of evidence encourages persuadees to *co-create* proof with the persuader. The result is powerful, and probably long-lasting, persuasion.

Several types of evidence lend themselves to the dramatic approach. For example, a good way to use dramatic evidence is through the narrative. In his book *People of the Lie: The Hope for Healing Human Evil*, noted author and psychotherapist M. Scott Peck (1983) relates "The Case of Bobby and His Parents." The narrative begins with Bobby, who had been admitted to the hospital emergency room the night before for depression. The admitting physician's notes read:

> Bobby's older brother Stuart, 16, committed suicide this past June, shooting himself in the head with his .22 caliber rifle. Bobby initially seemed to handle his sibling's death rather well. But from the beginning of school in September, his academic performance has been poor. Once a "B" student, he is now failing all his courses. By Thanksgiving he had become obviously depressed. His parents, who seem very concerned, tried to talk to him, but he has become more and more uncommunicative, particularly since Christmas. Although there is no previous record of antisocial behavior, yesterday Bobby stole a car by himself and crashed it (he had never driven before), and was apprehended by the police. . . . Because of his age, he was released into his parents' custody, and they were advised to seek immediate psychiatric evaluation for him (p. 48).

Peck goes on to observe that although Bobby appeared to be a typical fifteen-year-old, he stared at the floor and kept picking at several small sores on the back of his hand. When Peck asked Bobby if he felt nervous being in the hospital, he got no answer—"Bobby was really digging into that sore. Inwardly I winced at the damage he was doing to his flesh" (p. 48). After reassuring Bobby that the hospital was a safe place to be, he tried to draw Bobby out in conversation. But nothing seemed to work. Peck got "No reaction. Except that maybe he dug a little deeper into one of the sores on his forearm." Bobby admitted that he had hurt his parents by stealing the car. He only knew that he had hurt them because they yelled at him. When asked what they yelled at him about, he replied, "I don't know." "Bobby was feverishly picking at his sores now and . . . I felt it would be best if I steered my questions to more neutral subjects" (p. 50). They discussed the family pet—a German shepherd whom Bobby took care of but didn't play with because she was his father's dog. Peck then turned the conversation to Christmas, asking what sorts of gifts Bobby had gotten:

BOBBY: Nothing much.
PECK: Your parents must have given you something. What did they give you?
BOBBY: A gun.
PECK: A gun?
BOBBY: Yes.
PECK: What kind of a gun?
BOBBY: A twenty-two.
PECK: A twenty-two pistol.
BOBBY: No, a twenty-two rifle.
PECK: I understand that it was with a twenty-two rifle that your brother killed himself.
BOBBY: Yes.
PECK: Was that what you asked for for Christmas?
BOBBY: No.
PECK: What did you ask for?
BOBBY: A tennis racket.
PECK: But you got the gun instead?

BOBBY: Yes.
PECK: How did you feel, getting the same kind of gun that your brother had?
BOBBY: It wasn't the same kind of gun.
PECK: (I began to feel better. Maybe I was just confused.) I'm sorry, I thought they were the same kind of gun.
BOBBY: It wasn't the same kind of gun. It was *the* gun.
PECK: You mean it was your brother's gun? (I wanted to go home very badly now.) You mean your parents gave you your brother's gun for Christmas—the one he shot himself with?
BOBBY: Yes.
PECK: How did it make you feel getting your brother's gun for Christmas?
BOBBY: I don't know.
PECK: (I almost regretted the question: How could he know? How could he answer such a thing?) No, I don't expect you could know. (p. 52)

Peck then brought the parents in for counseling. However, they seemed unable to realize what message they had sent their remaining son by giving him his brother's gun. Bobby continued therapy until he was sent to live with a favorite aunt.

> By the time he was discharged to Helen's care, three weeks after his admission to the hospital, the sores on his arms and hands were only scars, and he was able to joke with the staff. Six months later I heard from Helen that he seemed to be doing well and that his grades had come up again. From his psychiatrist I heard that he had developed a trusting therapeutic relationship but was only barely beginning to approach facing the psychological reality of his parents and their treatment of him. (p. 59)

When I first read this dramatic example, I literally gasped as I discovered that Bobby's parents had given him a gun for Christmas, and I was totally dumbstruck to learn that it was *the* gun.

Although the story was emotionally charged, you would be hard put to call it "illogical." In fact, it is probably totally logical to conclude that such neglect of other people is harmful, even though that conclusion is based on a single case. If the evidence is dramatic enough or emotional enough, persuadees will not ask for more.

Most of the great preachers, orators, and politicians have also been great storytellers. They use the narrative skillfully to capture an audience's attention and to draw them into a topic. This effect is reinforced with other evidence, and more narratives might be worked in to keep us interested.

Chances are that you have heard speeches or sermons in which the story, or narrative, was skillfully used. Such speeches seem to have the most impact and are remembered the longest. The parables of the New Testament are easy to recall, whereas many of the other verses fade from our memory soon after we hear them. As Ralph G. Nichols, a professor of mine, once said, "The narrative will carry more persuasive freight than any other form of evidence."

Testimony. Another type of dramatic evidence is **testimony.** Here, the persuader might read an eyewitness account aloud or simply recount his or her personal experience. If the issue being discussed is unemployment, persuadees might be swayed if they hear from out-of-work persons. The details of having to wait in line for one's unemployment check, the embarrassment of having to take government-surplus foodstuffs, and other experiences of the unemployed will probably have dramatic persuasive power. As receivers, we vicariously live through what the witness experienced when we hear direct testimony.

Although eyewitness testimony is potent, studies have shown that it is often unreliable and even incorrect. Psychologist Elizabeth F. Loftus (1980) discusses the many cases in which persons have been wrongfully imprisoned on the basis of eyewitness testimony. (Loftus, 1984) As Figure 7.1 illustrates, witnesses often see and hear what they want to see and hear, and often give testimony from their idiosyncratic points of view.

As receivers, we need to carefully examine the testimony used to persuade us. Ask questions such as: Was the witness in a position to see what is claimed? Could the witness be mistaken in any way? Does the witness have a bias that might cloud his or her testimony? Might the witness have a motive for giving the testimony? Is the witness being paid for giving the testimony? What might he or she have to gain from testifying?

Anecdotes. **Anecdotes** are short narratives that make a point in a hurry—maybe in only a sentence or two. For example, there is the anecdote of the optimist who was asked to describe his philosophy: "That's simple. I'm nostalgic about the future." Anecdotes are often funny and are frequently hypothetical, so they are quite different from actual testimony. The key thing about anecdotes is that unlike testimony, we rarely take them as truth. Instead, we tend to process anecdotes as if they are the exclamation points of persuasion. Abraham Lincoln was once trying a case in which the opposing attorney was rather long-winded. Lincoln used this anecdote to make that point to the judge and jury:

> My friend is peculiarly constructed. When he begins to speak, his brain stops working. He makes me think of a little old steamboat we had on the Sangamon River in the early days. It had a five-foot boiler and a seven-foot whistle, and every time it whistled, it also stopped.

In discussing the NRA's opposition to the ban on assault weapons, President Clinton used the anecdote. He recounted the many hunting trips he had been on using standard hunting guns, not assault weapons, and ended by saying, "And you know something? I never saw a turkey or a deer wearing a flak jacket." The anecdote made the

Figure 7.1. *Witnesses see events or persons from their own point of view. (Reprinted by permission of John Jonik from Psychology Today.)*

point very clearly. Assault weapons aren't needed for any legitimate purposes like hunting—they are intended for warfare and for killing people.

Participation and Demonstration. There are several other ways in which persuaders can dramatize evidence. At an antismoking presentation, for instance, audiovisual materials can show cancerous lung tissue. Smokers can **participate** by exhaling cigarette smoke through a clean white tissue and observing the nicotine stains left behind.

Sometimes persuaders dramatize a point by using visual aids to demonstrate the problem and solution. One of my students spoke on the need for people to be aware of when stress is building up and of how to use jogging to reduce it. He displayed a large, deflated balloon that he said represented an average student at NIU. The "student" was inflated a little with the stress of settling into a new dorm room. Another puff of air represented the stress of registration. More air went in for the first exams and fraternity rush. Soon the balloon was ready to pop. The speaker then called on his audience to release their stress through exercise. He ended the speech saying, "Or else, do you know what could happen?" Whereupon he popped the balloon with a pin. The audience's attention never strayed from the balloon or the point of the speech.

Rational Evidence

Not all evidence is dramatic. Sometimes evidence appeals to our logical processes in nondramatic, intellectually oriented ways. For example, newspaper editorials frequently use evidence that appeals to the reader's logical processes. A good example comes from a series of editorials in the *Chicago Tribune* that promoted early childhood education ("The Payoffs for Preschooling," 1984). The lead sentence of the editorial made the major claim that "early childhood education is the surest way

to break the chain of chronic poverty." The case was developed with supportive claims, such as:

> Early childhood education reduces the costs of welfare, special education, and the criminal justice system. . . . Early learning programs reduce the risks of mental malnutrition. . . . These children [those going to preschools], then, need less special and remedial education. They are happier with themselves and their school environment. They get along better with teachers. . . . They are more likely to graduate from high school, get a job or go on to higher education. . . . They are less likely to get caught up in delinquency and crime. (p. 25)

What do you think?

How do you know when an argument is rational?

Research was reported that at-risk students having gone to preschool had

> better grades and fewer failing marks. They were absent less from school. They needed less special education. And they had a better attitude toward school than a group of similar youngsters who did not get the preschooling. (p. 25)

At age nineteen, the children with preschooling were

> more likely to finish high school and to score average or above on competency tests. More of them had jobs or were involved in higher education. And they were less likely to have been arrested, to be on welfare, or to become pregnant. (p. 25)

The logical argument then went on to cite the savings resulting from preschool education and the resulting cut in remedial programs:

> It actually cost less to educate the children who got the preschooling . . . even when the expenses of the early classes [were] included. . . . Preschool cut the cost per student of each succeeding year in school by about 20 percent—about $800 per child every year in savings.

In terms of reduced crime alone, taxpayers will save $3100 for every one of the youngsters who got the preschool training. . . . These are the direct costs and don't count the anguish, fear and suffering that criminals can inflict on victims. Nor does it attempt to measure the psychological benefits of a reduction in crime rate in a community. . . .

Taxpayers have already saved seven times the cost of one year of preschool in the Ypsilanti project and 3½ times the tab for two years. And the savings resulting from reduced needs in welfare, from less crime, and from greater ability to earn will continue for the rest of the lives of these young people — even reach into the lives of the following generation. (p. 25)

Notice how these claims appeal to our logical processes. The writer knows that we receivers have a major premise in our heads about costs versus benefits. We desire that any idea, product, or program have benefits that justify the costs. Knowing that we have this internal premise, the writer makes claims of great benefits for the preschool idea. The writer also knows that we expect to see some sort of evidence to back up such claims and that we will probably respect this evidence if it is reported "scientifically."

There are no narratives in the editorial. There are no anecdotes. The only testimony is the report of the Ypsilanti project, which is not testimony from an eyewitness but rather is a statistical summary.

Appeals to our logical processes can be seen in other persuasive messages — in advertising, for example. Look at Figure 7.2. The Campbell Soup Company knows that persons concerned with health and nutrition are aware of the much-publicized need for increasing the amount of fiber in the American diet. Most of the literature on this subject has recommended eating high-fiber foods such as whole wheat bread and bran cereals. However, many people don't like dry cereal,

let alone dry bran cereals. Campbell's offers similar benefits but with different costs — you can get fiber by eating Manhandler soups such as Bean with Bacon or Split Pea with Ham.

As you can see from these examples, the appeal to logical processes relies on a reasoning pattern such as "the past is a guide to the future" or "the cost is less than the benefits." What are some other logical patterns that persuaders often use?

Types of Reasoning

Recall our definition of proof: enough evidence *connected with reasoning* to lead an audience to believe or act on a persuader's advice. We will now explore the second step in the process of logical persuasion: connecting the pieces of evidence by reasoning.

Several patterns of reasoning seem to be deeply believed in our culture. One school of research suggests that there is a linguistic explanation for reasoning. The premise is that the "deep structure" of our language is accompanied by deep logical structures (Clark, 1969; Reynolds and Burgoon, 1983). This possibility is dramatically exhibited when people violate the accepted "deep structure" of logical reasoning and are hence labeled as "off the wall" or "way out in left field," or when a logical "deep structure" is violated and humor results. Most ethnic jokes are based on this kind of violation, like the one about Lars Larson, who was telling his friends about his favorite bar where he and his wife went every Wednesday for "Free Sex Nite." Each stool was numbered, he explained, and several times the owner would draw a number and the person occupying that stool got to go in back for free sex. His friends wondered if he had ever won. "No. But my wife has won 42 times this year already. I never saw such luck." The humor results from Lars's missing a deep structural logical premise.

MADE OF THE FINEST FIBER

If you're like most people who eat right, you probably give high fiber high priority.

And like most people, when you think of fiber, you probably automatically think of bran cereals.

Well, there's another good source of dietary fiber you should know about. Delicious Campbell's® Bean with Bacon Soup.

In fact, Campbell's has four soups that are high in fiber.

And you can see from the chart that follows exactly how each one measures up to bran cereals.

So now when you think of fiber, you don't have to think about having it just at breakfast.

Instead, you can do your body good any time during the day. With a hot, hearty bowl of one of these Campbell's Soups.

You just might feel better for it—right to the very fiber of your being.

FIBER IN A SUGGESTED SERVING			
CAMPBELL'S SOUP		BRAN CEREALS	
Bean with Bacon	9g	100% Brans	11g
Split Pea with Ham	6g	40% Brans	6g
Green Pea	5g	Raisin Brans	5g
Low Sodium Green Pea	7g	Others	5–10g
This comparison includes soluble and insoluble fiber			

CAMPBELL'S SOUP IS GOOD FOOD

Campbell's has a full line of low sodium soups for those people who are on a salt-restricted diet or have a concern about sodium.

Figure 7.2. *This appeals to our logic. What rational argument does it present? (Used by permission of the Campbell Soup Company.)*

Luck doesn't explain everything—sometimes there are other forces at work.

Or consider the following letter to the editor of a local newspaper regarding ways of removing nuisance deer from public parks in the area (Scott, 1989):

Let's look at some hard facts:

- It cost taxpayers $50,000 to shoot the deer at Ryerson Woods.
- It would cost taxpayers $30,000 a year to shoot the deer at Rock Cut Park.
- The Department of Conservation made $20,000 a year from hunting at Rock Cut.
- Hunters already have won the right to hunt on public land in the Supreme Court.
- Hunters pay millions of dollars annually to buy state parks.

Pretty good so far, even if you don't agree with the man's position. He has begun with what appears to be an inductive line of argument using "effect-to-cause" reasoning (that is, citing a set of effects and then concluding by identifying a probable cause). He shows the varying degrees of effectiveness of several alternative plans used in the past (his first three points), and then goes on to state a fact about the law relating to hunting on public lands. Finally, he makes a claim that hunters pay for state parks. This last point is a little unclear, but he probably means that state parks are at least partially funded by revenue from hunting licenses, the high federal and state taxes on guns and ammunition, and the hunter's own property, sales, and income taxes. We anticipate that he is about to claim something like

Therefore, hunters are positive persons and deserve to hunt in state parks, especially when their hunting helps remove nuisance deer from these parks in economic and even revenue-producing ways.

The fact that we anticipate such a "logical" conclusion is probably evidence of at least one type of deep logical structure. Now notice what happens when our expectations are unmet in the conclusions the author actually draws from the five points noted above:

If you were an animal, would you prefer to live ten years free, even if you died a slow death, or would you want to live it penned up, sleeping in your own manure? I think most Americans would want to be free. That's also the way God wanted it. That's why he said it is a good thing to be a hunter. For Jesus Christ is alive and well, but Bambi never was.

The conclusion is wacky; it seems befuddled and barely related to the evidence. What do living free and dying slowly have to do with the argument? How does sleeping in one's own manure relate to the issue? Where did God say that it was good to be a hunter? What does the Jesus Christ versus Bambi comparison mean? None of these conclusions flow from the evidence.

It is clear that the author's conclusion demonstrates several serious violations of the deep structural logical expectations held by most people; our preference for a line of reasoning has been violated. But what does this example have to do with our study of persuasion from the receiver's point of view? Remember, we are looking for content premises—logical patterns that serve as the first premises in enthymemes. The deep structural logical preferences serve in this way: We believe and act on what we perceive to be logical arguments presented to us by persuaders. As a result, it is useful for receivers to be aware of those deep structure logical patterns that most people prefer and that are used by persuaders every day. Let us explore some of these logical "deep structures" in more detail.

Cause-to-Effect Reasoning

Cause-to-effect reasoning is powerful in our culture; even our language depends on it. For example, we rarely say, "The ball was thrown and the window was broken," which is a passive-voice sentence. Instead we put the cause out front and let it create the effect. We say, "Johnny threw the ball and broke the window." This active-voice sentence tells us that Johnny *caused* the ball to go through the air and break the window. This construction gives us much more information; this is an active-voice sentence. It tells us *by whom* or *what*.

Persuaders frequently use cause-to-effect reasoning to identify events, trends, or facts that have caused certain effects. They tell us that if a cause is present, we can expect certain effects to follow. If the effects are bad and we want to do something about them, we usually try to remove the cause.

Cases of food poisoning are frequently solved this way. We know that something caused some people who ate at a restaurant to become violently sick, while others who ate at the same time didn't get ill. So we search for the one food item that the group that was struck ate and that the other group did not eat.

Advertising frequently uses the cause-to-effect form of reasoning. Consider an ad for a cellulite-reducing complex. It identifies a cause for the effect of dimpled-appearing thighs—a weak skin support system—and then goes on to offer a way to remove the cause and with it the undesirable effect—regular use of the product. The advertiser knows the audience has a deep logical structure for cause/effect reasoning and skillfully uses that structure as the first premise in the enthymeme underlying the ad.

What do you think?

Have you used cause-to-effect reasoning recently?

Effect-to-Cause Reasoning

Another type of reasoning that is less used (and sometimes flawed) is called **effect-to-cause reasoning.** Here, the persuader cites some known

effects and tries to work back to the cause. For example, in the world of the television spot commercial, Bob Garfield (1988), a staff writer for *Advertising Age,* gives high praise to a spot for Stokely's Singles, microwaveable single-serving vegetables. "Moms don't like heating and reheating broccoli for their busy families' various dinner shifts," writes Garfield. "They hate trying to please four finicky palates with one frozen vegetable dish. And they despise the grimaces that greet their bowls of succotash." Those are the effects. How to identify the cause, remove it, and substitute Stokely's Singles was the problem. In a "slice of life" ad, the family members would come off as ingrates who were lucky to be getting a meal at all. So Stokely's did an exaggerated "slice of life" ad using humor. "When mom dishes up the vegetables, Dad and the kids grimace outsize grimaces, Mom responds with an outlandish sneer and slings the whole bowl over her shoulder in disgust. The problem is real. The identification is immediate. The exaggeration is amusing. And the solution, lo and behold, is Stokely's" (p. 86).

Reasoning from Symptoms

Persuaders sometimes identify a series of **symptoms** or signs and then try to conclude something from them. For example, politicians may cite how much worse things are now than they were when their opponent took office: Unemployment is up, crime is rampant, and recent polls show that people have lost faith in their ability to control their own destinies. The hope is that the voters will blame the incumbent for the troubles.

Returning again to Garfield's high-quality TV spots, we find reasoning from symptoms in an ad for South Carolina Federal. The ad agency understood that "People pay no attention to disingenuous *ersatz* bankers. To persuade anybody that it is more human than the competition, a bank first must get their attention. Then it has to *act* more human" (p. 86). The usual bank ad relies on research to find out what people dislike about banking and then has some "bankerish-looking actor" claim that "Our bank is different because we value our customers." And because the ads all look alike, consumers overlook them. South Carolina Federal's approach was different. Instead of using humans, the bank used animals to react to the things consumers dislike about banking. One ad featured an orangutan in its opening spot. "How does your bank react when you ask for a home equity loan?" asks an offscreen wimpy voice. The orangutan yawns. Then the voice asks about bank hours: "Do they have all-day banking?" The orangutan shakes its head "No!" "Free checking?" The orangutan blows a raspberry at the camera. And so it goes, with the voice eliciting other symptoms of disliked banking practices followed by a humorous look or gesture by the orangutan until the final line: "Well, if we were you, we'd bank with us."

Criteria-to-Application Reasoning

Sometimes persuaders establish what appears to be a reasonable set of criteria for purchasing a product, voting for a candidate, or supporting a cause and then offer their product, candidate, or cause as one that meets these criteria. For example, following phone system deregulation, an ad for the Bell System established several criteria for good telephone service:

1. Reasonable rates and reliable service

2. Free information services for long-distance areas

3. Ability to handle calls to all parts of the country, not just those areas serviced by the system

The spokesman, a well-known TV actor, reminded viewers of the Bell System's past dependability and of its ability to reach anywhere in the country, as well as foreign countries. Finally, after noting the free information service Bell provides, he offered viewers the "ten-dollar hour"; they could get sixty minutes of long-distance telephone time anywhere in the country for only $10 if they called a special number and made the request. Note that by setting up what appears to be a reasonable set of criteria initially, the persuader has already won half the battle. Receivers, having accepted the criteria, logically infer that Bell is a good choice when they get the reminders of past dependability, free information services, international dialing, and—the final hook—the ten-dollar hour.

Reasoning from Comparison or Analogy

Sometimes persuaders use **comparison** as their logical reason for some conclusion. In this form of reasoning, an example is analyzed and described and conclusions are then drawn about that example or situation. The persuader then compares the example with another situation, pointing out similarities and reasons that the conclusions about the example apply to the current situation. During the 1996 presidential primaries, numerous candidates proposed revising the U.S. tax code in order to simplify its complex rate structure and to shift tax burdens. In arguments for various plans, argument by comparison was a frequent logical appeal. Tables, charts, and graphs were used to compare how much tax an individual would pay under the old system with how much he or she would pay under the new one. Supposedly, voters who saw their position improved as compared to their position under the old system would vote for the candidate whose plan seemed best.

We also frequently see argument by comparison in advertising: A product is compared with its competitors in terms of cost, effectiveness, safety, and so on. The big battle over the light beer market is largely an argument from comparison, with one brand claiming fewer calories and better taste than others. The same thing is seen in ads for low-tar and low-nicotine cigarettes.

In the case of reasoning by **analogy,** something familiar is used to demonstrate something that is unfamiliar or complex. For example, suppose we wanted to compare the military fighting still going on in the former Yugoslavia with the Vietnam War. We might point out that in both cases, guerrilla warfare was the predominant mode of fighting and that government leaders were corrupt. This is a *literal* analogy. In other words, we are comparing a familiar past war (Vietnam) with an unfamiliar present (and possibly future) war in Bosnia-Herzegovina.

Using a *figurative* analogy, we would compare a familiar but unrelated and simple thing to something that is unfamiliar and complex. For example, political races are often compared to horse races by using such expressions as "front-runners," "early starters," "late comers," and "dark horses." Either of these persuasive means of comparison can help simplify the issue or example being discussed. In either case, you as a receiver should ask yourself if the comparison or analogy is appro-priate. For example, in the Vietnam-Yugoslavia comparison, certain elements in the two situations are not really parallel. Vietnam was a jungle war; Yugoslavia is a mountain war. Vietnamese have oriental values; residents of the former Yugoslavia have a mixture of Ottoman and Catholic values. In the horse race analogy, there are numerous differences. In political races, there is only one winner, and those who "place" and "show" receive nothing. Not all candidates start from the same "gate," and so on.

Deductive Reasoning

A familiar form of appeal to logic is **deductive reasoning,** which can be defined as reasoning from the general to the specific. In a legislative body, a persuader might support a bill or a motion by saying something like "The legislation before us is desperately needed to prevent the state budget from going into a deficit situation." Then, the persuader goes on to provide the specifics. An editorial might begin, "Sycamore needs to pass this school-bond referendum in order to save its extracurricular sports, its music and art programs, its newspaper, and its dramatics program" and then go on to describe the details. One of the problems with the deductive approach is that receivers who feel the least bit negative about the persuader's general point may lose interest and not pay attention to the specifics that are at the heart of the issue. Or the initial generalization may prompt rebuttal before the persuader has the opportunity to provide the details of the case.

Inductive Reasoning

Inductive reasoning gets the specifics out on the table before bringing up the generalized conclusion. For example, in the school-bond case the persuader might begin by saying, "Many of you know that it costs over $60,000 just to run the athletic program. The budget for the marching band is over $12,000 for travel, instruction, and uniforms. I was surprised to learn that it cost over $2000 just to pay the royalties for the spring musical. We have cut and cut until there is nothing left to cut. The last referendum increase was fourteen years ago — inflation has risen over 200 percent since then. Unless we pass this referendum, the district now faces elimination of these valuable extracurricular programs." With the specific evidence apparent, the generalization flows logically from it.

Tests of Reasoning and Evidence

Of course, logical persuasion can be exploited by intentionally or unintentionally misusing either evidence or reasoning or perhaps by misusing both evidence *and* reasoning. Let's look at some examples of the misuse of evidence so that we can spot it when it occurs. The following examples of misuse of evidence and how to test evidence are not exhaustive.

Use of Statistics

One of the mainstays of logical persuasion is the use of statistics. We tend to believe statistics without questioning them. But several questions ought to be asked when statistical evidence is offered.

First ask, "Is the sample from which the statistics are drawn a representative one?" In other words, is the sample selected in any way that might bias the results? We need to know whether the statistic/sample is a reliable representation of reality. We might want to know how the sample was selected. From the phone directory? Not everyone has a telephone, some people have several, and others have unlisted phone numbers.

Another misuse of statistical evidence is using a single instance as an example of all instances. We hear of an enormously wealthy person who pays nothing in taxes and are led to believe no other enormously wealthy persons pay taxes.

Another misuse of statistics is biased sampling, which occurs when a nonrepresentative portion of the population is sampled. Responses from a sample drawn from subscribers to *The National Rifleman* will be very different from one drawn from subscribers to *Horticulture* or *The Organic Gardener*.

The mode of presentation can also misrepresent statistics. For example, the graph in Figure 7.3 was used to demonstrate the degree to which homosexuality exists in the general population. The shaded portion indicates persons who have had at least one homosexual encounter. These range from persons who have had just one such encounter to those for whom all sexual encounters are homosexual. The unshaded portion of the graph indicates heterosexual persons. The graph suggests that the proportion is at least 50 percent. Thus, it visually misrepresents the case and distorts the meaning of the statistics. What the graph fails to provide is information about the size of the sample in each segment.

There are many other ways to distort statistics using graphic presentations of the numbers, so receivers need to be alert not only to what statistics really mean — for example, the way they were sampled and the type of measurement used — but also to the mode of presentation.

Use of Testimony

As noted earlier, one problem with the use of testimonials is that the person "testifying" may not be reporting accurate information. Also, seemingly insignificant shifts in wording can "lead" a witness to certain answers. Most of the time we don't have the opportunity to "cross examine" the person giving the testimonial. Instead, when we see or hear a person endorsing a product, a candidate, or an organization, we are forced to make up our mind right away as to whether the person is qualified to give the testimonial. When testimonials are used to persuade you, ask is the person giving the testimonial an authority on the subject, and if so, how reliable is he or she? Was the person giving the testimonial close enough to have witnessed the evidence he or she is testifying about? Is it possible that the person giving the testimonial is biased for

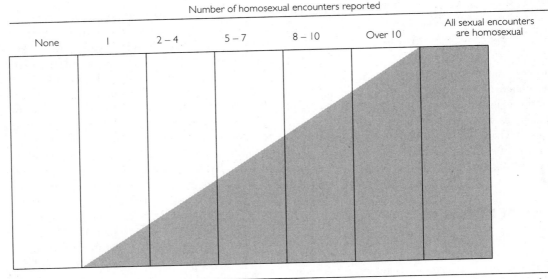

Figure 7.3. *This graph is misleading because it implies that half the population is homosexual, whereas the statistics being represented are much lower than that.*

some reason or another, and if so, is the bias pro or con?

As persuadees, we need to be alert to the ways in which testimonials can be distorted or misused. We know that in many cases the testimonial is being given only because the sponsor has paid the person to give it. So the next time you see a sports personality endorsing a product, don't assume that he or she uses it on a daily basis. And try to determine the degree of authority the person has about the product.

Use of Comparisons and Analogies

As noted earlier, the misuse of comparisons and analogies (sometimes labeled the fallacy of faulty comparison or faulty analogy) is common in persuasion. For example, politicians frequently compare the national budget to the budget necessities of the individual family. They argue that the family has to live within its resources, so the government should live within *its* resources. However, individuals can't create money like governments can, they don't have to provide for national defense, and they don't have to build the roads they drive on. If they did, there would be no money left for the necessities of life. Comparing the government's budget to the individual family's budget is like comparing apples to oranges.

The same thing applies to faulty analogies. For example, one father of a college freshman maintained that his college experience was analogous to that of his son: Since the father had gotten by on $5 a week spending money, the son should surely be able to make it on $10 a week. This faulty analogy has several dimensions: Inflation had quadrupled, not doubled in the years since the dad was in college; dormitories no longer provided clean towels and linens, so some of the spending money had to go to laundry costs; and athletic, theater, and concert tickets were no longer provided for a single low price but had to be purchased separately.

Figurative analogies like the horse race one noted above can also be confusing. Granted, there are some similarities, but the analogy is misleading, taken in its entirety. It is obvious that persuadees need to examine comparisons and analogies to see whether they do indeed lead to a certain conclusion or whether there is some faulty comparison or analogy being used.

Common Fallacies Used in Persuasion

Webster's Collegiate Dictionary Tenth Edition defines "fallacy" as "deceptive appearance . . . a false or mistaken idea . . . an often plausible argument using false or invalid inference." It is this last definition that concerns us here: believable arguments or premises that are based on invalid reasoning. In spite of the fact that these fallacies have been identified for centuries, they still pop up frequently in advertisements, political persuasion, interpersonal persuasion, and elsewhere. Briefly, here are the more common fallacies that we encounter almost daily.

Post Hoc Ergo Propter Hoc

"Post hoc ergo propter hoc," commonly called the *post hoc fallacy*, translates to "after this, therefore because of this." As the translation implies, because one event follows another, the first event is assumed to be the cause of the second. We run into this fallacy almost daily in the world of advertising. For example, in a recent radio ad for *TV Guide*, a salesman for computer hardware seated

next to a French businessman on an airplane describes how his firm could modify the Frenchman's computer system. The Frenchman wants to know about American television, so the salesman gives him a spare copy of *TV Guide* and makes a $30 million sale—all because of *TV Guide*.

In political persuasion, the *post hoc* fallacy is often used to blame the current state of affairs on the incumbent. For example, the reason the school system is out of money is that the superintendent and school board wasted all the money from the referendum eight years ago on unneeded frills. Not necessarily so.

A humorous use of the *post hoc* fallacy can be seen in Dana Carvey's impersonation of George Bush on *Saturday Night Live*. In one skit, he was shown standing in front of the torn-down Berlin Wall. "Before Bush, Wall," says Carvey, followed by "With Bush, No Wall." "After this, therefore because of this?" Not always.

Ad Hominem

The Latin term "ad hominem," translated "against the man," means any attack against the person instead of the person's argument. The purpose is to lead the audience to take certain actions just because of a character quirk or other flaw in a person presenting the opposite viewpoint. The cartoons in Figure 7.4 are good examples of the *ad hominem* being used against me. As faculty president of the policy-making body on my campus, I was responsible for implementing the recommendations of a task force on committee structure and size. One such recommendation was to alter the duties of the publication board of the student newspaper, the *Northern Star*, so that it would become involved in the selection of the editor and

What do you think?

Identify ad hominem as it is used in editorial cartoons.

Figure 7.4. *Cartoons using the* ad hominem *fallacy. (Reprinted by permission of Kevin Craver.)*

be responsible for periodic review of editorial policy. The paper's editors and cartoonist felt that this was an infringement on the First Amendment of the U.S. Constitution and set out on a campaign to attack me, not the proposed change, as can be seen from the cartoons. You can see that the target of the cartoons is a person, not an issue. They are a classic case of the use of the *ad hominem*. By the way, the reform was passed, and I sort of enjoyed the temporary notoriety. This tactic is not usually seen, read, or heard in advertising because products, not people, are being promoted. It is frequently used in ideological persuasion, where one leader attacks another. Whenever attacks are made on a person's character instead of on his or her stands on issues, be aware that the *ad hominem* fallacy is probably at work. If persuaders have nothing substantive to debate, they frequently turn to attacking the personality of the opponent.

Ad Populum

As its name implies, the *ad populum fallacy* is persuasion that relies on whatever happens to be in vogue at that time. There are many examples in our history of the use of the *ad populum*, some important, some tragic, and some trivial. For example, consider just a few trends that justified themselves at one time or another using the logic of the *ad populum* ("Do it now; everyone else is!"): Prohibition, the speakeasy, and flappers in the 1920s; the baby boom, rock 'n' roll, and the suburbs in the 1950s; yuppies, personal computers, the fall of communism in Eastern Europe, and recycling in the 1980s; and rap music, virtual reality/interactive media, the World Wide Web, and others in the 1990s.

Appeals using the *ad populum* also abound in the worlds of fashion, popular culture, and advertising and usually result in persuasion of the masses (wearing one's baseball cap backward, owning Air Jordan athletic shoes, body piercing, 900-number telephone "services," and e-mail erotica interest groups, to name a few). Whenever someone urges us to "get on the bandwagon" or to "follow the crowd," the *ad populum* fallacy is probably operating.

The Undistributed Middle

The fallacy of the *undistributed middle* occurs in most cases of what we call "guilt by association," whereby the persuader argues that just because an individual, group, or philosophy shares one aspect or attribute with another, it also shares all other aspects or attributes. Consider the following argument: "Gut Malloy is a member of Tappa Kanna Bru fraternity, and fraternity boys are heavy drinkers, so he must be a heavy drinker, too." Common sense tells us that there is something missing here. The heart of the fallacy lies in the middle of the argument, where the phrase "fraternity boys are heavy drinkers" is used to suggest that all fraternity members share all attributes beyond group membership with all other members of fraternities. In other words, the argument assumes that "heavy drinking" is equally distributed or practiced by all members of fraternities, when in fact, some members are moderate or infrequent drinkers or don't drink at all (Jensen, 1981). Of course, this example is trivial, but persuaders use the guilt-by-association or undistributed middle principle to sway opinion and alter behavior in significant ways. For example, in the 1992 presidential campaign, some persuaders suggested that because Bill Clinton had demonstrated against the Vietnam War during his college years, he was therefore unpatriotic. After all, since some antiwar demonstrators are unpatriotic, they must all be unpatriotic.

The fallacy of the undistributed middle also frequently persuades us to purchase products, vote for candidates, and support "good causes." The fallacy lies behind any appeal suggesting that buying and using a certain brand will make you like others who buy and use it.

The Straw Man Argument

In the *straw man fallacy*, persuaders set up a weak, or "straw man," case they know they can easily defeat. They then represent this case as the position of the other side of the debate. Finally, they bring out their key evidence and reasoning and defeat the bogus case, along with the opposition.

Political persuasion is riddled with this tactic. Candidate A says that candidate B's position on defense spending is thus and so, then promptly shows how wrong the straw man position is by presenting impressive statistics, examples, and so on. Clearly, anyone holding to such a weak position shouldn't even be considered for public office.

In the world of advertising, where it is usually considered bad strategy to mention your competition, we occasionally see, read, or hear a straw man case. A good example is a television ad in which the announcer says something like "Do you think this Chevy pickup truck can climb this tough mountain carrying a Dodge pickup on its back?" Then we see the Chevy climb the mountain with the Dodge on its back. Of course, if the Chevy couldn't do the job, they would never have aired the ad.

Most comparative advertising usually depends on the straw man fallacy. In the cola and burger wars, the opposition is often set up as a straw man waiting to be demolished by the advertiser's brand.

The straw man fallacy is also commonly used in ideological arguments. Antiabortion advocates frequently argue that abortion is an inhuman way to practice birth control and should thus be outlawed. However, pro-choice advocates have never recommended abortion as a means of birth control — that claim is a straw man argument that will naturally be demolished by pro-life advocates. Or consider the controversial antiabortion films *The Silent Scream* or *Conceived in Liberty*. The very titles seem to set up a straw man. In one scene, a fetus that is about to be aborted seems to be trying to desperately escape from a surgical instrument that has been inserted into the womb. The narrator, a medical doctor, uses powerful language to describe the struggle and the instrument. He relates what will happen when the fetus is removed, describing how its skull will be crushed by forceps. Naturally, the audience feels revulsion at the thought of the brutal crushing of the fetus. The natural response will be to reject abortion. What the narrator does not tell the audience is that they are seeing a third-trimester abortion, which represents only about 10 percent of all abortions. Again, a straw man argument has been set up so that it can be easily defeated.

Other Common Fallacies

Other types of fallacious reasoning include using partial or distorted facts (such as only telling one side of the story or quoting out of context); substituting ridicule or humor for argument (such as depicting the opposition candidate as "a slow-dancing bureaucrat"); appealing for sympathy (such as O. J. Simpson's video following his acquittal); using prejudices or stereotypes (such as that college professors are absentminded, so they can't be counted on); appealing to tradition, or the *ad verecundiam* ("That's the way we've always done it around here"); begging the question or evading the issue (such as "National health care is nothing less than socialism!"); using a *non sequitur* (an irrelevancy); using a false dilemma (such as "We either outlaw deficit spending or declare the country bankrupt"); and others (Kahane, 1992; Thompson, 1971).

Logical Syllogisms

There are three major types of syllogism that commonly form the foundations of content premise persuasion: conditional syllogisms, disjunctive syllogisms, and categorical syllogisms.

Conditional Syllogisms

Conditional syllogisms use "If A then B" reasoning. Like other syllogisms, they have a major premise, a minor premise, and a conclusion. The major premise states a condition or relationship that is presumed to exist in the world. Receivers are assumed to accept the existence of the condition or relationship in most cases. The following is a conditional syllogism in its classical form:

If the U.S. government can't control terrorism with our present laws, then we need to give it new laws that are tough enough to stop terrorism. (major premise)

The Oklahoma City and similar bombings as well as destruction of Flight 800 are proof that the government can't control terrorism with present laws. (minor premise)

Therefore, we need to give the government new tougher laws to stop terrorism. (conclusion)

The first element in the major premise is called the *antecedent,* and the second element is called the *consequent.* In affirming the antecedent, which is what we did in the minor premise by referring to the bombings and Flight 800, we can draw a *valid* conclusion that tough laws are needed.

I hope you are saying to yourself, "Hey! That's not necessarily the case." If so, you are making a distinction between **truth** and **validity.** The syllogism is valid, but the premises are not necessarily true. Validity depends on the general rules of reasoning and not on the truth of the premises. Advertisers know this and frequently make perfectly valid arguments using false premises. A good example is the statement on a package of Trilene fishing line: "If you are seeking a world record, you should use one of the pound tests coded in the chart at right." You can detect the *If . . . then . . .* format in the sentence. We all know that using the right line — Trilene — won't assure me of a world-record fish. But the advertiser uses the conditional form on the package because receivers tend to accept it as logical and

factual. In truth, no line can assure anyone of a world record.

With conditional syllogisms, there are two valid forms of conclusion drawing. First, you can affirm the *if* part of the major premise and conclude the *then* part of the major premise. A related but *invalid* procedure would be to deny the antecedent and conclude that the consequent has been denied. Suppose, in the terrorism example, that we had affirmed the consequent instead of the antecedent in the minor premise by saying, "We have given new tough laws to the U.S. government" (which did occur in the Anti-terrorism Act of 1995) and then concluded, "Therefore the U.S. government will be able to control terrorism." The fallacy becomes apparent immediately — the existence of tough laws doesn't necessarily indicate the ability to control terrorism. The reasoning here is invalid because there may be an *intervening cause.* In fact, there are several such intervening causes for the terrorist bombings, including the ready availability of fertilizer (for nitrogen) and diesel oil — the key ingredients for a bomb.

In a related but also invalid procedure, suppose we had denied the consequent in the minor premise by saying, "We have not given enough tough new laws to the U.S. government" and then concluded, "Therefore the U.S. government will not be able to control terrorism." The fallacy is less apparent but still there — the lack of tough laws doesn't necessarily indicate the inability to control terrorism. Again, there could be intervening causes, such as those previously noted. Although invalid, this form of syllogism is frequently used in advertisements. A romance is "saved" by a certain mouthwash or shampoo, or a family feels more loving toward the mother because she decides to use a certain product in her cooking.

Thus, although a conditional syllogism may be perfectly valid in a logical sense, it may be untrue. Be alert to this trap. Persuaders may use a logically valid syllogism to camouflage untrue premises. Ask yourself whether the premises are true *and* whether the argument is valid.

As you have probably noticed, the conditional syllogism is similar to the cause-effect linkage described earlier.

Disjunctive Syllogisms

The disjunctive syllogism has as its basic form "Either A is true or B is true." This is the major premise of a disjunctive syllogism and is usually accompanied by some set of proof or evidence that suggests the probable presence of A or B or the probable absence of A or B. The conclusion is then drawn on the basis of these probabilities. A school board could threaten to do away with extracurricular activities unless the voters approve a certain referendum increasing property taxes, saying, "Either you vote to increase property taxes or you lose the extracurricular activities." The voters then provide the minor premise of the syllogism through their vote. The strategy is often effective because the issue is so clear-cut.

Most disjunctive syllogisms have a key weakness. Few situations present a clear either-or, even in cases of life and death. For example, politicians often state that to deal with the problems of the national debt and deficit spending, we must **either** increase taxes **or** decrease spending, suggesting there are no other workable solutions. However, many economists argue that increasing the gross national product would generate more income for the government and hence reduce deficit spending, which could lead to a decrease in the national debt. Another solution might be to institute a national lottery (though some argue that this is nothing more than another form of taxation, albeit voluntary). Strict either-or logic cannot take into account other belief systems or more than two alternatives in a situation. Examine persuasion framed in the either-or mode to search for other alternatives or differing belief systems under which the disjunctive model would not work.

Categorical Syllogisms

Categorical syllogisms deal with parts and wholes or sets and subsets. Both the major and minor premises deal with membership or nonmembership in one of two categories or clusters. The conclusion relates the clusters of both premises into a new finding or result, as shown in the following:

> All men are included in the class of mortal beings. (major premises)
>
> Socrates is included in the class of men. (minor premise)
>
> Therefore, Socrates is a mortal being. (conclusion)

Although this example is frequently used to demonstrate the categorical syllogism, it is not one that you will find many opportunities to use, and it is not likely to be brought up in any controversial arguments or debates. Its format, however, is frequently seen, read, or heard in various kinds of persuasion. Take, for example, the U.S. Marines' recruiting slogan: "We're looking for a few good men." The implied categorical syllogism is as follows:

> All U.S. Marines are included in the class of good men. (major premise)
>
> You are a good man. (minor premise)
>
> Therefore, you should become a Marine. (conclusion)

Because you are a member of some category, it is assumed that you must or should be a member of another.

IBM recently used this technique when it ran a two-page public relations ad that featured two pairs of baby booties, one pink and one blue, and the question, "Guess which one will grow up to be the engineer?" The ad goes on to explain that boys are encouraged to excel in math and science, whereas girls are not, thus accounting for the discrepancy in the numbers of men and women engineers. The ad then points out that IBM has supported over ninety programs to strengthen women's skills in these areas and intends to continue such support. Two uses of the categorical syllogism can be seen here. First, there is one concerning engineers: "Persons encouraged to excel in math and science are likely to become engineers" (major premise); "Males are encouraged to excel in math and science" (minor premise); "Males are likely to become engineers" (conclusion). On another level, the ad says: "Good companies encourage women to excel" (major premise); "IBM encourages women to excel" (minor premise); "IBM is therefore a good company" (conclusion). Although the first syllogism is valid (and probably true as well), the second is invalid. IBM uses the illusion of a logical syllogism to make its case. While good companies do encourage women to excel, simply doing that does not necessarily guarantee the label "good."

The Toulmin Format

Most of us do not encounter persuasion that is overtly syllogistic. Instead, the syllogism often is the underlying structure in persuasive arguments. British philosopher Stephen Toulmin (1964) developed a model that identifies the kind of logical persuasion we encounter in everyday events. According to Toulmin, any argument aimed at our logical reasoning processes is divided into three basic parts: the claim, the data, and the warrant.

Basic Elements

First in Toulmin's model is the **claim** or the proposition that the persuader hopes will be believed, adopted, or followed. Claims usually need to be supported by evidence, or **data,** the second part of the model. Data give the receiver reasons for following the advice of the claim. However, sometimes the relationship between the claim and the data is not clear, so the persuader must explain the relationship. This Toulmin called the **warrant.** These three elements become clear as we examine persuasion at work.

Take, for example, the recent debate over cultural diversity and how the educational system should deal with non-English-speaking students. The following letter to the editor addressing the problem demonstrates the use of the claim, the data, and the warrant of Toulmin's system:

Recent articles, editorials, letters to the editor, and other commentary have argued that there is a need/right to have courses taught in one's own native language. A better alternative would be to require all students to be proficient in at least two languages, one of which must be English. Let me point out some relevant facts.

1. English is the international language of diplomacy, science, commerce, politics, literature, travel, and popular culture. Ninety percent of all computer files are in English as are 100 percent of the indexes to them. A Chinese pilot flying a Chinese airliner into Chinese airspace and in contact with a Chinese air traffic controller must communicate in English, not Chinese — it's international law.

2. With the exception of Chinese, English is the first language of more native users than any other language, and its users as a second language outnumber native users. It is the first language of forty-five countries, and nonnative users claim it is the easiest (and most fun) language to learn and use.

3. A recent study in Houston showed that Southeast Asians who are fluent speakers of English earn three times more than nonfluent speakers. The same holds true for native speakers of other languages.

As the child of immigrants, I understand the need to preserve the language and customs of the "old country," but I also understand the economic and social necessity of becoming proficient in the language and customs of the "new country." To advise persons to do otherwise is a cruel hoax that will doom them to jobs at minimum wage or less and will make them social outcasts. We live in a global economy in which the universal language is now English. If one isn't fluent in English, he or she can plan on a career in the fast food industry.

The author's *claim* is that *people should learn two languages, one of which must be English.* His *data* are the various *facts about English and fluency* that he presents. His *warrant* is the statement that *not teaching nonnatives to be fluent in English will doom them to low-paying jobs and make them social outcasts,* which he reasons from his own experience as the child of an immigrant.

If the audience accepts the persuader's claim, there is no need to present any data and hence there is no reason for a warrant. If the audience rejects the persuader's claim, again there is no need for data or a warrant. However, if the audience is unsure or if the persuader anticipates some doubt about the claim, then data must be presented. If the data are accepted or rejected outright, again there is no need for the persuader to proceed to the warrant. However, if the audience isn't entirely convinced, or if the persuader anticipates some doubt about the claim now supported by data, then it will be necessary to present a warrant that explains the reasoning by which the data support the claim. In this letter to the editor, it is apparent that the persuader anticipates audience resistance at each step of the way and thus presents a complete, three-part argument with claim, data, and warrant all apparent.

This pattern of moving the logical argument from claim to data to warrant and the resulting three kinds of responses (agree, disagree, and uncertain) is typical of almost every reasoned argument in the everyday marketplace of ideas. Figure 7.5 uses the claim that the United States must become the Globo-Cop in the world to show how the flow of argument goes in the Toulmin system. Trace the stages of argument in the figure.

Substantiating Elements

Toulmin's system has a number of secondary terms. For example, a claim may be modified by what is termed a **qualifier.** (Usually it is a simple qualifier — something like "In most cases" or "Probably" or "It is likely that.") The concession qualifies or limits the claim.

To continue our Globo-Cop example, you might ask the persuader to qualify the claim by pointing out the limits or boundaries beyond which the claim doesn't apply. For instance, the persuader might alter the claim to state "*In most cases*, the United States should become an international peacekeeper using military intervention and other assistance in world crises." Other examples of words or phrases that qualify or limit the applicability are "Probably," "It is likely that," and "Possibly." These and similar qualifiers limit the claim, thus allowing for the possibility that this is not a simple case of the either-or argument.

Another minor term in Toulmin's model is the **reservation,** a statement related to the warrant that states the conditions under which the warrant is valid. It is stated in words like "unless" or "only if there is a reason to believe that." In the Globo-Cop case, the reservation might indicate that there are some conditions under which the warrant becomes nonoperative or nonbinding.

For instance, suppose the warrant stated that *"Except in the case of revolutions*, the United States is the only remaining superpower capable of establishing and maintaining world stability." Another reservation is expressed with the word "Unless," in which case the warrant might state: *"Unless* the United States is not the only remaining superpower capable of establishing and maintaining world stability. . . ."

This aspect of the reservation is often overlooked by persuaders and persuadees alike; they assume that both parties begin from the same point, from the same frame of reference. Only when we begin at the same point or when we make allowances (such as reservations) for these differences can we really progress in any persuasive transaction. Coupled with the qualifier, the reservation allows for great flexibility in persuasion because both terms allow for dialogue; both provide the persuadee with an opportunity to object or agree to part but not all of the persuasion.

Advertisers are clever with the use of qualifiers. For example, the label on Cascade dishwasher detergent says that it will make your dishes "virtually spotless." Not spotless, but *virtually* spotless, and who can say whether one spot or three spots or twelve spots qualifies as being *"virtually* spotless"?

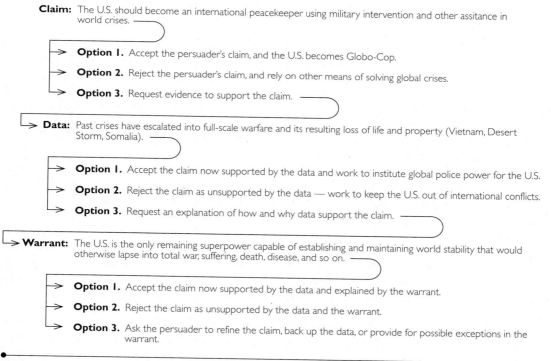

Claim: The U.S. should become an international peacekeeper using military intervention and other assitance in world crises.

    Option 1. Accept the persuader's claim, and the U.S. becomes Globo-Cop.

    Option 2. Reject the persuader's claim, and rely on other means of solving global crises.

    Option 3. Request evidence to support the claim.

Data: Past crises have escalated into full-scale warfare and its resulting loss of life and property (Vietnam, Desert Storm, Somalia).

    Option 1. Accept the claim now supported by the data and work to institute global police power for the U.S.

    Option 2. Reject the claim as unsupported by the data — work to keep the U.S. out of international conflicts.

    Option 3. Request an explanation of how and why data support the claim.

Warrant: The U.S. is the only remaining superpower capable of establishing and maintaining world stability that would otherwise lapse into total war, suffering, death, disease, and so on.

    Option 1. Accept the claim now supported by the data and explained by the warrant.

    Option 2. Reject the claim as unsupported by the data and the warrant.

    Option 3. Ask the persuader to refine the claim, back up the data, or provide for possible exceptions in the warrant.

Figure 7.5. Toulmin's basic elements of an argument, applied to the example of U.S. intervention in world crises.

So the persuadee needs to be aware of two problems connected with qualifiers or reservations. One is the absence of them, which can lock us into one course of action or belief. The other is the too vague qualifier, which allows persuaders to wriggle out of any commitment to a product, action, person, or idea. Persuaders may still try to interpret the qualifiers to their advantage, but it is much more difficult when specificity and details are given. Persuadees need to think twice when confronted with lack of details and lack of specificity in persuasive claims. If advertisers say that their tires will stop faster, we need to ask such questions as "Faster than what?" and "Under what conditions?" For all we know, they may be comparing the tires with wagon wheels or doughnuts.

The final element in Toulmin's system for showing the tactics of argument is the *backing* for the warrant. Suppose a persuadee does not consider a warrant to be valid or doubts some part of it. The persuader must then provide proof that supports the reasoning expressed in the warrant. What we have then is a whole separate argument with a separate claim, data, and warrant to support the original warrant. Essentially, persuaders claim that the warrant is acceptable because of the support.

We can now see that the tactics of persuasion are not usually parts of simple syllogisms. Instead, persuaders make claims that persuadees may respond to by (1) accepting them outright with no questions asked, (2) rejecting them outright, or (3) asking for proof. Persuaders then can provide data, which again can be accepted, rejected, or questioned. If the persuadee continues to request more, the persuader ultimately provides the warrant, or reason, for linking proof to request. Given enough time, three other elements may enter into the persuasive appeal: the qualifier, the reservation, and the backing. Finally, the job of persuadees is to dissect persuasion.

What matters is that persuadees are aware, critical, and fairly sophisticated and systematic as they are exposed to persuasion. Toulmin's system for analyzing the tactics of persuasion provides us with a simple but discriminating tool that operates well with the kind of persuasion we are exposed to every day.

Research on the Effects of Evidence

Some researchers use the scientific method to determine the effects of evidence on receivers. In such studies, presumably typical persuadees (for example, several hundred college students) are given attitude tests. Then they are exposed to various degrees or types of persuasion and evidence (for example, emotional versus logical evidence, good delivery of evidence versus poor delivery of the same evidence). Following this, the subjects' attitudes are reevaluated. The results are compared, by statistical methods, with pretreatment scores to determine the effects of varying types or amounts of evidence. Early studies demonstrated that although the relationship between evidence and attitude change is elusive and sometimes even fickle, several patterns seem to be stable.

In 1983, communication scholars Rodney Reynolds and Michael Burgoon reviewed the relationships among belief processing, reasoning, and evidence. They determined that some of the previously fickle or negative findings could be interpreted from a different perspective, one that suggests that there is a positive relationship between datalike assertions and what appears to be attitude change. These patterns led them to make a series of propositions that support the evidence-persuasion relationship, especially in cases in which other variables are present (such as credibility of the speaker).

Reynolds and Burgoon (1983) made the folloing assertions.

1. Using evidence produces more attitude change than not using evidence.

2. Using evidence produces more attitude change than using simple assertions.

3. Using irrelevant evidence from poorly qualified sources produces counter-to-advocated attitude change (in other words, produces the opposite effect) regardless of an advocate's credibility.

4. If advocates who have low to moderate credibility fail to use relevant evidence from qualified sources, the result may be counter-to-advocated attitude change.

What do you think?
Which finding about the effects of evidence seems most reasonable?

5. If advocates fail to cite relevant evidence in a message that follows an opposing message that *does* cite evidence, their credibility will be lowered.

6. Citing evidence produces more attitude change when the evidence source and source qualifications are provided or when evidence is presented without a source citation than when evidence is presented with only a source identification.

7. If an advocate who has low to moderate credibility cites evidence clearly, the advocate's credibility and success in persuasion will increase.

8. Using evidence from highly credible sources will, over time, increase an advocate's credibility.

9. If an advocate cites evidence from less credible sources after, rather than before, other evidence, message acceptance will improve.

10. Poor delivery of evidence citations by advocates who have low to moderate credibility reduces persuasive effects.

11. Using evidence results in attitude change when receivers have no prior knowledge of the evidence.

12. Using evidence increases attitude change over time, regardless of the credibility of the advocate.

13. Using evidence results in attitude change over time only when receivers hold extreme attitudes on an issue.

14. The credibility of an advocate increases the evaluation of message attributes.

15. The clarity of evidence citations increases evaluations of the evidence and the advocate.

16. Highly dogmatic people select persuasive messages containing highly documented, rather than undocumented, evidence.

17. People tend to evaluate evidence from the perspective of their own attitudes, regardless of the quality of the evidence.

18. Evidence that is inconsistent with the major propositions being advanced is more difficult to detect than is irrelevant evidence or evidence from unqualified sources.

These propositions make sense, especially when applied to familiar persuasive events.

In a review of the past fifty years of research on the effects of evidence on persuasion, communication scholar John C. Reinard (1988) used Petty and Cacioppo's elaboration likelihood model to identify a number of consistent trends. If you recall, that model suggests that there are two information-processing modes in persuasion:

the peripheral and the central processing paths. Persuasion in the peripheral path is typified by topics or issues that are not personally involving. The audience is often swayed by variables other than the message or good evidence. For example, persuasion may be affected by variables such as the attractiveness of the source, how discrepant the message is from the audience's own position, and so on. In the central processing route, however, the persuadee is highly involved with the issue or topic. You can persuade these persons only with compelling arguments that are well documented by evidence. Using the model, Reinard was able to identify the following trends:

1. Testimonials seem to be consistently persuasive as long as the source of the testimony is clearly documented.

2. Factual information such as reports of events or examples seems to be persuasive, but it can be affected by the mode of presentation. For example, on issues regarding policy ("The United States should stockpile petroleum for the next five years"), specific facts are more persuasive than general facts.

3. In spite of the almost reverent attitude that many people have toward statistical evidence, such evidence is not as persuasive as other factual evidence. (Reinard speculates that this may be because statistics are not vivid or dramatic.) However, when powerful, involving, and vivid examples are backed up by statistics that show the examples to be typical, the examples become more powerful.

4. Presenting audiences with evidence seems to "inoculate" or protect them against subsequent counterpersuasion.

5. Evidence seems to have long-term effectiveness when an issue is processed in the central path, but there is little long-term effective-

ness when the issue is processed in the peripheral path.

6. A source's credibility has persuasive effects — that is, credible sources are more persuasive than less credible ones. This is one of the most consistent patterns identified by Reinard.

7. Evidence that reinforces the receiver's beliefs is more persuasive than evidence that does not reinforce the receiver's position.

8. Strong evidence is more persuasive than weak evidence, especially when an issue is personally involving to the receiver, who then uses the central processing path.

9. Novel evidence is more persuasive than evidence the audience already knows.

10. Unless a topic is personally involving, credibility seems to be more persuasive than evidence, but even credible sources can enhance their persuasiveness by using evidence.

11. Evidence consistently increases speaker credibility.

12. Good delivery enhances the effectiveness of evidence unless the audience is distracted.

13. Evidence is most effective with highly intelligent receivers, those who are "hard-nosed about getting the facts."

14. People who are highly analytical are more likely to be persuaded by evidence, and intellectually sophisticated receivers prefer technically oriented evidence.

Reinard's overall conclusion is that evidence is persuasive, especially if we look at the past fifty years of research from the perspective of the elaboration likelihood model. As with the Reynolds and Burgoon conclusions, the patterns Reinard identified (especially those related to the model), make real sense when used to analyze "real world" persuasive examples.

In conclusion, several characteristics of the use of evidence in content premises in persuasion can be noted. First, evidence is probably most effective when it encourages audience participation. Earlier we noted that, in using emotionally oriented evidence, persuaders are most effective when they present audiences with a dramatic scene or setting and then ask the audience to empathize with the character acting within that setting. By participating with their imaginations, members of the audience co-create the proof— they incorporate the proof into their own frames of reference.

In using intellectually oriented evidence, effective persuaders present claims and perhaps data to support them. They hope that warrants will be provided by the audience, but even if listeners do not supply the necessary linkage and instead question the persuaders' conclusions, they are still participating in their own persuasion when they begin to play the game (that is, co-create a proof with the persuaders).

A second characteristic that seems to help in using evidence for "logical" or content-oriented persuasion is to highlight the evidence—either as part of a narrative or in some form of analogy.

Review and Conclusion

Content premises do not necessarily rely as much on the internal states of persuaders as do process premises. Instead, they rely more on universally agreed-on norms or rules.

Evidence tends to be either dramatically oriented or intellectually oriented. Users of dramatically oriented evidence may lead persuadees to a "logical" conclusion, drawn from a content premise, by creating a dramatic scene and then

inviting the audience to join in the drama. Persuadees thus "prove" the validity of the premise to themselves. Users of intellectually oriented evidence, on the other hand, may lead their persuadees to "logical" conclusions by presenting them with a set of data in support of a certain claim or content premise. The persuadees provide the connection between these data and the claim in the form of a warrant.

Both types of evidence rely on a kind of self-persuasion on the part of the persuadee. Persuadees ought to participate in some way in their own persuasion, whether the evidence is intellectual or dramatic. When we engage in self-persuasion, even if it runs counter to our own beliefs, the effect of the participation is powerful.

From a strategic point of view, the traditional syllogism usually forms the skeletal structure of an overall argument or content premise. Within this structure, the tactics or particular arguments or premises are represented by claims supported by data. Claims and data are linked by audiences through warrants.

Finally, of the types of evidence available to the persuader, several seem more important than others. First, probably, are those that support the three major linkages: cause-effect, symptoms, and congruency. Also, evidence that provides perspective for the audience is probably more effective than evidence that does not. We have focused on two particularly effective methods of providing this perspective: the use of analogy, which provides a comparative perspective, and the use of narrative, which has the same ability to provide a perspective within a dramatic frame of reference. Both are also "artistic" in the sense that neither merely presents information: Both depict evidence in dramatic or visual formats.

In sum, we are most effectively persuaded by our own experiences—real, vicarious, or imagined. Successful persuaders try to shape content premises, their linkages, claims, data, and warrants in terms of the audience's experience. If they can invite audiences to participate in drawing conclusions or in the drama of the proof, au-diences will share in their own persuasion, thus being affected by it.

Questions for Further Thought

1. What are the three types of syllogisms discussed in this chapter? Give examples of each from advertisements, political speeches, or some other source of persuasion.

2. Define *proof*. What constitutes adequate proof for you? Does it change from issue to issue? If so, in what ways?

3. Review some magazine commentary concerning a particular issue and attempt to identify the data that are offered. What kinds of evidence are they? Are they dramatic? If so, in what ways? If not, are they persuasive? Why or why not? What is the underlying syllogistic structure inherent in the discussions of the issue?

4. What is the difference between intellectually oriented evidence and emotionally oriented evidence? Give examples and explain how they differ.

5. Give examples from your own experience of (a) opinion, (b) attitudes, (c) beliefs, and (d) values that affect *behavior*. Give examples that do not affect behavior. Why is there a difference?

6. Why was "The Case of Bobby and His Parents" so persuasive? Was logic involved? Was the example an illogical one to prove the point Peck wanted to make?

7. What is the difference between a figurative and a literal analogy? Which is being used when a political campaign is compared to a horse race?

8. What are some of the ways in which statistics can be misused? Give examples.

9. What are some of the ways in which testimony can be misused? Give examples.

10. What is a *post hoc* fallacy? Give an example.

11. What is an *ad hominem* fallacy? Give an example.

12. How has the *ad hominem* been used in recent elections?

13. What are some contemporary examples of the *ad populum* being used in advertising?

14. How does the undistributed middle fallacy operate? Give examples.

15. How does the straw man fallacy operate? Give examples.

16. What is the false dilemma fallacy? How does it operate? Give examples.

References

Clark, H. H. (1969). Linguistic processes in deductive reasoning. *Psychological Review, 76,* 387–404.

Dowd, M. Bushpeak, *The Chicago Tribune.* April 1, 1990, sec. 5, p. 3.

Garfield, B. (1988). Ad review: Good commercials finally outnumber the bad ones on TV. *Advertising Age,* March 14, p. 86.

Jensen, J. V. (1981). *Argumentation: Reasoning in communication.* New York: Van Nostrand.

Kahane, H. (1992). *Logic and contemporary rhetoric: The use of reason in everyday life*. Belmont, CA: Wadsworth.

Loftus, E. F. (1980). *Eyewitness testimony*. Cambridge, MA: Harvard University Press.

Loftus, E. F. (1984). Eyewitness testimony. *Psychology Today*. February, p. 25.

Morganthau, T., et al. (1993). Globo-Cops: Deciding how and when to use the U.S. military. *Newsweek*, August 23, pp. 14–19.

The payoffs for preschooling. (1984). *The Chicago Tribune*, December 25, p. 25.

Peck, M. S. (1983). *People of the lie: The hope for healing human evil*. New York: Simon & Schuster.

Reinard, J. C. (1988). The empirical study of evidence: The status after fifty years of research. *Human Communication Research, 15,* Fall.

Reynolds, R., & Burgoon, M. (1983). Belief processing, reasoning and evidence. *Communication Yearbook, 7,* 83–104.

Scott, B. (1989). *The Rockford Register Star*. November 8, editorial page.

Thompson, W. N. (1971). *Modern argumentation and debate: Principles and practices*. New York: Harper & Row.

Toulmin, S. (1964). *The uses of argument*. Cambridge, Eng.: Cambridge University Press.

8

Cultural Premises in Persuasion

We are all prisoners of our own culture, and as a result we often overlook patterns of behavior that influence how and by what means we are persuaded. Anyone who has visited another culture (even another Western culture) immediately becomes aware of significant cultural differences between his or her patterns of behavior and those of the foreign culture. Not only are values, languages, and customs different, but hundreds, even thousands, of little things differ from our familiar American ways. For example, only one-third of the world's people use our kind of flatware to eat. Another third eat with chopsticks, and the rest eat with their fingers. Even in England, differences are apparent. People wait at bus stops in neat, orderly lines, or queues, to board a bus. We Americans usually crowd around the bus door.

If you happen to visit a formerly communist country in Eastern Europe, you will quickly understand the immense difference between "hard currency" and "soft currency"—even the hotel I stayed at in Prague refused to accept Czech currency. A thriving black market in currency is commonplace in the cities of Eastern Europe. A friend recently told me that taxis in Moscow will stop only if you hold up a pack of cigarettes; they don't want rubles. In Eastern European countries one always carries a shopping bag just in case one finds something available. In fact, the slang term for a shopping bag is a "perhaps." Such conditions make an incredible difference in a country's purchase patterns. You don't buy something there because you need it; you buy it because it happens to be available. This idea would never cross our minds back here in the United States, because we know full well that most items are in good supply.

Although many aspects of any given culture are permanent, cultures are also subject to constant change. In the United States, for example, the constant influx of different ethnic groups is reflected in a variety of ways. Diversity and multiculturalism are apparent everywhere—such as in supermarkets where you will find soybean curd, bean sprouts, wonton, corn and flour tortillas, and pita bread. You can buy a wok or futon at your department store. These minor cultural differences are, of course, only the tip of the iceberg. The important differences among cultures are values, beliefs, and patterns of behavior that are trained into us from early childhood through our language, the myths and tales we hear, and our observations of how those around us behave. Many of these values and beliefs are relatively permanent aspects of a culture, although over time they change in response to societal shifts.

This training, which we absorb from our culture and language, forms some of the premises we have been discussing. The cultural preferences we have, the cultural myths we believe in, and the cultural values we embrace are all missing premises in enthymemes that persuaders can construct. This kind of persuasion occurs at a low level of awareness; we often react subconsciously to various stimuli based on our cultural training. Consider the following instance of cultural patterning.

Cultural Patterns

Suppose you are a member of an Inuit tribe called "People of the Deer," whose sole food supply is caribou. You kill enough animals in the spring to last the tribe until the fall, when again the animals migrate south following the food supply. The custom is to kill and preserve these deer in a period of a week or two. Suppose that you have just finished your fall hunt and discover that you face a severe winter without having killed enough caribou to last until the spring migration. Death is certain without sufficient supplies of meat and fat. You attend a meeting called to consider the matter. What would you do?

In my persuasion classes, students brainstorm solutions to this problem and come up with the following suggestions usually in this approximate order:

1. Let's follow the deer and kill enough of them, and thus increase the supply.

2. Let's seek an alternative food supply—we can eat berries or fish or birds.

3. Let's send a band of the young and healthy to get help.

4. Let's ration food to make it last longer.

5. Let's eat all the parts of the caribou—skin, horns, everything—to increase the supply.

6. Let's send some of the people away to another place where food is more plentiful and thus decrease demand.

7. Let's kill some of us to decrease demand.

8. Let's kill the most useless persons—the old first, and the very young next.

9. Let's resort to cannibalism; let's eat those we kill.

The most practical solutions emerge first, and then the ideas become increasingly desperate to the point of cannibalism. The actual People of the Deer *do nothing*—they eat the food at their regular rates, knowing full well that they will not live through the winter. Then they sit and wait for death. In fact, they even refuse the help of their government. They simply do not enter into the problem-solving frame of mind typical of Western culture. They accept a situation and do nothing, whereas we try to find solutions for any problem, even though it may be insoluble. We are trained to *do something*. In our culture, persuaders succeed if they outline a problem and suggest solutions.

One of the problems of the Middle East/Gulf War crisis of 1990 was that there seemed to be no solutions available, yet diplomats and others scurried around dreaming up far-fetched compromises, offers, and counteroffers. Egypt's President Mubarak probably suggested the most realistic solution—offer Iraq a bribe: some of Kuwait's oil and a cash settlement. Bribes are commonplace in the Arab world where *baksheesh*, as it is called, is part and parcel of everyday life.

You can probably observe yourself and others, when faced with a problem, responding with an almost compulsive search for solutions of any kind. Unfortunately, this pattern can sometimes make us easy prey for unethical persuaders, or it may shunt our efforts away from certain problems.

The case of the People of the Deer reveals other cultural attributes that we have and that can be targeted by persuaders. Notice, for instance, that students' early solutions emphasized positive and assertive steps. These are always suggested first, indicating an American cultural bias in favor of the "pull-yourself-up-by-your-bootstraps" approach. Americans have always valued individualism and individual achievements. This country has always been a place where immigrants could come to make a new life *for and by themselves*. Persuaders market a whole host of products and services based on this "bootstraps" belief.

Another appeal to the value or potential of the individual and his or her ability to succeed is the many pyramid schemes for selling products. (One example is Amway, which stands for "the American way.") Such schemes persuade individuals that they can go into business for themselves, not only by selling products to their friends and neighbors but by recruiting others to do the same and getting a percentage of the recruit's sales as well. The recruit presumably recruits others and gets a percentage of what they sell, and so on down the line, until one develops a wide and complex "network." Success is measured by one's wealth and by the various symbols—awards, pins, jewelry, or whatever—that the company awards. At Mary Kay Cosmetics, for example, persons in the top levels in the pyramid get a pink Cadillac.

What do you think?

Is the value of the individual operating in your life?

But there is a flip side to the determined individual, as Robert Bellah and his associates (1985) point out in *Habits of the Heart: Individualism and Commitment in American Life*. As you will recall from an earlier chapter, Bellah and his colleagues did in-depth interviews with over 200 Americans from various walks of life, attempting to duplicate what Alexis de Tocqueville did in his book *Democracy in America*, written in the 1830s, in which he described core American values and mores as "habits of the heart." Key among them was the value of the individual. Bellah and his coauthors point out:

> The central problem of our book concerned the American individualism that Tocqueville described with a mixture of admiration and anxiety. It seems to us it is individualism and not equality, as Tocqueville thought, that has marched inexorably throughout our history. We are concerned that this individualism may have grown cancerous. (p. viii)

What they meant by "cancerous" is that individualism had by 1985 become "me-ism": emphasizing the individual at the cost of the community, thus drawing individuals inside themselves with little concern for others (see Figure 8.1). As they note:

> American cultural traditions define personality, achievement and the purpose of human life in ways that leave the individual suspended in glorious but terrifying isolation. (p. 6)

And others have echoed their theme. What we describe as "yuppie" values are those that Bellah and his associates see as the early signs of a cancerous individualism. If you carefully examine the responses of the People of the Deer example you will find that the early responses of my students are very positive and action oriented, reflecting the positive side of the American value of individualism. The middle

C. Barsotti

"Damn it, the eighties are over!"

Figure 8.1. *During the '80s — the "me" decade — high value was placed on the individual through the individual's symbols of success or conspicuous consumption. Competition was fierce, and mammoth mergers put many persons out of work for the sake of an individual's success. Apparently these expressions of the value of the individual and the value of success are persistent American cultural values, but like other cultural values, they ebb and flow with the times. What has replaced the means for expressing these values in the 1990s? (Drawing by C. Barsotti; © 1988 The New Yorker Magazine, Inc. Reprinted by permission.)*

portion of responses are more reflective of a sense of community and cooperation, while the last three reflect the malignant side of American individualism.

How do we identify these patterns of cultural values? Where do they come from? How do persuaders appeal to them? Questions such as these are the focus of our search for cultural premises.

To see how these premises relate to persuasion in general, we look first at how we get them (cultural training and pressure). Then we look at kinds of cultural premises: (1) cultural images or myths and (2) the American value system. Bear in mind that a *value* is an idea of the good or the desirable that people use as a standard for judging means or to motivate others. Examples of values are honesty, justice, beauty, efficiency, safety, and progress. Because our value system is a major source of persuasive leverage, you may be

interested in discovering how persuaders link proposals and arguments to our values.

Cultural and Societal Pressure

Everyone has heard stories about the children of various Native American groups who never cried because it was essential not to frighten off game. Anyone who has been around a newborn infant must doubt these stories. Children cry when they are lonely, hungry, or want exercise. How, then, did Native Americans train their children not to cry out?

During the first hour of life, whenever a Lakota baby cried, its mother clapped her hands over the child's mouth and nose. The hand was removed only if the child stopped crying or began to smother. If this was done within the first hour of life, the infant never again cried out loud.

Of course, as the child grew, it saw a pattern repeated over and over again. Parents and elders spoke of the power of silence. They valued quiet and stealth in stalking game. Young men were tested and proved their courage by experiencing pain and not crying out in a ritual dance. A leather thong was sewn into the young man's shoulder flesh. He was then tied to a symbolic tree at the center of a sacred circle or "medicine wheel." The test was to dance away from the pole until weariness and the pain of the thong forced him to fall (usually after several days of dancing). The fall usually tore out the thong from the shoulder. The young man was then a full-fledged warrior. Later he could do the Sun-Gazer's Dance. This involved dancing while staring directly into the sun. Sitting Bull is supposed to have done this for three days, after which he had a vision of the future massacre of Custer and his soldiers at the Little Big Horn. Thus, the pattern introduced at birth was seen at work throughout life.

In less dramatic terms, perhaps, each of us is trained in the ways of our culture. This training forms the core of our values, which then become rules for governing ourselves as we interact. We do not even notice that they are there. We respond instinctively to them. This training underlies each of the cultural premises we are going to study. It lurks beneath our surface thoughts and acts. Sophisticated persuaders appeal to these premises directly and cleverly. They can appeal to cultural and societal premises because they believe in them and expect that their audiences do also.

Cultural Images and Myths

Every culture has its own myths and heroes who do things valued by the culture. For example, early Greek society developed a series of myths surrounding the sin of pride. Eventually, the myths became institutionalized in such Greek dramas as *Oedipus Rex*.

Parts of the myths related to physical acts (such as trying to control one's own destiny) that were discouraged. Greeks placed a high value on avoiding prideful action. They valued modesty. They elected leaders who were modest. We have similar beliefs. You probably know that the overly proud student is less likely to be elected to office or chosen as team captain than the more humble person. We view the antics of a pompous person with disfavor. We ridicule needless pride.

What are some of the cultural myths or legends or images underlying American culture and society, and how do persuaders use them? Can these images be changed? If so, how? Are they being changed at present, and if so, how? Stereotypes and proverbs are good indicators of cultural myths. Let us consider a few of them.

Wisdom of the Rustic

One of the legends in American literature that has great persuasive appeal is that of the clever rustic. No matter how devious the opposition, the simple wisdom of the backwoods wins out. Numerous folk tales rely on this image. The Daniel Boone tales, the stories about the inventiveness of Paul Bunyan, and many Abraham Lincoln stories rely on the rustic image (see Figure 8.2). We have faith in humble persons when we look for leaders. The small-town boy is chosen team captain. We believe in humble beginnings, and we believe that difficulty teaches even the most uneducated of us to be wise in a worldly way.

Politicians across American history have tried to emphasize their humble origins. In fact,

What do you think?
Name a current persuader who uses the "wisdom of the rustic" myth.

"Of course, one of the more popular myths is that our 16th president was born in a little log cabin."

Figure 8.2. The wisdom of the rustic. (Reprinted by permission. © 1993 FarWorks, Inc./Dist. By Universal Press Syndicate. All rights reserved.)

public learns of their physical disabilities or emotional suffering.

Products are frequently marketed using a rustic as the spokesperson — Wilfred Brimley, for instance, serves as a rustic endorsing the value of good old-fashioned Quaker Oats.

At the same time that we seem to value the simple, commonsense rustic, our culture tends to devalue the intellectual or the educated. Alexis de Tocqueville, in *Democracy in America*, described this distrust:

> The nearer the people are drawn to the common level of an equal and similar condition, the less prone does each man become to place implicit faith in a certain man or a certain class of men [intellectuals]. But his readiness to believe the multitude increases, and opinion is more than ever mistress of the world. Not only is common opinion the only guide which private judgment retains . . . it possesses a power infinitely beyond what it has elsewhere.

Richard Hofstadter (1961) also wrote about this anti-intellectualism. Persuaders often use this reverse side of our value in the wisdom of the rustic: The intellectual is often the brunt of jokes, and the rustic often wins out over the smart guy.

Possibility of Success

The Horatio Alger myth is based on several novels written for boys by Alger in the nineteenth century. The protagonist of these novels was invariably a young man who, through hard work, sincerity, honesty, and a faith in the future, was able to make good. He might even rise to the top and own his own company, have a beautiful wife, live a fine life, and be able to do good for others. The myth was particularly appealing to immigrants, the poor, and the downtrodden. They passed it on to their children, admonishing them to work hard and achieve success. In more recent times,

many have manufactured myths about their rustic origins even to the point of constructing log cabins that they claimed as their birthplace, as did William Henry Harrison, or "Tippecanoe." Ronald Reagan emphasized his humble origin in Dixon, Illinois, and Bill Clinton lets it be known that he was born in a small house in Hope, Arkansas.

If the politician cannot claim humble beginnings, he or she must find some substitute for them — usually hardship or suffering. Thus we find patricians such as Franklin D. Roosevelt and John F. Kennedy are viewed as humble when the

the myth has been generalized to include women and has appeal for new groups of immigrants.

The myth incorporates the values of hard work, sincerity, honesty, and law and order. Again, this myth was observed by Alexis de Tocqueville:

> No Americans are devoid of a yearning desire to rise; . . . All are constantly seeking to acquire property, power, and reputation. . . . What chiefly diverts the men of democracies from lofty ambition is not the scantiness of their fortunes, but the vehemence of the exertions they daily make to improve them. . . . The same observation is applicable to the sons of such men; . . . their parents were humble; they have grown up amidst feelings and notions which they cannot afterwards easily get rid of; and it may be presumed that they will inherit the propensities of their father, as well as his wealth.

You probably can see your grandparents and parents in this description. If Tocqueville was right, you may also see yourself. You are thus ready for persuasion that promises the possibility of success. Products and services such as Internet access are marketed with the claim that they will result in success for the entire family, from Mom and Dad on down to the toddlers. Politicians promise a successful future to the voter who supports a commonsense approach to problems. This promise probably will continue to be a part of our political vision. After all, who would vote for a politician whose campaign promises don't offer a chance to improve ourselves? Expect to hear appeals made for the myth. Persuaders will offer success "just around the corner," if only you will follow them and not the false prophets. They will offer the "big break" and the chance to have a better life for you and your children. Whether it is a pyramid marketing scheme, a body-building machine, or a weight-loss club, the carrot is always the same—try and you will succeed.

Coming of a Messiah

A cultural myth that is related to the possibility of success is that of the coming of a messiah. Here the situational assumption is slightly different—the culture is near disaster or perhaps even already in the midst of an almost impossible mess, be it economic, religious, or political. It is a period of great uncertainty and pessimism; it is chaotic, confusing, and frightening. At such times, we expect to be rescued from the chaos and danger by some single great leader who projects a sense of confidence and who we believe can turn things around. Many leaders have served to fulfill this role. Lincoln emerged from obscurity to save the Union; despite his handicap, Franklin Delano Roosevelt saved the country from economic collapse; John F. Kennedy "rescued" the entire world for Democracy; Ronald Reagan delivered the country from double-digit inflation and worldwide scorn, and Bill Clinton promised to save the economy from stagnation and gridlock. Although circumstances may change, Americans seem to be always waiting for another messiah to come down the road and save them from one big bad wolf or another.

What makes us receptive to the messianic? First, we are action oriented. As shown by the values expressed in the People of the Deer solutions, we seem to want our saviors to be doers, not thinkers. Second, our solutions had better not be too theoretical or intellectual—we prefer simple and practical answers to the most complex problems. The messiah should also be vigorous, witty, and charming, and not afraid to try the unknown or unproven.

Presence of Conspiracy

Another cultural premise operant in our culture is the belief that big problems don't have simple causes. Richard Hofstadter (1967) calls this belief the *paranoid style*. This is the belief that when problems appear great, the only reasonable explanation is that a powerful group has conspired to cause them. This conspiracy argument has recurred throughout our history. Most recently, the conspiracy argument has been used to explain terrorist attacks such as the Oklahoma City bombing of the Murrah Building and the housing complex in Saudia Arabia. Some believe that groups such as the militia movement are currently conspiring to overthrow the government, many in the militia movement believe the government is in the hands of international conspirators, while others believe the Internet is really a governmental conspiracy to monitor our citizenry.

If Hofstadter is right, we can expect to hear the conspiracy offered as an explanation for problems any time three factors are operating for the audience:

1. They have something of value to lose — they are in possession of some kind of power or property.

2. They see themselves in danger of losing some or all of this power or property or as already having lost some of it.

3. They see themselves as helpless to prevent the loss.

It is easy to see how these beliefs in a conspiracy could link up with a messiah: The messiah can defeat the evil conspirators and thus save the culture. Here lies one of the dangers of the conspiracy argument: It invites mass hysteria and charismatic leaders. In times of trouble and confusion, we may see the rise of mass movements following leaders who are believed to be heroes or saviors combating those who conspire against us. Far-right fringe groups such as the Christian identity movement are examples.

Value of Challenge

The value of challenge myth is fairly simple and parallels tribal tests of strength and character. It suggests that there is a kind of wisdom gained only through great challenge and testing. There is a rite of passage or initiation that gives one power, character, and knowledge.

You are probably now going through such a test in college. People say that going to college is a test of endurance more than training for a specific job. College graduation shows that you can meet a challenge and handle it, that you have matured, and that you have learned how to learn. Employers hire college graduates and then train them for a job after college. Boot camp offers another example of belief in the value of overcoming difficulty and in meeting challenges.

The concept of the Outward Bound program rests on the value of challenge myth. Somehow, it says, the most problematic children will be restored to good behavior if they get through a mountain-climbing expedition, a rafting trip down the Colorado River, or a wilderness canoe trip. Even corporate America believes in this concept and often sends its executives on such Outward Bound experiences to shape them up.

Political persuaders frequently offer voters a dramatic challenge and paint their election as one of critical importance. Lincoln said his election would decide whether the nation could exist "half slave and half free." FDR said that the country under his leadership would have "a rendezvous with destiny." John F. Kennedy said that with his election a torch had been passed to a new generation and the light from the torch would "light the world." Ronald Reagan offered a "new beginning." And most recently, Bill Clinton declared that under his administration, there would be a "new covenant" between the governed and their leaders. Product appeals frequently present the consumer with a challenge — "Use the Soloflex machine regularly and lose 20 pounds in 30 days!" or "Get your MBA at Olivet College by attending classes one Saturday a month!"

In many cases, the value of challenge myth is presented as a rite of passage that underscores several cultural values that persuaders frequently use in their appeals. First, the myth suggests that there is something good about suffering or that nothing good was ever accomplished without pain. Second, the myth suggests that suffering begets maturity, humility, and wisdom — you learn and grow as you meet challenges and surmount them. Finally, the myth suggests that all great leaders have become great because they were tested and found equal to the challenge. Thus, defeats and failures can be explained away as tests that prepare you for the future. As you begin to catalog the persuasion aimed at you, you will find the value of challenge used frequently, whether for products, candidates, or ideologies (see Figure 8.3).

The Eternal Return

Mercia Eliade (1971), a professor of history at the Sorbonne, identified a historical myth persistent not only in Western culture but in other cultures as well. He called it the "myth of the eternal return." He said that people reject concrete historical time and instead yearn for and often reenact a "periodical return to the mythical time of the beginning of things, to the 'Great Time.'" American culture seems to embrace this myth, perhaps because our beginnings are so recent compared with those of other cultures. America was conceived with the perception that it was a "second Eden," a chance to start anew with no historical baggage to clutter up our purpose.

According to the myth of the eternal return, there was a time when things were perfect and harmonious; things could be shaped or molded as they were meant to be. This time of creation is usually associated with a specific geographical "center," where things are assumed to have begun. In the United States, this center is probably Philadelphia, where the Continental Congress signed the Declaration of Independence and where the memento of another myth is stored — the Liberty Bell that supposedly cracked while pealing out independence. Another potential symbolic center would be Washington, D.C., where our great historical documents are enshrined in the National Archives.

At the creation, there were heroes (George Washington, Benjamin Franklin, John Hancock, and so on). There were also villains (King George, the colonial governors, the British generals, and the redcoats). After suffering for some time, the heroes participated in some critical act that was redemptive — it released them from their former enslavement and permitted them to create the "Great Time" or the "Golden Age."

Included in the myth is the notion that society has lost sight of this archetypal beginning, and we must find our way back if we are to rid ourselves of the corruption, misplanning, and confusion that have developed since then. We accomplish this through reenactment of the original act in a ritual, usually held at the center where everything began (every Fourth of July). This periodic return to the origins of our beliefs reestablishes these values for us and is an act of redemption.

The rite freezes us in a mystical time that has power to transform us through the ritual. As Eliade notes:

> Time, too, like space is neither homogeneous nor continuous. On the one hand there are the intervals of a sacred time, the time of festivals (by far the greater part of which are periodical); on the other hand there is profane time, ordinary temporal duration. (Beane & Doty, 1975)

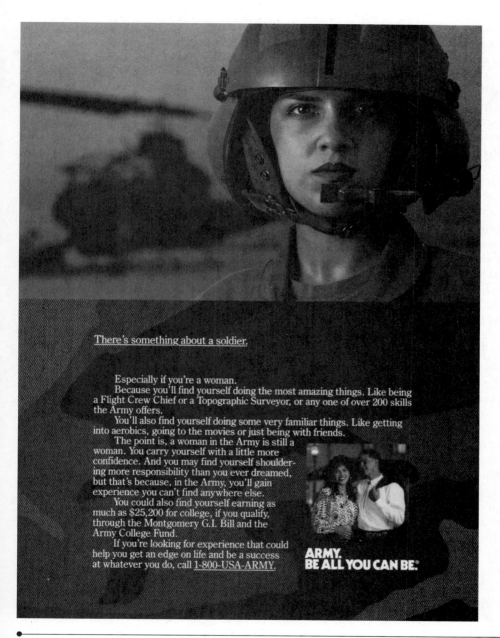

There's something about a soldier.

Especially if you're a woman.
Because you'll find yourself doing the most amazing things. Like being a Flight Crew Chief or a Topographic Surveyor, or any one of over 200 skills the Army offers.
You'll also find yourself doing some very familiar things. Like getting into aerobics, going to the movies or just being with friends.
The point is, a woman in the Army is still a woman. You carry yourself with a little more confidence. And you may find yourself shouldering more responsibility than you ever dreamed, but that's because, in the Army, you'll gain experience you can't find anywhere else.
You could also find yourself earning as much as $25,200 for college, if you qualify, through the Montgomery G.I. Bill and the Army College Fund.
If you're looking for experience that could help you get an edge on life and be a success at whatever you do, call 1-800-USA-ARMY.

ARMY.
BE ALL YOU CAN BE.®

Figure 8.3. *The U.S. Army's "Be All You Can Be" campaign exemplifies the persuasiveness of the value of challenge myth, especially for women in this advertisement. (Army photograph courtesy of U.S. Government, as represented by the Secretary of the Army.)*

Our contemporary language reflects this belief in the cyclical nature of things and of the two types of time. For example, when we say "What goes around comes around," we mean "This will come back to haunt you," "What ye sow, so shall ye reap," or "History repeats itself." Although we have a reverence for certain "sacred" times — historical holidays, ritualistic meals (such as Thanksgiving, Christmas, Passover), and governmental rites (the inaugural address, the oath of office, the state of the union address, among others) — we disdain persons who waste time, who are just "passing the time," or who are just "couch potatoes" living through "profane" time.

Commercial persuaders are aware of the importance of sacred time. They have special sales on historical holidays: a "Hatchet Days Sale" on Washington's birthday, an "Independence Day Sale" on the Fourth of July, a "Pre-Christmas Sale" the day following Thanksgiving. And in recent years, some stores have held a "Super Bowl Sale" in mid-January. The 1996 Olympics in Atlanta provided numerous instances of sacred time being celebrated.

Politicians are often skillful at challenging us to return to an earlier time — to reestablish and renew ourselves. Not only is this apparent in their speeches, but the inaugural ceremonies themselves are acts of renewal that promise to return to the untainted past. As noted earlier, Ronald Reagan offered a "new beginning," while George Bush offered a "kinder, gentler America," Bill Clinton offered a "new covenant" in 1992 and a "bridge to the future" in 1996. In his inaugural address, Clinton referred to renewal, the cycle of the seasons (his generation of voters would "force the spring"), and a national return to a more sacred time — the years of vigor and innovation experienced under former Democratic presidents.

In ideological campaigns and mass movements, the return and renewal theme is also persistent. Martin Luther King Jr. used it in his "I Have a Dream" speech, while Jesse Jackson used it to build his Rainbow Coalition. We hear strains of the myth even in the pro-life, antiabortion movement; one leader said, "People are going to look back on this era the way they look back on Nazi Germany. They'll say 'Thank God there were a few sane people' " ("America's Abortion Dilemma," 1985). This reference to profane time was echoed by moral majority leader Jerry Falwell, who said of abortion, "This criminal activity . . . sets us back to the Stone Age" (p. 22). In the antiabortion case, the focus is on the profane ground of the abortion clinics and the profane time following *Roe* v. *Wade* and symbolic acts such as the bombing of clinics. One pro-lifer called the Christmas 1984 bombings "a gift to Jesus on his birthday" (p. 23).

Even in product ads we can detect appeals to the new beginnings or to the return and renewal myth. NEC Corporation says, "The new information age is built on the merging of computers and communication . . . you deserve no less. NEC, the way it will be." The famous Virginia Slims "You've Come a Long Way, Baby" ads are based on a new beginning, which is contrasted with a tainted past. Mercedes-Benz reminds us that "This year, as for ninety-nine years, the automobiles of Mercedes-Benz are like no other cars in the world." In fact, one of the most frequent advertising appeals is a renewal idea: "New and Improved!"

This myth of the eternal return and the cyclical reenactments of the Golden Age — with its heroes, villains, and sacred and profane ground — is a powerful tool that persuaders use in a variety of circumstances (see Figure 8.4). It is reflected in a set of cultural myths described below.

Reich's Cultural Myths

In his book *Tales of a New America*, Robert Reich (1987) discusses the problems facing us in the

Figure 8.4. *This ad by Danner Boots appeals to the myth of the eternal return with its reference to a "Golden Age" when men were men and their boots stood the test of time. (Reprinted by permission of Danner Shoe Manufacturing Co.)*

1990s. He contends that the future appears chaotic for a variety of reasons: rapidly advancing technology, rising expectations for prosperity throughout the world, and a generalized confusion about where we are headed as a nation. Reich and his Harvard colleagues have identified what they call basic cultural parables for the United States. These parables convey

> lessons about the how and why of life through metaphor [which] may be a basic human trait, a universal characteristic of our intermittently rational, deeply emotional, meaning-seeking species. . . . In America the vehicles of public myth include the biographies of famous citizens, popular fiction and music, feature stories on the evening news and gossip. . . . They anchor our political understandings. . . . What gives them force is their capacity to make sense of, and bring coherence to, common experience. The lessons ring true, even if the illustration is fanciful. (p. 7)

Reich's work often echoes what has been emphasized earlier in our study of persuasion: Human beings are fascinated and driven by the power of the dramatic or the narrative.

Reich's myths are rooted in the vignette of a man named George, the son of immigrant parents who worked hard to provide a good home. George did well in school and worked long hours to bring home a few dollars for the family. He was good in sports, although he didn't have much time to participate. He never picked a fight, but on one occasion he did step in to stop the town bully and banker's son, Albert Wade, from beating up on the smallest kid in class. He let Albert have the first swing and then decked him with a single punch. George went off to fight Nazism in Europe and saved his squad by single-handedly destroying a machine gun nest, but he was too humble to wear or display the medal he received for heroism. After the war, he returned to his

hometown, married his childhood sweetheart, and became successful in the construction business. He gave his spare time to good causes and lived modestly. George kept pretty much to himself until his old nemesis, Albert Wade, inherited his father's bank and began to squander the depositors' savings by making shaky loans to his buddies and buying himself into the office of mayor. The only person to stand up and challenge the corrupt election was George. Then Wade's bank refused to loan any money on houses built by George. In a showdown town meeting, one of Wade's corrupt councilmen finally couldn't take George's accusatory gaze and broke down, spilling the beans on Wade, who ended up in jail while George went back to his quiet and modest life. It is *the* American morality play, according to Reich.

This brief story has been told over and over again in various versions, including Horatio Alger novels, films, and biographies of famous Americans. It contains Reich's four basic cultural parables, which are discussed next. As you read about these parables, note some of the similarities between the work of Reich and his colleagues and what we have been calling cultural myths.

The Mob at the Gates. The basic idea in this parable is that America stands alone in the world as the last, best remaining hope for a good, moral, and affluent life in a world that is filled with perilous possibilities and awesome problems. This parable creates an "us versus them" mentality, or mind-set. The mob may be drug traffickers, illegal aliens, or something more abstract: environmental polluters; the militia movement; foreign or slave labor that can provide goods at prices much lower than American companies; secular humanists; minorities; and others.

The parable has at least two sides—a liberal one and a conservative one. Both sides may defy the mob at the gates on one issue, such as

What do you think?

What is a current example of the "mob at the gates" myth?

foreign competition, but on other issues the mob may be acceptable for one side and not for the other. Such a case might be the issue of illegal aliens, which the liberals see as far less dangerous than the conservatives do.

Reich cites several events of central importance to our nation that rested on the mob at the gates parable. One example he gives is Franklin Roosevelt's "rotten apple" metaphor — several "rotten" nations could ruin the "whole barrel" of nations. Reich argues that the post–World War II "domino theory," in which nation after nation fell to the communists, was also an appeal to the mob at the gates myth. More recently, we have seen this myth used by the leadership of Russia, who are trying to institute a market economy in the face of hardline communists.

Advertisers base many of their ads for products on this parable. Millions of germs are lying in wait to infect you, but if you use Listerine mouthwash, you'll knock 'em for a loop. Hordes of mosquitoes will ruin your picnic unless you are vigilant enough to spray the area with long-lasting Raid insect fog. Orkin products can exterminate the mobs of termites and carpenter ants that are destroying your home.

The mob myth is a natural for ideological campaigns as well. For example, the secular humanists are ready to taint America's moral fiber with their approach to questions of morals, so it is absolutely essential to join the "moral majority." And of course politicians use the image in a variety of ways — the mob may be the other party, the threat of uncontrolled terrorism, a runaway national debt, the "heroin chic" crowd that threatens the future of all of our youth, or a maverick political organization, such as H. Ross Perot's Reform Party.

The Triumphant Individual. This parable has as its subject the humble person who works hard, takes risks but has faith in self, and eventually reaches or even exceeds goals of fame, honor, and financial success. It is the story of the self-made man or woman who demonstrates what hard work and determination combined with a gutsy approach to problems and a spunky style can do. Usually the individual is a loner, sometimes even a maverick who is willing to challenge the establishment and try to do something on a shoestring.

A modern example is Steven Jobs, the inventor of the Apple computer. Not only did Jobs begin building the Apple empire in his garage, but he went out and started over again when he left Apple to form NEXT. He was self-reliant, was hard-working, and believed in himself. Another example from the corporate world is Lee Iacocca, the maverick at Ford who bucked the odds and the office politics, fighting long and hard for a product he believed in and finally persuading the company to bring out its most successful product ever: the Mustang. After he was fired by Ford, Iacocca took over the nearly bankrupt Chrysler Corporation and turned the company around, paying off a $1.2 billion government "bailout" loan early; innovating with front-wheel drive and the mini-van; instituting customer rebates, driver and passenger airbags, the seven-year or 70,000-mile warranty; and bringing back the convertible. This myth strikes the same chord as the wisdom-of-the-rustic and possibility of success myths discussed earlier.

We frequently see the triumphant individual in a variety of persuasive arenas. In politics, self-made men or women are the ones to put your money on — they made it this far on a gutsy attitude and a belief in themselves, and as a result, they will come out winners on election day as well. Bill Clinton used this appeal in both the 1992 and 1996 campaigns.

The Benevolent Community. The myth or parable of the benevolent community is the story of the essential goodness of people and their willingness to help out the other guy in time of need. An ad for the Miller beer company portrayed this myth in action. A small town in Wisconsin was struck by a tornado that demolished several homes and nearby farms. But the men and women of surrounding communities joined forces and within two weeks had nearly rebuilt all that had been destroyed. Of course, at the end of a hard day of raising walls and rafters, they enjoyed the camaraderie of the event by drinking the sponsor's product. Groups of students help victims of flooding in the Midwest. Corporate America regularly enhances its image after various disasters by advertising that they have donated money and products to the victims, and thus the corporation becomes part of the benevolent community.

We find this cultural myth recurring throughout our history in struggles like abolition, women's suffrage, the civil rights movement, and the prolife demonstrations of recent times. As Reich notes, "The story celebrates America's tradition of civic improvement, philanthropy, and local boosterism" (p. 10). We can be sure persuaders will continue to use the lesson of the benevolent community to market products, candidates, and ideologies.

Rot at the Top. The "rot at the top" parable or myth has conspiratorial aspects and revolves around a number of subthemes: corruption, a lack of morals or ethics, decadence, and the malevolence of persons in high places. Like the presence-of-conspiracy myth, it seems to follow a cyclical pattern, which Reich calls "the cycles of righteous fulmination." First we trust the elite, then we find them lacking in trust or goodwill, and we end up distrusting or unseating them. Reich traces the myth to the founding fathers' sensitivity to the abuse of power experienced under King George and his designees, the colonial governors and English soldiers. There always exist abuses of power by elites who buy their power with money and favors (as did George's archenemy, Albert Wade) or whom power has made arrogant and corrupt.

Our history recounts numerous and varied types of rot at the top, but Reich believes that the myth usually has one or two targets: political corruption or economic exploitation. Politically, we have seen it in Teapot Dome in the 1920s, Watergate in the '70s, and Bill Clinton's Whitewatergate in the '90s. Economically, we often hear that big business has exploited the common man; Teddy Roosevelt was a "trust-buster" on behalf of the common man, while Franklin Roosevelt promised to "throw the money changers from the temple" in his first inaugural address. President Dwight Eisenhower warned of "the military-industrial complex" in his farewell address. And the late '80s had numerous Wall Street scandals based on insider trading by "stock market jackals" and "corporate barracudas," to use Jesse Jackson's term—all examples of rot at the top. The '90s will undoubtedly reveal more rot at the top.

The lesson of this myth is simple: "Power corrupts; privilege perverts." And the power of this myth is considerable, especially in politics: "When in doubt, vote the scoundrels out."

What do you think?

What is a current example of the "rot at the top" myth?

The "Man's Man" and the "Woman's Woman"

Another popular myth is that for a male to be a success, he must be a man's man. Schools, family, and television tell children that important males are those who do macho things: who compete in macho activities, use colognes with names like "Iron," are involved in sports, talk tough, and own guns, heavy-duty equipment, and four-wheel-drive vehicles. They never show their emotions, and they die with their boots on.

On the other hand, ideal women are soft spoken, kind, and nurturing. They may work, but they are also perfect wives and mothers, are immaculately groomed, and are vain.

These myths, of course, affect the way we treat our children—valuing certain things they do and devaluing others. It is "unfeminine" for a woman to engage in any sport except tennis, golf, or swimming; it is "unmasculine" for any man to take up gourmet cooking, needlepoint, or flower gardening (vegetables are okay). Boys shouldn't cry. Girls always do.

This myth of the distinctions between the sexes is obviously changing, however. High schools and colleges boast women's field hockey, basketball, and baseball teams. In many towns, you will find girls' softball leagues for seven-, eight-, and nine-year-olds. In fact, we now place great emphasis on athletic ability and health in both men and women. Female executives are featured in ads for hotels. Female pilots are shown using deodorant. At the same time, men are now expected to contribute their fair share of housework.

Old myths do not die easily, however, and we still see many examples of the stereotypical macho man and the "perfectly feminine" woman. Beer ads feature retired athletes engaged in a man's world, bragging to one another over beers. The makers of perfume know that Cindy Crawford, for example, epitomizes femininity. One look at any current magazine will show advertisers pitching their products at people who must believe these images of men and women.

Although gender-bound, stereotypical representations of men and women are changing, these images still have persuasive power and are still used to advertise products, push candidates, and promote ideas. Despite reductions in gender differences in job and political candidacy and in gender-related language use, the old stereotypes are still potent persuaders. The major change in attitude toward gender-related issues has occurred in young, college-educated, upper-middle-class, nonminority populations. But the far greater proportion of our population still seems to buy into the man's man and woman's woman myths. We can expect to see ads for macho four-wheel-drive Jeeps and super-powerful chainsaws for as long as we continue to see ads for Maidenform bras, Hanes pantyhose, and Emeraude perfume, along with their advice: "Want Him to Be More of a Man? Try Being More of a Woman."

Persuaders will adapt as Americans shift their values regarding gender and other human characteristics, such as age, single parenthood, and economic status, but their persuasion will reflect the premises that the audience believes. Persuasion is more often a reflection of a culture's values than a shaper of them (see Figure 8.5).

Image (Charisma) or Ethos as a Cultural Premise

Sometimes persuaders are successful because of their **image,** or **charisma.** We believe them because their presentations are convincing and dynamic or because they have a reputation for being truthful or knowledgeable. This kind of proof was recognized by Aristotle, as well as others. He called it *ethos*, or ethical proof. More recently, researchers have worked at identifying exactly what causes or creates high ethos in some persons and low ethos in others. One research technique is to have audiences rate various speakers on a variety of bipolar scales that have sets of opposing adjectives at either end.

Figure 8.5. *Here are examples of the myth of the "man's man" done tongue in cheek. (Making It copyright 1988 Keith Robinson. All rights reserved. Reprinted by permission of Making It Productions)*

Researchers have used several hundred such pairs of terms to determine which traits seemed to typify speakers considered persuasive and believable. They have discovered in repeated tests that the choices seem to cluster around three traits or three dimensions of **source credibility**: expertise, trustworthiness (sincerity), and dynamism.

Expertise

The *expertise* component of source credibility means that highly credible sources are perceived as having knowledge and experience regarding the topic they address. This makes sense; we tend to put more store in the ideas and advice that come from experts than those that come from nonexperts. Whom would you listen to for advice on auto racing—the winner of the Indy 500 or the kid down the block who drag-races on Friday nights? The clustering of items related to expertise has been verified by experiments in which a variety of groups listen to the same tape-recorded speaker giving the same speech. The speaker is introduced to some of the groups as an expert— say, the surgeon general, while to others the speaker is introduced as a college senior. The listeners find the "expert" much more believable than the nonexpert.

Berlo, Lemmert, and Davis (1969) found that three believability factors emerged from audience-generated words describing credible sources. These factors were *safety, qualification,* and *dynamism.* Qualification is similar to expertise. This dimension has been identified under various conditions repeatedly since then and seems to be one of the more stable factors in determining whether we believe someone.

Trustworthiness

Another dimension that recurs in studies of image is *trustworthiness* or *sincerity.* Over forty years

ago, researchers at Yale identified this factor in their studies, concluding that the credibility of any source is tied to "trust and confidence" attributes (Hovland, Janis, & Kelley, 1953). This dimension has reemerged in numerous studies over the years, although at times it may have been labeled *safety* or *personal integrity* (Baudhin & Davis, 1973).

An interesting indicator of trustworthiness occurs in situations where a biased source testifies against his or her own self-interest or bias. This may give us a clue to what is really involved in the trust dimension. Communication researchers Herbert Kelman and Carl Hovland (1953) wanted to know who would be believed in the following situation: A message promoting the need for stiffer penalties for juvenile delinquents was attributed in one case to a juvenile court judge and in another case to a drug-pushing juvenile delinquent. The audience believed the judge because of his expertise in dealing with juvenile cases, but their belief in the delinquent came from their trust in testimony that was obviously against the speaker's bias.

Trust involves receivers analyzing a speaker's motives or hidden agenda. A person's motivation is a key to his or her sincerity. The etymology of the word "sincerity" gives us some insights. It comes from the Latin *sincerus,* which literally means "without wax." This had a dual meaning in ancient times. The first meaning referred to the use of wax coatings as preservatives. To be without wax was to be fresh, pure, or unadulterated. The second meaning referred to a practice of unethical pillar carvers, who used wax to cover up their mistakes. Only after decades of weathering did the wax fall out to reveal the deception practiced by the long-gone carver. So a sincere person was *without wax* or uncamouflaged.

Audiences may believe speakers are sincere when they maintain good eye contact, don't shift back and forth on their feet, and lack a tremor in their voices. Or audiences may judge sincerity from the speaker's reputation. Trustworthiness or sincerity is also a fairly stable factor in credibility, as has been repeatedly demonstrated in research studies. Although its effects vary from situation to situation, receivers believe persons they trust, whether because of the sources' reputation, delivery, or supposed motivation.

Dynamism

A final dimension of credibility that has been demonstrated through experimental research is not as easy to describe or define. This factor has been labeled *dynamism, compliance,* or *image* by various researchers; it is the degree to which the audience admires and identifies with the source's attractiveness, power or forcefulness, and energy. The following word pairs have been linked in testing to the dynamism factor: *aggressive* as opposed to *meek; emphatic* as opposed to *hesitant; frank* as opposed to *reserved; bold* as opposed to *passive; energetic* as opposed to *tired;* and *fast* as opposed to *slow.*

This characteristic is clearly related to charisma, and although it is influenced by a speaker's attractiveness, unattractive persons can be charismatic or dynamic, too. Dynamic speakers don't necessarily move about or wave their arms to give off dynamism cues. They just seem to take up a lot of psychological space. They enter a room and people expect them to be in charge.

There are other dimensions of source credibility that could be investigated, and some already have been. A tall speaker, for example, is generally more likely to be believed than a short one. Timid or shy and reserved persons are likely to have low credibility, whereas authoritative and self-assured ones have high credibility. Bossy and egotistical persuaders lose credibility, whereas pleasant and warm persuaders do not. These and many other dimensions of source credibility interact and affect the three fundamental dimensions of trust: sincerity, expertise, and dynamism, or potency.

These values are not shared by all cultures. In cultures where the bribe or "baksheesh" is the order of the day, people are admired for being *untrustworthy.* Haggling over prices in the bazaars and markets of other cultures is based on *insincerity,* not sincerity. In some cultures, a religious leader who perhaps lacks expertise in economics and diplomacy becomes the head of state, whereas the experts are ejected from government.

Presence of an American Value System

The myths we have just examined are actually fantasy forms of deep and enduring values that most Americans hold. They are expressed in myths in order to simplify them. This makes them seem less lofty. For example, Americans have a belief or value that all persons are to be treated equally and that in the eyes of God they *are* equal. This value has been debated for more than two centuries through such issues as slavery, women's suffrage, civil rights, desegregation, and affirmative action programs. The value is acted out or dramatized in the possibility of success myth. We see the myth portrayed in print and TV ads. For example, a recent image ad for the DuPont Chemical Company featured a black man who was still able to play top-notch basketball even though he had lost both legs in Vietnam, thanks to the good folks at DuPont who sold the raw materials for making the artificial limbs that now enable him to be successful in the world of amateur sports (see Figure 8.6).

One of the early speech communication studies that explored values was conducted by

For Bill Demby, *the difference means getting another shot.*

When Bill Demby was in Vietnam, he used to dream of coming home and playing a little basketball with the guys.

A dream that all but died when he lost both his legs to a Viet Cong rocket.

But then, a group of researchers discovered that a remarkable DuPont plastic could help make artificial limbs that were more resilient, more flexible, more like life itself.

Thanks to these efforts, Bill Demby is back. And some say, he hasn't lost a step.

At DuPont, we make the things that make a difference.

Better things for better living.

REG. U.S. PAT. & TM. OFF.

Figure 8.6. *This ad enhances DuPont's ethos by implying that the company is responsible for Bill Demby's "getting another shot" at life. (DuPont Company photograph. Used by permission of DuPont.)*

Edward Steele and W. Charles Redding (1962). They looked at the communication of several presidential election campaigns and tried to extract core and secondary values. Below are descriptions of the core values observed by Steele and Redding.

Puritan and Pioneer Morality

This moral value involves the willingness to cast the world into categories of foul and fair, good and evil, and so forth. Although we tend to think of this value as outdated, it has merely been reworded. The advocates and foes of marijuana laws and of legal abortion both call on moral values such as just/unjust, right/wrong, and moral/immoral to make their cases.

Value of the Individual

This value involves the ranking of the rights and welfare of the individual above those of government or other groups. This value seems to persist. All politicians claim to be interested in the individual. Cosmetics are made "especially for you." We protect individuality, and Burger King lets you "Have It Your Way."

Achievement and Success

This value entails the accumulation of power, status, wealth, and property. In the late 1960s and 1970s young Americans seemed to reject this value, favoring communal living and refusing to dress up for school, church, or even job interviews. Many of those same young people are now the upwardly mobile, achievement-oriented, and graying yuppies. People today seem to evaluate others by symbols or emblems of success — whether BMWs or Mercedes-Benz's, Rolex watches, Mont Blanc pens, or even pinky "success" rings.

Persuaders frequently appeal to this need for achievement or success. Most of the military recruitment posters, advertisements, and slogans promise that by starting a career in the Army, Navy, Air Force, or Marines, one will be able to climb the ladder to success faster. If you read the *Wall Street Journal*, success and status will be yours. First impressions count, so be sure to "dress for success" by shopping at Neiman Marcus.

The achievement and success value, like the cultural myths, seems to wax and wane or ebb and flow with time. All of the self-help courses and pyramid schemes that we noted earlier will continue to be marketed, even when the values of achievement and success seem most dormant.

Change and Progress

This value is typified by the belief that change (of almost any kind) will lead to progress and that progress is inherently good for us. This is the appeal of any product that is either "new" or "new and improved." The product life cycle theory almost dictates "change" and "progress" in the form of "improvement" to delay the eventual decline of product sales. From a legal point of view, the producer of a laundry product, for example, can claim that its product is new and improved merely by changing the color of the "beads of bleach" or by slightly altering the ratio of ingredients.

Because we as a culture value change and progress, we go for new and improved products as trout go for red worms. This is not to say that all such products are

What do you think?

Which of the core American values seems most out-of-date?

230

bad—only that the appeal has great power. Indeed, many changes have been obviously beneficial: the downsizing of the American automobile and the increase in its fuel efficiency; the development of new generations of home and business computers; the use of the dish antenna; the many new medical technologies that have been recently developed, and the Internet, which has made available an enormous quantity of information on any and every topic as well as making communication with people all over the globe instantaneous.

Ethical Equality

The equality value expresses the belief that all persons ought to be treated equally. They should have an equal opportunity to get an education, to work and be paid a fair wage, to live where they choose, and to hold political office. We all know that although this value may be laudable, the reality is that not everyone is born equal, nor do they all have an equal opportunity for jobs, education, or decent housing. Nonetheless, attempts to create a situation of equality are a part of American history.

Effort and Optimism

This value expresses the belief that even the most unattainable goals can be reached if one works hard and "keeps smilin'." The myths of the triumphant individual and the possibility of success are examples of these values in action. Many optimistic self-help books and programs are further evidence of the ongoing belief in these values. And in today's business world, it is important to be a "striver" or a "self-starter." Folk wisdoms such as "Every cloud *must have* a silver lining," "If at first you don't succeed, try again," "Keep on the sunny side," and "Lighten up" serve as cultural

metaphors of the value we place on effort and optimism.

Efficiency, Practicality, and Pragmatism

Americans are a practical people. A key question often asked of any piece of legislation is "Will it work?" This value extends to other parts of our lives, too. We want to know whether a microwave oven is energy efficient, practical, or handy. We want to know whether our schooling will lead to a job. We are fascinated by questions of efficiency—fuel efficiency in our cars, energy efficiency in our appliances, and efficiency of movement on the job. We go for practical solutions, as was demonstrated in the film *Apollo Thirteen,* in which the crew was able to use various pieces of equipment and supplies to jerry-rig a repair of their malfunctioning spacecraft. In other words, we value what is quick, workable, and practical.

Even though these values were catalogued over forty years ago, they still have a great deal of relevance. This, if nothing else, suggests their basic validity. The fact that political position has less to do with the strength of these values than with the method of enacting them underscores the probability that these are core values for Americans. Our culture is effective in instilling a set of values in nearly all of its members; radicals, moderates, and reactionaries all believe in the same things but apply them differently. The power of a social system or culture to train its members is immense, even though the members do not often realize this as they react to the dictates deeply ingrained in them.

Does this mean that values remain essentially static and cannot be changed? Not necessarily. It means only that values are so deeply ingrained in a culture that its members often forget how strong these pressures are.

Review and Conclusion

By this time, you know that the world of the persuadee in an information age is not an easy one. There are so many things to be aware of: the persuader's self-revelation using language and stylistic choices, the internal or process premises operating within each of us, and the interactive rules for content premises. Now we have glimpsed societal and cultural predispositions for persuasion that may also act as premises in persuasive arguments. Persuaders instinctively appeal to values that rely on the societal training in the target audience. On at least three separate levels, this training has an effect on each of us — in the cultural myths or images to which we respond, in the sets of values we consciously articulate, and in the nonverbal cues to which we react (artifacts, space, and touch, to mention a few).

Questions for Further Thought

1. What are the three types of culturally or socially learned predispositions for persuasion? Give examples of each from your own experience.

2. How does a culture or society train its members? Give examples from your own experience.

3. How do you rank the core values mentioned in this chapter? How do you put them into practice? Are there other values in your value system not mentioned here? What are they? Are they restatements of the core values? If so, how? If not, how do they differ?

4. Considering today's headlines, is there a mob at the gates present? Explain.

5. To what degree can you identify a benevolent community in your life? Explain.

6. In the award-winning film *Witness*, there clearly is rot at the top. If you have seen the film, identify the critical moment when the "narrator" of the film discovers the "rot," and describe what he does about it.

7. Explain the ethos of the hosts of the various talk shows. How does their ethos differ from the others' (for example, does Jay Leno seem more or less sincere, expert, or dynamic than David Letterman)?

8. How have the core values described by Steele and Redding operated on your campus? in your own life?

References

"America's Abortion Dilemma." (1985). *Newsweek,* January 14, pp. 20–23.

Baudhin, S., & Davis, M. (1972). Scales for the measurement of ethos: Another attempt. *Speech monographs, 39,* 296–301.

Beane, W. C., & Doty, W. G. (1975). *Myths, rites, and symbols: A Mercia Eliade reader.* New York: Harper Colophon Books.

Bellah, R. N., Madsen, R., Sullivan, W. M., Swidler, A., & Tipton, S. M. (1985). *Habits of the heart: Individualism and commitment in American life.* New York: Harper & Row.

Berlo, D., Lemmert, J., & Davis, M. (1969). Dimensions for evaluating the acceptability of message sources. *Public Opinion Quarterly, 33,* 563–576.

Eliade, M. (1971). *The myth of the eternal return: Of cosmos and history*. Princeton, NJ: Princeton University Press.

Hofstadter, R. (1963). *Anti-intellectualism in America*. New York: Knopf.

Hofstadter, R. (1967). *The paranoid style in American politics and other essays*. New York: Vintage Books.

Hovland, C., Janis, I., & Kelley, H. (1953). *Communication and persuasion*. New Haven, CT: Yale University Press.

Kelman, H., & Hovland, C. (1953). Reinstatement of the communicator: Delayed measurement of opinion changes. *Journal of Abnormal and Social Psychology, 48*, 327–335.

Reich, R. (1987). *Tales of a new America*. New York: Times Books.

Steele, E. D., & Redding, W. C. (1962). The American value system: Premises for persuasion. *Western Speech, 26*, 83–91.

9

Nonverbal Messages in Persuasion

Videotapes of persons shopping in stores during the devastating 1989 earthquake in San Francisco show that the first thing people did after checking the environmental symptoms of the earthquake—whether objects fell from shelves, or windows and walls cracked—was to check out the nonverbal behavior of the people around them. They looked for facial expressions, movement, and probably a host of other cues of impending danger. During the Middle East crisis of the early nineties, Iraqi strongman Saddam Hussein tried to win worldwide public approval for his actions by being photographed and televised talking with young Western children who were being "detained" (or held hostage) in Iraq (see Figure 9.1). During his interviews he stroked the children and, as a result, prompted worldwide criticism. Fictional hero Jason Bourne, in Robert Ludlum's best-seller *The Bourne Ultimatum,* is able to identify disguised assassin and terrorist "Carlos the Jackal" by the way the villain walks. Advertising researchers observe and record the dilation of the pupil and the eye's path as it surveys a print advertisement to determine the ad's effectiveness. And *Saturday Night Live* actor Dana Carvey clev-

erly mimics the nonverbal gestures, facial expressions, and vocal qualities of politicians and celebrities in his hilarious impressions.

These are but a few of many examples of nonverbal communication that occur around us every day. You and I produce and process hundreds—perhaps thousands—of nonverbal messages daily. In fact, researcher Albert Mehrabian (1971) once estimated that nonverbal communication accounts for over 80 percent of the meaning transferred between people. Usually, these nonverbal messages are part and parcel of the appeals we process in our world of persuasion.

Nonverbal premises in persuasion resemble cultural premises in that both are culturally taught, and both are consistent across and within cultures. A major difference between the two is that many nonverbal premises exist at a very low level of awareness and so aren't readily apparent. Neither are they carefully examined and analyzed. We may sense that a certain persuader seems disreputable and that it may have something to do with his shifty eyes, but we don't analytically dissect our interaction to find out exactly what it is that causes us to distrust or why. One of the more

Figure 9.1. *What kinds of meaning do you derive from this photograph? How is the meaning communicated? (Photo by AFP. © 1990 Newsweek, Inc. Reprinted by permission of Newsweek.)*

valuable strategies persuadees can use to deal with the barrage of persuasion aimed at them is to sensitize themselves to some of the nonverbal factors that enter in whenever someone tries to persuade another. This sensitivity serves a dual purpose: It increases the amount of information on which to base decisions, and, more important, it provides "tipoffs" to the persuader's "hidden agenda" and ultimate goals. You see, most nonverbal communication occurs almost instinctively or automatically. It is hard to fake, and even when faked, the persuader's intent seems to "leak" through nonverbal channels.

Nonverbal Channels

There are several channels through which we can communicate nonverbal meaning. Communication researcher Dale G. Leathers (1986) identifies nine nonverbal channels, including facial expression; eye behavior; bodily communication; proxemics (the use of space); personal appearance; vocalic factors such as voice stress, timbre, and volume; and, finally, tactile communication (the use of touch). Mark Knapp (1978) identifies eight channels: the environment (including architecture and furniture), proxemics and territoriality, physical appearance and dress, physical behavior and movement, touching, facial expression, eye behavior, and vocal cues. Other researchers identify similar categories, with some, such as Ekman and Friesen (1975), focusing only on various aspects of facial communication. Gender differences are the focus of study for some researchers (Hall, 1984), whereas others study nonverbal cues of deception and the nonverbal behavior of liars (Knapp and Comendena, 1985). We can't begin to examine all of these fascinating topics in a single chapter, but we can focus on some of them, especially those that affect persuasive messages in a variety of ways. For our purposes, let's

use the categories suggested by Leathers, as well as considering gender differences in nonverbal communication.

Facial Expression and Eye Behavior

The first nonverbal message channel identified by Leathers is **facial expression** (sometimes called "affect displays") and **eye behavior.** He claims that the face is "the most important source of nonverbal information" (1986, p. 19). Facial expression is familiar and readily noticed, and subtle nuances in facial expression can make a world of difference in perceived meaning. Such variables as the amount and rate of dilation of the pupil or eyeblink rates can communicate a great deal of information about one's attention, emotion, and interest.

Knapp (1978) notes that, correctly or not, people often use the face as a measure of personality, judging high foreheads to indicate intelligence, thin lips to indicate conscientiousness, a bulbous nose to indicate drunkenness, and close-together eyes to indicate low intelligence.

Leathers identified ten general classes or categories of facial expression (and many more specific kinds of facial meaning), including disgust, happiness, interest, sadness, bewilderment, contempt, surprise, anger, determination, and fear. Among his more specific kinds of expressions, Leathers includes rage, amazement, terror, hate, arrogance, astonishment, stupidity, amusement, pensiveness, and belligerence, to name a few.

Ekman and Friesen (1975) identify only six categories of facial expression on which there is universal researcher agreement, including happiness, sadness, surprise, fear, anger, and disgust. Interestingly, they have found that some of these facial expressions are consistent across cultures (for example, 95 percent to 100 percent agreement among American, Brazilian, Chilean, Argentinian, and Japanese subjects on the expression of happiness, but only 54 percent to 85 percent agreement on the expression of fear). The key facial expressions used to convey meaning include eyebrow raising or drooping, smiling or frowning, forehead knitting or relaxing, eye closing or widening (thus exposing more or less white), nose wrinkling, lip pursing, teeth baring, and jaw dropping.

Leathers (1986) identifies six functions that the eye serves. One is the *attention function*, indicated by mutual gazing. You have probably noticed persons who continually look over your shoulder and past you as if they are looking for more interesting possibilities. Some eye behavior serves a *regulatory function*, by indicating when conversation is to begin or stop. When speakers look back at a person or audience, this is generally taken as a signal for them to take their turn talking. Eyes can also serve a *power function*, as when a leader stares at an audience. Many have remarked on the power expressed in the eyes of convicted murderer and cult leader, Charles Manson. Eye behavior also serves an *affective function* by indicating positive and negative emotions. You probably know what your parents' eyes look like when they are angry or what the eyes of someone "in love" look like; both are examples of the eyes' affective function. Eyes are also used in *impression formation*, as when persons communicate a winning image or a lack of self-esteem. Finally, Leathers notes the *persuasive function* of eye behavior. We rate speakers who maintain eye contact as credible, and we suspect those whose gaze is continually shifting about. If people avert their eyes when talking to us, we assume that they are either shy or hiding something from us.

What do you think?

Does eye contact ever make you feel uncomfortable? When? Why?

Bodily Communication

Bodily nonverbal communication has several dimensions, one of which is *kinesics,* or physical movements of the body, such as gestures, the way one holds one's body (tense or relaxed posture), and how one uses the body in given contexts. For example, Leathers reports that former Vice President Nelson Rockefeller, a power seeker, had a set of stairs rigged to his office desk so that he could climb up onto the desk when he wanted to command attention. Powerful persuaders want to be physically or perceptually "above" their audience. They also demonstrate relaxed but erect posture, dynamic gestures, good eye contact, and variation in speaking rate and inflection. Bill Clinton is a master of these nonverbal cues. Powerless persuaders behave more submissively and exhibit lots of body tension, little direct eye contact, "closed" postures (for example, legs and arms crossed), and few gestures.

Knapp identifies several head movements that convey meaning: cocking of the head, tilting or nodding of the head, and the thrusting out of the jaw or the shaking of the head. And, of course, there are other movements that convey meaning: clenching one's fist, having one's arms akimbo on the waist, and standing in an "open" stance with legs spread apart. These movements can indicate anger, intensity, and degree of commitment or dedication.

In some cases, gestures and bodily movements are emblematic—they stand for a particular meaning. For example, stroking the index finger while pointing it at someone is emblematic of "shame on you," crossed fingers indicate "good luck," and the hitchhiker's closed fist and extended thumb are emblematic of wanting a ride (although the same gesture means "gig 'em" to a student of Texas A&M). And there are many obscene gestures that can quickly arouse anger or other emotions.

Proxemic Communication

Proxemic communication (or how one uses physical space) is the fourth category of nonverbal channels in Leathers' system. You have undoubtedly noticed how most people fall silent and don't look at one another when they are in crowded elevators or public restrooms, for example. Edward T. Hall (1959) identifies four kinds of space in his book *The Silent Language:*

1. *Public distance.* This type of distance is often found in public speaking situations where speakers are fifteen to twenty-five or more feet from their audiences. Informal persuasion probably will not work in these circumstances. Persuaders who try to be informal in a formal situation meet with little success.

> **What do you think?**
>
> How do people behave in the intimate distance of a crowded elevator?

2. *Social or formal distance.* This type of distance is used in formal but nonpublic situations, such as interviews or committee reports. The persuader in these situations, although formal in style, need not be oratorical. Formal distance ranges from about seven to twelve feet between persuader and persuadee. Persuaders never become chummy in this kind of situation, yet they do not deliver a "speech" either.

3. *Personal or informal distance.* Two colleagues might use this distance when discussing a matter of mutual concern. Roommates discussing a class or a problem they share use this distance. In these situations, communication is less structured than in the formal situation; both persuadee and persuader relax and interact often with each other, bringing up and questioning evidence or asking for clarification. In our culture, informal distance is about three and one-half to four feet—the eye-to-eye distance when sitting at the corner of a teacher's desk as opposed to the formal distance created when you sit across the desk.

4. *Intimate distance.* People use this distance when they mutter or lovingly whisper messages they do not want others to overhear. Persuasion may or may not occur in these instances; usually the message is one that will not be questioned by the receiver—he or she will nod in agreement, follow the suggestion given, or respond to the question asked. When two communicators are in this kind of close relation to one another, their aims are similar, in all probability. The distance ranges from six to eighteen inches.

How do persuaders use these distance boundaries? Are you and I vulnerable to persuasion using proxemics? The examples that surround us often escape our notice because proxemic communication is transmitted at such a low level of awareness. Take automobile sales as an example. When customers come into a new-car showroom, imagine the results if the salesperson rushed over to them and within personal or even intimate distance asked something like, "What can I do for you folks today?" The customers would probably retreat from the showroom or at least from the salesperson, saying something like, "Well, we're just looking around." Clever sales representatives stay within public distance of the customer until they get an indication of interest or a verbal or nonverbal signal that the customer wants help. Only then will the salesperson move into informal or even formal distance.

Look at the advertisements in any popular magazine and you will notice the use of proxemics as a persuasive device (see Figure 9.2). The young adults who "Go for It" in the beer ads are having fun and enjoying one another in personal or intimate space.

ENJOY

Savor a spectacular weekend at a sensational rate.

Hotel Inter-Continental Chicago invites you to enjoy the perfect weekend getaway at an enticing weekend rate, good any Thursday through Sunday... up to December 30. Ideally located at 505 North Michigan Avenue, this historic landmark presides right on the "Magnificent Mile." Surrounded by splendid shops, theaters, galleries and museums, the hotel is also home to The Boulevard Restaurant, Chicago's finest new dining establishment.

Hotel Inter-Continental Chicago... offering elegant accommodations, incomparable dining and impeccable service. Not to mention a spectacular weekend rate on a luxurious single or double guest room, a refreshingly low... **$125***

For reservations contact your travel agent or call (312) 944-4100, toll-free 800-327-0200.

HOTEL INTER·CONTINENTAL CHICAGO
505 North Michigan Avenue • Chicago, Illinois 60611

* Single or double occupancy, per night. Stay must include a Friday or Saturday night. Subject to availability and advance reservations. Not to be used in conjunction with any other program. Local taxes and gratuities not included. Not available to groups.

Figure 9.2. Which of Hall's four types of communication distance seems to be operating in this ad? Why do you suppose this distance was used? (Reprinted by permission of Hotel Intercontinental, Chicago.)

Recently, people in the real estate business became interested in the communicative power of the correct and strategic use of space. Industry publications have discussed such questions as how close a real estate agent should be to the prospective buyer during a tour of a home or whether the agent should lead or follow the buyer. In many other contexts — offices, hospitals, banks, prisons, and factories — serious consideration is given to the use of space as a communicative device or as a communication facilitator.

Try to be alert to the uses of space in your life. How have you arranged your room or apartment? Does the arrangement facilitate or deter communication? How do various people with whom you interact use their space? Do foreigners use space differently than you? You will soon discover how important this nonverbal channel of communication is to persuasion.

Physical Appearance

During a recent faculty externship at a major advertising agency, I learned that the agency had just fired a female employee because of her appearance; they simply couldn't expose their clients to her unprofessional and sloppy looks. And it is always easy to guess what's going on toward the middle of the spring semester when my students come to class dressed "fit to kill": It is interview time on campus, and everyone knows that appearance sends a message to the interviewer. But **physical appearance** goes much further than just good grooming and proper attire, according to Leathers. For example, his sources maintain that larger-than-normal facial features — nose, ears, and lips — are generally considered unattractive.

Knapp reports other interesting studies regarding physical appearance. For instance, first-born females who are attractive tend to sit toward the front of the class and make more comments during class. They also tended to get better grades. Attractive females are also more likely to persuade male audiences than unattractive females are. You probably wonder what is meant by "attractiveness" in these cases. The research used the same female in both the attractive and unattractive conditions, but in the unattractive condition she wore loose-fitting clothing, had no makeup on, had messy hair, and appeared ungroomed (p. 155).

Another element in physical appearance is bodily attractiveness, according to Leathers. His sources show that slenderness is considered attractive in females, while waist and hip measurements correlate negatively with ratings of attractiveness (that is, larger-waisted and hippier females are perceived as less attractive). A recent fashion trend called "heroin chic" features attractive but emaciated-appearing female models who should be taken to an "all you can eat" buffet as soon as possible. For males, broad shoulders, a well-muscled upper body, and a tapering upper trunk correlate positively with attractiveness ratings. Leathers also found that one's self-image has a lot to do with ratings of attractiveness; if you feel good about yourself, you will probably engage in good grooming and keep your body in good physical condition.

Clothing and adornments such as jewelry also contribute to one's physical appearance (see Figure 9.3). In the case of the dismissed ad agency employee, she tended to dress too casually for the workplace, and her clothing wasn't always clean or pressed. Jewelry also communicates. Think of the different evaluations you might make of a person wearing a Rolex as opposed to a Timex watch or the degree to which gold jewelry can attract your attention. East European businessmen appeared threadbare to me, and I wondered what triggered that evaluation. After some analysis I realized that all of them carried imitation leather attaché cases and that the quality of their shoes rated below that of the specials at cheap discount stores.

Who says charm isn't hereditary? We've been helping it along for 172 years. And while change is inevitable, a tradition of quality is our legacy. And yours.

Grandfather, tuxedo from Brooks Brothers formal wear collection, from $495, and exclusive furnishings. *Grandson*, classic navy blazer, $95.

THE MAN IN THE BROOKS BROTHERS SUIT

Brooks Brothers

Figure 9.3. *Clothing is used to communicate. What message is being communicated in this ad? (Reprinted by permission of Brooks Brothers Clothing.)*

Artifactual Communication

Although birds feather their nests with bits of string, straw, hair, and wood, they do it for purely functional reasons: to keep their nests intact and cozy. We humans feather our nests not only for these reasons but also for highly symbolic reasons. The best way of discovering how this happens is to look at your work area or at that of your roommate or other friend. You will find that it is arranged not only for work. People feather their nests with objects—**artifacts**—that symbolize their sense of self. Arrangement is also symbolic (certain kinds of people have messy desks, whereas others have extremely neat desks, with each pencil sharpened and papers stacked in neat piles). Our culture has taught us to react in certain ways to the artifacts of others and how they are used. These patterns of responses form premises for persuasion.

A common type of artifactual cosmetology is revealed in the objects surrounding a persuader in a message situation. For example, in a public speech situation, the banners, bunting, use of flags, and insignias all contribute to the ultimate success (or failure) of the persuasive attempt. Clothing is another type of artifact. What people wear sends signals about what they are like and about what they believe or represent (for example, a priest's collar or an army officer's uniform).

Another type of artifact is exemplified in the personal objects surrounding a persuader. Consider how you feel when you go into a doctor's office that has diplomas on the walls—no art, no colorful posters, no other kind of decoration, just diplomas. What kind of person is the doctor likely to be? Compare that with the feeling you have as you enter a college professor's office that has posters or abstract art on the walls. These artifacts symbolize the kind of persuasion you will be likely to hear—in the one case, professional, concrete, and probably prescriptive, while in the other, abstract and probably informal.

Large objects such as furniture also give off signals. We expect a certain kind of communication to occur when we are told to sit down at a table and the persuader sits at the opposite side. Persuaders who put a lectern between themselves and the audience will probably engage in a certain kind of communication—formal. If they step out from behind the lectern or walk around while talking, they may be more informal. Types of furniture can also symbolize certain characteristics. What kinds of persuasion and what kinds of persons would you associate with French Provincial furniture? What kind of persuasion is likely to occur in a room with metal office furniture?

These artifactual messages vary among cultures and even subcultures. Frequently, artifactual communication makes the difference between successful and unsuccessful persuasion. Try to identify the most effective kinds of artifacts for persuading you.

What do you think?

What kinds of artifacts do you use in your room or on yourself?

Vocalic Communication

Each of us has had the experience of answering the phone and not being quite able to figure out who is calling. We listen carefully and ask innocuous questions until something the person says matches his or her vocal patterns; then we recognize who it is and carry on as if we had known all along.

Leathers (1986) notes that there is a **semantics of sound** that affects how we respond to a persuader's message. Some of the factors he identifies include volume or loudness, pitch, rate, vocal quality, clarity of pronunciation, intonation pattern, and the use of silence. These elements enable you to recognize the voice on the phone. More important, these vocalic factors influence you to be or not to be persuaded by a given source, and they frequently indicate a lot about persuaders and their emotions, goals, and sincerity.

Monotonic persuaders bore the audience and lose most of their persuasiveness. High-pitched voices indicate excitement; sometimes low-pitched but tense voices indicate anger. Rate of speech can indicate nervousness or confidence. Vocal quality communicates a number of things; breathy voices in females, for example, communicate a stereotype of simplicity and shallowness, whereas breathy voices in males may indicate that the speaker is effeminate. Screeching or tense voices indicate stress and concern. Nasality is often associated with being stuck up and maybe even sissified. Persons who articulate poorly and who mispronounce words generally lose some of their credibility and effectiveness.

Knapp (1978) reports research indicating that people can fairly reliably identify certain stereotypes from vocal cues. These stereotypes include such characteristics as masculinity/femininity, age, enthusiasm/apathy, activeness/laziness, and good looks/ugliness. He also reports research that identifies the following correlations: breathiness in males indicates youth and an artistic nature; a thin voice in females indicates social, physical, and emotional insecurity; vocal flatness indicates sluggishness for both males and females; and nasality is associated with a number of undesirable traits in both males and females. He also reports that most listeners are quite sensitive to vocal cues.

It is clear from the foregoing discussion that one feature of oral persuasion that receivers must pay attention to is the vocalic qualities of communication coming from the persuader.

Tactile Communication

Some of the more important nonverbal message carriers are the ways in which and the degree to which people **touch** one another. We know that infants genuinely *need* to be touched and cuddled. We also know that this need doesn't diminish as the child matures, but that in our culture the number, type, and duration of touches a child gets are greatly reduced as he or she matures. Children may substitute other kinds of touches for the touches they received from their parents: socking a pal, shoving someone, tickling, holding hands with someone, and so on.

There are gender-related differences in the use of touch. Women are more likely to use touch to communicate than are men. In fact, the average woman touches someone else about twelve times per day, whereas the average man touches someone only eight times a day (Kotulak, 1985). Touches by both males and females are more likely to be with a person of the opposite sex, which is the reverse of what occurs in some other cultures. In Western culture, touch between men generally is limited to shaking hands or backslapping.

Persuaders who are too "touchy" with persons around them probably offend not only the person touched but also those observing the touch. Credibility can be drastically undermined if persuaders misread a relationship and respond inappropriately with touch.

Leathers makes the point that we live in a "noncontact" society, with touch noticeably absent in public places, particularly between men. We probably would not accept the vice-president hugging and kissing the president on the president's return from abroad, yet that is perfectly acceptable in many countries of the world. These norms for the use of touch, Leathers notes, usually relate to two general factors: the part of the body that is touched and the demographic characteristics of the interactants (age, gender, social class, race, and status). He also reports that research shows the head, shoulders, and arms to be the most frequently touched parts of the body, with other parts being more or less "off limits" to public touch, and that the use of touch is more frequent among minorities. In terms of persuasion, research shows that persuaders who touch persuadees are the most successful persuaders (Kotulak, 1985).

Touch seems to be a good way to convey special kinds of emotional persuasion, such as empathy, warmth, and reassurance. For firefighters, the only acceptable touch from another male was the handshake or backslap. However, a firefighter must sometimes calm frantic men, women, and children to get them out of a burning building, so willingness to touch varies depending on the situation. The laying on of hands used in some religions is sometimes given credit for conversions; it is possible that touch is persuasive enough to prompt people to come forward and convert.

Sometimes touch is extremely important in facilitating certain kinds of communication. Terminal cancer patients, for example, need more touch than less ill patients, according to some experts. Touch helps to express sympathy when one attends a funeral service. Recent studies showed the importance of touch. Strangers were asked to give information to a researcher on a street corner. In half of the cases, the researcher lightly touched the stranger before saying, "Excuse me, but I'm sort of lost. Can you tell me where . . . ?" The researcher got much more information and even conversation when using the light touch. Observe printed ads in magazines. Look at the kinds of touches used in them. You will discover that the persuasive potential of touch has many dimensions.

Some touches are taboo. Researchers Stanley Jones and Elaine Yarborough identified taboo touches including (1) touching strangers; (2) touching that inflicts pain, as when someone touches someone else's sunburn; (3) touching that interferes with another's activities or conversation; (4) touching that moves others aside; (5) playful touching that is too aggressive, as in mock wrestling or pinching; and (6) what they call "double-whammy" touching, in which touch is used to emphasize a negative point (as in touching someone's belly when mentioning that they have put on weight) (Kotulak, 1985).

As you continue to improve your abilities as a receiver, one of the nonverbal channels of communication to observe closely is the use of touch, whether it occurs at the first meeting one has with a stranger, punctuates the closing of a business deal, represents the empathic sensitivity one has for another, or provides the assurance that can help move people out of a dangerous situation.

Chronemics: The Use of Time

There is good evidence to suggest that our use of time sends many signals about how we evaluate others. A saying in our culture goes, "Time is money—don't waste it!" Time can communicate many messages to others. Let's suppose that you have set a time and reserved a place for a meeting of a work group. Because you are arranging the meeting, you show up ten minutes early to make sure things will go well. A few minutes before the meeting is to start, two members of the group arrive and begin to chat. Right on time, to the minute, comes another group member. Now only two people are missing. You probably will say something like "Let's wait a few minutes before starting." After five minutes, one of your missing persons shows up and you start the meeting. Nearly a half hour after the meeting has started, the missing member arrives. What messages were sent by each member of the group? In our culture, it is permissible to arrive at a meeting up to five or six minutes late, but arrive later than that and you'd better have a good excuse, such as a flat tire, a stalled elevator, or a speeding ticket. By coming late, you "persuade" the others that you really don't care much about the appointment, that you are a thoughtless person, and that you are probably an arrogant prima donna.

What do you think?

What message do you get when your professor shows up for class five minutes late?

If, on the other hand, you are invited to a party, be sure to show up at least forty-five minutes late if it is a college party and at least twenty minutes late if it is a business cocktail party. If you show up on time, the host and hostess may still be grooming themselves or putting the final touches on the place settings.

If you really want to put people in their place, make sure they have to wait to get in to see you—a favorite trick of some college professors. On one campus, students must wait at least five minutes for an "instructor" to arrive at class, ten minutes for a "professor," and twenty minutes for a "Dr." before assuming there will be no class. So time is not only money; it is often also status. Begin to observe how time works in your culture or subculture, and don't be surprised if it doesn't operate the same way in other cultures or even in subcultures within our culture.

Gender Differences in Nonverbal Communication

Recently, researchers have investigated gender differences in nonverbal communication. For example, in a 1989 study of attitudes toward the use of touch, researchers found that women are sig-nificantly more comfortable with touch than are men and that higher levels of "touch comfort" are signs of a greater level of socialization (Fromme et al., 1989). Brenda Major (1984) noted significant gender differences in how individuals touch others and in how they receive such touches, and she found that these differences are exhibited very shortly after birth. Whereas men tend to initiate touching in cross-gender encounters, they are less likely to initiate touch in same-gender encounters. Women, on the other hand, are less hung up about touching other women. Although touch often cues warmth and intimacy (especially among women), it can also communicate power or status relationships. In this case, men tend to use touch more frequently, indicating that they perceive themselves to be superior.

Major also reported on gender differences in reactions to touch. If, for example, the toucher is of the same status as the touchee, women react more positively and men more negatively, particularly when the toucher is a woman. Major concludes that, overall, women tend to react more positively to touch than men do and that this probably stems from the fact that girls are touched more frequently from birth on and are perceived as being more fragile and passive than boys.

Porter and Geis (1984) wondered whether gender and nonverbal communication are related to leadership in small groups. They found that in both all-male and all-female groups, geographical position at the head of the table is the best predictor of leadership. In mixed-gender groups, males emerge as the leader if they sit in the leadership position, while women do not.

Ellyson, Dovidio, and Fehr (1984) investigated dominance in men and women as it relates to visual behavior. They found that dominance is usually indicated by what they called "look/speak" rather than "look/listen" behavior (that is, attempting to dominate by speaking rather than listening when catching the eyes of others). Further, they found no gender-related factors; that is, if women use the "look/speak" strategy, they are just as likely to be evaluated as dominant as are men who use the same strategy.

Judy Hall (1984) found that women have more expressive faces than men and smile and laugh more often than men, especially when they are in all-female groups. She speculates that smiling and laughing may be seen as unmasculine, which tends to discourage males from exhibiting these behaviors.

Regarding "gaze" and "gaze holding," Hall found that women tend to gaze more at other persons than do men and that women are more uncomfortable than men when they cannot see the person being spoken to. They also seem to be gazed at more frequently than men (which makes perfect sense to me). Hall hints that gaze differences between males and females exist because females are perceived as having more warmth than males. Also, males avoid the gazes of other males to bypass the potential implications of such gazing.

Regarding proxemics, Hall finds that men maintain greater distances from others when in conversation and that women are approached more closely than men. Women tend to face more directly toward the person with whom they are interacting. When given the choice of sitting adjacent to or across from others, men tend to sit in the "across" position, whereas women prefer the "adjacent" position. Finally, females are also more approachable than males, which Hall attributes to real or perceived "warmth, affiliativeness, and/or size," rather than any perception of lower status, as is the case when gender is not a variable. She also found that women initiate touching more than men. Hall speculates that this may be due to women's appreciation for being touched more and that there may be gender-related differences for various kinds of touch (for example, where on the body, how emphatic the touch, and so on).

Regarding body movement and position, Hall found little research on which to base generalizations. However, it does appear that men are more relaxed than women, more physically expansive (for example, spreading arms and legs, leaning back in chairs with legs forward, and so on), and more restless (for example, fidgeting, playing with objects, and shifting the body in various ways). Another difference is that whereas women tend to carry things in front of their chest, men carry things at their side.

Hall finds several gender-related differences in the use of the voice in nonverbal ways. Men, for example, seem to be less fluent than women, make more verbal errors, and use more vocalized pauses such as "uh" or "um." Women's voices tend to have higher pitches, even though their vocal mechanism permits them to use lower ones. At the same time, women's voices have more variability in pitch, are more musical, and are more expressive than men's voices. Women's voices are also softer than men's voices, and, on a global basis, women's voices are judged to be *more* positive, pleasant, honest, meek, respectful, delicate, enthusiastic, and anxious and *less* confident, domineering, and awkward. Male voices, on the other hand, tend to be demanding, blunt, dominant, forceful, and militant.

Using an entirely different perspective and methodology, Jean Umiker-Sebeok (1984) studied women as they appear in magazine advertisements. Among other things, she found that in ads showing women in a professional role (for example, wearing a doctor's smock and taking someone's blood pressure, or dressed in a suit at a business conference), their hair is always in place, they always wear makeup, their posture and gestures are feminine, and the setting is usually "feminized" by the use of houseplants, floral arrangements, flouncy curtains, or mirrors. The result is women who are dressed *for* someone — usually a man — and defined, in the words of Roland Barthes, as "entirely constituted by the gaze of man."

Umiker-Sebeok's major findings relate to how women are depicted at each of five life stages: infancy and childhood, adolescence, young adulthood, middle age, and old age and senility.

Ads depict gender differences beginning in the toddler stage. Females are depicted as being interested in appearance; they are smaller than males in the same ads; they are subordinate and passive; they are rounder; and they are emotional, displaying smiles, laughter, fear, surprise, innocence, and dismay. In childhood, females are rarely depicted away from home, in contrast to boys. Shopping seems to be one of the few "away from home" settings in which female children appear, and then they are usually seen being helped by a kindly older male. They are rarely pictured in independent roles; rather, they usually are seen close to Mom and doing things in the kitchen, the laundry, or flower garden. Umiker-Sebeok speculates that these settings associate female children with productivity and fertility. Fathers and sons, on the other hand, are more frequently depicted outside the home enjoying some sort of competitive activity: sports, contests, or daring adventures.

In adolescence, females are depicted in extremes, vacillating between independence and being protected, usually by Dad now. They might be seen in or away from the home, trying on roles and the accompanying "costumes." They seem to be in a second infancy, with soft, hairless complexions, pink cheeks, rounded body contours, and wide eyes as they sleep, stroke themselves, or smile demurely at the camera while they lick or suck something. If they are associated with athletics, female adolescents are usually in an auxiliary role, such as that of cheerleader.

In young adulthood, females are depicted as seeking independence along with one of two "paths": the glamour and sophistication path or the wholesome, girl-next-door path. They will be shown as either young, beautiful, and narcissistic women or somewhat older but happy housewives, presumably caring for a family. If a young woman is on the glamorous and sophisticated path, she may choose an aggressive lifestyle (posing in an aggressive male stance, fists on hips, chin held high, and staring at the camera, perhaps with one foot propped up with the knee at a right angle — a male phallic display posture). She might, however, appear appealing and alluring (for example, kneeling or sitting, head tilted to one side, and smiling). If she is seen on the job, her office is "feminized"; she might be sitting on the edge of her desk or standing in a doorway or at the outline of buildings, which Freud thought symbolized the womb.

If a woman opts for the wholesome role, she is depicted as a pretty doll in a shop window, presenting herself for her hubby's approval or involved in courtship. In this life stage, men look at women more often than women gaze at men. Women gaze off into the distance with their hair blown back, eyes closed, perhaps involved in a fantasy or daydream — often about a male — as in Chanel perfume ads. If pictured with a male, he is holding her hand, and she is generally being protected by the male to whom she "belongs" (see Figure 9.4). She is almost always positioned lower than the male: seated while he stands, shorter, or lying down. In courtship, she is a highly polished object who is being "traded" from her father to her husband. As a bride, she is innocent, angelic, vulnerable, and childish as she is "given away" by her dad. The groom usually dresses and stands like Dad during the exchange.

Umiker-Sebeok found that middle-aged females are depicted as awkward, bumbly, somewhat overweight, and sometimes comical. Usually the middle-aged female is unattractive, but if she is attractive, she is featured because she

Figure 9.4. *This wholesome "girl next door" is "owned" and "protected" by her man in this photo from an ad by Aquascutum. (Reprinted by permission of Aquascutum Shop.)*

doesn't look her age. The middle-aged female is often shown caring for a pet—a substitute child—and is pictured in the home more often than away from it. Again, if she is away from home, she is often shopping. If the middle-aged female is upper middle class, she will be more angular, will be thinner, and will probably wear glasses as she engages in some information-seeking activity such as talking on the telephone or reading. She might offer women advice about personal-hygiene products. If she is lower middle class, she will be plumper, more submissive, serving homemade food, or offering advice about housekeeping duties such as cleaning, cooking, or the laundry. When she talks to hubby, she frequently is discussing health-related topics such as high-fiber or low-sodium diets. She is usually in a servant/master relationship with her husband.

In old age and senility, both males and females undergo radical changes; their hair turns to silver and they "return to the earth" by moving from the city to the country, where they like sitting on the porch, walking in nature, or gardening. Machines (even cars) are rare. Everything is peaceful and stable. Grandma and Grandpa give instructions in cooking or whittling, tend to look like one another, and frequently fall asleep while babysitting the grandchildren. They represent the values of stability and the home.

Thus, even our life stages are reflected by nonverbal cues, and we have become culturally trained to read these cues, even in advertisements. In fact the nonverbal cues in an ad may be more persuasive than the verbal messages in the ad.

Dialect

Dialect, or one's pronunciation and usage, is culture-bound and often indicates one's socio-economic or regional background. We learn dialect culturally. It can communicate many things about us and can affect our persuasion, too. Many of my students come from Chicago or its suburbs—often from the South Side. They get angry with me when I tell some of them to stop "talking like steel workers." They do not hear themselves saying "dis" for "this" and "dat" for "that" and "dem" for "them." Yet they will be discriminated against if they keep their dialect. At the same time, others from the North Side and some suburbs have another dialect that may cause equal problems for them. They say "Dubbie" for "Debbie," "Shovie" for "Chevy," and "newahht" for "north." And it would be easy to document the kind of discrimination that occurs when black or Spanish dialect is used. Be aware of your responses to various dialects, and see whether people respond to your dialect in certain ways. I still have a Minnesota dialect and get certain responses because of my frequent use of "Yup" and "You betcha." People start looking for hayseeds in my hair.

Communication professor Norman Heap (1976) observed that we tend to regard dialect as signaling educational background and communication context, resulting in a four-category system:

1. *Formal context/educated speaker.* This category is typified by proper pronunciation and usage, such as that used in the courtroom, in governmental bodies, and on TV news programs.

2. *Informal context/educated speaker.* This category includes proper pronunciation accompanied by slang usages, which signal the informal context. It includes localisms like my "You betcha" or profanity. Once this usage is exposed in formal contexts, it is sometimes viewed as unacceptable, as was the case with the release of Nixon's taped conversations during the Watergate debacle.

Figure 9.5. *Which socioeconomic class is shown here? (Reproduced with the permission of Kraft General Foods, Inc.)*

3. *Formal context/uneducated speaker.* This category is marked by attempts at proper pronunciation and usage, such as might be heard when an uneducated person testifies in court or at some sort of governmental hearing. It is like the custodian saying at an elegant dinner party, "This spoon is entirely too large for my mouth." The speaker is trying *too hard* to sound correct.

4. *Informal context/uneducated speaker.* This category includes pronunciation and usage such as we might expect in steel mills: the "dese" and "dem" and "dose" pronunciations. These vary from locale to locale but usually are associated with blue-collar job settings or informal outings. Educated speakers can lose credibility by being too formal or correct in such settings.

Use of Nonverbal Tactics

Nonverbal message carriers can be manipulated by persuaders in a process that Erving Goffman (1957) called **impression management.** This involves using powerful verbal and nonverbal signals to convince the audience that the source is a certain kind of person. Governor Lamar Alexander, a candidate for the 1996 GOP presidential nomination, wore red-and-black checked "lumberjack" shirts when he campaigned in New Hampshire and hip boots when his opponents began to engage in mudslinging. President Clinton manages our impressions of him by wearing jogging suits and other casual clothing in the White House.

The use of clothing to communicate nonverbally in impression management is a popular topic in the corporate world. In her book *The Power of Dress,* Jacqueline Murray (1989) provides a number of case studies to demonstrate the communicative use of dress. For example, at Electronic Data Systems ("cowboy capitalist" H. Ross Perot's company) everyone has a military look: clean-shaven face; shiny, black, plain-toed shoes; white shirts and dark suits; and army haircuts.

Murray identifies three categories of business dress: *corporate dress* (most often used by bankers, attorneys, and executives), *communication dress* (most often used by persons in sales, marketing, education, personnel, or new, high-growth industries), and *creative dress* (used most frequently by interior decorators, commercial artists, people in advertising, some retailers, such as boutique owners, and entrepreneurs). Corporate dress is simple in line, shape, and design; tends to be tailored; features gray and blue colors for suits and off-white or light blue for shirts and blouses; and uses fabrics such as silks, herringbones, tweeds, and flannels in suits or dresses and plain cottons, wools, or linens in shirts and blouses. Communication dress features suits and dresses that are practical, relaxed, semi-traditional, as well as blazers and sports coats. Communicators use a mix of colors for their blouses and shirts, are willing to wear stripes or relaxed prints, and choose fabrics such as knits, loose or bulky weaves, and fabrics preferred by the corporate types. Creative dress tends to be loose fitting, with elongated line and exaggerated design in both suits and dresses and blouses and shirts. The preferred colors in this category are striking, dramatic colors, as well as understated taupes, peaches, and basics. Although some may question Murray's conclusions, few would argue that dress is unimportant as a nonverbal channel of communication.

Other Nonverbal Messages

Eye movements and other movements of the head can also communicate. We are all aware of the

Top view

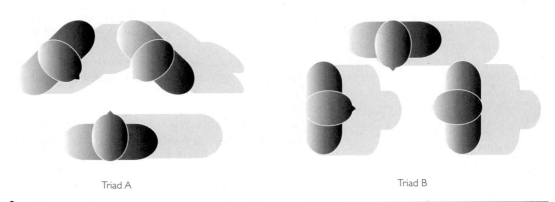

Triad A   Triad B

Figure 9.6. *Notice the difference between the body positions of the persons in each triad. Which is involved in "blocking" behavior?*

negative impression we get of persons whose eyes are continuously moving or who can't look you in the eye for more than a brief moment. Completely different meaning can come about from what is called "gaze holding," or maintaining eye contact with another person. Usually this conveys sexual interest. Even the *rate* of eyeblinks can communicate. Vance Packard (1964) reports in *The Hidden Persuaders* that grocery shoppers' eyeblinks slow down as they proceed up and down the aisles — to the point that they are almost mesmerized, approaching the early stages of hypnotism.

There are other movements and uses of the body that carry nonverbal meaning. Albert Scheflen (1973) a researcher in the use of gestures during psychotherapy, found that when a psychiatrist uses "the bowl gesture," patients often open up and reveal more about themselves and their problems. We are familiar with the use of this gesture in persuasion: It is the logo for a large insurance company — that's right, "You're in good hands with Allstate."

People can use their bodies to invite or inhibit communication. Notice the two configurations in Figure 9.6. In triad A, the body positions of the three persons would *inhibit* a fourth person from joining in the conversation, whereas in triad B, the body positions *invite* participation. The use of the body to discourage communication or interaction could be called "blocking" behavior, and the use of the body to encourage communication or interaction could be called "inviting" behavior Scheflen (1973) came to call these and other nonverbal invitations or blocks "quasi-courtship behavior" when he observed the behaviors in pairs of persons of opposite genders.

Related to the use of the body to block or invite communication is the use of objects such as furniture, piles of books on a library table, a podium, and so on, to either encourage or dis-

What do you think?

Do you ever use blocking behavior? When? Why?

courage communication. The incidence of violence on the New York City subway system increased radically when the folio newspaper then being published went on strike. Apparently, many persons had been using the newspaper to "block" themselves from fellow passengers by holding it up in front of their faces. When the paper was no longer available to discourage interaction, there were more opportunities for confrontation to occur, which resulted in the increase in violent interchanges.

Other types of body movement send nonverbal messages. For example, research shows that lifting or lowering one's chin at the ends of sentences serves as a signal that the person is intending to continue to speak or that he or she is done speaking and someone else can join in. And of course, we are all aware of the communicative power of head nodding, winking, and various obscene gestures, which may vary in meaning from culture to culture.

As you begin to observe the nonverbal messages occurring around you, you will discover an almost infinite number of potential nonverbal message carriers: the color of a room or of one's clothing; seating and furniture arrangements; who reaches for the check at a restaurant first; nervous gestures or twitches; volume, stress, and tone of verbal messages; the use of pauses; and curious habits, such as cracking one's knuckles or doodling, which may communicate subconscious tensions.

Even the sense of smell seems to be an important carrier of information. We are all aware, for example, of the person who uses too much cologne or aftershave lotion or of the person with body odor, but apparently we can detect more subtle odors as well. For example, some persons claim to be able to smell hostility or tension on entering a room. In the popular film *Scent of a Woman*, Al Pacino's character bases his judgments about women on the scent of their perfume and other olfactory cues. He uses scent to plan his strategies of romance. Many homes have unique and characteristic odors caused by the kinds of food cooked in them, the kinds of cleaning solutions used, or the kinds of wood used in their construction. The fragrance of a new car is now available in aerosol cans to spray in used cars, thus making them seem newer and "fresher."

Review and Conclusion

By this time, you know that the world of the persuadee in an information age is not an easy one. There are so many things to be aware of: the persuader's self-revelation using language and stylistic choices; the internal or process premises operating within each of us; and the interactive rules for content premises. In this chapter we also learned about the world of nonverbal premises, which can be communicated by a variety of channels, including facial expression, eye behavior, and bodily communication (gestures and posture; proxemics, or the use of space; physical appearance and the use of artifacts; vocalic communication; tactile communication, or the use of touch; chronemics, or the use of time; gender and life stage differences; dialect; and dress and other nonverbal communicators). These premises do not make receivers' tasks any easier, especially since they operate at particularly low levels of awareness and frequently are overlooked as we analyze persuasion. You will have to train yourself to be more sensitive to nonverbal elements in the persuasive process, not only so you can skillfully use these channels in your own communication, but, more important, so you can more accurately decode the real meaning of the messages aimed at you every day.

Questions for Further Thought

1. What are some of the facial expressions you find easiest to identify? Which are most difficult?

2. What is kinesics? Give some examples and explain how and what they communicate.

3. Which of your friends uses gestures most effectively? What does he or she do that makes the gestures so effective?

4. What are some examples of the ways physical appearance sends messages in your world? What are some examples of how physical appearance identifies a contemporary musical artist or group?

5. With what artifacts do you surround yourself? What do they mean to you? (Some students have reported that the first thing they do after unpacking for dormitory living is to purchase "conversation pieces" or artifacts that symbolize themselves.) What about your roommate? What artifacts does he or she use?

What do they symbolize about him or her? What about your family members' artifacts?

6. How often do you touch others? Try to increase the number of touches you use and observe the responses of others. Does the increase cause a different effect? If so, how?

7. Give examples of how chronemics operates in your life — on campus, in the dorm, in the classroom, and at home.

8. Identify some of the gender differences in nonverbal communication as they appear in contemporary advertising.

9. What is the predominant dialect where you live? Are there any other dialects that you can identify in your community? What effects do they have on people's attitudes and behaviors?

10. What is "blocking" behavior? Give examples from your everyday life.

References

Ekman, P., & Friesen, W. V. (1975). *Unmasking the face: A guide to recognizing emotions from facial expression.* Englewood Cliffs, NJ: Prentice-Hall.

Ellyson, S., Dovidio, J., & Fehr, B. J. (1984). Visual behavior and dominance in men and women. In C. Mayo & N. Henley (Eds.), *Gender and nonverbal behavior.* New York: Springer-Verlag.

Fromme, D., Jaynes, W., Taylor, D., Hanhold, E., Daniell, J., Rountree, R., & Fromme, M. (1989). Nonverbal behavior and attitude toward touch. *Journal of Nonverbal Behavior, 13,* 3–13.

Goffman, E. (1957). *The presentation of self in everyday life.* New York: Anchor Books.

Hall, E. T. (1959). *The silent language.* Garden City, NY: Doubleday.

Hall, J. A. (1984). *Nonverbal sexual differences: Communication accuracy and expressive style.* Baltimore: Johns Hopkins press.

Heap, N. A. (1976). Private correspondence.

Knapp, M. L. (1978). *Nonverbal communication in human interaction.* New York: Holt, Rinehart & Winston.

Knapp, M. L., & Comendena, M. E. (1985). Telling it like it isn't: A review of theory and research on deceptive communication. *Human Communication Research, 5,* 270–285.

Kotulak, R. (1985). Researchers decipher a powerful "language." *Chicago Tribune,* April 7, sec. 6.

Leathers, D. (1986). *Successful nonverbal communication: Principles and applications.* New York: Macmillan.

Major, B. (1984). Gender patterns in touching behavior. In C. Mayo & N. Henley (Eds.), *Gender and nonverbal behavior.* New York: Springer-Verlag.

Mehrabian, A. (1971). *Silent messages.* Belmont, CA: Wadsworth.

Murray, J. (1989). *The power of dress.* Minneapolis: Semiotics Press.

Packard, V. (1964). *The hidden persuaders*. New York: Pocket Books.

Porter, N., & Geis, F. (1984). Women and nonverbal leadership cues: When seeing is not believing. In C. Mayo & N. Henley (Eds.), *Gender and nonverbal behavior*. New York: Springer-Verlag.

Scheflen, A. (1973). *Communicational structure: Analysis of a psychotherapy session*. Bloomington: Indiana University Press.

Umiker-Sebeok, J. (1984). The seven ages of women: A view from American magazine advertisements. In C. Mayo & N. Henley (Eds.), *Gender and nonverbal behavior*. New York: Springer-Verlag.

PART THREE

Applications of Persuasive Premises

In Part I, we examined some of the definitions of persuasion and the underlying theoretical foundations for persuasion, with a special emphasis on language. We focused on receivers and noted how we could use a knowledge of persuasion to critically process the persuasion that bombards us every day. In Part II, we explored sources for the various premises that persuaders use to develop their pitches. These are the unstated but powerful first premises in the enthymeme, a form of argument in which persuadees provide a missing part (usually a major premise), thereby participating in their own persuasion.

In Part III, we look at applications of these theories and audience-held premises in a variety of contexts. We maintain the receiver focus, always asking how our analyses of these applications can assist us to make critical judgments about whether to buy, to elect, to join, to quit, to give, to believe in, or to support.

Chapter 10 explores a familiar application, the persuasive campaign—a series of messages designed to lead receivers to specific ends. Chapter 11 focuses on the source of persuasion and dis-

cusses how to become a persuader. In addition to helping you persuade others, what you learn enables you to critically process the persuasive messages aimed at you. Knowing what kind of proof or organization a persuader uses helps you judge the validity of the message.

In Chapter 12, we explore the most dominant channels for persuasive messages: the mass media. Mass-mediated messages range from the brief but influential TV or radio commercial to more extensive advertisements, speeches, documentaries, and news reports. We will discover that the media of our time may be the determining factor in deciding which problems we, as a culture, should concentrate on. In some cases media take over the role of the family or parent in shaping values.

In Chapter 13, we explore the ways in which propaganda, foreign and domestic, operates to persuade us and to shape our opinions. Finally, Chapter 14 investigates a particular form of persuasion—print and electronic advertising—and how they have come to dominate contemporary American society.

10

The Persuasive Campaign or Movement

For many years the study of persuasion focused mainly on the public speech and the "single-shot" perspective on persuasion. As a result, persuaders, researchers, students, and teachers overlooked the impact of artistically coordinated multiple messages that ultimately lead to product adoption, voting decisions, or support of various kinds of movements. This kind of persuasion — campaign or social movement persuasion — was not carefully examined by communication researchers until recently.

Political scientists had, for the most part, also ignored the communication dimensions of political campaigns, with the possible exception of research on campaign financing. They remained focused on the nature and structure of government. Meanwhile, most of the research done on campaigns had occurred in advertising or marketing departments and was proprietary — it belonged to the client — who naturally refused to make it public. Only relatively recently has communication teaching and research been devoted to the persuasive campaign. Yet it is probably the most prevalent form of persuasion today. In fact, one of the hottest "buzz words" in marketing and adver-

tising today is "integrated marketing communications," which refers to the carefully planned melding of advertising, P.R., sales promotion, personal selling, packaging, Internet homepages, and a host of other elements of persuasion into a single integrated campaign. In this chapter we look at three general types of persuasive campaigns: product-oriented campaigns, person- or candidate-oriented campaigns, and idea- or ideologically oriented campaigns. We look at these types of campaigns from several perspectives.

Of course, a single chapter can't possibly cover all there is to say about persuasive campaigns. All that can be hoped for is that you become more aware of campaign persuasion as you receive it and as you produce it. Yes, as you produce it, because as an individual you wage your own campaigns — for the purchase of a new appliance, for a desired change in the behavior of someone you know or love, on behalf of some organization you belong to, and on other public and personal issues.

The impact of advancing technology in computers, the Internet, digital audio, and videographics on a campaigner's ability to convey powerfully persuasive messages cannot be underestimated. Consider what a changed world we face in the 1990s and as we approach the year 2000. The number of persuasive campaigns will increase—and so will their sophistication. With satellite, cable television, and Internet options increasing, costs for media time will drop, and market segmentation will become much easier to accomplish. It will be critical to understand something about persuasive campaigns for products, persons/ candidates, and ideas to avoid being completely taken in.

The Role of Communication in Campaigns

Campaigns and mass movements are classic examples of communication systems at work. The first **communication system** discussed in this text was the Shannon and Weaver SMCR model, including a feedback loop. This model is a good example of a communication system because it produces a predictable flow of symbolic information and a means of evaluating the success or failure of the attempted communication. All communication systems have some means of feedback or evaluation.

The systematic and predictable flow of persuasive information in campaigns includes all of its auditory and visual symbols, both verbal and nonverbal: words printed on a sign, page, or screen; graphics, typeface, pictures, symbols, or scenes in an ad; auditory words; and auditory "pictures" created by music, words, sound effects, and silence. For example, during radio's early years, listeners were persuaded that scenes took place at night by playing the sound of chirping crickets.

An example of a visual symbol within the systematic flow of campaign information comes from the initial ad campaign for the Infiniti automobile. The vehicle was never shown throughout the entire campaign. Instead, the advertiser used various visual symbols of the concept of infinity—a flock of geese migrating or rushing water in a stream, accompanied by classical music. Then the scene faded to the word "Infiniti" printed on the screen—nothing else. Understandably, the campaign created a lot of interest in the unveiling of the first models.

In both cases, the systematic flow and evaluation of persuasive information had measurable effects on either the audience or the environment. In most integrated campaigns, teams of workers who are experts in various aspects of campaigns carefully research their target audience. Using the research, they plan campaign messages in such formats as press releases and print and electronic ads, and painstakingly test them at each stage in their development. Using research on the audiences of various media, they schedule time or space in magazines, newspapers, and radio and television networks and stations. When the nationwide "rollout" of the campaign finally takes place, the systemic nature of the campaign shifts to an evaluation mode using sophisticated polling techniques, focus groups, and other means of measuring the effect of the campaign. The results of the evaluation are then fed back to the campaign staff and midflight corrections are made, tested, tried, and evaluated in an ongoing process that doesn't cease until long after the campaign is over.

One way to think of this flow is to imagine yourself moving into, passing through, and moving out of a huge block of "information bits" of the campaign and coming into contact with some but not all of them—for example, ads, news conferences, bumper stickers, direct-mail pieces, and news programs featuring the product, candidate, or idea. This happens to us many times daily with numerous distinctly different campaigns. If a campaign is well-designed, we will pass through it several times, being exposed to different information bits each time. These information bits will differ from those our fellow consumers are exposed to during their passages.

The rule of thumb in advertising agencies is that it takes at least three exposures for an ad to create brand awareness. The first exposure passes by almost unnoticed by the consumer. The second exposure alerts consumers to the existence of the product and triggers their unconscious memories of the first exposure. It also creates curiosity about the product. If it is well designed and properly timed, the third exposure either prompts a preexisting need for the product or creates a new need. The consumer, voter, donor, or joiner now is aware of the product, candidate, or good cause, and, if the campaign is properly orchestrated, will begin to evaluate the appeal and may ultimately buy, vote, donate, or join.

Campaigns Versus "Single-Shot" Persuasive Messages

How do campaigns differ from other kinds of persuasion? Campaigns are not just a series of messages sent to audiences over time about the same product, candidate, or cause. Nor are they debates over a specific issue. Campaigns differ from single shots of persuasion or from "collections" of persuasive messages delivered over time in three major ways. They

1. systematically create "positions" in the audience's mind for the product, candidate, or idea

2. are intentionally designed to develop over time (in other words, campaigns are composed of stages for getting the audience's attention, preparing the audience for action, and, finally, for calling the audience to action)

3. dramatize the product, candidate, idea, or ideology for the audience, inviting receivers

to participate in real or symbolic ways with the campaign and its goal

Following movements or campaigns is like watching a TV series. Although the episodes can stand alone (each has its own beginning, middle, and end), they rely on one another to form a collage of messages that meld together until an entire image or picture of the campaign is perceived and stored in the minds of the consumer, voter, or joiner. By the end of the campaign, if it is well designed, large segments of the population will have been exposed to enough "episodes" that a similar image of the product, candidate, or idea emerges.

Types of Campaigns

As noted earlier, three kinds of movements or campaigns predominate: (1) the *product-oriented* advertising campaign, (2) the *politically oriented* campaign for office, and (3) the *ideological*, or *cause-oriented*, campaign (sometimes called mass or social movements).

These three campaign types have many similarities. For instance, high-profile individuals can be prominent in both the second and third types. However, the person-oriented political campaign centers on the individual's name (see Figure 10.1). The focus of such campaigns may be on electing *someone* to office, getting *someone* out of prison, or raising enough money to pay for *someone's* organ transplant. The slogan might feature a candidate's name—"Be Sure to Vote for John Countryman"—or it may feature a person needing financial support—"Dollars for Jimmy, Our Country's Liver Transplant Candidate." In issue- or "cause"-

What do you think?

What idea-oriented campaign(s) is/are presently being conducted on your campus?

"I'd like to thank my Mom, my Dad, my kids and
most of all . . . my media consultant!"

Figure 10.1. *Person-oriented campaigns—especially political campaigns—rely heavily on sophisticated
uses of media. (Reprinted by permission of Bill Whitehead.)*

oriented campaigns, on the other hand, the slogan or theme always features the cause—"Guns don't kill. People kill."

Often the kinds of campaigns may overlap, and sometimes it is difficult to draw exact distinctions among them. A good example would be Jesse Jackson's 1988 campaign for the Democratic nomination for President in which he promoted the idea of establishing a "rainbow coalition" of the poor, minorities, and the underprivileged to influence government. Thus, within his political campaign was also an idea-oriented subcampaign.

Goals, Strategies, and Tactics in Product, Person, and Ideological Campaigns

The successful campaign is not a case of "salesmanship in print," as it has sometimes been defined. Campaigns don't sell; instead, they deliver a prospective consumer, voter, or joiner to the point of sale, the voting booth, or the headquarters of the good cause. And if the campaign is to succeed, it must educate and prepare the consumer, voter, or joiner to be ready to take action, be it purchasing, voting, or joining/donating behavior. To accomplish this task, campaigns must zero in on well-defined *goals*, create appropriate *strategies* to accomplish the goals, and then use various *tactics* to put the strategy into action.

This pattern of goals/strategies/tactics applies to advertising and election campaigns as well as to campaigns for causes or ideologies. For example, the advertising agency for Claussen's refrigerated dill pickles, in conjunction with the manufacturer, might set as a goal to "increase sales in specified test markets by 10 percent in the fourth quarter of the year." The campaign staff and the manager then work out a promising strategy. In the case of Claussen's, one strategy was to use television spot advertisements to emphasize the unique feature of the brand: It is refrigerated rather than cooked. The benefit to the consumer is that Claussen's are crisper and crunchier than the competition. The product had previously been advertised only in print media—not a very effective way to communicate crispness or crunchiness. Hence, Claussen's hadn't been successful in communicating the benefits of the brand. To implement the strategy, the agency used the tactic of comparative advertising, matching Claussen's against the competition, Vlasic's pickles. The agency prepared several ads in which the competitor's cooked pickle was bent in half without breaking, while Claussen's pickle couldn't be bent without snapping in two, giving off a spray of brine and cucumber.

The goal of Carol Moseley-Braun's primary election campaign for an Illinois senate seat was obviously to win the Democratic nomination for the general election. Her strategy during the campaign was to avoid mentioning her two opponents, the incumbent and a multimillionaire, both of whom were busy attacking each other's character in speeches, news conferences, and especially expensive negative advertising. The challenger spent millions of his personal fortune. This was a clever strategy for Moseley-Braun because she couldn't begin to match the spending levels of either of her opponents. And by not attacking either of them, she appeared to be above the fray and was identified as the candidate who was taking the "high road" of debating the issues instead of engaging in mudslinging. Moseley-Braun won the nomination by attracting the votes of women, minorities, students, and nontraditional Democratic voters, as well as independent voters and even some Republicans. She ultimately defeated a weak Republican candidate.

A church music committee had as a goal to raise $100,000 to rebuild a fifty-year-old pipe organ. Their strategy was to educate the congregation about the wisdom of rebuilding a pipe organ instead of purchasing a new electric one and to challenge the congregation's sense of pride. The tactics included several presentations during services plus postservice demonstrations of the difference in sound between a pipe organ and an electric organ. Further, the music committee offered individual members of the congregation the "opportunity" to "buy" variously priced parts of the organ (a rank of pipes, an octave of pipes, the console, the keyboard, the motor, and so on). A final tactic was to sell the pipes that were being replaced for a nominal sum—they made decorative conversation pieces to hang on one's wall.

As we have noted, product, person, and ideological cause campaigns are similar in some ways and quite different in others. These similarities and differences are highlighted in the following survey of models or explanations for successful and unsuccessful campaigns. In some cases only one or a few elements of the model apply to more than one of the types of campaigns. Your task is to use these models (or subelements of the models) to help you make decisions about whether to make a purchase, vote, or join/support a cause or ideology.

Developmental Stages of Successful Campaigns

All three types of campaigns are developmental—they pass through a series of predictable stages as they grow and mature and adapt to audience feedback, the competition, the issues, and the demands of the persuasive situation. For example, one campaign goal of a new product, candidate, or idea is to establish itself in the audience's mind or consciousness. (A variety of strategies can be used to accomplish this identification: The product maker may give out free samples, the candidate may announce his or her candidacy at a press conference, and advocates might stage a dramatic protest in some highly symbolic location.) This initial stage may succeed or fail, but no matter what the outcome, the campaigner learns about the audience. Perhaps the customers seem to be buying the brand because of its warranty, not because of its price. Maybe the voters don't want to hear much about increasing taxes on gasoline but do respond to the issue of deficit reductions. And some animal rights activists may respond to some issues but not others. So, in all three types of campaigns, strategies are tried and kept, altered, or dropped as the campaign develops. Additional elements are common to all three types of campaign.

What do you think?
What is the difference among goals, strategies, and tactics in campaigns?

The Yale Five-Stage Developmental Model

Most campaigns pass through at least some if not all stages of a model developed by researchers at Yale while observing the growth of national identity (Binder, 1971). Although the model was originally used in this international political context, it is highly applicable to product, person, and idea campaigns in other contexts as well. The five functional stages noted by the researchers are *identification* (including but not limited to name identification), *legitimacy*, *participation* (real and symbolic), *penetration*, and *distribution*.

Identification. As we've briefly noted, one thing all campaigns must do is to develop an identity in the minds of consumers, voters, and potential converts or donors. Many products and causes develop a *graphic symbol* or *logotype* to create identification in the audience's mind. For example, in the well-established logo of The Goodyear Tire and Rubber Company shown in Figure 10.2, the winged foot of Mercury is inserted between the two syllables of "Goodyear," probably to suggest that the company's products are swift and safe. Another well-known product logo is the Golden Arches of McDonald's, but what this symbol is supposed to communicate is less obvious. The small letter "e" used to identify the environmental movement was inserted inside the capital letter "C" to create the logo of Commonwealth Edison electric company, suggesting that the company is environmentally conscientious, a good identification for an energy monopoly. A series of arrows in a triangle with the point of each arrow bent to point at the next arrow is the logo for any kind of recycling, and is used by many cause campaigners. And you will notice hundreds of other logotypes that are supposed to communicate something about the product or cause to you.

Closely related to the logo in creating an identity is the *name* associated with the product, candidate, or cause. For example, the name of the magazine *Newsweek* suggests that it contains the news of the past week, while the name of the LeBaron automobile was probably meant to suggest good taste, classiness, and distinction. The name of the fast-food franchise Burger King also communicates about the quality of the food you

Figure 10.2. *Many devices are used to gain product, person, or idea identification in campaigns. Logos such as this one are one kind of device. Why is the winged foot of Mercury used? What does it communicate? Why put it between "GOOD" and "YEAR"? Answers to these questions help explain how product image or identification develops. (Used by permission of The Goodyear Tire and Rubber Company.)*

will find there—it will be "fit for a king." Some candidates for office label themselves "The People's Candidate" or a similar term to create an identification. In the abortion controversy, antiabortion advocates selected a particularly strategic label—pro-life—for their cause, and the name is persuasive. It suggests that advocates are in favor of life—something everyone could agree with. And it also implies that opponents of the movement are either "anti-life" or "pro-death," neither of which is very positive. Upstaged by the "pro-life" label, abortion rights advocates had to settle for the less effective "pro-choice." Try this experiment to demonstrate the potency of a good name. Ask a sample of people to name three brands of turkey that are available for Thanksgiving dinner. You will find that the name "Butterball" will be on everyone's list, while competitors' names will not occur as consistently if at all. Then ask them what the key benefit of a Butterball turkey is, and they will tell you that it is the most moist turkey on the market. Its name is key to this perception. And there are other examples of the persuasive power of the name one selects for a product, a political organization, or a cause. Figure 10.3 shows an ad for NameLab, a company that designs and tests various names to help organizations establish an identity for a product, political entity, or cause.

Another device that helps identify a product, candidate, or cause is *color coding*. The campaigner picks a color or colors and consistently uses them in packaging, in advertising, on letterheads, and perhaps in uniforms. United Parcel Service carriers wear dark brown uniforms, and their trucks are painted dark brown. Candidates usually select some combination of red, white, and blue. Camouflage and drab olive green are associated with the "Be All You Can Be—In the Army" campaign. And Century 21 real-estate agents wear gold blazers. Further identification can be achieved by using the same color and typeface in all ads, signs, buttons, and bumper stickers. The successful "Stop ERA" movement to defeat the Equal Rights Amendment adopted the color red, probably to associate with its connotations of "Danger" and "Stop!" among others.

Slogans also help identification and frequently become part of our cultural heritage if they are catchy enough: "Folgers—The Mountain Grown Coffee," "When You Care Enough to Send the Very Best," "You're in good hands with Allstate," "We Try Harder," and "Smart. Very Smart" are all good examples. Finally, jingles, uniforms, salutes, and all sorts of campaign paraphernalia (balloons, buttons, hats, and so on) can help establish name and purpose identification. Logos, slogans, jingles, color codes, and other

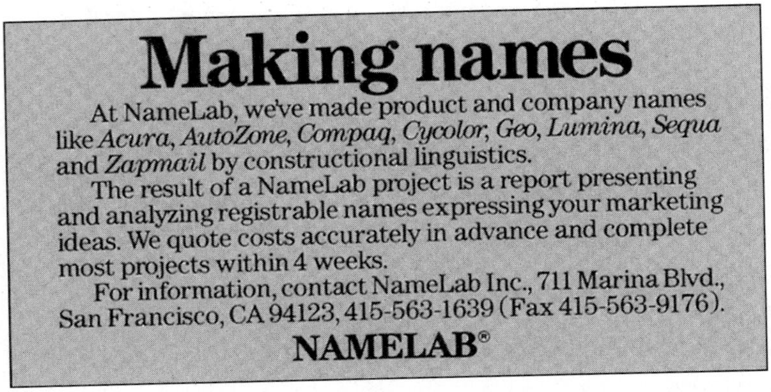

Making names

At NameLab, we've made product and company names like *Acura, AutoZone, Compaq, Cycolor, Geo, Lumina, Sequa* and *Zapmail* by constructional linguistics.

The result of a NameLab project is a report presenting and analyzing registrable names expressing your marketing ideas. We quote costs accurately in advance and complete most projects within 4 weeks.

For information, contact NameLab Inc., 711 Marina Blvd., San Francisco, CA 94123, 415-563-1639 (Fax 415-563-9176).

NAMELAB®

Figure 10.3. *The name of a product, political entity, or cause is part of the mix of factors that create identification for the campaigner. (Used by permission of NameLab.)*

identification-producing devices are then communicated to the target market or audience using a variety of media ranging from simple signs to electronic spot advertisements to sophisticated home-pages on the World Wide Web.

Legitimacy. The second functional stage entails the establishment of **legitimacy.** Candidates usually achieve this by getting the party endorsement or by winning primary election battles. Legitimacy can be thought of as a power base. Candidates may choose to demonstrate how power works using rallies, being pictured with well-known supporters (who are usually celebrities), or being photo-graphed in front of some national symbol of legitimacy, such as the U.S. Capitol building, the Lincoln Memorial, or the White House. In political campaigns, incumbents have automatic legitimacy (unless they have bumbled and botched the job), so challengers have a major task. They must try to discredit and erode the legitimacy of the incumbent and develop their own. Further, they may have to do this while running in primary elections against fellow poitical leaders who are also emphasizing the shortcomings of the incumbent.

Mudslinging in political campaigns is usually an attempt to destroy another candidate's legitimacy. A challenger finds out that the incumbent gave government contracts to friends. The incumbent points out the nasty tactics of the challenger. The real question is which candidate the voters will consider the most legitimate.

Products can demonstrate legitimacy in several ways. One way, of course, is to show that the product is effective. Patent-medicine shows frequently used testimonials from persons who had been cured using the product. Testimonials are frequently used in advertising. Model Cindy Crawford symbolizes the legitimacy of the "New Generation" of Pepsi drinkers, pro-athletes demonstrate the legitimacy of various shoes. Established endorsements can also help products demonstrate legitimacy—the Underwriter's Laboratory seal of approval is an example, as is the Good Housekeeping seal. Demonstrations can create legitimacy by showing how effective the product is at solving the consumer's problems. Brands can also develop legitimacy by associating themselves with good causes, such as by sponsoring community events (see Figure 10.4).

She makes it look effortless.

Reflecting the thousands of hours she's practiced and honed her skills, until every muscle responds in unison

to the command for perfection. It is this dedication, this courage to face competition boldly and without compromise, that has inspired Phillips Petroleum to proudly sponsor United States Swimming since 1973.

And we'll be national sponsor for years to come. Because we believe that with every leap of grace and form, we are watching the future of our nation take shape.

PHILLIPS PETROLEUM COMPANY

Figure 10.4. Phillips Petroleum established its legitimacy by sponsoring U.S. Olympic teams. (Reprinted by permission of the Phillips Petroleum Company.)

In idea campaigns, large numbers of participants or amounts of money are used to demonstrate legitimacy. Such tactics as newspaper ads with the names of known supporters who endorse the movement can establish legitimacy. Large numbers of angry citizens show up at a council meeting and demonstrate their displeasure. In one high school, students who objected to the lunch program demonstrated the legitimacy of their movement by the number of students uniting in nonviolent and effective tactics. One day, several hundred students boycotted the lunches, leaving the school with tons of leftovers. The next day, all students bought the hot lunch, leaving the school short of supplies. The following day, everyone paid with a $5 bill, running the cashiers out of change. The next day, the students paid in pennies, creating havoc in the checkout lines as cashiers counted each cent. On the fifth day, school officials negotiated with student representatives about improving the lunch program.

Participation. The legitimacy stage of campaigns usually blends so smoothly with the **participation** stage that it is almost impossible to tell when one ends and the next begins. In the legitimacy stage, the participants are *known supporters*. In the participation stage, the leaders seek to involve previously *uncommitted persons*. There are many techniques for doing this. Some involve effort by participants, whereas others require minimal or only symbolic participation.

The distributors and users of products *participate* in the use and profit of the product. In some instances, stores are paid to allow some of their space to be used for special displays of certain soaps, wines, and so forth. The dealer may get an extra discount for pushing a certain product. Coupon offers are made to product users, who buy and use the product and get money or gifts. Various brands provide merchandise (T-shirts, caps, coolers, etc.) imprinted with the logo, slogan and/or name of the brand, thus producing walking advertisements as well as audience participation with the brand. Other participation-producing devices are being developed continually.

A movement may urge participation in real or symbolic ways. People may be asked to wear armbands or badges, to yell slogans at rallies, or to put signs on their lawns or on their cars. Candidates running for student president may ask others to canvass dormitory floors or student groups. This kind of activity gets people involved in the campaign or movement and guarantees further active support. As previously mentioned, people who put bumper stickers on their cars will vote for the name on the sticker most of the time. Movements ask supporters to *do* something, even if it is only symbolic. Supporters can march, hold a vigil, or salute. The effect of these activities is to increase commitment to the cause.

As new technologies develop, they are used to encourage participation. Examples include the "scratch and sniff" perfume strips in magazine ads, holograms, interactive media (Seagram's ads often have a supposedly "subliminal" message, and the reader is told where in the ad the message is located), or photographic enhancement or alteration, and we will surely see participation on the WWW. Of course, there are always the old reliable techniques for prompting participation—giving free samples, offering trial use of the product, getting people to canvass their precinct on behalf of the candidate, or enlisting people to sign a petition supporting the ideological or good cause campaign. All these devices are designed to get the audience involved with the product, candidate, or cause, as symbolic behavior represents a commitment to the product, candidate, or cause. As Figure 10.5 demonstrates, participation can include "playing" with the ad.

Penetration. The **penetration** stage can be thought of as the stage where a person, product,

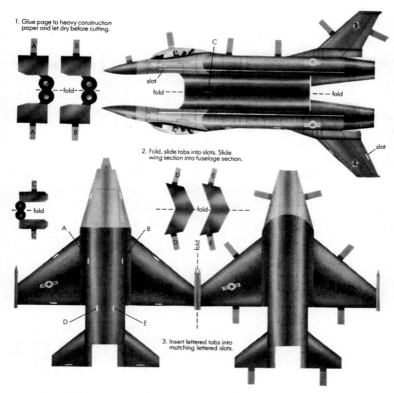

One of two ways to get your hands on an F-16.

If you think you're too young to fly, cut it out.

Fold. Assemble. And prepare for take-off.

While your paper airplane may not quite reach the speed of sound, use it as a reminder of just how fast the Air National Guard can help you get your future off the ground.

And we're not just talking about a military career. Air Guard training can prepare you for a civilian career in over 200 fields of technical expertise. Every-thing from meteorology to security. Tele-communications to computer technology.

We'll even pay part of your college tuition. What's more, you'll have the chance to take part in exciting adventures that can lead you around the world.

All you have to do is serve as little as two days a month and two weeks a year.

Want to learn more? Call your local recruiter. And find out if you're cut out for the Air National Guard.

AIR NATIONAL GUARD

Americans At Their Best.

88-501

Figure 10.5. *This ad for the Air National Guard encourages real, not symbolic, participation. (Courtesy Air National Guard.)*

or idea has "made it" in the market; that is, it has successfully established a meaningful share of the market, electorate, or constituency.

For products, gaining a significant share of the market is enough to achieve the penetration stage. Crest and Gleem dominated the toothpaste market for years by offering fluoridation as a feature and decay prevention as the resulting product benefit. Then, in the 1970s, new toothpastes such as MacLeans, Pearl Drops, and others offered the benefits of whiteness and sexiness in place of decay prevention, thus segmenting and penetrating the market. This resulted in several other "me-too" toothpaste campaigns that offered the white and sexy benefits, while both Gleem and Crest lost sales.

Chrysler's innovations enabled it to penetrate the auto market, with front-wheel drive in 1980, the minivan in 1984, the seven-year/70,000-mile warranty in 1988, and others in the '90s. The share of the market that these innovations captured was significant enough to force the competition to follow suit; front-wheel-drive cars, minivans, extended warranties, and convertibles were being marketed by several manufacturers by the mid '90s. When you see a successful penetration stage in campaigns for products, you can be almost certain that the competition will begin to market their own versions of the newly dominating product.

In presidential politics, especially in the early primaries, a candidate doesn't have to win the most delegates to establish penetration. Running third may be enough. Other indications of political penetration include ratings in public opinion polls, increases in the number and size of financial contributions, increases in the number of persons volunteering to help the candidate, and sizable crowds showing up for campaign events. Just as in the product campaign, penetration of the market in political campaigns usually prompts a response from the "competition" or other candidates in the race.

In idea-oriented campaigns, penetration is achieved when those in power find that they are hearing about a campaign often enough or when it is "costing" them a lot (such as when legislators are barraged by mail or have to repeatedly answer questions about the campaign topic at news conferences). Other indicators of penetration in idea campaigns include large enough rally crowds to cause serious inconvenience to those supporting the status quo, an increase in the number of persons joining the cause, increased financial and volunteer support, and, as in product and political campaigns, significant responses from the "competition" or those in power.

Distribution. In the fifth and final stage of development — **distribution** — the campaign or movement succeeds and becomes institutionalized. Having achieved the control, votes, or market share they sought, the campaign or movement leaders must now live up to their promises in some way. They must signal the people that change is going to occur. The likely moves are the designation of subgroups of the campaign staff or the movement's leadership to positions of power with tasks to complete. These tasks fit with the promises made in the campaign and with the goals of the movement. Patronage jobs are used to distribute the "winnings" achieved in the campaign. This stage does not always occur in product campaigns. However, devices such as rebates, money-back coupons, and incentives to store owners (such as discounts, prizes for most sales, and premiums or other gifts) are kinds of distribution that we see in product campaigns.

One problem with idea-oriented campaigns and, to some degree, political campaigns is that the persuaders don't always live up to their promises. For example, Fidel Castro never enacted the land reforms he promised. The populace then becomes cynical about the movement or politicians. This is how many people come to believe that all politicians are crooks. As Cicero put it, "Politicians are not born; they are excreted."

Product-Focused Models

While some campaign models can be used to describe all of the three types of campaign, other models are more focused on one of them. Let's examine several models that are more appropriate for product-oriented campaigns.

The Hierarchy of Effects Model. Advertising and marketing experts Robert Lavidge and Gary Steiner (1961) suggested a model that for many decades has been the basis for setting goals in many marketing departments and advertising agencies. It is a developmental model in that it assumes that the potential customer must pass through a series of stages in roughly sequential order, from initial awareness to ultimate purchase. Their **hierarchy of effects model** has subsequently been altered and adapted by various theorists, but it remains as valid today as when first suggested (Schultz, 1990). The model comprises seven distinct stages or phases, and various communication, advertising, research, and promotional strategies and techniques can be used in each stage.

At the bottom of the hierarchy, consumers are completely unaware of the product, brand, or service being promoted. As a result, the persuader's first task is to learn about consumers' current patterns of use of similar products, brands, or services before spending time or money on advertising. So consumer research precedes the entire campaign and is the first step the advertiser takes, using focus groups, surveys, and other research methods. For example, suppose the marketers of Oreo cookies are considering adding a new product to the Oreo and Double Stuffs brand family but wonder what consumer response might be to a third Oreo cookie. They do research using focus groups, as well as observe people eating the regular Oreo cookies and the Double Stuffs. A pattern emerges—many people start eating the Oreo or the Double Stuff by splitting the cookie in half and eating the filling, then they eat the chocolate portion—a pattern that had inspired Double Stuffs (Fortini-Campbell, 1992). Consumer attitude tests reveal that the filling is rated as the "best" part of Oreos and Double Stuffs and that a cookie with a different flavored filling would sell. Viola! The Double Chocolate Stuff by Oreo.

Now, with a "consumer driven" product to promote, we move on to steps 2 and 3—*creating consumer awareness* of the product and *developing consumer knowledge* about it. The advertiser can begin to create product or brand awareness in a variety of ways. For example, the product/brand gets a name. The agency creates a slogan and jingle, and public relations specialists send out press releases inviting the media to the premiere taste-testing press conference. Then "teaser" ads communicate that "Double Chocolate Stuff is coming soon! Watch for it on your grocer's shelves!" Descriptive copy is prepared, and various promotional devices are used (skywriting, coupons, and so on). Researchers continue testing brand awareness, and as the awareness stage merges with the third step in the model—developing knowledge—the advertiser informs and "teaches" the consumer about the product or brand using print, electronic, and direct-marketing techniques. Researchers then test consumers' knowledge level using surveys, mall intercepts, and unaided and aided recall.

In the fourth and fifth steps—*liking* and *preferring*—the advertiser uses image ads that communicate status and glamour as being associated with the product or brand. Spokespersons appear and tell why they like and prefer the brand. If the brand has competition, the advertiser might use comparative ads to demonstrate

What do you think?

What is a "consumer-driven" product and campaign

how Double Chocolate Stuffs are better than the competing cookies. The customer is now aware of the product/brand and has reason to like and even prefer it; the only thing remaining is to convince him or her to purchase the brand.

The final two stages of the hierarchy are *conviction* and ultimate *purchase*. Researchers might measure "intention to purchase" among potential consumers to determine whether they are ready for that final nudge that will move them to the store shelves. They encourage retailers to feature the product/brand in retail advertising. Testimonial ads are continued in the hope that conviction will increase if consumers become confident that the testimonial is sincere. Price appeals are usually made during this stage (two for the price of one, cents-off coupons with a tight expiration date, cross-couponing with another product), as are "last-chance" offers. This is the time to prepare and distribute sales promotional material, such as in-store coupons, free end-of-aisle displays for retailers, shelf or shopping cart signs, premiums, and in-store sampling on certain days. A combination of these tactics should not only deliver the prospect to the retail outlet but also prompt him or her to make that first purchase. Repeat purchase and ultimate brand loyalty now become the focus of the advertising/promotion activities, using on-package coupons, brand-image advertising, and special prices to induce continued use of the brand.

The Lavidge and Steiner hierarchy of effects model is one of several models that help us to understand the goals, strategies, and tactics of product-oriented campaigns. Let's examine some others.

The Positioning Model. Trout and Ries (1986) offer their **positioning model** as a way to attract prospects to a campaign. The model begins with the premise that consumers, swamped with information, can only maintain "top of mind" awareness of a few brands in a product category. Research shows that, depending on the complexity of the product, consumers can usually remember only five to nine brands. The campaign's goal is to establish such an awareness for the brand in the prospect's conscious mind. They advise searching for unoccupied *niches* in the marketplace and then *positioning* the brand in that psychological space. Here are some ways to position a brand in the marketplace.

1. *Being first.* The first brand to appear in a product class has a natural advantage of being the "pioneer" in that class. Lunchables by Oscar Meyer — conveniently packaged single servings of crackers/cheese/lunchmeat "snacks" — are such a brand and were positioned in "first" niche throughout their introductory and subsequent campaigns. Other snack-pack brands followed but couldn't claim pioneer status. Chrysler Motors innovated several brand features and even new product types during the 1980s and '90s. Chrysler "reinvented" the convertible — the style hadn't been produced by any company for many years. And Chrysler was the first to offer both driver and passenger air bags. Not surprisingly, the company was able to position itself and its products as being first.

2. *Being best.* Consumers repeatedly shop for good quality and are usually willing to pay a reasonable price for high-quality brands. In fact, one indicator of quality *is* price (see Figure 10.6). This niche is filled by the brand that can claim to be the "best" brand in the product category. As noted earlier, Swift's Butterball turkey, one of the most expensive brands, claims to be best because a full pound of butter is injected into each turkey, resulting in "butter basting" throughout the baking process. This feature is associated with the benefits of juiciness, moistness, and good taste. The brand name is also fortunate in that it is linked to the feature being promoted. Not surprisingly, Swift's can ask a premium price for their "best" brand. Furthermore, research shows that the typical Butterball consumer spends more time in the supermarket and buys more premium

Figure 10.6. *Here, Canadian Club is positioning itself as "the best." (Reprinted by permission of Hiram Walker & Sons, Inc., Farmington Hills, MI.)*

accoutrements (cranberry relishes, bakery not frozen pies, and so on) than consumers selecting a different brand. Retailers are glad to prominently display the brand. Over the years, several imported car brands have tried to claim the "best" position. Initially, Mercedes-Benz seemed to be the permanent occupant of the position. Later, other existing brands (Jaguar and BMW) as well as several new brands (Infiniti and Lexus) also claimed to be "best," resulting in a crowded niche. The American Express Gold card, Rolex watches, and Mont Blanc pens are examples of other brands positioning themselves as being the best on the market.

3. *Being the least expensive.* Besides shopping for quality, consumers often shop for price, so being able to claim that one's brand is the least expensive in the product category is a definite advantage. Not surprisingly, as a product class becomes crowded, some brands will be offered as the least expensive. A good example can be seen in the burger and cola wars that have typified the fast-food marketplace since the 1980s. Even with high-ticket items such as cars, computers, and camcorders, the price wars proliferate. The Geo, the Hyundai, and other brands in the automobile market compete to offer the best value for the price. The introduction of generic branding for products such as napkins, facial tissue, sugar, and flour prompted food chains to come up with their own versions of generic branding. Various service products also claim the "least expensive" slot. The airline industry goes through regular cycles of fare wars, with various airlines claiming to have the lowest fares. More recently, various bank and credit cards have engaged in price wars related to annual fees and low finance rates. We will probably continue to see various kinds of price wars as the wholesale and retail business markets become increasingly price competitive.

4. *Being the most expensive.* Status in relation to others is critical to some people, and one way of demonstrating status is by buying the most expensive brand on the market. The Visa Gold card could claim that its steep annual fee and high finance rates are worth the highest price in the credit card market because Visa Gold is the most universally accepted form of credit. Coco Chanel, the French clothing designer and *parfumeuse*, made it a point to sell the most expensive brand in the marketplace. With most products involving fashion (designer clothes, perfumes, shoes), one or more brands eagerly claim to be the most expensive and hence the best indicator of status.

5. *What we're not.* Another means of positioning a brand is by telling the consumer what the brand *is not*. For example, the makers of Seven-Up, on the brink of bankruptcy at one time, were saved by claiming that the soft drink is the "Uncola." Dr. Pepper imitated this strategy and was also able to capture a portion of the cola market. Claussen pickles claim to be "uncooked" and hence crisper and crunchier. With the recent interest in various health issues, numerous brands claim to be "fat free," which suggests that they will also be low calorie—something that is not necessarily the case. Not having artificial dyes is another way to claim "what we're not." And now we are seeing many brands of "clear" products—clear cola, clear dish detergent, and even clear gasoline.

6. *Positioning by gender.* Many brands compete by purposely appealing to only one gender. They position themselves as the woman's brand or the man's brand. Few right-thinking males would ever smoke Virginia Slims or Eve cigarettes, while few women smoke Camel or Lucky Strike nonfilter cigarettes. One company considered marketing a male version of pantyhose. It seems that pro football players and many males who work outdoors use pantyhose for warmth. Among the company's strategies of positioning by gender were the brand's name, Mach-Hose, and packaging the hose in "six packs." Calvin Klein's Obsession for Men and the magazine *Gentleman's Quarterly* are obviously positioned by gender. A risk is involved in offering a brand only for males or only for females, but if the strategy is well

Figure 10.7. *Here is an example of positioning by gender, even though males aren't the only purchasers of condoms. (Used by permission of Jeff McElhaney.)*

executed, a brand can capture a huge segment of the market.

7. *Positioning by age.* Advertisers often target a given *cohort* as the most likely prospect for a product or brand. Cohorts can be defined either as those born in the same year or those born in a certain set of years. That is what Trout and Ries mean by positioning by age. Targeting a specific set or group of potential consumers has many advantages. For example, one of the most targeted cohorts is the baby boom generation. The baby boomers were born between 1946 and 1964. Generation Xers like yourselves are another cohort that advertisers have decided to target. Yet another highly targeted age group is senior citizens, many of whom belong to the American Association of Retired Persons (AARP). Benefits of joining include lobbying efforts on behalf of retired persons, discounts on certain products (such as motel bills and car rentals), group activities (such as travel), and information about such topics as retirement programs, exercise equipment, and so on (you can now join at age 45!). Joiners also receive a subscription to *Modern Maturity*, which has the largest circulation among U.S. magazines, making it an ideal advertising vehicle for targeting this affluent and growing cohort in our population. Positioning by age is used to market such varying products as soft drinks, designer jeans, bookbags, hair tints, and medicines. You can imagine how targeting of cohorts focuses an advertiser's packaging, slogans, message strategies, media buys, and other communication efforts in product-oriented campaigns.

What do you think?

What is a "cohort" and to which one do you belong?

Politically Oriented Campaigns

While they share some characteristics with product-oriented campaigns, politically oriented campaigns differ in many ways from the marketing of products or brands. For example, the research data available to candidates are much more limited, and politically oriented campaigns must communicate more sophisticated information. Let us now turn to developmental models that help explain political campaigns.

The Communicative Functions Model. Communication researchers Judith Trent and Robert Friedenberg (1983) describe four stages that a political campaign must achieve if it is to be successful. They call their model the **communicative functions** approach.

In the first stage, the candidate lays a lot of groundwork by mapping out the district, organizing financial committees, developing contacts in key areas of the district, and so on. This process is usually accompanied or preceded by a formal announcement of candidacy. This stage is called the *surfacing*, or *winnowing*, stage. During this stage, the major campaign themes are tested and focused, the candidate's image is tested and promoted, and, with luck, adequate funds are raised. In presidential politics, this may begin for the out-of-power party as early as the day after losing the previous election.

In stage 2 of this model, the *primaries* serve to narrow the field of candidates and to focus issues. More people get involved, as in the participation stage of the Yale model. These persons may pass out leaflets, attend rallies, sponsor fund raisers, or perform some other overt activity that gets them involved.

In presidential politics, this stage is extremely expensive, even with the matching funds the government gives to candidates. Twenty million dollars would not be an unbelievable sum to spend in pursuing a presidential nomination. Of course, the costs are smaller with lower offices, but even senate primaries can cost several million dollars. This is a dangerous stage for candidates because they may make promises that they later can't fulfill, may reveal plans that later come back to haunt them, and may make mistakes or gaffes that can topple their candidacy.

During stage 3 — the *nomination* — the candidate is legitimized in front of the press and the corresponding media audience, and so are the party's platform and themes. The final stage — the *election* — is that period between nomination and election day when candidates wear themselves to a frazzle going from crowd to crowd saying basically the same thing over and over. Here, the use of the press is critical in both paid-for political promotions (billboards, signs, bumper stickers, buttons, TV ads, radio spots, newspaper ads, and so on) and unpaid media coverage (interview programs, short "sound bites" on the evening news, and so on). Candidates must be covered by the press so that they get key items broadcast or quoted. They must purchase their TV and radio times carefully to get the messages to the target audience at the right time and in the right way. As we will see in Chapter 12, this use of media is sophisticated and complex.

Idea/Ideological Campaigns

In a third kind of campaign — the idea/ideological campaign — neither a product nor a person/candidate is being promoted. Instead, the persuaders are trying to get an audience to engage in or change some behavior or to embrace some religion or other ideology. For example, some campaigns promote preventive measures that individuals might take to avoid contracting sexually transmitted diseases. Other campaigns urge making donations to various not-for-profit charities or other good causes. Idea campaigns are also used to urge people to help the environment, such as by recycling aluminum, glass, tin cans, plastic containers, and so on. A protest campaign might persuade people to wear black armbands on a certain day to indicate their displeasure with a policy or law. Many of the elements in the Yale model help explain the strategies of such campaigns, and some elements of the product/person campaign models can also apply. But other models have originated specifically to explain idea/ideological campaigns.

The Social Movements Model. Communication researchers Charles J. Stewart, Craig A. Smith, and Robert E. Denton, Jr. (1989) define and describe the **social movement** model of idea/ideological campaigns. They maintain that social movements have seven unique characteristics that set them apart from product- or person-oriented campaigns. First, social movements are *organized groups* of people, with leaders who usually act as the spokespersons for the movement. Second, although they are organized, *they are not "institutionalized" or recognized* by those in power. Third, social movements attract *large numbers of persons* and are large in scope either geographically or historically. Thus, "pro-lifers" would qualify as a social movement, whereas those promoting radon-free drinking water probably wouldn't, because of the limited scope.

Fourth, social movements either *promote or oppose social change.* Stewart, Smith, and Denton identify three subtypes of groups promoting or opposing change: The *innovative* movement wants to totally replace existing social values and norms (examples: gay liberation, radical feminism); the *revivalistic* movement seeks only partial change in society and a return to past values (example: breakaway religious sects); and the *resistance* movement seeks to block instead of oppose change (examples: the pro-choice movement wants *Roe v Wade* to remain the law of the land, the NRA opposes limitations on the right to own guns). Fifth, *social movements are moralistic,* preaching good versus evil, right versus wrong, patriotism versus treason. Sixth, social movements *encounter opposition* from those in power. The power may be held by formal groups (the military, police, a regulatory body), office holders (senators, judges), or "beneficiaries" of the status quo (small business owners, religious or patriotic groups). This opposition often leads to symbolic and then real violence (initially sending movement members to "havens" and then starving, raping, or killing them). Finally, *persuasion is the essential tool* used for attracting new converts, changing people's minds, and ultimately motivating those supporting the movement to take action.

Social movements also have their own set of developmental steps or "stages" through which they seem to pass, according to Stewart, Smith, and Denton. Their model of social movement outlines five stages: genesis, social unrest, enthusiastic mobilization, maintenance, and termination. In the *genesis* stage, ideologues preach about shortcomings or injustices in the status quo. These early prophets may go unheard for a long time as did those who warned that terrorism would soon spread to the United States. Finally, like-minded persons are drawn to them, and the first stage creates a hard core of devoted supporters. Then, usually, a dramatic event (like the bombing of the World Trade Center in New York City) catapults the issue into the public spotlight.

In the second stage — *social unrest* — growing numbers of people identify with the movement and feel displaced by the shortcomings described by the prophets, who now agitate these frustrated people by identifying the devils and gods of the movement and its sacred and profane grounds and acts. This leads to the third stage — *enthusiastic mobilization* — in which the true believers of the movement begin to convert more and more people and begin to encounter opposition from those in power. These are active converts now, not merely persons who identify with the movement, as in the social unrest stage. They are willing to "help" fight terrorism. Sometimes, competing organizations promoting similar ideas spring up, and there may be internal bickering and disagreements. The overall message of this stage is that there is a "we-they" world out there and "you" had better join "us" so "we" can take care of "you" and defeat "them."

In the *maintenance* stage, the movement adopts a lower profile as the media turn to other events and as some successes are perceived by converts. These successes may dull enthusiasm and siphon spirit from the movement, so it must bide its time until some crucial event or perhaps a charismatic spokesperson emerges to rekindle enthusiasm. In some cases, the movement achieves its goal(s), or it may merely wither and die in the *termination* stage. Perhaps supporters lose faith and patience, the movement may be outlawed or become outmoded, or its leaders may be co-opted by or assimilated into the establishment.

The Agitation and Control Mode. In their book *The Rhetoric of Agitation and Control*, John Bowers, Donovan Ochs, and R. J. Jensen (1993) described several stages or strategies through which most ideological movements pass before ultimately failing or succeeding. In the first stage, agitators **petition** the sources of power (the government, the corporation, or the school district), making demands that are constructed to just barely exceed the level that the power source can or will give up. This makes the power source appear unreasonable and assists the agitators in their second stage, which is called **promulgation,** or the marketing of the movement. Using handbills, leaflets, or rallies, the agitators develop their movement by informing outsiders of the unreasonableness of the power source. At this stage, the movement leaders hope to gain recruits and to get publicity that will attract even more recruits. If this stage is successful, the movement grows and moves into a third stage called **solidification.** Now the newly recruited members are educated and hyped up through rallies, protest songs (for example, "Solidarity Forever," "We Shall Overcome," and "We Shall Not Be Moved"), salutes (for example, the Nazi "Heil," or the "V" for victory and, later, for peace), or symbols (for example, the swastika, the picture of a fetus with the "forbidden" symbol superimposed on it, or the uniforms worn by militia members).

In the fourth stage, with a now-committed and educated following, the movement leaders seek **polarization** of the uncommitted population. They do this by focusing on a *flag* issue or person. The reason they are called "flag" issues or persons is that they will epitomize the ultimate enemy or may become the most easily recognized symbol of what the movement or ideology hates. Past flag issues have been the use of napalm, the extinction of some species of fish, the development of a nuclear site, or the aborting of fetuses. Flag persons personify the issue. Past flag persons have included Iraqi strongman Saddam Hussein, the head of the FBI, and, in local politics, various mayors, councilpersons, senators, representatives, or any leader who is depicted as the root of the problem. Polarization forces the onlookers to choose between "us" and "them."

In the fifth stage, **nonviolent resistance** is used. Police call in sick with the "blue flue." Students occupy a building, claiming that they have "liberated" it. There is a rent strike or an illegal march. The militia stages "war games." Some militia members and others on the far Right refuse to obtain driver's licenses or license plates for their vehicles; when charged with crimes, they refuse to enter a plea because they do not acknowledge the legitimacy of the government. These and other devices call attention to the mass movement and are meant to prompt some sort of response from the power source. Agitators may hope that the power sources will call out the army or police and that the press will cover the confrontation. Then agitators may claim repression or gestapo tactics. Usually this leads to the sixth stage—**escalation**—which is intended to increase tension in the power sources. Perhaps threats are made—rumors of planted bombs or public displays of weapons. Perhaps some violent act occurs, such as a strike with fights, a killing or

kidnapping, or a symbolic bombing, such as that at the 1996 Olympics.

If the forces in power try to repress the movement at this time, there usually is a split inside the movement between those who favor violence and those who favor nonviolence. Bowers, Ochs, and Jensen call this stage **Ghandi versus guerrilla.** Usually, the nonviolent segment of the movement goes to the power source and argues that unless the power source gives in, the guerrillas will take over. Depending on the outcome of this stage, the final stage may or may not emerge. This last stage is **revolution.**

So far in the 1990s, a number of ideological campaigns have followed this sequence of stages. Some examples of such agitation and control movements include the overthrow and ultimate dissolution of the Soviet Union; both pro-life and pro-choice movements; the gay liberation movement; and many religious movements. With the end of the cold war and the new role of the United Nations as a police force in the world, we will very likely see such agitation and control tactics used in campaigns throughout the world and in ideological campaigns here at home as well. The ability of the agitation and control model to describe, explain, and even predict stages in movements across time testifies to both its validity and its reliability.

The Diffusion of Innovation Model. Some idea campaigns do not seek to promote an alternative ideology. Rather, these campaigns hope to induce their audience to adopt new practices or change their behaviors, such as instituting safer procedures in a factory, reducing intake of red meats and fats, or conserving energy. Everett Rogers (1962) studied the stages through which people approach the adoption of any new technology (computers, cellular phones, e-mail, the Web, and so on), practice (recycling various kinds of waste), or value (gays in the military). His **diffusion of innovation model** also has some applicability to product- and person-oriented campaigns. He outlines four stages through which people must pass on the way to adopting change.

In the first stage—*information and knowledge*—the potential adoptee acquires or actively seeks information about the innovation (How does it work? What are its features and benefits? How much will it cost? How have other adopters rated it? and so on). When people first became aware of the practice of recycling—a time-consuming activity with little direct payoff—few rushed out and got containers for aluminum, glass, tin cans, newsprint, and mixed paper. It sounded like a lot of bother. However, being made aware of recycling drew people's attention to various pieces of information (the life expectancy of local landfills, the effects of deforestation on climate) that increased their knowledge about the value of recycling.

In the second stage—*persuasion*—the potential adopters process persuasion aimed at inducing them to actually try the new practice. With major changes in practice, this takes longer than when the change is only minor. Those advocating the change may use testimonials from well-known persons who have adopted the new practice. When the Beef Council, for example, wanted to change the frequency of people's use of their product, they hired two well-known and attractive stars, Cybill Shepard and James Garner, to appear in television commercials. Both testified that, contrary to popular opinion, beef isn't necessarily high in calories if one chooses lean cuts and prepares them in new and exciting ways. The council further promoted beef by running full-page ads in gourmet magazines, featuring recipes and appetizing pictures, as well as noting the low level of fat and calories in each serv-ing. Overall the campaign was successful, although it did run into difficulty when Shepard made it known in private that she really didn't eat much beef, and Garner had a heart attack.

In the third stage in Roger's model—*decision, adoption, and trial*—the potential adopters decide to try the new practice. They get the recycling containers, go to a trade show to try the new handheld computer, or order the innovation on a "money-back guaranteed trial basis," then actually use the new technology, product, or practice. A key element in most innovation campaigns is to "induce trial," which is why in the initial stages of such campaigns free samples, free trial periods, low prices, or some other technique is used to get prospects to try the product for themselves. An automobile manufacturer, for example, might induce trial by offering new models to car rental firms at below cost just so the potential adopter will be exposed to and will try the brand. Sometimes marketers might request the user to respond to the product/brand/practice by mailing back a rating survey. This technique moves the potential adopter into the next stage in the model.

In the *confirmation and evaluation* stage, the new adopter reconsiders the adoption and measures its performance against his or her expectations. "Did it deliver what it promised?" "Did I like it?" "Was it worth the price?" and similar questions are raised in the adopter's mind and, if confirmed, more permanently cement the adoption decision. If one decides to continue usage of a product or practice, he or she then searches for information that confirms or "okays" its adoption. Studies have shown that the person most likely to read an ad for a particular brand of automobile is the person who most recently purchased the brand. As adopters of innovations, we seek confirmation of our decision.

The Rogers model is helpful in considering campaigns that offer new and innovative practices to consumers. With the rate of change accelerating in our technocracy as we approach the millennium, we will undoubtedly go through these stages ourselves or observe them in others many times over. Most recently, we have seen the process at work in getting people to try e-mail or "surfing" the Web. Knowing what is happening in such situations helps put decisions to adopt new practices into a clearer perspective that should result in making wiser choices.

Other Communication Characteristics of Campaigns

Besides these developmental models of campaigns, several other theories help explain the ultimate success or failure of a given product-oriented, person-oriented, or idea/ideological campaign. We now examine some of these explanatory tools or characteristics.

Symbolic Convergence Theory

Most of us like to affiliate with people with whom we agree and who are like us in "substantial" ways (to borrow and adapt terminology from Burke). This means that we seek to find "communities of agreement," or sets of people who share the same meanings for basic values and who have the same lifestyle as we do. Such agreement necessitates the merging of my meanings for events and values with your meanings for those same things. We don't need to be identical twins, just similar persons. Having similar values and lifestyles identifies us as a "particular audience"—or to use the marketing term "a market segment"—to whom advertisers, politicians, and ideologues try to appeal. A theory developed by E. G. Bormann (1985), his students, and followers helps explain how shared meanings begin, develop, continue, and finally motivate us to action. The theory is called **symbolic convergency theory,** and the methodology is called **fantasy theme analysis.** They have been applied to small-group, interpersonal, corporate, institutional, and organizational communication, and, for our purposes, for doing audience analysis for product, idea, and political

campaigns. When combined with focus-group interviews and a statistical technique called *Q-sort analysis*, the theory and method have great power for analyzing the kinds of dramas to which specified groups of consumers and voters respond (Cragan & Shields, 1994, 1995).

A basic premise of symbolic convergence theory is that reality is socially based and socially constructed. That is, the way each of us perceives the world is the result of our interactions with others and our adoption of and addition to the meanings of these interactions. Because we share our inputs and interpretations with others in our social groups, we come to believe them even more devotedly than if we had been told what to believe from some respected authority. When this sharing occurs fully, we have a "symbolic convergence" of meaning.

The first clues to the power inherent in the social creation of realities came from the work of Robert F. Bales (1970), a professor of sociology at Harvard. His initial interest was in identifying the kind of interactions that occurred in small, task-oriented groups, and he noticed that in one category of interaction, much tension reduction was being accomplished through the telling of stories in which the group seemed to participate. He called this category "dramatizes." He began to describe the way these stories or minidramas seemed to develop, or, as he called it, "chain out" in the group, resulting in what he came to call **fantasy themes.**

At this point, Bales's work caught the attention of Bormann and later of Bormann's students and colleagues. They, too, had noticed the sharing of fantasies in small groups at the University of Minnesota, and thought that the process of reality building in small groups had a wider application. In a series of studies, Bormann and his followers identified the operation of symbolic convergence in presidential election campaigns. Using a variety of techniques, they discovered that "a number of communities of voters shared differing configurations or dramatizations and thus shared statistically different visions of the campaign" (Bormann, 1985). These visions were later checked against actual voting behavior and were found to be reliable predictors of voter behavior.

The researchers also discovered that those covering the campaign for the media developed their own "rhetorical vision" of the campaign, in which the role of the reporter was to dig out the truth. It was in this process of investigative reporting that "fantasy types" emerged—favorite topics, themes, or images discovered by reporters trying to dig out the "truth." One fantasy theme is that of "the front-runner," the candidate who, according to the polls or because of incumbency, has the kind of legitimacy discussed earlier in the Yale five-stage campaign model. This candidate is focused on by the media, which cover such issues as how far ahead the candidate is, whether he or she is showing signs of stumbling, is hiding something, or is acting as a stalking horse for other candidates. This dramatic presentation of the "truth" about the campaign makes for good reporting, bonuses, and other perks to the reporter.

Another fantasy theme is that of the baseball game, with the candidates being in "the early or final innings" or unable to "get to first base" with the electorate. Another theme makes use of boxing images, with candidates "being on the ropes" or delivering "knockout blows" to the opposition, who is "just a lightweight" and not a real "contender."

Another fantasy type is the "crucial blunder or gaffe" in which a candidate makes a mistake that endangers his or her candidacy. The blunder may be misspeaking oneself in some embarrassing way, being caught in some questionable activity (sexual promiscuity, getting "kickbacks," having some past event like pot smoking brought up). The gaffe may ruin a candidacy or, if skillfully handled, can demonstrate how cunning and "political" the candidate is.

There is also the fantasy theme of the "spin doctor," a media expert attached to the candidate's campaign staff. The spin doctor's job is to see to it that the press gives the proper interpretation to the candidate's words and deeds. In this fantasy, the candidate tends to be a bumbler in need of propping up by "behind-the-scenes manipulators" who will put the perfect "spin" on his or her statements or actions.

In product-oriented advertising, the ad agency or an advertising huckster puts "spin" on the product using press releases about the product's introduction, by getting press coverage for giving the product away to some worthy group, or by emphasizing the product's astounding benefits. Bert Metter, chairman of J. Walter Thompson USA advertising agency and part-time columnist for *Advertising Age*, defines it this way:

> We are in the age of spin. The art and science of creating images is out of the closet. . . . As spin becomes more common . . . we've got to deliver more effectiveness. . . . The agencies with the answers will succeed. Others will have a lot of spinning to do. (1990, p. 36)

Naturally, this kind of spin doctoring for products is bound to raise criticism from those who believe that the ad industry is responsible for conspicuous consumption and all of its accompanying ills: pollution, easy credit, and "keeping up with the Joneses." "Spin" operates in idea/ideological campaigns as well. For example, pro-life advocates use interpretations of when life begins that have a pro-life "spin."

Hoffer's Model

Throughout American history, various populist movements have focused on such issues as the gold standard, the prices paid to farmers for their goods, the right to form a union and bargain collectively with management, the right to vote, abolition of slavery, and the prohibition of alcohol. These movements have always formed around "men [and women] of words," to use Eric

Hoffer's (1966) term. One of the common fears in this country is that a talented persuader might be able to agitate the common man into a movement or perhaps even into revolution. The rhetorical vision that seems to emerge from this fear might be labeled "the demagogue takes over." Hoffer identifies fanaticism as one characteristic of such leaders.

It is this fanatical zeal that most average citizens fear, because the "true believers" will say anything, believe anything, do anything, and sacrifice anything—even their own lives on occasion—on behalf of the movement. The followers cease to be individuals, as Hoffer points out, and instead become melded into a powerful entity—the movement. It is the basis for the individuals' collective and individual identities.

The "men [and women] of words" use several unifying devices to forge the collective power of the movement. It is clear that the offer of change and of hope can be a means of developing unity among followers. It is no accident that the leaders of mass movements of the past promised their followers "a better tomorrow." This kind of ideological campaign rhetoric catches the imagination of the audience and can unify them in zealous action. As Figure 10.8 demonstrates, wordsmiths often use words to confuse the audience.

Hoffer points out several unifying devices that seem to be characteristic of the ideological campaign. In many ways they are the reality links in the fantasies, which ultimately create the rhetorical visions of mass movements. These reality links have led to, for example, the abolition of slavery movement, the union movement, and the civil rights movement in their positive forms or to terrorism and racism in their negative forms.

Hatred is a powerful unifying device. In fact, Hoffer says, "Hatred is the most accessible and comprehensive of all unifying agents. . . . Mass movements can rise and spread without belief in God, but never without a belief in a devil" (pp. 85–86). We know that Hitler used Jews as the hate device, and abolitionists used slaveholders. Today, Palestinian terrorists use Israel. Hoffer speculates that this unifying hatred frequently springs from self-contempt and guilt or feelings of impotency, ineffectiveness, and worthlessness. At the same time, the unified hatred removes individual guilt and permits the individuals to do things they would never do if they were acting on their own. As Hoffer notes, "When we lose our individual independence in the corporateness of a mass movement, we find a new freedom—freedom to hate, bully, lie, torture, murder, and betray without remorse or shame" (p. 85). This helps explain the insanity of racism and terrorism. The terrorist experiences no fear, guilt, or remorse for blowing up the building or airplane and its occupants—it was done in the name of the movement and not in the name of the individual terrorist.

Imitation is another unifying device in the ideological movement, according to Hoffer. It helps to make the fantasy seem more real when there is tangible evidence of the power of the movement. He says there must be a "diffusion of uniformity" (p. 94). This accounts for the chanting of the crowd at a rally, the salutes frequently adopted by mass movements, the adoption of official uniforms in some movements, the use of bumper stickers or pins bearing a symbol of the movement, and numerous other real and symbolic means of imitation.

Persuasion and **coercion** also are unifying agents that help to spread and maintain the fantasy of the movement. What Hoffer refers to here is the kind of propaganda that is used within the movement to build emotion and develop loyalty in its membership. As Hoffer puts it, "Propaganda by itself succeeds mainly with the frustrated. Their throbbing fears, hopes, and passions crowd at the portals of their senses. . . . It is the music of their own souls they hear in the impassioned words of the propagandist" (p. 98). Hitler could easily raise the emotions of the crowds with his

Wordsmiths

Figure 10.8. *These are the wordsmiths for the politically oriented campaign. How effective would they be for an idea-oriented campaign? Why? (Drawing by W. B. Park; © The New Yorker Magazine, Inc. Reprinted by permission.)*

anti-Semitism—they already hated Jews. According to Hoffer, if fanaticism begets violence, it is equally true that violence begets fanaticism or at least reinforces it. Also, persuasion and coercion frequently result in a powerful need to proselytize, or "spread the word," to the uncommitted.

Leadership is a critical unifying element that can spark powerful fantasies in audiences' minds. They can visualize themselves doing great things and enacting noble and historical deeds through the leader. The circumstances must be ripe for such leadership to emerge, according to Hoffer. "Once the stage is set, the presence of an outstanding leader is indispensable" (p. 104).

Suspicion is another excellent unifying device in sparking fantasies in the audiences of mass-movement rhetoric. If you suspect that someone is planning to harm you, you naturally turn to a movement for assistance. Hoffer asserts that it is the dissatisfaction with ourselves that leads us to identify the same sort of shortcomings in others.

Hoffer says that suspicion "acts yet as a marvelous slime to cement the embittered and disaffected into one compact whole. Suspicion too is an ingredient of this acrid slime, and it too can act as a unifying agent" (p. 114).

Action is a final unifying agent in the ideological campaign, according to Hoffer. He notes how important a simple action like marching together can unify people, and how the Nazis recognized that "Marching diverts men's thoughts. Marching kills thought. Marching makes an end of individuality" (p. 112). Small wonder that so many mass movements have relied on the rally followed by a demonstration, many times in the form of a march.

Other forms of action used in some campaigns include boycotts, candlelight vigils, destruction of physical property, and even the maiming and killing of "the enemy" who is to blame for the state of affairs.

Thus in our understanding of ideological and other campaigns, symbolic convergence theory and the ideas of Hoffer help explain why some campaigns succeed and others fail.

Campaign Message Characteristics

Several other characteristics of campaigns relate to how they communicate — what messages they send overtly and what messages they send covertly. We will now look briefly at some of these communication characteristics of the successful persuasive campaign.

Credibility. Successful campaigns usually communicate a sense of *credibility* about their product, person, or idea. We follow the advice of those in whom we have faith — those we feel we can believe. As noted earlier, credibility relates to a number of factors discussed earlier, such as *dynamism, trustworthiness,* and *expertise* or *competence.* Some candidates build credibility by show-

ing their expertise on some issue or another, whereas others focus on their dynamism or honesty. In one Senate campaign in Illinois, a long-time incumbent who was physically attractive and dynamic was defeated by professional congressman Paul Simon, who wore a bow tie. The incumbent was depicted as insincere through ads that called him a "chameleon" while emphasizing that Simon had always been consistent and was an expert on downstate problems. In other states, rugged, active, macho types seemed to win the day. Credibility — whether communicated through expertise, sincerity, or dynamism — is essential to the successful campaign.

Climate of Opinion. Successful campaigns tie in with the prevailing *climate of opinion.* Public opinion is a fickle thing in our culture, and many critics have observed the pendulum effect, wherein popular opinion moves from one side of the political continuum to the other. These shifting sands of public opinion are critical to the successful persuader and need to be identified and then worked into the campaign.

In product-oriented campaigns, we have seen this many times. Seven-Up, for example, was nearly bankrupt when it asked the J. Walter Thompson ad agency to design an ad campaign. The agency hooked Seven-Up into the then-prevailing idea of being different and non-conformist, launching the "Uncola" campaign and turning Seven-Up's fortunes around. We see a similar thing in ads aimed at the "me generation," members of which are now reaching child-bearing years. The ads stress being good to yourself even if you are going to balance holding a job with raising a family and pursuing your private interest in skydiving.

Some recent examples of climates of opinion are the disturbing militia movement, which plays

What do you think?

What is the "prevailing climate of opinion" on your campus today?

on governmental distrust, the graying of the baby boomers which is being used by many advertisers, and the concern for preserving the environment.

Opinion Leaders. Successful campaigns seem to aim their messages at *opinion leaders*. Studies done over thirty years ago to discover how farmers adopted new farm methods (contour plowing or crop rotation) found an interesting phenomenon. Most farmers did not respond to direct appeals from the Department of Agriculture. Instead, they seemed to adopt the new methods only after a highly respected farmer or an opinion leader did. This pattern was labeled the *two-step flow* theory of communication. We are most persuaded when an opinion leader does something in response to what a persuader says. Later studies demonstrated that this flow had many levels, and the two-step notion was elaborated to a *multistep flow* of information. The Successful Farmers, who followed the lead of the Super Farmers, were leaders in turn to the Good Farmers, who were opinion leaders to the OK Farmers. Even OK Farmers were opinion leaders to the Unsuccessful Farmers.

Prompting Messages out of the Audience. Successful campaigns usually rely on information, experiences, or memories that are already inside persuadees rather than trying to teach the audience new information. This idea comes from Tony Schwartz's book *The Responsive Chord* (1973).

Schwartz has been a media consultant to several presidents and presidential nominees as well as to many state and local politicians. His basic idea is that campaigners should try to identify the internal state of the target audience: What are poignant memories or experiences for them? Then the campaigner determines how these can be prompted or cued.

A good way to sell a drain cleaner is to show someone sticking his or her hands into a stopped-up sink full of greasy water filled with food bits,

coffee grounds, and the like. Most people have had to do that at least once in their lives and so already have the feeling embedded in their experiential storehouse. Then the person pours some Liquid Plumber in the drain and we watch the sink unclog and drain out as clean fresh water washes away the muck. This is another feeling to which those of us who have had to unclog sinks can relate. In this ad, the persuader *gets the meaning out of* the viewer. Contrast this ad with a commercial that might explain how traps in sinks get clogged with grease and hair. The ad then shows a cutaway of such a trap and goes on to explain that the grease can be cut by either an acid or an alkalyde. Because acids can damage plumbing, the announcer suggests that we use Drano, an alkaline-based product, to dissolve the grease and unclog the sink. The ad then shows that happening. This ad is busy trying to *get something into* the viewer.

As noted, all persuasion involves self-persuasion. We must agree to be persuaded and then find good reasons for deciding. Many of these good reasons are already embedded in our conscious or subconscious memory pool. Clever persuaders identify ways to cue these memories and connect them to a product, candidate, or idea/ideology. They tune the persuadee's ear to the kind of messages that will be carried in campaigns seeking new buyers, new voters, or new joiners.

Review and Conclusion

Person/candidate, product, and idea/ideology campaigns demonstrate both permanence and change. The formal and functional characteristics of campaigns that we have explored seem to persist over time, forming permanent patterns. The ever-shifting issues and increasingly sophisticated technologies of product testing, public opinion polling, media production, and direct marketing are the elements of change. Among the recurring aspects of campaigns are:

1. a systematic flow of communication from the persuader to the audience and back to the persuader via a feedback loop — something that typifies all communication systems

2. the establishment of formal goals, strategies, and tactics

3. the creation of a "position" or "niche" in the audience's mind

4. stages through which most campaigns must pass

5. a participatory dramatization of the product, candidate, or idea/ideology; the audience is invited to participate in the campaign drama in real or symbolic ways

6. the kinds of appeals that unify and recruit zealots for the mass movement

7. the "chaining out" of rhetorical visions in campaigns/social movements that ultimately involve mass audiences

You need to prepare to be a critical receiver who makes responsible decisions about which product to buy, which candidate to vote for, and which ideas or ideologies to endorse. These decisions are appropriate only after thorough analysis of the campaigns. Ask yourself how the campaign responds to feedback; what its objectives, strategies, and tactics are; how the campaign positions the product, person, or idea; what developmental stages emerge; and in what kind of drama you are being invited to participate. When you have answered these questions, you will be ready to make a responsible decision.

Questions for Further Thought

1. Choose a present-day campaign for a product, person, or idea/ideology. What appear to be its objectives, strategies, and tactics?

2. Define each of the Yale developmental terms and identify examples of the first three stages in some magazine or newspaper campaign.

3. In the agitation/control model, what stage of a campaign or movement is represented when we vote for or against a particular candidate or proposition? Why?

4. What are some ways now being used to position products you are currently using? candidates currently running for office? idea campaigns requesting your active or financial support? mass movements currently seeking converts?

5. Identify a social movement that is either going on or seems to be developing. Use the social movements model and agitation/control model to trace its development. Which most accurately describes what is happening?

6. Using Bormann's symbolic convergence theory, explain the same social movement identified in question 5. Which of the methodologies seems most message oriented? Which is most audience related?

7. Identify several "fantasy types" in a campaign for a product made popular in the 1980s. Are they similar to those for products of the 1990s?

8. What are some of Hoffer's "unifying devices"? How have they worked in past campaigns? Where do they seem to be working now?

References

Bales, R. F. (1970). *Personality and interpersonal behavior*. New York: Holt, Rinehart & Winston.

Binder, L. (1971). *Crisis and sequence in political development*. Princeton, NJ: Princeton University Press.

Bormann, E. G. (1985). *The force of fantasy*. Carbondale and Edwardsville: Southern Illinois University Press.

Bowers, J. W., Ochs, D. J., & Jensen, R. J. (1993). *The rhetoric of agitation and control*. Prospect Heights, IL: Waveland.

Cragan, J. F., & Shields, D. C. (1994). *Applied communication research: A dramatistic approach*. Washington, DC: Speech Communication Association.

Cragan, J. F., & Shields, D. C. (1995). *Symbolic theories in applied communication research: Bormann, Burke, and Fisher*. Creskill, NJ: Hampton Press.

Fortini-Campbell, (1992). *The consumer insight book*. Chicago: The Copy Workshop.

Hoffer, E. (1966). *The true believer*. New York: Harper & Row.

Lavidge, R. J., & Steiner, G. A. (1961). A model for predictive measurements of advertising effectiveness. *Journal of Marketing, 24*, October, 59–62.

Metter, B. (1990). Advertising in the age of spin. *Advertising Age*, September 17, p. 36.

Nimmo, D., & Combs, J. (1990). *Mediated political realities*. White Plains, NY: Longman.

Novak, M. (1974). *Choosing our king: Powerful symbols in presidential politics*. New York: Macmillan.

Rogers, E. (1962). *The diffusion of innovation*. New York: Free Press.

Schultz, D. E. (1994). *Strategic advertising campaigns*. Lincolnwood, IL: NTC Business Books.

Schwartz, T. (1973). *The responsive chord*. New York: Anchor Press/Doubleday.

Stewart, C. J., Smith, C. A., & Denton, R. E., Jr. (1989). *Persuasion and social movements* (2nd ed.). Prospect Heights, IL: Waveland.

Trent, J. S. & Friedenberg, R. V. (1983). *Political campaign communication*. New York: Praeger.

Trout, J., & Ries, A. (1986). *Positioning: The battle for your mind*. New York: Harper & Row.

11

Becoming a Persuader

Thus far we have focused on receiver skills: how to be a critical, responsible, and ethical consumer of persuasion. However, we all must become a persuader from time to time. Luckily, the knowledge gained in our role as a persuadee can be applied to our occasional role as a persuader. We can use tactics of intensification and downplaying; we can mold our persuasion using process, content, cultural, and nonverbal premises; and we can apply our knowledge of what is ethical in persuasion. As a persuader, your first step in preparing your message is *knowing your audience*. A second stage in becoming a persuader is *shaping your message*. Here, considerations such as patterns of organization, kinds of proof, and styling of messages will be important. Finally, you must choose how to go about *delivering your message*. This will involve not only the physical characteristics of how you speak (eye contact, posture, and so on) but also choosing a channel through which to deliver the message, timing the message delivery, and so on. Finally, you will want to be aware of some common persuasive tactics.

Knowing Your Audience

It is easy to assert that persuaders should know as much as possible about their audience, but it is not so easy to prescribe specific ways you can get to know your target. One of the best ways is to *listen to them as they persuade*. When they persuade, they use tactics that would be persuasive to them. I, for example, am most persuaded when the source uses narratives and examples. I often use the narrative example to get you to take my advice. If you want to persuade me, fill your message with narratives and examples. At the present time, I am in my third term as president of our faculty senate. During my first term I observed those key persons who I knew I would need to persuade—the president of the university, the provost, the chair of the board of trustees, various faculty senators, and others. I watched them in their attempts to persuade others for about a semester before trying to persuade them of many things. After that I realized where some wanted the facts—just the facts—others wanted the story behind the story. "What do the faculty think about that?" And another party needed to be complimented profusely before becoming open to persuasion. I became a better persuader by observing my audiences carefully.

Know your audience, observe them, listen to them, and analyze what they say and how they say it. When your parents try to persuade, how do they go about it? What kinds of evidence do they use? Some people, for example, are most easily persuaded when they think that *they are the ones who came up with the idea for change*. It is best to give such persons several alternatives and let *them* make the choice. Then they "own" the idea or innovation. The president was such a persuadee—I let him "come up" with my ideas.

Demographics and Audience Analysis

When persuasion is aimed at larger audiences, persuaders can use **demographics** to analyze their audience. In demographics, people are grouped via their shared attributes—their likes, dislikes, habits, and values. A good indicator of demographic clustering is the magazine subscriptions people have. If you subscribe to *Outdoor Life, Field and Stream* and *Sports Illustrated*, you are likely to be different from the person who subscribes to *Atlantic, Horticulture, Organic Gardening,* and *Bon Appétit*. Both of you would be good bets for catalogs featuring outdoor clothing. In all likelihood, only you are interested in hunting or fishing gear and would be a good candidate for a catalog for lures or decoys. Probably neither of you is interested in rock music or MTV.

Your affiliations (church, fraternal, or community groups) are another demographic index, as are your credit cards. Through these means as well as the census, the state driver's license department, returned warranty information, and many other sources, all of us have been identified demographically as good candidates for certain pitches.

Most of us don't do this kind of elaborate analysis of a potential audience, but we can do a lot even if we are limited in time and resources. For example, suppose you have been asked to make a presentation to the governing board of your college or university. Your goal is to get them to provide enough funding so that each student can have access to the Internet and WWW either via computer labs, computers in dorm rooms, or student-owned computers using modems. You need to find out who the board's members are, what they do for a living, and where they live. Information about how your audience has acted in the past is critical. What kinds of past funding have they used? What kinds of alternatives have they allowed? Why? These are the kinds of questions that can help you analyze your audience.

What are some of the demographic factors to look at in preparing a formal persuasive presentation? The first step is to decide which factors will be significant for your audience. Audience factors that make a critical difference vary with the goal of the persuader. Age is important if you are discussing tax planning for retirement, but not if your topic is recycling. Gender is important for some topics but not for others. The same thing goes for income, religion, or politics.

Return to our WWW access situation. Which of the following will be among the factors you will want to explore about your audience?

1. *Average age*. Will it matter if they are all over fifty or if they are all under thirty-five? Probably.

2. *Income*. Will it matter if they are well-to-do or just struggling along?

3. *Gender*. Are the board members likely to be male or female, and does that matter?

What do you think?

Describe an audience you need to persuade in the near future.

4. *Religion*. This factor is one you can probably ignore.

5. *Family size*. Will it matter if your audience members have two or five children? Probably, since children frequently influence parents on matters of technology.

6. *Political party*. In this case political affiliation would have little bearing.

7. *Type of occupation*. If the audience members are white-collar workers, they may be convinced by a solid set of statistics and a tightly reasoned presentation done in a formal manner. Plan to use graphs, charts, and informational handouts, and remind them of the importance of technology and computer literacy on the job. Your request is not designed to provide students with access to merely useless, "fun," or "erotic" materials, but rather it will provide hands-on training that will make students better employees and citizens upon graduation.

Once you know the key demographic factors for your group/topic/context, the next stage is to explore them. The president will be able to tell you about some of the board members. The P.R. folks at your school can provide information about where they live, which can cue you to income and age. If they have turned down past requests from students, you need to know why. Sometimes just talking to one or two typical members of a group before you attempt to persuade can be helpful. Any characteristics they share as a group can be useful in shaping your message for that audience.

Determining Audience Needs

Some audience touchstones are emotional, some are logical, some are cultural, and some are nonverbal. We could do some pretty sophisticated analysis on our target to determine their needs.

We could focus on the human need for self-improvement and confidence to sell our idea. Or we could talk about the need to constantly keep up with technology.

All audiences have some sets of shared experiences. You can probably recall where you were when the *Challenger* space shuttle tragedy occurred. All parents remember the birth of their first baby. An interesting example of such shared experiences and emotions for college students is the classic examination dream first identified by Freud. Apparently it is common for college graduates to dream about showing up for a final examination only to be unable to recall anything about the class. In other variations, students cannot find the examination room or realize that they never studied for the exam or perhaps never even went to class or purchased the texts. Most college graduates remember the stress of their college years. All these stored memories can be persuasive building blocks. What might be some of these stored experiences for the members of the governing board? Probably they all can remember getting their own first PC and trying to learn how to use it. The value of getting hands-on training is an argument that will resonate with them. They probably all also remember coming to the realization that you will not have to learn how to use the PC just once but rather that it will be a lifelong process since the "half-life" of technology is constantly shrinking.

Thus, in the process of audience analysis, we can also try to locate the key experiences that relate to our topic or goal. The next time you need to persuade someone, try to list the experiences he or she is likely to have had. Can some of these be tied into your message?

Another factor in audience analysis is also suggested by Tony Schwartz (1973) in his book *The Responsive Chord*. Schwartz favors messages that are built for the time and place, when and where they will be heard. If you were trying to send a message to people telling them to vote for someone, and you knew that they would hear it on Labor Day weekend, how would you design the message? You would want to plug into the picnic mood, the out-of-doors experience, and the family fun that people are having on that weekend. You might have the candidate talk about conservation for us and for our children or about the need to make it easy for friends to be together. Schwartz calls this the **task-oriented approach** to persuading. You can use it, too.

First ask yourself whether your goal fits with the audience's ability to follow your advice. If you are going to ask them to quit smoking, you'd better do it in such a way as to make it easy for them. Give them brochures that offer helpful hints on quitting. Try to find out the state of mind of your persuadees — the board, the sales force, or the job interviewer. What is the likely mood? Will they be relaxed? Will they have doubts? Take these things into account and design your message to do its task. Remind them of the good feeling of knowing that you are computer literate. Then tell them that there is a chance to make that kind of feeling available to more students through the universal access to the Web.

Once you know something about your target group and how its members feel about your topic, you can shape the message. There are many steps in the shaping process. First you need to *organize* the message in the most useful way. People are more likely to recall messages that are well organized.

Forms of Organization

There are a number of ways to organize messages to make sure they are persuasive and easy to remember. We will look at five such formats here: the topic format, the space format, the chronological format, the stock issues format, and the motivated sequence format. In the first three of these formats, we will use the following example: A student group on my campus wanted to bring Bob Zemeckis, a highly successful filmmaker and former student, back to campus as a guest speaker. He was willing to donate his honorarium to the sponsoring student group to be used for field trips, travel to national conferences, and funding for a career day. The persuasive presentation to the student speakers committee could be organized in several ways.

Organization by Topic

The topical format is most useful when the message that you want to convey covers several topics or issues. Here is a list of topics that might be used in the guest-speaker example:

1. Zemeckis' fame and success as a reason to bring him to campus

2. The kind of role model he would provide

3. The special offer of previewing the speaker's latest unreleased film

4. The degree to which he is in demand on the speaking circuit

5. Bob's generosity in donating his fee to the student group

6. The other benefits to be derived from Zemeckis' presence on campus: publicity for the school, the added programming made possible by his donation, the career counseling he might be able to give to aspiring student filmmakers

By presenting the six topics with supporting evidence, you give the student government a variety of good reasons to fund the speaker. The topic format is a good choice when presenting specific reasons for some suggested action.

Organization by Space

The spatial format is a good choice when we want to compare our topic to the larger picture. The spatial idea relates to the comparative size of our proposal. In the Zemeckis example, we might compare his relative cost to that of speakers invited by other departments. His fee might be only a quarter of that asked for by a similar student group and for a less well-known speaker. Furthermore, this speaker's fee represented only 5 percent of the total guest speaker budget for the semester, and our student group is only one of more than forty similar groups in the university. In the spatial format, we might draw several pie graphs. In one, we could visually depict our speaker's fee as one-twentieth of the pie and label the remainder "Other Speaker Fees." Another graph might show our 5 percent share as only a fraction of those allocated to other student groups. In all of these examples, we would be using space as an organizing principle.

Organization by Chronology

Sometimes the essential message in persuasive communication is best relayed to the audience by taking them through the issues in historical sequence. We might relate our speaker's career as follows:

1. In 1975 the speaker became a major in our department.

2. Two years later he transferred to the USC film school, eventually graduating in film. But he still values the basics of filmmaking he learned while he was with us.

3. He made his first picture, *Caddy Shack*, as an independent a year later.

4. It was released the next June, and as a minor summer hit, it recaptured the initial investment plus a small profit.

5. Later that year, the film got several "honorable mentions" at film festivals, and our speaker then signed a contract to make pictures for Stephen Spielberg and one of the largest film studios.

6. In the next few years he turned out several moneymakers, such as *Romancing the Stone*.

7. Then in 1982 he made his first blockbuster, *Back to the Future*, which went on to win several Academy Awards.

8. Since then he has been independently turning out hits like *Back to the Future II, Who Framed Roger Rabbit?* and *Forrest Gump*, and is now one of the best-known writer/producers in Hollywood.

Organization by Stock Issues

The stock-issues organizational format is most frequently seen in cases where a major policy change is being considered. Its name refers to the fact that there are several universal issues that need to be addressed when major policy changes are considered. Our Bob Zemeckis example doesn't involve a policy change, so we will look at a different example.

In the Broadway musical comedy *The Music Man*, band instrument and uniform salesman Harold Hill sells an entire town on a need for a boys band complete with uniforms on the flimsiest of logical appeals. He points out numerous symptoms of trouble in the town (kids are smoking, reading "dirty" books, cussing, dressing outrageously, and so on). He then concludes with these words, "There's trouble, my friends, right here in River City. I said trouble, and that starts with T and rhymes with P and that stands for 'Pool'!" He goes on to point out that with a band to busy them, the boys will make no more visits to the pool hall where the bad habits are all learned. In this example, an overkill of symptomatic evidence enables the persuader to short-circuit the reasoning process. Hill's "proof" relies on a rhyme scheme — P rhymes with T; therefore pool means trouble — but P also rhymes with B, C, D, E, G, P, V, and Z — a fact Hill ignores.

Hill is successful because he plays on the stock issues expected whenever a policy such as supporting a city band is addressed. In a stock-issues approach, two sides debate an issue. One side wants change, and the other prefers the status quo. In our law courts, the side wanting change is the prosecution, and the side favoring the status quo is the defense. In our legal system, you are presumed innocent (the status quo) unless the prosecution can show that you are guilty beyond reasonable doubt (change). We say that the **burden of proof** rests with the prosecution, the side that wants to change the status of the defendant. The status quo is presumed to be wise or true until proven otherwise.

What do you think?

What organizational format is used in a criminal trial?

The side with the burden of proof must show serious shortcomings with the status quo, usually by indicating *symptoms* of a problem. These symptoms are then tied to a supposed cause to create a cause-effect or problem-solution frame of reference. The political persuader might tie the unemployment to deficit spending and say that reducing the deficit will increase investment and hence employment.

Once the persuader has presented an adequate **need for change,** the focus of the argument shifts to the necessity for some **plan of action** that we can reasonably assume will somehow solve a problem. In other words, effective persuaders can't just point out shortcomings in the status quo and leave it at that. Neither can they offer a ludicrous plan of action that obviously cannot solve the problem or that has no possibility of being enacted. A critic of the status quo can't offer to solve the federal deficit problem by having the government print trillions of dollars in unbacked paper money. Such a plan could never pass Congress; further, it would create runaway inflation. The critic might suggest that marijuana be made legal and its manufacture and sale be operated by the federal government, thus generating $30 billion in revenue. Or the persuader might suggest a national lottery, like the Irish Sweepstakes, that could generate another $20 billion to be set aside for debt service and deficit reduction. Having shown a need for change and a realistic plan for change, the persuader can now move to the stage of stock issues, demonstrating that the need shown can be dealt with through the suggested plan.

This third stage, the **plan-meets-need** stage, involves demonstrating that the suggested plan could be enacted, could generate the needed revenues, and additionally, would not create other problems that would be worse than the status quo. Here, the side defending the status quo might bring up such issues as the possible side effects of marijuana legalization, such as increased drug-related automobile and other accidents. The critic of the status quo might point out the realistic nature of the plan and its supposed effects by presenting examples of places where the plan has worked, and might go further and point out added benefits, such as reduced costs for the criminal justice system. This give-and-take is sometimes called *comparative advantages or comparative disadvantages.* The status quo defender may grant that there is a need for change and move directly to this plan-meets-need stage, comparing a repaired status quo with the proposed plan or offering a totally different plan and then debating the comparative advantages and disadvantages of the two.

We see stock issues frequently used as content premises in the world of politics and business, and in other policymaking forums. As a receiver, you should also be aware of the stock issues. Any time you are the target of persuasion focused on policy change, identify the side suggesting change and the side supporting the status quo.

As a persuader attempting to bring about a change in policy, you need to begin by addressing the need for a change. Like Harold Hill, you need to be specific about the "trouble" being caused by the status quo. *You* have the burden of proof. Start by citing symptoms of the problem. You should research specific instances that demonstrate to the audience that they are suffering something, losing something, or are in danger of losing it. Tie symptoms to a cause that, if removed and replaced, will solve the problem. Then present a reasonable alternative to the status quo—the plan or the new policy. Finally, show that "plan meets need." One way to do so is to show that the plan has been successful in other places.

At each stage of the stock-issues format, expect some kind of rebuttal. In some cases it will be openly stated, as in a policy debate in your student government. If you are giving a speech covering all three stock issues—need, plan, and plan meets need—anticipate such rebuttals and be ready to counter them. You might also short-circuit anticipated rebuttals by presenting a two-sided message stating the anticipated rebuttals and answering them then and there.

The stock-issues format is useful for persuaders who are proposing a change in policy from the status quo. Just remember the steps of the stock-issues format. Remember that Harold Hill was able to persuade River City to fund a boys band simply because the letter T rhymed with P, but only after he made them aware of troublesome symptoms in the actions of the young people of the town.

Organization by the Motivated Sequence*

Another organizational pattern that resembles the stock-issues approach is the **motivated sequence format,** suggested by communication scholars Alan Monroe, Douglas Ehninger, and Bruce Gronbeck (1982). This format involves five steps used by persuaders to get persuadees to attend to their message, to feel a need to follow their advice and, most important, to take action related to the advice. The motivated sequence is a good pattern to use in sales, recruitment, politics, and many other situations.

The first step in the motivated sequence—the **attention step**—aims at capturing the attention of the audience. There are hundreds of ways to do this. You could begin your message with a question or a startling statistic.

> How clean is your mouth? Think about it. There are over 300 kinds of microorganisms that thrive in the human mouth and most persons just brush their teeth once or twice a day. Furthermore they "clean" the mouth with the same toothbrush for months without ever thoroughly cleaning it and while storing it in warm moist conditions a few feet from the toilet! People need to change their toothbrush every two weeks and at the beginning and end of any infection or respiratory disease. (Woods, 1993)

Or you could use a quotation (for example, "I ain't got no philosophy—I calls 'em like I sees 'em." Will Rogers), a joke, or an anecdote. Another approach is to make an important announcement in the first few moments of the message.

Our old friend the narrative can also serve to capture audience attention, as can visual aids that arouse curiosity.

*Portions of this material are used by permission of Scott, Foresman.

In the second part of the motivated sequence you try to convince the audience that they are losing something, are about to lose something, or could be gaining something but aren't. This is the **need step.** You might use a real or hypothetical case to show the need:

> How would you like to get out of college and have a sizable nest egg? In his sophomore year, Bill Smith used his student loan as a down payment on a student rooming house. He lived there all four years rent-free and was able to charge rent for the other nine rooms using the rents to make mortgage payments *and* to pay tuition and fees. After selling the rooming house on graduation, he paid off all of his student loans and had a $50,000 profit on his investment. You can follow his example and not only graduate debt-free but end up with a nest egg.

This need step could easily be tied to the attention-getting step (for example, use a "reward poster" that offers a $50,000 nest egg), thus creating a smooth flow from step to step for the audience.

Steps 3 and 4 are the **visualization** and **satisfaction steps.** In them, the persuader gives examples, data, testimony, or some other form of proof to induce the audience to visualize either what life will be like for them if they follow the persuader's advice (if they go ahead and invest part of their student loan in student housing) or what life will be like if they don't. Following this visualization step, the persuader then offers some way to satisfy the positive need or to avoid some negative consequences.

Finally, the persuader needs to give a definite, specific, and realistic **action step.** It probably will do no good to ask audience members to alter their attitudes on the topic. Attitudes are fickle, as we have seen, and, furthermore, it is hard to know whether an audience has changed. It is far better to give the audience specific things it can do to avoid tooth decay, save energy, make wise investments, or earn good grades. In one re-search study, people given a booklet with specific action steps to cut electricity consumption registered less use of electricity on their meters in the following two weeks than did those not given the specific action steps (Cantola, Syme, & Campbell, 1985). If you want the audience to write to their elected representative, it would be a good idea to have a petition on hand that the student audience could sign or to announce the phone number and e-mail address of the legislator's local office. (Phoning or e-mailing is easier than writing a letter.)

In effective persuasion, it is essential to give persuadees a realistic action step, whether it is signing a sales contract, phoning a representative, or boycotting a certain food. Build such steps into your persuasive attempts, and you will find your percentage of success increasing dramatically.

A related model for making a persuasive appeal is called the **AIDA approach** (AIDA is an acronym that stands for *attention, interest, desire,* and *action*). In this model, as in the motivated sequence, the first step is to capture the audience's *attention* using any of the tactics cited earlier. In the second step, the persuader's goal is to heighten the audience's interest in his or her topic or proposal. This might be done using a satisfaction or a visualization process, as in the motivated sequence, but other techniques might be used. For example, you might tell how many persons have already tried the product or used the new procedure and found it to be useful, or you might point out unforeseen problems with continuing the present practice.

Once attention and interest have been gained, the next task is to create *desire* in the persuadee to purchase the product or service, vote for the candidate, or follow the persuader's advice. There are several ways to create such desire. In product-related persuasion, it usually is done by providing some product benefit or product promise. For example, Chrysler advertised a safety feature that was standard in their cars: a built-in air bag. The obvious benefit of this feature was that it could save one's life in an accident. By mentioning research that proved how well the bag cushioned the driver's body, Chrysler created desire for the product in the audience. In their action step, they asked the customer to go to their nearest Chrysler dealer to learn more about the air bag and take a test drive.

Communications professor Hugh Rank (1982) has offered a simple four-part model for creating desire. Although it can be used in promoting products, it also can be used in a variety of other persuasive situations. Persuaders can use four kinds of desire-stimulating tactics with this model (see Figure 11.1). First, they can promise the audience security or protection by demonstrating that their advice will allow the audience "to keep a 'good'" they already have but might be in danger of losing. Crest and other fluoridated toothpastes, for example, promise that regular use of their toothpaste will help keep your teeth free from decay—you keep a "good." Politicians frequently point out all of the funding they have brought to their districts. They then claim that their reelection means keeping this "good."

A second set of desire-stimulating tactics relates to "bad" or uncomfortable symptoms or feelings. Persuaders who use these tactics promise that by following their advice one can either get rid of a "bad" or experience relief from it. Rank calls these two approaches the "prevention" and "relief" appeals. Advertisers often promise that their products will prevent the embarrassments of bad breath, body odor, or dandruff. Or they promise that their products will give you relief from headaches, heartburn, flyaway hair, or acne. Such "scare and sell" approaches can also be used in nonproduct persuasion. For example, a persuader can promise that by passing the school bond referendum we can "avoid" losing the athletics and music programs and other extracurric-

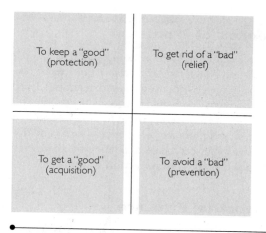

| To keep a "good" (protection) | To get rid of a "bad" (relief) |
| To get a "good" (acquisition) | To avoid a "bad" (prevention) |

Figure 11.1. *Rank's model for ways to create desire in audiences.*

ular activities. You will discover ways to use any or all of these desire-creating tactics when you choose to become a persuader.

The last stage in the AIDA model is to present the audience with a clear and effective *action* step, as in the motivated sequence. Action steps can be prompted by stressing concepts such as timeliness (for example, "Deadline is March 15" or "24-hour sale!") or limited supplies or opportunities (for instance, "While supplies last!" or "This may be your last chance to . . ."). Action steps can also be prompted by using the competition or opposition as foils. For example, the manager can appeal to employees to adopt a new technology (robotics, computerized typesetting, superconductors, or whatever) in order to beat the competition or to avoid being beaten by the competition. And there are other ways to stimulate action on the part of audiences.

What do you think?

Which of Rank's techniques for creating desire in audiences affects you most?

Forms of Proof

People want good reasons for changing their attitudes and beliefs, and the proof requisites for taking action steps are even more demanding. Even if the advocated change is a good one, people still need proof to motivate them to act. Let's look at the forms of proof available to persuaders and discuss how they can be used to prompt audiences to change attitudes or take action.

Statistical Evidence

Sometimes the most effective support is statistical. For instance, car buyers want to get good gas mileage. In this case, EPA figures probably persuade them to choose a car model more than a salesperson's reassurances that the car is a real gas saver. Statistics persuade best when they are simple and easy to understand.

When you decide to use statistics, make them clear, and provide a reference point for the numbers. If you are warning persuaders about the increasing national debt, make it real to them. Tell them that the interest on the debt amounts to $1800 per year for every man, woman, and child in the country.

Narratives and Anecdotes

Earlier we noted the power of drama, stories, and jokes. Narratives make examples come alive and make them easy to recall and relate to. The story of a person rising from rags to riches persuades more than a set of statistics.

Testimony

We suspect people who attempt to persuade using only their own feelings or brainstorms. This is why the testimony of another person is valuable. Even unqualified testimony has influence.

Of course, it is much better to have an expert witness testifying as to the value of a person, product, or idea.

Visual Evidence

Walk into a department store where a salesperson is demonstrating a food processor or a pasta machine, and you will see the power of visual data. Of course, actual demonstrations of a product are not always feasible, but persuaders can develop various kinds of visual evidence (such as graphs or charts) to help the audience understand the problem. Visuals should be large enough that everyone can see them. They should be simple. Complex charts will confuse the audience. For example, a student advocating a trip to Jamaica sponsored by the student association effectively used travel posters, large pictures of Jamaican cuisine, easily seen cutouts from magazines depicting sandy beaches, and other pictures of tropical life to motivate her audience.

Keep visual evidence unobtrusive. It may be better to use drawings of how to fend off an attacking dog than to bring your dog to class and have it pretend to attack you. One student who did so was embarrassed when his dog relieved itself instead of attacking on command.

Comparison and Contrast

Sometimes it is hard to see a problem in perspective. We see the issue from a single viewpoint and cannot judge it accurately. So it is wise to provide something with which to compare or contrast your point. Comparisons should help the audience see the difference between two sides of the issue or between two cases. It doesn't help them much to know that OPEC decided to increase production by 550,000 barrels per day. It will be more meaningful to mention that this is an increase of 20 percent over previous production levels. Make your comparisons and contrasts meaningful by elaborating on them and by explaining the *relative difference* in the things being compared.

Analogy

We have discussed analogies as a form of proof and noted that although they can be effective, a risk is involved in using analogies — particularly figurative ones — because they can be turned around on the persuader. Analogies must be chosen carefully.

Building Your Credibility

All the evidence in the world, organized perfectly and delivered well, will not persuade if listeners do not trust the persuader. In matters such as persuading the boss to give us a promotion or parents to let us marry before graduation, credibility is a key factor. What makes some people credible while others are not? How can we build our own credibility before and during persuasion? In earlier chapters we discussed the idea of credibility using Aristotle's ideas about the reputation of the speaker, the speaker's delivery during the speech, and the audience's response to the speaker's image. In more modern times, this has translated into several dimensions of credibility.

Reputation is roughly equated with the known *expertise* of the speaker. For example, when an identical speech is attributed to experts in some cases and to novices in others, the expert's speech is always more persuasive than the novice's.

Delivery and charisma are related to sincerity and dynamism. We don't believe speakers who cannot maintain eye contact. Tall speakers have more persuasive potential than do short ones. Speakers with an animated delivery persuade more effectively than those who are frozen at the podium. Exciting language usually

helps make the speech more persuasive. A well-groomed speaker is more persuasive than an unkempt one.

Most of these points seem obvious, yet they are overlooked daily by sales reps, politicians, spouses, teachers, students, and parents. Here are some examples from everyday life in which the elements of credibility can be used.

Trust

We trust people for many reasons. We trust them because they have been trustworthy in the past; because they have made direct eye contact; because they have a calm voice; and so forth. We also try to give off trust cues. We look at our persuadees directly. We try to sound sincere. We remind our audience of our past record for trust. We refer to times when it would have been easy to break that trust. We might, for example, remind our boss that there have been many times when she was out of town and we could have slacked off but didn't. Or you might remind your parents of the many opportunities you had to party but instead studied. All these devices and others help build credibility.

Expertise

How do we know whether someone is a true expert on a topic or job? Mostly we look for past success at a task. If a person was a good treasurer for the fraternity or sorority, he or she will probably be a good treasurer for the student government. Sales representatives who did well in the Midwest should also do well in the more complex East. A person who has had experience in many areas of the company — shipping, sales, and so on — is much more credible to co-workers than the person who has had experience in only one area.

Even if we do not have direct expertise on a given topic, we can borrow it by referring to known experts in our presentation. It is always useful to refer to your sources' background so receivers can judge the credibility of their testimony.

Clothing consultant John Molloy (1977) believes that you can create credibility by giving off competence cues. He has written several books and a syndicated column dealing with how one's clothes can give off messages that say "I am competent and in charge," or "I am a threat." Molloy says that the color of our clothing communicates, too. And there are other nonverbal signs that can further develop your credibility. Finally, you can signal expertise by being well prepared, by demonstrating knowledge about the topic. Being willing to engage in question/answer sessions when you have finished speaking also communicates credibility.

Dynamism

The dynamism factor of credibility is elusive. It is sometimes related to physical appearance, in that attractive people tend to hold attention better. Dynamism or "charisma" probably cannot be developed much. However, other factors can. Many people who aren't particularly attractive are nonetheless persuasive and dynamic. Dynamic speakers seem to take up a lot of psychic space — they have "stage presence." Each of us can project a dynamic image in several ways. One is to speak with authority — use your voice with good projection and volume and choose words that indicate certainty. Posture and appearance also signal dynamism, as do gestures, facial expression, and eye contact.

Wording Your Message

Stylistic speeches and exciting language choices persuade better than dull speeches. How do persuaders develop style in their presentations?

Variety in Word Choice

Most of us need to improve our vocabulary. You should try to rewrite your speeches using word variety to make them livelier, flashier, sexier, more dramatic, or more humorous. It helps to develop an interest in puns and other word games, as they can help you get the attention and friendship of your audience. Study the eloquence of other people. Read some of the great addresses of past presidents. Pay attention to the language used in government news releases or in speeches by politicians. Finally, study uses of humor.

Figures of Speech

Enhance your style by using proper figures of speech at the right time. Metaphors and similes help your audience visualize a point. The audience ties information to the metaphorical structure and remembers the information better as a result.

Alliteration or assonance can also liven style. Alliteration is repetition of consonant sounds; assonance is repetition of vowel sounds. Both create a kind of internal rhythm in the message, which makes it more lively and memorable. We see this device used in advertising frequently to aid in brand name recall. Satin cigarettes are "smooth, slender, and sensuous," and the Parker pen is "wrought from pure silver and writes like pure silk." Both alliteration and assonance can be heard in "A portable phone system? Gee! No, GTE." Both devices help improve your style.

Vividness

Choose vivid words to catch your audience's interest. Although vividness can be overdone, it is more frequently overlooked in favor of dull and uninteresting language. Which of the following is more vivid?

I'm offended by your representation of lutefisk. It is not rubbery!

Lutefisk may be "a rubbery and repulsive ethnic dish" to the socially deprived, but to the properly initiated it is the nearest thing to ambrosia this Earth has ever produced.

Vivid and colorful language helps make a persuasive presentation memorable and effective.

Conciseness

Be as economical with your words as possible. Go over your presentation and pretend you are paying fifty cents per word to telegraph it. Then see how much excess baggage you can cut. Often, a straightforward statement is most effective.

You should state your point in a short introductory declaration. Elaborate on it later when and if necessary. Once when Lincoln was trying to justify a pardon he was granting to a deserter, he said, "I think the boy can do us more good above ground than underground," thus stating his case concisely.

You don't have to say everything in one sentence; you have an entire speech. Make your major point as a concise assertion or frame it in a provoking question. Then follow up with elaboration. If you try to say everything in the opening sentence, you will confuse your audience.

Parallel Structure

Parallel structure involves using similar or even identical wordings or sentence structures. For example, in a speech to the American Legion in 1992, President Clinton said, "I am not the only American whose life has been made better by your continuing service here at home. From baseball to Boy Scouts; from keeping veterans hospitals open to keeping kids off drugs; from addressing homelessness to preventing child abuse to instilling a deep sense of patriotism into still another generation of Americans, a grateful nation owes you a debt of gratitude" (Chicago, August 25). His repeated use of the "From . . . to . . ." format makes for parallel structure and symmetry in the speech.

Imagery

Imagery appeals to our senses, experiences, and impressions. Perhaps you can't bring the smell, taste, touch, sight, or sound of an object to the audience, but you can use words that conjure up memories of a "tall, cool glass of chilled beer dripping with beads of perspiration" or of the "fragrant smell of Mom's pot roast, ready to fall apart, with its juices making a savory gravy that starts your mouth watering." Think about the sensory experiences your audience has had that you can evoke. State your points so that they appeal to one or more of the senses. A good way to develop this skill is to take a given product and try to restate its appeals in terms of the various senses. For instance, Campbell's soups are "Mmm, Mmm, Good." How can they be described using the other senses? As one salesperson put it, "Don't sell the steak; sell the sizzle."

Humor

The effective use of humor in persuasion is an obvious stylistic asset. How can you develop humorous examples, comparisons, anecdotes, and stories? People who regularly engage in public speaking usually have a ready supply of humorous material with which to embellish their speeches. They develop the use of humor as they work up other materials for their speeches. You may be the kind of person who can never remember a story or joke. If so, keep a file of stories or jokes or even punchlines for your humor file. When you need the anecdote, the file will trigger your memory, and you will be able to relate those to-the-point humorous examples. Some sources for humorous examples and anecdotes include *Reader's Digest* (browse it while you're waiting at a doctor's office); collections of stories or jokes from the library; television shows such as *Saturday Night Live, David Letterman,* or *The Tonight Show*; your daily newspaper; and people who frequently tell jokes (bartenders, barbers, and others). Get yourself a supply of humorous material to improve your style; it will make your persuasion more effective and memorable.

Delivering Your Message

Usually we think of delivery as a source factor. To some degree, this is true. However, there are several other factors that can affect the delivery of your message, such as the appropriate channel and the means of audience involvement. Persuaders often overlook these. In the following consideration of delivery, we will look both at those things that the source does during delivery and at those that are not tied to delivery.

The Persuader

Among the factors that persuaders adjust before and during delivery are posture, eye contact, body movement and gesture, articulation, and vocal quality. Other factors under the speaker's control are the use of visual aids and other nonverbal cues.

Posture. Some persuaders are so nervous about their speeches that they cannot stop pacing back and forth. When they do stop, they stand ramrod stiff and look as if they might freeze into statues. Other speakers are so relaxed that they seem uninterested in their own messages. They slouch lazily across a podium or slide down into their chairs during a meeting. They rarely look up, and

sometimes nod off. Clearly posture can signal the audience that you are either too relaxed or too nervous. The ideal posture lies somewhere in between. Be alert and erect. Your shoulders should not tense or slump. Avoid looking nervous or tense (I wiggle my toes, but no one can see that). Overall, the message should communicate confidence. Observe persuaders in differing contexts — interviews, speeches, arguments — and you will see that the effective ones avoid both the nervous and the "nearly asleep" extremes.

Eye Contact. Most people believe that a person cannot lie to you while looking you straight in the eyes. You will be more believable if you maintain eye contact with your audience. You don't need to look at everyone. Instead look at various areas in the audience. In a one-on-one context, establish repeated eye contact with your persuadee. Politicians make sure to look directly into the TV camera and hence to have apparent eye contact with each viewer. In a meeting, establish eye contact with many people, or maybe even everyone, at the meeting.

Body Movement and Gesture. Movement livens up a speech, if it doesn't distract. Likewise, gestures during a speech keep audience attention. However, it is a mistake to overrehearse gestures, body movements, and facial expressions. These nonverbal elements in delivery must appear natural or they will have a negative effect. We all use gestures every day without thinking about them. Let your natural impulses guide you in your use of gestures in formal and interpersonal exchanges. Nothing can add more to your message than a natural gesture, movement, or facial expression. The naturally prompted gesture is the most effective (Scheflen, 1964).

Articulation and Vocal Quality. Everyone has heard people who pronounce words incorrectly. As a result, the audience focuses on the error and not on the message. Successful persuaders listen carefully to themselves and work on articulation. Listening to yourself on tape will help you pinpoint your mistakes and focus on your vocal quality. If you are interested in persuading others, spend some time working on your voice and your articulation.

The Channel

In a rural political campaign, the candidate put most of his money into billboard space. This was a surprise, as in a TV age, the major advertising expenditure would most likely be for TV. In this case, however, the candidate's district was large, stretching nearly half the length of the state, so no single TV channel reached all of it. Using TV would mean paying a triple load to get a single message across. But because the district was large, all residents had to drive to do shopping, business, or farming. Thus the billboard was the one channel that could touch nearly all voters in the district.

Our recent presidents have returned to using radio for regular weekly persuasive talks. Why is radio such an appropriate channel for political persuasion? Well, people listen to the radio while they are doing something else — driving, reading, mowing the lawn, or exercising. They also usually do these things during the daylight hours, so by choosing the relatively inexpensive medium of radio, the presidents were able to reach people they otherwise might not have.

Ask yourself what is the best way to inform your boss that you will look for another job if you don't get a raise or promotion. The grapevine might be best. Or maybe a straightforward memo will do the job. Maybe asking her to be a reference so she will not get an out-of-the-blue inquiry will be best. Start by listing all the potential channels that could be used to send your message. Then try to match them with your audience.

The Audience

Sometimes persuaders encourage audience participation, which can increase audience energy and activity. For example, at the 1992 Democratic national convention, Vice-President Al Gore got the delegates to yell out in unison the phrase "It's time for them to go!" referring to the Republicans.

Get your audience involved by asking direct questions and calling people by name if possible. You can also get the audience involved by leaving sentences incomplete and letting them supply examples. One speaker got audience involvement right away by asking the audience to stand up before he even began his speech. He then asked them to become aware of the muscles they are using in their feet, ankles, calves, and thighs at that moment and tied this awareness to his topic — the need to develop communication awareness on the job.

One word of caution: Don't distribute any reading material until the end of the speech. Audiences start reading right away, and the speaker loses their attention and interest. Hand out such materials at the end of your presentation.

Some Common Tactics of Persuasion

Successful persuaders spend time finding out what the audience already believes, then they use various tactics to tie their points to audience beliefs. Here are some of those tactics.

The Yes-Yes Technique

A common tactic used in sales and other persuasive appeals is called **yes-yes**. The source attempts to get the target group or person to respond "yes" to several parts of the appeal, holding the key request until last. Having agreed to most parts of the appeal, the persuadee is likely to say yes to the key and final request. For example, suppose that you were trying to sell a lawn service. You might ask the homeowner, "You would like to have a beautiful lawn, wouldn't you?" The answer is going to be yes. Then you ask, "And you'd like to get rid of the weeds?" Another yes is likely. "And wouldn't it be nice if these things could be effort free?" A yes answer is likely again. Now that the homeowner has accepted all your points in favor of the service, it is nearly impossible to respond with a no answer. "Then you'll want to sign up for our lawn service, won't you?" By accepting the yes pattern, the buyer responds "yes" to your final request. The same technique is useful in a meeting, where a persuader gets the group members to agree with all but the final point in favor of the change in work schedules, for instance. They agree that flexibility is good, that more free time for workers is good, and so on. They are then likely to agree that the change is a good one.

Persuaders use the yes-yes technique to lead their target group or person through stages to a final "yes" answer when the persuader requests purchase, change, or a vote for a candidate.

Don't Ask If, Ask Which

It is easier to make a choice between two alternatives than from among many. This is the strategy behind the "don't-ask-if, ask-which" persuasive tactic. I learned as a parent of young children that the worst thing to ask them on Saturday mornings was "What would you like for breakfast today?" I got all kinds of requests. It was better to say, "Which would you like for breakfast today — Dad's blueberry pancakes or Dad's blueberry coffee-cake?" The same thing applies in persuasion. Don't ask your audience to choose from too many options; ask them to choose from only a few or maybe only between two — "Would you rather have us undercoat your new car, Mr. Jones, or do

you want to take it elsewhere?" "Would you rather meet on your promotion this week or next?" "Do you want guns or butter?"

Although the don't-ask-if, ask-which tactic can be manipulative, it has the value of forcing action when buyers, voters, or others are stubborn and try to avoid making decisions.

Answering a Question with a Question

A tactic that some people use to throw you off guard is to respond to a request by asking a question. For example, they say, "Why do you think I would like to do that?" or "What gave you that idea?" or a similar response. We are expecting them to come to the point, to make a statement that relates to the discussion or the request. This throws us off.

The tactic of responding with another question is useful because it usually catches other people off guard and gives you time to think. Even asking people to repeat themselves or to elaborate can have these effects. This puts the ball back in their court. People who question you sometimes are trying to discredit or annoy you. Turn the tables — answer with another question.

Getting Partial Commitment

Evangelists often close their pitches by asking members in the tent or auditorium to bow their heads and close their eyes for prayer. This gets a **partial commitment** from all the audience. The preacher then asks the Lord to enter the hearts of all and asks those who want God to come into their lives to raise their hands. The final request may then be "Those of you with your hands up come to the front and be saved." The tactic is seen elsewhere, too. Trying a sample of a product is a kind of partial commitment, as is clipping a coupon. Once we are partially committed, we are good prospects for full commitment.

Of course, other kinds of commitment are used to persuade. A politician asks you to sign a petition to put his or her name on the ballot. The act is a form of commitment to that politician.

The tactic resembles the yes-yes technique but uses *acts* instead of *words* to lead the persuadee to the final request. Persuaders can use it with neutral or negative audiences.

Ask More, So They Settle for Less

Ask more, so they settle for less involves setting a price or level of commitment in people's minds that is higher than what they are willing to pay or do. When the persuader backs off, the buyers or voters think they are getting a special offer. For example, suppose I bring in a set of test scores to my class and write on the chalkboard the curve that the computer suggests. Now I distribute the answer sheets; students moan because the curve is so high. Then I say that because I think the computer's curve is unreasonably high, I am making my own curve. I write a lower curve on the board. Students cheer and sigh with relief. I set a high expectation. Then I back off from that high level, and my curve, compared with the machine's curve, is like a gift from Santa Claus. Contemporary retailing is built on the notion of setting prices that can be marked down. No one buys anything at the regular price nowadays. It's always "marked down."

Persuaders can use this tactic when they have a product or goal that is hard to sell. Better to ask for more than your audience will stand for, so that, in compromising, you will persuade.

Planting

The device called **planting** uses one of the five senses to open a channel to the audience's memory. We want the target group or person to recall our product, idea, or candidate. Memory responds best, it seems, to messages that have sensory data as raw material. Restaurant ads often appeal to several senses, not just the sense of taste. They describe the "crisp and crunchy garden salad" to appeal to the sense of touch, offer "sizzling hot steaks seared on a grill" to appeal to the sense of hearing, describe the "thick red tomato sauce" to appeal to the sense of vision, and use the words "a steaming fragrance of garlic and spices" to appeal to the sense of smell.

> **What do you think?**
>
> Can you use "planting" in any persuasion you are presently contemplating? How?

In a classic case of using the sense of touch, Mr. Whipple of Charmin toilet tissue fame was regularly caught squeezing a pack of Charmin when he thought no one was looking. An ad for an automobile may have someone slam the door shut so the audience hears the solid "thunk" and mentally compares it with the rattles of their own five-year-old car. Tie your persuasion to one of the five senses, and you'll find that the audience will remember your message better and longer.

Getting an IOU

Sometimes called the *swap* or *trade-off* tactic, the technique of **getting an IOU** tries to get listeners to feel that they owe you something. For instance, the insurance rep spends several hours doing a complex assets-and-debts analysis for a prospect. The goal is to prove to the prospect that he or she needs more insurance. The sales rep then spends more hours explaining the figures to the spouse, perhaps taking the couple out to lunch or dinner. By the end of all the special treatment, the couple may feel that they really *ought* to buy something, even though they may not need it or cannot afford it. They respond to the obligation — the IOU — that was built by the salesperson's effort.

Persuaders find this tactic useful when it is hard to make a first contact with buyers, voters, or joiners. You can place your audience in your debt by giving them free samples or offers of help. The old adage "There's no such thing as a free lunch" is a pretty good warning in our doublespeak world.

Review and Conclusion

We all have to persuade at some point. To be effective, we must plan how our format will affect the message. We must develop our forms of support and think about which would be most persuasive. We must control factors in delivery. We need to use source factors, such as posture, eye contact, and dress. Channel factors are subject to our control also. Receiver factors can be used to get the target group involved in its own persuasion. As you are called on to persuade, use these skills in preparing. Rely on the audience analysis that the receiver-oriented approach teaches—listen to your audience. Get messages out of them, not into them.

Questions for Further Thought

1. What demographic clusters can you identify for the people in your class? in your dorm? in your club? elsewhere?

2. What is a task-oriented message? Give examples from ads in which persuaders have used this technique effectively. Give other examples from ads in which they have failed.

3. What are the forms of organization? How do they differ from the forms of support? What might be other ways to organize a message?

4. What is AIDA, and how does it differ from the motivated sequence?

5. What are Rank's desire-building tactics? How do they work?

6. What are the factors in credibility? Give examples of people who have them. Find ads that rely on each factor. Describe the person and the ad in terms of the factors.

7. Where does humor fit into the persuasion process? Give examples of sources who use humor. Does it relate to the audience? How?

8. How can a persuader get his or her audience more involved? What are some examples you have seen or heard recently?

9. What is the difference between the forms of proof discussed here and those discussed in Chapter 7?

10. How does "planting" work? What about "getting an IOU"?

References

Cantola, S. J., Syme, G. I., & Campbell, N. A. (1985). Creating conflict to conserve energy. *Psychology Today*, February, p. 14.

Faries, C. J. (1977). Teaching rhetorical criticism: It's our responsibility. *Journal of the Illinois Speech and Theatre Association, 33,* 7–15.

Greene, B. (1982). Exam dream never fails to panic. *Chicago Tribune*, October 19, sec. 1, p. 5.

Howell, W. S., & Bormann, E. G. (1988). *The process of presentational speaking.* New York: Harper & Row.

Molloy, J. T. (1977). *The dress for success book.* Chicago: Reardon and Walsh.

Monroe, A., Ehninger, D., & Gronbeck, B. (1982). *Principles and types of speech communication*. Chicago: Scott, Foresman.

Rank, H. (1982). *The pitch*. Park Forest South, IL: The Counter Propaganda Press.

Scheflen, A. E. (1964). The significance of posture in communication systems. *Psychiatry, 27*, 316–331.

Schwartz, T. (1973). *The responsive chord*. Garden City, NY: Anchor Books.

Selby, P. (1902). *Lincoln's life story and speeches*. Chicago: Thompson and Thomas.

Woods, M. (1993). Toothbrush tips for wellness. *Chicago Tribune*, September 12, sec. 5, p. 3.

12

Modern Media
and Persuasion

There have been four major communication innovations in the history of humankind, each tied to the development of a new medium for communicating with others. Each innovation/medium has shaped and changed the world and the destiny of humanity forever after. And each has allowed humans to see the world in vastly different ways and to interact with one another more efficiently and with varying degrees of permanence. And another is on the way.

Media Innovations

These four media innovations are the spoken word, the written word, the printed word, and the electronic word, and we are poised on the verge of a fifth great medium—the interactive electronic word. The first three innovations took us thousands of years. The fourth began over 150 years ago, but began to develop its current dominance only 75 years ago, and the fifth may be realized within a few years.

The Spoken Word

While we were still only *hominoids*, or humanlike creatures, we used grunts and gestures to communicate. Over thousands of years, we developed the first communication innovation in human history: the power to speak and to symbolize. This permitted humanity to gather into groups or tribes. Speech also led us to develop labor specialization, rituals and religions, and a kind of history, embodied in myths, ballads, and legends.

We sense the immense power of this development in the reverence with which the spoken word is held in most religions and in our everyday lives. For example, in the Book of Genesis, the story of the Creation indicates that with each creative act, God *spoke*. *Speaking* was the catalyst for the creation of night and day ("Let there be light"); earth and seas; fishes, animals, and birds; and ultimately man and woman. Later in the Old Testament, God again *speaks* to the various characters: Jacob, Moses, and David. In the New Testament, almost all of Christ's miracles are brought about by His *speaking* some words, and Christ is also referred to as the "Word made flesh." In our daily social life, this religious attitude toward the spoken word continues. We must be sworn in to *testify*, or to *speak* to the court. At baptisms, the child's name must be *spoken*. At weddings, the vows must be *said* aloud. The judge must *speak* the sentence before the defendant can be taken to prison. Even in death, we *speak* words of absolution and commit the body to the grave using the *spoken* word.

The spoken word permitted humans to become *social animals* and to work together for the common good. It allowed one generation to pass down the history of the tribal society in the form of myths or legends. It provided a means for the society to pass information down from generation to generation, thus allowing progress to occur: The wheel didn't have to be reinvented in each generation. In a sense, the development of the spoken word led to the recognition of *information* that could be shared by everyone. In oral/aural cultures, such as Native American tribes, information or knowledge is most frequently and fully held by the old. Thus, age is valued and honored. And because wisdom or knowledge increases with age, the older one becomes, the more important he or she is to the tribe. Among the Lakota it was the custom to give every newly married couple an "Old One," perhaps a relative, to live in the couple's tepee to do the simple chores of tending the fire, comforting the babies, and being available for advice when asked. Not only did this help the young couple but it provided the Old One with a home. There were no "bag ladies" among the Lakota.

The spoken word still exists, of course, but not in the same way it did in an oral/aural world, as Father Walter J. Ong (1982) has pointed out. In the oral/aural culture and even after, the spoken word was an experience—an event. It occupied time, not space. It was ephemeral; the beginning of the word was gone before the end of

the same word was uttered. Its only permanence was in the human mind and memory, and you re-experienced it only by reuttering it. The spoken word had magical qualities and continues to have them today.

The Written Word

The next major communication innovation was the development of the phonetic alphabet, an alphabet tied to *speech sounds*, and not an ideographic one tied to vision (e.g., hieroglyphics). It had equally profound effects. With the alphabet, one could collect knowledge and store it. Advances of various kinds could be based on these stored records of what others had tried to do and how. The written word allowed us to develop complex legal systems and to assign or deed land and other possessions. That led to the centralization of power. Knowledge was power, obtained and held only by those who controlled the written word: kings, emperors, feudal lords, and the church.

In ancient Greece and Rome, few people could read or write, and only the rich could afford scribes. Thus, information came to be thought of as *individual property* that could be "owned" and not shared with others. The great ancient libraries (such as the Greek library at Alexandria) were the repositories of these societies' knowledge and information. But they weren't "lending libraries" as we know them—that would have to wait until Benjamin Franklin invented them in the eighteenth century. These libraries were private, so not everyone had access to the knowledge or information. Without this access, the average person remained ignorant of much of society's knowledge and thus remained at the bottom of the social order as fiefs, peasants, or slaves.

Not long after writing made the "ownership" of knowledge possible, the concept of ownership was applied to other property—land, cattle, horses, jewelry, buildings, and so on. Such ownership could be officially recorded in deeds to property, for example, which made the lawyer, or official interpreter of the deed, a necessary evil. No such concept existed in the oral/aural cultures of the American Indians, for example. As a result, they had no concept of land ownership. This accounts for much of the misunderstanding associated with the land treaties of our history. To the white man, they represented the legal contracts through which land ownership was transferred. To the Indians, the treaties were "worthless scraps of paper."

Ong (1967) points out that whereas the spoken word took up time, the written word took up *space* and was not ephemeral—it lasted across generations—making us more likely to rely on written records for the "last word" on an issue. Indeed, the written word came to be thought of as more trustworthy than the spoken word. Even if they couldn't read, people wanted to see things "in writing" before they would believe them.

Ownership of knowledge as property also made knowledge a key ingredient for establishing and maintaining power. The written word allowed powerful persons to develop "nations" over which they ruled. It is no accident that the Romans attacked and destroyed the great Greek library at Alexandria.

Yet the word as an experience persisted in societies where writing was invented. As Ong (1967) points out:

> Ancient Hebrews and Christians knew not only the spoken word but the alphabet as well. . . . But for them and all men of early times, the word, even when written, was much closer to the spoken word than it normally is for twentieth-century technological man. Today we have often to labor to regain the awareness that the word is still always at root the spoken word. Early man had no such problem: he felt the word, even when written, as primarily an event in sound. (p. ix)

So the word remained an experiential phenomenon, even when it was written. And it was to continue to be so perceived.

The Printed Word

The third major communication innovation was Gutenberg's invention of printing using movable type in the late 1400s. The effects of spreading the power of the written word to the common people were immense. Within a short time, the release of this power led to the Renaissance. Because information could be spread and shared, science developed rapidly. Scientists could read about one another's work and build on what others had done.

Knowledge was no longer limited to clerics, although religion itself was greatly affected by the printing press. Before the printing press, few people outside the church could read or write. Books were expensive, and knowledge was power, held mainly by the church. But when one could cheaply and accurately reproduce the Bible and other books, pamphlets, and tracts, this power became diffused. The Reformation, like the Renaissance, was the inevitable outcome of this diffusion of knowledge and thus power. People could read the writings of Martin Luther, and because the printing press was available, his objections to certain features of Church practice were duplicated and spread to many people. Many decided to start their own churches. The process continued with factions fragmenting off to form various Protestant religions.

What do you think? Why did the printed word lead to the middle class?

Governments weren't immune to this diffusion of knowledge either, and soon most of them set up a censorship policy to help them control information and thus maintain power. Not until

John Peter Zenger, a German printer in the American Colonies, was tried for sedition because he had printed a tract criticizing the British Colonial governor did the notion of *freedom of the press* gain credibility. Curiously, Zenger was not tried for *writing* the criticism but for *printing* it. The British government held all printers responsible for what they published, in effect making every printer an unofficial censor. Zenger may never even have read the seditious pamphlet.

Like the power of the spoken word, the power of the printed word has diminished to some degree. Although the number of newspapers published in the United States has risen since the advent of television, readership of newspapers and news magazines is down. Nearly 30 percent of the U.S. population is functionally illiterate, which means they can't read such simple things as menus, directions in phone booths, and street signs (Kaplan, Wingert, and Chideya, 1993). Of those who do read newspapers, some estimates show that they devote only about eight minutes a day to the daily paper. The per capita consumption of books is down to less than a third of a book per year per person.

So the printed word gave us the Reformation, the Renaissance, and their many effects: the "New Science," because scientists could share the results of experiments in learned societies; the "New Art," because artists did not need to devote their energies to religious subjects alone; and the "New Music," because musical scores could be printed accurately and cheaply and exchanged among composers, who learned from one another's works. But most important, in terms of persuasion, the printed word gave us *literacy*, which was to greatly influence the way we formulated and shared our thoughts and ideas. It led to a conception of humans as unique because they could think and reason and write down their thoughts and logic. Logic became the password of literacy, and the emotions of experience were demoted.

Literacy led to great discoveries and inventions in Europe and America. As noted earlier, Benjamin Franklin invented the "lending library"—a remarkably generous concept when you think of it. He also invented the postal service, the fire department, bifocals, central heating, the lightning rod, the rocking chair, the *Saturday Evening Post*, and a host of other inventions. It is probably no accident that Franklin's background was as a printer's apprentice.

Literacy opened the remarkable door of opportunity for Franklin and for many others, but it also enslaved us to some degree. We had to set aside a certain number of years of our lives to "learn" all the things that literacy had led to, and as a result we had to invent "childhood"—that time when a person gets an education. Naturally, the length of childhood has had to be expanded several times as the amount of information to be learned has increased. Today, we talk of "lifelong learning" and frantically try to read as much as we can, falling further and further behind all the while.

The Electronic Word

The electronic word began in 1844 with the first demonstration of the telegraph. The telegraph used electrical impulses that were turned on and off by the telegrapher's key to signal the various letters and spaces, thus allowing words to be sent as a series of dots and dashes. Then, in 1876, came the telephone, which transformed the spoken word into electronic impulses. Shortly thereafter came the radio, or wireless telegraph, which transformed written and later spoken words into electronically produced sound waves.

We looked briefly at the changes brought by the electronic word when we discussed technological determinism in Chapter 3. As noted there, we are only dimly aware of the influence of these electronic words—the telegraph, radio, and telephone—but it is possible to get a glimmering of

Figure 12.1. *Certain aspects of modern electronic media are causes of concern, as this cartoon demonstrates.* (Frank and Ernest *reprinted by permission of NEA, Inc.*)

their effect with a hundred-year perspective. For example, the telegraph greatly sped up the communication process. Instead of relying on the Pony Express to get a message across the country (which took ten days), people could telegraph the message in minutes. In a sense, the electronic word not only wiped out space but time as well. For example, with telegraphs you could know the results of the game or horse race almost immediately—think what that means if you are a bookie. The same was true of election results, catastrophes, joyous and sad family events, and a host of other areas of social life.

Of course, there exist other versions of the electronic word—television, personal computers, video games, and more. Most of them have occurred only recently, and the changes they are bringing about are probably unnoticed by us. The changes are there, however, and the critical consumer of persuasion should be alert to the ways the electronic word influences us and our culture.

Some people are concerned that these media will adversely affect us. For example, many critics are worried that the home computer will drive Western culture inward, making us unable to interact with others on an interpersonal level. Anyone who has used a PC knows that time can evaporate on you in the twinkling of an eye—you just

started on the document a minute ago and now three hours are gone. People regularly complain about the way society is becoming depersonalized by electronic technology. Likewise, many people are concerned about the amount of television being watched each day by the average American child—and adult (see Figure 12.1). We worry about the effects of television violence. We wonder whether America's youth may go prematurely deaf because of the volume used on radio headsets, tape players, or compact disc players.

The most common kind of electronic persuasion that we receive is advertising—in TV and radio spot commercials. As noted before, most college freshmen have seen more than 22,000 hours of TV programming. We live in a world in which electronic and print messages literally surround us—on billboards and in newsletters, magazines, catalogs, signs on shopping carts, electronic catalog kiosks in air terminals, videos in supermarkets, and so on. The mass media are the most effective channels to persuade people. Mass media persuade us to buy products, to vote, and to take up causes. Why is this? One reason may be that there is no real feedback in mass message systems (you cannot question, applaud, or respond), so certain ploys work that will not work in an open arena.

Another reason that modern mass media, particularly electronic media such as radio, television, video games, and the personal computer, are able to persuade so effectively is that they are inherently oral/aural in nature. That is, in the same way that spoken words are fleeting, electronic signals or images are heard or seen for only an instant and then disappear from the screen or speaker never to be recalled unless we have "saved" them on an audio- or videotape or a computer disc. These electronic signals are "experienced" more than they are logically thought out, reasoned with, or subjected to tests of proof.

For example, one can't ask whether Candice Bergen is true or false in her roles as Murphy Brown and spokesperson for Sprint. She is neither, and she is both. Our experience with this week's episode or ad is not necessarily logical. In fact, it is more likely to be emotional.

The same holds true of many other electronic media messages: Like the spoken word, they are events meant to be experienced before being recorded or analyzed. Future technological developments suggest that such messages will become even more emotional—perhaps not as experiential as the "Feelies" of Aldous Huxley's *Brave New World*, in which people *really* "experience" movies.

The Interactive Electronic Word

We are on the verge of having to deal with a new kind of communication innovation—the **interactive electronic word.** Previously the electronic word has affected our lives as receivers for the most part. These media are consumed more than they are produced by the average person. In interactive electronic media, the receiver gets into the act much more.

Although only in its infancy, one such experiential medium beginning to affect society is virtual reality. In one form it resembles a video battle game and costs about $1 per minute to play. A player either enters a "cockpit" or dons a helmet and glove,

whereupon the battle begins. Unlike traditional video games where the player "looks in" at the battle occurring on a video screen, virtual reality puts players "inside" the battle game. The players each have 360-degree vision (that is, the picture surrounds them), and they can "see" the full 360-degree battlefield by either "revolving" their cockpits or turning their heads/helmets. In some versions as many as eight players divided into "teams" can fight it out with the enemy for ten minutes. At the end of the session, each player receives a printout that gives a blow-by-blow description of what happened plus scores for all the players. As a result, the battle seems to be almost real.

Such game versions of virtual reality have little practical applicability. However, the potential uses of developing virtual reality technology are breathtaking. For example, surgeons might conduct "virtual operations" for training purposes, then laser scalpels might be programmed for the virtual operation to the real one—after, of course, redoing the mistakes. Used in retailing, virtual reality might replace the showroom floor or retail outlet. Charles Madigan (1993), a researcher into potential applications for the technology, describes a potential "virtual purchase." A customer in his or her own living room facing a bigger-than-life fully digitized television screen will say,

"Shop Ralph Lauren." After a pause of only a few seconds, the image of Ralph Lauren will come, smiling to life on the screen. . . . Ralph will ask for some particulars. . . . Perhaps price will be discussed. . . . It won't really be Ralph Lauren. . . . More accurately, it will be virtual Ralph having a virtual conversation.

Other possible uses for virtual reality technol-ogy include virtual golf lessons at home taught by virtual Arnold Palmer; virtual concerts after dinner by famous string quartets; virtual physical therapy or psychiatry in the privacy of your own home; virtual exercise led by a holographic three-dimensional Cindy Crawford;

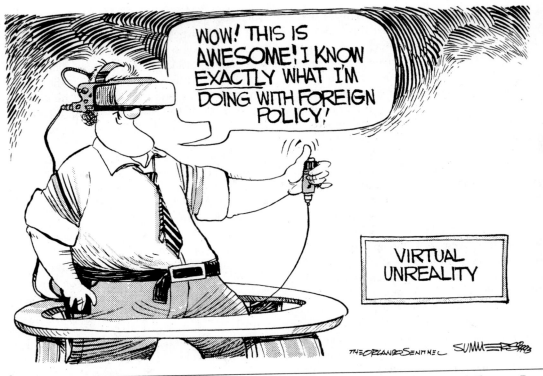

Figure 12.2. *The newest of the electronic buzz words is "virtual reality." (© 1994 The Washington Post Writers Group. Reprinted with permission.)*

virtual holidays in foreign countries; and not surprisingly, "teledildonics" a term coined to describe virtual sex with holographic lovers—not far from Huxley's "Feelies" (Madigan, 1993).

The potential implications of this new medium are awesome. Imagine virtual television spot advertisements, virtual propaganda, or virtual politicians and virtual elections (see Figure 12.2). Sounds like some far-fetched fantasy? Perhaps, but Madigan poses an important question when he asks, "Who could have anticipated the impact that television would have on a society back when it was still a novelty? Information technology is moving so rapidly, developing so exponentially, that no one knows quite where it will lead" (p. 16). In another example, when we engage in electronic mail or Internet "chat groups," we are consumers but also potential producers of persuasion. By being involved in interactive media, we may be forming virtual communities of like-minded persons. We have just begun to process the implications of this new kind of word through phenomena such as the militia movements, the stalking of crime victims on the Internet, the possibilities of interactive fraud on

What do you think?

What percentage of students on your campus use e-mail? the Internet?

the WWW, and the implications of privacy in cyberspace.

And we need to consider what is going on in research labs around the world (most notably in Japan, Germany, and England) that delve into possible technological innovations. Consider Stewart Brand's (1987) description of some of the developments at the Media Lab at M.I.T. that occurred while he was there on sabbatical. The $45 million lab was established and funded by the leading corporations in three communication fields: the print industry, the film/video/audio industry, and the computer industry. Each corporation and industry realized that phenomenal changes in communication technology were imminent and that to develop them most effectively and prudently was far beyond the financial and research capabilities of any single corporation or industry. So they pooled their resources and sought out the brightest and best media researchers, technicians, engineers, and theorists in various communication fields and asked them to literally "invent the future" in the various communications industries.

The Media Lab's director, Nicholas Negroponte, knew that the three industries were already beginning to converge, as shown in Figure 12.3. Some examples of this convergence include print that is computer typeset and enhanced visually by video technology; video graphics that are computer generated and produced; electronic mail, fax, and digital audio; recent print ads that incorporate appropriate electronic music; and 3-D IMAX theatres, to name but a few.

Negroponte foresees a much broader convergence of the three technologies, which will look more like Figure 12.4 by the year 2000. The predicted kinds of changes exceed our wildest dreams. A brief example demonstrates the immensity of these changes:

> Negroponte bases all of his plans on the growing computer intelligence of the TV set itself. "... twenty years from now your TV set will prob-

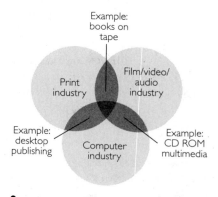

Figure 12.3. *The convergence of the print, film/video/audio, and computer industries and technology today.*

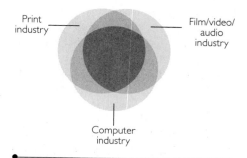

Figure 12.4. *The convergence of the print, film/video/audio, and computer industries and technology in the year 2000.*

ably have 50 megabytes of random access memory and run at 40 to 50 MIPS [millions of information pieces per second]. It'll basically be a Cray computer" (Brand, 1987, pp. 77–78).

It is not our intent here to survey and hypothesize over future developments of the interactive electronic word, but it is our purpose to try to understand how they will affect us and to prepare for the ways in which these new mass media will try to persuade us. Here, the work of two important media theorists, Tony Schwartz and Marshall McLuhan, can help us understand the experiential nature of the current level of technology and prepare ourselves for the developments we will encounter in the next decade.

Schwartz's Perspectives on Media Use

Although over 20 years old, the ideas found in Tony Schwartz's book *The Responsive Chord* (1973) have been used by sources ranging from a presidential media staff to hundreds of firms and ad agencies selling everything from baby powder to booze. Schwartz offers two competing models for explaining the way media work to persuade: the evoked recall, or resonance, model and the transportation, or teaching, model. Schwartz favors the first approach and offers reasons why.

The **evoked recall** (or **resonance**) model rests on the idea that it is better to get a message out of receivers than to try to put one into them. In other words, it relies on the set of experiences and memories that people have stored inside themselves. Schwartz's initial interests were in radio and how various sounds could trigger responses in audiences. For example, an early client wanted the sound of a newborn crying in order to cue feelings of fear, concern, and even guilt in expectant mothers in order to sell the client's baby powder. The sound of crying **resonated** with real **experiences** that the expectant mothers had had with other of their children or with infants of family and friends. There is nothing quite so piercing as the cry of a newborn, and they cry on the average of four

What do you think?

Why does Schwartz advise getting messages "out of" versus "into" audiences?

hours a day. When and if you have children you will understand just how effective the strategy was in persuading the mothers to make a purchase. Later, Schwartz's interests expanded to television, which he felt closely resembled radio and the oral/aural means of communication in its ephemeral nature and its reliance on cuing experiential meaning out of receivers. The basic tactic in eliciting these data is to cue them in some way. Using this approach, persuaders might want to think of the problems people have with, say, a stalled car. Knowing that the potential buyer of the product—an AAA membership—knows what a stall is like, the source can build a message around the feelings people have when their car stalls. Actors in an ad can show frustration, signaling the anxiety target buyers have felt when they knew a stall would make them late. The music or score can heighten the feelings. The voiceover at the end can say soothingly, "When you've got to be there, Triple A gets you there."

Schwartz observes that most experiential meaning is not cued symbolically because it is not stored as a symbol. Instead, it is stored as a feeling—a sense of ease or dis-ease. The best way to cue these feelings out is drama: The source acts out the feeling in the listener's head. Many times, the cueing occurs through music, color, sound effects, the actors' facial expressions or tone of voice, the acoustics, or some other nonverbal message.

What are some stored experiences and emotions that are common to large numbers of people and that media can prompt out of us? The examination dream mentioned in Chapter 11 is one example; the frustration over a clogged sink is another; and car trouble is another. Any event or situation to which people respond with something like "Boy, are you touching a nerve there" or "You're getting awfully close to home" probably resonates with large numbers of people. Mass-media persuaders, especially advertisers, have identified many of these resonating experiences and use the media to cue them out of us. For example, an automobile company advertised its sporty convertible on billboards. The boards showed a teal-colored convertible model heading off into an unclear "future" in the background and the words on the board said "Go Ahead— Have a Midlife Crisis." The ad was targeted at baby boomers approaching midlife. Teal was a popular "boomer" color; the convertible resonated with experiences in their youths; and the unseen future resonated with their fears of mortality. The words were merely the action step for achieving the nostalgia and offered a "cure" for the disease being **experienced** by the target market. As you examine the media persuasion aimed at you in magazine ads, TV and radio spots, and billboards, try to identify the common experiences being aimed at.

You probably won't find these experiential or emotional roots for media persuasion in the *verbal script*, since it most often contains the logical and discursive part of the message. The messages that tug at the heartstrings instead of the mind probably occur elsewhere. One place is in the *auditory script*, which goes beyond verbal symbols. This involves such things as the musical score, the lyrics of the jingle, the sound effects, and maybe even the subliminal cues. Another place where common experiences might be identified is in the *visual script*—the images, editing, montages, camera movement, use of lenses, and other visual effects such as computer graphics. Each of these media "languages" can be critical in plucking a responsive chord.

The Verbal Script

Of course, Schwartz's idea runs counter to what many ad agencies believe. It is also counter to much of the theory about persuasion that emphasizes being specific, logical, and clever with words. That view looks only at the verbal script, which *is* the message. When ad agencies test their ads, they do just that. They ask people to look at

ads and then to respond by recalling the words, images, numbers, and names in the ad. Rarely are viewers asked about their feelings or about the characters in the ads. Often a quirk of fate brings out such data, as in the case of the people who resented the idea that their suitcase would survive a plane crash and they would not.

The Auditory Script

A typical TV spot includes more than just its verbal script. It usually has a sound script—things you hear that are not words. The "language" of sound—sizzles, pops, grinds, klunks, plops, and buzzes—can sometimes cue powerful, unconscious, emotional feelings. For instance, good feelings about parties are cued by the sounds of beer being poured. The gurgle of the first mug being filled triggers the experience of good times. Then the advertiser simply adds words: "We've got beer in a can that's as good as beer from a keg— Hamm's Draft in the new aluminum can." The can is shaped like a barrel or keg to reinforce the good feelings most people have about past keg parties.

This type of auditory-script message can be reinforced by the musical score and sound effects and can also prompt feelings and emotions. We have all had experiences cued out of our collective storehouses of experience in the same way that small cues prompt what we call a déjà vu experience. For example, take an ad for Diet Coke entitled "Break time," which was targeted at working women ages 18–34—the typical Pepsi drinker. We see a group of women gathered at the drinking fountain at break time. One says something like "O.K. It's time," and a handsome, muscular male construction worker across the street begins to peel off his T-shirt for his break. The women ogle him through the office window and we hear sighs. The worker pops a Diet Coke and leans back to swig it down. More sighs are heard. The words are practically irrelevant—it is what the women look like, what the male looks like, and the sighs that make the ad work. These act as cues for the experience of voyeuristic lusting in the minds of the target market. There is nothing logical about the ad or the response it cues from viewers, nor is the ad particularly true or false in any way. It simply "is."

The same kinds of experiences can be cued in an entertainment program, a radio spot ad, or a foldout 3-D print ad. They all rely on stored experiential memories associated with a particular sound cue — a sound effect, a musical score, or the experience of opening a surprise. In fact, some of the scores for jingles have been so effective that they have become popular songs. For instance, the Coca-Cola jingle "I'd Like to Buy the World a Coke" was transformed into a popular song titled "I'd Like to Teach the World to Sing."

The Sight Script

The sight script also serves as an important source of cues. The keg-shaped beer can and the packing of certain cleaners in drum-shaped bottles to give the feeling of heavy-duty power are examples. Another way the sight script cues feelings is by camera angle. A low angle that looks up to a leader distorts size somewhat and "says" that this person is one to be looked up to — a cut above most people. A wide-angle shot with crowds of people thronging to see a leader and shouting salutes sends the message that this is a great leader of a great movement. Hitler used this technique in the famous Nazi propaganda film *Triumph of the Will*. It was outlawed in Germany for many years after World War II because of its power to raise emotions and feelings.

Close-up or zoom-in shots of people convey the idea that we need to take a closer look, to find out what sort of stuff they are made of. Editing can call out feelings that are then used to persuade. Quick cut edits convey the feeling of action. A camera pans from left to right in a slow revelation of the immensity of a scene or crowd. Frequently,

when there are few people in a crowd, the camera hides the fact by dollying (moving or rolling forward) up to the back of the last row of spectators, giving the illusion of a crowded room when actually there are many empty seats. If news editors want to show the sparsity of a crowd for a certain politician, however, they can take a shot from behind the speaker and can pan the empty seats.

A quick cut builds excitement and gives a sense of speed. For example, a snowmobile leaping across the screen and cutting through a huge snowdrift would represent action and excitement. If the view then cuts quickly to downhill racers carving their way through a tough slalom course, and we end with a final quick cut to ice-boat racers zooming across a frozen lake, the sense of excitement is maintained. Only the end would need to include some verbal script, such as "Warm Up Winter This Year. Come to the Winter Wonderland of Lake Geneva" and close with an attractive couple nuzzling one another in front of the fireplace in the after-ski lounge. The visual script does most of the work here. It builds the excitement and prompts out the experiential memories from the audience's subconscious. The verbal script merely tells the viewer where the memories can be brought to life. Look at Figure 12.5. What elements of the visual (not verbal) script are used in this ad to cue out the "relaxed" experience?

Other aspects of the sight script continue the job of pulling messages out of us. Many newscasts convey a newsroom atmosphere. Computer printers churn out page after page, people rush around the set carrying pieces of paper meant to be news flashes, and so on. The network anchorpersons are then superimposed on the set from another studio, giving the visual impression that they are in the middle of the hustle and bustle of the newsroom. You feel that you won't miss any news if you stay tuned to that channel.

Similarly, the background shots for political candidates can signal sophisticated nuances of meaning. If the candidate is standing in front of

Figure 12.5. Why is there a busy street scene in the background? What makes the model look so relaxed? What do the words do here? Do they reinforce the feeling of relaxation and enjoyment or do they try to move the consumer to action? (Reprinted by permission of Grey Advertising.)

WHAT DO YOU CALL A WOMAN WHO'S MADE IT TO THE TOP?

Ms.

She's a better prospect than ever. Because we've turned the old *Ms.* upside down to reflect how women are living today. And you're going to love the results.

The new *Ms.* is witty and bold, with a large-size format that's full of surprises. Whether it's money, politics, business, technology, clothing trends, humor, or late-breaking news — if it's up-to-the-minute, it's part of the new *Ms.*

So if you want to reach the top women consumers in America, reach for the phone. And call Linda Lucht, Advertising Director, *Ms. Magazine*, One Times Square, New York, N.Y. 10036. Tel: (212) 704-8581.

The new Ms. As impressive as the woman who reads it.

Figure 12.6. Here is the ad for Ms. magazine that prompted the angry letter to the editors of Advertising Age. Is the ad true or false? Is it realistic or unrealistic? At whom was the ad probably targeted? What do you think would be Tony Schwartz's response to the ad, to our semiotic analysis of it in Chapter 5, and to the letter to the editors? (Used by permission.)

the Lincoln Memorial with the president, we know he or she is devoted to issues of equality and justice.

Props, jewelry, furniture, artworks, costumes, and other visible effects are part of the sight script, too. Look at the ad for *Ms.* magazine in Figure 12.6. Each visual element adds a new layer of meaning suggesting that the *Ms.* reader is a sophisticated and attractive woman, approaching middle age, well dressed, bejeweled, a world traveler, and a mother. She uses cosmetics, carries cash, and drives an Audi, all the while being sentimental but open to new technologies. These elements are all part of the sight script. Are they true or false? One reader had some strong feelings about the ad, which she put in a letter to the editors of *Advertising Age* magazine, where the ad appeared:

[The] ad on behalf of *Ms.* magazine is one of the most unrealistic, off-target ads I've seen in a long time, and probably succeeds in irritating, if not aggravating, the very reader it was targeted at.

No woman of any note, especially one who's "made it to the top" would ever carry around most of the objects "falling" out of her pocket. . . . Guys gimme a break: A passport? A champagne cork? A $100 bill? Not to mention "cute" kid drawings, credit cards and pills or breath mints. Why do you think women carry purses? . . . Women are lucky to find velvet pants with pockets in the first place. . . . My second objection is that any woman worth her gender and deserving of making it to the top would never find herself in this "falling out of pockets" position in the first place if she DID have stuff in her pockets. Any reader of *Ms.* magazine would have been prepared and removed this stuff before becoming comfy in an upside-down mode. (Victory, 1988, p. 20)

The tone of the letter and several phrases in it make it clear that the author assumes that the intended targets of the ad are the readers of *Ms.* magazine (for example, "any woman worth her gender" and "any reader of *Ms.*"). The criticisms

she raises in her letter would probably be accurate if that was the intended target. However the target was *potential advertisers* in *Ms.* magazine. *Ms.* had been sold to the same company that publishes *Sassy.* They tried to reposition *Ms.* by shifting its image from a magazine for ardent feminists to one for successful, upscale women in their middle years—the baby boomers, yuppies, and muppies ("mature urban professionals"). They hoped to get airlines to advertise in the new *Ms.* magazine, hence the passport. They wanted cosmetics companies to advertise, hence the lipstick. They wanted computer companies to advertise, hence the solar calculator. They wanted companies that market sentimental products to advertise, hence the champagne cork and the florist's card with her husband's name on it. Of course the ad was unrealistic; it was intended to be that way in order to be explicit about the readership of the NEW *Ms.* magazine. The strategy failed, however, and the new *Ms.* went bankrupt.

Thus, the most real, most true advertisements are those that *resonate* most closely with the experiences in the audience, and the title of Schwartz's book, *The Responsive Chord*, reflects that relationship between the audience and the persuasive message, whether the message is the advertisements, the articles printed in magazines, or programs heard on radio or seen on TV. The degree to which they resonate with the experiences stored in the conscious or unconscious minds of the audience predicts their success or failure.

In fact, Schwartz says that the issue of truth is irrelevant in examining the programming or the advertising of electronic media. I suspect that he would say much the same thing about many of the print ads we see in contemporary magazines and newspapers. In a sense, they have become more like the video medium in the past decade. Today we see ads with little or no copy that present a potential dramatic script that could be brought to life on a television screen. A recent example of the resonance principle being used by advertisers can be seen in the storyboard for an ad for the 1994 Acura Integra shown in Figure 12.7. The ad aims at young baby boomers (thirty-one to thirty-five-year-old males) who recalled having played with Hot Wheels, a racetrack toy by Mattel. The Integra runs on a giant Hot Wheels track and negotiates the loop-the-loop part of the track just as the boomers' old toy did. In a bit of clever humor at the end of the ad, an announcer says "Track sold separately."

Or take, for example, the Chivas ad in Figure 12.8. The visual script is effective because it resonates with the experiences of many parents of young children. The couple in the Chivas ad are treating themselves to the best restaurant dinner, the finest scotch whiskey, and probably a night of lovemaking. Many consumers identify with the plot, characters, and setting in the visual script. In other words, the script resonates with the experiences consumers have stored in their conscious or unconscious minds. Persuaders need to identify such common experiences and then design print or electronic messages that prompt the audience to recall the experience while also mentioning the product, candidate, or organization seeking support.

What if the audience doesn't have such a stored experience? Schwartz recommends "planting" the experience in ads early in the campaign. For example, show macho guys in whitewater rafts being bounced up and down and getting doused with water until they reach a slack pool, paddle to the shore, and open their cooler to enjoy a cold can of Miller. Even someone who has never whitewater rafted now has the experience planted in his or her mind. The next step is to reinforce that experience in print ads, focusing on the final scene, and with shorter television and perhaps radio ads. Then, at the point of purchase, voting, or joining, some cue prompts the recall. The shape of the product's packaging, the candidate's name on the ballot, the organization's logo on a billboard or package—all help to prompt meanings at the point of purchase.

In a clever use of graphics and superimposition, *TV Guide* highlighted the "new" svelte Oprah Winfrey following one of her many diets. The cover of the magazine showed a composite photo of Ann-Margaret's body in a sexy Las Vegas show costume with Oprah's head (see Figure 12.9). The message being planted (Oprah looks like this after her diet) is neither true nor untrue; it is simply memorable and can be cued, using Schwartz's resonance principle, at a later time for a variety of reasons (such as to increase Winfrey's ratings or to prompt recall of the publication itself).

Schwartz's resonance principle, as it is used in contemporary advertising, presents receivers of persuasion with several challenges: identifying the common experience that the persuasion aims to prompt from us; identifying persuasive messages that are used to "plant" experiences that are to be triggered later at the point of purchase; and the symbiotic relationship between the verbal, auditory, and visual elements in any mass-mediated persuasion.

McLuhan's Perspective on Media Use

Marshall McLuhan (1963) was another theorist who studied media use in our times. His ideas resemble Schwartz's in many ways. McLuhan believed that we relate to media in two ways. First, every medium is an extension of one of our senses or body parts. Second, media can change our way of thinking about our world, as when the telegraph gave people the idea that they could communicate quickly across long distances thus "destroying" space. The invention of the wireless helped bring David Sarnoff to power as president of NBC. As a young man, he was broadcasting from high atop a New York hotel on the

Figure 12.7. *This ad for the Acura Integra taps into men's experience of having played with a Hot Wheels racetrack, thus resonating with the experiences of its target audience — male baby boomers born in the early 1960s. (Reprinted by permission of American Honda Motor Co.)*

Sometimes life begins
when the babysitter arrives.

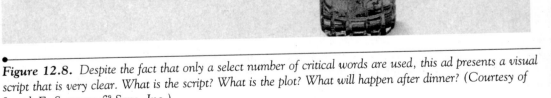

What are you saving the Chivas for?

Figure 12.8. *Despite the fact that only a select number of critical words are used, this ad presents a visual script that is very clear. What is the script? What is the plot? What will happen after dinner? (Courtesy of Joseph E. Seagram & Sons, Inc.)*

Figure 12.9. An Ann-Margaret publicity "still" similar to this photo served as the basis for Oprah Winfrey's "new" image. The clever use of graphics and superimposition helped "plant" the image of the "new" Oprah and promote recall of TV Guide. (Reprinted by permission of AP/Wide World Photos.)

night the *Titanic* struck an iceberg and slowly sank. He heard her distress message and contacted her, serving as a key liaison between people aboard the ship and their families, business associates, and attorneys. Essential directions about where wills were located, what to buy and sell, and so on were exchanged through Sarnoff, thus providing him entré to the rich and powerful who help promote radio and radio programming—the arenas that gave Sarnoff both wealth and influence.

And radio revolutionized the reporting of news and helped create what we call "popular culture" through its entertainment programming (dramas, variety shows), its news reporting (national, state, and local coverage, on-the-spot reporting, play-by-play sports reporting, and foreign coverage by correspondents such as Edward R. Murrow, especially during World War II), its cultural offerings (the Metropolitan Opera, documentaries, classical music), and most important its broadcasts of several types of popular music (big bands, country/western, rock 'n' roll, rhythm and blues, and so on).

Television changed and expanded popular culture in similar ways. Instead of reading a newspaper account or listening to a radio report of a news event, we are transported via television to see and hear the actual story unfolding anywhere in the world. TV news announcers (such as Barbara Walters, Dan Rather, Connie Chung, and Ted Koppel) ultimately became universally recognized icons. Investigative television journalism changed the concept of what is newsworthy and what is credible in news reporting (for example, the reporting of dramatic scandals beginning with Watergate and continuing to today's Whitewater reports and regular "special reports" on local scandals or issues). Today most Americans report that their primary source of news is television — not the newspaper or news weeklies, and more recently, "fluff" journalism, in which "nonstories" are reported.

Television has also effected changes in the world of sports. Take the two-minute drill in football. It didn't exist in the days of radio or even in television's early years. It was "invented" by the networks to create more opportunities to run spot advertisements. The game was stopped by the officials in an artificial time out that teams could use in conjunction with other time outs and plays that "kill" the ball to get quick and often game-saving scores. Television also changed the nature of family and individual lifestyles (think of the "TV Dinner" instead of regular meals, and of models of "good" or "typical" families in sitcoms such as *The Brady Bunch* and more recently *Roseanne*, *The Simpsons*, or *Home Improvement*. Television also gave us new ways of organizing our lives around its programming. It gave us the six o'clock or the ten o'clock news at night, *The Today Show* and its clones in the morning, and *Sesame Street* in the afternoon. Some people schedule their lives around certain shows, such as *Monday Night Football* or *Seinfeld*. In many homes television serves as a "clock" used in determining the time of day and the day of the week ("If *Murphy Brown* is on, it must be Monday at 9 P.M.").

Television surely altered our sense of community and belonging as well. With TVs on more than seven hours a day in the average American home, there simply is not enough time to do the kind of socializing that occurred prior to its existence. This has created what one critic labels "the lonely crowd," in which people in neighborhoods (and even more so in dense living quarters such as apartment complexes) rarely know one another. You probably experience the feeling of the lonely crowd both on and off campus. In some third-world countries, on the other hand, televisions and VCRs are owned by the entire village or community and serve as entertainment, a political debate forum, education, and more.

Because television has an easy "access code" (that is, we don't have to learn to watch television in the same way we have to learn to read a book), it may have contributed to the growing illiteracy in our country. MTV clearly altered American pop culture and provided new and sometimes disturbing role models (Madonna and Beavis and Butt-Head) and actions (violence against women). And we could go on to discuss many other changes wrought by television in the past fifty years. Most of these changes have important implications for persuasion, and they demonstrate what McLuhan meant when he said, "The medium is the message."

Computers have also transformed our culture in revolutionary ways that have given us a new "information society." The computer has changed the way we think about literacy. One must now be "computer literate," which means literate in several computer "languages." The computer has certainly changed our language, giving new or changed meanings to such words as "backup," "boot," "mouse," "hacker," "menu," "window," or "virus"

What do you think?

Does the interactive word have an easy or a difficult "access code"?

Medium	Source of Information	Definition	Participation	Type of Medium
Television	Lighted dots	Low	High	Cool
Books	Completed letters	High	Low	Hot
Cartoons	Dots on paper	Low	High	Cool
Photographs	Image on film	High	Low	Hot
Telephone	Low-fidelity sound wave	Low	High	Cool
Movie	Moving image on film	High	Low	Hot
Telegraph	Dots and dashes in sound	Low	High	Cool
Digital audio	High-fidelity sound wave	High	Low	Hot
Personal Computer and Internet	Lighted dots	Low	High	Cool

Table 12.1. *Hot and Cool Media*

(Lederer, 1991). The half-life of computer technology (the "power" you get for your money) is now under three years, creating a marketing and persuasion gold mine.

The computer drives us inward to a world occupied only by the self, the machine, and the task at hand. It also alters one's sense of community and further isolates one from others (for example, someone at the computer usually resents being interrupted, especially just to "shoot the breeze"). More and more, computers make us become members of "the lonely crowd" and simultaneously determine the scale and pace of our lives.

One of the ways in which media tend to affect the way we look at our lives, according to McLuhan, is by the *form* or *fidelity* of their *signals*. Some media signals come to us in a complete, high-fidelity form. Others come to us in an incomplete, or low-fidelity, form. High-fidelity forms require little of us in assembling the signals into complete messages. Low-fidelity forms require us to use our senses and to convert incomplete signals into complete messages. The telegraph was such an incomplete, low-fidelity form or signal (that is, the message was encoded in

Morse code), whereas radio broadcasts complete words and sentences. The same message sent via the two forms would be different, according to McLuhan. The high-fidelity form, by requiring little participation, results in *little physiological* or *sensory involvement*. The low-fidelity form, requiring much participation, results in *high physiological* or *sensory participation*. McLuhan called the high-fidelity, or complete, message signals "hot" and the low-fidelity, or incomplete, ones "cool" (see Table 12.1).

Hot Media

As noted above, McLuhan used "hot" to refer to media and messages that have high fidelity or definition and are easy to perceive. Their images are well drawn or recorded. We do not have to work to process the image or the sound through the central nervous system. It is like the difference between the old wind-up phonograph that scratched out the sounds of the 1920s and today's digitized sound that makes you feel as if you are right in the middle of an orchestra. The digital sound is hot because it has high fidelity or definition. Hot messages have the same quality. A good example is the hard-sell advertiser who comes on during the late movie and tries to sell three rooms of carpeting for only $599.99. The message is distinct and comes through crystal clear. Or consider the hot political candidate Patrick Buchanan, who said that delegates attending the 1992 Democratic nominating convention represented "the greatest single exhibition of cross dressing in political history." Buchanan is the kind of persuader, Schwartz said, who would blow out audience fuses because he was too hot.

Another example of a "hot" persuader on a "cool" medium is Jerry Springer, who regularly invites controversial guests to his show and then prompts the audience to get into verbal combat with them, and vice versa. Jerry sits on the sideline fanning the flames with his commentary. In contrast, Jay Leno is a cool spokesperson on a cool medium, and the audience is less "fired up" by his program format, style, and guests. Other hot persuaders include Rush Limbaugh, David Letterman, and Howard Stern, while Ted Koppel, Jenny Jones, and Oprah Winfrey are cool persuaders.

Cool Media

Cool media have low fidelity or definition. We must work to process these messages. On TV, for example, at any given instant only half of the lines of resolution are lit. We must put together these "half-images" we see on TV, just as we must imagine a lot of sound quality with the wind-up Victrola. Low-fidelity sounds come out of a telephone, and cartoons are cooler than photos. What kinds of messages are best for these media? McLuhan said that cool media breed cool messages, or vague and ill-defined images. He saw the politician of the TV-dominated future as abstract, fuzzy, shaggy around the edges, and not needing to say everything at gut level. Instead, the candidate lets the voter fill in or put together a meaning or image. What affect will HDTV have?

McLuhan was right, judging by the growth in image politics since his theory first appeared. The politicians who seem to catch on are those with an easy-going approach. That is why the addition of Jack Kemp (a "cool" persuader) to the 1996 GOP ticket did so much to lift poll results in favor of Bob Dole (a much "hotter" persuader). "Cool" is abstract to the voter, not distinct. Likewise, we see more TV commercials that rely less on words or scripts than on giving a mood or feeling. Viewers add to or subtract from such commercials and arrive at a final meaning. Think of the many commercials that get us anticipating through the use of music or sets or lighting. We hear the sounds of a love ballad. Then we see a well-dressed man and woman slowly walking down the stairs at the opera house. The man asks the valet to get his car. Up drives a Volkswagen Jetta. Only then does the voiceover tell us that the Jetta is in good taste anywhere.

So cool media have low fidelity or signal quality and high audience participation. The participation is usually physiological—we use our senses to "complete" the message. The message itself may be insipid and not worth processing, but it still results in high levels of interaction between the *signal* and the receiver.

McLuhan also said that we spend an increasing portion of our days involved with cool compared to hot media. In addition to the hours we spend with the TV, we may spend hours at work in front of a computer terminal and screen. Those who don't, say that a great portion of their workdays is spent on the telephone, another cool medium. And many homes have video recorders and computers, which also involve family members with the cool medium of television.

McLuhan predicted that this great increase in the use of cool media and the corresponding increase in audience participation, coupled with satellite transmission of television, radio, and telephone signals, would lead to a "Global Village" in which everyone is interested in everyone else's business. That prediction has come true most dramatically with the Internet, electronic mail, and the WWW. Here McLuhan and Schwartz overlap and enhance each other. The involving and participatory trend, coupled with the notion of identifying experiences that can be prompted by mini-cues allowing people to add their own meanings provide a powerful set of tools in the hands of creative and insightful persuaders.

Agenda Setting by the Media

One explanation of how mass media persuade is called the **agenda-setting function** of mass media (McCombs & Shaw, 1972). According to this theory, the public agenda—the kinds of issues people discuss, think about, and worry about (and sometimes ultimately press for legislation on)—is powerfully shaped and directed by what the news media choose to publicize. As theorists put it, mass media do not tell us what to think; they tell us what to think about (see Figure 12.10). How many persons would have followed the testimony at the O. J. Simpson trial if the media hadn't continually reported on it, thus putting it on the "front burner" of the American agenda? Would we be thinking about the militia movement if the media hadn't kept running stories about various bombings involving persons affiliated with militia-type groups? Deciding what to focus on and, equally important, what *not* to focus on in reporting the day's news falls to small groups of "gatekeepers."

How do gatekeepers make programming decisions and by what criteria? Not much is known about this process, but there are some hints of how and why the decisions are made. Meyrowitz (1985) refers to one criterion called LOP, or "least objectionable programming." This means that "the key is to design a program that is least likely to be turned *off*, rather than a program

Figure 12.10. *Although media may not tell us what to think, they can tell us what to think about.* (Berry's World *reprinted by permission of NEA, Inc.*)

viewers will actively seek out" (p. 73). Some media critics note that while media advertisements purportedly *sell products* to viewers, the economic design of mass media *sells audiences* to advertisers. In terms of television, for example, we tend to think of programs as "products" for which we pay a price—we have to watch ads from the program's sponsors. In reality *we* are the products, and *we* are being sold to the advertisers. Therefore, the goal is to design programming that will capture and "hold" the attention of the largest number of people or of a certain segment of people, such as upscale spenders.

Berry's World

© 1988 by NEA, Inc. 3-D

"You're talking in 30-second bites again."

Figure 12.11. *The 30-second news bite is one criterion that affects gatekeepers' decisions as to what is newsworthy and what is not. As this cartoon implies, the news bite may even be affecting our conversational styles. (Berry's World reprinted by permission of NEA, Inc.)*

Recently, CBS, finding itself at the bottom of the ratings, determined that henceforth the "news" programming had to make a profit. The news division at CBS had been a sacred cow, but that went out the window when ratings dropped and profits entered the picture, particularly after the purchase of CBS by the Westinghouse Corporation. Perhaps this explains the ever-increasing incidence of what has come to be called "fluff journalism."

Another criterion for deciding what is to be broadcast on television is whether or not a piece can be delivered as a 20- to 30-second "news bite," defined by Jamieson and Kohrs-Campbell (1983) as a piece of news less than 35 seconds long, delivered by a credible source in an energetic way. Meyrowitz explains that viewers actually may prefer short "bites" because they report whether anything important has happened that day (see Figure 12.11). For example, if the first story or bite in the broadcast is not earth-shattering, then it hasn't been an important news day. On the other hand, if the first story is of a crisis nature, viewers know that an in-depth report will follow.

Newspapers, since they generally provide us with yesterday's news, frequently follow the gatekeeping decisions of television. They run stories that the television news programmer chose the day before. News weeklies are caught in the same bind, presenting last week's news in this week's issue. Both the newspaper and the news weekly can do in-depth coverage of issues. However, fewer people are reading them, and those who do are spending less time reading them.

Another criterion used to determine which story gets broadcast and subsequently printed is the expressiveness or dramatic quality of both the video and the audio elements in the message (Meyrowitz, 1985). "Newsworthy" stories include the instantaneous reactions of a mother who has just heard that her son has been kidnapped. A mike is shoved under her chin, the camera zooms up to her face, and supposedly the audience "experiences" how she must feel at that moment. McLuhan once observed of newspapers that the only good news in them nowadays is advertising and P.R., and that it took an awful lot of bad news to sell all that good news.

As critical receivers of persuasion, we need to diversify our reading, listening, and viewing of news and information to expose ourselves to as many divergent sources as possible. You might

Berry's World

"Seventeen years ago, he was just a BABY. Now, he's watched more than 15,000 HOURS OF TV."

Figure 12.12. The hours we spend watching TV strongly influence our agenda. Note also that the average seventeen-year-old now may have watched 20,000 or more hours. (Berry's World reprinted by permission of NEA, Inc.)

want to listen to the news as reported on public television or public radio. Try adding *Morning Edition* and *All Things Considered* to your radio selections and *Washington Week in Review* or the *News Hour with Jim Lehrer* to your TV viewing. Above all, don't let one medium—such as TV—so dominate your awareness of the world that you overlook other sources of news and information. Even if you watch as much TV as the student

in Figure 12.12, delve into other sources such as radio, books, periodicals, and newspapers. Widen the range of the agenda being set for you. With *several* sources telling you what to think about, you can decide both what to think and what to think about.

Role Modeling and the Media

In earlier times, people learned to model themselves after those with whom they worked or lived. Girls learned to be homemakers by watching their mothers. Boys learned to be farmers by watching their fathers and the other farmers in the community. Today, the media exert a much more potent force on role modeling than the immediate world around us does. Cultivation theory offers a good explanation for this media-centered role modeling. The media "cultivates" or "grows" favorable predispositions to preferred lifestyles, personal images, patterns of acceptable and unacceptable behavior, and value systems, among other things. As a result we learn what it is like to be a parent, child, lover, employee, police officer, and so on from media, and then we model the roles we enact on those examples.

We adopt such roles in two ways. Sometimes we take on a certain role because the scene or setting demands it of us. For example, people expect certain roles at funerals, and others at weddings. These are **assigned roles.** The scene assigns a president the role of leader, and shows of emotion are not called for in leaders. At other times, the setting demands a role that we reject, and we choose another role. For example, a pro football player should be tough and burly. He makes a show of proving that he is "all man." Big, tough, burly he-men don't hurt, and they don't cry. The football-field scene assigns this role. However, suppose that players know that a teammate is dying of some disease. Now the tough guys show emotion and cry at the end of the final game of the stricken player's final season. These actions come from roles dictated by the players, not the scene. These are **assumed roles.** They are taken on at the will of the role player and often run counter to the demands of the scene. Again and again throughout our lives, we choose between these two options — assumed and assigned roles. We have varying degrees of success and failure in playing roles, and we learn from them.

How do we learn which roles to emulate and which to reject? Here is where mass media come in. Ask yourself what a working mother is like. Your responses may come from watching your own working mother, but they will also come from characters in ads or in situation comedies or in other TV and radio programs. This explains why the critics of the mass media express such concern about programs, ads, and other messages that feature sex or violence such as we frequently see on MTV. While current programming does present characters and situations that more closely approximate the real world rather than the MTV world, there are still major objections to what is referred to as "jiggly programming" such as *Baywatch* and *Baywatch II*, and there is also concern over the glamorizing of teenage motherhood on many soap operas. Successful women don't always have to be beautiful, shapely, and ready to tumble into the sack. Successful men don't always have to be aggressive and macho or look like Brad Pitt.

When *The Simpsons* first debuted on evening prime time, many parents wouldn't let their children watch it. Why not? After all, it was all in good fun, and the barrage of Simpsons paraphernalia (T-shirts, lunchboxes, stickers, and so on) on the market showed the program's popularity. Communication researcher Mary Larson observed that parents' objections related to the role models depicted by the Simpson family members (Ramhoff, 1990). Bart is an underachiever with an "attitude problem," which means that he is

disrespectful of parents and authority figures. He also uses smart aleck slang words and phrases such as "dude" and "Don't have a cow!" Marge Simpson yells at her kids and sometimes uses earthy language: "Get your butts down here: we're going to be late for church!" and Homer Simpson is a glutton and a lout who is incompetent at his job.

News Manipulation and Persuasion

In his book *Don't Blame the People*, Robert Cirino (1971) observes that the role of the news industry is to do business with business. After all, the media stand to profit from the success of their clients and customers. Does news manipulation really occur, or are people such as Cirino supersensitive and paranoid about the power of the networks, the wire services, and the major newspapers and newsmagazines? If there is any manipulation, we ought to acquaint ourselves with the possible tactics that can make or unmake news. That will allow us an extra safeguard against possible "hidden persuasion" in news programs. Let us look at some of these tactics and at our news system.

Three major wire services (AP, UPI, and Reuters) supply most of the news we see, hear, and read. Go through your daily newspaper and see how many stories are run from each service. In a way, we are all getting the same news. There is nothing wrong with that, as long as the news is accurate and as long as the key news items get printed or broadcast. This is the problem. The key items don't always get on the front page.

The problem is more severe with broadcast news. The evening news shown on TV contains only about twenty-two minutes of news. Furthermore, the messages are sent through the aural/oral channel. Speech speed on broadcast news is about 125 words per minute, or about 3000 total words. The average 400-words-per-minute reader can cover that in only seven to eight minutes. Thus, we miss a lot of important information if we rely only on electronic media for news.

Even this truncated news became diluted by the pressure of the ratings. The news as "show business" began with male and later female anchors, and continued with slick "news teams" and now "fluff" journalism. According to Ron Powers (1978), the result is news that caters to audiences instead of educating or informing them. As he noted:

> People did not want complicated, disturbing newscasts any more. . . . People were sick of unpleasant news. The new "mood of the country" . . . was no longer "issue-oriented" but "people-oriented." The very term "Pee-pull" to denote a news genre became oracular; it was spoken in hushed italics; it bore the tintinnabulation of cash register bells.

The result is a news *program*, not a news *broadcast*. The news is manipulated, selected, shaped, and massaged to attract the largest share of the audience — to please the most and offend the fewest.

Since 1980, with the advent of *Nightline* (which grew out of the hostage crisis in Iran), television news has seen great change. All-news channels such as CNN, all-sports channels such as ESPN, special-interest channels such as The History Channel, The Weather Channel, and a major new network — Fox — have all come online in recent times and provide viewers with more in-depth coverage of not only news but other areas of interest.

Barbara Matusow (1983) agrees in her book *The Evening Stars*: "The triumph of the Anchor is, in fact, the logical outgrowth of a system almost totally unfettered by any consideration except the need to maximize profits (p. 40). Her

account of the struggle by CBS to land Dan Rather to replace retiring Walter Cronkite makes the point clearly. After lots of bumping and shoving among CBS management, Rather, and other networks, CBS offered Rather the anchor spot for a fee of approximately $25 million, spread over ten years, plus other perks. Matusow quotes Roone Arledge of ABC News, which was competing for Rather's services, as saying, "It's hard to put a value on Dan Rather. If he . . . brings viewers to the *World News Tonight*, how much he is worth over ten years is incalculable."

When you are trying to gain a certain segment of the market, the temptation is to manipulate the news, to make it more interesting, sexier, more sensational, and more entertaining. Your tactics are limitless, and bias is bound to creep in. As Edward R. Murrow, the first electronic news star, put it:

> One of the basic troubles with radio and television news is that both instruments have grown up as an incompatible combination of show business, advertising and news. Each of the three is a rather bizarre and demanding profession, and when you get all three under one roof, the dust never settles. (Matusow, 1983, p. 304).

The show-business aspects of electronic news distorts electronic news just as yellow journalism distorted print news. Here are some ways news can be manipulated.

Ignoring

One way gatekeepers distort the news is by simply ignoring it. Officials ignored the danger of buildings containing asbestos until one school district in Virginia finally brought suit. Asbestos without a lawsuit apparently wasn't an interesting story. More recently, the news media ignored warnings about the breakup of the former

Yugoslavia until it was too late to shape public opinion and influence U.S. and UN policies regarding the breakup. The breakup of the Soviet Union and its satellite states made much better news.

Favoring the Sponsor

Because every commercial news program has sponsors, it's possible that news reporters and editors will soft-pedal any negative news about these sponsors. Good examples are the number of years it took to get broadcasters to refuse advertising from cigarette manufacturers, and the campaign to keep beer and wine ads from being banned. It is always wise to ask who the sponsor is for a newscast. Getting your news from several sources helps us to avoid sponsor-favoring editing. This method is getting more complicated as a few large corporations buy up communication outlets and corporations owning such outlets; General Electric owns the NBC network, Westinghouse owns CBS, and Disney owns ABC, to give just a few examples.

The Pseudoevent

Although there is an overabundance of news each day, not all of it is interesting or entertaining, so news reporters are often drawn to highly drama-tic or bizarre events. Daniel Boorstin (1961) called these "pseudoevents" or "planned news." This occurs with the announcement of stock dividends, contract settlements, or grand openings. Reporting them falls somewhere between public relations and hard news. Various mass movements use pseudoevents to draw media

What do you think?

Can you think of a recent pseudoevent?

attention to their cause by holding marches, rallies, or vigils, or even using violent tactics such as bombings, lootings, or other dramatic events. Most corporations, banks, major not-for-profits, and so on, maintain sophisticated public relations offices that frequently have "events" coordinators whose job it is to plan pseudoevents to "make news" for the organization.

Bias: Verbal and Nonverbal

We previously noted several kinds of bias, such as gatekeeping and ignoring; there are numerous others. A skillful interviewer can make an interviewee seem to be quite different from his or her real self. Larry King is an expert at drawing out the interviewee in selective ways. News reporters can make the candidates seem controversial by dubbing an audio track of booing on a video track of cheering and then having the announcer say that the candidate faces opposition from left and right. Or an editor might superimpose two or more conflicting images: angry farmers and grain dealers; college students and college loan officers; homemakers and supermarket owners; starving children and people wasting food or gorging themselves. They can select who is featured, choosing only pro or only con advocates. The reporter can say that so-and-so refused to comment on the issue, thus making it seem that so-and-so must be guilty.

Finally, news can be biased by simply taking things out of context or by misquoting a source. As Black Muslim leader Malcolm X put it, "I don't care what points I made . . . it practically never gets printed the way I said it" (Cirino, 1971, p. 147).

We can't possibly look at and listen to all the print and electronic news available. But we can diversify our exposure, not relying on any one medium such as television or on any one network, newspaper, or magazine.

Review and Conclusion

The average eighteen-year-old American has seen 22,000 hours of television and hundreds of thousands of commercials. And TV is just one media channel being used for persuasion. Most of us are affected by billboards, films, magazines, and newspapers. Labels, bumper stickers, T-shirts, and other paraphernalia persuade us. Although, on the average, Americans buy less than one-third of a book per person per year (we don't know whether they are ever read), books may sometimes persuade us (Schwartz, 1973).

All in all, we live in a highly persuasive, media-rich environment. You need to be persuaded about some things, and media persuasion is sometimes the best way to get information about your alternatives. You can protect yourself from persuasive attempts made by the media by beginning to look beyond the surface meanings in media messages. Look for the responsive chords being plucked and decide whether the messages that elicit them are hot or cool. Look for the agenda being set. Also, consider the immense changes we are facing because of the development of new communications media such as the Internet and virtual reality (Larson, 1996; Gumpert & Drucker, 1996; Postman, 1996; and Zettl, 1996).

Questions for Further Thought

1. What are some similarities between primitive oral/aural cultures and the electronic culture in which we now live?

2. Why is information associated with power? Give examples.

3. How was the concept of "ownership" associated with the development of writing?

4. What changes in society resulted from the development of print?

5. How did literacy free us and also "enslave" us?

6. What are some of the developments at the Media Lab at M.I.T.? How will they affect us in the future?

7. Could you use virtual reality to persuade people? If so, how?

8. According to Schwartz, are symbols used to store the experiences we have?

9. Which of your values or experiences can be evoked by persuaders and then tied to their product, idea, or candidate? Think of favorite experiences you have had that relate to a product. Recall some unpleasant experiences that relate to a product.

10. What does Schwartz mean by "evoked recall"? Give several examples.

11. What is a hot medium? Give an example. Why is it *hot*? What kinds of messages go best with a hot medium?

12. What "mistake" did the writer of the letter to the editors of *Advertising Age* make about the target audience of the *Ms.* magazine ad?

13. Which media type—hot or cool—dominates our times?

14. Give examples of the criteria gatekeepers may be using to determine what will be put on the evening TV news.

15. What is the agenda-setting function of mass media?

References

Boorstin, D. (1961). *The image: A guide to pseudo-events in America*. New York: Harper & Row.

Brand, S. (1987). *The media lab: Inventing the future at M.I.T.* New York: Viking Penguin.

Cirino, R. (1971). *Don't blame the people*. Los Angeles: Diversity Press.

Greene, R. (1985). Less violence would be a big hit on TV. *Chicago Tribune*, January 15, sec. 2, p. 1.

Gumpert, G., & Drucker, S. J. (1996). From locomotion to telecommunication, or paths of safety, streets of gore. In *Communication in cyberspace: Social interaction in an electronic environment*. Eds. Strate, L., Jacobson, R., & Gibsen, S. J. Cresskill, NJ: Hampton Press.

Jamieson, K. & Kohrs-Campbell, K. (1983). *The interplay of influence*. Belmont: Wadsworth.

Kaplan, D., Wingert, P., & Chideya, F. (1993). Dumber than we thought. *Newsweek*, September 20, pp. 44–45.

Larson, C. U. (1996). Dramatism and virtual reality: Implications and predictions. In *Communication and cyberspace: Social interaction in an electronic environment*. Eds. Strate, L., Jacobson, R., & Gibsen, S. J. Cresskill, NJ: Hampton Press.

Lederer, R. (1991). *The miracle of language*. New York: Pocket Books.

Madigan, C. M. (1993). Going with the flow. *Chicago Tribune Magazine*. May 2, pp. 14–26.

Matusow, B. (1983). *The evening stars: The making of a network news anchor*. New York: Ballantine.

McCombs, M., & Shaw, D. (1972). The agenda-setting function of the media. *Public Opinion Quarterly, 36,* 176–187.

McLuhan, M. (1963). *Understanding media: The extensions of man*. New York: Signet Books.

Meyrowitz, J. (1985). *No sense of place: The impact of electronic media on social behavior*. New York: Oxford University Press.

Ong, W. S. (1967). *The presence of the word*. New Haven, CT: Yale University Press.

Ong, W. S. (1977). *Interfaces of the word*. Ithaca, NY: Cornell University.

Ong, W. S. (1982). *Orality and literacy: The technologizing of the word*. London: Metheun.

Postman, N. (1996). Cyberspace, schmyberspace. In *Communication and cyberspace: Social interaction in an electronic environment*. Eds. Strate, L., Jacobson, R., & Gibsen, S. J. Cresskill, NJ: Hampton Press.

Powers, R. (1978). *The newscasters: The news business as show business*. New York: St. Martin's Press.

Ramhoff, R. (1990). Bart's not as bad as he seems: Simpsons as positive as other family. *Rockford Register Star*, October 18, sec. 2, p. 1.

Schwartz, T. (1973). *The responsive chord*. Garden City, NY: Anchor/Doubleday.

Victory, V. B. (1988). Pocket veto. *Advertising Age*, April 25, p. 20.

Zettl, H. (1996). Back to Plato's cave: Virtual reality. In *Communication and cyberspace: Social interaction in an electronic environment*. Eds. Strate, L., Jacobson, R., & Gibsen, S. J. Cresskill, NJ: Hampton Press.

13

The Techniques of Propaganda

For many years, the idea of studying propaganda in a communication class was deemed laughable. Aside from wartime, which was often typified by heavy-handed propagandistic techniques, propaganda didn't seem to be operating. Only a few cheered the addition of this propaganda chapter over a decade ago. Many thought it a waste of time to cover an antiquated topic. At about that same time, however, a new focus in propaganda emerged, and the communication discipline began to investigate ideological communication in its various forms — especially as it operates in popular culture.

Since that time, we have witnessed dramatic examples of the powers of modern propaganda including the fall of the Shah of Iran and of Ferdinand Marcos of the Philippines. In our own country, the Reagan/Bush administrations used propaganda to dismantle longstanding liberal programs in social welfare. Propaganda was also used to justify the invasion of Grenada — a minuscule Caribbean Island — to "protect American interests in the area." In 1990 propaganda reversed the seventy-five-year-old ideology of Leninist/Marxist communism in the Soviet Union. Earlier, Amer-

ican propaganda had been used to paint the USSR as an "Evil Empire." Propaganda forced the South African government to free Nelson Mandela and helped reverse the longstanding practice of *apartheid*. Propaganda was central in toppling the socialist states of Eastern Europe, setting them on the path to free-market systems. Sophisticated and massive propaganda warfare on both sides was used to justify as well as condemn the Iraqi invasion of Kuwait. More recently, both sides of the national health insurance issue have used propaganda to sway public opinion, as have the pro-life, pro-choice, and gun lobbies. And we can expect more propaganda coming to us from religious, political, and economic ideologues as they try to sell their systems of beliefs and values.

As you can see, far from being a rickety and antiquated concept, propaganda is alive and well and quite active in this last decade of the twentieth century. As receivers, we need to recognize propaganda when we encounter it and respond accordingly. This chapter outlines the dimensions of modern propaganda and offers some tools for recognizing and responding to it.

What Propaganda Isn't

What do you think of when you hear someone say, "That's just propaganda"? How do you differentiate it from the word "persuasion"? How does it differ from "coercion" or "education" or "culture" or "advertising" or "public relations"? Some people would say that they are all one and the same — that virtually everything involving communication to persuade is in some way propagandistic. The problem with defining propaganda as "everything" is that it gets you nowhere. It doesn't allow you to say the words "I love you" or "I'm sorry" or "I think I understand, but please go over it once more for me" without spreading propaganda. If you have a definition that cannot distinguish one kind of persuasive communication from another, you don't have much of a definition. Let's look at the origin of the word and at its denotation or dictionary definition.

The word "propaganda" comes from the Latin *propagare*, which means "to spread or grow," much as the word "propagate" (which comes from the same Latin root) indicates growth or spreading. Originally instituted formally by Pope Gregory XV in the *Sacra Congregatio de Propaganda Fide* in the seventeenth century, its purpose was to spread the faith and Christianize the world. It was a noble cause to be a true and successful propagandist in 1623.

Webster's Collegiate Dictionary Tenth Edition defines propaganda as "ideas, facts, or allegations spread deliberately to further one's cause or to damage an opposing cause." Three key words in this definition help distinguish propaganda from other kinds of communication. The most important is the word "cause," which implies some sort of dogma or ideology that one is trying to propagate, whether religious dogma, political dogma, economic dogma, vegetarian dogma, antivivisectionist dogma, pro-life dogma, pro-choice dogma, or a host of other "causes" that people hope to promote. This helps us rule out many kinds of communication that aren't dogmatic or related to a cause. For example, while advertising promotes a brand, it doesn't promote a **cause** or ideology; and the same holds true for most public relations — they may promote a new bank in town, the "Pumpkin Fest" in my town or a hometown hospital, but they usually aren't used to promote a **cause** or ideology unless they are promoting a candidate or some religious organization. The second most important word in the definition is "deliberately," because it helps us rule out a great many kinds of communication in which we don't intend to spread any cause and in which we are simply trying to discover information or to express our feelings. The third most important word in the definition is "spread," which carries with it the idea of affecting many persons with communication about the cause. This helps us distinguish propaganda from instances in which we are trying to affect one or only a few other persons — our family, dorm floor, fraternity, sorority, or friend. The 1993 *American Heritage College Dictionary* echoes this approach, defining "propagandize" as "to engage in propaganda for (a doctrine or cause)." Thus, not all communication is propaganda — propaganda deliberately spreads a doctrine or a cause.

Now what about all those negative connotations that pop up when the word "propaganda" is mentioned? Where did all that negativity come from? Well, some of it has come from the overzealousness of certain religious propagandists who come knocking on our doors or who grab us by the arm and ask us whether we have been reborn. Some of it comes from deep-seated prejudices about race, gender, social class, or ethnicity. But most of the negativity associated with the word "propaganda" stems from wartime propaganda used by

What do you think?

Do you think propaganda is alive and well? Why?

"us" and "them" in this country. And much of the paranoia about propaganda stems from the tremendous communication power made possible by current and future technologies. As Garth Jowatt and Victoria O'Donnell (1986) note in their book *Propaganda and Persuasion:*

> The late nineteenth and early twentieth centuries were periods of great expansion of propaganda activities. The growth of the mass media and improvements in transportation led to the development of mass audiences. . . . Each of the mass media — print, movies, radio and then television — contributed its unique qualities to new techniques of propaganda. Radio, in particular, brought into existence the possibility of continuous international propaganda, whereas television has increased the problem of "cultural imperialism," where one nation's culture is imposed upon another nation. (p. 63)

A Definition

It is essential to define the object of one's study as specifically as can be done to distinguish it from similar but not identical concepts. We need a definition that will allow us to identify the critical differences between, for example, propaganda and debate or propaganda and advertising. If we defined everything as propaganda, it would be both easy and impossible to identify it.

Propaganda Is Ideological. For our purposes, propaganda is first and foremost **ideological.** It tries to sell a *belief system* or *dogma.* Propaganda can be religious, political, or economic.

Propaganda Uses Mass Media. Second, propaganda **uses some form of mass communication** to sell ideology. Media that could be used in the propaganda process include speeches; documentary films, TV programs, and radio shows; posters and billboards; mass mailings; and so on. Postage stamps, coins, paper currency, music, art, and drama have all been used for propaganda. This fits with the key words "deliberately" and "spread" from the dictionary definition. Beliefs that are spread interpersonally do not affect large numbers and so do not qualify as propaganda under our definition even though they may be propagandistic in terms of the other elements of the definition.

Propaganda Conceals. Third, one or some combination of the following must be **concealed from the target audience** (Taylor, 1979):

1. The **source** of the communication

2. The source's **goal**

3. The **other side** of the story — various perspectives

4. The **techniques** being used by the source in sending the message

5. The **results** of the propaganda if successful

Propaganda Aims at Uniformity. Propaganda **aims at uniformity** in the *beliefs, attitudes,* and *behaviors* of its receivers. So while most ads want you to believe something "about" the brand — say, Fords — they generally don't try to make you believe "in" the brand. However, internal communication at Ford that is aimed at employee morale tries to do just that, and it *is* propaganda.

Propaganda Circumvents the Reasoning Process. Usually, propaganda appeals to the heart and not the mind of the audience. If the propagandist gave both sides of the issues, people would make up their own minds, and the propaganda would probably fail. In order to bypass logical thinking, propaganda uses biased information that is aimed at stirring up audience emotions and that "forces" the audience to an opinion or conclusion that is already known by the propagandist. For example, television evangelists use their (biased) sources to work on audience fears, loves, hates, and so on in order to move the television audience to a foregone conclusion (e.g., repentance, making a donation, or going out to convert others).

Using this definition, we can see that not all advertisements are propaganda: They usually are not ideological and we usually know the source and the goal. However, some advertisements *are* propaganda. In an obvious case, an ad for an "Awareness Weekend" sponsored by an organization having the acronym CARP (which is actually the Unification Church of Reverend Moon) was clearly propaganda: It espoused a dogma, it used some form of mass communication, and it did not reveal information such as the source, the other side of the story, the techniques to be used (for example, sleep deprivation), and the probable results (being "converted"). Finally, it certainly aimed at uniformity of behavior.

The pro-life film *Silent Scream* is an example of filmic propaganda. It uses all the terms and techniques discussed thus far to "suggest" to the audience that an aborted fetus was a living human being until the abortionist's forceps crushed its skull. On the other side of the issue, the pro-choice forces made similarly emotional suggestions in a recent magazine ad showing an unbent coat hanger with its sharp ends, along with the headline "To Many of Our Daughters, This Looks Like A Coat Hanger." Subheadlines then asked the reader to "Please Sign The Pledge to Keep It That Way" and "Add Your Name To Mine — After Sixteen Years of Safety, Time Is Running Out."

A computer program entitled "Womb with a View" probably qualifies as propaganda by our definition. It suggests that it is merely information about pregnancy and baby's development in the womb, but it is sponsored by Project Reality, which is a pro-life organization that is affiliated with another organization, Birthright of Chicago, whose slogan is ". . . and the right of every child to be born." It clearly **spreads** an **ideology** using **mass media** while it **conceals** its real intention

through its self-characterization as "educational," and it **aims at uniform behavior** (carrying the fetus to term) by involving the target audience in **emotional versus logical** appeals (notice that all references are to "baby," not to the fetus, and that "mother" learns about what she is experiencing while recording her "personal thoughts" and "special moments."

Let's look at what some experts on modern propaganda have to say and compare their views with our definition.

Views of Modern Propaganda

Modern propaganda began with the development of the modern mass media of communication (see Chapter 12 for more on this point). With the advent of the loudspeaker, radio, film, and later television, persuaders and demagogues learned to turn these media to their advantage. In the United States, people such as Huey Long and Franklin Roosevelt used these new media to gain the support of millions. Elsewhere, Adolf Hitler in Germany and Joseph Stalin in the Soviet Union used the new technology to great advantage. Scholars and social critics became concerned about the influence of propaganda coupled with electronic media.

Early investigators also tried to define propaganda. For example, L. W. Doob (1935), a world-famous sociologist in the middle of this century, said that the use of **suggestion** is the key. If suggestion is used, "then this process may be called propaganda, regardless of whether or not the propagandist intends to exercise control." On the other hand, Doob said that if the same result would have occurred with or without the use of suggestion "then this process may be called education regardless of the intention of the educator" (p. 20). Doob used the word "suggestion" very explicitly. He did not mean everyday suggestions like "I suggest trying the burritos here" or "I suggest trying the pumpkin-colored sweater with those slacks." Instead he was referring to emotional appeals and the "predetermined conclusion." In Doob's definition, propaganda refers to a well-planned campaign of carefully orchestrated messages and cues that would lead the ordinary person to a specified conclusion. Take, for example, Leni Reifenstahl's 1934 pro-Nazi film *Triumph of the Will*. Throughout the film we see row upon row and rank upon rank of German troops as far as the camera's eye can see. The ranks and columns are all giving the "Heil Hitler" salute and raising their flags and banners. All of this is accompanied by stirring martial music, marching troops, Hitler Youth brigades beating drums, and flames burning from "eternal" torches. Above it all stands Adolf Hitler, looking out over the crowds as if to fix each person with his gaze. He begins to speak, quietly at first, but then building volume until he is almost screaming his message. The crowd roars back, "Seig Heil!" as the camera focuses on Hitler's emotion-laden face, dripping with sweat from his exertion. Even viewers who didn't know either German or history would understand the "suggestion" given by the filmic cues. A less spectacular example of suggestion might be a picture of a car wreck accompanied by the words "Don't let a friend drink and drive."

J. Driencourt, a French student of political science, defined propaganda this way: "Propaganda is everything" (Taylor, 1979). Of course, that isn't very helpful in distinguishing propaganda from other communication forms, as we have noted. To Joseph Goebbels, the Nazi minister of propaganda, it had to be covert: "Propaganda becomes ineffective the moment we are aware of it" (Taylor, 1979, p. 23).

J. A. C. Brown (1963), a British scholar interested in propaganda, emphasized several critical points as he developed a definition. First, he said propaganda is a "scheme for propagating a doctrine or practice for influencing the emotional attitudes" (p. 12). So, not all communication is propaganda—it must propose a doctrine,

a dogma, or an ideology aimed at people's emotional state, not their rational state. Under this definition, most advertising is not propagandistic *unless* it promotes an ideology. (Some would argue that advertising does promote an ideology: conspicuous consumption.) Under Brown's definition, most religious communication would be considered propagandistic because it espouses a dogma and makes use of emotional, not logical, appeals. Under this definition, most governmental communication would be considered propaganda, since it promotes the ideologies of democracy and capitalism.

Brown adds another stipulation to distinguish propaganda from argumentation. He says that in propaganda, the "answers are determined in advance" (p. 13). All propaganda attempts to change people's minds, but not all mind changing is propaganda; if there is an honest interchange of argument, or group discussions without hidden agendas, that is not propaganda. A court trial is not propaganda either—it espouses no dogma, and the final outcome isn't predetermined. Legislative debate over policy issues may use some of the techniques of propaganda, but as a whole, it is not propaganda, as the outcome isn't known in advance.

Propaganda is always *against* something at the same time that it is *for* something else—the communication isn't propaganda if there are no alternatives. There can be propaganda by censorship also. Brown points out that it wouldn't have been propaganda to teach that the Earth is the center of the solar system in pre-Copernican times, but it would have been propaganda to suppress, censor, or conceal the ideas of Copernicus or Galileo, as was done by the Catholic Church until 1822. Propaganda nearly always conceals something: the purpose of the propagandist, the means used to achieve the purpose, and so on. The distinction between education and propaganda is this: "The former tells people *how* to think; the latter tells them *what* to think" (Brown, p. 21). However, according to the *Soviet Political Dictionary* of the

1960s, propaganda and education are equivalent: Propaganda is "the intensive elucidation of the writings of Marx, Engels, Lenin and Stalin and of the history of the Bolshevik Party and its tasks" (Brown, p. 21). Doesn't that sound like education? Brown points out how this blurring could be carried out even in such "bias-free" subjects as mathematics. He reported the research of one social scientist who found that in a widely used American math textbook there were over 600 problems that focused on such "capitalistic" concepts as rent, interest, and investments. Yet you and I would be unlikely to think that the math book was propagandistic. Finally, propaganda has to be "part of a deliberate scheme for indoctrination" (Brown, p. 22).

What do you think?

What are some advantages of Brown's definition of propaganda?

Other people (including Jacques Ellul, whose theory we will examine later) maintain that in a technocracy propaganda is the combined rules, ordinances, administrative directives, patterns of living and learning, and social graces of the modern political state. It also is an automatic extension of a technological society and may be covert or overt (Ellul, 1979). In other words, much of the contemporary technocratic culture is propaganda in their view. Figure 13.1 demonstrates the use of propaganda during the American Revolution.

Propaganda scholar Dierdre Johnson (1994) suggests that propaganda messages fall along a continuum, ranging from pure propaganda to no propaganda; many messages are only partially propaganda, using some propaganda devices. She does agree with our definition here, noting that three critical elements in any propaganda message are concealment, manipulation, and the short-circuiting of logical reasoning by using emotional arguments and suggestion. As she notes, "It's a matter of degree."

Propaganda experts Anthony Pratkanis and Elliot Aronson (1992) agree with Johnson that "not all persuasion is propaganda," and they remind us that the conception of propaganda has developed from the view that it was something that only the "villains" used to a more contemporary view that it means "mass 'suggestion' or influence through the manipulation of symbols and the psychology of the individual" (p. 9).

Jowatt and O'Donnell (1992) support the views of Johnson and of Pratkanis and Aronson. They trace the development of propaganda from its official, rather benign beginnings in the seventeenth century with the Vatican's *Sacra Congregatio de Propaganda Fide,* to the idea that only the bad guys use propaganda, to a more current communication perspective focusing on all the elements of the SMCR model, showing that propaganda is "a subcategory of persuasion as well as information" (p. 3). Jowatt and O'Donnell also identify terms often used as substitutes for propaganda (such as deceit, brainwashing, psychological warfare, and distortion), but they note that these words really just describe the characteristics of propaganda messages, not the goal of the propaganda — the crucial element to focus on. The propagandist's goal or purpose implies deliberate intent, which, they say, "is linked with a clear institutional ideology. . . . In fact, the purpose of propaganda is to send out an ideology to an audience with a related objective" (p. 2). What might be the ideology in Figure 13.2?

So, not all communication we get via the mass media is propaganda by our definition. You can identify messages that clearly are propaganda or that border on being propaganda. Being able to identify propaganda reduces its effectiveness and perhaps even makes it harmless. Knowing *what* propaganda is is only a part of the story; we also need to know *how* the propagandist works. What tactics are used and how can we identify them?

Figure 13.1. *Here is an early use of propaganda: a depiction of the Boston Massacre engraved, printed, and sold by Paul Revere. It tells only one side of the story, and Revere's goal is not clear. (Used by permission of The New York Historical Society, New York City.)*

MOSCOW, 1993

For Jews in the former Soviet Union, the exit signs are clearly marked.

The signs are all too familiar. Brown-shirted fascists march. Synagogues mysteriously go up in flames. Right-wing extremist Vladimir Zhirinovsky rants against Jews and "Zionist plots." And his party wins more votes than any other in Russia.

Once again, opportunists blame terrible conditions on their traditional scapegoat—the Jews.

And for Jews, anti–Semitism just adds to the misery of life in the former Soviet Union: Severe economic hardship. Political instability. The depressing lack of opportunity for an education, for a better life.

But there is hope. Operation Exodus.

So far, the UJA–Federation Operation Exodus Campaign has helped rescue 500,000 Jews from the former Soviet Union—69,132 in 1993 alone. And brought them home to Israel.

Yet, 1.4 million Jews remain. With your support, they can leave the hatred and despair behind. Before it's too late.

Please give generously to Operation Exodus and the Annual Campaign. This time we can clearly see what's happening over there. And all the signs point in the same direction. Out.

Figure 13.2. *This ad uses emotional language in describing what it is like to live in a totalitarian state. What parts of the description fit the definition of propaganda given in this chapter? (Reprinted with permission of United Jewish Appeal, Inc.)*

The Tactics of Propaganda

From the early concern over propaganda and its power to move entire nations in World Wars I and II up to the present, people have made numerous attempts to identify the tactics propagandists use. The Institute for Propaganda Analysis identified certain devices, and many teachers taught them (Miller, 1937). In fact, some of you may be familiar with them. They are a good place to begin the study of propaganda tactics.

Plain Folks

The "**plain folks**" tactic is used by propagandists to convince the audience that the public figures or groups they represent are not well trained, shrewd, and manipulative but are just "plain folks" like you and me. Politicians are using this device when they put on bib overalls, don work boots, and wipe their brow with a red bandanna while talking with a back-country drawl. Sometimes the technique is as simple as using common language to appeal to the audience. The tactic might take the form of plain, everyday actions such as splitting wood or driving a tractor.

These devices use pretense to create identification between source and receiver. Such sources are not plain folks at all. Instead, they are trying to manipulate the audience into following their call through a false feeling of kinship. A recent example of the plain folks technique can be seen in the campaign that billionaire (and definitely not "plain") H. Ross Perot waged while seeking the presidency in 1992 and that he continues to wage under the banner of the Reform Party. He uses sentences and phrases reminiscent of backwoods common sense. For example, during the campaign he referred to politicians as a bunch of "slow dancin' bureaucrats," and during the televised debate over the North American Free Trade Agreement (NAFTA), he referred to the un-workability of the treaty by saying "This huntin' dog just won't hunt." Public relations appeals frequently use the plain folks technique. In the face of falling enrollments and complaints that my university was not "user friendly," the president, all his staff, and the deans of colleges showed up at the dorms on "move-in" day dressed in N.I.U. T-shirts to "help" the students unload and move into their rooms. While not propaganda, because no ideology was being promoted and nothing was concealed (though the photo opportunity was used to publicize the event), this public relations appeal did use the plain folks approach.

Testimonial

The **testimonial** is a familiar device in today's world of advertising, where well-known celebrities or athletes tell us why we should buy this product or that. Under our definition of propaganda, this use of the testimonial is not propagandistic, but other uses of testimonials are clearly propaganda. Brief examples include refugees who testify about atrocities committed by the government in their homeland, persons held captive by terrorists relating their experience, or a prime minister testifying as to the difficulties of dismantling apartheid in South Africa.

In all these examples, the audience cannot tell whether the people giving the testimony are actually reliable sources of information. They might be dupes of some government. Furthermore, we do not know for certain what the goal of the source is. Did the hostage become converted to the terrorists' ideology? (This sometimes happens.) Have the refugees been duped by their spokespersons? and what will be the outcome if we follow the advice of the testimonials? These are but a few of the concealed elements in these testimonials. Of course, there are also many testimonials that do not promote any particular ideology or dogma: A customer of the bank tells of the great service he or she got, or a recent purchaser of a muffler tells about how much she saved by going to Magic Muffler instead of Midas. Neither of these qualifies as propaganda by our definition, although both are probably effective advertising P.R.

Bandwagon

Propagandists, like some advertisers, try to convince the audience that it is *almost* too late to take advantage of the offer, to join the organization, to follow the fad, to vote for the candidate, to be contemporary — to get on the **bandwagon.** The history of the word "bandwagon" gives us a clue to the basic intent behind the appeal. When the circus came to town in the nineteenth century, part of the razzmatazz used to attract customers was the circus parade along the village main street. The first wagon in the parade was always the bandwagon. Being on the bandwagon became synonymous with being a leader — a person who was "out in front" of an idea or a fashion. When you receive a pitch such as "Sign the petition now! Send a wake-up call to the legislature! The people's rights before the rights of capitalistic corporations!" Those phrases are tipoffs. The time limit and the stress on joining "the people" suggest that everyone is getting on the "bandwagon" — don't miss out.

Again, H. Ross Perot's 1992 and 1996 presidential campaigns are examples of the power of the bandwagon effect. Initially his cause went unnoticed, but as he bought more and more television time, individuals in almost every community circulated petitions to put Perot and his Reform Party on the ballot in their state. Urgency was stressed, and many persons signed the petitions simply because many of their friends and neighbors had signed. Signing the petition didn't necessarily mean that you supported Perot — only that he and his party should have the right to be considered on the ballot. The petitions were appeals to "get on the bandwagon."

Card Stacking

Building an overwhelming case on one side of an issue while concealing another, perhaps equally persuasive, side is called **card stacking.** Of course, few persuaders try to tell both sides of a story, but responsible persuaders at least suggest that there *are* other sides. With card stacking, however, the other side may not even be recognized, or it may be downplayed or possibly denigrated. Thus, the audience gets only one version of the story. A good example is the Clinton Administration's promotion of its national health care plan — no mention was made of the drawbacks cited by critics or of other proposals for reforming health care. The abortion issue is another example — clearly both sides "stack the cards" with overwhelming evidence. Another example is the current debate over cigarette advertising aimed at teenagers. Both sides of the debate tell *their* side of the story with *overwhelming* mountains of facts and testimony. Public relations firms often use scads of evidence to stack the cards on behalf of their clients also. Critical receivers try to identify at least the existence of another side.

Transfer

The propaganda technique called **transfer** is similar to Rank's "association" tactic for intensification. For example, a politician is photographed in front of the U.S. Capitol Building, and the aura of the U.S. government and historic Washington, D.C., is transferred to the candidate. The transfer implies that the candidate is a patriot who will follow in the footsteps of the great leaders of the past.

Transfer also resembles an endorsement or a testimonial in that the credibility of the endorser transfers to the product. In international politics, Saddam Hussein was compared to Hitler. Hitler's negative aspects transferred to the Saudi dictator. In Illinois, calling a politician a "machine democrat" links him or her with Chicago and transfers the negativity of the Chicago political machine to the candidate. On the other hand, calling the candidate a "downstate" politician dissociates him or her from the Chicago machine and transfers the positive aspects of small-town Illinois to the candidate.

To destroy credibility, the opposition is linked to an undesirable action, person, or organization. The candidate is linked to big business, lobbyists, the CIA, or organized crime, and any negative loading for these groups transfers to the candidate and ruins his or her credibility. In the mid-nineties, PLO leader and terrorist Yasir Arafat used transfer to build his credibility and to initiate a return to Palestine of lands won by Israel in the 1967 war. He discussed the problem with high-visibility world-class politicians — the U.S. secretary of state, prime ministers, and presidents. Their reputations, suggestions, and actions transferred their credibility to Arafat. The transfer was so effective that he was denounced by and targeted for assassination by leaders of PLO splinter groups. His success may have contributed to the assassination of Israeli prime minister Yitzhak Rabin. Again the transfer technique is used in public relations. The credibility/ visibility of some celebrity is used to transfer credibility/visibility to a particular brand, candidate, good cause, or organization.

Glittering Generalities

Abstract language, highly charged with emotion and cultural values, is used by propagandists because of its power. Such words seem to "glitter" with high purpose and energy that can short-circuit people's reasoning process and make them jump to conclusions. Words such as "justice," "freedom," "dignity," "equality," "patriot," "integrity," and "wisdom" are actually not very specific, yet they pluck at powerful emotions in audiences. Who hasn't heard some political speaker introducing a candidate who is "*dedicated* to the con-

tinuance of *justice* for all in this great nation of ours; who has worked *diligently* for our *freedom* and *dignity*, fighting for *equality*. My friends, I give you a *patriot* of great *integrity* and *wisdom* — Senator Fogbound!" Later, of course, the voters may discover that Fogbound drinks too much, sexually harasses his assistants, and has been videotaped taking bribes.

The **glittering generalities** of the advertising world are only slightly less emotional and vague. Some examples are "*heavy duty*," "*youthful*," "*vitality*," "*jumbo*," "*old-fashioned*," "*homemade*," and "*glamorous*." No one has ever heard of a *light-duty* battery or a *medium-duty* vacuum cleaner, just as no one has ever heard of a *small* or *medium* shrimp — they come in only three sizes: *colossal*, *mammoth*, and *jumbo*. Leaf through any popular magazine and you will find hundreds of glittering generalities like these. Of course, in these cases the glittering generalities aren't being used to market an ideology or dogma, so, under our definition, they don't qualify as propaganda.

Name Calling

The other side of glittering generalities is **name calling:** using words that have high negative loadings to smear another person or group. For example, we might call a certain religious group "a bunch of zealous, fanatical Jesus freaks" to make the group seem on the fringe and unpredictable or wild-eyed. During World War II, Germans were called *huns*, *krauts*, or *heinies* and Japanese were called *Japs* or *nips*; during the Korean and Vietnam wars, the enemies were called *gooks*, *slants*, *slopes*, or *Charlies*. Why? These names reduced the enemy to the level of brutes with low intelligence and apelike behavior. The current controversy over "political correctness" called attention to the power of name calling. For example, at Penn State University a student was almost dismissed under the campus speech code's ban on "hate speech" (a term that turns up frequently in speech codes). He had called a group of black women "water buffaloes," and though the charges were ultimately dismissed, his case drew national attention to the political correctness issue and to the name calling.

Contemporary Perspectives on Propaganda

With the advances of research on the formation and alteration of attitudes, theorists took a new look at propaganda during the 1960s and 1970s. J. A. C. Brown, whom we met earlier in this chapter, took a look at propaganda from this more modern perspective. He identified several prerequisites for propaganda and the stages through which propaganda passes. Brown surprised many critics of propaganda because he rejected the "propaganda as deceit" and "brainwashing" approaches. Instead, he held that to be truly successful, propaganda has to tell not lies but the truth. What makes the propaganda effective is the way in which the truth is interpreted by the propagandist. Brown (1963) quoted an official of the British Broadcasting Corporation (BBC) commenting on British propaganda in the war:

> Do not say anything which you do not believe to correspond with the facts as known to you; and secondly do not say anything to one country, or audience, which is or looks inconsistent with what you are saying to any other country or audience. (p. 94)

This makes perfect sense in terms of our old friend credibility. If you use lies and are caught, you destroy your credibility. However, if you interpret the truth to your own advantage, only your interpretation can be questioned. We know that during World War II many persons in occupied Europe and even Germany itself listened to the BBC because it was the most credible source of news. There was a Nazi news service, but it had been caught lying too many times, and the public distrusted it. A similar shortcoming helped the overthrow of communism in the former Soviet Union. With the easing of communications restrictions, many Russians saw for the first time that they were not the country with the highest standard of living in the world — a lie they had been told for decades by their leaders.

Brown also described the stages through which propaganda passes. In the **prepropaganda stage,** propagandists want to make their messages stand out among all the competing messages. The propagandist may spend time distributing leaflets, knocking on doors, or displaying posters. The purpose of this stage is to catch the audience's *attention* by appealing to the powerful emotions already in the audience: hatred, jealousy, envy, love, fear, hope, guilt, and so on. Frequently, this is done by creating *guilt* feelings in the audience. Hitler repeatedly told his audiences that it was Germans who had *betrayed* Germany at the end of World War I. Guilt is most powerfully called up in the audience using *suggestion*. During the 1996 Democratic National Convention, actor Christopher Reeve was a key speaker. He had been paralyzed from the waist down during a horse riding accident. He reminded the convention and television audiences that one in five persons suffered from some sort of disability and that the Democratic party had always been for taking care of the downtrodden. He reminded them that Franklin Roosevelt, who could hardly lift himself from his wheelchair, had lifted the country out of the depths of the Great Depression. All of these references served to raise feelings of guilt in those who didn't have a disability or who hadn't helped someone who did have a disability, thus setting the stage for major planks in the Democratic platform — clearly a piece of propaganda by our definition.

After drawing the audience's attention and interest, the propagandist then creates *emotional tension*. Perhaps the audience is told that it has been kept from some opportunity, that its legal rights have been trampled, that its heritage has been stained, or that it has been lied to. The powerful emotional tension that is developed is *identified* with some enemy—usually an **outgroup** such as the Jews in Nazi Germany, "camel jockeys" in Iraq, the Redcoats in colonial times, or "niggers" or "honkies" in America. According to Brown, this outgroup is identified in a number of ways:

1. *Stereotyping.* Using powerful descriptive language, the outgroup is characterized with negative attributes and qualities. Thus, in propaganda the Jew is conniving, exploitative, clannish, and cheap. The black is lazy, dull, and interested only in mating. The Irish are drunkards, are dumb, and have criminal instincts. Of course there are, no doubt, some Jews, blacks, and Irish who have some of those characteristics and even some who have all of them, but the propagandist asserts that *all* Jews, blacks, or Irish have *all* these qualities.

2. *Substitution of names.* Again using powerful language, the propagandist substitutes unfavorable names for neutral ones. For example, the Jew becomes a *kike*, a *sheeny*, or a *hymie*; the black becomes a *nigger*, a *spook*, or a *coon*; and the Irish become *micks*, *lace-curtain Irish*, or *shanty Irish*. Other epithets include *redneck*, *capitalist pig*, *dirty communist*, and *diaper head*.

3. *Repetition.* Propaganda tells the same tale over and over again using similar language, examples, and references. Goebbels thought that the masses would believe anything if you told the "big lie" enough times. We see this approach used all the time in slogans and jingles.

4. *Pinpointing the enemy.* Specific members of the outgroup are selected as representing the worst aspects of the stereotype: Jewish bankers or pawnshop owners; black rapists, pimps, or whores; Irish drunks, cops, or mobsters. These are especially powerful if they fit with the preexisting patterns in the audience's experience, thus explaining why using the Jew as an enemy scapegoat worked so well in Europe, where there existed a long pattern of anti-Semitism, and why blacks are so frequently used as scapegoats here in America.

With the emotional tension built up and identified with an outgroup that has been properly denigrated and dehumanized, the propagandist can then impel the audience to action by giving them a way to relieve their tension. This almost always involves the real or symbolic destruction of the outgroup. Real destruction can involve torture, killing, and even genocide. In symbolic destruction, the outgroup is stigmatized in some way. The outgroup is segregated physically (having to step down into the gutter instead of walking on the sidewalk, or having to move to the back of the bus). They must wear some sign of negative caste (a yellow Star of David, a sign labeling them a traitor, or some other negative tattoo). Their businesses may be boycotted, and their homes, places of worship, and even their bodies may be violated in some way. The tension thus is relieved through the real or symbolic destruction.

Brown explains this process in terms of Freud's ego defense mechanisms. The symbolic killing involves *projection*, or characterizing the outgroup as having one's own weaknesses or sins. The outgroup may be the victim of *compensation*, making up for a frustrated drive by finding a substitute goal (for example, if you fail in business, you become a successful villain, and thus villainy compensates for failure). *Conformity* and *identification* permit large numbers of persons to follow a charismatic leader because they believe he or she is their voice. This sanctions whatever the leader decides to do.

Finally, propaganda is most likely to emerge in the *modern state*, in which individuals are isolated (as you may now feel if you are on a large campus), unknown, and helpless to control their own destiny. The supporters of many propagandistic mass movements are the uneducated or the unemployed—those who feel helpless and hence find the movement attractive because it promises change. Feelings of loneliness are removed by becoming a member of a group. The group offers individuals substitute identification and value. Furthermore, a group, and especially a crowd, is likely to behave more emotionally than any single individual. *Mob psychology* can take over, and violent acts (lynchings, gang rapes, stonings, riots, and so on) are committed in the hysteria. Further, since the guilt is shared by the group, no one individual need feel remorse. As Brown says, "Each society has its own kind of circus and hopes that after the performance is ended, the participants will return less reluctantly to their dull round of daily life" (p. 73). Propaganda provides the tickets to the circus.

Jowatt and O'Donnell's Perspective

Propaganda scholars Garth Jowatt and Victoria O'Donnell (1992) helped us define propaganda earlier in this chapter. Having defined the beast, they provide us with a ten-stage model that helps us identify and analyze propaganda. Let us explore these stages.

Determining the Ideology and Purpose of the Propaganda Campaign. In the first stage, the propaganda analyst looks for statements and images that express a set of attitudes, beliefs, and values and any other evidence that might indicate a world view—in other words, an ideology. Persuasion scholars Martha Cooper and William Nothstine (1992) maintain that ideology "consists of a multiplicity of messages that . . . func-

tion ideologically if they instill or strengthen a particular view of the world in the minds of their receivers" (p. 339) and that such world views combine to create culture. Any statements or images that give the target audience a way to judge good from evil or rightness from wrongness or that suggest there are certain classes or conducts that are desirable or undesirable should tip us off to the presence of a propaganda campaign.

Examining the Context in Which the Propaganda Occurs. The second stage for propaganda analysis is to look at the context in which the propaganda occurs. One aspect of context is the prevailing climate of opinion. For example, during the late 1980s and early 1990s, many programs and practices were justified in terms of the degree to which they were ecologically sound or were healthful. "Reuse, Reduce, and Recycle" became bywords, as did "high fiber," "low sodium," and "no fat." In this stage the propaganda analyst looks for what the public expects from society, what sorts of issues concern people, how the issues can be resolved, and what will the resolution cost in human and material ways. Evidently, Bill Clinton identified American concern over the mushrooming costs of health care (especially for the elderly) as making up part of the prevailing climate of opinion and thus focused parts of his candidacy and presidency on repairing the health system. Climates of opinion are constantly shifting. Japan was our enemy in World War II, our dependent during its postwar rebuilding, our source for inexpensive labor and productivity in the 1950s and 1960s, our competitor in the 1970s and 1980s, and perhaps even our economic enemy in the 1990s. According to Jowatt and O'Donnell, cultural myths, such as those explored in Chapter 9, are another indication of a propaganda campaign being under way.

Identifying the Propagandist. In the third stage we are urged to pinpoint the source of the propaganda. Is it coming from some sort of institution (a church, a political party, or any other group attempting to affect public policy)? Jowatt and O'Donnell suggest asking "Who or what has the most to gain from this?" any time you suspect that propaganda is present. Of course, the ultimate beneficiaries may not be evident until years hence. However, asking the question is sometimes like turning over a stone—you may find something creepy or crawly. When the propagandist is a person, Jowatt and O'Donnell advise looking at his or her style, or as Doob (1966) called it, the person's "verbal compulsions" (p. 274). Another thing to question is the individual propagandist's affiliations—he or she may be acting as a "front" for an institution. With whom, for example, does Rush Limbaugh affiliate? Which politicians or political parties? Which industries? Which churches?

> **What do you think?**
>
> Could rap music be used for propaganda?

Analyzing the Structure of the Propaganda Organization.

This stage of analysis is probably one of the most difficult to accomplish. Many organizations consider their goals and practices to be private and proprietary. Nonetheless, there are several ways we can study the structure of the propaganda organization. We should look for any hint of a hierarchy and investigate how those at the top got there. For example, in my community there is an organization that uses propaganda; known as D.A.R.E., or the Dekalb Alliance for Responsible Energy, it wants to severely restrict and even cut back on the use of nuclear energy. The group's leadership is known and can be studied.

Another element in the structure of the propaganda organization, according to Jowatt and O'Donnell, is the propagandist's specific goals and the means being used to achieve them. These would include both long- and short-term goals as well as the media or other techniques used to disseminate the propaganda. Why, for example, does Pat Robertson's 700 Club choose television as its medium of dissemination? To generate funds? To make the propaganda seem more personalized? Or could it be that Robertson wants to "maintain a presence in the market" so he can run for president of the United States? We could also look at an organization's slogans, emblems (such as the swastika), uniforms (Fidel Castro and his supporters wear army fatigues), rituals and rules, and any other ways in which the member of the organization behaves uniformly.

Determining the Target Audience.

Just as our whole society has become fragmented, so has the process of identifying the target audience of any propaganda. Suppose that you were working for the NRA to recruit new members and to get support for opposing handgun legislation. Who would be your target audience, and how could you get your propaganda to them? In all probability, the most likely targets are persons who already own handguns, which must be registered in many states. You could possibly purchase lists of handgun owners in these states. State governments frequently "sell" their data on a variety of dimensions, and their handgun registrants might be such a dimension. Another target would be persons who own shotguns or rifles—they might be sympathetic to your cause. Again, many state governments sell their lists of persons who have bought a hunting license, and you could target those persons. You might also purchase subscriber lists from magazines such as *Outdoor Life*, *Sports Afield*, *Pheasants Forever*, and *Fin and Feather*. There are also fishing and hunting programs on specialized television stations like ESPN, and fishing often goes hand-in-hand with hunting among people's interests. When we get down to this kind of targeting, the propagandist is using a "rifle" instead of a "shotgun" approach to market segmentation.

Identifying Media Utilization Techniques. We need to know not only which media are being used in the propaganda campaign but also how they are being used. For example, during both the '92 and '96 presidential campaigns, H. Ross Perot's use of television featured the technique of the infomercial—a half-hour or longer "show" in which the propagandist/persuader can go into detail on a variety of issues. Another medium of choice is the documentary. We tend to respond to documentaries as if they represent objective reality when frequently they only represent the documentary maker's point of view. Propagandists usually try to appeal to the emotions, through the use of music and explicit images of emotion-laden situations or places (such as showing fetuses in the wastebasket of an abortion clinic, starving prisoners in Serbian concentration camps, gaunt-looking homeless persons). Other media techniques that propagandists use include camera and lens movement and editing techniques to give a "documentary" feel.

Noting Special Techniques to Maximize Effect. Jowatt and O'Donnell note that Joseph Goebbels, Hitler's propaganda minister, believed that any means that could be used to propagate Nazism was acceptable. One such technique was using the school classroom as a propaganda device, with instructors "teaching" their students to be good Nazis, even if it meant betraying family and friends. Another was the formation of the *Hitler Jugend* (Hitler Youth) and the *Schulerbund*, or Students' League. Chanting, singing, and saluting are other unifying techniques, as are many of the methods described by Eric Hoffer in Chapter 10.

Another special technique used in propaganda is brainwashing, in which the targets of propaganda are prisoners of war. In the Korean war, for example, prisoners were forced to repeat communist ideology over and over again and to humiliate themselves by "confessing" to be filthy American capitalists. More recently, religious groups like the Moonies, Branch Davidians, or Hare Krishnas would entice college students and others to awareness weekends during which brainwashing was used to convert the unsuspecting attendees. They were isolated at the session, then questioned and induced to renounce their previous religion, their parents, and so on. Once thoroughly indoctrinated, they were sent out to beg for money at airports, on city streets, and so on. Some parents of these converts ultimately resorted to having their child "kidnapped" away from the religious groups and then having them "deprogrammed" back to normality.

Identifying Predispositions of the Audience. You have seen the famous "Daisy" ad in which several verbal and nonverbal as well as audio and video techniques resonated with the average voter of 1964 when the ad was aired. The ad featured a little girl walking on a flowery hillside picking the petals from a daisy while counting to ten. At the count of ten, the action froze, and the camera zoomed into her face and ultimately to her eye as the audio track played a "countdown" for a nuclear detonation. At the end of the countdown, detonation occurred and a huge mushroom cloud rose to take over the whole screen. The announcer then said something like "Vote for President Johnson on November 4th—The stakes are too great not to." Voters had experienced being afraid of the possibility of nuclear war, and the ad played on these predispositions to convince them to reject Barry Goldwater as being "trigger happy" with nuclear weapons. As Jowatt and O'Donnell (1992) put it:

> The propagandist uses belief to create belief by linking or reinforcing audience predispositions to reinforce propagandistic philosophy. . . . Rather than change political loyalties, racial and religious

attitudes, and other deeply held beliefs, the propagandist voices the propagandee's feelings about these things. (p. 222)

In propaganda analysis, one must try to gauge audience reactions to the various techniques being used. These reactions indicate the success or failure of the techniques. Jowatt and O'Donnell stress the need to look at audience behaviors rather than at opinion polls. Does the propagandees' voting behavior indicate success? Do they donate time or money to the cause? Are they willing to form local groups or suborganizations to carry out the work of the propaganda? Do they take on a new symbolic identity (as is the case with many cults, where joiners even get new names)? How do they talk about the propaganda? These are all behaviors that can be assessed if one suspects that propaganda is being used successfully.

Identifying Counterpropaganda.

When we discussed successful campaigns back in Chapter 10, we noted that those promoting a product, candidate, or cause knew they were successful at the penetration stage of the Yale model when their competitors responded by bringing out a "me-too" version of the product or when competing candidates or causes addressed messages to them. The same holds true for propaganda: An indicator that propaganda exists and is succeeding is that it gets a response. The Polish union "Solidarity" knew that its propaganda was succeeding when it was outlawed, and the populace was propagandized by the then-ruling Communist Party of Poland. Forced underground by the official government, Solidarity continued its propaganda battle, and as we now know, it was ultimately successful in ending communism in Poland. Jowatt and O'Donnell point out that democratic reformers in both Poland and Czechoslovakia used satellite broadcasting to propagandize the people to resist the state, and as in Poland, they were ul-

timately able to unseat the existing governments. Certainly the emergence of the pro-life movement indicated the success of pro-choice advocates, especially in the face of *Roe v. Wade*. Pro-life counterpropaganda emerged to compete with abortion rights propaganda.

Assessing Effects.

Finally, as Jowatt and O'Donnell suggest, the propaganda analyst should try to assess the immediate and long-range effects of the propaganda under consideration. For example, the immediate effects of pro-life propaganda were initially limited. However, in the long term, some states passed legislation limiting abortion rights, requiring that parents of minors be informed of and agree to the abortion, and so on. The long-range effects of pro-life propaganda may ultimately be revision of the *Roe v. Wade* decision. The short-range effects of the propaganda urging U.S. withdrawal from the Vietnam war seemed minimal at first, but the long-range effects of that propaganda were influential in many ways. The United States finally did withdraw from the war, President Johnson decided not to run again, exemptions from compulsory military service were done away with, and compulsory military service was then abolished. We still feel many long-range effects of this propaganda, such as serious questioning of sending military forces to any country, even if the action is sanctioned by the United Nations. The propaganda currently being used to promote "diversity" and "multiculturalism" has not had very major effects, but ten years from now we may discover major changes in our social fabric as a result.

Jowatt and O'Donnell suggest examining a number of possible symptoms of the success or failure of any propaganda. Growth or decline in membership of the organization sponsoring the propaganda is one symptom. Other symptoms include adjustments in mainstream society (such as no prayer in public schools or no more segregated restrooms); changes in personal and social behaviors (such as no longer sitting in the back of the bus); and changes in the use of language throughout society (saying or writing "Native American" instead of "Indian")." Of course, the most significant effect (other than a revolution) is the passing of legislation favoring the propagandist's position (such as passage of the Civil Rights Act of 1964).

In Jowatt and O'Donnell's eyes, there are several ways to limit the results of any propaganda, even when the entire story and some details are not unearthed until years later. The most important thing is for receivers to alert themselves to the presence of potential propaganda and then to study it in depth, using these ten and other possible approaches to propaganda analysis.

Jacques Ellul's Perspective

A common feeling in the final decade of the twentieth century seems to be that everything is out of control—the machine is about to go smash. We are all familiar with the incredible mountains of information—more then we can handle—available to us on a variety of fronts. We know only too well the insignificance of our individual efforts to reduce the deficit, clean up the environment, help the poor, or *really* make a difference. We all realize that change is occurring so fast that it is impossible to keep up. It is like a bad dream I have. My shoes are made of lead, and they stick to the ground. I can't catch the departing train, no matter how hard I try to run. These feelings are apparently common for persons living in highly sophisticated technological societies. Jacques Ellul, a French sociopolitician and theologian, has discussed these feelings and their causes using a concept he calls **la technique.** La technique includes all the rules, ordinances, patterns of behavior, forms to be filled out, directions, values, administrative orders, and so on

that characterize any modern bureaucracy. Then add all the technology that is necessary for efficiently carrying out the orders. Then you have la technique, or the modern political **technocracy.** As Ellul says:

> The first great fact which emerges from our civilization is that today everything has become means. There is no longer an end; we do not know whither we are going. We have forgotten our collective ends and we possess great means: we set huge machines in motion in order to arrive nowhere. (Christians & Van Hook, 1981, p. 21)

La technique has at least three aspects. First are **economic techniques** (investment, capital, profit, loss, inflation, deflation, taxes, welfare, and budgeting, to name a few). Then there are **political techniques** (laws, electoral processes, the courts, organizations, government, administrators, and so on). Finally, there are **human techniques** (advertising, public opinion polling, attitude testing, evangelism, time study, and demographics are a few examples). Each of these aspects of la technique is essential to the others, and each is typical of the modern technocracy in which we live.

How different this view of propaganda is when compared with earlier views—even ones as contemporary and well conceived as J. A. C. Brown's. Here, propaganda is frightening not because of its use of deceptive gimmicks or the power of modern media but because it is so pervasive, ever present, and at the same time so apparently benign. It is not something *they* do; it is rather something *we* do. Each of us experiences propaganda every day from childhood on, and we probably approve of it. This makes it all the more difficult for us to identify, evaluate, and accept or reject. Furthermore, the technology binge we are on seems endless—no one can turn it off. Critics of Ellul have said that facing la technique is like saying, "The kitchen has burned, and the intellectuals keep writing cookbooks; the boats have sunk, and the people on the life rafts still worry about time schedules" (Jowatt & O'Donnell, 1986, pp. 69–70).

Propaganda and Technology

Ellul's description of propaganda comes closer to what Jowatt and O'Donnell describe as "The New Audience" influenced by "The Emergence of Mass Society," which seems to devour and believe everything "The New Media" tells them is true. They trace this depersonalizing process beginning with the penny press of the 1830s. During the Civil War, media were used by the North and the South to propagandize against each other. Following the war, the print medium was repeatedly used for propaganda—the sinking of the battleship *Maine* and the resulting Spanish American War is a good example.

Particularly interesting are the ways in which the technology of film was used for propaganda purposes from its earliest years. A few of the titles of propaganda films during these early years give one a feel for how they might have appeared. *Tearing Down the Spanish Flag,* produced during the Spanish American War, was nothing more than a flagpole flying the Spanish flag, whereupon it was torn down and the American flag was raised in its stead, which had "sensational" effects on the audiences. During World War I, films such as *The Kaiser, The Beast of Berlin,* and *Battle Cry of Peace* (1915) showed Germans attacking and demolishing New York City. The most famous propaganda film of the early years was the Russian-produced *Potemkin* (1925), which justified the Bolshevik Revolution to the Russian people, most of whom couldn't read but all of whom could look at a movie screen and see the brutality of the czar and his troops.

What do you think?
What are the possible propaganda uses of the Internet?

In the years between the world wars, Hollywood dominated the movie screens around the world—a precursor of the "cultural imperialism" noted previously. My father's decision to come to this country in 1929 was partially influenced by the vision of America and its tremendous economic opportunities that he saw on movie screens. Also, the new wave of immigration that began at the turn of the century and continued until the Great Depression provided an eager audience for whatever American filmmakers could produce. Immigrants were illiterate but could still watch the screen. This example recalls Meyrowitz's observations about literacy and television: Media with simple access codes can be powerful in influencing people who have minimal or no literacy.

With the rise of nazism in Germany, the Soviet film industry turned out large numbers of anti-fascist propaganda films. Not until 1939 did Hollywood produce its first anti-fascist propaganda film, *Confessions of a Nazi Spy,* and until the United States entered the war in late 1941, "propaganda" films were mainly recruiting devices, such as *Devil Dogs of the Air* and *Here Comes the Navy.* And even after we got into the war, less than a third of the films produced actually dealt with it. Jowatt and O'Donnell note of this period that "American films were most successful when they stressed positive themes particularly as they depicted normal life on the home-front or the inner strength of the ordinary fighting men."

Radio, developing at the same time as film, was recognized early on as a potential propaganda medium. Lenin described it as a "newspaper without paper . . . and without boundaries" and directed its development to communicate Communist ideology to the illiterate peasants at home and in other countries. By 1922 Moscow had the most powerful radio station in the world, broadcasting its propaganda in a variety of languages. The fascist governments of Germany and Italy soon broadcast in a variety of languages aimed at North and South America, Africa, and Asia. Radio Tokyo began propaganda broadcasting in 1936. During World War II, the BBC was the major broadcaster of Allied propaganda. Soon more than eighty nations were broadcasting some kind of radio propaganda (for example, the Voice of America, Radio Moscow, the BBC, Radio Peking, and All Asia Service out of Sri Lanka). Radio as an economical and efficient propaganda technology has great impact in third-world countries, where it is not uncommon to see a peasant listening to a Walkman while plowing the land with oxen.

Although television has not been frequently used for direct propaganda, its impact in the area of "cultural imperialism" has been immense. Most third-world programming comes from the United States, Great Britain, and West Germany. Each year the United States alone sells 150,000 hours of programming to other countries, conveying American values, fashions, and capitalist ideology. The programming area that is most propagandistic is news reporting, which has raised the issue of the "free flow" of information between the Western world and developing nations. Here is where the third world becomes distorted. We see pictures of famines, revolutions, fanatical dictators, and conflict, instead of stories about positive developments. We naturally come to believe that the negative situations are the entire "third-world story."

One of the most potentially exploitable communication technologies is the 8mm videotape/camcorder. In many countries, American films are outlawed. However, copies can be smuggled in easily and dubbed onto multiple tapes. Thus begins a flourishing underground trade in these "forbidden" films. In the late 1980s, for example, an X-rated video called *Playboy Lovers* was brought into the Philippines. On it most of the pornography had been erased and replaced by a documentary on the assassination of opposition leader Benigno Aquino. The tape was duplicated many times over

and was seen by large numbers of people, thus helping to shape their attitudes toward the Marcos regime. The X-rated video became an "envelope" for anti-Marcos propaganda, which eventually led to the revolution and expulsion of the dictator.

This brief history of examples of how technological developments lead to increased and more efficient propaganda underscores what Ellul is saying.

What can you and I do about propaganda having the dimensions of la technique? More important, what can we *realistically* do? Ellul (1973) describes la technique as "an indispensable condition for the development of technical progress and the establishment of a technological civilization" and says it "has become an inescapable necessity for everyone" (p. 95).

A brief example of the dilemma may help. One of the major myths put forward by la technique is that *progress* is good—it is desirable to improve our products, our processes, our bodies, our minds, our lot in life, and a host of other things—and progress is seen as improvement. You and I have no future without progress. That piece of propaganda is essential to you and me. At the same time, I know I should do something about the myth of progress—accept it, reject it, or something. Most of us find ways to anesthetize our dependency (and la technique frequently supplies them): television, narcotics, family, alcohol, pleasure, the "me generation," careers, sex, "surfing" the Web, and the cult of the self are all ways.

Ellul (1973) emphasizes, however, that just because la technique is necessary doesn't mean it is therefore good and to be fostered. Rather,

necessity never establishes legitimacy; the world of necessity is a world of weakness, a world that denies man. To say that a phenomenon is *necessary* means, for me, that it denies man; its necessity is proof of its power, not proof of its excellence. However, confronted by a necessity, man must become *aware* of it if he is to master it. . . . Only when he realizes his delusion will he experience the beginning of genuine freedom—in the act of realization itself. (pp. xv–xvi)

Can we do this? Can we step back from our hectic culture and at least identify the many myths that keep us twitching? Ellul seems to think so; he says the probable alternative is a life in which

> man will be fully adapted to this technological society, when he will end by obeying with enthusiasm, convinced of the excellence of what he is forced to do, the constraint of the organization will no longer . . . be a constraint, and the police will have nothing to do. (p. xviii)

All propaganda, according to Ellul, relies to some degree on one of two basic psychological devices, the **conditioned reflex** (or the automatic, knee-jerk response) and the **myth.** "Let's put it to a vote!" might stimulate a conditioned response. Stereotypes such as that of the prissy English schoolboy, the impatient and emotional Italian, the authority-driven German, or the inscrutable Oriental might also be used to evoke conditioned responses. By a "myth," Ellul means "an all-encompassing image: a sort of vision of desirable objectives . . . [which] pushes a man to action precisely because it includes all he feels is good, just, and true" (1973, p. 30). Examples he notes are the myths of race, progress, wealth, and productivity.

According to Ellul, both the conditioned reflex and the myth are part of a *prepropaganda phase* in which people are prepared for action by being conditioned into accepting the values of a culture. When the time comes for action, the leader or the "establishment" can prompt a reflex response by appealing to people's mythic beliefs. For example, our American culture treasures the myth of democracy, which says that the wisdom of the people, when operating in a democratic fashion, leads to the best decisions and will prevail. This myth explains our overwhelmingly positive reactions to the student demonstrations in Beijing's Tienanmen Square and to the collapse of Leninism-Marxism

in former Soviet countries. The assumption is that democracy, coupled with a free marketplace, will reverse the economic and political slavery experienced by these countries. Events seem to demonstrate that the answer isn't nearly that simplistic, yet our trust in the myth of democracy continues to lead us to recommend democracy as the "best" political system for other countries.

Another myth of la technique is that efficiency is good. As long as we buy the legitimacy of this myth, we are conforming with the propaganda of la technique. What does such conformity imply? What can we do about efficiency-related issues when we disagree? An interesting example is the inefficiency of the family farm. In the film *Country*, a young family tries to make it on a family farm in the 1980s and find themselves facing the myth of efficiency. Those who believe in the myth help the bureaucracy foreclose on the loans and dispose of family belongings by bidding at auctions. However, la technique is blunted by individual action and by rephrasing the questions implied by the myth. In *Country*, instead of asking of the family farm, "Will it work?" the heroine, Jewel Ivy, asks "Is it a healthy way to bring up children? Is it a humane way to relate to other people?" Her questions turn the myth of efficiency on its head and ultimately lead the local administrator of the Farm Home Administration to quit his job rather than pursue the myth of efficiency to foreclose on the Ivy farm. Soon, however, la technique seems to work its will over the Ivys, when a bureaucrat from Washington supervises an auction of the Ivy's belongings, machinery, and tools. However, a critical action and statement is made by Jewel's son as he bids all his savings on his grandfather's horse harnesses—the ultimate symbol of inefficiency in modern farming. This act spurs the rest of the crowd to recognize that it has been duped by the myth of efficiency. They refuse to cooperate in the auction and bid ridiculously low prices—seven cents for a combine, a dime for a tractor, and so on. The bureaucrat tries to reassert the myth by threatening to haul the belongings to another county to auction them. Jewel retorts, "When you try to auction off this land and get no bids, you can't take *it* to another Goddamned county!" La technique loses.

As long as people respond with a conditioned reflex to what they have been taught about efficiency and pragmatism in the prepropaganda phase, la technique is the obvious victor. But once the questions have been rephrased to focus on *people* instead of *production*, la technique is relatively toothless. Thus, the technocracy of the federal government had to reverse its position and aid farm families in refinancing their debts.

The same approach could be used with the many other myths we embrace: the myth of progress, the myth of pleasure, the myth of production, the myth of the individual, the myth of status, the myth of success, and others. Are they humane? healthy? rewarding? These are the kinds of questions Ellul wants us to ask once we have identified the propaganda of la technique.

Eight Characteristics of Modern Propaganda

Ellul's theories of propaganda were analyzed by Clifford Christians and Michael Real (1979). On the basis of their analysis, Ellul's work can be seen as revolving around eight central ideas that help identify the propaganda of la technique.

1. Propaganda is always associated with industrialized societies in which la technique (or the quest for ever more efficiency through technology) supersedes human social interaction.

2. Propaganda is not a set of tricks but is an ongoing, ever-present, interrelated system of methods, technologies, or "techniques" that pervade modern society.

3. Propaganda inevitably occurs in societies in which people are depersonalized and unknowingly forced into *masses* while at the same time isolated as individuals. They derive their identity from the mass, which is united through propaganda.

4. The purpose of modern propaganda is not to agitate the masses to action but to integrate them into society. This is done through peer pressure, social norms, and collective standards — usually expressed by a leader.

5. International propaganda tends to come from "propaganda blocs" such as the United States, China, the Arabs, the Israelis, and the third world. Propaganda is intended for internal consumption to calm, not agitate, the masses and can come from governments, corporations, political parties, or religions.

6. Propaganda in a highly technological society is *totalitarian*. Everything is infused with some element of a propagandistic message. Totalitarian propaganda also infuses our social interactions. We find flags in church, pledges of allegiance at the Lions Club, patriotic songs sung at school and church, and mealtime prayers in many homes.

7. Contemporary propaganda isolates the individual, stereotypes public opinion, and offers simplistic answers to complex social questions.

8. Propaganda in Ellul's terms is everywhere. Our art and music — even antipatriotic and nonpolitical art and music — identify our cultural values and beliefs. In fact, this book, which asks you to be a conscientious receiver of persuasion, would be but another example of propaganda if seen through Ellul's eyes.

What Can We Do?

If all of this sounds negative and depressing, don't be surprised. It is. In fact, this is one of the recurring criticisms of Ellul's work — it offers so little hope and is nihilistic. Ellul's own words often prompt such criticism:

The individual is in a dilemma: either he decides to safeguard his freedom of choice . . . thereby entering into competition with a power against which there is no efficacious defense and before which he must suffer defeat; or he decides to accept a technical necessity, in which case he will himself be the victor, but only by submitting irreparably to technical slavery. In effect, he has no choice. (1979, p. 84)

However, a closer reading of Ellul's work and that of his critics reveals a position that is not totally hopeless. Ellul sees the solution in a three-step process (Christians & Van Hook, 1981). In stage one, we *recognize* the existence and dangers of la technique in its many forms: bureaucracy, isolation of the individual, and its various myths. This phase also involves resisting standardization, whether brought on us by the media, government, economics, or some other force.

Stage two is the *transformation* of the self into a nontechnological human. This requires us to identify ways in which our life can be changed. In Ellul's view, we need to identify the ways in which we are influenced by the propaganda of la technique and reject as much technology as possible. Ellul is certain that realization of the dangers of la technique, coupled with disengagement from technology, will lead to stage three — the *action* stage. Here Ellul advocates "creative nonconformity . . . spontaneous movement . . . and tangible acts which *ipso facto* circumvent the sociotechnological order (1979, p. 154). He is not prescriptive about specific actions and instead advocates a "passion to play" or a return to festivals and rituals that emphasize humane values.

Even Ellul recognizes that stage three is extremely difficult and potentially dangerous. For our purposes, realization, reflection, and then avoidance may suffice. If we accept Ellul's ideas, asking humane questions of technological institutions seems to be the most promising action we can take. At least it has the potential of raising the consciousness of others in regard to the dangers of la technique.

Review and Conclusion

Our interest in propaganda and its uses always appears during times of war or national crisis. When we are not faced with war or national crisis, our interest in propaganda diminishes, and we become more concerned with the events of the day and with personal problems. Yet, as we have seen, the absence of war does not mean the absence of propaganda. A major difficulty arises in identifying just what propaganda is, in determining its sources and intent, and in determining how and why it affects us.

It is clear that even if Ellul overstates his case, his theory is useful. It jars us. It forces us to look deeper — to take a second and even a third look at many of the things that are happening around us. In those second or third looks, we often can identify propaganda that we might otherwise have overlooked.

Questions for Further Thought

1. Are you being persuaded through a technique of which you are only dimly aware (for example, telemarketing)? If so, what is it?

2. What is the plain folks device? Identify its use in several examples of persuasion.

3. What is card stacking? Identify uses of it.

4. What is the transfer device? Identify uses of it.

5. What is the glittering generalities device? Identify uses of it.

6. Which medium discussed by Jowatt and O'Donnell is the most underused for propaganda purposes? Which has the most potential?

7. Look back at the cultural values discussion in Chapter 8. Are any of these values being urged on you? If so, can you identify the source of the urging?

8. Where in your world is the value of efficiency espoused? Look at advertisements, editorials, campaigns, and so on.

9. In what ways do you agree and disagree with Jacques Ellul's ideas on propaganda?

10. What can we expect in the future regarding propaganda?

References

Brown, J. A. C. (1963). *Techniques of persuasion: From propaganda to brainwashing.* Baltimore: Penguin Books.

Christians, C., & Real, M. (1979). Jacques Ellul's contributions to critical media theory. *Journal of Communication, 29,* 83–93.

Christians, C. G., & Van Hook, J. M. (1981). *Jacques Ellul: Interpretive essays.* Champaign: University of Illinois Press.

Cooper, M. D., & Nothstine, W. L. (1992). *Power persuasion: Moving an ancient art into the media age.* Greenwood, IN.: The Educational Video Group.

Doob, L. W. (1935). *Propaganda—Its psychology and techniques.* New York: Barnes & Noble.

Doob, L. W. (1966). *Opinion and propaganda.* Hamden, CT: Archon Press.

Ellul, J. (1973). *Propaganda: The formation of men's attitudes.* New York: Vintage Books.

Ellul, J. (1979). *The technological society.* New York: Knopf.

Johnson, D. (1994). *The art and science of persuasion.* Dubuque, IA: William C. Brown/Benchmark.

Jowatt, G., & O'Donnell, V. (1986). *Propaganda and persuasion.* Beverly Hills, CA: Sage Publications.

Jowatt G., & O'Donnell, V. (1992). *Propaganda and persuasion* (2nd ed.). Newbury Park, CA: Sage Publications.

Miller, C. P. (1937). How to detect propaganda. *Propaganda analysis.* New York: Institute for Propaganda Analysis.

National Report (1993). Controversial speech policy ends at Penn. *Chicago Tribune.* November 18, sec. 1, p. 8.

Pratkanis, A., & Aronson, E. (1992). *The age of propaganda: The everyday use and abuse of persuasion.* New York: Freeman.

Taylor, R. (1979). *Film propaganda.* Baltimore: Barnes & Noble.

14

The Use of Persuasive Premises in Advertising

The most dominant, and perhaps the most effective, forms of persuasion in contemporary culture are print and electronic advertising. Although we may feel smug about not running out and buying every product we learn about from advertisements, product ads still have a dramatic impact on us. They shape not only our purchasing behavior but other behaviors as well (for example, becoming aware of a product's existence, developing attitudes toward products, and even making changes in our values and preferred lifestyles). The field of advertising has a long and frequently sordid history, but it is also a fascinating area of persuasion to study. I hope that this chapter will provide insights into how you and your culture behave in response to and because of advertising.

To give you an idea of how much impact advertising has on Western consumers (particularly those in the United States) and thus how it helps shape our culture, consider the following:

1. The average expenditure on advertising in the United States exceeds $400 per person per year (Ries & Trout, 1986). This includes all kinds of print and electronic advertising. It doesn't sound like so much, does it—a little more than a dollar a day?

2. The average American is exposed to over 1700 advertising messages every day. Again, this includes all kinds of advertising. Now that's more impressive! It gives us a feel for what the word "clutter" means to persons in the advertising industry, and it explains why it is so hard to "break through the clutter."

3. The average expenditure on advertising in the rest of the world (including such Western democracies as Canada, Great Britain, Mexico, and all of Western Europe, where advertising expenditures are also great) is only *$17 per person per year*. That's about $.32 per week, or $.04 per day.

No wonder many people from other countries come to the conclusion that Americans are the most compulsive, selfish, and greedy consumers of goods and services in the world.

Advertising and Culture

As we analyze "the world's second oldest profession," as advertising has been referred to by some of its critics, you will find yourself evaluating our culture in various ways, too. No matter where you look in human history, there have been sellers and promoters of one kind or another. Of course, advertising is most evident in contemporary American life. And even though we Americans aren't unique in the use of advertising, we are highly effective in producing and consuming it. Some of it ranks as pop art and is extremely creative and even entertaining. Some of it isn't even good enough to rank as schlock.

The real lesson to learn from studying the persuasive appeals of advertising is how they affect human society and our behavior and whether none, all, or even just *some* of those effects are bad or good, ethical or unethical for humankind in general and for you in particular. A final value in studying advertising is that it can help each of us understand ourselves as consumers.

Also keep in mind that any discussion of the topic is really an interpretation of events as seen through the eyes of the beholder. Thus Marxist critics see advertisements as tools of the upper classes used to exploit the lower classes. Advertising executives see ads as better or worse than those of the competition. My perspective is both as a teacher of persuasion (especially as seen in advertising principles) and as a practitioner of various advertising techniques in the real world. But my perspective also contains a concern for consumers as they face the cluttered world of advertising in their lives. If this chapter is at all worthwhile, you should come away from it as a much more critical, insightful, and selective consumer of today's barrage of advertising appeals.

Advertising, Sales Promotion, and Positioning

All of us are targets of advertising and sales promotion at various times of our lives. We ought to be aware of the kinds of appeals that are targeted at us in order to wisely decide whether to buy or not. We are usually only aware of brand advertising, and even there, we usually are conscious of the big picture — the slogan or jingle, the spokesperson, the main "pitch" — and overlook numerous smaller yet persuasive details such as brand naming, packaging, and positioning.

One thing to keep in mind is that a product is not a brand, though the terms are often used interchangeably. Brands compete with one another *within* a product category (e.g., Folgers and Maxwell House in the coffee category). Products compete with one another *across* product categories according to the need they are supposed to fill (e.g., coffees also compete with teas among hot drinks). Also, in the newest approach to marketing — integrated marketing communication — advertising is intimately connected with sales promotion, personal selling, direct marketing, and public relations, among other things, to achieve the ultimate marketing goal — sales of goods and services.

Branding and Brand Names

Contemporary advertising grew out of the establishment of branded, packaged foods in the nineteenth century (Nabisco put its crackers into boxes, not barrels in 1899) and the early twentieth century. Before that, people went to the general store in their area and bought unbranded flour, sugar, coffee, beans, salt, and other products. With the growth and development of brands, producers had to differentiate their version of a product from the competition's. Some ways to differentiate were via packaging, means of distribution, and, of course, advertising the brand in memorable ways, emphasizing its distinctiveness from other brands in the same product class. Until the 1920s advertising was limited to the print medium — newspapers, magazines, in-store signs, packages, and (with the growth of the automobile) outdoor billboards.

Several strategies emerged in those early years to communicate the brand more effectively. For instance, the naming of a brand makes a major difference in how it is perceived and is embedded in the consumer's memory. Consider the case of Allegheny Airlines, a regional brand, as the name implies. When Allegheny wanted to change its image to that of a national carrier, its marketers researched various new names and ultimately settled on an ideal name: USAir. That name was already trademarked by an air freight company, so Allegheny bought the brand name. As we all know now, the choice of USAir was excellent and served to change the airline's image.

Consider other brand names to see whether they persuasively communicate their differences from competing brands. For starters, compare the competitors in the frozen turkey market. If you ask friends and acquaintances to name a brand of frozen turkey, most will say "Butterball," the brand with the greatest name recognition. Note that not only is the name memorable, but it says something about the brand's attributes and benefits: Butterball turkeys have the reputation of being the moistest brand because they are basted with a pound of butter prior to freezing (Dollas, 1986b). A few other examples will get you going: DieHard auto batteries, Easy Off oven cleaner, No Pest Strip insecticide, Taster's Choice instant coffee, and Energizer batteries. How do these brand names compare with those of their competitors in the product category?

McNeill and Zeren (1981) found several criteria being used as guides in brand-name selection. A good brand name should describe product benefits, be memorable, fit with company image, be "trademarkable," be easy to promote/advertise, be unique among the competition, be easy to pronounce, be suited to the package, be contemporary, be understandable, and be persuasive, to name a few characteristics. Research on shopping lists demonstrates that consumers frequently list brand, not product, names (Rothschild, 1987).

Packaging

Packaging persuades and reinforces the brand name. Not only does the package protect the product, but it makes the brand more attractive and easy to see, and it should make it easier to store and display. Most important, packaging "says something" about the brand and is a cost-efficient way to make "impressions" on the consumer. The goods have to be packaged anyway, so why not make the package attractive and memorable in as many ways as possible? Showing the package in advertising also helps the consumer recall brand characteristics and advantages at the P.O.P. (point of purchase). Packages can also carry a sales promotion, such as a coupon for future purchases of the brand, and can be valuable in and of themselves (e.g., metal containers for soda crackers).

Consider the case of Taster's Choice instant coffee in terms of its naming, advertising, and packaging. Instant coffees have been around for a long time (soldiers in World War II got packets of instant coffee in their K-rations, and Sanka and Nescafe have been on the market since just after the war), but they never did well because they didn't taste like brewed coffee. In the late 1960s and early 1970s "freeze-dried" instant coffees came on the market and demonstrated that an instant coffee could taste almost like the real thing. The brand positioned as being "first" with a real coffee taste was Maxim by Maxwell House, an established brand known for being "good to the last drop." Maxim maintained an early market share, but in 1971 Taster's Choice came on the market and soon replaced Maxim as the market leader.

Taster's Choice was made by Nestlé, which had no identification with the coffee market. Yet the brand succeeded. Why? It obviously had a better name than Maxim (which sounded modern and technological but said nothing about the brand or its benefits. The name Taster's Choice was also unusual and made a claim about the brand's benefits — it was a good-tasting brand.

Furthermore, the jar, unlike Maxim's (which was cylindrical and feminine looking), was almost square, and its wide "shoulders" communicated masculinity, another attribute that reinforced the "robust" and "stronger tasting" benefits. Taster's Choice labels further underscored the masculinity message by picturing a man "tasting his choice" from a steaming mug. Also, the label was smaller than the competition's and thus allowed the consumer to see the "coffee crystals," which appeared significantly different from powdered instant coffees. In its early electronic advertising, the Taster's Choice jar was magically fitted with a handle and spout to resemble an old-fashioned coffeepot. The consumer could see the "pot" give off wonderful-smelling aromas, which drew a masculine fellow to sniff it and then pour and savor a cup of the stuff. Perceptual maps of the brand showed that it was perceived as "easy to use" and as having a "strong, rich taste," compared to the perception of Maxim as "easy to use" but with a "weak taste." Proof positive of the effectiveness of the brand name, brand packaging, and brand advertising were Taster's Choice's capture of a significant share of the market and the fact that Maxim soon changed the shape of its jar and used a smaller label.

As you go about being a critical consumer, try to identify the effects of brand naming, packaging and labeling and how they interact with brand advertising. A few examples will get you started here, too—look at the naming and packaging/labeling of Janitor in a Drum, Paul Newman's Spaghetti Sauce, and L'eggs panty hose.

P.O.P. and Sales Promotion

As consumers, we are usually more aware of P.O.P. advertising and sales promotion appeals than we are of the details of naming, packaging, and labeling. Point-of-purchase appeals include signs that tell us the brand is available at that location, and they frequently announce special "in-store" bargain prices. Other P.O.P. approaches include displays showing the product in use, signs on shopping carts, sample taste testings, promotional buttons or signs, "shelf talkers," in-store coupons, fliers, in-package "gifts," and reduced-price premiums (appliances, dish sets, or sets of books/tapes/CDs in end-of-aisle or checkout counter displays). All these methods are aimed at reinforcing the brand name and may also "teach" the consumer about brand benefits as well as increase purchase behavior, particularly impulse purchasing. Research shows that P.O.P. displays and signs can increase sales by margins of 20 to 90 percent, depending on product category. This is not so surprising when you consider that research shows that almost half of all purchases are unplanned (even when consumers are shopping with a list) and that 65 percent of all purchases are based on in-store decisions (Rothschild, 1987).

Sales promotion can be defined as "temporary inducements to encourage immediate purchase decisions." One example that has been around for a long time and that exemplifies the power of sales promotion is the "free prizes" in each box of Crackerjacks. It is safe to say that in all its years of sales, Crackerjacks has never contained a prize worth very much. Yet whether consumers are nine or ninety, the first thing they do is search for the prize rather than eat the product.

Consumer-targeted sales promotions include special sale pricing ("two for the price of one"), short-term price reductions ("special 6 hour sale!"), coupons, rebates, "extra" product in the package, premiums (e.g., steak knives), contests, sweepstakes, recipes on the packaging, and bonus packs, to name a few. All are designed to increase demand. They try to "pull" the products through the supply pipeline using consumer demand for the brand as the "carrot" and short-term appeals (coupon expiration dates or limited supplies available) as the "stick" to prompt purchase.

Most of us are aware of consumer-targeted sales promotions, but few are aware of the retailer-targeted promotions that account for the lion's share of all sales promotion spending. Although manufacturers want to move the *brand* onto store shelves, retailers want to move *products* off the shelves. To induce the retailer to put the brand on the shelves, manufacturers use such retailer-targeted promotions as special buying allowances, advertising allowances, and direct stimulus of the retailers or salespersons. A buying allowance is a special "on-deal" offer to the retailer, who gets a certain number of "free" cases with the purchase of a certain number of cases at the regular price. Advertising allowances and co-op advertising offer the retailer high-quality camera-ready ads or video/audio clips and frequently include sharing the costs of advertising time or space to promote the brand. Interestingly enough, many retailers are unaware of or choose not to use co-op advertising or allowances (the amount of unused co-op ad dollars exceeds all other advertising expenditures). Direct stimulus appeals (sometimes called "spiffs") are aimed at the retailer or salespeople to get them to stock or to "pitch" the brand. A common tactic is free merchandise (such as appliances or jewelry) for stocking or selling a certain amount of the brand. Spectacular vacation trips can also be "earned" by selling a target amount of the brand.

> **What do you think?**
>
> What is the connection among advertising, packaging, and sales promotion?

Positioning

Finally, marketers believe that every brand should occupy a "position" in the consumer's mind. We live in a world filled with too many products and brands to remember. Research shows that we are able to remember only a finite number of brands in each product category. Some theorists speculate that this "top-of-mind" awareness is limited to 7± 2 brands. For complex product categories such as computers, most consumers can recall only about five brands, whereas they can recall as many as nine brands in less complex product categories such as beer or breakfast food (Ries & Trout,

1986). As a result, a brand needs to stand out so it will be remembered at the point of purchase.

Most contemporary professionals in the field agree that advertising is a *tool of marketing*. In other words, you don't come up with a product and then try to sell it to consumers through advertising messages. Rather, the successful marketer begins with the minds of consumers and tries to identify potentially unmet needs. If one or more are discovered, then either a product is designed to fill the need or an existing product is "redefined" to fill the need. This approach of beginning with the consumer was made popular by the work of Al Ries and Jack Trout. In their articles, speeches, and best-selling book, they deal with the idea of **positioning**—finding a niche in the minds of consumers that a given product might fill. For example, Taster's Choice is positioned as the "freeze-dried" instant coffee, thereby preempting that position for other brands. Chrysler is positioned as the "most innovative" automaker because it was first to bring out front-wheel drive, consumer rebates, the extended warranty, the minivan, the convertible, and the air-bag safety device in the 1980s.

Once a position is established for a product, advertising is used to prepare the customer for trial and purchase. It lays the groundwork for sales by increasing product or **brand awareness** (for example, repeating slogans or jingles), by communicating and improving the **product image or personality** (for example, Chrysler's innovative image), and by making an **offer** that will move the consumer to the point of purchase. Once the consumer is at the grocery store, the auto dealership, or the clothing store, sales promotion and/or personal selling are used to close the deal.

Problems of an Overcommunicated Society

One of Ries and Trout's (1986) main contentions is that we live in an overcommunicated society. They claim that the usual defense consumers have in our overcommunicated society is to develop an "oversimplified mind," by which they mean a mind that largely ignores most of the information to which it is exposed. Most people select products they think are appropriate for their purposes and then generally stick with those products. We call this *brand loyalty*. Brand loyalty makes it easier to live in an overcommunicated society, because you never have to change your mind, and you can easily ignore the ads for competing brands in that product category.

Interestingly enough, brand loyalty is most strongly developed in consumers like yourselves between the ages of eighteen and thirty-four. Brand loyalty is portable—you can take it with you wherever you go (Pizza Huts are found across the country, and you can get Coca-Cola anywhere in the world), and brand loyalty helps the consumer predict quality and value from place to place. This is appealing to those in the early years of their careers facing frequent job and location moves.

Advertising agents and agencies frequently face the criticism that their efforts amount to selling people products that they don't need or that may even be harmful (such as tobacco, alcohol, and foods high in sodium or fat). As Michael Schudson notes in his book *Advertising, The Uneasy Persuasion* (1984), advertisers defend themselves from this criticism by claiming that their aim is "not to change people's product choices but to change their brand choices. Advertising . . . is a competitive war against commercial rivals for a share of a market."

In order to break through oversimplified minds, advertisers must find something that is already in the audience's mind and then "retie the cords" to their products in ways similar to Schwartz's evoked recall model, which gets messages out of audiences, not into them. Ries and Trout (1986) suggest that the best way to do so is to use an "oversimplified message." They report the results of a survey of name recognition that showed that only 44 percent of supermarket shoppers knew then-Vice President George Bush. At the same time, 93 percent of them easily recognized Mr. Clean.

The overcommunication problem is extended by what Ries and Trout call the *media explosion*, which we looked at in Chapter 12: TV, cable, satellites, AM and FM radio, morning and evening newspapers, news weeklies, magazines, catalogs, direct mail, billboards, bus signs, and interactive media (see Figure 14.1). Even the human body carries trademarks: Calvin Klein, Gucci, Benetton, Guess, and other product names.

The Product Explosion

Besides the overcommunication problem and the media explosion, we also have what Ries and Trout call the *product explosion*. For example, the average supermarket contains 12,000 products or brands; in Europe, and now in the United States, there are super-supermarkets that contain over 60,000 or more products or brands from which to choose. To further complicate the situation, each year 25,000 new trademarks are registered at the U.S. Patent Office, with "hundreds of thousands of products and brands being sold without trademarks" (Ries & Trout, 1986, p. 14).

More products coming on the market results in more advertising. Ries and Trout call this the *advertising explosion*—a problem not only in the sheer increase in the volume of advertising but in the many new types of professionals (lawyers, dentists, doctors) and institutions (hospitals, nonprofit organizations, governments) being forced to turn to advertising.

Breaking Through the Clutter

How do advertisers break through the triple whammy of exploding media, products, and advertisements? In other words, how do they break through the clutter? The techniques of positioning provide one way to break through clutter.

Figure 14.1. One of the major problems for advertisers today is what Ries and Trout call the advertising explosion, by which they mean not only the increased volume of advertising but also the new advertising "vehicles," or places where advertising can occur. (Freeze Frame cartoon from Advertising Age, April 25, 1988. Copyright Crain Communications, Inc. Reprinted by permission of Crain Communications and Sidney Harris)

We encountered some of these tactics in Chapter 10, which covered market segmentation in persuasive campaigns. "Being first" has helped products such as Jell-O, Kleenex, and Xerox break the clutter. These products have become "imprinted" in consumers' minds to the extent that the brand names are almost generic for the product category. As Ries and Trout note, "You build brand loyalty in a supermarket in the same way you build mate loyalty in a marriage. You get there first and then be careful not to give them a reason to switch" (p. 21). Not only were Apple personal computers the *first* in the PC market but they were also first at being "user friendly." This realization let them get the jump on IBM and thus gave consumers reason to remain loyal to Apple.

But what if you're not first in the market? Then positioning becomes even more important. You don't want to be a "me too" brand. In earlier advertising eras — the *product benefit era* of the USP (or "unique selling proposition"), innovated by Rosser Reeves, and the *product image era*, innovated by David Ogilvy — the competition wasn't nearly as fierce as it is in the 1990s. With more and more "me too!" products on the market, neither product benefits nor product images could beat the competition. Products have to be unique in the marketplace, and usually advertisers rely on simple but distinctive copy to communicate uniqueness.

The poetry of product benefit or product image ad copy (such as "99 and 44/100% Pure — it floats" or "Magnavox. Smart. Very Smart") doesn't seem to work so well anymore. We still encounter colorful "poetic" ad copy, as Figure 14.2 demonstrates. And just as effective was the slogan "First class is Michelob" which positioned Michelob as "unique" in the market — a premium-priced beer actually produced in America.

A variety of techniques can be used to make a product seem to be the only brand in the product category with a certain benefit. You are exposed to these kinds of pitches every day. For example, which coffee is "mountain grown"? The chances are that you said "Folgers." You are wrong — all coffees are grown in the mountains, but Folgers preempted that product claim, thus carving out its unique niche in the coffee market. It would be advertising suicide to say, for example, "Maxwell House is mountain grown,

too." Instead, other brands of coffee need to find different niches — like "Good to the last drop."

And there aren't many niches in a given product category. So if the competitors are firmly entrenched in the audience's mind, what can be done? One possibility is to go up against one of them with *comparative advertising*. Ries and Trout give an example of this approach in the Avis Rent-a-Car campaign, whose slogan was "Avis is only number 2 in rent-a-cars so why go with us? We try harder." After thirteen years of losing money, Avis made $1.2 million the first year after admitting to being second, $2.6 million the second year, and $5 million the third year before being acquired by ITT, which ditched the number 2 idea and promptly began losing money. Interestingly enough, the "We're #2, so we try harder" campaign didn't hurt the market leader, Hertz — in fact, it increased their business. Rather, the campaign took business away from the third- and fourth-place brands in the market — National and Budget.

One way a brand can break through clutter is by telling consumers what it "is not." In 1968, Seven-Up was near bankruptcy. Its advertising agency, J. Walter Thompson, came up with one of the most successful "Tell 'em what you're not" campaigns in history with the "invention" of the word "un-cola," which the agency then used in very creative ways. The Seven-Up delivery trucks were labeled "The Man from Un-cola," which played on a popular TV series, *The Man from U.N.C.L.E.* And there was a series of ads in various languages in which the only word most viewers could understand was "un-cola." The campaign positioned Seven-Up third in the soft-drink market right behind Coca-Cola and Pepsi. The only way to come up with an idea such as "un-cola" is to get into the consumer's mind: "You won't find an 'un-cola' idea inside a Seven-Up can. You find it inside the cola drinker's head" (Ries & Trout, 1986, p. 34).

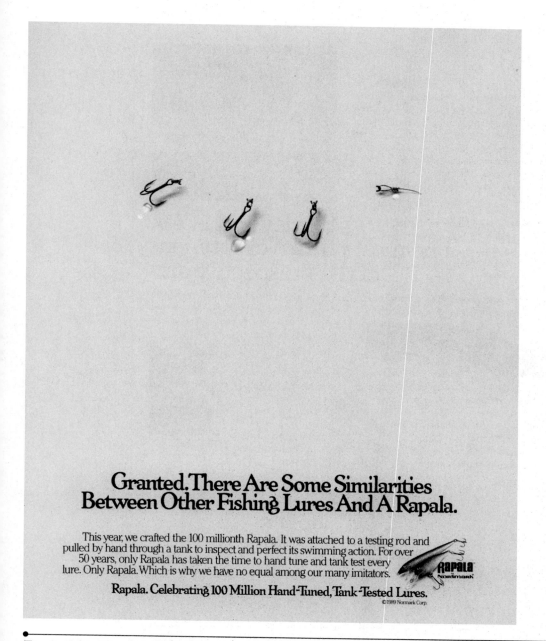

Granted. There Are Some Similarities Between Other Fishing Lures And A Rapala.

This year, we crafted the 100 millionth Rapala. It was attached to a testing rod and pulled by hand through a tank to inspect and perfect its swimming action. For over 50 years, only Rapala has taken the time to hand tune and tank test every lure. Only Rapala. Which is why we have no equal among our many imitators.

Rapala. Celebrating 100 Million Hand-Tuned, Tank-Tested Lures.

© 1989 Normark Corp.

Figure 14.2. How did this hard-hitting product ad by Rapala break through the clutter? (Reprinted by permission of Normark Corp.)

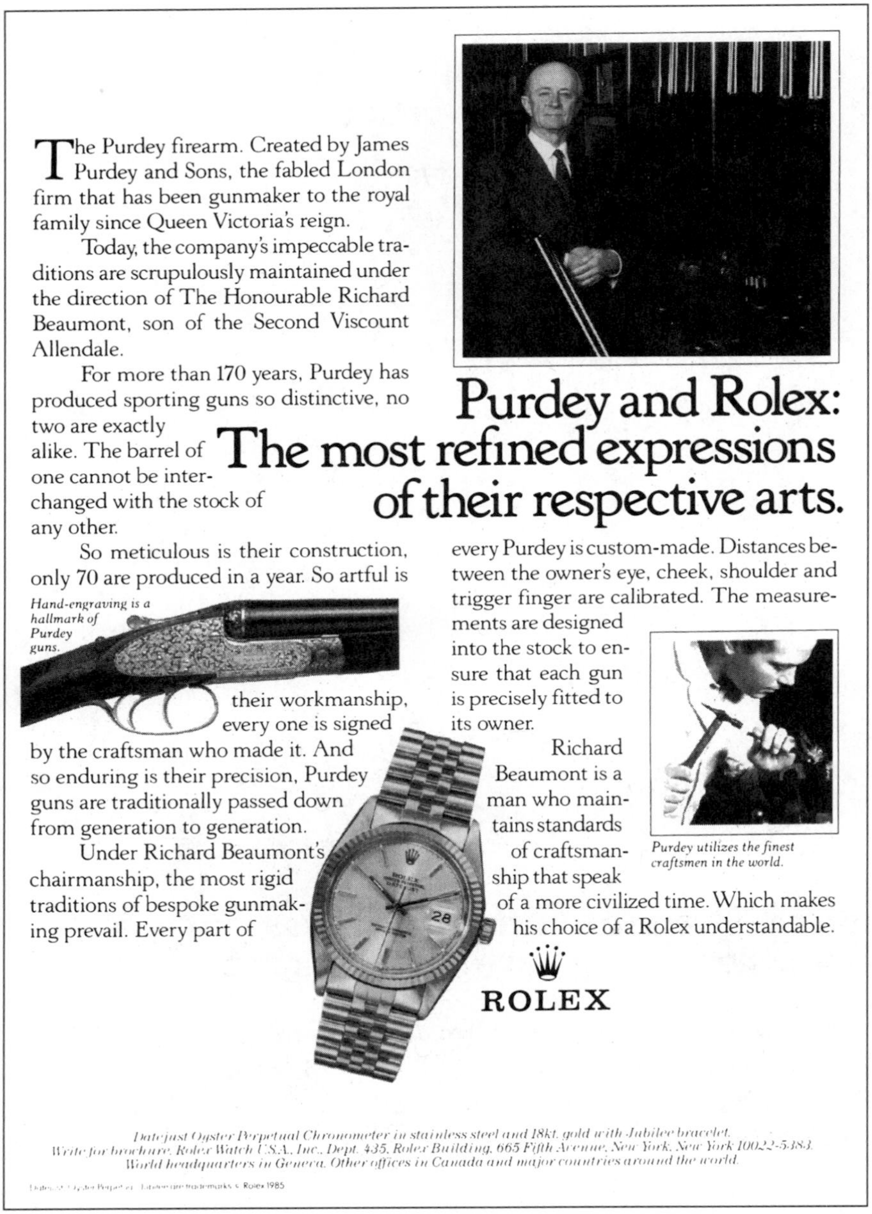
The Purdey firearm. Created by James Purdey and Sons, the fabled London firm that has been gunmaker to the royal family since Queen Victoria's reign.
Today, the company's impeccable traditions are scrupulously maintained under the direction of The Honourable Richard Beaumont, son of the Second Viscount Allendale.
For more than 170 years, Purdey has produced sporting guns so distinctive, no two are exactly alike. The barrel of one cannot be interchanged with the stock of any other.
So meticulous is their construction, only 70 are produced in a year. So artful is their workmanship, every one is signed by the craftsman who made it. And so enduring is their precision, Purdey guns are traditionally passed down from generation to generation.
Under Richard Beaumont's chairmanship, the most rigid traditions of bespoke gunmaking prevail. Every part of every Purdey is custom-made. Distances between the owner's eye, cheek, shoulder and trigger finger are calibrated. The measurements are designed into the stock to ensure that each gun is precisely fitted to its owner.
Richard Beaumont is a man who maintains standards of craftsmanship that speak of a more civilized time. Which makes his choice of a Rolex understandable.
Purdey and Rolex:
The most refined expressions of their respective arts.
Hand-engraving is a hallmark of Purdey guns.
Purdey utilizes the finest craftsmen in the world.
ROLEX
Datejust Oyster Perpetual Chronometer in stainless steel and 18kt. gold with Jubilee bracelet.
Write for brochure. Rolex Watch U.S.A., Inc., Dept. 435, Rolex Building, 665 Fifth Avenue, New York, New York 10022-5383.
World headquarters in Geneva. Other offices in Canada and major countries around the world.
Rolex 1985

Figure 14.3. *This product image ad breaks through the clutter using a copy-heavy strategy to tell Rolex's product story. The comparison between Rolex watches and Purdey shotguns relies on both the price and quality niches. (Reprinted by permission of Rolex Watch U.S.A., Inc.)*

Another approach is to take advantage of one's existing image or reputation. For example, Arm & Hammer is known for producing baking soda, but did you know that it also makes and sells sodium bicarbonates to cattle raisers? Arm & Hammer took advantage of its already established reputation to market, in a very competitive marketplace, a new product—cattle feed supplements that aided digestion and resulted in weight gain. This is called *line extension*. So, relying on one's strength and reputation can be an effective means of breaking clutter.

Many "me too" products claim to be "better." The problem is that it's hard to convince the consumer that a product is better. A company may waste inordinate amounts of *time* and *money* trying to increase demonstrable product quality, thus allowing the competition to catch up and out-advertise and out-sell the new "me too" product. This happened when Volkswagen broke into the U.S. compact-car market in the late 1950s. Because few compact cars were available in the American market at the time, VW preempted the "small" niche using the two simple words "Think small" as its slogan. American automakers countered by making smaller cars than they had been making, but none were as small or as successful as the VW beetle.

Price can be another clutter breaker. A product can find a lower-priced niche, such as that filled by the Yugo, or it can find a high-priced one like that of Mont Blanc pens, Rolex wristwatches, and BMWs (see Figure 14.3). Other clutter breakers are gender and age. The largest-selling perfume is not Arpege or Chanel No. 5 but Charlie—the first perfume to advertise using a masculine name. Examples of products occupying the age niche are Geritol and high-fiber foods. Distribution and packaging can break clutter, too. L'eggs was the first hosiery to be distributed in supermarkets, and its packaging gave it a unique position in the market (Ries & Trout, 1986). Hosiery is usually packaged in a thin square envelope with a window in it to show the consumer the shade of the hose. There are high labor costs involved in folding the hose around a cardboard sheet inside the envelope. L'eggs hosiery, on the other hand, can simply be "stuffed" into the container, thus eliminating this labor cost and bringing the price down. And the egg-shaped container is not only visually unique but also appealing for secondary uses, such as for storage of small items and for various crafts (Dollas, 1986b).

Advertisers can also break through clutter by repositioning an existing brand (for example, changing Cheerios from a "children's" product to an "adult" product by stressing its high-fiber content. Finally, clutter can be broken by choosing the right name or slogan for the product. A powerful bathroom cleaner named "The Works" fits with the idea of trying the ultimate—"Give it the works!" Compare the clutter-breaking abilities of Buick's slogan "Buick Builds It Better" with Pontiac's slogan "We Build Excitement!" Which cuts through the clutter? Giving examples of the product's benefits, as in the California avocado ad in Figure 14.4, helps break through the clutter.

All of these examples of clutter-breaking techniques grow out of various kinds of advertising research that permit the advertiser to get into your head and resonate with your needs. Let's explore some research of this kind.

Getting into the Consumer's Head: Advertising Research

Three kinds of advertising or marketing research are most frequently used: *demographics* (which we discussed in Chapter 11), *psychographics*, and *sociographics*. Sometimes one is used alone; sometimes two of them may be used in conjunction with each other; and sometimes all three may be used.

There are also a variety of ways of conducting these kinds of research, including using census data, surveys, and questionnaires; focus-group

Figure 14.4. *How many product benefits are pointed out in this ad? Will they "break the clutter"?*

interviews (which we briefly explored in Chapter 10); a pupilometer, which measures the dilation of the pupil of the eye as it scans a printed ad; the tachistoscope, which gives viewers "miniglimpses" of ads, after which they are asked to recall the visuals and copy; galvanic skin response, which measures electric resistance (sweat) in the palm of the hand when a person gets excited; heart rate; and others too numerous to mention. All of these techniques have the same purpose: to identify the consumer's "hot buttons" and "cold buttons." Ad expert Terry Gallonoy (1970) says that successful commercials have to "make people shut up or stop eating or freeze on the way to the bathroom. . . . 'Stop the lady with the full bladder for just one full minute' is the order of the day."

Demographics

Demographics are used in the study of groups of consumers, or *market segments*, on the basis of some quantifiable variable or variables, including annual income, religious affiliation, political preferences, age, family size, gender, purchase patterns, or any combination of demographic factors. Based on these statistics, advertisers design ads that feature certain kinds of characters or have certain settings, props, and so on. One recently identified pattern is the growing number of DINK ("double-income, no-kids") households (see Figure 14.5), using two demographic variables — number of persons working in the household and family size. DINKs divide into two subgroups: those who intentionally have no children and are largely self-indulgent (the yuppie segment of the baby boomers), and those whose children have left home and are now independent of their parents (formerly called "empty nesters" before Mom decided to go back to work). This second group is sometimes called "muppies," or "mature urban professionals" — the now-aging front edge of the

Figure 14.5. *Demographics identified one segment of DINKs as older couples with no dependent children. Advertisers need to appeal to this group in different ways than they advertise to other groups.* (Berry's World *reprinted by permission of NEA, Inc.*)

yuppies. Quite obviously, an advertiser needs to appeal to these two subgroups in very different ways, using very different characters, settings, music, props, and so on.

The muppie segment is increasing at the rate of 5500 persons per day, which adds up to over 2 million new consumers a year. Advertisers know a lot about this segment: There are about 157 women for every 102 men in this age group; the average age of the group is increasing; they have a 76.8-year average life expectancy; their rate of divorce is increasing at three times the national rate. Persons in this segment tend to get up earlier in the day and to retire earlier at night — perhaps just after the evening news. They have more discretionary income available than previously, but they spend a good amount of it on children and especially grandchildren. They are concerned about health issues and are exercising more and more. They travel more than the average person does. About half of them live in seven states — California and New York, with over 2 million each, and Florida, Illinois, Michigan, Ohio, and Pennsylvania.

Now, you play advertising executive with these data and tell when, where, and how you would appeal to the muppie market segment. Your product is a nationwide travel network that permits older persons to travel in groups at special low rates during the off season. Would you advertise in *Modern Maturity,* or would you make your appeal during local evening news shows, which have a much smaller "reach" or population that could potentially see or hear the message? Or would you use direct mail to persons over 65 in the seven major states? Whom would you pick to be your spokesperson — Angela Lansbury, Burt Reynolds, Mike Ditka, Roseanne Barr, or Tina Turner? There are a host of other factors that could make a difference with one segment and not the other. As you can see, even the dullest demographic facts can lead advertisers to target someone as part of the market segment they want to reach with their messages.

Psychographics

Psychographics is the study of consumers' lifestyles. It provides quantitative data as to how consumers spend their time, in what kinds of activities they engage, what their interests are, and what

their opinions are on any given set of issues. The shorthand term for these factors is AIO, or "activities, interests, and opinions." Some examples of **activities** are work, social events, vacations, hobbies, entertainment, club membership, community activities, shopping, and sporting events.

Even this category of activities can be subdivided providing even more narrowly focused market segments. For example, there can be sports and leisure activities (e.g., golf, bowling, tennis, watching sports on TV). Another subcategory might be labeled good life activities (e.g., cultural events, gourmet cooking, investing, or wine tastings), and advertisers could look at outdoor activities (e.g., skeet shooting, fishing, or motorcycling) or at high-tech activities (e.g., video games, home computers, photography, or watching science channels on cable TV). In each and all of these categories, marketing and advertising pitches need to be tailored to fit the consumer. A golfer who is interested in gourmet cooking, skeet shooting, and photography is a different consumer from a bowler who is interested in the same things. And both need to receive their own idiosyncratic advertising messages, tailored to them specifically. This is the aim of data-base marketing, the newest development in the field.

Interests include the family and home, one's achievements, recreation, fashion, technology, food, and media. **Opinions** can be held about oneself, social and political issues, business and economics, religion and culture, education, and the future. A psychographic study is done by having large numbers of persons respond to questions about activities, interests, and opinions that relate to a particular product. From these answers, the advertiser infers what the respondents' lifestyles are like and how they are likely to respond to the product. In some cases, the results may dictate points to be used in the ad copy — and even specific language to be used.

The items in psychographic questionnaires may be general or specific. For example, a study could be conducted to determine what type of consumer would be most likely to bring a malpractice suit against a physician. Items in the questionnaire would be something like:

- I have a great deal of confidence in my own doctor.

- Many physicians are out-of-date.

- Physicians are overpaid.

- Malpractice is hard to prove.

- You are your own best doctor.

Responses may range from "strongly agree" to "strongly disagree." Trends in responses are then correlated to persons actually bringing malpractice suits.

In an example directly related to product advertising, persons strongly agreeing with the following items are highly likely to use Listerine mouthwash rather than Listermint mouthwash and are more likely to use mouthwash in general (Rothschild, 1987).

- I do not feel clean without a daily bath.

- Everyone should use a deodorant.

- A house should be dusted three times a week.

- Odors in the house embarrass me.

- The kind of dirt you can't see is worse than the kind you can see.

- I am a very neat person.

- Dirty dishes should be washed after every meal.

- It is very important for people to wash their hands before eating each meal.

- I use one or more household disinfectants.

You can imagine several effective advertisements that could be developed just by knowing that Listerine users respond this way to cleanliness.

Appeals could be made to the germ-killing and antiseptic qualities in the product. You could justify Listerine's antiseptic taste by intimating that "clean doesn't mean 'good tasting' in mouthwashes" and go on to point out that "flavored mouthwashes" compromise cleanliness for the sake of taste.

So, knowing about the activities, interests, and opinions of consumers provides advertisers with critical psychographic data about their potential customers. Keep in mind that no matter how ineffective you think a given national print or electronic advertisement is, it probably had to pass rigorous research tests before ever going on the air or into print.

Another psychographic model widely used in advertising and marketing is known as VALS ("Values And Life-Styles"), developed by Arnold Mitchell (1983) at Stanford Research Institute. It is very relevant for the '90s. Mitchell describes three general lifestyles and then breaks them down into subcategories having certain values, demographics, and buying patterns (Engel, Blackwell & Miniard, 1986). The three general categories are persons who are *need driven*, persons who are *outer directed*, and persons who are *inner directed* (see Table 14.1).

Need-Driven Consumers. These consumers are living on the edge of or in the midst of poverty. They represent only 11 percent of the population, and advertisers do not often target them because need-driven consumers have little discretionary income. They are forced to use most, if not all, of their income to buy the minimum essentials.

There are two subcategories of need-driven consumers: survivors (4 percent) and sustainers (7 percent). *Survivors* struggle to provide the daily necessities of life, tend to mistrust people and products, and are usually social misfits. They live

> **What do you think?**
> What might a psychographic study of you reveal?

Percentage of Population (age 18 and over)	Consumer Type	Values and Lifestyles	Demographics	Buying Patterns
Need-Driven Consumers				
4%	Survivors	Struggle for survival Distrustful Socially misfitted Ruled by appetites	Poverty-level income Little education Many minority members Many live in city slums	Price dominant Focused on basics Buying for immediate needs
7	Sustainers	Concern with safety, security Insecure, compulsive Dependent, following Streetwise, determined to get ahead	Low income Low education Much unemployment Live in country as well as cities	Price important Want warranty Cautious buyers
Outer-Directed Consumers				
35%	Belongers	Conforming, conventional Unexperimental Traditional, formal Nostalgic	Low to middle income Low to average education Blue-collar jobs Tend toward noncity living	Family Home Fads Middle and lower mass markets
10	Emulators	Ambitious, show-off Status conscious Upwardly mobile Macho, competitive	Good to excellent income Youngish Highly urban Traditionally male, but changing	Conspicuous consumption "In" items Imitative Popular fashion
22	Achievers	Achievement, success, fame Materialism Leadership, efficiency Comfort	Excellent income Leaders in business, politics, etc. Suburban and city living	Give evidence of success Top of the line Luxury and gift markets "New and improved" products

(continued)

Table 14.1. *VALS Lifestyle Segmentation*

Percentage of Population (age 18 and over)	Consumer Type	Values and Lifestyles	Demographics	Buying Patterns
Inner-Directed Consumers				
5%	I-Am-Me	Fiercely individualistic Dramatic, impulsive Experimental Volatile	Young Many single Student or starting job Affluent background	Display one's taste Experimental fads Source of far-out fads Clique buying
7	Experiential	Drive to direct experience Active, participative Person-centered Artistic	Bimodal income Most under 40 Many young families Good education	Process over product Vigorous, outdoor sports "Making" home pursuits Crafts and introspection
8	Societally Conscious	Societal responsibility Simple living Smallness of scale Inner growth	Bimodal low and high incomes Excellent education Diverse ages and places of residence Largely white	Conservation emphasis Simplicity Frugality Environmental concerns
2	Integrated	Psychological maturity Sense of fittingness Tolerant, self-actualizing World perspective	Good to excellent incomes Bimodal in age Excellent education Diverse jobs and residential patterns	Varied self-expression Esthetically oriented Ecologically aware One-of-a-kind items

SOURCE: Reprinted with permission of Macmillan Publishing Company from Arnold Mitchell, *Nine American Lifestyles: Who We Are and Where We Are Going* (New York: Macmillan, 1983). Copyright © 1983 by Arnold Mitchell.

Table 14.1. VALS Lifestyle Segmentation *(continued)*

in slums, have low educational backgrounds and poverty-level incomes, and most likely are members of a racial or ethnic minority. As you would expect, survivors' buying patterns are dominated by price and immediate needs.

Sustainers are a little better off. They are very concerned with security and safety; they really want to get ahead and think they can because of their "street savvy." Like survivors, they have low educational backgrounds and low income levels, but they may live in the country as well as the city and aren't necessarily members of minority groups. Although price is important to sustainers, they also want warranties and are cautious. But their desire to get ahead may make them targets for get-rich-quick schemes such as pyramid marketing (e.g., Amway or Mary Kaye) or lottery tickets.

Outer-Directed Consumers. This category makes up 67 percent of the marketplace and is an important target for all advertisers. Outer-directed consumers are divided into three subcategories. *Belongers* (35 percent) are very conventional and traditional. They do not usually experiment with new products or services, and they conform to traditional patterns. They tend to be blue-collar workers with low to middle educational levels. They are family oriented, focusing on products with domestic appeal. Belongers are also nostalgic and are good targets for direct-response television ads for "Great Music of the 50s" or "Patsy Cline's Greatest Hits" and other nostalgic products and slogans ("Bread like Grandma used to make"). They are also affected by fads.

Emulators (10 percent) are upwardly mobile and ambitious persons who are status conscious and competitive. Sometimes they try to project a macho image. They have good incomes, tend to be young, and live in urban areas. They have traditionally been males, but that is changing as more and more women enter the workplace. Emulators are into "conspicuous consumption" and purchase "in" products that represent popular fashion. They are good targets for the newest styles in clothing, automobiles, and leisure activities (health clubs, racquetball, cross-country skiing, and so on).

Achievers (22 percent) have "made it" in today's world. They are interested in efficiency, leadership, achievement, success, fame, comfort, and conspicuous con-

What do you think?

Give an example of someone you know who is an achiever.

sumption. They have excellent incomes and high degrees of education. They live in suburbs and "trendy" parts of large cities. They tend to be leaders in politics, business, and community activities. Achievers' buying patterns reflect their success — they always buy top-of-the-line products. They are willing to try "new" products and are good targets for luxury items such as Rolex watches, BMWs, "success rings," and spun-aluminum briefcases.

Inner-Directed Consumers. These consumers represent a small but distinctive slice of the market (22 percent) and are divided into four subcategories. *I-am-me* consumers (5 percent) are very individualistic and reject traditional possessions or ways of behaving. They are experimental and impulsive and tend to be dramatic and volatile (see Figure 14.6). I-am-me's come from affluent backgrounds, even though they themselves may not have much discretionary income. Many are students or are just starting on the occupational ladder. Their buy-ing patterns are more related to "taste" than high price — just the opposite of emulators and achievers. In fact, I-am-me's may be "far out" as consumers and go for faddish items.

As their name implies, *experientials* (7 percent) want to have many and varied experiences. They participate in many activities, are introspective, and are frequently artistic. They may have high or low incomes depending on their decisions about living standards. They have good educations and are likely to have families and be under 40 years of age. Experientials' buying habits focus on vigorous outdoor sports — mountain climbing, backpacking, wilderness camping, whitewater canoeing, and rafting. They are also into "do-it-yourself" projects if they relate to making a home. Experiential consumers would be good targets for products from L. L. Bean, hot-air balloon or glider rides, and advertising for the arts.

Societally conscious consumers are into simple living and have great concern over environmen-

Figure 14.6. *I-am-me's resent being labeled and want to be individualistic. They are also volatile and dramatic, as this cartoon shows. They usually are "early" baby boomers (born between 1946 and 1955). (*Arlo and Janis *reproduced by permission of NEA, Inc.)*

tal issues. They have a strong sense of societal responsibility and are likely to join the Sierra Club, Greenpeace, the nuclear freeze movement, or Salmon Unlimited. They are interested in smallness of scale and inner growth. They are mainly white and have excellent educations but bimodal incomes (that is, they cluster around the low and high ends of the income scale). These consumers are as likely to live in cities and towns as in villages or the country. Their buying habits have a conservation emphasis, focusing on simplicity and frugality. They would be good targets for energy-saving devices, cars that get good gas mileage, solar heating, recycling aluminum cans, and the human potential movement. They might be interested in organic gardening, wine making, and freezing home-grown garden produce.

Integrated consumers (2 percent) feel good about themselves and their niche in life. They are tolerant and have a sense of psychological maturity. They are also self-actualizers who take a world view on products and issues, so they would be concerned with the issue of acid rain and might boycott certain products that pollute. They have good to excellent incomes but are bimodal in age. Like societally conscious consumers, their residential pattern is variable. Their occupations

are diverse. They want to express themselves and do so in their buying habits, focusing on the uniqueness of the product in the marketplace. They would be good targets for products that allow for self-expression (for example, pottery throwing). They might also be interested in restoring historic homes, refinishing antiques, or collecting unique things. They are also aesthetically inclined and might be good targets for "artistic products" (statuary, art, music, drama, and so on). Integrated consumers are usually "early" baby boomers, that is, born between 1946 and 1955. This market segment is growing rapidly, whereas the numbers of need-driven consumers are declining and the numbers of outer-directed consumers are remaining stable.

How do advertisers use such research models and results to target us, the consumers of this country? Engle, Blackwell, and Miniard offer an illuminating case study of how VALS were used to shape not only advertising and sales promotion but brand image as well. As they report it, a midwestern chain of restaurants called Max and Erma's analyzed over 400 of their frequent customers (customers who visited the chain twice or more a month), using the VALS categories. Their core customers fell primarily in the inner-directed group (38 percent compared with 20 percent for the overall population). They were typical DINKs who ate out frequently and who were willing to try anything. They were sophisticated nonconformists who liked to express themselves and favored personal tastes rather than status or what other people think of them. They were also success oriented, hardworking, and interested in quality versus price. They probably wouldn't choose Wendy's, Bob Evans, or Shoney's. Based on these and other data, Max and Erma's reoriented its advertising, its sales promotion, and even its menus by featuring ways in which the inner-directed consumer could express his or her individuality. Menus now carried such items as "Name your own burger," "Top your own pasta," and "Build your own sundae." Local franchises offered various special promotions using direct-mail lists of potential customers and various sales promotions, including coupons and special events. In one case, local television ads feature a well-known, successful attorney and his spouse, a well-known, inner-directed community leader who was also an attorney. The couple was shown eating frequently at Max and Erma's on occasions when they wanted or needed such benefits as "time convenience," "informality," "fun times," and "quality items on the menu," all of which had been rated high by the VALS subjects/participants. Max and Erma's also provided sales training for franchise managers and staff. The result of the new approach was a turnaround in sales at a time when the industry as a whole was experiencing either further losses or at best flat levels of profits. New locations for the chain were established, whereas competing chains experienced essentially no growth or even losses.

Sociographics

Sociographics is the study of how, why, and where people gather. Its basic assumption is that "birds of a feather flock together"; that is, people choose to live with or near persons whom they find to be similar to themselves. It is something of a combination of geographics (where people live), demographics (the clusterings of variables), and psychographics (lifestyles). Research in sociographics is done by sampling persons from a zip code area that resembles the kind of neighborhood to which the advertiser believes a product will appeal. Then the ad researchers bring subjects together in focus groups to answer a survey that relates to the product and its competitors. A leader directs the groups to discuss the product, its competitors, advantages, disadvantages, and their attitudes toward it.

The researchers then analyze the data and look for patterns in the survey responses and in the focus groups' use of language. They look for recurring words, phrases, or images. These results are then turned over to the ad agency's creative staff, who design messages around the consumer-generated copy points. Sometimes they even use the exact language of the participants for the ad copy.

Some market research companies compile demographics about a variety of "typical" neighborhoods and sell these data to persons who then can confirm and add to their knowledge about the demographics of a target community. For example, the ACORN ("A Classification of Residential Neighborhoods") system identifies forty-four residential types and then categorizes subsets of each. Market segment A2, for instance, is composed of "newer suburbs, professionals, and middle-aged families," and the demographics are "similar to A1's but with slightly younger families. Middle-aged and older white families. Children are in their teens." The housing in A2 is "newer than in A1, but still has extremely high values. Almost exclusively single family, owner occupied." The lifestyle and marketing implications are as follows:

> Households in market segment A2 are second only to A1 in terms of investments, leisure activ-

ities, and travel. They are heavy spenders on their children, home furnishings, and clothing. They are the heaviest consumers of imported wines and mixed drinks. They drive expensive cars which are sportier than those of A1 households; the second car tends to be a mid-size American car, sometimes a station wagon. They are high on fitness and travel to warm climates.

Knowing this about a market segment tells the advertisers which of its products can most likely be marketed to the segment.

Sociographics also show media-use patterns, what parts of the day are devoted to which media, radio format preferences, and so on. All of these data fall into place in designing the ads using sophisticated research techniques. Think how much research goes into ads that are nationally broadcast or printed. Sophisticated persuaders using demographics, psychographics, and sociographics know a great deal about us and our consumer behavior. Nothing—well, almost nothing—in a national ad is accidental. It is all based on highly sophisticated "audience analysis."

VALS is but one kind of psychographic research model or system. All such devices try to get into the consumer's head in order to strategically develop salable products and to design advertisements that will move consumers to take sales-related action (product trial, coupon clipping, going to the point of purchase).

Another psychographic/sociographic system is based on Michael Weiss's book *The Clustering of America* (1989), and is marketed by the Claritas Corporation under the brand name PRIZM. The system has identified fifty-six distinct psychographic/sociographic neighborhood types that have names such as "Two More Rungs," or the young emulators on their way up the corporate ladder; "Pools and Patios," or achievers enjoying the good life as they approach retirement; or "Shotguns and Pickups," or high-school-educated blue-collar craftsworkers who live in modest homes or mobile home parks where one will always find a large screen TV, a dusty pickup in the driveway, and powdered soft drinks. Companies like Claritas know an amazing amount about these clusters. For example, take "Towns and Gowns," the typical college town. They are populated largely by white singles who are college grads or students who voted Republican and jogged throughout the '80s, and who are unlikely to have a van, toy-sized dogs, mutual funds, or burglar alarm systems. However, they do have personal loans, like to water and snow ski, read *Modern Bride* or *GQ*, drive Sables, Subaru DL4s, Toyota Tercels, Mazda GLCs, or Volkswagen Jettas. They like watching *David Letterman* but hate *Night Court* and Sunday morning interview programs.

What do you think?

Why is sociographics like "birds of a feather flock together"?

Imagine what knowing this kind of detail can do for an advertiser in terms of targeting the audience, ad design, media selection, and so on. And these are but a few of the details available through PRIZM. As critical consumers of persuasion, we need to be alert to the degree to which advertisers have psychographically designed ads aimed at us or our market segment.

From Research to Copy: The Languages of Advertising

Once the research department has done its job, the results are brought to the agency's creative staff for conversion into attention-getting and "memorable" ad copy. It must not only be believable but should also "sell" the product in the midst of a sea of other ads that clutter print and airwaves. Here is where our interest in persuasion should be greatest. If you have been fine-tuning your ability to analyze persuasive appeals of various types, and if you have become more aware of the nuances of meaning that both verbal and nonverbal communication can carry, then you should be able to get a sense of what copywriters are doing to us each and every day.

John O'Toole, former chairman of the board at Foote, Cone, and Belding (the eighth largest ad agency in the world) makes some interesting observations about reaching the audience in believable ways in his book *The Trouble with Advertising* (1985). His basic idea is that the consumer is at the center of the process. O'Toole believes that the only kind of language — verbal and nonverbal — that can effectively persuade in an advertisement is that which is targeted at the consumer *as an individual and not just one of the masses*. At Foote, Cone, and Belding, the first task for a new product or account is to develop a "personal profile" of the consumer. The consumer is considered a unique individual with whom the client carries on an interpersonal dialogue using advertising as the means of communicating. To quote O'Toole on this: "Advertising works best when it most closely approximates a dialogue between two human beings" (p. 122). He also says, "Regarding the other party as a person rather than as people . . . making that person know you recognize him as an individual rather than as a face in the crowd, is going to cause him to respond more positively to you" (pp. 110–111).

O'Toole gives several examples of this kind of personal language and copy, including: "Aren't you glad you use Dial? Don't you wish everyone did?" This slogan addresses the consumer much more personally than the one for another deodorant: "Get off the can. Get on the stick." Or take the Sears DieHard battery ad copy that follows a demonstration of the battery in action: "The DieHard. Starts your car when most other batteries won't." What about "You're not getting older; you're getting better"? These copy lines are aimed at an individual, not at just another cipher in the masses. They fulfill Fairfax Cone's memo to O'Toole: "Let us make every advertisement that we make *personal*. Let us aim it at just *one* person, just as we would in face-to-face contact."

That kind of ad copy gets what O'Toole calls "the nod of agreement." This phrase is close to what Schwartz means by resonance: Consumers recognize some part of themselves or their experiences in the words or visuals of the ad. The nod of agreement is part of what O'Toole calls "the implicit contract" between advertiser and consumer. Although the contract is unwritten, it is clearly understood by even the most naive consumer. The implied contract is simply that advertisers will try to promote a product but won't tell you about their competitors. They will try to present their product in its best light, but they won't mislead you, lie to you, or bore you. In return for the opportunity to promote their product, advertisers subsidize programs, journalism, documentaries, the news, music, sports events, entertainment, and more. Sometimes we are fooled and purchase a product that is not all it has been "puffed up" to be. In that case, we may return the product or never buy it again, and we can warn other consumers not to buy the product. O'Toole admits that there have been misleading and even outright false advertisements across the years, but he is quick to point out that consumers soon identify those ads and then ignore them.

O'Toole contends that "American consumers are the canniest of creatures. . . . And they are powerful [because of] their refusal to repurchase" (p. 21). That is why 80 percent of the new products brought out on the market in any given year *fail*.

Although O'Toole's assurances are sincere, consumers should still be aware of some of the kinds of appeals advertisers make that do not actually "lie" or that are not obviously "fraudulent," but that "bend" the truth without actually fracturing it. Several of the more interesting, useful, and lively discussions of the topic of "misleading" advertising are found in the work done by Carl Wrighter and Hugh Rank.

Language Use in Advertising: Wrighter's Model

We have been looking at how advertisers use words in media messages. We know that symbols are the basic raw material of persuasion, and we know that words are central carriers of symbolic meaning. So we need to look at how clever persuaders use words and at how these words work in ad messages. Carl Wrighter, a former adman, in his book *I Can Sell You Anything* (1972), focuses on some of the key words that he thinks are used to deceive us. He calls them *weasel words* because they allow persuaders to seem to say something without ever really saying it. These words let sources weasel their way out of a promise. They are key tipoffs to the kind of pitch we need to guard against. Here are some to watch for.

"Helps"

The word "helps" is a clever one. It seems to offer aid or perhaps even a cure. We hear that Listerine mouthwash *helps* prevent colds. Even if you get a cold, it *helps* you feel better right away. What is the promise here? Can you expect that you will feel better in a few days if you use Listerine? If you did, could you say your improvement resulted from the *help* Listerine gave? These questions point up the problem with a word such as "helps." We need to be alert to this often-used weasel word.

"Like"

Another weasel word used in ads is "like." For instance, there on the printed page is a famous tennis star telling us that driving a Honda Prelude is *like* driving one of those expensive European cars—but for a lot less in overall costs. Or the house brand is *like* the expensive name brands—"we just don't advertise."

You can easily see the deception that can be floated with a word that has as many loopholes as "like." Cindy Crawford is supposed to be *like* women all over the world. A prepared food tastes just *like* homemade. A jug wine tastes *like* the expensive French wines. Geritol will make you feel *like* you are a kid again. A BMW hugs the road *like* a cat.

"Virtually"

The weasel word "virtually" resembles "like," except that it seems to promise even more. The new cotton chamois shirts are *virtually* indestructible. Leatherette feels *virtually like* cowhide. Cascade leaves your dishes and glassware *virtually* spotless. The promise seems so specific. There is only a tiny loophole. But that loophole widens as much as is needed when the customer says that the leatherette wore out after several months or when we find a few spots here and there on the dishes and stemware. If the product did what is claimed, the word "virtually" would not be needed.

What do you think?
Find examples of weasel words at work.

Deceptive Claims in Advertising

Another kind of deception to which we are exposed in ads is found in claims. Clever promoters use claims to attract our attention and to prompt us to buy products, to vote for candidates, or to adopt certain practices. Let us look at several kinds of claims identified by Wrighter.

The Irrelevant Claim

Some persuaders use ad messages to make claims that sound impressive but are irrelevant if you look at them closely.

You are exposed to such claims whenever you turn on your TV, open a magazine, or tune in your radio. The basic tactic is to make a truthful claim that has little to do with the purpose of the product, plan for change, or idea. Then that claim is dramatized in such a way that the people link the claim with the product, candidate, or movement.

J&B scotch claims to be "rare" and "natural." Why would you want "rare" scotch? What is "natural" about J&B? Are other scotch whiskeys unnatural? If you can't find an answer, chances are you have identified an irrelevant claim.

The Question Claim

Wrighter notes a kind of claim we often see beamed at us through the media: the claim that is hidden by a question. "If you can't trust Prestone, who can you trust?" "Why not buy the original?" "Why not send the best?" "Would a bunch of guys really go at it this hard just for a Michelob?" and "Why not catch a lunker — with Stren monofilament?" are all examples of the question claim. Notice that the product advantage is only implied. Trusting one's antifreeze is OK, but the question implies that dependability is to be found *only* in Prestone. But we know that other brands of antifreeze are also dependable. Why buy the original? It may be overpriced. Maybe the Michelob is just an afterthought. Will using Stren guarantee that I'll catch a lunker? When you see or hear a question claim, the best response is to ask for details and guarantees.

The Advantage Claim

Wrighter also noted the type of claim that seems to offer some advantage for a product or idea. Mother's noodles claim to be made with 100 percent semolina wheat — but so are all the other brands. If you compare the levels of vitamins in several types of breakfast cereal, you will discover that they are

all about the same. Most of the protein comes from the milk you add and not from the cereal. Thus, there is no advantage in Corn Chex's claim that it is "fortified with six important vitamins and minerals." These are advantages that aren't.

Politicians often claim to have come from humble beginnings, which is supposed to be an advantage. It may be a real disadvantage from one perspective: People who had humble beginnings may be insecure. They probably had to compete for everyday things, which may limit their educational sophistication, sense of diplomacy, social skills, and ability to communicate with leaders in higher social strata.

Whenever we are faced with a person, product, or idea that claims some significant advantage, we need to ask whether the advantage is real; whether it is exclusive to that person, product, or idea; and whether certain disadvantages might not accompany it.

The Hazy Claim

The hazy claim confuses the buyer or voter. If persuaders can confuse you, you will follow their advice just to be on the safe side. Consider the ad for Dannon yogurt shown in Figure 14.7. It confuses the reader by implying that yogurt eaters live longer. As you read more of the ad copy, you see that the only health claim Dannon can make is that its yogurt, unlike some others (how many? which brands? so what?), has active cultures. The consumer does not know whether it is good to eat Dannon Yogurt, yogurt of any kind, or no yogurt. Out of this confusion, Dannon persuades through its slogan: "If you don't always eat right, Dannon yogurt is the right thing to eat." We ought to ask, "Why is it right?" "Who says?" and "With what proof?" when a hazy claim appears.

Again, we can see hazy claims widely used in the world of politics. For example, a politician says that she supports the economic policies of free trade and protective tariffs. These policies, however, are 180 degrees apart, so the result for voters is confusion. If voters watch images, the problem becomes worse. What does it prove when a politician kisses babies or plays baseball or talks about the price of pork? These activities do not tell us much about an elected official's ability to construct policies on education, leisure time, or farm prices. They are likely to confuse the voter and draw attention away from the issues.

The Magic Ingredient Claim

Wrighter calls this the *mysterious* claim because it refers to a mysterious ingredient or device that makes a better product. I prefer to call it the magic ingredient claim.

Noxzema, for example, has a product called "Acne 12," which is claimed to contain a magic, secret ingredient that dermatologists prescribe most. Oxy-Clean contains "a powerful yet gentle medication no ordinary cleanser has." If the manufacturers had a real secret ingredient, they would not tell about it.

Many other kinds of claims are made through the mass media. Wrighter's book points out several. You will discover others as you begin to evaluate advertising messages you receive. The important thing is to maintain a critical attitude. Ask key questions of the claim.

Rank's 30-Second-Spot Quiz

Hugh Rank, who originated the intensify/downplay model discussed in Chapter 1, has outlined an easy-to-apply set of key questions to ask about advertising appeals. His system, "The 30-Second-Spot Quiz," is based on his book *The Pitch* (1982).

Rank begins by pointing out that any advertisement, but especially a television spot advertise-

Dannon Yogurt may not help you live as long as Soviet Georgians. But it couldn't hurt.

Bagrat Topagua, age 89.

His mother.

There are two curious things about the people of Soviet Georgia. A large part of their diet is yogurt. And a large number of them live to be well over 100.

Of course, many factors affect longevity, and we are not saying Dannon Yogurt will help you live longer. But we will say that all-natural Dannon is high in nutrients, low in fat, reasonable in calories. And quite satisfying at lunch or as a snack.

Another thing about Dannon. It contains active yogurt cultures (many pre-mixed or

Swiss style brands don't). They make yogurt one of the easiest foods to digest and have been credited with other healthful benefits.

Which is why we've been advising this: If you don't always eat right, Dannon Yogurt is the right thing to eat.

By the way, Bagrat Topagua thought Dannon was "dzelian kargia." Which means he loved it.

Dannon Milk Products, 22-11 38th Ave. Long Island City, N.Y. 11101.

Figure 14.7. The hazy claims about longevity and yogurt may confuse the persuadee enough to try the product, just to be on the safe side. (Used by permission of Dannon Milk Products.)

ment, is a *synthesis* of complex variables — research, scripting, settings, camera angles, acting, props, costumes, colors, and so on. Any analysis of such a complex synthesis demands that consumers look at the spots in a sequential way.

This can be accomplished, Rank suggests, by listing, in order, the "shots" or visual frames that make up a 30-second spot, remembering that there might be as many as forty quick-cut shots. For example, most spots have an "establishing shot," or the shot that "sets the stage" for the ad. Various versions of an ad for Miller's Reserve lager and ale used views of some familiar sight in the city in which the advertising was tested. The San Francisco version used the Golden Gate bridge and the Chicago version used the Sears Tower. Other kinds of shots continue to further the "story" of the ad. A medium shot showing a couple from the waist up involved in an argument tells us that conflict is central to the story. We hear the audio come up and discover that they are arguing about whether to buy an American or foreign-made automobile. The camera moves in for a close-up shot of the man's face, and we hear musical tension increasing as we see and hear the tension in his face and voice. Then the close-up shifts to the woman's face and we hear her say "You know, you're cute when you're serious like this?" and we hear a giggle and see a nuzzle. The shots tell the story. Your job as a receiver using Ranks' 30-second-spot quiz is to continue listing the shots in order until the ad is completely described. Try to distinguish the "surface variations" that occur as well as the "underlying structure" of the spot. For example, the underlying structure of the ad just described is conflict resolution, but a surface variation could have used two males for the argument. This surface variation would alter the dialogue, tension, drama, and, finally, the meaning of the ad.

Rank also suggests recognizing the audience's involvement in the spot. What benefits are we seeking, and what benefits are being promised by the brand? For example, the Ford Escort advertises that it has "aerodynamic styling," "independent wheel suspension," and "rack and pinion steering." These are "features" of the Escort and not benefits. Features should offer some benefit to the consumer. For instance, "aerodynamic styling" offers the benefits of better handling, less wind resistance, better gas mileage, and a quieter interior. This is the key kind of question to ask.

Once these preparatory steps are taken, Rank suggests asking five basic analytical questions:

1. What **attention-getting techniques** are being used? For example, most ads appeal to one or more of the five senses (see Figure 14.8). Most also appeal to our emotions and may use the unexpected, the interesting, and the noticeable (such as famous athletes) to capture consumers' attention.

2. What **confidence-building techniques** are being used to convince consumers that they can trust the brand? The use of authority figures, repetition, references to the amount of time the brand has been successful, appeals to trust and sincerity, the use of expert testimony such as from a doctor or other authority, satisfaction and service guarantees, warranties, and a host of other techniques help build consumer confidence.

3. What **desire-stimulating techniques** are being used to motivate the consumer to try the brand? Rank suggests that identifying the benefits being offered is a good way to discover these techniques. He suggests that most ads offer one or more of the following as desire-stimulating reasons to try the brand: (a) to *prevent or avoid* some bad thing (disease, discomfort, embarrassment), (b) to *protect or keep* some good thing (health, status, appearance, wealth), (c) to gain *relief or get rid of* some bad thing (bad breath, dandruff, financial worry), or (d) to *acquire or get* some good thing (a new car, a cash card).

4. What **urgency-stressing techniques** are being used to get the consumer to "act now" (expiration dates, deadlines, "while supplies last")?

5. What **response-seeking techniques** are being used to tell the consumer what kind of action is being sought (purchase, brand shifting, joining, calling)?

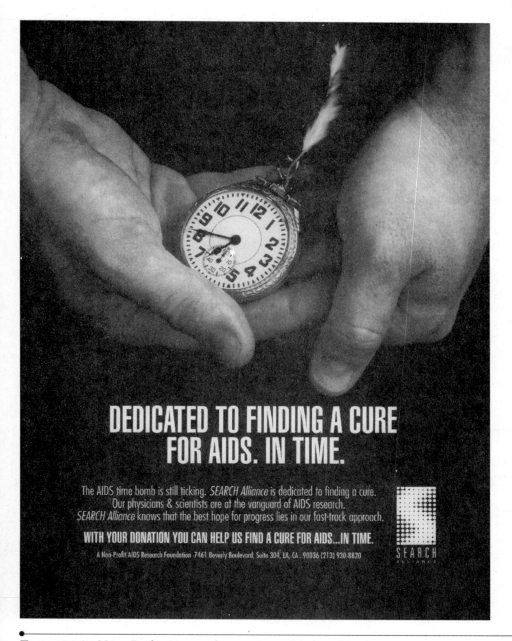

Figure 14.8. Using Rank's 30-second-spot quiz, explain how this ad gets consumer attention. (By permission of Search Alliance.)

Changes in Our World: Implications for Advertising

Since the first edition of this book, twenty-five years ago, a number of societal changes have occurred that have had enormous effects on the way we behave as consumers and how critics of persuasion—especially advertising persuasion—have come to look at this field. Consider a few trends. More families than ever now rely on two incomes per household. This trend has led to many new products. For example: Campbell's "Soup for One" is a single-sized serving of the product, just as Stokely's Singles are servings of vegetables for one person. Who are the targets of such products? Widows and widowers? Single persons? Divorced persons? To some extent yes, but research demonstrated to Campbell's that the eating habits of Americans were in a rapid state of change. Because of the two-income family pattern, meals were not the traditional "family around the dinner table" anymore. Dad went off to his late meeting while Mom was not yet home from her job; Bobby rode his bike to soccer practice, and his older sister Susie had to rehearse for the high school play. The perfect solution? Give both Bobby and Susie their choice of a sandwich and their favorite "Soup for One."

Another change has been the introduction of 1-800 and later 1-900 dialing, which makes it much easier to purchase anything from clothing to ammo to phone sex. For two-income families, time is a commodity to be "spent" carefully, and mail-order purchasing for oneself or for gifts for others saves time. As a result we have an explosion in cataloging—*it saves time.* So does eating out, and as a result fast- and specialty-food establishments have proliferated. The average American eats more than half of his or her meals out.

Retail square footage increased by about 70 percent in the last decade, while disposable consumer income grew only about 14 percent in that same period. This resulted in a very competitive marketplace, especially given the amount of disposable income being used for catalog and other direct-marketed products. We now see "pre-Christmas sales," as well as the traditional "post-Christmas sales." The number of large discount chains has increased as well, which has important implications for advertising. For one thing, the amount of advertising will increase simply because one of the ways to try to beat the competition is to out-advertise them. There will be more sales promotions—coupons, rebates, sweepstakes, celebrities at point of purchase, shelf-talkers, product demonstrations, displays, and so on—a persuasion approach closely related to advertising.

A new video-equipped grocery cart is being tested in several markets by Information Resources, Inc., whose chairman says that whereas most "in-store selling techniques are aimed at selling something without providing any benefits to the consumers, Videocart makes shopping more informative and fun for consumers" (Storch, 1988). The local supermarket's satellite dish antenna receives a new product's advertisement, which replaces the old ad on the store manager's computer. This new ad is transmitted to the shelf space where the product is on display. When a cart passes the transmitter, it triggers the coffee ad on the screen that is part of the cart. At the checkout counter, the cash register/computer tells which ads triggered a purchase and what path the cart took through the store. In short, there will be more "clutter" for advertisers to try to "break through" and for us to try to sift through. And we are just on the cutting edge of interactive computer and Internet advertising. As people spend more and more time on PCs, advertisers will surely target the new technology as an additional way to promote their brands. *Advertising Age* began to include an "Interactive" section in its weekly issues in the early '90s, and ad execs and others took notice. No successful corporation would think of operating without a home page.

Academic Analysis of Advertising

From an academic viewpoint, it has finally been recognized that television is a topic worthy of study and criticism and that even the lowly TV spot is a kind of "rhetoric" that needs to be critically analyzed instead of being dismissed out of hand (Williamson, 1977; Postman, 1987; Diamond, 1984; Leiss, Kline, & Jhally, 1986).

The Language of Advertising by Torben Vestergaard and Kim Schroder (1985) is an excellent resource for analyzing advertising. They point out that advertising is senseless unless goods are sufficiently overproduced so that sell-ers need to "beat the competition." They note that material needs and social status are frequently communicated through habits of consumption. In other words, the purchased objects have become *semanticized*. The kind of clothing, cars, audio equipment, and so on that we buy has a "meaning" to others with whom we socialize. This permits advertisers to exploit our needs for group affiliation, self-identification, and status.

Vestergaard and Schroder go on to define advertising as a "text" that is meant to be "read" in all its verbal and nonverbal nuances, and describe it as having three dimensions:

1. It exists in a particular communication situation.

2. It is a structured unit and has texture.

3. It communicates meaning.

Perhaps the most difficult dimension to understand is the idea of a text having structure and texture. Vestergaard and Schroder provide helpful examples. Take the structure or sense of the information content of this copy from an ad in *Cosmopolitan:*

> An automatic applicator gently smooths on soft cream or high-shine colour, for a smooth silky finish that lasts. And lasts.

and

> . . . colours that look lastingly tempting. Longer.

Here, we have two sentence fragments—"And lasts" and "Longer"—which could have as easily been included in the sentences that precede them. Why split them up? Because the advertiser has cut two sense-making units into four, thus encouraging the reader to focus on the product benefits four times instead of two.

Another technique that can give an ad structure or texture is the drama implied. Vestergaard and Schroder use the work of A. J. Griemas and his pairs of teams, which are used to describe a fundamental drama in folk tales and myths:

> subject—object
>
> helper—opponent
>
> giver—receiver

To see how this model can be used in analyzing the verbal and nonverbal languages of an ad, consider an ad for Avon. The visual, or nonverbal, part takes up the upper two-thirds of the page. It shows a mature woman standing behind a younger woman who is trying to put on make-up. The headline reads, "I enjoy helping other women to look good," and the copy then goes on to explain that by being an Avon representative, you can bring all of the wonderful Avon products into customers' homes. Furthermore, Avon products have a "no quibble guarantee."

The "subject" is the young woman, and her "opponent" is her uncertainty. The "helper"—the Avon representative—solves this problem by bringing a "giver"—Avon products—to her door. The "receiver" is thus "rescued" from the opponent by the product.

Vestergaard and Schroder point out several other concepts that contribute to the structure and texture of advertisements. The important thing is to try to take the ad apart, bit by bit, verbally and nonverbally, and see what it is *really* saying and how it works—to "deconstruct" the ad, in other words.

They go on to point out the traditional task of the ad copywriter as having five steps:

1. Attract attention.

2. Arouse interest.

3. Stimulate desire.

4. Create conviction.

5. Get action.

Attracting Attention. The easiest way to attract attention is by putting the product's name next to a visual of the product. Far more effective is to also describe a product benefit.

Another way to attract attention is to ask a question of the reader/viewer ("Why don't you come back to Folgers?") or to use the word "when" (as in "When the day is done, have a cold one—Coors, the Rocky Mountain reward"). Naming the user also captures attention ("Contact lens users—Now you can have all-day comfort with Comfordrops"). Naming the consumer is even more effective when coupled with some kind of flattering statement about the user ("For the outdoorsman who has everything: give him a Schrade Knife"). Certain words are attention getters—Free, New, More, Now, You, and Act are just a few examples. Ads that have people in them pull better than those that just show the brand, and attention improves if children, puppies, or kittens are seen. Recipes included in the ad also help attract attention and get consumer involvement. Seductive and sexy models also boost ratings, and other attention-getting and -maintaining devices are being developed almost daily at the advertising agencies of the '90s.

Creating Interest, Desire, and Conviction. Vestergaard and Schroder also say that a good way to get audience attention and then to create inter-est is to ask a question that the reader or viewer probably cannot answer. This provokes curiosity and usually leads the audience to interact with the advertisement in some way: reading the copy, looking at the visuals, or even physically interacting with it (scratch 'n sniff, for example).

One example of this tactic is to ask a question that leads to a true/false "quiz" that the reader is supposed to answer. For example, the headline of a full-page, four-color ad by General Motors Parts asks, "Do you know where your next fender is coming from?" GM satisfies the reader's curiosity by answering, "America's body shops are being flooded with imitation parts. Look-alike doors. Copycat hoods. Imitation bumpers, grilles, fenders and more. . . . These not-so-exact replicas seldom measure up to General Motors original specifications. . . . Insist on genuine GM parts." This ad copy is designed not only to answer the attention-getting headline but also to create interest, desire, and conviction in the reader/viewer by pointing out product benefits—the *unique selling proposition* (USP) mentioned earlier. Again, notice the use of sentence fragments—"Look-alike doors" and "Copycat hoods"—to give the advertiser extra "shots" at the reader.

A problem in today's crowded marketplace is that most products are "me too" imitations of the original, and most of the USPs tend to be aesthetic. All dog food, for instance, looks pretty much alike—either like pebbles if it is dry or like glop if it is canned. But look at what Gaines Burger did. In the first place, its name sounds like and the product looks like hamburger—the all-American favorite food. Of course, its redness is not natural—it comes from an additive. It won't hurt your dog, but it will cause you to make a link with a past experience: buying fresh red hamburger (which is also not naturally red).

Another tactic used for creating interest, desire, and conviction is to stress the "high quality" of the product if it is a "me too" product. High quality is a slippery thing to prove, which is why the word is used so often in ads. If an advertiser says its product is the lowest priced in town, that can be verified as true or false, which is why you do not often see that statement. Instead, advertisers more frequently say that they will "meet or beat" any price. But if they say the product has the best quality for the price, they are not likely to be called on to prove their claim. We all know that quality is not "Job 1" at Ford — productivity and resulting profit are the real Job 1.

Another approach is to appeal to the reverence we hold toward anything scientific by including some scientific-sounding ingredient such as "Platformate," "retsyn," or "DZM-21." An advertiser can also make a "scientific" claim: "The pain reliever recommended most by doctors and hospitals" is one example. Or the spokesperson might be dressed in a laboratory coat and standing in a lab with microscopes, test tubes, and so on, in the background. This "scientist" then tells us about the product benefits.

Getting Action. Any salesperson will tell you that the critical and usually the hardest thing to do is to "close" the sale — in other words, to get action. "Buy now" would seem to be the most direct call to action, but Vestergaard and Schroder found the word "buy" in only two advertisements in their analysis of the ten magazine issues on which their book is based. However, there are other ways to say "buy now" without using the word "buy." For example, "act now," "phone now," and "send now" say the same thing as "buy now" but avoid the negative connotations of the word "buy." Other urgency-stressing words and phrases can be the call to action: "While supplies last," "Offer good until . . .," "24-hour sale," and so on. These are what Vestergaard and Schroder call *directive language*. they found that 32 percent of the

> **What do you think?**
> What are some good ways for advertising to get action?

ads they studied used one form or another of this type of language. Directive language falls into three categories:

1. *The imperative clause, which gives an order.* "Get some today" is one example. Another can be found in an ad for a fishing lure supposedly in short supply — the Shadrap. The ad copy for it reads: "The Rapala company was only able to send 125,000 Shadraps to the U.S. — If you see one, grab it!"

2. *Other less directive and more suggestive language to encourage the reader or viewer to buy.* An example is the "negated interrogative," as in "Isn't it time you tried Dial?" A softer version is "Why not try Dial?" Even less directive is "Dial is worth a try." And in the weakest version, the directions are not directly attributed to the reader or viewer but to a reference group: "For people who believe a deodorant bath soap should also be gentle on the skin, there's Dial with lanolin."

3. *Directive language that invites the reader or viewer to send for details, use the trial sample, or remember the product.* Sometimes these appeals are designed to get a sale, but more often they are used to create "qualified leads" that can be followed up by a telephone call or a visit by the salesforce. If a person sends in for a free pamphlet on energy saving, for example, he or she is probably a good prospect ("qualified lead") for storm windows, aluminum siding, and energy-efficient furnaces.

Although only two of the ads investigated by Vestergaard and Schroder used the word *buy*, only twenty other verbs made up most of the directive appeals. They were

try, ask for, take, send for, call/make, come on, hurry, come/see/give/remember/discover, serve/introduce, choose/look for.

Sexual Appeals and Subliminal Persuasion in Advertising

The issues of sexual appeals and subliminal advertising appeals are controversial ones. Criticisms arise from diverse constituencies. For example, feminists are concerned about advertising's exploitation of the female body. Others are concerned about increases in sexually transmitted diseases, high rates of teenage pregnancy, and increasing promiscuity on the part of all levels of society. And still others question the ethics of subliminal appeals and maintain that such appeals violate the individual's right to know what messages are being targeted at them.

Sexual appeals in advertising range from the obvious and blatant ones that almost *promise* sexual success for users of the product to the less obvious and more symbolic ads that seem to only *suggest* instead of promise sexual success. In addition there may be subliminal ads that seem to only suggest sexual success on the surface but that promise it at the unconscious or subliminal level.

Of course, the work of Sigmund Freud and his followers is applicable here. Freud maintained that sexual impulses and the resulting procreative urge are among the most powerful motivators of human action. Not only do they alter physical behavior, they also affect symbolic behavior, giving sexual meanings to a wide variety of objects and actions. For example, the Freudians saw cylindrical objects (pens, pencils, cigars, bottles, guns, and so on) as being symbolic of an erect phallus, while they saw round or open objects (goblets, vases, bowls, open windows and doors, flowers, and so on) as symbolic of the vagina. Thus, all sorts of ordinary everyday activities (washing one's hands, fiddling with objects) might become symbolic substitutes for human sexual activities — intercourse or masturbation. Freud's work was ridiculed by many, but it was taken very seriously by a number of psychologists and, more importantly for our

purposes, by many people in the field of advertising, as we learned from Vance Packard back in Chapter 6.

Even putting Freudian explanations aside, simple observation of the power of the human sexual impulse makes the reason for the use of sexual appeals in advertising perfectly apparent. After all, one of the major goals of advertising is to gain and maintain the attention of prospective users, so why not use one of the most powerful and hence "interesting" topics in the world? The question facing persuaders is not *whether* to use sexual appeals in advertising but *how* to use them. We'll examine some obvious, some more sophisticated and not so obvious, and some unconscious and possibly subliminal uses of sexual appeals in advertising and try to derive some idea of how such appeals work on us. We are limited to print examples in this book, but electronic advertising obviously uses sexual appeals as well. For instance, in a TV commercial for Pepsi, two young boys make apparently suggestive comments about Cindy Crawford as they ogle her from afar while she buys a drink from a vending machine; they turn out to really be talking about the Pepsi. Try to become aware of how pervasive and persuasive sexual appeals are in all kinds of advertising, whether the appeals are blatant, sophisticated, or subliminal.

Obvious Sexual Appeals

In the use of obvious sexual appeals in advertising, the advertiser usually *promises* sexual success or satisfaction to the person using the product. The promise is carried in both the verbal (words, phrases, sentences) and the nonverbal (pictures, layout, typeface, etc.) elements in the ad. For instance, consider the ad for Royal Copenhagen Cologne for Men shown in Figure 14.9. The appeal is quite obvious: Use the product and you will experience sexual success and satisfaction.

Figure 14.9. *Blatant uses of sexual appeals in advertising promise sexual success to the user of the product. (Reprinted by permission of Tsumura International.)*

With the exception of the play on the words "wildest storms," the reader would have to be pretty slow not to get the meaning here. Some more subtle sexual appeals are at work as well. A Freudian would immediately point out the phallic prow of the ship and bottles of cologne. The use of two bottles — one boxed and one un-boxed — might also suggest intercourse. And the fact that we are seeing the love scene through a secret *window* makes us all voyeurs. You might try to do some analyses of other obvious sexual appeals in advertising in such magazines as *Vanity Fair, Cosmopolitan,* and GQ.

More Sophisticated Sexual Appeals

In more sophisticated sexual appeals, the advertiser seems to only *suggest* that the product will lead to sexual satisfaction instead of virtually promising sexual success. Such appeals may also contain subtle cues to indicate successful sexual prowess. For example, consider an ad by Tiffany and Company for a sterling silver flask pendant by Elsa Peretti. A close-up photo shows the pendant, dripping water, hanging by a silver chain, and resting in the cleavage of a well-endowed, wet, and nearly nude woman. Inserted in the flask is the stem of an orchid on which a preying mantis is perched. Aside from naming the product and the retail store where it is available, the ad contains no verbal appeals — no promise of sexual success, prowess, or satisfaction. Yet the ad clearly uses the sexual urge as an appeal to the customer. Again, Freudians would be quick to point out the symbolism of the phallic orchid stem inserted into the vaginally shaped flask. Freudians would also see the abundance of water as symbolic of completed intercourse. But why put a preying mantis on the orchid — what do you think it symbolizes or communicates?

Subliminal Appeals

Subliminal appeals are a highly controversial topic (Phillips & Goodkin, 1983). Many doubt their very existence. In fact, some reviewers of this book have suggested that this section on subliminal persuasion be dropped. Why should this topic stir up so much controversy? Probably because it runs counter to the idea that human beings are by nature logical, not emotional, and are certainly not totally preoccupied by sex. Then, too, the controversy also probably occurs because subliminal persuasion smacks of sensationalism and the kind of witch-doctory of which the Freudians were accused. Let us examine the arguments made by those who claim that subliminal messages do exist and the controversy over whether the technique works. We will also look at some ads that seem to be using subliminal or nearly subliminal appeals.

Support for the Existence of Subliminal Messages. The basic claim in subliminal persuasion rests on Freud's notion of the id, a component of personality that is completely unconscious. He saw the id as powerful and creative but unruly, full of antisocial impulses. In his view, the impulses of the id are so powerful that they must be enacted in conscious life, even if only in symbolic ways. Freud also believed that the unconscious mind is constantly working at processing "information" that the conscious mind simply ignores, and that it stores this information from the moment of birth on. Those who believe in the existence of subliminal appeals maintain that such appeals are sometimes so short or so disguised that the conscious mind ignores them, yet at the subconscious level of the id they are extremely powerful.

The interest in subliminal persuasion dates back to the late 1950s, when James Vicary, the owner of a failing research business, claimed that he had increased Coca-Cola and popcorn sales at a local theater by flashing the words "Drink Coke" and "Eat Popcorn" for brief instants on the movie screen during a film. He claimed that the messages bypassed the conscious mind but were embedded in the unconscious mind. Sales of Coke and popcorn supposedly increased by over 50 percent. However, his results could not be replicated. Nevertheless, the technique seemed to be so powerful that it was barred from use in the radio and television industry following pressure from the Federal Communications Commission.

This ruling did not forbid the use of subliminal messages in print and film media. In 1972 a corporation marketing movies to airlines announced that it would be selling spots for subliminal ads. Over a dozen commercial research firms in Chicago and New York offer services in producing subliminal messages to advertisers. Subliminal messages were used in the film *The Exorcist,* leading to a personal injury lawsuit against Warner Brothers over an alleged accident during a screening that was attributed to a subliminally embedded message (Goodkin & Phillips, 1983). Subliminal researcher Hal Becker used auditory subliminal messages to treat a number of psychological problems. Becker argued that subliminal persuasion could be used nationwide to reduce alcoholism, drug abuse, dangerous driving, and various phobias. He also recommended using subliminal messages to discourage shoplifting in stores by mixing messages about honesty and getting caught if you shoplift with the piped-in music (Becker & Glanzer, 1978). The CIA has had a long and continuing interest in how subliminal communication might be used in intelligence work, especially in espionage and counterespionage (Goodkin & Phillips, 1983).

In the mid 1970s a researcher and professor of advertising, Wilson Bryan Key, popularized the issue in three books: *Subliminal Seduction* (1973), *Media Sexploitation* (1977), and *Clambake Orgy* (1980). All of the books claimed that subliminal cues — usually erotic ones — were "embedded" in

magazine ads that appealed to subconscious and repressed sex drives. These messages usually occurred in ads for liquor and cigarettes, he claimed. These "embeds," as he called them, were faintly airbrushed into ads in the final stages of production and were subconsciously "remembered" some time later when cued by a chance to buy the product or brand.

Key was originally struck by the need to retouch photos used in the production of certain magazine advertisements. For example, Key notes that most liquor ads needed airbrushing because the ice cubes in the glasses would melt under the hot lights needed for magazine-quality photos. As long as the persuaders were airbrushing in the ice cubes, Key reasoned, why wouldn't they consider airbrushing in a subtle message such as the words "buy" or "good"?

Advertisers need to get maximum effect for their dollar. They know that basic human needs are the most motivating and that themes of sex and combat are central in most people's fantasy worlds. Key tested his hypothesis by studying a Gilby's gin ad; he found what seemed to be the word "sex" airbrushed into the ice cubes, and he thought he detected phallic symbols, reflections that depicted various stages in seduction, and so on. Because these vague airbrushed words and symbols might all have been in Key's head, he tested 1000 people by showing them the ad and asking them to put into words the feelings they had while looking at the ad. None of the 1000 was told what to look for, and none had heard of or knew of subliminal techniques. Although 38 percent did not respond at all, the remaining 62 percent reported that the ad made them feel "sensual," "aroused," "romantic," "sexy," and even "horny" in several cases. It is possible that this finding was accidental, but Key reports having replicated the test with several ads with similar results. It is also possible that the advertiser does not consciously put subliminal messages into ads —

that they are accidental. I suppose it really does not matter as long as receiver effects occur.

Of course, if the advertisers really were trying to persuade by manipulating the subconscious, that would raise some ethical issues. However, if an advertising agency did use subliminal techniques, they would probably deny it, as many agencies have done since the publication of Key's books. So whether or not the messages are there as a strategy of the source, the message has effects that correlate with Key's hypothesis that symbolic embeds (usually sexually oriented) affect audiences.

Key advises us to become critical receivers by looking beyond the surface message in any ad and searching for elements in the background, in the lighting, in the potential symbolic messages. This will alert you to an ad's hidden meaning and may train you as an "embed spotter." He says that the ad copy, layout, and characters should tip you off to any potential embeds. Whether or not you see the embedded sex symbols, you can get cued to possible subliminal persuasion by looking at ads more critically and by trying to determine what they suggest without saying.

Some Possible Subliminal Ads. Let's explore some advertisements that are possible candidates for using subliminal or near-subliminal persuasion. In all cases, their appeals seem to promise sexual success, prowess, and satisfaction.

Consider the two perfume ads in Figures 14.10 and 14.11. The first is called "The Promise Made." The second is called "The Promise Kept." Observe what has changed between "The Promise Made" and "The Promise Kept." The champagne bottle is empty, the phone is off the hook, the fire has died down, the woman's shoes are on the dais, the flowers on the left seem to have bloomed in the heat, and the woman's earrings are off, as is her stole. Use Key's technique to see whether you find any subtle messages here. First, note the actual words included in the ad. Do they imply any dual meanings? If so, search for visual clues

in the ad that would substantiate the implied meaning.

In the early 1980s, the "dancing" logo of the Danskin Company was "hidden" in each of its ads, much as *Playboy* "hides" its rabbit motif on each *Playboy* cover. Subliminal persuasion devices are being marketed as aids in self-improvement, as seen in Figure 14.12.

Now turn your attention to Figures 14.13, 14.14, and 14.15. They are part of an ongoing series of ads on behalf of Seagram's Gin called the "Hidden Pleasure" campaign. The ads use embeds, but instead of hiding them, the folks at Seagram's point them out to you. They are, in a sense, spoofing Wilson Bryan Key's claims. The appeals in them are not directly sexual but rather are only benignly romantic.

In the ad in Figure 14.13, the key words turn out to be "Hidden Pleasures," "Serve one," and "It's a hit" because embedded in the ice cubes and drops of moisture on the glasses are two tennis players, one male and one female. The one at the left has his racquet lifted as in serving a tennis ball. The one on the right has her racquet in the ready position. In Figure 14.14, the ad designers have once again given the reader a clue for finding the embed: The words "Hint. It's as smooth as a moonlit waltz" are at the left of the goblet, and an arrow points to a waltzing couple emerging out of the air bubbles in the martini glass. In Figure 14.15, you'd have to be blind not to see a couple sitting next to one another, holding hands, embedded in the ice cube.

What do you think?

Do you think subliminal techniques are used in the advertising you see and hear?

Are Subliminals Effective? If subliminal messages are used, can they be effective in persuasion? The president of the American Psychological Association's Division of Consumer Psychology says, "Absolutely. . . . The controversy has always been over *changing* people's attitudes. That you can't do.

Figure **14.10.** *What kind of promise is being made? (Courtesy Lanvin Parfums Co., New York.)*

Figure 14.11. *What differences imply that the promise was kept? (Courtesy Lanvin Parfums Co., New York.)*

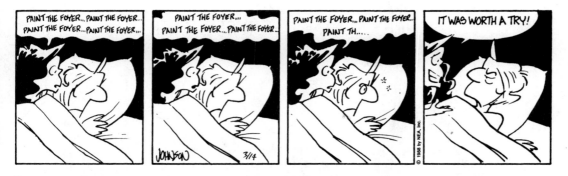

Figure 14.12. *Subliminal behavior modification is now a multibillion-dollar business, with many users testifying to its effectiveness.* (Arlo and Janis *reprinted by permission of NEA, Inc.*)

What you can do is *trigger* a prior attitude or predisposition" (Lander, 1981). Note how familiar to us that statement is — the most effective persuasion uses information already in the audience. Effective persuaders get messages out of their audiences, not into them.

There are several sides to the subliminal persuasion controversy. The ad people say they never use the stuff, and people such as Key say that our world is loaded with subliminal seducers. Interested observers also differ. Some say that Key is like the man who responded with "sex" to every inkblot presented by the psychiatrist. When accused of being preoccupied with sex, the patient countered that it was the doctor who collected all the "dirty" pictures. My position is that if it is possible to persuade through subliminal messages — sexual or otherwise — then someone is probably doing it.

I am not alone in my belief. A University of Utah professor of chemistry and president of Innovations Consulting, Inc., has tested the use of subliminal suggestion during sleep and recently advised Oak Ridge, Tennessee, nuclear scientists that they could use the method to increase productivity and creativity. Subliminal tapes have become a multibillion-dollar business, with many

users being "true believers" in the method ("Success . . . ," 1987). In another case, Dallas radio station KMEZ AM-FM regularly broadcast subliminal messages to "stop smoking" as part of the American Cancer Society's "Great American Smokeout" after checking it out with the FCC. The FCC doesn't consider paid announcements containing subliminals exactly illegal but as "against the public interest." In the Dallas case, however, the message was considered a socially desirable one (Subliminals used . . . ," 1987).

Of course, certain ads that use sex aren't at all subliminal about their messages. The Calvin Klein ads for Obsession for men are good examples. Others border on the subliminal: The message is hazy but clear enough to give you the idea the advertiser wants you to get. A good example is the campaign to promote Travel Fox sneakers. With a tiny budget and facing competition such as Nike and Reebok, the company hired a Swedish agency, Hall & Cederquist, to create ads for Travel Fox sneakers that had little ad copy. The visuals showed various permutations of a man and woman wearing the shoes and in various "positions" just sexually distinguishable. The ad shown in Figure 14.16 clearly shows the man and woman in a suggestive position. Sales in the

Figure 14.13. *Can you see the "hidden" image? (Reprinted with permission from Ogilvy & Mather.)*

Figure 14.14. *What hidden picture can you find in this ad? (Reprinted with permission from Ogilvy & Mather.)*

Figure 14.15. *Obvious enough for you? (Reprinted with permission from Ogilvy & Mather.)*

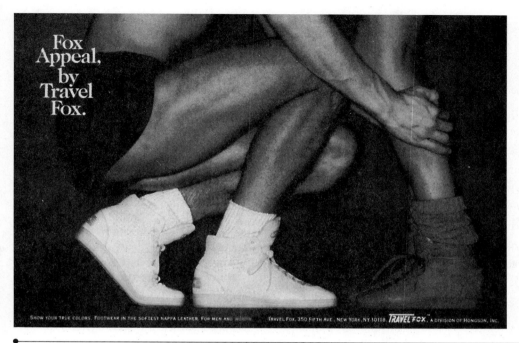

Figure 14.16. *In this ad for Travel Fox sneakers, the words* Fox *and* appeal *tell you what is going on as we see a man and woman obviously in a sexual position. (Used by permission of Hall & Cederquist Advertising, Inc.)*

and woman in a suggestive position. Sales in the New York test market tripled in a year.

Review and Conclusion

As noted earlier in this chapter, Americans live in a world exploding with new products and brands. This world is even more cluttered with advertising for those products and brands—probably many times more cluttered than other Western democracies. Yet the advertisers continue to try to catch our attention; they then educate us about their brand's benefits and advantages; and finally, they use clever cues and sales promotional material to prompt us to buy at the point of purchase. They use sophisticated kinds of research, including demographics, sociographics, and psychographics. Moving from this research they develop ad copy, layouts, and scripts to appeal to our various needs and desires. As Carl Wrighter pointed out in his 1972 book *I Can Sell You Anything*, they often use misleading and even deceptive "weasel" words and claims to hype their products and brands. We have explored a few of these possibilities, including sexual appeals of various degrees and some "subliminal" examples. All of them should put us on guard as consumers.

Questions for Further Thought

1. How much money is spent for advertising in the United States per person compared to that spent in other countries?

2. Why might advertising reflect the values and norms of a culture?

3. What might a Marxist critic say about the purpose of advertising?

4. What is "positioning," and how does it relate to the niche?

5. What product features can serve as niches?

6. What are some of the problems of an "over-communicated society"?

7. What is the "product explosion," and how does it affect us?

8. What does "breaking through the clutter" mean?

9. Why is "American-made" an example of positioning?

10. Explain the difference between demographics, sociographics, and psychographics.

11. What is the "muppie" market segment?

12. What is a DINK?

13. What is the VALS system, and how does it work?

14. What are focus groups, and what is their purpose?

15. What is the ACORN system, and how does it work?

16. What are some of the "languages" of advertising? Give examples.

17. How does advertising research lead to advertising copy? Give examples.

18. What are "weasel words"? Give examples.

19. What are some deceptive claims? Give examples.

20. What is meant when we say that a product has become "semanticized"? Give examples.

21. What differentiates blatant sexual appeals in advertising from sophisticated ones? Give examples.

22. How are subliminals used in advertising? How effective do you think they are?

References

Becker, H., & Glanzer, N. (1978). Subliminal communication: Advances in audiovisual engineering applications. *Proceedings of the 1978 institute of electronical and electronics engineers: Region 3*. Atlanta: Institute of Electronical and Electronics Engineers.

Dollas, C. (1986a). A description of packaging design as a medium of communication. Unpublished starred paper, Department of Journalism, Northern Illinois University, Dekalb.

Dollas, C. (1986b). Butterball turkeys: An examination of advertising theory and practice. Unpublished starred paper, Department of Journalism, Northern Illinois University, Dekalb.

Diamond, E., & Bates, S. (1984). *The spot: The rise of political advertising on television*. Cambridge, MA: MIT Press.

Engel, J., Blackwell, D., & Miniard, P. (1986). *Consumer behavior*. Chicago: Dryden.

Gallonoy, T. (1970). *Down the tube: Or making television commercials is such a dog-eat-dog business, it's no wonder they're called spots*. Chicago: Regenery.

Goodkin, O., & Phillips, M. (1983). The subconscious taken captive. *Southern California Law Review, 54,* 1077–1140.

Happy 65th birthday to 5,500 Americans — daily. (1988). *The Chicago Tribune,* April 20, sec. 8, p. 10.

Kaid, L., Nimmo, D., & Sanders, K. (1986). *New perspectives on political advertising*. Carbondale: Southern Illinois University Press.

Key, W. B. (1973). *Subliminal seduction: Ad media's manipulation of a not so innocent America*. New York: Signet Books.

Key, W. B. (1977). *Media sexploitation*. New York: Signet Books.

Key, W. B. (1980). *The clambake orgy*. New York: Signet Books.

Leiss, W., Kline, S., & Jhally, S. (1986). *Social communication in advertising: Persons, products and images of well-being*. New York: Methuen.

Mitchell, A. (1983). *Nine American lifestyles: Who we are and where we're going*. New York: Macmillan.

O'Toole, J. (1985). *The trouble with advertising*. New York: Times Books/Random House.

Postman, N. (1987). *Amusing ourselves to death: Public discourse in the age of show business*. New York: Penguin.

Rank, H. (1982). *The pitch*. Park Forest, IL: The Counter Propaganda Press.

Ries, A., & Trout, J. (1986). *Positioning: The battle for your mind*. New York: McGraw-Hill.

Rothschild, M. (1987). *Advertising: From fundamentals to strategies*. Lexington, MA: D. C. Health.

Schudson, M. (1984). *Advertising, the uneasy persuasion: Its dubious impact on American society*. New York: Basic Books.

Subliminals used to fight smoking. (1987). *Dekalb Daily Chronicle*, November 18.

Success through the subconscious: Subliminal tapes help people improve. (1987). *The Chicago Tribune,* October 1, sec. 1A, p. 28.

Storch, C. (1988). Humble grocery cart now a video ad vehicle. *The Chicago Tribune,* May 1, Tempo Section, pp. 1, 5.

Vestergaard, T., & Schroeder, K. (1985). *The language of advertising*. London: Basil Blackwell Press.

Weiss, M. J. (1989). *The clustering of America: A vivid portrait of the nation's 40 neighborhood types — their values, lifestyles, and eccentricities*. New York: Harper & Row.

Williamson, J. (1977). *Decoding advertising: Meaning and ideology in advertising*. London: Marion Boyers Ltd.

Epilogue

One recurring phenomenon I have noted as I revised *Persuasion: Reception and Responsibility* over the years is the continually accelerating rate of change in many arenas. Change is fascinating — even if it leads to chaos, confusion, or even violence. Consider just a few of the changes that have occurred since the seventh edition of this book was published in 1995, three short years ago. It is clear that Leninist-Marxism is utterly bankrupt. The 1980s — the decade of greed — has been supplanted by a new concern for the environment. The baby boomers who put an end to the Vietnam War now are getting AARP cards. The same boomers who rejected American society in favor of the counterculture and who evolved from yippies to yuppies now face midlife as muppies. They are returning to church in droves as they seek the meaning of life; 80 percent of them consider themselves religious. We still haven't come to grips with the national debt, the energy crisis, AIDS, or the role of American influence in the rest of the world. The balance of power in both houses of the U.S. Congress has shifted; homegrown terrorism has displaced the foreign variety on our national agenda; we are still trying to come to terms with the divisiveness caused by the most widely publicized murder trial in our history; and we are becoming ever more diverse as a society. As all of these changes unfold, the number of persuasive messages confronting us continues to mushroom, and not only are the messages more numerous, they are infinitely more sophisticated.

Many of the themes emphasized in this book seem to foretell a bleak world for receivers in the twenty-first century: a loss of individual identity for most of us, deterioration of a sense of community in American culture, and an increasing volume of and sophistication in the development and distribution of persuasive messages. Robert Bellah and his colleagues, in *Habits of the Heart: Individualism and Commitment in American Life* (1985), describe our predicament this way:

> But we have never faced a situation that called our deepest assumptions so radically into question. Our problems today are not just political. They are moral and have to do with the meaning of life. . . . we are beginning to understand that our common life requires more than an exclusive concern for material accumulation.

Perhaps life is not a race whose only goal is being foremost. Perhaps the truth lies in what most of the world outside the modern West has always believed. That . . . work that is intrinsically rewarding is better for human beings than work that is only extrinsically rewarded. Perhaps enduring commitment to those we love and civic friendship toward our fellow citizens are preferable to restless competition and anxious self-defense. . . .

We have imagined ourselves as a special creation, set apart from other humans. In the late twentieth century, we see that our poverty is as absolute as the poorest of nations. We have attempted to deny the human condition in our quest for power after power. It would be well for us to rejoin the human race.

Perhaps these words are overly critical of contemporary American culture and too pessimistic about the future. But it seems that the remainder of the 1990s bodes ill for us. With such challenges to face, isn't it more important than ever that we train ourselves to be truly *responsible* receivers of persuasion? I think so, and my feelings are reinforced by communication researcher and professor Rod Hart (1990) of the University of Texas at Austin. He describes the dramatic appeal he makes to his students each term:

On the first day of class, I observe to my students that all persuaders ask to borrow just a bit of their minds, just for a little while. . . . I tell my students that my course will return their minds to them. I tell them that the cups-full of themselves they willingly loan out to teachers and preachers and cheerleaders in the bleachers can lead to an empty cupboard. I tell them that if they keep giving portions of themselves away that there will be nothing left when they need themselves most — when confused, when frightened, when pressured for a decision. I tell them that persuasion is a science that moves by increments, that it happens most powerfully when it least seems to happen at all. . . . I try to instill a kind of arrogant humility in my students, a mindset that gives them the courage to disassemble rhetoric but also the wisdom never to underestimate it. . . . the persuasion course is the most important course they will take in college.

As you conclude this course, I hope you will *not* conclude your practice of the reception skills discussed here. I hope you will try to expand your skills and your ability to critically "disassemble rhetoric" and get at its obvious and hidden meanings. I hope you will recognize the complexities of the world we live in and the many persuasive messages we receive. I trust your instinctive suspicion of persuasive appeals. Together with Professor Hart, I "trust, mostly, in the critical mind's wondrous capacity to call a spade a spade and a rhetoric a rhetoric, to depuff puffery and to make mortals of gods, and to maintain a tenacious resolve that we shall not all fall, lemminglike into the sea."

References

Bellah, R. N., Madsen, R., Sullivan, W., Swidler, A., & Tipton, S. M. (1985). *Habits of the Heart: Individualism and Commitment in American Life*. New York: Harper & Row.

Hart, R. P. (1990). Teaching the undergraduate persuasion course: Why? In Daly, J., Friedrich, G., & Vangelisti, A. (Eds.), *Teaching Communication*. Hillsdale, NJ: Lawrence Erlbaum.

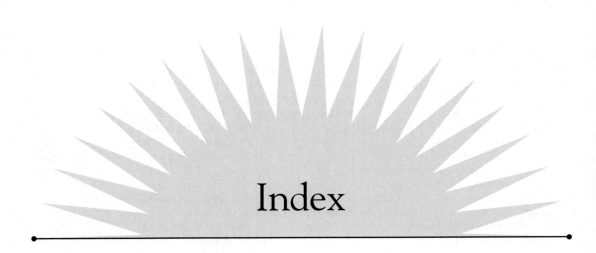

Index